A FIERY &
FURIOUS PEOPLE

A FIERY & FURIOUS PEOPLE

A History of Violence in England

JAMES SHARPE

BOOKS

1 3 5 7 9 10 8 6 4 2

Random House Books
20 Vauxhall Bridge Road
London SW1V 2SA

Random House Books is part of the Penguin Random House
group of companies whose addresses can be found at
global.penguinrandomhouse.com.

Penguin
Random House
UK

First published by Random House Books in 2016

www.penguin.co.uk

A CIP catalogue record for this book is available from the British Library.

ISBN 9781847945136

Typeset in 12/15.25 pt Dante MT
by Jouve (UK), Milton Keynes
Printed and bound by Clays Ltd, St Ives plc

Penguin Random House is committed to a sustainable future
for our business, our readers and our planet. This book is made
from Forest Stewardship Council® certified paper.

MIX
Paper from
responsible sources
FSC
www.fsc.org   FSC® C018179

CONTENTS

Preface   vii

Introduction: the Death of Roger Crockett   1

PART I

'NO MAN WAS SURE OF HIS LIFE': ENGLAND IN THE MIDDLE AGES

1.	The Violent Middle Ages?	43
2.	Church and State: the Forces of Restraint	77

PART II

'A POLITE AND COMMERCIAL PEOPLE': FROM THE TUDORS TO THE VICTORIANS

3.	The Retreat from Killing	107
4.	Violence in Print: from Murder Pamphlets to Revenge Tragedies	139
5.	Domestic Violence: Wives, Husbands and Servants	169
6.	Mothers and Infanticide	197
7.	Verbal Violence: Scolding, Slander and Libel	223
8.	The Rise and Fall of the Duel	255
9.	Sport and the Decline of Casual Violence	283

CONTENTS

10. Violence and Organised Crime:
    Highwaymen and Smugglers 309
11. The Georgian Mob 337
12. State Violence and the End of the
    Old Punishment Regime 373

PART III

'VIOLENCE IS ALWAYS ON THE AGENDA':
THE MODERN AGE

13. An English Miracle? 407
14. Partners and Children,
    Victims and Killers 443
15. Women and Sexual Violence 477
16. The Serial Killer: a Very Modern
    Murderer? 507
17. Public Violence: from Football
    Hooliganism to Inner-city Riots 541
18. A Culture of Violence? Film and
    Television 575
19. Peaks and Troughs: Patterns of
    Violence Today 605

Appendix: Crime Statistics 639

Further Reading 645

Notes 659

Index 721

Picture Acknowledgments 751

PREFACE

Most of my research and publication since I began work on my
Oxford DPhil thesis in 1968 has been on the history of crime in early
modern England, and as that research developed I became increasingly interested in violence as a historical phenomenon. At the same
time, teaching the social history of the early modern period led me
to take an interest in peasant revolt and other forms of popular disturbance, while the burgeoning of gender history from the early
1980s onwards encouraged me to deepen my understanding of
domestic violence and rape as historical phenomena. I had also, via
working on pamphlets dealing with murder (and latterly witchcraft)
trials, begun to ponder on some of the broader, longer-term implications of media representations of violence. These various interests
were brought together when I was successful in obtaining funding,
under the aegis of the Economic and Social Research Council's Violence Research Programme, for a research project on violence in
Lancashire and Cheshire between 1600 and 1800. While I was working on the project between 1998 and 2000, I found myself in productive
scholarly debate with historians working on more recent periods,
and with sociologists and criminologists. These experiences helped
me decide to try to put together a book on the long-term history of
violence in England between the late middle ages and the present
day. I am also acutely aware that violence remains a major preoccu-
pation of modern society, in the United Kingdom as elsewhere, and

I was intrigued by what resonances the study of violent behaviour in the past, and representations of it, might have for our current situation.

I have engaged with a number of historians and their publications while formulating my ideas on the history of violence, notably Robert Muchembled, Randolph Roth, Pieter Spierenburg and John Carter Wood, while I have also received unfailing support from my wife, Krista Cowman, my literary agent, Jane Turnbull, and Nigel Wilcockson at Random House. I have further benefitted from discussing this book as it progressed with my York colleagues Mark Roodhouse and Craig Taylor, and from giving papers as my research on violence developed to conferences at Bern, Brussels, Jyväskylä, Leicester, Leiden, Liverpool, Lyon, Montpellier, Oxford and Rotterdam. Most of the research for this book has been carried out in the J. B. Morrell and Raymond Burton Libraries of the University of York, or on electronic resources made available by them. I have also made use of the holdings of the Borthwick Institute for Archives, York; Cheshire Archives and Local Studies; and The National Archives (TNA) Kew, London. I acknowledge Crown copyright in TNA documents and modern government publications cited.

The title of the book is derived from one of the possible translations of the chronicler Jean Froissart's description 'gens foursenés et esragiés' which he applied to the rebels in London in June 1381, during that mass-uprising we know as the Peasants' Revolt. In a sense, this book describes how, over the long term, the English people became less fiery and furious. One has to hope that they will not become so again.

James Sharpe
University of York
July 2016

The Genesis story of Cain and Abel – here depicted by Albrecht Dürer – is one of the most ancient and enduring tales of murder. Violence, the Bible suggests, has been part of the human condition since Adam and Eve's expulsion from the Garden of Eden.

THE DEATH OF ROGER CROCKETT

I

Everyone agreed on the way that Roger Crockett received the injuries that caused his death on that December morning, but very few of the 116 witnesses who subsequently gave evidence were willing to identify the person (or persons) who had actually inflicted them. Not even Margaret Parker, into whose lap Crockett almost fell when he was struck on the head from behind with a staff, was prepared to give an opinion. As so often in the aftermath of a brutal attack, some people may have had more than an inkling who was responsible, but were either too afraid to name the perpetrator or else had a vested interest in keeping his identity a secret.

At the time of his death in 1572, Crockett was the owner of the Crown Inn at Nantwich in Cheshire, a bustling market town of about 1,800 inhabitants that prospered on the profits from salt production as well as passing trade attracted from travellers on the London–Chester road. Crockett was a shrewd, up-and-coming businessman, who was gradually acquiring land in the area and had become interested in securing the lease to a potentially very profitable piece of pasture – known as Ridley Field – from its owner, a Leicestershire gentleman named Edward Leigh. But while this may have been a shrewd financial decision, it was also a move guaranteed to bring him into direct conflict with the Halsalls. They were a prominent local family already on bad terms with Crockett: on one occasion he and Richard Halsall had been overheard hurling that most colourful of sixteenth-century insults, 'tird [turd] in thy teeth', at each other. Now the Halsalls were furious that Crockett should seek the lease to a field that Richard Halsall currently held and that had previously been in the possession of Halsall's father.

Widespread local gossip suggested that if there were to be trouble, it would occur on Wednesday 19 December, the day Crockett was due to take possession of his new land. At the subsequent inquest Ralph Ince told how he 'heard a little girl of his own coming in from play out of the street from other children say that there would be mischief and if Crockett came to Ridley Lane he would be beaten'. Ince's wife Ellen confirmed the story, saying that the twelve-year-old girl 'as she played with Halsall's children and others heard them say, that if Crockett purchased Ridley Field, he should be killed for it'.

Sure enough, on 19 December tension spilled over into violence. First Thomas Wilson, one of a group of men the Halsalls had gathered together, assaulted Thomas Wettenhall, who, along with his brother Roger, was an associate of Crockett. Then, a little later, Roger Wettenhall and Richard Halsall encountered each other, and a fight ensued. Young Alice Inpley described its early stages:

> Being sent on an errand by her father into the town, & coming back again being about 8 of the clock in the morning she saw Richard Halsall come out of the gate of his own house, and going down as far as Woodstreet Lane end saw Roger Wettenhall meet the said Halsall, and cross over the channel [presumably a drainage channel] and strike at him, and so they struck there 20 blows before anybody came to him.

The two men fought with staves, Wettenhall receiving a head injury and collapsing into a hedge. Halsall, his brother William and Thomas Wilson, who had joined him, were contemplating inflicting further injuries on him, but were dissuaded by Halsall's father, who told them Wettenhall had suffered enough, and that they should stop.

By now a large crowd had gathered, witness after witness later testifying how they had heard a commotion in the street, and left their houses or workshops to find out what was going on. And it was at this moment that Crockett appeared, carrying a staff, but signalling his unwillingness to fight by not having it raised ready for use (there was evidently a code of conduct in such matters). He made his way through the crowd, trying to get to his friend Roger Wettenhall. Halsall's men, however, attacked him and knocked him to the ground with a blow to the head. (Crockett's widow and his associates were later to claim that more than a single blow to the head had been involved, and that Crockett had been savagely assaulted.)

At this point Richard Wilbraham, probably the most important man in Nantwich and certainly a member of one of Cheshire's most prominent families, intervened. He had been in bed when the fighting started, and his haste to get to the scene was reflected in his appearance: he arrived half dressed, holding up his hose with one hand and clutching a staff in the other; his points (the laces which held the various parts of Elizabethan clothing together) were undone and he was shoeless. He was no friend of the Wettenhalls or of Crockett: indeed Crockett's wife Bridget was later to allege that he had been involved in a conspiracy in the town against her dead husband whose business success, as already suggested, had ruffled the feathers of some of Nantwich's leading residents. On the other hand, Wilbraham clearly felt that his social status required him to act as peacemaker. Accordingly, with the encouragement of several members of the crowd, he quietened things down. Halsall and his men went back to Halsall's house, presumably to celebrate. Crockett was helped up, taken to the nearby house of Roger Gorse, cleaned up and then led home, where he was put to bed. His injuries, according to some of the witnesses who saw him at that stage, were horrific. He had a bad head wound, one of his eyes had been almost knocked out, and he had also suffered injuries to his legs, arms and torso. From time to time he coughed up blood and brains. He died between eight and nine o'clock that night.

The two warring parties swiftly circulated their own – very different – versions of what had happened. Although the evidence from witness statements and the subsequent coroner's inquest suggested that Crockett had received multiple wounds, the Halsall faction argued that he had been hit only once, and that this had merely left a 'dalke' or depression on his head. Their hope, presumably, was that if this account became the accepted one and the case ever came to trial, a verdict of manslaughter rather than murder would be brought in. To counter this, the Wettenhalls and Crockett's widow Bridget took the extraordinary course of displaying the dead man's body, naked except for a cloth over his private parts, on the streets of Nantwich, and on the Saturday after the killing took it to Nantwich Market. They also enlisted the services of a painter named John Sinter, who, as he explained later, was sent for by Thomas Wettenhall and asked to

> Draw out on paper the picture of the body & the signs & marks thereupon and upon his oath deposeth that as near as he could in every respect he did the same according as appeareth in the same paper now being shewed before him, saving only at that time there was no blood about his nose or ears, until it was the day he was carried to church.

Sinter claimed that a number of men in the town, including Richard Wilbraham, expressed their displeasure with the painter for making this record.

On the afternoon of the day Crockett's corpse was carried to the market, a coroner's inquest was held in a packed Nantwich church (so packed, in fact, that the two coroners had to clear many spectators out of the building). The body was inspected by both coroners and by the sixteen-man inquest jury. One coroner, John Maisterson, expressed the view that the injuries sustained had been minimal. Since Maisterson happened to be Richard Wilbraham's brother-in-law, Bridget Crockett not surprisingly alleged that he was far from being a disinterested official.

And then the key witness, Roger Wettenhall, made an intervention that introduces us to a curious contemporary belief. It was widely held in sixteenth- and seventeenth-century England that the corpse of a murdered person would bleed if it were touched by the murderer (there are scattered examples of this practice being used as a means of establishing proof in murder cases during the period). Wettenhall demanded, in the Queen's name, that this test should be applied to those he held to be Crockett's murderers (these men are not named in the records that survive), quoting Aristotle in support of his argument (and thereby providing an interesting example of how classical education had spread to the English provincial gentry by the late sixteenth century). The coroners were not impressed. According to John Gryffin, a gentleman who was present at the inquest, one of them

> . . . said to Wettenhall if you can show me a book case [i.e. legal precedent], that they ought to be sent for I will send for them or else, not, and then Wettenhall answered that he thought Mr Coroner was both wise & learned according to his office, and he in humble manner required it for the prince [i.e. the Queen].

Having failed in his bid to have the corpse touched, Wettenhall was asked to state the names of those he considered to be Crockett's killers. He equivocated. The coroners initially refused to release the corpse for burial, possibly because they did not wish it to be examined further, but after some argument agreed to do so. Crockett's body was taken away, and presumably buried in Nantwich churchyard.

II

The events of 19 December 1572 offer a tantalising glimpse of a society where violence, if not exactly taken for granted, was very much part of the normal order of things. It was a world in which a dispute over a relatively trivial property matter could end in a man's death. It was also a world in which those involved in such a brawl, far from being the lower-class element who, since Victorian times, have rightly or wrongly been regarded as most prone to violence, were actually 'respectable' citizens of the town.

It's also very apparent from the witness statements just how many Nantwich citizens carried weapons around with them as a matter of course – or, at least, how many had easy recourse to them. The fight itself, according to one of the witnesses, William Jackson, involved 'the great clash of staves'. Practically all of the men who came along to see what was going on bore a staff or some other weapon that they were fully prepared to use. A townsman named Richard Bally was one such. On that morning he was in Richard Wilkes's house, and

> . . . hearing a woman make an outcry that there was a fray in the street sent out the wife of the house to see who it was; and she came and said she could see nobody, and then Peers Crewe said it may be some friend of ours, let us not sit here for shame and so stepped up and took the examinant's staff standing in the entry and this examinant took a bill [a type of halberd] out of Wilkes's chamber and Wilkes took a skull [a metal helmet of a pretty basic design] and put it upon his head and a staff in his hand and so came all three together until Peers Crewe was stayed by his own wife and maid and carried into his own house.

Another witness, Thomas Palen, gave a detailed description of the weaponry carried by the company the Halsalls had gathered together to fight for Ridley Field. Most of them were armed with some type of staff, Thomas Wilson having one twelve feet long and with a metal pike head. One had a dagger and a staff, one had a pickerel (a short pike), another had a bill. Palen claimed that he saw 'all the company in battle array'.

Yet there are also clear indications that many of those drawn into the melee, or witnesses to it, were opposed to violence. Peers Crewe's wife dissuaded him from going to see what was happening – an interesting glimpse of the inner workings of an Elizabethan marriage. The three men he knew who did go along, did so to see if any of their friends needed help. Others who ventured out with their staves were clearly motivated by a desire to defuse the situation rather than become involved in it. One such was John Lovett who, on hearing 'a clattering like the felling of wood' and then women crying out 'help, help', went into the street carrying only a 'cloth yard' (a form of measuring rod) for protection. He later described how he saw a number of women and children watching two men fighting. Noticing that Thomas Wilson and William Halsall were armed and approaching the combatants, he tried to stop them, and seized hold of Halsall. He broke free but Lovett ran after him, caught, disarmed and then restrained him.

Women were also involved – as so often throughout history – as potential peacemakers. Ellen Turner intervened to save Roger Wettenhall, and claimed to have held back one of the men attacking him. Another woman, identified variously as 'Joan of Love Lane' or 'Joan of the Lane', also tried to protect Wettenhall, putting herself between him and his would-be assailants. Richard Halsall's father intervened to save Roger Wettenhall from worse punishment at the hands of Richard, his brother William and Thomas Wilson. And, of course, Richard Wilbraham, as one of the town grandees, clearly felt that it was incumbent on him to bring the violence to an end. On the one hand, then, there were those who were prepared to attack and kill a man over a property dispute. On the other, there were many who instinctively felt this to be wrong.

We will never know who really was responsible for the death of Roger Crockett. Early rumours, encouraged by the pro-Crockett faction, suggested that it had been Richard Wilbraham, an unlikely claim given the evidence of his role as peacemaker, but one clearly put forward to cause trouble for a man perceived to be an enemy. Suspicion then fell on Edmund Crewe, a local shoemaker, who, according to the Halsall faction, admitted striking the fatal blow.

However, they also seem to have been able to spirit him away – or, at least, he conveniently fled the area and was never put on trial.

Bridget Crockett and the Wettenhalls were clearly and understandably dissatisfied with the coroner's inquest and later proceedings at Cheshire Court of Great Sessions. They therefore took matters further, invoking an antique procedure rarely used by the late sixteenth century: an appeal of felony. This was, in effect, a civil suit that could be brought if the appellant felt the normal course of justice had been perverted. It was a hazardous process to undertake – it was very easy to lose on a technicality and, if you lost, you could be sued for damages – so the fact that Bridget Crockett should have resorted to it shows just how passionately she felt about the justice of her cause – or, alternatively, how much she hated the Halsalls. At any rate, at the Court of Great Sessions at Chester in July 1573 Edmund Crewe was indicted in his absence, along with twenty-one other people. Six (among them Richard Wilbraham and Richard, Anne and William Halsall) were bound over until the next convening of the court in February 1574, at which point they were discharged. Bridget Crockett's attempt to prove that there had been a conspiracy to murder her husband had come to nothing.

So we are left uncertain as to the identity of the man who struck the blow that killed Roger Crockett. But we do have a very clear impression of how a violent incident was played out nearly four and a half centuries ago, and a sense of the ways in which actions and attitudes differed from those of today, as well as of the many parallels.[1] The Nantwich incident thus forms a useful piece in the complex jigsaw puzzle of half a millennium or so of violence in England.

III

Violence is currently a major source of concern in England as it is in most other countries of the world.[2] We are constantly being told by our press and politicians that we live in a 'violent society'; many people in inner-city areas live in fear of violence; we hear tales of widespread aggression within the home; and its alleged prevalence is seen as an important indicator of a wider social malaise. Yet at the same time we are fascinated by violence; we watch movies and television programmes and play video games that all depend very heavily on depictions of it. Besides that there is still the widespread belief that a willingness to fight is a badge of masculinity: some might argue that this is restricted to certain classes and age groups, but nevertheless fighting is something most men have experienced at some point in their lives. Violence is therefore an established social problem, even if there is no consensus on the point at which it shades into aggression or aggression into mere assertiveness.

It certainly seems to be part of the human condition.[3] The Judeo-Christian tradition dates it back to the second generation of mankind. *Genesis*, 4:1–14 tells us the first murder story, involving two brothers, Cain and Abel, the sons of Adam and Eve. Abel was a pastoralist, 'a keeper of sheep', and Cain, the elder brother, an agriculturalist, 'a tiller of the ground'. Both made appropriate offerings to the Almighty, in Cain's case an offering 'of the fruit of the ground'; in Abel's 'the first-lings of his flock and the fat thereof'. God accepted Abel's offering, but rejected Cain's ('But unto Cain and his offering He had not respect'). Cain was angry. He 'talked with Abel his brother, and it came to pass, when they were in the field, that Cain rose up against Abel, and slew him'. When the Lord returned, found Abel missing and enquired as to his whereabouts, Cain replied: 'I know not. Am I my brother's keeper?' 'What hast thou done?' came the response. 'The voice of thy brother's blood crieth unto me from the ground. And now art thou cursed from the earth, which hath opened her mouth to receive thy brother's blood from thy hand'. And so the first agriculturalist was turned into 'a fugitive and vagabond', cursed to wander the world (in fact Cain made off to 'the land of Nod, on the east of Eden'). But Cain pointed out that his vagabond status would mean he could be killed by anybody whom he encountered, so God put his mark on him, promising seven-fold vengeance upon anyone who harmed him.

Some might object that this account of the first murder is scarcely a historical one. It is, however, a very ancient one and there is plenty of evidence of a more scientific nature that humans have always had a propensity to violence. We know, for example, that the first inventors of pebble tools, the African Australopithecines, used this technical innovation not only to hunt, but also to kill their fellows.[4]

Violence, of course, encompasses a wide range of human behaviour, from killing, through non-fatal forms of interpersonal violence, to threats and intimidation. Some social scientists take the broadest possible view of it. The philosopher Slavoj Žižek, for example, has argued that all social and political systems based on inequality and exploitation are inherently violent, and he ends his book on violence by commenting that sometimes doing nothing is the most violent act possible.[5] My own working definition is rather narrower. I would argue that at its core, violence is the use of physical force to injure or damage people and property, or involves language or behaviour that threatens to do so. I'm aware, though, that even this definition leaves us with a very fluid concept. Violence can be prompted by a wide range of drives and emotions: self-defence, frustration, a desire for revenge, a desire to retaliate, a desire to dominate, a desire to maintain honour. It is subject to different cultural interpretations, and views of it change over time. Even a single culture at one particular moment in its development may have an ambivalent attitude to aspects of violence, unsure whether certain acts are legitimate or not. Thus wife-beating was widely regarded as acceptable in the past, but it was also of questionable legality and drew the opprobrium of some social commentators. Likewise, between the sixteenth and nineteenth centuries, the duel was regarded as being of central importance to the honour code of at least some members of the aristocracy and gentry; yet it was also illegal and, almost from the moment of its arrival in England from the continent, attracted hostile comment.

Then there are areas of licensed violence to be considered. Formerly, masters and mistresses of apprentices and servants (and people a fair way down the social scale might keep a live-in servant or two) were entitled to use physical chastisement, as, of course, were parents and schoolteachers. Even then (to reiterate the role of culture) there were widely held beliefs regarding appropriate levels of 'correction', and local opinion might intervene if it judged that the line had been crossed between acceptable practice and the outright abuse of an individual.

An added complication is that acts of violence normally involve three people or sets of people: the perpetrator and the victim, of course, but also, in many cases, an audience. And as the events surrounding Roger Crockett's death show, the audience can play much more than an observational role: its attitudes and behaviour can be crucial in defining whether or not an act of violence is deemed legitimate, and hence at what stage it should be brought to an end.[6] To make matters even more complicated, while violence may sometimes be spur of the moment, it can just as easily be carefully orchestrated and regulated. In the past, fights between men were subject to rules of engagement; both the men involved, and certainly those watching them, had a clear idea of how much physical force would be appropriate to the occasion (not, of course, that this necessarily stopped things getting out of hand). Indeed, as the presence of an audience suggests, and as anyone who has seen two men squaring up to each other and trading insults as a prelude to fighting will understand, violence can be performative. So while the popular view of violence is of unrestrained and unthinking force, it can just as easily be carefully choreographed and bound by unwritten rules.

This can be seen among those unlikeliest of theatrical performers, football hooligans. Here, for example, is a description of the actions of Sheffield United supporters – or 'Blades':

> Blades play to various audiences and, like thespians worldwide, they and their fellow performers need to adhere to the boundaries of the plot and understand the script. That said, some fluff their lines, while others ham; still others fail to

respond on cue, and some have to improvise constantly. The outcome is hooligan dramas that are contextual, negotiated and improvised . . .

Continuing his metaphor, the commentator also draws attention to 'the theatre critics – journalists and police – who report on what they see as the appalling performance'. [7]

Football hooliganism shows that violence can be a performance. It also demonstrates that it can involve ritual. On one famous occasion fighting broke out between opposing football fans during a match, and the police had to be called in to restore order. During the fighting it appeared that some of the fans were directing kung-fu kicks at their opponents – clear evidence to those who saw the match televised that what was unfolding before their eyes was one of the worst cases of football hooliganism yet. Closer inspection of the relevant footage, however, showed that the kicks were directed into the air about three feet away from rival fans. The football hooligans may have been intent on shows of bravado, but they were also generally keeping to well-established rules. That doesn't mean of course that ritual violence can't get out of hand and boundaries be transgressed. [8] But it does suggest that, even in the case of apparently aggressive kung-fu football hooligans, what initially appeared to be extreme acts of violent and random provocation were actually carefully considered and did not involve physical contact. Newspapers often talk of 'meaningless' or 'mindless' violence. In fact, most violence takes place for a reason: it normally has a meaning, even if that meaning is obscure, or distasteful to many outside observers. So we need to recognise that violence can be 'instrumental' – a calculated act to bring about a calculated end.

One common feature of violent behaviour, which can be traced back as far as records go (and, indeed, to Cain and Abel), is that it tends to be performed by men. The driving force here is a sense of male honour. As the anthropologist Julian Pitt-Rivers put it, 'The ultimate vindication of honour lies in physical violence, and when other means fail the obligation exists . . . to resort to it.'[9] The willingness to fight and changes in attitudes to fighting are therefore very much related to changing notions of masculinity. To us, the reasons why eighteenth-century labourers got into pub brawls or their social superiors fought duels may seem trivial, but both groups were working within an honour code that stipulated that violence was an acceptable – perhaps the only – way of vindicating reputation and regaining status. For certain – especially young – men, then, a willingness to demonstrate hardness and a taste for fighting was an important way of demonstrating masculinity.

Shifting views of masculinity gradually led to the widespread rejection of interpersonal violence between men, except among those elements of society deemed 'rough'. Attitudes to other forms of violence also changed over the years. Wife-beating, which I have already touched on, is a case in point. At one time it was pretty widely accepted, and although there were always voices raised against it, both in local communities and in print, it was rare for this kind of abuse to result in a formal charge and conviction. Over the course of the twentieth century, however, domestic violence came increasingly to be recognised as a major social evil and, as such, a matter for the police and for the courts. Condemnation of sexual assaults on women has also grown in force over time, resulting in an increased willingness on the part of victims to see their assailants brought to trial (between 1897 and 1901 an average of 759 cases each year were reported to the police in England and Wales; between 1965 and 1969 that figure had risen to 11,293, and in the year from September 2013 to September 2014 to 24,043).[10] It's a similar picture with bullying. Two generations ago it was certainly known about and disliked, but in general those suffering from it (especially at school) would be advised either to fight back on the basis that bullies are cowards (a rather questionable premise) or to accept it as part of the normal course of things. Today, however, bullying, both at school and in the workplace, has, like domestic violence, been identified as a serious social issue.

IV

So far I have touched on violence among individuals and small groups. Collective violence is also an important strand of English history. In the summer of 2011 a number of cities were afflicted by a brief but serious outbreak of rioting and looting, which destroyed property and led to confrontations with the police. In the summer of 1780 central London suffered the infinitely more destructive Gordon Riots, during which the mob went almost unchecked for several days. In the summer of 1381 London was the target of peasant rebel armies, which looted the property of unpopular political figures, massacred foreigners, and executed the medieval equivalents of the Prime Minister and the Chancellor of the Exchequer.

There is a tradition of popular unrest and popular protest in England, which encompasses not only these large-scale outbreaks, but also numerous smaller outbreaks during which Englishmen and women demonstrated, sometimes violently, over the price of grain, over landlords enclosing their common land, over pay and conditions at the workplace, and over trades union rights. Things sometimes got out of hand and there were certainly instances of spontaneous aggression, but – as with many other forms of violence – there was often a structure to the apparent mayhem: rioters were frequently motivated by legitimate grievances, and they could demonstrate a surprising degree of 'order within disorder'. In so far as riots were violent, they were clearly demonstrating a form of violence other than that manifested in purely interpersonal violence.[11]

V

The violence of war is beyond the scope of this book, but it is interesting to speculate what effect everyday violence has had on the way in which the wars that have intermittently punctuated English history have been fought. Some historians have suggested, for example, that the grim living conditions of the pre-1914 working class made their experience of the First World War less daunting than it would otherwise have been. Set against this is the view of the historian Dan Todman, who commented that 'The inhabitants of urban Glasgow might regularly have set about each other on sectarian lines, but they did not employ trench mortars, machine guns and flame-throwers.'[12] It is also interesting to speculate as to whether wars have tended to worsen everyday violence – whether, in other words, people who are given the task of killing become intrinsically more violent as a result. We are certainly now aware of the post-traumatic stress that wars can cause – we know that war can take a terrible mental toll – but it has to be admitted that when it comes to earlier periods the evidence is very patchy. John Keegan's brilliant reconstructions of the experience of fighting at Agincourt and Waterloo have given us some sense of what it was like to be in combat before the twentieth century, but that doesn't mean we can be sure of the impact of that experience on those doing the fighting.[13] And linking the experience of war to greater levels of violence among returning soldiers is very problematic.

At the end of the First World War it was anticipated that there would be a wave of violent crime among ex-servicemen, who had been brutalised at the Front by their experiences. The fear proved to be misplaced. Some British battalions in the Normandy campaign of 1944 were noted to be suffering from worryingly high levels of combat fatigue, possibly a sign of what today we would call post-traumatic stress – a psychological condition that can leave ex-combatants ill-fitted for a return to civilian life.[14] Yet post-war crime statistics do not decisively demonstrate a rise in violence after these soldiers returned home.[15]

VI

War occupies an unusual place in the annals of violence because it is legitimate: it is fought at the behest of the state. This can lead to some surreal judgements. President Johnson, for example, could deplore rising levels of violence in the United States at the same time as his B52s were raining down bombs on North Vietnam. But it's also a reminder that, as Max Weber pointed out many years ago, one of the defining characteristics of the modern state is its claim to maintain a monopoly on legitimate violence in the society it governs.[16] A state can declare war, kill tens of thousands of people, and argue that it is acting legally. Similarly, in times of peace, it can mutilate or take the lives of those who have transgressed its laws. In England up until 1868 criminals could still be executed in public. Up until well into the nineteenth century petty offenders, men and women alike, could be stripped to the waist and publicly whipped. In the case of public corporal punishment, the practice slowly declined in the course of that century, just as the taste for public execution dwindled in Victorian times. Both trends could be said to illustrate something, not just about the workings of the state but about changing attitudes among the public to pain and suffering, and hence, perhaps, violence, though it is always dangerous to assume an inexorable trend: just as flogging subsided, for example, one of England's periodic moral panics led to its almost immediate revival for men convicted of robbery.

The fact of state-sponsored violence has inevitably led some to question its legitimacy. One influential theorist was Frantz Fanon, whose book *The Wretched of the Earth*, first published in France in 1961, was a key text for rebels against colonialism and, a little later, for some leftist groups. It was written while the Algerian War of Independence was still being fought. (Fanon did not live to see either a free Algeria or to enjoy the book's success. In the year of publication he was diagnosed as having leukaemia, and died in Washington in December.)

For Fanon, violence is an essential part of the anti-colonial struggle:

But it so happens that for the colonised people this violence, because it constitutes their only work, invests their characters

> with positive and creative qualities. The practice of violence
> binds them together as a whole, since each individual forms a
> violent link in the great chain, a part of the great organism
> of violence which has surged upwards in reaction to the set-
> tler's violence in the beginning . . . At the level of individuals,
> violence is a cleansing force. It frees the native from his in-
> feriority complex and his despair and inaction; it makes him
> fearless and restores his self-respect.[17]

Fanon, then, raises an important point about the legitimacy, and morality, of violence in pursuit of a struggle against oppression. His writings
had comparatively little impact in England, although they were
espoused by elements within the New Left. The 1960s engendered
another classic work lodged firmly in contemporary politics, Hannah
Arendt's On Violence, which inter alia reminded its readers that, by the
time of the Cold War, state violence could obliterate humankind.[18]

And yet if the state is the arbiter of violence, most would argue that
it is also the guarantor against it. After all, the law – an expression of
state authority – helps restrain those violent passions to which, it
seems, humankind is prone. This was certainly the viewpoint of the
philosopher Thomas Hobbes, in his Leviathan of 1651. Writing in the
wake of the Civil War, Hobbes understandably felt that a strong, and
unchallengeable, central authority – a sovereign power – was essential
to the existence of civil society. Like many political theorists of the
seventeenth and eighteenth centuries, he imagined humans before the
installation of government living in a state of nature, which, for him,
was a grim place, 'a time of war, where every man is enemy to every
man . . . and the life of man solitary, poor, nasty, brutish and short.'
This is 'what manner of life there would be, where there were no common power to fear'. And for Hobbes it was the emergence of that
common, sovereign power which prevented the war of all against all,
and made civil society possible.[19] Hobbes took an unusually pessimistic
view of human nature but, as post-apocalyptic movie after post-apocalyptic movie has demonstrated, there is a strong conviction among

many that the existence of the state and its law-and-order apparatus is our main guarantor against the descent into violent anarchy.

A second major restraint is – or certainly has been – religion. Throughout the period covered in this book England was, in formal terms at least, a Christian country, and for most Christian thinkers violence is a bad thing. That doesn't necessarily make Christianity a peaceful religion, as various Middle Eastern peoples confronted by Crusaders in the high middle ages found to their cost, and as is suggested by the doctrine of the just war, developed as early as the fifth century by St Augustine. But the fact nevertheless remains that the Christian message is essentially one opposed to interpersonal violence.

Family ties, too, play a part in steering people away from violence. At the height of the Roger Crockett affair, Peers Crewe, keen to go and find where the fighting was in case any of his friends needed assistance, was pulled into his house by his prudent wife aided by their maidservant. The theme of responsibility to family is often to be found in writings on violence, notably tracts written against the practice of duelling. John Bennett, preaching a sermon against duelling in Manchester in 1783, reminded would-be duellists of their responsibilities to 'parents, perhaps tottering with age, who have nursed thee in infancy, guided thee through youth, and watched thee to manhood'. He pointed out that the duellist might also have 'a tender partner of thy cares': 'wilt thou plunge her into such inexpressible distress?' And then there might be children to be considered:

Thou hast children, who cry for help, and cling round thee for support. Wilt thou not hear their cries? Wilt thou not pity their helpless sorrows? Wilt thou not wipe their trickling tears, and wilt thou turn them into the world – comfortless and uninstructed – not only without a parent – but (what is infinitely worse) with the remembrance of one who *might* have lived the counsellor of their infancy, and the 'guide of their youth' – but who fell – hear it in conscience – hear it sensibility [sic] – who fell, untimely, by his own determination.[20]

Being married did not automatically stop a man from getting into fights. But for many it must have inculcated a sense of responsibility sufficient to lead them away from violence and other forms of criminality.

So if violence is a constant in human behaviour, its nature and extent – as well as attitudes towards it – have clearly changed over time. Until the nineteenth century, for example, men had licence to chastise their wives, their children and their servants. But as the Victorian era drew towards its close, such behaviour had become increasingly frowned upon. Even at a single given moment in time different people might hold very disparate, sometimes very muddled, views about violence. An eighteenth-century gentleman would be horrified to read about a labourer beating his wife to death, but prob-. ably would not think twice about involving himself in a potentially fatal duel. And there is plenty of evidence to suggest that even at the level of the individual, attitudes to violence can change over the course of the years: young, aggressive unmarried men could – and still can – turn very easily into more docile middle-aged husbands.

VII

When it comes to theories about violence, there is certainly no shortage of ideas. There are biological explanations, which concentrate on such fundamental issues as the genetic make-up of human beings, especially men, and on how aspects of the functioning of the human brain might inhibit or encourage violence among individuals. There are psychological theories, which concentrate on the impact of (to take the most obvious example) neglectful, abusive, or violent parenting, or the loss of parents or other important adults early in life. And there are sociological theories, which look at the social conditions likely to fuel violent behaviour, and at how violent individuals react to the world around them and to their fellow human beings. For the moment let me focus on two theoretical positions that are currently exercising historians who write on violence. The first of these is evolutionary psychology; the second is the concept of the 'civilising process' put forward by the German sociologist Norbert Elias.

The historian who has made the most sustained attempt to derive insights from evolutionary psychology is John Carter Wood. His ideas were set out in developed form in an article of 2007 in which he argued for a fundamental unity of human psychology: just as all human beings have a basically similar physical make-up, he suggests, so their mental processes are fairly uniform. Accordingly, Carter Wood cites Leda Cosmides and John Tooby to the effect that 'rather than a "blank slate" or all-purpose thinking machine, the brain is theorised as a collection of modular "regulatory circuits" that organise the way we interpret our experiences, inject certain recurrent concepts and motivations into our mental life, and provide universal frames of meaning that allow us to understand the actions and meanings of others'. Among the 'regulatory circuits' are those governing the human propensity to violence. And since it is present in all societies, even if at varying levels and inspiring different reactions, it's fair to assume that a tendency to violence is part of human evolution – a factor in the survival of the human race.[21]

Violence, then, comes down to the basic concept of the survival of the fittest, the term being applied not, as it so often is currently, to individuals, but rather to species, and corresponding closely to the Darwinian concept of natural selection. All males, it is argued, are programmed to compete for resources, of which perhaps the most important are sexual partners for reproductive purposes. Males will therefore fight to gain access to females. Only the strongest will manage to mate, and because the strongest prevail the species is thereby strengthened. Male competitiveness and consequently violence are thus a core part of the male psyche for evolutionary purposes. All successful species are adaptive, and this is one of the key ways in which the human race has adapted to survive.

There are problems with this theory – not least that evolutionary change occurs too slowly to explain the changes in patterns of

violence that can be traced in the historical record. But the theory
does seem to address one fundamental issue. As I have already
noted, it is predominantly men who are violent. Most historians
would see this as the outcome of cultures which are patriarchal, in
which male control is taken for granted, and in which at least some
men see a willingness to fight as an important component of masculinity and the maintenance of masculine honour. But the idea of the
part played in natural selection by male aggressiveness helps explain
why, historically, culture after culture has shared the attribute. Both
historically and currently, many male-on-male killings can be understood in terms of this evolutionary imperative. The pretexts may
sometimes be very trivial, but they are bound up with the maintenance of status and respect, part of a competitive struggle that has its
psychological and biological origins in the imperative for men to be
more aggressive over reproduction. This also explains why men
have a tendency to be risk-takers, and to become involved in violent
confrontations. The view that male violence has its roots not in culture, but in what was necessary for the human race to achieve
success in the selection process, therefore seems a tenable one.

   That said, most historians would still argue that culture is of fundamental importance to an understanding of violence. Surely, for
example, it is culture that helps explain the sometimes massive variations in homicide rates between different (and often adjacent)
regions of the world. Take, for example, some of the research in
what is perhaps the most important work arguing for the connection between evolutionary psychology and modern homicide,
Martin Daly and Margo Wilson's *Homicide*, published in 1988.[22] The
evidential base of Daly and Wilson's research is an analysis of murders committed in Detroit in 1972. At that time, over the nearby
Canadian border, homicides were running at a fiftieth of the rate
afflicting Detroit. Assuming that the Canadian authorities were as
good at detecting homicide as were their Detroit counterparts, the
explanation for this massive divergence can only be cultural. Even
within the United States, there are some striking variations in

murder rates between different cities. In 1996 Simi Valley, California, with a population of 107,000, suffered no homicides. San Antonio, Texas, a city with a population the same size, had a homicide rate of 55.3 per 100,000. As I explain later, the homicide rate in medieval England was massively higher than at present. Given that six or seven centuries is a mere blip in evolutionary terms, we have to assume that cultural differences determined this change. Even if we accept that human beings, and especially male human beings, are programmed to be aggressive or violent as an outcome of the dictates of natural selection in the human race's pre-history, it would appear that the consequences of that programming emerge through a set of very strong cultural filters.

This tension between evolutionary psychology on the one hand and studies of the influence of culture on the other has also been explored by those interested in primates: creatures whose behaviour (like that of many animal species) depends on that mix of basic programming, evolved traits, adjustment to the environment, the ability to learn and the ability to think that affects human action. Primates can, like humans, be seen as rational actors, whose behaviour is shaped by emotions and instincts, but there is considerable disagreement as to just how far their underlying make-up controls group behaviour. And the findings of one of the leading exponents of primate studies, the Canadian scholar Linda Marie Fedigan, add an interesting dimension to the problems of primate studies that are relevant to the historians of violence. She finds that primatologists face the same sort of problems defining animal aggression as historians and social scientists have in defining human violence, and also notes that studies of aggression among primates, more than most other areas of animal research, can be affected by 'the prevailing cultural attitudes of the period and the advocacy positions of researchers'.[23] In other words, even in apparently scientifically objective studies, the intellectual and cultural assumptions of those undertaking the research have a tendency to shape their findings. If it's a problem for animal behaviouralists, it's certainly an issue for historians.

Evolutionary psychology and primate studies, then, can certainly shed interesting light on human violence. But historians have tended to engage more with the work of the German sociologist Norbert Elias, best known for his two-volume work *The Civilising Process*, the first volume of which appeared, with a certain grim irony, in September 1939.[24] Elias was born into a comfortably off Jewish middle-class family in Breslau in Silesia (now the Polish city of Wroclaw) in 1897. He volunteered for war service in 1915, entering the German signal corps. In 1916 he was on the front line on the Somme, suffered a nervous breakdown as a result, and was posted back to Breslau as a medical orderly. There he resumed his education, and following a brief period of medical studies decided to focus on sociology. By 1930, after various vicissitudes, he was an assistant to Karl Mannheim, an associate of the Frankfurt School, a grouping of communist and leftist scholars. But in 1933 Hitler came to power, and Germany became an inhospitable place for Jewish intellectuals with leftist leanings: Elias's mother was to be killed in Auschwitz in 1941.

After a spell in Paris, Elias moved to Britain, where he was supported by a Jewish relief fund while he wrote *The Civilising Process*. Following a period of internment as an enemy alien after the Second World War broke out and several years teaching WEA classes at Cambridge, he moved to Leicester, teaching evening extension classes there and finally gaining a post at Leicester University in 1954, where he worked until his retirement in 1962. From 1965 he based himself at Amsterdam, and also held visiting fellowships and professorships at a number of German universities. He died in 1990.

His paradigm of the civilising process, virtually forgotten since 1939, enjoyed something of a vogue among Dutch and German academics and students after his move to Amsterdam, perhaps its most notable adherent being the Dutch historian Pieter Spierenburg, who has researched and published extensively on the history of violence.[25] And although his ideas have certainly not won universal acceptance, they have proved too influential to be ignored. Spierenburg and the Swiss criminologist Manuel Eisner, author of a remarkable synthesis of evidence of European homicide over the last seven centuries, would go further. Both have suggested that Elias's paradigm is the one that seems to offer a way forward in organising the available data.[26]

Elias's objective was to provide a coherent theoretical framework that would explain what appeared to be a long-term increase in individual self-control within European societies between the middle ages and Elias's own time. Any summary of his views is bound to be somewhat simplistic, but essentially his argument was that changes in attitude resulted from the processes of state formation. He traced a gradual transition from societies based on knightly concepts of honour, which he saw as characteristic of the middle ages, to the relatively pacified courtly societies of the sixteenth and seventeenth centuries when the state, to employ that concept of Max Weber's, achieved a monopoly of violence. The decisive factor in all this was the rise of monarchical absolutism. Under absolute monarchies the nobility sloughed off their bellicose proclivities, in particular as part of their reconfiguration as courtiers. As institutions enforcing the authority of the state became more stable, so the enhanced levels of stability and security in society at large facilitated economic development and brought about more sophisticated, peaceful interactions, motivated by self-interest, between different social groups and individuals. Capitalism thus played its own crucial role in the formation of the modern nation state: it not only broadened and developed social networks, but also fostered those qualities of prudence and calculation that Elias considered to have been absent from the middle ages. The psychological corollary of these processes was the emergence of a personality that shied away from open displays of aggression and regarded spontaneous emotions with suspicion. Elias's was a paradigm of the transition from medieval to modern society to set against those of Karl Marx and Max Weber.

Anybody reading Elias for the first time will be struck by the resonances between what he says about the development of psychological controls and those proposed by Freud – scarcely surprising, of course, given that Elias came to intellectual maturity in the progressive intellectual circles of the 1920s and early 1930s. When discussing those psychic controls which characterise modernity, for example, he in effect regards the functioning of something very like the Freudian 'super-ego' – that is, the element of our minds that restrains our instinctive behaviour – as one of the essential driving forces. What differentiates his approach from that of Freud is that he was concerned with the historical processes which permitted the construction of modern mentality, and that he saw the development of greater psychological controls over sexuality as only one aspect of the 'civilising process'.

Although it provides a useful framework for discussion, there are a number of problems with Elias's civilising process. The first is that it is based on a view of history that is un-nuanced, not to say simplistic, particularly when Elias is describing the supposed omnipresent violence of medieval times.[27] One suspects that he was unduly influenced by a book that we shall meet properly in the next chapter, Johan Huizinga's *The Waning of the Middle Ages*, probably the most influential work on medieval history published in the twentieth century, and one that stressed – arguably, hugely over-stressed – the uncontrolled passions and spontaneity of medieval people. A further objection is that Elias's model of change is essentially a top-down one. His focus is on the elite, and he has little to say on how changes in the social psychology of those at the top of society permeated through the rest of the population. His assumption is that the population at large simply adopted the ideas of their betters. Although the chronology of this process is left rather vague, Elias seems to regard it as a fairly recent development. (If so, his view runs counter to the evidence of much recent research into local English history from the sixteenth century onwards, which persuasively suggests that, however violent certain individuals might have been, their communities generally craved peace and stability, and that the creation of law and order stemmed as much as from the community as from those in positions of authority.) It could also be argued that Elias's theory is too Eurocentric. Certainly, it would be interesting to see if it could be applied to the Ottoman Empire, Mughal India, or Tokugawa Japan. And, finally, the argument has a certain circularity to it: people seem more civilised as the centuries move on, Elias argues, so there must be a civilising process at work to make them so. Nevertheless, and even accepting all the problems that exist with Elias's theory, his concept of a civilising process does provide us with more than an interesting overarching, if flawed, interpretation: often it provides a very useful paradigm for understanding how social developments in England took place.

I've already touched on the links between Elias and Freud, and it is worth saying a little more here about psychoanalytic theory and the analysis of violence. Freud himself had little to say about violence in his early writings, his focus being more on the implications of sex and sexual repression on the development of human beings and civilisation more generally. But – probably in reaction to the horrors of the First World War – the themes of aggression, destructiveness, and what Freud called the death wish, became more salient in his later works, receiving detailed treatment in his *Civilisation and its Discontents* of 1930. Here he described aggression as an essential element in the human (or, to be more accurate, male) psyche. 'A powerful measure of desire for aggression has to be reckoned as part of their instinctive endowment', he wrote of his fellow humans, slipping into almost Hobbesian mode as he added that 'civilised society is perpetually menaced with disintegration through this primary hostility of men one to another'. Only culture, along with what Freud termed 'reaction-formations in men's minds', could keep aggression in check – the culture and behaviour that comes with the realisation that violent urges have to be curbed if civil society is to flourish.[28]

One does not have to be a Freudian to recognise the power of an approach that views violence as an innate human quality that has to be controlled. According to this interpretation, violence can be characterised as a psychological phenomenon with behavioural consequences, rather than a form of behaviour with psychological consequences. There is, in other words, tucked away in all of us, a potential for aggression, destructiveness, violence and cruelty, which most of us manage – for the most part – to suppress. We might be able to do so because we feel empathy with our potential victim. We might be able to do so because we feel that it is in our interest to live by the code that you should do as you would be done by. We might have ethical or religious objections to violence. We might fear the legal consequences of a breach of the peace. Or we might nurse the suspicion that our adversary is more powerful than we are. Obviously these restraints don't always work: there are plenty of otherwise perfectly reasonable people who commit acts of violence, just as there are hardened aggressors we label criminals, psychopaths or sadists.

In Anthony Burgess's *A Clockwork Orange* the state controls violence through drugs and aversion therapy. In the real world, fortunately, its decline has been as much willed as dictated, and where attempts have been made to deal with violent or abusive offenders by encouraging them to adopt the habits of responsibility and restraint, these attempts have at least been permissive.[29] But has violence within the community really declined in the way Elias thought it to have done, particularly bearing in mind that evidence for our propensity to aggression: two world wars fought within the last century? How can we be sure and how can we measure that decline?

VIII

Historians of violence can draw on a plethora of historical documents and literature, but their starting point tends to be national crime statistics. And, of course, it is crime statistics that inform the perceptions that politicians, senior police officers, newspaper editorials, and the public at large have of the state and extent of crime in Britain. First published early in the nineteenth century, from 1857 crime statistics were collected by the police, collated by the Home Office, and then published annually as the *Judicial Statistics*. Changes in the way offences were categorised can sometimes make straightforward historical comparison tricky. Nevertheless, a number of categories of violent offence stayed broadly unchanged from the late nineteenth century to the 1960s, which means that for that period at least it is possible to establish and examine trends. The categories in question are murder (victim aged one or over), murder (victim aged under one), attempted murder, threats and conspiracy to murder, manslaughter, felonious wounding, malicious wounding, rape, indecent assault on a female, and robbery. Many of these categories remain part of criminal law today.

There are no similar officially generated statistics for earlier periods, but we are fortunate that England enjoyed a precociously developed legal system that allows us to trace patterns of homicide back at least into the thirteenth century. This system was gradually formalised into one whereby serious offences – felonies – including homicide, were usually tried at the assizes.[30] These courts, operating between the late thirteenth century and 1971, were perhaps the longest running of all legal institutions, and the assize system was a very neat method of bringing central, royal justice into the provinces. Criminals would be apprehended locally, given a pre-trial investigation by a justice of the peace, and either sent to the county gaol (normally a ruinous castle) to await trial, or be bound over to appear in court. England was divided for the purposes of the assizes into groupings of counties known as circuits. Two senior judges from Westminster would be allotted to each of these circuits and would, quite literally, 'ride' round them twice a year, trying criminals in the county towns where the assizes were normally held. The assizes, then, were national in scope and regular in their occurrence. They nevertheless pose certain problems for historians.

Unfortunately, many records have been lost: for the period between about 1550 and 1650, for example, they exist only for the Home Circuit, comprising the counties of Essex, Hertfordshire, Kent, Surrey and Sussex. What's more the records that do survive are difficult to use (indictments, for example, were written in Latin until 1733) and sometimes damaged. And, of course, they generally allow us only to make comparisons on a county basis: creating anything like a national pattern of serious crime from assize records is simply impossible before the late eighteenth century.

Although serious crime was tried at the assizes, there were many other courts in medieval and early modern England at which violent offences might be tried. At a very local level, in the middle ages through to the seventeenth century, the manor court might try cases of simple assault. Assaults were also tried at the quarter sessions, held four times a year for each county, and the occasional homicide might be tried at these tribunals as late as the seventeenth century. Up to about that point homicides might also be tried at local borough courts, which had a right of gaol delivery, and these could also try assault. There was, moreover, a system of ecclesiastical courts. These would not normally be empowered to try violent offences, but the odd case of, for example, brawling in a churchyard might come to them, while their jurisdiction over marital issues meant that they dealt with cases of violence or abuse within marriage. Given perfect record survival, it would in theory be possible to gain an impression of the total levels of prosecuted violence in a given county over a given time period: but record survival is never perfect, and working through all of the records if it were would in any case be an impossible task.

For this reason statistically based discussion of long-term trends in violence in England has tended to centre on figures for homicides. There are strong grounds for regarding these as inherently reliable. Murder, it could be argued, has always been regarded as a heinous crime, and is therefore more likely than most to be reported. There is much to say about the historical record of homicide statistics, but, in brief, the generally accepted pattern is that levels of homicide were high (maybe averaging 20 per 100,000 of population) in the middle ages, and then dropped gradually to about 1 per 100,000 of population by 1800. Rates stayed low over the nineteenth and first half of the twentieth century, and then rose again in the late twentieth century.

Our knowledge of homicide has been enhanced by the fact that from the late twelfth century (the first reference comes in 1194) there existed in the form of the coroner an official whose duties included, and over time came mainly to focus upon, violent or suspicious deaths.[31] We know little about the detail of coroners' inquests before the eighteenth century (the 1572 Nantwich episode gives us a rare glimpse of a coroner's inquest in action) but we do at least have, from the middle ages onwards, the bare bones of their records. These at first were normally single parchment strips with the details of the inquest given in closely written Latin, recording not just murders but also suicides and accidental deaths. Among this latter category we find an unfortunate medieval Londoner who died when the seat of a privy he was using collapsed beneath him, casting him into the cesspit below, and a bell ringer at Chester Cathedral who died after he became caught up in the bell-ropes.[32]

There are inevitably complications attached to using homicide statistics to determine fluctuations in homicide over the long term or comparisons between the past and the present. One such is the issue of medical intervention: advances in medicine mean that a large, and unknowable, proportion of those who died through interpersonal violence in the middle ages would survive under current conditions, so that what might have been recorded as murder then would be designated assault today. It is also not an absolute given that every homicide was regarded with such horror that it was automatically reported. Nor are even seemingly reliable statistics always what they seem. On the one hand, for example, the well-recorded homicide rates in Victorian England seem to point to an inherently stable society; on the other, there is evidence to suggest that the reason for their consistent nature is that funds were available to prosecute only a limited number of homicide cases each year. Many possible murders were, therefore, categorised otherwise, most frequently as accidental deaths.

And, of course, categorising murder is not always a straightforward proposition. In 1892, for example, three-year-old Ann

Concannon was found dead with her head in a privy in Liverpool. At first it was thought that she had suffocated to death. Her mother, however, reported that the girl had been wearing new boots and a pair of gold earrings the day she died, and none of these had been recovered when the body was found. The conclusion of the police and the local coroner was therefore that she had been robbed and then left next to the privy into which she had fallen accidentally. (An alternative, more sinister theory was advanced by one of the surgeons involved in the inquest, who thought he had found evidence of sexual assault.) Thus we have a death that could have been the result of an accident or the outcome of a robbery or the consequence of a sexual assault. We also happen to have a case that never made its way into official police statistics: we only know about it because it was reported in the *Liverpool Mercury*.[33]

If murder statistics can sometimes be somewhat tricky to interpret, those for other forms of violent crime are frequently deeply problematic. In cases of sexual assault and rape, perhaps more so in earlier periods than at present, victims might be prevented by feelings of shame from bringing a prosecution. Assault might also be seriously under-reported, certainly when it occurred in 'rough' working-class cultures where fighting was regarded as a normal part of life. Thus recorded cases of assault, even today, must be assumed to fall massively below actual numbers of assaults committed. The Islington Crime Survey, for example, based on victim interviews rather than police statistics, suggests that only about a third of assault cases are reported to the police, and that only 6 per cent of all assaults actually enter the official record.[34] And, before the official categorisation of violent offences, which came into being in the nineteenth century, assault was an impossibly wide category, covering everything from being shaken by the lapels to being brutally beaten. In most instances, the indictments preserved among the assize and quarter sessions rolls provide little indication of what exactly the circumstances of a pre-modern assault were, and what level of violence occurred.

The nature of surviving documents also makes it difficult to trace recidivism in pre-modern periods. Today, computerised records allow us very easily to identify re-offenders and build criminal biographies. Equivalent mechanisms simply didn't exist in the past, and it's by chance alone that we get a glimpse of someone who made a career of violence, and then often only because the violence involved was so frequent or so extreme. The Smith family who lived in Eccles in Lancashire in the early seventeenth century are a rare case in point. William Smith and his two sons, Robert and another William, although already bound over to be of good behaviour, variously tried to pick a fight with John Woodward, fell out with and struck another man over a bar bill, threatened another man for the same reason, and threatened a further man with a knife. In May 1611 six members of the Smith family stormed into the house of Thomas Peele in Eccles, armed with staves, pitchforks, swords and daggers, and threatened two men who were there, one of whom was menaced again on a separate occasion by a gang of Smiths, who included William the elder's wife, Margery. In total, forty-four violent offences (generally described as assaults or affrays) were alleged against William Smith the elder and his sons together, a further twelve were listed against Robert Smith, and a further six against William Smith the younger. Living in the same community as these people must have been a trying experience.[35]

IX

Criminal statistics are, then, a very imperfect guide to levels of violence in both past and present society; but they clearly have their uses, and can provide some very helpful insights into what proportion of offenders and victims were male or female, what their occupational background or social status was, and what punishments they received. Such information can play an important role when it comes to assessing the imposing range of other documents still in existence that give us anecdotal or qualitative impressions of violence.

Court records can on occasion provide fascinating glimpses into the personalities and society of earlier periods, as the evidence gathered about the death of Roger Crockett demonstrates. The key document here, used by the law enforcement system from the mid sixteenth century onwards, was known as the deposition or the examination. It was the forerunner of the modern witness statement. Unfortunately the deposition was not what was technically known as a 'matter of record', and consequently most depositions, usually written during the pre-trial investigations by justices of the peace, and often very short, terse documents, were simply thrown away later. Among those that survive, though, there are some that are astonishingly graphic and dramatic. Consider the depositions given by Alice Compton of Newton township in Manchester, raped by two soldiers named Murray and Wroe in 1729. According to Alice, the two men demanded bread from her as she walked on the highway, and when she said she had none Murray threw her to the ground 'and swore he would f—k her'. She struggled, and begged them not to 'meddle' with her, 'but all her stratagems and endeavours proved in vain for the said Murray in the highway forced this deponent down and pull'd up this deponents clothes to her naked belly'. She was screaming, but the men threatened to cut her throat if she made any more noise after which

> the said Murray did then with force and violence enter this deponent and with force enter'd this deponent's body and actually debauch'd her. But the said Wroe lay a good time on the said deponent and swore damn her he never saw such a woman in his life he could not get his prick to stand whereupon Murray said damn thee get done don't lie long on the poor woman or some such.

After this the two men demanded money from her, and took all she had: threepence halfpenny. We do not know if the men were ever apprehended and convicted. What we do have is a powerful account of the experience of a rape victim nearly three centuries ago.[36]

Outside the realm of court records, information about early cases is often hard to come by. Medieval chronicles are useful for general accounts of major local and national events, but they rarely deal with specific instances of interpersonal violence and, when they do, tend to use them as a springboard for a moral commentary. That said, there are occasional beams of light in the darkness, as for example this superbly evocative passage from Thomas Walsingham's *Historia Anglicana* that describes the mayhem in London accompanying the 1381 outbreak of civil disorder known as the Peasants' Revolt:

> For to them it was a solemn game, if they could seize anyone who did not make fealty to them or failed to co-operate with them or who was especially hated by an individual rebel, to drag off his hood immediately and to rush into the street with their usual clamour to kill him. Nor did they show any reverence to holy places but killed those whom they hated even if they were within churches and in sanctuary. I have heard from a trustworthy witness that thirty Flemings [foreign merchants were targeted by the rebels] were violently dragged out of the church of the Austin friars in London and executed in the open street. Seventeen others were taken from another parish church in London. All these, to the contempt of holy sanctuary and by a cursed mob who at that time feared neither God nor man, paid the like penalty of losing their heads.[37]

Walsingham was a monk at St Albans, which was one of the local centres of unrest in 1381. It's tempting to think that the vividness of his account of events in London was in part informed by his own local experiences.

By the late sixteenth century a new literary form had arisen: the murder pamphlet – popular, sensational, and up to the early eighteenth century, at least, characterised by a distinctly moralistic tone that placed murder and its detection and punishment very firmly in the context of the workings of divine providence and the Christian worldview. Its rather more secular nineteenth-century successor was to be the penny dreadful. But both were increasingly to give ground to the popular newspaper, which started to take hold in the eighteenth century and which achieved mass circulation by the middle of Queen Victoria's reign. Originating in the seventeenth-century *coranto*, it was initially, like its medieval chronicle forebear, principally concerned with 'important' and, above all, international events. But by early-Georgian times, as a network of national newspapers started to develop, and, alongside it, a lively provincial press (most county towns had at least one newspaper by the mid-century), attention was increasingly paid to accounts of local crimes and trials of note. The *York Courant* for 10 April 1781, for example, includes the following description of an attack made by one Joseph Linwood on Margaret Lee as she made her way home to Huntingdon, a village just outside York:

> Not satisfied with taking the woman's property, he used every argument, every threat to force her compliance with his desires. Finding himself so strongly opposed to obtain his wish, he took her by the feet and dragged her for a considerable way on a plowed field, adjoining to the road which leads to Huntington, till her clothes were almost torn off, and himself out of breath. He exercised more cruelties than this, but finding them equally abortive, he at last asked her if she knew him; but being answered in the negative (tho' at the same time she perfectly recollected him, yet afraid to confess it) he permitted her to depart.

Having described the crime in these comparatively brief and restrained terms (popular Victorian newspaper accounts would be far more extensive and lurid), the paper tells us that Linwood was arrested, tried and sentenced to death, and that the judge expressed the view that the attempted rape was as serious an offence as the robbery (itself a capital crime). The twenty-seven year old left behind a widow and three small children.

X

Outside the realm of legal documents and records, and journalists' accounts of individual cases, there is much to be gleaned about contemporary attitudes to violence from the substantial body of literature, written between the middle ages and Victorian times, that was designed to inculcate good Christian conduct in gentlemen and gentlewomen. By its very nature it tended to offer an idealised view of how society might be, but, apart from anything else, it often serves as a useful corrective to the temptation to believe that because a certain type of behaviour was widespread at a particular time, it was also universally accepted. Duelling, for example, might have been quite common among those in the upper echelons of society, but it's clear from the moralising literature of the time that not all contemporaries approved. Thus when the former lawyer and would-be poet Richard Brathwaite published his *The English Gentleman* in 1630, he was at pains not only to condemn revenge in general (it was, he said, one of the 'three violent passions incident to youth', the other two being lust and ambition) but to criticise duelling in particular:

> O Gentlemen, how many of your rank and quality have perished by standing upon these terms; how many, and those of the choicest and selected'st rank, have exposed themselves to the extremist danger, whereby they might gain themselves the style of valiant! How many, even on trifling occasions, have gone into the field, and in their heat of blood have fallen? Sure I am, that their dear country hath felt their loss, to whom in all due respect they should have tendered both love and life, and not have made prodigal expense of that, which might have been a means to strengthen and support her state.[38]

Other advice books took a similar line, while more general observations on the ungodliness of violence could be found in commentaries on the Ten Commandments, another literary genre which flourished between the sixteenth and nineteenth centuries. And it was not just young gentlemen to whom books of advice were directed. Heads of households could also read books, written from a godly perspective, that would tell them how to run their families and discipline their servants. *Inter alia*, these works discussed under what circumstances servants or children could be physically chastised and, interestingly, contained some of the earliest suggestions that wife-beating was an unacceptable practice.

Imaginative literature can similarly give us useful insights into contemporary views and prejudices, from medieval *chansons de geste*, to Elizabethan and Jacobean revenge tragedies, to novels and contemporary films and dramas. And then there are the snippets that can be garnered from more personal literature, such as autobiographies, diaries and letters. Pepys's famous diary is a case in point. Its author was not, as a rule, a violent man (though he admits to hitting his wife on occasion). His diary, however, is peppered with mentions of duels and brawls, often involving very highly placed people, and sometimes – to us, at least – almost farcical in their level of triviality. In an entry for September 1661, for example, Pepys records how a dispute over precedence between the French and the Spanish Ambassadors spiralled into a street fight between their servants in which a number of Frenchmen, two Spaniards and several of the French Ambassador's coach horses were killed, along with an unfortunate English bystander who was shot accidentally.

Reporting on events further down the social scale, he describes in July 1664 what seems to have been an institutionalised conflict between London's butchers and weavers, 'between whom hath been ever an old competition for mastery'. He talks of a prize fight he witnessed, conducted with swords, between a butcher and a waterman, which ended in a general brawl when the watermen who had been watching thought the butcher had acted unfairly and stormed the stage the two men were fighting on. He also notes a violent altercation that took place between two coachmen, one employed by Sir Henry Finch, the other by the King, at the end of which the King's coachman was struck with a whip and lost an eye as a result. Pepys's London was not a tranquil place.[39]

His reference to a prize fight reminds us that it's not just written records that can provide us with windows on to aspects of past violence. The changing ways in which popular games and sports were played and observed can be revealing of underlying attitudes, too. Take, for example, the folk-football match, formerly played on Shrove Tuesday or at Whitsun. Essentially, it was a free-for-all involving men of opposing villages, or from different ends of the same village, who would turn out and spend a day getting a ball to some point in the rival team's territory. In its time it enjoyed great popularity. As the nineteenth century progressed, however, local authorities and respectable opinion began to view its waywardness with increasing disquiet. Simultaneously, various sports – including football – became increasingly bound by rules of conduct. That doesn't mean that aggression was written out of sport. The perceived virtues of manliness and 'pluck' continued to hold sway, attributes which were connected with an ability to take and give out violence. The Regency man about town Pierce Egan even went so far as to suggest that boxing demonstrated the superiority of the Englishman over the knife- or stiletto-wielding foreigner:

In England, the FIST only is used, where malice is not suffered to engender and poison the composition, and induce the inhabitants to deeds which their souls abhor and shudder at – but an immediate appeal to boxing – the bystanders make a ring, and where no unfair advantage is to be taken of each other. The fight done, the hand is given, in token of peace; resentment vanishes; and the cause generally buried in oblivion. This generous mode of conduct is not owing to any particular rule laid down by education – it is an inherent principle – the impulse of the moment – acted upon by the most ignorant and inferior ranks of the people.[40]

This is a fascinating insight into one man's view of 'good' and 'bad' violence – both very slippery categories that have shifted constantly over the centuries.

XI

One final point remains to be made. It has to be recognised that, whatever the mores of a particular era, every period contains some individuals who are by nature very gentle, and others who are extraordinarily violent. A number of modern studies have shown that people who were aggressive as youngsters are three times more likely to acquire convictions for violent offences as adults than those who were not. Some, like the seventeenth-century Smith family of Eccles, enjoy violence, are good at it, and are willing to deploy it with minimal justification. And, at the very least, as a student of football hooliganism has put it, 'there will always be young men who, when honour has been felt to be transgressed, take a punch and give two in return'.[41]

My intention in this book is not to give what might be termed a 'punch by punch' account of six and a half centuries of violent conduct in England. Instead I shall be taking a number of running themes and, in large measure, grouping my analysis around these. I shall also be looking at types of violence that flourished in particular periods: the duel in the seventeenth and eighteenth centuries; the killing of newborn children in the same period; serial killers from Victorian times onwards. At times I will illustrate my arguments with statistics, but as a rule I have preferred to adopt a more anecdotal approach, selecting stories that point up what violence has felt like and meant at specific times in our history, and how its nature has changed. Apart from anything else, I feel this approach helps throw light on what is happening today.

I should add that the English experience lies at the core of this work. The experiences of the other countries within the British Isles have been different. Moreover the vagaries of the survival of court

records and other sources make it difficult to trace the history of violence in Scotland or Ireland over the same time-span. That said,
since criminal statistics from the nineteenth century have lumped
England and Wales together, aspects of the Welsh experience do feature in this study.

I have said that my ultimate goal is to shed some light on long-
term changes and patterns. But, as I have also intimated, any history
of violence is also formed from a welter of individual stories. Not
only do these have much to tell us about the human condition and
the nature of society in earlier times, they also have a compelling
immediacy. So let me close this introduction with a tantalisingly
bizarre one.

William Moore, a draper living in Lewes in Sussex, suffered, as
the coroner's inquest describing his death in 1682 put it, from 'stink-
ing breath', which he was anxious to cure. Three men, Robert
Brinkhurst, Thomas Lester and Samuel Driver, all from Lewes,
obtained some arsenic, and sent it to Moore with a forged covering
letter purporting to come from a friend of his, John Newton, assur-
ing him that the arsenic was a medicine appropriate for the curing of
halitosis. Moore took the arsenic mixed with sugar, and died five
days later. Only Brinkhurst was identified as a killer by the coroner's
jury, and we do not know if he ever stood trial.[42] Nor do we have any
idea why he and his confederates should have wanted to kill William
Moore. The account of Moore's death, held in the King's Bench
records in the National Archives, remains shrouded in mystery. But
it reminds us that behind the overviews, the trends and the theories
are individuals and individual tragedies.

PART I

'NO MAN WAS SURE OF HIS LIFE': ENGLAND IN THE MIDDLE AGES

In 1381 an army of peasants from Kent and Essex marched on London, destroying buildings, freeing prisoners, and killing the Archbishop of Canterbury and the Lord Treasurer. The 'Peasants' Revolt' was the largest popular uprising that took place in medieval England and contributed to the myth of the country's 'violent Middle Ages'.

CHAPTER I

THE VIOLENT MIDDLE AGES?

I

In 2002 the former Serbian leader Slobodan Milošević, on trial at the War Crimes Tribunal at The Hague for his part in the atrocities committed in Bosnia, Croatia and Kosovo in the 1990s, was accused by the prosecutor Carla Del Ponte of having acted with 'medieval savagery'. He was, it was alleged, guilty of charges that ranged from genocide, to complicity in genocide, to the deportation and murder of civilians, to attacks on individuals, to the plunder of private and public property, to the destruction or damage of historical monuments and educational and religious institutions. It was a grim roll call of appalling crimes. And it came at the end of a century that had already seen more than its fair share of violence and suffering: the First World War had resulted in the deaths of upwards of 9 million fighting men;[1] the Second had witnessed the loss of around 50 million combatants and civilians; the Nazi regime in Germany had murdered 6 million Jews, and similarly condemned to death gipsies, homosexuals, communists, socialists, trades unionists, and people judged to be mentally sub-normal. Stalin's regime in Russia had killed perhaps 10 million people in the 1930s, Mao's in Communist China even more than that in the 1950s and 1960s; further such atrocities were committed by the Khmer Rouge in Cambodia (2 million murdered) and the Hutu in Rwanda (800,000 killed). Yet, strangely, it was 'medieval savagery', rather than, as would surely have been wholly appropriate, 'twentieth-century savagery', that was held to characterise Milošević's conduct. Clearly, Carla Del Ponte's choice of words was meant to strike a responsive chord among those listening.

There is certainly no doubt that the popular view of the middle ages is that it was a peculiarly violent period. Many scholars have claimed as much, too. The first chapter of Johan Huizinga's hugely influential *The Waning of the Middle Ages*, originally published in Dutch in 1919, is entitled 'The Violent Tenor of Life' in the English translation.[2] A few years earlier, Achille Luchaire wrote a book on the reign of Philip Augustus in which he argued that medieval France was a country in which there was so little personal security that individuals were left with no option but to protect themselves and their property as best they could.

Luchaire's views were echoed a generation later by the great French historian Marc Bloch (himself a victim of twentieth-century savagery when he was shot by the Gestapo for Resistance activities in 1944), and then again in the following generation by the eminent French medieval historian Georges Duby. English medieval historians since T. F. Tout, in the early 1900s, have held a similar view.[3] John Keegan, for example, in his ground-breaking study of the experience of armed combat, suggested that 'the commonplace character of violence in medieval life' would have made those English soldiers fighting at the Battle of Agincourt in 1415 much less sensitive to killing at close quarters than their modern equivalents would be.[4] For many, the medieval world is the one evoked by Barbara W. Tuchman in her popular history of the fourteenth century, in which casual violence, cruel punishments for criminals watched by appreciative crowds, torture and violent sports often involving cruelty to animals were commonplace, and brutally reared parents passed on similar treatment to their own offspring.[5]

For Huizinga what was telling was not medieval violence *per se* but the violence of medieval emotions, an insight that takes us back to the psychological approach of Norbert Elias touched on in the Introduction to this book (Elias did, in fact, draw heavily on Huizinga). And Elias, for his part, was at pains in *The Civilising Process* to stress what he felt to be the unpredictability of medieval people, and their tendency to indulge in sudden and marked mood swings:

> Not that people were always going around with fierce looks, drawn brows, and martial countenances as the clearly visible symbols of their warlike prowess. On the contrary, a moment ago they were joking, now they mock each other, one word leads to another, and suddenly from the midst of laughter they find themselves in the fiercest feud.

He goes on to describe 'the sudden flaring and uncontrollable force of their hatred and belligerence'.[6] For him, as for so many other commentators, medieval men and women had yet to acquire the inhibitions characteristic of the modern psyche. Quite simply, they had less self-control; they were directly driven by their feelings. And Elias was in no doubt as to the general nastiness of the middle ages. For him, this was a world where, to judge from contemporary manuscript illuminations, a ragged peasant might well disembowel a horse while a pig sniffed at his half-exposed bottom; where men laboured dolefully at the plough in place of beasts; where after public executions the bodies of dead criminals were left to rot on the gallows. In such a world violence was only to be expected.

So much, then, for popular impressions of the medieval world in all its violence. But is it possible to create a more nuanced picture? It has to be admitted at the outset that there are considerable obstacles in the way of this: many contemporary records have been lost or are incomplete, and creating any sort of statistical analysis that might give us a sense of shifting patterns of behaviour is fraught with problems (we cannot even be sure, for instance, what the true population of England was at any given point in the middle ages). That said, though, thanks to the precocity of the country's royal justice system, we do at least have court records dating back to the thirteenth century (England is the only country to have such an early sequence), and these can be very revealing, not only when it comes to trying to establish just how violent society was at particular periods, but also in reviewing the sorts of violent crime being committed.

A pioneer researcher here was the American historian James Buchanan Given who, in 1977, published a study of medieval homicide based on surviving court records, especially those hundred or so surviving parchment rolls produced by the royal justices on eyre (eyres were itinerant courts aimed at bringing royal justice into the regions, and eyre rolls recorded their proceedings). His particular focus was on records dating from between 1201 and 1276 relating to Bedfordshire, Kent, Norfolk, Oxfordshire, Warwickshire and the cities of London and Bristol, involving 2,434 victims of homicide and 3,492 alleged perpetrators.

One of the most striking findings to emerge from Given's research was just how widely homicide rates seemed to vary from area to area. Rural Norfolk, for example, appeared to have a very low average of 9 homicides per 100,000, while at the other extreme the level of killings in Warwickshire ran at 47 per 100,000 (why this should have been remains a mystery). The figures for Bedfordshire, Kent and Oxfordshire were, by contrast, closer together at 22, 23 and 18 per 100,000 respectively.[7] While it's dangerous to extrapolate too confidently from all this, Given's research – broadly supported by the findings of others – does seem to suggest that a conservative working average for rural England in the thirteenth century was about 20 homicides per 100,000.[8] By any standards this is an astonishingly high number. After all, by 1800 the countrywide average had fallen to 1 in 100,000. Today, the figure for England and Wales is 1.15 per 100,000. As early as 1873 that pioneering historian of crime Luke Owen Pike, comparing the 88 homicide cases recorded in Yorkshire alone in 1348 with the 250 homicides recorded annually in England and Wales in his own time, commented that 'the security of life is now at least eighteen times as great as it was in the age of chivalry'.[9]

One might have expected homicide rates to be higher in medieval towns than in the countryside of that time – just as they are today – but Given's research did not support this. In London, for example, the eyre rolls for 1244 and 1276 recorded 199 victims or 12 per 100,000, while in Bristol the rolls for 1227 and 1248 listed a mere 16 murders – just 4 per 100,000 of population. It has to be said, though, that other research does not always support these findings. While, for example, one analysis of a London eyre roll of 1278 is broadly in line with Given's findings, suggesting that there were about 6 cases of homicide a year, or (assuming that London's population at the time was about 40,000) about 15 cases per 100,000 of population annually, a generation later the annual level appears to have been as high as 52 – or 36 per 100,000.

And then there was Oxford. The first of England's university towns, it was, very early on, prey to simmering tensions between town and gown, which came to a head in the St Scholastica's Day riot of 1355.[10] The cause of these was trivial enough: a dispute between a group of students and the landlord of a tavern at Carfax, during which the students threw a quart pot of wine in his face and beat him up. Three days of full-blown riots followed, at the end of which the townsfolk, reinforced by local villagers, worsted the students. In the process several people were killed, a number injured, and considerable damage was done to university property.

This was, of course, an exceptional event but Carl I. Hammer Jr.'s pioneering study of fourteenth-century Oxford suggests that there was a violent undertow to town life even in apparently quieter times.[11] By his calculations, Oxford in the years before the Black Death (1348–9) was inhabited by around 5,500 townspeople, university servants and employees, and by 1,500 or so 'scholars' – in other words, its total population was in the region of 6,000 to 6,500. If this was so, then Hammer's study of a run of 66 inquests between 1342 and 1348 suggests that Oxford's homicide rate during this period might have been as high as 120 per 100,000 thousand of population. As ever, there are problems with this apparently scientific figure.

Hammer's sample is a very small one: only 36 of the inquests he looked at actually involved homicide, suggesting quite a low annual frequency, ranging from 2 in 1347/8 to 9 in 1346/7. Nevertheless, relative to the size of Oxford's population, the homicide rate was strikingly high.

All the evidence indicates that what made the town so volatile was its student population – in other words, its high proportion of young males. Hammer certainly came across instances of violence perpetrated by women – for example, a woman who was accused of drowning her baby girl – and occasionally of killings that occurred within families or households, though not among affluent ones (even at this early date killings rarely happened in the more affluent parts of town). But most homicides seem to have involved men in non-domestic situations. Stabbing caused the majority; a few deaths were inflicted by arrows; and a few by staffs. In 1298, for example, a riot broke out between students and university servants on the High, following an earlier incident during which students had assaulted the town bailiffs and some of their number had been arrested. Shops were wrecked, passing townsfolk were assaulted, and in the midst of all this a shop owner, Edward of Hales, fired an arrow from his upstairs window, fatally wounding a student named Fulk Nermit.

Throughout this period, Oxford undergraduates were divided along geographical lines between 'Northerners' and 'Southerners', and this division, like that between town and gown, could on occasion lead to fatal internecine conflict. The undergraduate Luke de Horton, for example, died at the hands of a fellow student in the course of a brawl in which he almost certainly played no part – he happened to step out of his house into Catte Street to pass water at precisely the wrong moment.[12] One way or another what emerges from Hammer's research is a picture of a medieval town in which it was highly likely that you would witness or become involved in a killing if you were a young man with university connections, resident in eastern Oxford and given to visiting alehouses at the weekend.

Given's research, like Hammer's, shows that medieval historians are not only able to come up with approximate homicide statistics for the period, but also hint at patterns of behaviour. Hammer gives us a sense of the confident, aggressive young Oxford student, prone to quarrel when he'd had too much to drink. Looking at English society more generally, Given suggests that while murders within the family occurred at about the same level as they do today in the UK and USA, in proportional terms they were far outweighed by killings among people who were not related to one another. When family strife was involved, husbands were more likely to kill wives than wives to kill their husbands, although there are certainly well-documented examples of wives doing away with their spouses. Hugh Dobin's wife Marjorie, for instance – a Herefordshire woman with a reputation locally as an adulteress – was alleged to have grown so weary of her husband's complaints about her conduct that in 1207 she arranged to have him murdered.

Generally, though, women played a relatively minor role in violent crime, either as perpetrators (9 per cent of the 3,492 accused) or victims (20 per cent of the 2,434 homicides recorded). Brothers, by contrast, often seem to have been involved in family arguments, some third of homicides committed within groups of relatives being recorded as having been perpetrated by them. In 1268 William killed his brother Henry (both are described simply as sons of Richard the carpenter of Goldington in Bedfordshire) by a blow to the head with a staff in a dispute over a halfpenny debt.[13]

So far as crimes in the wider community were concerned, there was a tendency for homicides to be committed by small groups, usually headed by a man assisted by relations, servants or neighbours. Unfortunately, the terse nature of contemporary documentation means that it is rarely possible for us to gain an insight into the background of these group killings. Some, presumably, were the outcome of long-standing vendettas, others the result of individuals coming together to perform a more spontaneous act of violence. Some murders were carried out by criminal gangs (the lower-class equivalents of the gentry robber bands discussed later). Such gangs – often, one assumes, ad hoc affairs – seem to have figured prominently in the 10 per cent of murders carried out as part of another crime (usually theft or robbery). An extreme instance of this occurred in the late afternoon of 1 September 1267 when a gang of robbers ran riot in the Bedfordshire village of Honeydon.

First they captured a boy who was returning from working in his father's sheepfold, using him to gain entry to a neighbour's house where they knifed the owner and killed his mother and servant; then they wounded and robbed another man in his own house; entered a widow's house and killed her; wounded a married couple in their home; killed another woman and stole items from her house; and then robbed another house before moving on to a neighbouring village and fatally wounding a man whose house they burned down. They then made off, successfully evading justice. Otherwise, most of the killings detailed on thirteenth-century eyre rolls were of the more mundane type so familiar in all periods of English history, a typical example being that of Margery de Karl, a London prostitute, killed in 1263 or 1264 by a man who claimed that she, along with two other prostitutes, had been trying to rob him.

This violent undercurrent to life continued into the fourteenth and early fifteenth centuries. According to the historian Barbara Hanawalt, who focussed on a sample of 575 homicides in Northamptonshire occurring in seventy years of relatively complete records between 1300 and 1420, murder remained not only an almost ubiquitous activity but an overwhelmingly male one: 99 per cent of the accused and 94 per cent of the victims were men. (Interestingly, though, in London during the same period Hanawalt established that women figured more frequently, both as perpetrators (7 per cent) and as victims (10 per cent). The Northamptonshire killers tended to come from the middle ranks of society, and contained a high number of what might be termed 'middling peasants', along with tradesmen (tailors, brewers, porters), a fair number of clergy, and more than a sprinkling of servants (constituting 12 per cent of suspects and 25 per cent of those accused). As in the thirteenth century, the records were dominated by killings outside the family, a quarter of which occurred during thefts or burglaries.

Hanawalt also established that people were most likely to kill on a Sunday (21 per cent of the Northamptonshire cases and 38 per cent of those in London) or Monday (15.4 per cent of killings in North-amptonshire and 23 per cent of those occurring in London). It's tempting to speculate that the heavy drinking that might have accompanied leisure on Sunday continued to affect people's behav-iour the following day. Certainly, and hardly surprisingly, drink played its part in outbreaks of violent behaviour in medieval times: in one well-documented (and not untypical) case from fourteenth-century London, Walter de Benington and seventeen companions came to the brewhouse of Gilbert de Mordone, refused to leave when asked to do so having consumed four gallons of beer, made it clear that they intended to carry on drinking, molested a young girl who was present and then assaulted Gilbert de Mordone and his brewer. The brewer took up a staff and killed Walter. The inquest jury returned a verdict of self-defence.[14]

There was a seasonal nature to violent crime, too. Perhaps not surprisingly, rural Northamptonshire was at its most dangerous in the spring and summer months: this was, after all, the period of the year when people were out and about the most, whether at work or enjoying themselves, and so they simply had more opportunity to meet others with whom they might end up quarrelling. Given this, it's also not surprising that just a third of killings occurred indoors, while over half took place in the fields or the street – mostly in the evenings or at night time (86 per cent of Northamptonshire and 90 per cent of London cases). Knives were the weapons of choice, being used in nearly 42 per cent of the Northamptonshire killings; staves were wielded in just over a quarter of the cases recorded; and a mere 0.6 per cent of victims met their death through blows from fists or feet. Around half of the Northamptonshire killings that Hanawalt looked at were the result of sudden altercations.[15]

It must have been reassuring to those who did commit

homicide – and of little comfort to the families of their victims – that the chances were that the culprit would never be brought to justice. In the middle ages charges of homicide could be brought in one of two ways: through an appeal, in essence a private prosecution; or through indictment, analogous to the modern criminal process. However, Given's research shows that medieval justice was a very hit or miss affair. More than half of those suspected of homicide in his survey never actually turned up in court, and were therefore outlawed. Of those who did appear, only 31 of the 529 who came to trial via the appeal process were executed (5.9 per cent), while just 216 (30 per cent) of the 722 who were indicted met the same fate. Similarly Hanawalt showed that in Northamptonshire a hundred or so years later, only about a third of those named as killers in coroners' inquests were actually brought to trial, and only a minority of these were executed. Evidence suggests that people who killed a relative were more likely to be convicted and executed than those who had killed a neighbour or a stranger, but the generally low conviction rate is striking. One reason for this may have been that juries, weighing up degrees of culpability, were often unwilling to bring in a verdict that carried with it the death penalty (the concept of manslaughter did not exist at this time). Another reason may have been that in those cases involving a group of assailants, juries found it difficult to establish who was most and least to blame. Whatever the reason, one is left with an image of a country where violence was never far away and where the perpetrators of violence were all too often at large.

II

Anyone looking for the violent middle ages would certainly have found them in London in June 1381. On the evening of Wednesday 12th two rebel peasant armies, one from Essex and one from Kent, reached the outskirts of the capital.[16] The Kentish men, who had already attacked people and property linked with government and church in their native county, stormed the Marshalsea prison in Southwark, wrecking it and releasing the prisoners detained there (its governor was subsequently murdered). On Thursday, after destroying other property in Southwark, the mob attacked the Archbishop of Canterbury's palace at Lambeth and also a brothel staffed by Flemish prostitutes. The same day Essex rebels attacked buildings associated with the legal profession, the House of the Knights Templar (owned by now by the Hospitallers) and a house owned by the Order of St John.

And now Londoners joined in, helping to wreck buildings in Fleet Street and attacking the Fleet prison in order to release its prisoners. Then they moved on to the Savoy Palace, the London residence of one of the most hated men in the country, John of Gaunt, Duke of Lancaster. Thomas Walsingham, author of a chronicle that was generally hostile to the rebels, described what happened next. He related how people ran 'like madmen' to the Savoy and 'set fire to the place on all sides and so destroyed it', but he also noted how the rebels destroyed rather than looted the goods they found there 'in order that the whole community of the realm should know that they were not motivated by avarice'. Walsingham recounted how, in an act of symbolic violence, the insurgents took one of Gaunt's 'most precious vestments', described by the chroniclers as a 'jakke' (that is, an upper garment), put it on a lance and fired arrows at it before destroying it with swords.[17]

It was not just property that was attacked that Thursday in June. As some of the events the previous day had shown, the rebels had a special hatred for lawyers and what were described as 'quest-mongers' – men who made a business of conducting various forms of legal proceedings, who had acquired an unenviable reputation for partiality and corruption. One such, Roger Legett, was dragged from the church where he had sought sanctuary and beheaded at Cheapside (a location which became the rebels' favoured execution site). His property was then burned down. Aliens were also singled out for attention. London, as an important trading centre, contained small colonies of foreign merchants, notably Flemings and Italians (normally described as Lombards): men who not only traded, but also helped London merchants, and indeed the English Crown, gain access to continental money markets. Many were now attacked, and in one particularly horrific incident on Friday 14 June thirty-five Flemings were dragged from the church of St Martin Vintry (that lay in an area favoured by alien merchants) and beheaded in the street. The chronicler who described this incident estimated that the rebels beheaded between 140 and 160 people that day.

Up until then the authorities had seemed frozen into inaction – something all the chroniclers criticised them for – but on the Friday the King, fourteen-year-old Richard II, attempted to assert his authority. Leaving the safety of the Tower of London, where he had stayed as the capital descended into chaos, he went to confront the rebels at Mile End and listened to their demands: the execution of men the rebels deemed to be traitors, a general pardon for themselves, and the abolition of serfdom and the labour services associated with it. Richard felt he had no choice other than to appear compliant, and he duly issued charters (which were revoked once royal power was re-established) abolishing serfdom in the rebels' native counties. Many were placated by this gesture, the Essex men in particular appearing happy to go home. This, however, left the initiative to the possibly more radical Kentish rebels, whose principal leader appears to have been Wat Tyler (probably a native of Maidstone), and their London allies.

Now high-ranking government officials became targets. A number of them had joined the King in the Tower of London for safety, but once Richard departed for Mile End they became vulnerable. The rebels attacked the Tower, seized five influential men, dragged them to Tower Hill and executed them. Foremost among the five was Simon Sudbury, Archbishop of Canterbury and Chancellor of England, whose beheading was botched so badly that it took eight strokes of a sword to sever his head from his body. The others were Sir Robert Hales, the Lord Treasurer; John Legge, a royal official and tax commissioner, who had narrowly avoided being lynched in Kent a few days previously; William Appleton, who was John of Gaunt's physician; and a tax-collector named Richard Somenour. The killing of Sudbury and

Hales was particularly incendiary – the equivalent of rioters today dispatching the Prime Minister and the Chancellor of the Exchequer.

Friday 14 June may have witnessed the rebels at the height of their success, but the following day saw their sudden collapse after one of the most noteworthy set-pieces in English medieval history: the meeting of Wat Tyler and Richard II at Smithfield. Accounts vary, but all agree that Richard arrived with a strong entourage and confronted many thousands of rebels, for whom Tyler acted as spokesman. They also generally agree that Tyler showed remarkable over-familiarity with the King. What happened next is a matter of dispute. Some chroniclers claim that Tyler played with a dagger as he talked with Richard, arousing fears among the King's supporters that he would stab the monarch; others say that he pulled a weapon in response to an insult from one of the royal entourage; some claim that orders were given to arrest him; there is also a possibility that Tyler might have been set up to be killed. In any case, all sources agree that he was wounded by William Walworth, Lord Mayor of London, and finished off with a sword by one of the royal entourage, Richard Standish. Many of the rebels wished to avenge Tyler's death. Richard, however, calmed the situation by intervening personally and undertaking to become the leader of the rebels. No doubt his persuasive powers were enhanced by the arrival of royal reinforcements.

And so the rebellion in London seems simply to have collapsed. The men of Kent, like those of Essex and the representatives of other counties who had joined the rebellion, returned home, many of them soon to face indictment and execution there. By November 1381, despite reports and rumours of further insurrections, it seemed safe for Parliament to meet, and the Lords and Commons set to pondering on the events of the summer.

III

London was not the only place to be convulsed by rebellion. We know, for example, that in Essex, where the revolt began, there were some 200 local incidents, ranging from violent physical attacks to the burning of manorial records. At St Osyth Nicholas Davenant, 'auditor' (that is, financial officer) for a local knight, was taken from the local abbey on 13 June and beheaded at Brentwood. The abbot was imprisoned for three days, his charters and other records burned and his rent collectors assaulted, while another man, Adam Dyer, was forced to 'make fine' with the rebels who entered his house – in effect buying them off. At Wennington, some of whose inhabitants had been involved in an attack on justices of the peace at Brentwood on 30 May, the house of Sir John Gildesborough was attacked. Indictments relating to this incident show that men from several settlements in Kent were involved, which suggests that the rebels were co-ordinating their efforts with those in other counties. And in an echo of events in London, Flemings were beheaded at the small Essex ports of Maldon and Manningtree.

Specific local scores were settled, too. In Southchurch, for example, it was later recorded that court rolls relating to a type of tenancy known as bondland had been destroyed during the uprising. This had clearly been the source of considerable friction between the local lord and the manor's peasantry, and when order was subsequently restored those involved were punished by having their land confiscated and only being allowed to reclaim it on the payment of entry fines (that is, money payable when a new tenancy was taken up).[18]

In Suffolk meanwhile, John Wrawe, believed to be an ex-priest from the Sudbury area, raised the county – initially with the aid of a group of men from Essex – and came to enjoy sufficient support to be able to style himself King of Suffolk. In Norfolk, Geoffrey Litster, a weaver from Felmingham near Norwich, emerged as a local leader. After Sir Robert Salle, sent out from Norwich to parley with the rebels, had been killed, Litster and his men were admitted to the city where they inaugurated a reign of terror that included the killing of a justice of the peace and the sacking of the houses of local notables. We get a sense of just how violent the rebels in East Anglia could be from the fate of John Cambridge, Prior of the Abbey at Bury St Edmunds, and Sir John Cavendish, Chief Justice of the King's Bench, Chancellor of the University of Cambridge, and owner of considerable lands in East Anglia. The two men had independently attempted to escape from the rebels, but were recognised, captured and beheaded. They had been friends, and so when the rebels put their heads on lances they pressed them together 'as if they were talking or kissing each other – an absurdly improper action'.[19]

Given the antagonism I have already described between town and gown in Oxford, it is scarcely surprising that there should have been similar tensions in Cambridge, and as the East Anglian revolt took root, so, on 15 June, the latent conflict between the town and the university exploded. Corpus Christi College, owner of numerous properties in the town and, through Lancastrian connections, associated with the hated John of Gaunt, was ransacked; other buildings were attacked; and the contents of the university library and university charters were burned in the market square.

St Albans – where one of the key chroniclers of the 1381 revolt, Thomas Walsingham, was a monk – proved to be another flashpoint, but here events took a less violent turn. As at Cambridge, particular local circumstances proved the spur to rebellion – in the case of St Albans, long-standing tension between the townspeople and the abbot of the large Benedictine abbey. In 1327, during an earlier period of political instability, the townsfolk, desperate to be free from ecclesiastical rule, had managed to secure a royal charter declaring St Albans a borough and so free from the overlordship of the abbey. However, this was revoked four years later. In 1381 the townspeople tried again, this time championed by another of those remarkable leaders thrown up that year, a man named William Grindecobbe. Grindecobbe led a delegation of St Albans men to London, and was among those who on 14 June at Mile End received a royal charter freeing his town. To make doubly sure, he also entered into an alliance with Wat Tyler (evidence of the Kentish leader's growing power). Grindecobbe and his associates then proceeded to use peaceful means (no monk of St Albans was killed) to establish their freedom. They redefined boundaries to reclaim common land enclosed by the abbey, tore down fences, and in one symbolic act that displayed their resentment of the abbey's attempt to deny them the right to hunt rabbits, secured a live rabbit to the town pillory.

IV

The Peasants' Revolt (given the social composition of the rebels, the popular name is actually something of a misnomer) was an exceptional event in medieval England. But by very virtue of being exceptional it loomed large in contemporary accounts, and that means that we know quite a lot about the nature of the grievances that drove a large number of people in the last quarter of the fourteenth century to rebellion and violence. As anecdotes from London and elsewhere show, these grievances ranged from expressions of general discontent to what amounted almost to a personal settling of scores. On the one hand, Wat Tyler's demand that serfdom be abolished, and the attacks on royal officials and on John of Gaunt's palace, suggest an overarching frustration with the status quo. On the other, the attacks on aliens, lawyers and particular individuals – not least the wretched Roger Legett who died at Cheapside – are evidence of more local, even personal disputes. And this mixture of general discontent and specific anger also characterised events in those areas of southern, eastern and midland England that were swept up in the summer unrest, and in the most northerly locations to be affected, the towns of York, Scarborough and Beverley, where the uncertainty of the times allowed long-standing political faction fighting to blossom.[20]

V

There is no doubt that one of the most significant causes of the revolt was the rapidly changing nature of the country's predominantly agrarian society. The population of England, which stood at roughly 2 million at the time of the Norman Conquest, had reached 5 or 6 million by 1300, and there is clear evidence that by this point the economy was struggling to support so many people. Then, in 1348, the Black Death struck, killing 40 per cent of the population, and at a stroke the balance of society changed. In the early fourteenth century the high population figures had favoured the more affluent: it was a sellers' market for tenancies, so landlords were in a strong position to bargain with their tenants, while a glutted labour market meant that wages could be kept low. Afterwards – not surprisingly – the less affluent who had survived the plague attempted to exploit an economic situation that was working in their favour. Peasant farmers negotiated for the best conditions when taking up new tenancies or reviewing existing ones. In particular, they sought to evade the labour services and other relics of serfdom that still encumbered so many tenancy agreements. Manorial court rolls of the period contain numerous references to tenants of the manor, individually or collectively, fighting against what they considered to be obsolete customs. Poorer peasants and agricultural labourers likewise felt themselves to be in a position to demand higher wages.

Parliament's response, however, was to pass the 1349 Ordinance of Labourers, and then the 1351 Statute of Labourers, both intended to keep wages at 1348 levels. A clear division thus became apparent between the men of property in Parliament, who passed these restrictive laws, as well as their propertied agents and the justices of the peace who enforced them, and the less-well-off tenants and wage-earners, who had felt themselves to be in a strong bargaining position. Serfdom had, in fact, already begun to dissolve before the Black Death; the pestilence simply gave the process further impetus. But it remained a symbol of a world which landlords wanted to preserve, a world where labour services were enforced and wages tightly controlled. Hardly surprising, then, that chroniclers of the events of 1381 should mention widespread attacks on manor houses and the burning of manorial documents. It was as if the peasants felt that destroying the written record of their servitude would destroy the servitude itself.

What tipped this general discontent into open revolt were events on the political stage. During the final years of his reign, Edward III, once a proud and effective monarch, had started to lose his grip. On his death he was succeeded by a mere child, his nine-year-old grandson Richard II. This led to a power vacuum and political infighting, and things were made considerably worse by a series of setbacks in England's long war against France. In the 1370s and early 1380s a number of naval and military expeditions were launched and botched; so feeble were English efforts, indeed, that in 1377 a Franco-Castilian fleet was able to raid the south coast (it is interesting to note that when the Kentish peasants marched on London in June 1381 they left men to guard their coastline). By 1381, therefore, there were very real worries about government incompetence.

Alongside these were rumours of corruption in high places. In 1376 Parliament investigated a major scandal involving William Latimer, the King's chamberlain, Richard Lyons, a city financier, and Edward III's mistress, Alice Perrers. Lyons (who was beheaded by rebels in London on 14 June 1381) and Latimer were accused of mishandling tax money and other corrupt practices, while Perrers was accused of collusion. In the event the trio were pardoned, largely due to the influence of John of Gaunt, Duke of Lancaster. Gaunt, who was already regarded as an over-mighty subject, was now therefore also associated with misgovernment and corruption, and his popularity was dented further when, in a political dispute of 1377, he was involved in an attack on the Liberties of the City of London. It was fortunate for him that in the summer of 1381 he was in Berwick, holding the Anglo-Scottish frontier.

Lack of military success and suspicions of corruption and weak government would have been bad enough; what made matters far worse was that because the war with France proved so expensive, the government had to find new ways to raise money. Most notorious of their methods was a series of three poll taxes, the first levied in early 1377, the second in the spring of 1379, and then, in spring 1381, in the face of severe financial problems, came a third poll tax, levying a flat rate of 12d on all men and women. The public response was mass tax evasion. In Essex, for example, 48,000 taxpayers were listed in 1377, but only about 30,000 in 1381. Accordingly, in early 1381 commissions were appointed to seek out evaders and enforce payment of tax. On or around 30 May one of those commissions, headed by a John de Bamptoun, sat in Brentwood in Essex. The negotiations with local villagers were clearly badly handled, and de Bamptoun soon found himself facing an uprising by the inhabitants of three settlements, Fobbing, Corringham and Stanford-le-Hope. He fled back to London, at which point Sir Robert Bealknap, Chief Justice of the Common Bench, was sent to stabilise the situation and arrest those who had resisted de Bamptoun. His arrival prompted a full-scale rebellion, during which three of de Bamptoun's men were beheaded. The Essex rebels began to attack manor houses in the county, not least, as already mentioned, that of Sir John Gildesborough who had been Speaker of the 1380 Parliament that had voted in the third poll tax and a member of the commission trying to enforce its collection when trouble broke out. The rebels also contacted the men of Kent, Suffolk and Norfolk in the hope that they would join them. Within days, the South East of the country erupted into rebellion.

There is one other background factor that also needs to be considered, however tentatively. One of the men identified by contemporaries as a leader of the Peasants' Revolt was John Ball, a priest eventually executed at St Albans on 15 July 1381. Ball, who had been a chantry priest at York and who later lived in Colchester, had been in trouble for preaching unorthodox doctrine from 1364 onwards, and at the time of the outbreak of the Revolt in June 1381 was in prison at Maidstone, whence he was freed by the rebels. Scholarly religious dissent in fourteenth-century England tended to coalesce around the ideas and teaching of John Wyclif, or Wycliffe (c.1320–84), who was, interestingly, a protégé of John of Gaunt.

Wyclif distanced himself from the Revolt, and it is impossible to demonstrate any direct link between his criticisms of the Church establishment and the rebels' actions, but with Ball we possibly have a proponent of religious radicalism.

Although we tend to think of the medieval Church as a bastion of wealth and power, there existed what might be termed a clerical proletariat of unbeneficed priests, who were drawn from the peasant and artisan classes, and who sympathised with the political and social outlook of the social groups they came from. The most famous saying attributed to Ball: 'When Adam delved and Eve span, who was then a gentleman?' was probably already proverbial when he used it as the text for a sermon in 1381. Nevertheless, Ball's employment of it indicates, as the scandalised chronicler Thomas Walsingham put it, that Ball felt 'all men were created equal by nature, and that servitude had been introduced by the unjust and evil oppression of men, against the will of God', and that he expected such words to strike a responsive chord in at least some of his listeners.[21] Walsingham was not the only chronicler to record Ball's words, and this suggests both that there were those involved in the revolt who espoused a radicalised view of Christianity, and that their views were sufficiently widespread to cause official concern.

All these profound sources of discontent seem to have come together in that fateful meeting on 15 June between Wat Tyler and his followers and Richard II and his entourage. The various accounts that survive all suggest that the rebels envisaged an egalitarian society, albeit one in which there was still a king. Landlordism and serfdom were to be abolished, as was the Church hierarchy, with the exception of one bishop and one 'prelate' for the whole of England. Church lands, like those of secular landlords, were henceforth to be held in common. The rebels also wanted a decentralised, community-based legal system, free from the corruption they felt was prevalent in the capital and personified by those legal figures the rebels had singled out for execution. It was an extraordinarily radical and wide-ranging worldview, though, of course, we cannot be sure just how accurately the chroniclers recorded Wat Tyler's words. But it's interesting to note that the leader of the St Albans rebels, William Grindecobbe, should, like Tyler, also have dwelt on the notion of liberty at his trial, at least according to the hostile chronicler Thomas Walsingham:

> Fellow citizens, for whom a little liberty has now relieved the long years of oppression, stand firm while you can and do not be afraid because of my persecution. For if it should happen that I die in the cause of seeking to acquire liberty, I will count myself happy to end my life as such a martyr ... They had accused me of many things and had a judge partial to themselves and eager to shed my blood.[22]

VI

The concept of the martyr for liberty's sake was one that was to recur throughout the centuries to follow, even though these martyrs and their followers were frequently to commit savage acts of violence. And, as the aftermath of the 1381 rising demonstrates, the state itself could display a similar taste for violence when it felt threatened. Once the rebellion in London had collapsed, order was swiftly restored elsewhere. Norfolk and Cambridge were pacified by Henry le Despenser, Bishop of Norwich, who donned armour and led troops against the rebels. Suffolk was occupied by a large body of royal troops on 23 June. In October of the same year, William Grindecobbe and fifteen of his associates were executed after a trial that showed scant regard for due legal process, and another eighty men were imprisoned. Needless to say, the concessions that they had secured during the revolt were revoked.

Nothing on the scale of the Peasants' Revolt ever occurred again. In 1450 Kent experienced a rebellion led by a man called Jack Cade that had strong overtones of 1381: grievances sparked by popular discontent at what was perceived as misgovernment, followed by the targeting and beheading of a number of royal ministers. This time round, though, attempts by the rebels to take London failed, there were no massacres of foreign merchants, and the area affected was comparatively limited.[23] In 1497 a peasant army set out from Cornwall, angered by royal demands for taxes to finance war against the Scots – which the men of Cornwall understandably regarded as a very distant threat. The Cornishmen and their adherents marched on London, but were defeated just south of the city.[24] The peasant rebellion of 1549 came closest in scale to that of 1381, affecting most of the midland and southern counties (in East Anglia 1549 was remembered as 'commotion time') and even causing East Anglia and the South West (where the grievance was the introduction of Protestantism) to pass out of government control for a short period.[25] But it was also the last of the old-style peasant risings.

The reason for this lay in the changing outlooks and aspirations of potential rebel leaders. In 1381 men like Wat Tyler and William Grindecobbe were fully prepared to step up to the mark. But the 1549 risings seem to have marked something of a watershed. In Norfolk that year the rebels were led by Robert Kett (by whose name the rebellion came to be known), a prosperous butcher and grazier, who enjoyed a status verging on that of a gentleman.

We know rather less about rebel leaders in other regions, but what we can glean suggests that they were men of similar social standing. In other words, those heading the revolt were the natural leaders in their communities. They were prosperous, frequently serving as parish constables, church wardens and manorial jurors; they were thus used to taking responsibility for community affairs, and also had experience of negotiating with landlords and outside authority. But as the population increased in the later sixteenth and early seventeenth centuries, and as prices rose (enhancing profits for men such as Robert Kett), so a division, both economic and cultural, grew between the local leaders who might once have thrown in their lot with their less prosperous brethren and the growing mass of the poor.

Now what by the late seventeenth century were to be known as the 'middling sort' were able to build better houses for themselves or, at least, to improve existing ones, to invest in larger-scale and more productive farming, perhaps even to send one of their sons to university. Their role as local government officials gradually exposed them to the values of an ever-more intrusive state. And increasing literacy among those in this stratum not only enhanced their sense of cultural differentiation from the poor, but also, in some places at least, made them more receptive to that great cultural shift which the English Reformation represented. Accordingly, these natural leaders of village and small-town society came to see themselves as what, in modern parlance, would be described as stakeholders in the national regime. Quite simply, they were no longer willing to lead popular risings as they had done in 1381 and 1549. Popular risings therefore dwindled. In the future they would be typified by the grain riot: localised, limited in its aims, and involving men and women from the lower social strata rather than the community as a whole. A profound shift had taken place in collective violence in England.

VII

Assumptions about the violent tenor of life in the middle ages do not rest solely on the high levels of homicide reported during the period, or an isolated large-scale rebellion such as the Peasants' Revolt. They are also fuelled by accounts of constant breakdowns of law and order as weak or inadequate monarchs (Stephen, John, Edward II, Henry III, Richard II) came and went, or as belligerent nobles and knights and their retinues fought each other beyond the reach of royal writ. And thanks to Shakespeare no era seems more emblematic of this constant turmoil, and the appalling bloodshed to which it could lead, than that of the Wars of the Roses.[26] The occasion for the conflict was the dynastic rivalry between the houses of York and Lancaster set in motion by the deposition of Richard II in the autumn of 1399 (and his death in February 1400), that degenerated into civil war in the mid fifteenth century and culminated in Henry Tudor's victory over Richard III at Bosworth in 1485.

To readers or audiences of the three parts of Shakespeare's *Henry VI* and of *Richard III*, the climate in which this conflict was fought seems to have been one of ambition, treachery, violence, usurpations, the murder of innocents, fathers killing their sons and sons murdering their fathers. Such a view, which was shared by most sixteenth-century commentators, was sustained by later historians. Thus William Denton, in his *England in the Fifteenth Century* of 1888, described how the Wars of the Roses wiped out the English aristocracy, caused more deaths among ordinary citizens than any other civil conflict in English history, wrecked the economy, destroyed most provincial towns, and pitched the country into a state of complete moral degeneracy matched by a corresponding physical degeneracy.[27] Denton's view may seem extreme but it echoes some documents of the time. Edward IV, for example, newly arrived on the throne after a coup d'état in 1471, characterised the period immediately preceding his taking power as one when

> No man was sure of his life, land, nor livelihood, nor of his wife, daughter, nor servant, every good woman standing in dread to be ravished and defouled. And besides this, what discords, inward battles, effusion of Christian men's blood, and namely by the destruction of the noble blood of this land, was had and committed within the same, it is evident and notorious through all this realm, to the great sorrow and heaviness of all true Englishmen.[28]

Edward was scarcely unbiased. But his claim goes hand in hand with the traditional view that late-medieval England was a mess waiting to be cleared up by the Tudors.

It is, of course, a rather broad-brush picture, not least because it implies that England in the later fifteenth century was a country constantly at war with itself. In fact, in the years between the first Battle of St Albans in 1455 and the Battle of Bosworth in 1485, only fifteen weeks of actual fighting occurred. It would therefore be more accurate to regard the Wars of the Roses (and some historians would even dispute whether that is a useful term for what happened) not as a period of continuous warfare (there was, for example, little fighting for four years after the first Battle of St Albans), but as two periods of very sporadic conflict between 1459 and 1471, and 1483 and 1487 (when a Yorkist army was defeated at the Battle of Stoke). Nor would it be true to say that the conflict devastated trade, which appears only occasionally to have been affected by war and was probably hit harder by a general economic depression that occurred during the period. It should also be borne in mind that new churches continued to be built, old ones refurbished, and unfortified domestic buildings constructed throughout the conflict – ventures that would not have been undertaken if there had been a complete breakdown in law and order.

That said, the Wars of the Roses should not be written off entirely. There may have been only fifteen weeks of actual fighting, but the fear of war, and the disruption caused by armies on the move, lasted much longer. The old feudal nobility might not have been wiped out as Victorian history books suggested, but even so the second half of the fifteenth century was not the safest time to be a nobleman in England. Between 1459 and 1471 twenty-two noblemen perished in battle and a further thirteen were executed.

It's harder to calculate what the casualty rate was among the ordinary soldiery, although as many of them were local levies, with little in the way of armour or protective clothing, we may reasonably speculate that it was high. It is commonly believed that the bloodiest battle ever fought on English soil was at Towton in North Yorkshire on Palm Sunday, 29 March 1461. An estimate immediately after the battle gave the death toll at 28,000, or roughly 1 per cent of England's then population (extrapolated on to a First World War battlefield, this would translate into 400,000 English deaths in one day). This seems very high. Nevertheless it does appear likely that perhaps 50,000 troops fought at Towton, and that at the end of a bloody ten-hour slogging match in recurrent snowstorms, followed by a rout of the Lancastrian forces when newly arrived Yorkist troops made a devastating flank attack on them, perhaps 15,000 men died. In 1996 a mass grave was found a mile or so from the main battlefield containing fifty-one bodies. These were surely the remains of ordinary soldiers who during the battle had worn only light armour – or none. Most of the bodies had multiple head wounds, suggesting perhaps that they had been killed in the rout that ended the battle, or were massacred after they had surrendered.[29]

As the events of the Peasants' Revolt demonstrate, law and order in the middle ages tended to deteriorate at times of weak royal authority, and the same was true during the Wars of the Roses. By now noblemen had formed indentured retinues, paying or offering material benefits to followers in return for their service – particularly their military service (an arrangement known as bastard feudalism, a term coined by the historian Charles Plummer in 1885).[30] In practice, this meant that in areas beyond royal control or at times of general instability, the nobility and lesser knights and gentry could resort to what was in effect gang violence to achieve their ends. In some cases, disputes even degenerated into prolonged family vendettas. The political instability created by the Wars of the Roses allowed the frequency of such conflicts to rise to an abnormal level, while the general dilution of authority encouraged local abuses of justice and acts of intimidation by a broad swathe of the landed orders and their retainers – the retainers, of course, being perfectly capable of creating mayhem in their own right if left unchecked, so creating a situation that might best be described as illegitimate bastard feudalism. Faction fighting among the aristocracy was a major factor in the outbreak of war in the first place, and as the dynastic struggle dragged on, the disorder created a local environment in which existing feuds and enmities could flourish.

A prime example of this interplay between national power politics and local disorder is provided by the career – and misdeeds – of Thomas Courtenay, 5th Earl of Devon. In the couple of generations before the outbreak of war, the Courtenays had seen their local influence eroded by the rise of a group of gentry families headed by the Bonvilles. Then in 1437 William Bonville was appointed royal steward in Cornwall for life. For Thomas Courtenay this was the last straw. He therefore initiated a campaign of violence against Bonville's supporters and tenants, and when in 1450 Richard, Duke of York, launched his campaign against Henry VI's councillors, the malcontent earl decided to attach himself to York's interest. In the short term this proved a foolish move, for when York had to capitulate to royal forces in 1452, it was the Bonville supporters who gained the upper hand, achieving positions of local power in Devon and the surrounding counties.

In 1453 York was rehabilitated, and the following year made Protector and Defender of the Realm. A by-now desperate Courtenay therefore felt sufficiently confident to embark on a new campaign of mayhem against Bonville and his supporters, culminating in the murder of one of their advisers, Nicholas Radford, an aged lawyer and a man of considerable local standing. In October 1455 the earl's retainers ransacked Radford's house, even throwing his wife out of bed so they could take the bedclothes. Radford himself was butchered at the earl's command by six men wielding swords and daggers. A few days later the earl sent his retainers back to Radford's house, where his body was laid out in the chapel. They held a mock coroner's inquest on the corpse, declared his death a suicide, and dumped the body in a grave in a local churchyard, adding further insult by throwing stones that Radford had gathered for the making of his tomb on top of the corpse.

By now the earl had a force of 1,000 men and they proceeded to advance on and then occupy Exeter, extorting from the cathedral clergy treasure that Nicholas Radford had left with them for safe keeping. They also besieged Powderham Castle, which was held by one of Bonville's associates. Bonville's forces were defeated in a minor battle at Clyst in mid-December, but fighting and the disruption of normal local administration continued well into 1456, although conflict between the two families had come to an end by

the autumn of that year. Fate caught up with all of the main participants in the struggle. Earl Thomas died in February 1458 (it was
rumoured that Henry VI's queen, Margaret of Anjou, had poisoned
him). William Bonville's son and grandson, along with the Duke of
York, were killed at the Battle of Wakefield in December 1460, and
Bonville himself was executed for treason after the second Battle of
St Albans in 1461. The 5th Earl of Devon's son and successor to the
title, also called Thomas, was himself executed as a traitor after
being captured at the Battle of Towton.

The social disorders that permeated the Wars of the Roses are,
thanks to Shakespeare, familiar to us. But although upper-class violence may have flourished in late-fifteenth-century England, it was
nothing new. Gentry criminal bands can be traced far back into the
previous century. In the 1330s, for example, a gang based in Leicestershire, led by Eustace de Folville, entered historical record when it
murdered Roger Bellers (or Belers), a royal official who had threatened, and possibly inflicted, physical injury on gang members. In
the same decade, another gang, headed by a James Coterel, was
operating in north Derbyshire and north Nottinghamshire.[31] At the
core of both gangs were groups of brothers. There were six Folville
brothers, only one of whom seems to have led an honest life; another,
when he wasn't conspiring with the others, was a minister of the
church at Teigh in Rutland. James Coterel's closest associates were
his two brothers and three or four local men. Both gangs, when
necessary, would recruit additional members for large-scale under-
takings. When, for example, the Folvilles kidnapped and ransomed
another royal official, Sir Richard Wylughby, they took with them a
group of between twenty and thirty men, including the Coterels
(there seems generally to have been a loose alliance of interlocking
criminal bands).

The gangs also relied on the support of what were known at the
time as 'receivers', people who gave support through providing food
and shelter, or by carrying messages, or through acting as guides in
areas with which the gang members were unfamiliar. These two

gangs, and many others besides, stole, poached, kidnapped people for ransom, and extorted money. One medieval gang leader even sent his intended victims threatening letters, an interesting use of the then rare skill of literacy. All were out to make money. Sir Richard Wylughby, kidnapped by the Folvilles and their associates, was ransomed for 1,300 marks (just under £867). They also used violence to punish and intimidate: Eustace Folville was reputed to have killed five men.

As I have already hinted, the social status of these medieval gang leaders could be fairly high. The Folvilles were minor gentry, the Coterels owned land, while another gang leader around 1330, who operated in Lancashire and Staffordshire, was a knight called Sir William de Chetulton. Other gangs might include retainers of knights or noblemen. Thus Charles Nowell, who around 1450 led a gang that caused endless problems in Norfolk, was, along with some of his associates, a retainer of the Duke of Norfolk. There were even occasions when criminal gangs were hired as strong-arm men by the eminently respectable: the canons of Lichfield Cathedral employed the Coterels at one point to remove the Vicar of Bakewell from his church and to collect tithes and protect their ecclesiastical jurisdiction in parts of the Peak District. And, as all these interconnections suggest, relations with legitimate authority were not necessarily hostile. The Coterels apparently had a highly placed undercover ally in the person of Sir Robert Ingram, at various times Mayor of Nottingham, Sheriff of Nottingham and Member of Parliament for both the city and the county.

Just as the authorities struggled to bring individuals to justice, so they found it difficult to control organised gangs. Members rarely appeared in court to answer the indictments levelled against them, and the worst that usually happened to them therefore was to be outlawed. Richard de Folville, the delinquent clergyman, ended his life in the winter of 1340–1 by being dragged from his church by a pursuing posse, which then executed him, but such moments of retribution were rare. Besides, most gangs did not stay together long.

The Coterels, for example, were involved in criminal activity for just five years between 1328 and 1333. Possibly tiring of a criminal lifestyle, many gang members were willing to buy pardons (in effect pay a fine) and settle down to a more or less honest lifestyle. Some of them subsequently served the Crown as soldiers (Eustace Folville was pardoned on condition he perform military service against the Scots), others in an administrative capacity. This apparent willingness to return to normal society after a period of deviance was obviously to the Crown's advantage.

Sadly, these criminal gangs bore little resemblance to those most celebrated of fictional medieval outlaws, Robin Hood and his Merry Men: they were, like most people involved in organised crime, dangerous and on occasion vicious. But there is one shard of evidence which demonstrates that Nottingham's most celebrated mythical son was indeed seen as a prototype outlaw in the middle ages: in 1439 Parliament was petitioned to the effect that a wrongdoer from Derbyshire called Piers Venables had gathered together a band of criminals, and that they had taken to the woods 'like it hadde be[en] Robyn Hode and his meynee [i.e. associates]'.[32]

The system of bastard feudalism whereby noblemen kept retainers, possessed arms (including artillery) and lived in fortified houses, or indeed traditional castles, persisted into Tudor times and beyond (castles still played a role when Civil War broke out in 1642). And the violent conduct that sometimes accompanied this way of life persisted, too. The historian Lawrence Stone describes an incident in 1573 when Lord Grey of Wilton and ten of his retinue let John Fortescue pass them in Fleet Street and then attacked him from behind, Lord Grey beating his victim senseless with a cudgel.[33] Fortescue was an up-and-coming royal official (he was later knighted for services to the Crown), who was amassing property in Oxfordshire and Buckinghamshire, counties where Grey's family – currently down on its luck – had traditionally been influential. That in itself was scarcely likely to make the two men friends. But Grey also had a tendency to allow his deer-hunting expeditions to trespass on

Fortescue's lands at Sladen. A little while before the London confrontation Fortescue had asked him to stop doing this, to which Grey had retorted: 'Stuffe a turde in your teethe, I will hunt it, and it shall be hunted in spite of all you can do.' Fortescue had brought a prosecution, the Privy Council had intervened to try and defuse the situation, and Grey's assault on his rival in Fleet Street was the ill-considered response. He was briefly incarcerated in the Fleet prison, and fined £350.[34]

This was a far from isolated case. Nevertheless, by the second decade of the seventeenth century violent gangs of the well-to-do were becoming both far less frequent and less socially acceptable, as new concepts of gentlemanly conduct took over from the more militaristic medieval concepts of chivalry.

VIII

All the indications, then, are that the middle ages were a comparatively violent period, with high homicide rates, a rebellion that brought in its wake considerable loss of life, and times of political instability that allowed nobles, gentry and their retainers to act without restraint. But whether that justifies Carla Del Ponte's 'medieval savagery' label is still open to question. For a start, to describe medieval England simply as a 'violent society', we need to define what 'violent society' actually means if we know that, on a day-to-day basis, most people were getting on with their lives and with each other. Furthermore, even supposedly objective evidence from the period can be interpreted in different ways: we know, for example, that many of the narrative or qualitative accounts we rely on were written by moralists or propagandists (like Edward IV) with a point to prove.

As historian Philippa Maddern has commented of what has frequently been portrayed as an unusually difficult period: 'it is almost as if faith in a high level of violence has become necessary to historians, to support their interpretation both of the state of government and of the nature of social structure in fifteenth-century England'.[35] Maddern may overstate her case when she suggests that to regard all medieval violence as illegal or destructive is to take too modern a view of the past: after all, being punched in the face or stabbed was probably no less unpleasant in the fifteenth century than it is today. Her findings, too, may have been shaped by her reliance on records from courts whose main focus was not trying cases of criminal violence (for example, documents from King's Bench rather than eyre rolls). But her painstaking study of East Anglia in the second quarter of the fifteenth century reminds us that for every violent person there were many who wished to lead a peaceful life; that accounts of violence coming to us via legal records are not always accurate; and that although violence was more widespread than at present, the East Anglian gentry do not seem to have been particularly violence-prone and indulged in few vendettas.

In this context it is worth remembering that the famous letter-writing Paston family, who, after all, lived through the years of the Wars of the Roses, espoused an outlook that was shaped by a strong concept of honour ('worship' as it was often termed) in which the welfare of the family, the maintenance of personal and family integrity, and the protection of family, servants, friends and associates, were paramount. And all this was to be achieved, as far as possible, without recourse to violence.[36]

The opening page of Henry de Bracton's *On the Laws and Customs of England*, written c.1220–50. A survey of royal enactments and court judgments, Bracton's work demonstrates the increasing role taken by the state in the suppression of violent crime in the thirteenth and fourteenth centuries.

CHAPTER 2

CHURCH AND STATE:
THE FORCES OF RESTRAINT

I

Some time between 1208 and 1213 Robert of Flamborough, a canon of
the Abbey of St Victor in Paris but, as his name suggests, probably
originally from Flamborough in Yorkshire, wrote a Penitential in
which he set out details of the penance that should be performed by
someone who had committed homicide. For the first forty days,
Robert stated, the murderer should be barred from entering a
church, should walk barefooted and bare-legged wearing only woollen garments, should live on bread, salt and water, and should not
have sexual congress with any woman, including his wife (it was, of
course, assumed that the penitent would be a man). Once that period
had elapsed he could wear full clothing and shoes but should abstain
from alcohol as well as meat, cheese and oily fish for twelve months.
Thereafter, he was expected to observe a gradually dwindling level
of expiation over several years, ultimately performing an act of penance every sixth day.

Other forms of violence itemised by Robert carried slightly different penalties according to the perceived severity of the original
crime. A greater display of contrition was expected, for example,
from someone who plotted the death of another than from someone who killed out of vengeance (though Robert noted that

vengeance was God's, not man's, prerogative), while the lightest punishment went to the person who killed by accident.[1] The overall message, however, was a clear one: God, and therefore his human agency the Church, could ultimately forgive wrong-doing, and exhort people to forgive one another; but murder was nevertheless a sin.

Ironically, Robert of Flamborough's painstaking rules and admonitions were something of an anachronism even as he penned them, for by the early thirteenth century murder was being categorised as a felony and so a matter for the royal courts rather than for ecclesiastical penance. Yet the Christian message, with its injunction to love one's neighbour as oneself, to turn the other cheek if provoked, and to turn away wrath with soft answers, retained its power. Nor, given how central Christianity was to everyday life in medieval Europe, is it remarkable that violence should have been a matter not just for the secular authorities to deal with but for the Church as well. Indeed, in continental Europe there was even a period during which the Church took more or less sole responsibility for the suppression of violence.

In the late tenth century, after the final collapse of the Carolingian Empire, political power fragmented and much of France and the areas adjacent to it descended into chaos. Authority, such as it was, was wielded by local petty aristocrats (*castellans*) and their mounted warriors (*milites*), a stratum of men who were the antecedents of what were later to be classified as knights. According to contemporary accounts, these men came near to creating a Hobbesian war of all against all, with violent self-help as their preferred means of conflict resolution. From about 975 the Church therefore stepped into the power vacuum, seeking initially to use its moral and religious authority to persuade individuals to protect churchmen, Church estates and the peasants living on them, and later to get people to abstain more generally from violence. In 1033 the chronicler Rodulphus Glaber described this 'Peace of God' movement in these terms:

Bishops, abbots and other men devoted to holy religion first began to gather councils of the whole people [*populus*]. At these gatherings the bodies of many saints and shrines containing holy relics were assembled. From there through the provinces of Arles and Lyon, then through all of Burgundy and finally the farthest corners of Frankland, it was proclaimed in every diocese that councils would be summoned in fixed places by bishops and by the magnates of the whole land for the purpose of reforming both the peace and the institutions of the holy faith.[2]

The meetings (usually held in a large field) were attended not just by leading churchmen and the general population but by local nobles, who would be required to swear oaths that they would desist from violence. Slowly the remit of this 'Peace of God' movement expanded. The Council of Narbonne of 1054, for example, declared that 'No Christian should kill another Christian, since whoever kills a Christian sheds the blood of Christ.' And alongside it grew the 'Truce of God', which, in honour of Christ's passion, sought to ban fighting between Wednesday evening and Monday morning, as well as during Advent, Lent, Easter and Pentecost. The aspirations of the Peace of God were not matched by its achievements, yet even if cause and effect are impossible to untangle, the fact remains that those decades around 1000 were the ones that witnessed the growth of more stable feudal states, the revival of urban life and significant Church reform.

No popular religious movement like the Peace or Truce of God ever made an appearance in England, not least because the country never experienced political breakdown and social chaos on the same scale. But the religious faith – and such instruments of faith as saints' relics – that on occasion prevented or restrained violence in regions of the former Carolingian Empire exercised a similar power in its island neighbour. Several descriptions survive, for instance, of priests restoring order by displaying the Host: its central role in the

Mass gave it a powerful symbolic force, serving to remind trouble-makers that they were endangering their eternal souls by their violent behaviour.

One such account describes how on a Sunday in 1453 a certain Laurence Caterall was set upon at Mass in the parish church at Gargrave in Yorkshire by a gang of armed men led by Richard Percy, brother of Thomas Percy, Baron Egremont – probably because Caterall was a client (that is, a dependent, supporter and protégé) of the Percys' great enemies the Neville family. The clergyman initially tried to protect Caterall by pushing him into a vestibule by the altar, but Percy and his men continued their pursuit, some even standing on the altar as they tried to hem in Caterall. So the clergyman picked up the Host, and ordered all present to desist from wickedness in the name of God. His injunction worked. Percy's cohorts climbed off the altar, and though they took Caterall prisoner they did so without any further violence.

Five years later the Host was employed to even more spectacular effect in London. On this occasion a quarrel had broken out in Fleet Street between local residents and a group of lawyers, and had rapidly degenerated into a three-hour brawl during which bows and arrows were used and several people were killed or wounded. Further violence was only averted when a procession of clergymen appeared carrying the Eucharist, at which point the fight broke up and people returned to their houses.[3]

If the Church condemned violence, it also condemned what it regarded as the root cause of violent behaviour – the sin of wrath – citing a number of biblical passages that warned of its dangers: 'A wrathful man stirs up strife, but he who is slow to anger allays contention' (*Proverbs*, 15:18); 'A man of great wrath will suffer punishment' (*Proverbs*, 19:19); 'He who is slow to wrath has great understanding, but he who is impulsive exalts folly' (*Proverbs*, 14:29). And popular literature picked up the theme, too, notably in one of the most familiar of medieval texts, William Langland's *Piers Plowman*. Langland himself was a clerk in minor orders. His book, written c.1360–90 and subsequently revised, is a didactic work with a strong Christian message at its core. In one extended passage it describes the Seven Deadly Sins, and offers this view of wrath (translated here into modern English):

> I am wrath . . . I'll gladly strike both with stone and staff, and sneak up on my enemy; I craftily think how to kill him with cunning. Though I sat and talked seven years I couldn't begin to tell the harm I've done with my hand and tongue.

Wrath, Langland tells us, lives among all sorts of people, both women and men: he has spent time among monks and has been a cook in a convent. He recollects how he encouraged two women to quarrel until, in a scenario closely akin to those often found in late-medieval and early modern court records, they called each other a whore, pulled off each other's headdress, and scratched each other's cheeks.

Wrath is also depicted at considerable length in *Jacob's Well*, a work thought to date from the first quarter of the fifteenth century, which survives in a single manuscript in Salisbury Cathedral. Divided into ninety-two chapters, and probably designed to be delivered as a series of sermons, *Jacob's Well* provides the Christian, whether lay or cleric, with a comprehensive devotional guide; and in Chapters 14 and 15 turns its attention to *Ira*, wrath, which it compares with a wolf. Wrath, it tells us, comes in three degrees. The first takes the form of hatred in the heart or malice, which is regarded as being as serious a sin as physical violence; the person guilty of malice is worthy to be tried in the court of heaven before God. The second degree is 'malice of the mouth' – verbal violence – which is worthy of heavy punishment in heaven. The third, which renders its practitioners 'guilty to the fire of hell', is 'when thou, with thy tongue, or with thy deed, avenges thee of thine enemy for wrath'; it's interesting to note here that the author views verbal violence ('he that . . . speeketh reproof, shame, or slander') as being as worthy of the torments of hell as actual physical violence. Wrath is regarded as being at the

centre of a whole range of offences, from manslaughter to vengeance to false imprisonment to defamation (which again, interestingly,
is equated with manslaughter) to damage to goods. The moral is a
very clear one: avoid the inner harbouring or outward display of ill
temper and the temptation to disparage others. It is a sin in itself,
and it may well lead to actual physical violence.[4] The ideal evoked
here is of a Christian society in which people live together in peace
and good fellowship.

Piers Plowman and *Jacob's Well* were not isolated literary examples.
Numerous other written guides circulated in manuscript form and,
from the late fifteenth century, in print. Their readership was, admittedly, a small and elite one: most medieval people, after all, were
illiterate. But sermons of the *Jacob's Well* type were becoming increasingly popular in the late middle ages, as were the morality plays
performed in many towns, such as York and Chester, and villages.
And at a very immediate, visual level church congregations would
have been surrounded by elaborate wall paintings (cheaper to create
and install than stained glass), depicting the Seven Deadly Sins or
scenes from the Old and New Testaments, and the Last Judgement.
No contemporary could have been unaware of the torments that
awaited them if they were found guilty at the last day of the sins of
pride, greed, envy, gluttony, lust, sloth and, of course, wrath.

Judging from a wall painting that survives at St Thomas Canterbury church at Capel and stained glass in the Lady Chapel of York
Minster, some would also have been fully familiar with the story of
Cain, who murdered his brother Abel with the jawbone of an ass.
Just how effective these verbal and visual admonitions were is a moot
point. It remains one of those paradoxes of history that medieval
England was both deeply devout and violent, and although ecclesiastical sanction, or the threat of ecclesiastical sanction, clearly worked
in many cases, indications that a simple reminder of the eternal price
to be paid for wrong-doing was sufficient to keep people on the
straight and narrow are distinctly lacking. At the same time, it's hard
to believe that the constant admonitions made by the late-medieval

Church – written, spoken and visual – had no effect on their target audience.[5]

II

But if one strand of Christian thought preached the end of all violence, another made allowance for it in particular circumstances, and this juxtaposition caused a constant tension in the medieval mind. God Himself was an ambiguous figure. He was the benign entity whose son had died for mankind's sins. But from the early middle ages until at least the seventeenth century he was also depicted as a vengeful figure, who punished sinners and the unrighteous not just in the hereafter but often on earth, too. The chronicler Orderic Vitalis, for example, describing the brutal 'harrying of the North' that William of Normandy conducted against English rebels in the winter of 1069–70, was confident that God would exact retribution:

I declare that assuredly such brutal slaughter cannot remain unpunished. For the Almighty Judge watches over high and low alike. He will weigh the deeds of all in a fair balance, and as a just avenger will punish wrongdoing, as the eternal law makes clear to all men.[6]

Medieval literature is packed with instances of divine retribution. In his *Golden Legend*, for example, Jacobus de Voragine tells us that after the death of St John Chrysostom not only was the city of Constantinople hit by a massive hailstorm (widely interpreted as a token of divine wrath), but the Empress Eudoxia, who had been a great opponent of the saint, died suddenly. Similarly, the death of St Juliana was swiftly followed by the drowning of her persecutor Eulogius, Prefect of Nicodemia. His body was later washed ashore, only to be devoured by beasts and birds of prey. As for the pagan priest who suggested that St Vitalis should be martyred by being buried alive head downwards, he was tormented for seven days by a demon, and then cast to his death in a river.[7]

It might be argued that divine wrath scarcely sanctioned human wrath – after all, *Romans,* 12:19 explicitly states: 'Vengeance is mine; I will repay, saith the Lord.' But the reality was more complicated. Once the notion of divine vengeance was allowed, that power could very easily be devolved to God's lieutenants on earth. Thus theologians fully accepted that monarchs had a right to punish criminals and rebels. At a practical everyday level, the clergy would readily offer the consolations of religion to those found guilty of a serious crime while being perfectly willing to go along with any retributive actions the secular authorities might choose to take.

Theologians also accepted that when it came to the most extreme form of human strife there was such a thing as a 'just war'. This was ultimately a Roman notion, which entered mainstream Christianity through the writings of St Augustine, the fifth-century church father whose works were to enjoy enormous prestige throughout the middle ages. For Augustine war was both the consequence of sin and the remedy for it, so while he believed individuals should not inflict violence, both he and many thinkers who came after him argued that in certain circumstances war was the appropriate way to restore moral order when it had been upset. In some circumstances this idea could also be invoked to address that most thorny of political issues, how to deal with a tyrant. Medieval political theory, deeply underpinned as it was by theological concerns, developed two opposing views of kingship, one of which was to lead by the seventeenth century to the idea of the absolute monarch, the other of which argued that in extreme cases it was acceptable to overthrow a tyrannical ruler (the general proviso was that those leading the rebellion should be men of note). Clerical backing for this latter stance is apparent in the decision taken by Stephen Langton, Archbishop of Canterbury, to support the baronial opposition to King John that was to lead to the imposition of Magna Carta in 1215, and in the actions taken by Walter de Cantilupe, Bishop of Worcester, between 1195 and 1266, to support the baronial opposition to Henry III.

Once an act as extreme as war was allowed, all sorts of

contradictions crept into medieval society. Thus it was accepted that soldiers were necessary and that they could fight and kill, though war theorists hoped that they would fight on sound moral principles and not for love of violence or expectation of gain – but it was also suggested that soldiers returning from war should do penance for the deaths they had caused. Those who served the Church preached the gospel of love and peace, yet they might also occasionally arm themselves for battle. Henry le Despenser, Bishop of Norwich, whom we encountered in the previous chapter enthusiastically putting down the Peasants' Revolt in East Anglia, enjoyed a dual career as high-ranking churchman and soldier.

He first saw active service in Italy when, as a resident in the papal curia, he fought on behalf of Pope Urban V against Milan. In 1383, at the instigation of Pope Urban VI, he led an initially successful military expedition to Flanders that then became bogged down, and this was followed a little later by a no more successful attack on Picardy. In 1385 le Despenser accompanied Richard II on his invasion of Scotland, and in 1402 was ordered to array the clergy in his diocese against an anticipated French attack on the Suffolk coast. Rumours circulated at the time that he was also contemplating another assault on Flanders. When a Scottish bishop, Thomas de Rossy of Galloway, offered to take on any English bishop in single combat as a means of settling religious differences between the two countries, he specifically challenged le Despenser 'who takes such delight in deeds of arms'. Judging from such accounts as we have of him, le Despenser was a rather unpleasant character and comes across as an unlikely servant of the Prince of Peace.[8]

He, at least, had official sanction for what he did. But there are also plenty of examples from the middle ages of clergyman who engaged in violent activities that were, quite simply, illegal. We have records of clergy who were members of criminal bands – on one occasion a group of clergy robbed a lone cleric of money, arms, clothing, and two papal bulls. If (as we have seen with the Coterels) a clergyman was unwilling to indulge in violent behaviour himself, he might have no qualms about getting others to do it for him. Thus when in 1304 Godfrey of Crombe, Rector of Weston-sub-Edge in Gloucestershire, was faced with the prospect of being removed from his living in favour of another clergyman supported by an incoming bishop, he hired a well-known gentleman malefactor, Sir Malcolm Musard, to lead a gang (which included other clergymen) to beat up the priest who replaced him, wreck his fish ponds, and cause other damage to property.[9]

Members of the clergy were also regularly indicted for murder: in fourteenth-century London about 8 per cent of both perpetrators and victims of murder were clergymen.[10] Many of these were drawn from the lower clerical orders, or from that clerical proletariat of unbeneficed priests or itinerant friars who were such a feature of the medieval Church. But their seniors and (theoretically, at least) their betters were sometimes no better. Perhaps the most spectacular, and certainly the most highly placed, of violent medieval clerics was Thomas de Lisle, appointed Bishop of Ely in 1345. In 1354 de Lisle was accused of attacking Blanche, Lady Wake, widow of Thomas, Lord Wake and sister of the Duke of Lancaster, of burning down some of her houses, and of complicity in the death of one of her servants. Further indictments indicated that the bishop had been heading a criminal gang whose inner core was a group of episcopal estate officials (de Lisle's brother John among them), and with a number of clergy as peripheral members. The gang, in the best traditions of medieval criminal gangs, involved itself in petty theft, kidnapping, extortion, arson, assault and murder. De Lisle was stripped of his temporalities and exiled to the papal court at Avignon.[11]

For English monarchs such cases were a real legal headache. How did you balance the requirements and traditions of royal justice with those of the secular and ecclesiastical courts? The issue of what to do with 'criminous clerks' had famously been a bone of contention between Henry II and Thomas Becket, formerly the King's chancellor but from 1162 Archbishop of Canterbury. Henry's view, enshrined in the Constitutions of Clarendon of 1164, was that a criminous clerk should, after initial investigation by a royal court, be transferred to the ecclesiastical courts for trial and, if found guilty, be defrocked and then returned to the royal court for punishment as a layman. Becket had initially agreed to this, and then swiftly back-pedalled. After his murder at the hands of four of Henry's knights in 1170, the King had had to accept the status quo, leaving an unresolved problem that rumbled on through the next century or so. The net result, though, was that by the late sixteenth century it was very unusual indeed to see a clergyman charged with crimes of violence.

III

If the restraining influence on violence of the Church was patchy and ambiguous, the same went for that most secular of codes of theoretically virtuous conduct: chivalry. Concepts of chivalry had developed in step with the rise of the mounted knight and they are of particular interest to the historian of violence because they show the tensions between ideals and reality in an era when aggressive behaviour was rife among the upper echelons of society.[12] The scope and nature of chivalry has been usefully summarised by one of its more recent historians, Craig Taylor:

> . . . it encompasses the full scope of aristocratic culture during the high and late Middle Ages, including not just the literature but all aspects of both court and martial life and lifestyle, including tournaments, feasts and knightly orders, heraldry and knighting ceremonies. From such a perspective, chivalry is not merely the literary representation of knighthood but also the social practices and rituals of knights and men-at-arms, and the values and ethos that informed these practices. In other words, chivalry constituted the norms, values, practices and rituals of medieval aristocratic society from the high Middle Ages onwards.[13]

Chivalry was a complex phenomenon, and our understanding of it has not been helped by some later interpretations. But what is clear is that at its core lay the intertwined concepts of honour, fame and reputation. In chivalric theory the knight's main objective in life was the gaining and maintaining of honour. And, as has so often been the case in English history, maintaining masculine honour involved fighting. This created a considerable tension between chivalry and Christian values, although most knights would have regarded the two sets of tenets as being perfectly compatible. In the same way, they would have argued that there was no tension between chivalry and royal justice, even though an aristocratic ethos which regarded violence as desirable, indeed in some contexts as essential, sat uneasily with a system of royal justice that was increasingly striving towards a more ordered society.

Given that fighting was central to the concept of chivalry, it's scarcely surprising that the celebration of chivalry in literary form, the romance or *chanson de geste*, should have been astonishingly violent. Take, for example, the cycle of romances known as *Lancelot* (originally written in Old French), as analysed by the American scholar Richard W. Kaeuper. He notes that the work contains about a hundred descriptions – some of them very elaborate – of combats between knights, usually involving an initial stage when they fight on horseback with lances, followed by combat on foot if one or both of the men become unhorsed. Kaeuper comments:

> Limiting ourselves to quantifiable instances – at least eight skulls are split (some to the eyes, some to the teeth, some to the chin), eight unhorsed men are deliberately crushed by the huge hooves of the victor's war-horse (so that they faint in agony, repeatedly), five decapitations take place, two entire shoulders are hewn away, three hands are cut off, three arms are severed at various lengths, one knight is thrown into a blazing fire and two knights are catapulted to sudden death. One woman is painfully bound in iron bands by a knight; one is kept for years in a tub of boiling water by God, one is narrowly missed by a

hurled lance. Women are frequently abducted and we hear at one point of forty rapes. Four knights are wounded by miraculous weapons.[14]

Kaeuper also finds the text refers to three private wars, one of them involving 500 deaths through poisoning, and four tournaments which, in this genre, have very much the flavour of minimally diluted warfare. Violence is obviously an integral element in the adventures these fictional knights experience, and is the problem-solving method of choice.

The *chansons de geste* were written in French, a language that was probably accessible to most of the nobility and gentry, perhaps less so to the population at large. But from 1485 English-language readers had an Arthurian work of their very own. In that year William Caxton, pioneer of printing in England, published a book by an obscure English knight called Sir Thomas Malory. The work drew together a number of continental and English Arthurian sources, and became known (this was apparently not its intended title) as *Le Morte Darthur*. The book enjoyed lasting popularity, being regularly reprinted until 1634 and encouraging a massive vogue for all things Arthurian in Tudor England. Elizabethan knights fought tournaments decked out as figures from the tales of the Knights of the Round Table, and Edmund Spenser's epic poem *The Faerie Queen* is shot through with Arthurian references and motifs.[15] *Le Morte Darthur* then went out of favour for a while, before being taken up again in Victorian times when it became the inspiration for many poets and painters (the Pre-Raphaelite Dante Gabriel Rossetti declared it to be the most important book in English after the Bible), part of a broader nineteenth-century vogue for idealising the middle ages in a reaction against industrialisation and materialism.[16]

These later retellings of Malory and his Arthurian legends have tended to obscure just how violent a work it is, although to a modern reader much of the mayhem comes over as cartoon violence. Early in the narrative Arthur fights with a giant (the 'foulest freke that ever was formed'), whose genitals he severs before cutting his belly open so that its bloody contents fall upon the grass. A little later Sir Lancelot takes on two giants, having previously cleft the head of the porter of their castle, who had offended him. He cuts off one giant's head and splits the other with his sword from the shoulders to the navel as he attempts to flee. Elsewhere, knights fight for an hour or two until the ground they stand on is covered with their blood, their injuries never being quite bad enough to stop them. So, for example, when Sir Bors fights Sir Pridam, the two knights shatter their lances at the first encounter and continue fighting on foot, giving each other severe head wounds, but nevertheless continuing to smite each other with their swords until Pridam eventually collapses. At this point Bors removes the fallen knight's helmet, beats him about the face with the flat of his sword, and tells him either to yield or be killed. Sir Pridam prudently chooses the former option. Whatever else chivalry might involve, then, for Malory and his readers it was centred on the notion of fighting.

There are certainly instances in Malory of what we would regard as 'chivalric' behaviour. His knights (or at least the virtuous ones) have a clear notion, for instance, that there are circumstances under which an opponent should not be attacked. Thus we find Sir Tristram, ordered by King Mark of Cornwall to fight on his behalf with Sir Lamorak de Gales, arguing that it would be contrary to the rules of knighthood to fight with one who has already been tired by combat. Later, when Sir Tristram has been wounded in another fray, Sir Palomides unchivalrously attacks him and, quite rightly, perishes in the attempt. Elsewhere we find instances of mercy being shown to a vanquished opponent, particularly if, as they lie on the ground with their helmets removed, they ask for mercy. When Sir Tristram defeats Sir Blamor after a lengthy fight, Sir Blamor begs to be killed, stating that he prefers death to dishonour. Tristram, unwilling to kill so valiant a knight, appeals to a number of knights who agree with him that Blamor should be spared (his brother Sir Bleoberis, however, agrees with Blamor's view that death is preferable to dishonour). Bleoberis and Tristram then help Blamor up, the two brothers kiss Tristram, and all make a vow of peace. The idea of death before dishonour that informs this story can also be found in another episode involving Sir Tristram. He and Sir Dinadan meet a damsel who informs them that Sir Lancelot needs rescuing from thirty knights. When Dinadan expresses reluctance to take on such odds, Tristram appeals to his sense of shame, and threatens to kill him himself if he does not join in the fight (later the tables are turned, when a disguised Tristram refuses to fight Dinadan). Individual honour, then, is of vital importance, even if at certain points in *Le Morte Darthur* it sits uncomfortably with the teachings of Christianity.[17]

For subsequent generations, the chivalric code conjured up not only images of knights on horseback but of knights rushing to the aid of damsels in distress. Indeed when in 1885 the artist Frank Dicksee exhibited a painting at the Royal Academy in which a young lady tied to a tree looks apprehensively over her naked shoulder at a knight sheathing the word with which he has just killed another knight (presumably her assailant), he entitled it, quite simply, *Chivalry*.[18] But while gallantry towards women may have been an element of knightly behaviour heavily romanticised by the Victorians, it is not entirely a later invention. Knights of the Round Table, Malory tells us, have to swear that they 'should always do ladies, damosels, and gentlewomen and widows succour; strengthen them in their rights, and never to enforce them, upon pain of death'.

Courtly love also sublimates much passion and the dangerous impulses to which passion can give rise: a knight who is not a lover cannot perform knightly deeds; but conversely, knights who are adulterous or lecherous or who keep paramours should not go on adventures. That said, courtly love does not preclude odd instances of casual sex in the *Morte Darthur*, nor morally dubious acts of dynasty building, as when King Pelles uses magic to get Lancelot to sleep with his daughter Elaine and father a son by her. Rape, too, is a persistent if minor theme, although it is largely committed by those who are already outside, or whose actions put them outside, the chivalric code. Among the former is the ogre whose genitals Arthur splits asunder: he has raped a duchess and cleaved her to her navel, and clearly has similar designs on three other maidens in his charge. Among the latter are the three brothers who plan to rape their sister, and then kill her when she calls out for their father.[19] The wording of the Arthurian oath instructing knights not to 'enforce' women also seems to exclude women of the lower orders; so, for example, Sir Tor's mother, the wife of a cowherd, relates how she lost her virginity and became pregnant with Sir Tor before her marriage when a knight (in fact, King Pellinore) had intercourse with her 'half by force'. And different moral standards seem to apply to women who misbehave than to men. When Sir Gaheris finds his mother, the widowed Queen of Orkney, in bed with a knight called Sir Lamorak, Gaheris promptly beheads his mother, but he does not kill Lamorak as he feels it is shameful to kill a naked knight.[20]

In fact illicit sex is a constant theme of Malory's work, and with it the suggestion that it can have a violent outcome. Arthur's nemesis, Mordred, is fathered by Arthur himself in an unwitting act of incest with his sister. The adulterous love affairs between Lancelot and Guenevere, and Tristan and Isolde, both have disastrous results.[21] (As medieval legal records show, the potentially calamitous consequences of adultery were not just the stuff of fiction – nor only the concerns of those at the top of society: there was the Herefordshire case from 1207 in which a woman named Marjorie, with a local reputation as an adulteress, was accused of murdering her husband who had remonstrated with her about her conduct; twenty years later, the disappearance of a man from Kent, Robert Fortin, was attributed to his wife who had transferred her affections to another and then got her servant to murder her husband.[22])

How far the world of the *chansons de geste* was reflected in reality is a moot point, although one suspects that medieval knights and their womenfolk (among whom these works were popular) were as competent as modern consumers of culture at distinguishing between fiction and reality. That said, the works of Malory and his like clearly struck a chord with contemporaries, and occasional actions redolent of chivalric romance can be found in real life, notably in that central concern of the knightly class, warfare.

One remarkable incident occurred early in the fourteenth century when a young Lincolnshire knight, Sir William Marmion, came to Norham Castle in Northumberland to see service against the Scots. He arrived with a gilt helmet, the gift of his lady who had given him instructions that it should only be worn where finding honour would be most dangerous. A small party of Scots approached the castle, and, after receiving approval from his garrison commander, Sir William rode off wearing the helmet, to take on the Scots single-handed. His commander waited until the knight was in danger of being killed, and then, honour being satisfied, intervened with the castle garrison to save him. A few years later, in the opening stages of the Hundred Years War between England and France, a French chronicler noted that a number of young English knights serving at Valenciennes were wearing patches over one eye, which would not be removed until they had impressed their womenfolk through feats of arms.[23] And while the fate of those captured in battle could be a precarious one, particularly if they were taken in the midst of a conflict whose outcome at that moment was uncertain, the general view was that knights should be spared: the assumption was that well-to-do prisoners would subsequently be held for ransom; the fate of ordinary soldiers was more uncertain.[24]

That said, a few isolated incidents apart, it's hard to find much that was chivalric about late-medieval warfare. It was brutal, hand-to-hand slaughter. The great English victory at Agincourt in 1415 is a case in point.[25] It opened with an attack by the French cavalry, followed by an onslaught of around 8,000 heavily armoured men-at-arms. Many slipped in the mud of the battlefield or fell over the bodies of fallen comrades in the front ranks as pressure from their comrades behind them forced them on. Others, who had become isolated from the mass, were attacked by groups of lightly equipped

English archers. Those who fell had their helmets beaten in with mallets, or their throats cut after helmets and defensive armour had been removed, or their heads and bodies pierced by thrusts through the eye slits in helmets or gaps in armour at the armpits or groin. Those French soldiers taken prisoner in the course of battle were, on this occasion, slaughtered.

Civilian populations also suffered from the brutality of medieval warfare. During the Hundred Years War the English mounted a number of *chevauchées*: large-scale mounted expeditions whose objectives, like those of strategic bombing in the Second World War, were to break the will and capacity of the enemy to fight. Towns and villages were devastated, homesteads and crops were burned, people and animals were slaughtered, and women were raped. As the historian Maurice Keen observes in his *The Laws of War in the Late Middle Ages*: 'in this light the whole theory of chivalry, of an order of knighthood whose Christian duty is the protection of the needy and defenceless, becomes meaningless.'[26] In any case, over time the organisation of warfare moved away from the ideal of chivalric service under a feudal overlord to a system based on indentures – in effect contracts setting out terms of service and payment to professional soldiers. And although most knights still fought in pursuit of fame through feats of prowess, they also wanted to turn a profit. This might come through plunder, or through the capture and subsequent ransoming of important members of the enemy army. In the Hundred Years War it was customary for captors to in effect sell highly placed prisoners of war to the Crown so that they could be used in subsequent negotiations. Sir Thomas Holland, for example, secured £12,000 in 1346 when he sold on a French count he had captured at the Battle of Caen.

Nor was fighting at its most brutal restricted to wars abroad. The battles of the Wars of the Roses were grim affairs, too, as is clear from the contents of the mass grave of fifty-one soldiers found at Towton, the scene of a battle in 1461. The skeletons (each known simply by a burial number) show a range of injuries, many of them to the head. One, Towton 18, has nine blade and two puncture wounds to his head, and a blade wound to his right femur. Another, Towton 32, has ten blade and three blunt-force wounds to his head and other wounds to his arms and hands. Yet another, Towton 41, has five blade and three puncture wounds to his head, and extensive blade wounds on other parts of his body. Towton 9 suffered only one wound, but its impact on his skull must have been massive: it is a square hole probably made by the beak of a war hammer.[27] There was nothing chivalric about the way these men met their deaths.

If there's one individual who encapsulates both the art of chivalry and its contradictions it is John Talbot, 1st Earl of Shrewsbury from May 1442, one of the most remarkable English military leaders of the fifteenth century. Born in around 1387, the second son of Richard, Lord Talbot, he was a pious man, who employed priests and chaplains in his household and went so far as to obtain a licence from the Pope to carry a portable altar with him on campaign. He was also a man steeped in chivalric values, who maintained a team of heralds and whose choice of present for Henry VI's newly arrived queen, Margaret of Anjou, in 1445 was a sumptuously bound and produced collection of fourteen works on chivalry, ranging from *chansons de geste* to the statutes of the Order of the Garter, of which – of course – he was a member. His death in 1453 at the age of sixty-six was suitably heroic.

In 1449 he had had to surrender to the French and offer himself as a hostage in order to avoid a pitched battle his forces were not in a position to fight. Released in 1450, he promised the French monarch Charles VII that he would never again bear arms against France. Consequently, when his soldiers engaged in battle with a massively superior French force in Gascony in 1453, he kept to his word by riding into battle without arms or armour, wearing a magenta-coloured robe that the French monarch had given him. Various accounts of how he died were given, but those that claimed he was felled by a blow to the head from a battle-axe were to be vindicated many years later when, in the nineteenth century, his tomb was opened and his skull inspected. A mouse was found nesting in the cranium – a poignant demonstration of the transitory nature of fame and chivalric glory.[28]

Yet the fact remains that in his military career spanning some fifty years – most of them spent rather fruitlessly defending English possessions in Normandy – he was a brutally efficient soldier, dubbed 'The Terror of the French', and a figure of fear even into the nineteenth century when mothers in rural France would invoke the name of 'le roi Talbot' to scare troublesome children into submission. In 1428, for example, as Governor of Maine and Anjou, he led a punitive expedition against anti-English rebels in Maine during which, as well as destroying castles and burning villages, he massacred the inhabitants of Le Mans who had had the temerity to hand their town over to the French. There is indeed little to suggest that he was ever particularly solicitous about the fate of civilians who crossed his path, and while his motivation to fight stemmed from loyalty to his king, there was a strong financial incentive to it as well. Between 1434 and 1444, as commander of the English troops in Normandy, he earned the considerable sum of £500 a year.

Even that arch celebrator of chivalric values Sir Thomas Malory was scarcely a paragon of chivalric virtue. Born some time between 1415 and 1418 to a Warwickshire gentleman of local importance, he pursued quite a successful early career, being knighted in 1441, possibly seeing military service in Gascony in 1442, and serving as MP for Warwickshire in 1445 (as his father had done). But in 1451 he was accused of being party to a plot to murder the Duke of Buckingham, and then of extortion, rape, theft, cattle stealing, deer stealing, and wrecking a hunting lodge belonging to the Duke of Norfolk and apparently used by Buckingham. Caught up in the power politics of the period he spent long stretches in prison, punctuated by occasional escapes and periods on bail, until the Yorkist triumph of 1460–1. He was then pardoned in 1462, and threw in his lot with the recently returned Yorkist monarch, Edward IV. Later in the 1460s, however, he became implicated in plotting against Edward by his erstwhile supporters, and in 1468 was imprisoned in the Tower of London. His was a fairly easy imprisonment which, *inter alia*, allowed him access to one of the best libraries in England, and it was under these conditions that he wrote the *Morte Darthur*, which was completed around 1470. A Lancastrian coup in that year led to Malory's being freed, and he died in London in March 1471 just as the return of Edward IV was about to reignite the Wars of the Roses. It was scarcely the career one would expect of the author of England's major work of chivalric romance, and it is ironic that he wrote the *Morte Darthur* while imprisoned on the distinctly unchivalric charge of treason.[29]

If there is one manifestation of the age of chivalry that displays an unequivocal, if gradual, move away from – or, at least, a moderating of – violence, it is the tournament.[30] A form of simulated combat designed to train heavy cavalrymen for combat, it seems to have originated in northern France and contiguous areas of the Holy Roman Empire in the decades around 1000, where it was linked with two other contemporary developments. The first was the growing practice among knights of fighting with their lances couched, that is, held under their arm when charging. The second was the rise of heraldry, whose original basic intent was to allow the easy identification of friend and foe on the battlefield, but which over time became a key and highly sophisticated aspect of knightly culture: since the right to possess coats of arms was restricted, heraldic crests imparted status on their bearers.

It took a while before the tournament made its way to England, and it was actually banned by the Crown for much of the twelfth century, but once it was legalised after 1194 (though in theory restricted to licensed locations) it became very popular and over time underwent significant change. Early tournaments took the form of melees, mock (and sometimes not so mock) battles fought with maybe hundreds of combatants on each side over a wide and undefined area. But gradually they became more regulated: locations were fixed and restricted, heralds and other officials took control, rules governing combat became more complex, melees gave way to single combat. The military impulse for the tournament became overlaid by a sporting impulse, as there emerged what we would now describe as celebrity sportsmen: knights (some of whom became well known and were feted) who became fixtures on the European tournament circuit. Combat also became safer as armour improved.

A powerful influence of the changing nature of the tournament was the growing involvement of the monarchy. Royal patronage of tournaments began in the reign of the warlike Edward I, but it was in the reign of his equally warlike grandson Edward III that it became particularly marked. Edward III certainly made sure that the tournament lived up to its original function – during the run-up to the outbreak of the Hundred Years War with the French during the 1330s, for example, it was a means of ensuring that the English knightly elite were fit for combat. But he was also fascinated by the trappings of chivalry – he was, after all, the king who in 1348 founded the Order of the Garter, a select body of twenty-six knights (including himself and his son Edward the Black Prince) that represented the flower of English chivalry.

Gradually tournaments became more ceremonial – by the end of their long history almost exclusively so. Crowds of men and women would gather to watch both the main event and the parades of participants that preceded it. Knights would wear their ladies' favours, anxious to perform feats of prowess that would honour them and, more generally, delight the other women present. Well into the sixteenth century Henry VIII proved a keen jouster, and a possessor of ever-larger suits of jousting armour that bear testimony to his increasing girth. During his daughter Elizabeth I's reign tilts were held to mark the anniversary of her accession, her courtiers assuming the identity of Arthurian characters or other exotic figures for the occasion. Tilts were then revived early in James I's reign by the young Prince Henry, who before his death in November 1612 was being identified, and was obviously fancying himself, as the model of a revived chivalric spirit. On Twelfth Night 1610, for example, the banqueting house at Whitehall witnessed the launch of the prince's career as a public figure with a celebration called 'the Barriers', halfway between a tournament and a court masque, in which Arthurian elements played a major part.[31] Thus over the centuries the tournament, and the jousting that was its central element, was transformed from a free-for-all melee over an ill-defined stretch of land to a tightly controlled formal celebration held at the royal court. It was a remarkable transformation.

IV

The teachings of the Church certainly provided medieval people with a moral compass, just as the chivalric code gave the warlike nobility some sense of a secular code of righteous behaviour, but in practical terms what ultimately proved the most effective constraint on violent behaviour was the increasing effectiveness of the justice system. In medieval England that meant the increasing effectiveness of royal justice. The roots and branches of the legal system were complex. At its heart was the common law, derived from Anglo-Saxon and Anglo-Norman laws and customs, and given greater coherence by the powerful and reforming Henry II. Then there were the customary law codes observed by individual manors and boroughs; and the canon law operated by the Church in its sophisticated system of ecclesiastical courts. There were more specialist areas of the law, too, such as that which operated when disputes occurred between English and foreign merchants and which was handled, by the end of the middle ages, by the Court of Admiralty. But ultimately what held the legal system together, at least in all non-ecclesiastical matters, was the authority of the monarch, and as that authority grew and spread, so did the concept of royal justice.

It was the legally minded Henry II who really started this process, giving England the most advanced royal justice system in Europe by the end of the twelfth century. Those involved in, say, land disputes were now less likely to seek their resolution through informal and often violent means and more likely to turn to the courts. Moreover Henry II established a near-monopoly over the right to try and to punish those suspected of serious crime. It was the Crown that selected judges to be sent out into the shires, where they would co-opt local men into jury service. It was the Crown that, through Parliament, amended existing laws and made new ones. And it was the Crown that, by reinforcing the prerogative it held over the granting of mercy in particular cases, not only helped to ameliorate the operation of a harsh system of punishment but also made it absolutely clear that mercy and justice alike came from the monarch. By the end of the fifteenth century the courts of Common Pleas, King's Bench, Equity and Chancery had, all at Westminster – the epicentre of royal power – established themselves as important arenas for litigation. In 1487 a statute was passed formalising the operations of what was in essence the King's council sitting as a court, the Star Chamber. When Englishmen were indicted for assault, riot, or forced entry into the property of another, the wording of the indictments reminded them that they were offending against not only their victims, but also the King's peace.

Of course, the quality of the justice administered varied according to the royal legal official overseeing it – and there were plenty of instances of corrupt officers and packed juries. It also suffered under weak or ineffective monarchs (as, for example, during the reign of Edward II or at various points in the second half of the fifteenth century), at which juncture over-mighty subjects had a tendency to take the law into their own hands.[32] But the basic idea of settling disputes by law nevertheless gained ground, and an increasing number of people came to see the law, rather than private retribution, as the upholder and arbiter of peace, whether they were litigants or witnesses.

Those slightly higher up the social ladder might serve as jurors in the criminal courts, coroners' inquests and manorial courts, and in the course of the early fourteenth century local gentry came to serve in various local offices, which were to coalesce in the office of justice of the peace. In the course of the fifteenth century the powers of justices were extended, to the point where they came to occupy a position of central importance in the exercise of law and order at a local level.[33] Obviously, being a justice of the peace did not stop some gentry from committing acts of violence, just as jury service did not guarantee morally upstanding individuals among their less prosperous neighbours, but the principle of royal justice nevertheless proved an increasingly powerful one. Its effectiveness was also regarded as a direct reflection of the King's authority.

In late-medieval times, rather than pursue cases through the courts, feuding gentry might sometimes opt to turn instead to informal arbitration. In the past this has been viewed as evidence of the shortcomings of the legal system – and of the limits of royal authority. But the truth is more complex. Arbitration, which appears to have been common in fourteenth- and fifteenth-century Europe, might seem to have been a rather ad hoc affair, but it offered the potential for a settlement to which both sides could be reconciled. The fact that lawyers were quite often involved alongside the great magnates who presided over these proceedings suggests that arbitration and litigation could go hand in hand. And it does seem to have been quite an effective way to settle feuds that might otherwise have ground on for years. A case in point was a property dispute between two fifteenth-century Cheshire gentlemen which was finally settled by arbitration, after which over sixty members of the local gentry were invited to Macclesfield church in April 1412 to witness the formal reconciliation of the two parties.[34]

An inevitable consequence of the rise of legal processes in medieval England was the growth of the legal profession. At first this was unregulated, and lawyers were left to learn their trade from the various law books that were circulating in manuscript from the twelfth century onwards or from service with an established lawyer. Early judges tended to be clergymen. From the beginning of the thirteenth century, though, the judiciary started to become a more secular affair, and, consequently, a career in itself. It also, and very quickly, came to be a profession the Crown was keen to regulate. In the summer of 1298, for example, Edward I, newly returned to England after three years abroad, launched investigations into allegations of corruption and malfeasance against various royal officials, among whom were a number of judges. Eventually, eleven judges suspected of misconduct were either dismissed and fined or compelled to buy their way to forgiveness.[35]

Over the course of the fourteenth century various benefactors helped fund legal studies at Oxford and Cambridge, while two colleges, King's Hall and Trinity Hall, were founded at Cambridge specifically to provide legal training. The two universities primarily offered training in the civil (or Roman) law widely practised on the continent, or the related canon law that operated in ecclesiastical courts. Meanwhile, in London the inns of court emerged, offering training in English common law and so providing the graduates from among whom royal judges (barristers in modern terminology) and common lawyers more generally were recruited. Soon a legal career became an attractive proposition for ambitious men keen to make their way in the world.

The careers of Sir Geoffrey Scrope and his brother Sir Henry are typical in this regard. The sons of a minor Yorkshire landholder who had been knighted in 1298 for military service, both ended up with substantial holdings of land and property. Geoffrey was particularly successful. He not only rose high in the legal profession but also served in diplomatic and military capacities, dying at Ghent in 1340 while accompanying Edward III on an expedition to Flanders. Of his five sons, the eldest became Baron Scrope of Masham, one became a canon of Lincoln Cathedral, and one saw extensive military service, while his two daughters married into a well-known gentry family, the Luttrells of Lincolnshire, a further reminder of the ways in which the law insinuated itself into the wider society.[36]

Of course, the rise of the law carried with it certain problems and abuses. Justice, as noted in the previous chapter, could be a very hit or miss affair. It was not axiomatic that wrongdoers would receive the punishment they deserved, even, that is, if they could be got to court in the first place, and there was always a risk of partisan justices or packed juries or both. Malicious and vexatious litigation could also rear their heads – something contemporary commentators frequently bemoaned. There were always going to be people who regarded litigation as being as satisfying as violence when it came to getting even with others, and who indeed might operate both approaches in parallel. Nevertheless, all social ranks, from those who used the local manorial court to those who took their cases to the Courts of Common Law and Equity at Westminster, were becoming used to the idea that disputes could be settled in a peaceful, legal way.

To take a typical sample: between 1422 and 1442 inhabitants of six eastern counties entered 3,194 suits in the Court of King's Bench at Westminster, the annual average rising from about 40 at the beginning of this period to 120 at its end. Some 616 of these cases involved violence, among them 521 instances of alleged assault, many of which may not have involved much by way of violence, and 61 of homicide. The overwhelming majority of these cases were suits between parties to settle disputes of one sort or another, most frequently over land or other forms of property. In this sample we know the status of 839 plaintiffs, and of these 469 (or 56 per cent) were knights, esquires, or gentlemen or -women. This indicates clearly that those very social groups whose habits of violence have been so often portrayed as a threat to order were by this date seeing the use of the law as a means of settling disputes.[37]

Invoking the law was, of course, not necessarily free from social disruption, and knights and other gentlemen, and indeed many of their social inferiors, might think it better to turn to the law in some circumstances yet resort to violence in others. But legal systems cannot survive unless sufficient people are willing to make use of them. Medieval monarchs may have passed laws, created court systems, and regarded the provision and dispensation of justice as one of the important functions of kingship, but it was their subjects who made the decision to move increasingly from rough to royal justice. And, arguably, this became a virtuous circle: as legal systems expanded, so they became more effective and so more people decided to turn to them or to become involved as jurors, justices, parish constables or other local officers. The increasing vigour of England's administration of justice in the high middle ages, coupled with its complexity (combining as it did common law, statute law, the canon law of the Church and the customary law of the local manor), belies the lazy stereotype of 'medieval savagery'.[38]

PART II

'A POLITE AND COMMERCIAL PEOPLE': FROM THE TUDORS TO THE VICTORIANS

CRUELTY IN PERFECTION.

William Hogarth's 1751 series of engravings *The Four Stages of Cruelty* tells the life story of Tom Nero, who becomes more and more sadistic as the story unfolds. He develops from a boy who enjoys torturing animals, into a coachman who violently beats his horse, into a criminal who (in the engraving shown here) seduces and murders a woman. Although Hogarth's prints conjure up images of a violent society, homicide rates were actually in decline by Georgian times.

CHAPTER 3

THE RETREAT FROM KILLING

Throughout the sixteenth and seventeenth centuries, Sussex was something of a backwater. Poorly served by roads, it contained only two urban centres of any consequence: the cathedral city of Chichester, with a population of 2,500; and Lewes, which numbered perhaps 2,000 inhabitants at the turn of the seventeenth century.[1] Otherwise the county was a patchwork of farmland, with a sprinkling of ports along its coast. To the north was the high wooded ground of the Weald, home to a thriving iron industry that employed as many as 7,000 people at the turn of the seventeenth century, but which also formed something of a natural barrier between London and lowland Sussex. It is scarcely surprising, then, that Sussex had a contemporary reputation for being isolated, backward and wild.

When it comes to crime and punishment in the county, though, posterity has been left with a remarkably vivid picture of life there, thanks largely to the high survival rate of key records, such as assize records and coroners' inquests. Obscure Sussex may have been to many contemporary Englishmen and women – and, of course, therefore not necessarily typical of the country as a whole – but, thanks to these survivals, we are able to glimpse into its seedy underbelly. And doing so gives us some fascinating insights, particularly into the patterns of homicide between about 1560 and 1620 – in other words the period of the reigns of Elizabeth I and James I.[2]

Between 1560 and 1619 surviving records list 153 homicides in Sussex, involving 169 suspects, the vast majority of them male (150 out of the 169). Cases of infanticide are not included in the figures: were they to be, the number of women accused of homicide would, of course, be significantly higher. Victims, too, were predominantly male – only 26 female victims are listed, of whom 10 were killed by other women. As in medieval times, comparatively few cases appear to have involved killings within the family or the home. True, it is not always clear from indictments and coroners' reports whether victim and perpetrator were related. Nor is it clear what other connection the victim might have had with his or her killer. Throughout this period, many households, even a fair way down the social scale, had live-in servants or apprentices, who were subject to physical correction by their masters and mistresses. Despite contemporary strictures that such correction should be 'moderate', some, we know, were maltreated, and a few died as a result. This situation was probably made worse by the expedient, enshrined in Tudor poor-law legislation, of forcing householders to take in parish apprentices, that is poor boys or girls whom the parish could not otherwise support.

But even when all these complicating factors are allowed for, it still seems to be the case that the violence between closely related or connected people that is such a feature of present-day society formed a smaller proportion of overall killings in Elizabethan and Stuart Sussex: those cases where the records state a definite household or familial link – or allow us to infer one – account for only 18 of the 153 homicide indictments. In other words, killings within the family were a fact of life in the sixteenth and seventeenth centuries, but their numbers were outweighed by killings of men unrelated to their (almost exclusively male) attackers.

Of the various domestic killings recorded, six involved husbands killing their wives. Four men went on to be hanged, including a gentleman named Thomas Alderton, who confessed to stabbing his spouse to death. Those spared the noose were Henry Pellyng, who in 1565 beat his wife's brains out with an axe but was found to be insane (the court record terms him 'a frantick man'); and Richard Juden, who was accused of killing his wife with an apple laced with arsenic ('ratsbane') but was ultimately acquitted. The one wife accused of killing her husband – Joan Cholle, who allegedly strangled Henry Cholle in his sleep one night in 1564 – was acquitted. Others hanged for domestic or family killings included Thomas Sheppard, executed in 1608 after being convicted of killing his mother; Thomas Roberts, found guilty of killing his master, Thomas Geering; and Joan Farnecombe, who drowned ten-year-old Leonard Farnecombe (their exact relationship is not stated) in a pond in 1578. Perhaps the most chilling case involving master (in this case, mistress) and servant is that of Isabel, the wife of Robert Woodgate, a gentleman, who in 1616 was accused of killing young Joan Gyles, having routinely subjected her to beatings with staves and straps, and burned her hands with hot tongs. Isabel's case, as presumably befitted her husband's status, was removed to the Court of King's Bench at Westminster, and she was exonerated two years later.

That lethal violence in this period was by no means the sole preserve of the 'lower orders' is demonstrated not just by this case but by the fact that 9 of the 150 men who were accused of homicide were described by the epithet 'gentleman' (to whom might be added the clergyman William Stanbridge, sentenced to be hanged after he was convicted of murdering Richard Burcher by stabbing him to death with a dagger in Singleton churchyard in 1578). Few of these 'gentlemen', though, were found guilty of murder. Most were either convicted of manslaughter, or, if a plea of self-defence was accepted, were pardoned. Their fatal encounters generally seem to have taken the form of an altercation during which they drew their sword. In one instance – involving a tanner named John Kennet – the altercation was clearly a duel: he died at the hand of Sir Thomas Tapper, a gentleman from Portsmouth, who thrust a rapier into him in the fields outside Chichester in 1597.

Assize indictments and coroners' inquests rarely give us more than a bare outline of the circumstances surrounding a killing, but occasionally we receive a slightly closer glimpse. We know, for example, that when in December 1589 two Penhurst labourers, Roland Meadowe and Nicholas Gower, murdered a woman named Alice Smyth, they cut her throat, and then sliced open her belly and removed the unborn child from her womb; both of them were hanged. We know that six-year-old Agnes Newe's death in 1600 came as a result of injuries sustained several months before when a petty chapman named Richard ap Beavans raped her. And we know that when a criminal gang attacked the house of Alice Holmes in 1581, one of the gang, Richard Haward, was badly injured by a sword thrust by one of Holmes's servants, and that, when they had reached a quiet spot away from the house, his associates bludgeoned him to death with their cudgels for fear he would be captured and reveal their identities.

Occasionally it is possible to trace underlying sexual or amatory tensions in a case. In 1572 William Harman, who had for some time been enjoying adulterous relations with Alice, the wife of Robert Thomas of Warbleton (the coroner's jury alleged that they had long plotted Thomas's death), went to her asking her to make a poultice for an ulcer from which he was suffering. Alice did so, and he stripped naked so that the poultice could be applied. Unfortunately Robert Thomas appeared at this juncture, and the two men fought, Harman eventually knocking Thomas's brains out with a mallet he found in an outbuilding. He was executed. Alice claimed that she was pregnant (see below, page 113), but her plea was rejected and she, too, was executed.

Other cases are a little more bizarre, or contain details that offer intriguing insights into everyday life at the time. Nicholas Spynner, for example, who arrived at John Symon's house with a gang of people intent on stealing a maypole that stood outside, was killed instantly when an arrow fired from a window of the house by a certain John Hayward hit him in the neck. In 1576 a man was fatally injured when he stood too near a target during an archery contest, and in the same year, during a bout of throwing the hammer ('sledge') and despite instructions from the master of ceremonies that people should stand well back, one spectator was fatally injured. The verdict was accidental death. A few years before, in 1567, another unfortunate bystander had been killed during a local equivalent of the modern Scottish sport of tossing the caber, 'a throwing of the bar'. Again, the verdict was accidental death. More deliberate was a killing at a football match in 1614, when Richard Longly inflicted fatal wounds on George Hosmer by striking him on the nose with a stone. Hosmer died the following day. The verdict, however, was death by natural causes. And, to round off this catalogue of sport-related deaths, this time from a case that came to the Sussex assizes in 1624, an account survives of a match at Horsted Keynes in which twenty-four-year-old Jasper Vinall was accidentally struck on the head by a cricket bat wielded by Edward Tye and died of his injuries some two weeks later.

If the Sussex records are representative of the country as a whole, it would appear that cases of homicide were spread across all classes and conditions of men in Elizabethan and Jacobean England. Fifty of those accused in Sussex for whom we have a record of their status were labourers. Thirty-six were crafts- or tradesmen. A slightly smaller number – 26 – were husbandmen, that is small to middling farmers, and the same number were described as yeomen, a label which by this period was being applied to richer farmers: men who through their own business acumen, luck or inheritance were benefiting from the general boom that agriculture was enjoying at this time. Of the 169 accused, 45 (33 men and 12 women) were acquitted, and one man and one woman had the charges against them thrown out following an initial screening by the assize grand jury that ruled the evidence too weak to justify a trial. Fifteen others (all male) were described as being 'at large': in other words, they had not been apprehended. For 13 offenders we simply have no details at all either of verdict or subsequent fate.

That leaves a balance of 21 cases that resulted in pardons, reprieves, verdicts of killing in self-defence, or the attribution of a killing to what appears to have been a fictitious perpetrator. Forty of the offenders were hanged (36 men and 4 women); 33 men were found guilty but escaped death by claiming benefit of clergy; and one woman was able to avoid being hanged by pleading pregnancy (see Appendix, Table 1).

What will perhaps come as a surprise, given the popular perception that Elizabethan and Jacobean justice was a blood-soaked affair, is that well over a quarter of those accused were ultimately acquitted (women were far more likely than the men to be found not guilty). Unfortunately, because assize indictments and coroners' inquests tend to be fairly terse documents, it impossible to tell why one case should end in conviction and execution, while another virtually identical one should result in an acquittal. But we do know that, thanks to an intriguing contemporary legal norm (found in other counties on the South-east assize circuit), if the defendant were not found guilty, the death would then be ascribed to a fictitious killer. In some cases, this may have been because the identity of the real killer just wasn't known. In others, though, it's tempting to conclude that it was a means of removing a suspect from the danger of possible execution (on the basis that the punishment dictated by law outweighed the offence committed).

Thus, for example, when Elizabeth Reader was acquitted in 1589 of killing ten-year-old Edward Cooper by beating him with a staff, the boy's death was attributed instead to Thomas Staff. When three cases heard at the Hilary 1592 assizes failed to result in convictions, the killings were attributed to John Atdeath. And when, a year later, Catherine Lucas was acquitted of killing Alice Tuppen with a 'wool card' (a wooden board used for 'carding' wool before it was spun), John Card was named as the culprit. At the same assizes William Anoke was blamed for another homicide, Anoke being a compressed form of the surname 'At the oak' sometimes applied to these fictional killers.

As I have already pointed out, even for those found guilty a death sentence was not inevitable. Indeed of the 169 accused in this period, only around a quarter – 36 men and 4 women – are recorded as having actually been hanged. This may seem surprising given the severe nature of the letter of the law, but the fact is that in practice a degree of leniency was allowed. In some cases, for example, it was possible to escape the noose by claiming benefit of clergy. This was a legal tradition that had its roots in medieval disputes over whether clergymen accused of a felony should be tried in church or in royal courts (a dispute that in part informed Thomas Becket's quarrel with Henry II), and that by the late fifteenth century had settled into a general acceptance that clergymen should be exempt from execution for felony for a first offence.

By this time, too, the definition of a clergyman had been extended from someone who bore a tonsure (in other words, had had the crown of their head shaved) to someone who could demonstrate that they could read – in other words, it theoretically included not just clergy but lay servants and others attached to clerical establishments. Such people, if convicted of a lesser felony, would be branded on the left hand with a hot iron, and would only suffer the ultimate punishment of execution if they were found guilty of a second offence. By the late sixteenth century, however, it's apparent that large numbers of illiterate convicted men were being granted benefit of clergy. In other words, courts were manipulating the system: if they felt there were mitigating circumstances, they could make use of a loophole to spare someone found guilty of a capital offence. Benefit of clergy had become a useful and humanitarian legal fiction, though from the mid sixteenth century onwards, certain felonies (notably rape) were no longer covered by this loophole.

Women, too, could similarly be spared – benefit of clergy for certain forms of larceny, which previously would have carried a capital punishment, being extended to them in 1623. But their best chance of escaping the gallows was to claim that they were pregnant. Under English law pregnant women could not be executed until after they had given birth. In theory, therefore, if a 'jury of matrons' established that a convicted woman was indeed expecting, she would be remanded until the child was born and only then be executed. In practice the plea of pregnancy, like claiming benefit of clergy, seems to have been regarded by the courts as a means of ensuring that 'deserving' offenders did not have to suffer the ultimate sanction. Indeed records suggest that even when convicted prisoners did finally give birth they might well be spared execution.

A handful of such cases appear in the Sussex records, of which one from 1592 involving Katharine Hinton and Susan Roffe, both described as spinsters, is fairly representative. The two were accused of beating Jane Roffe around the head with a staff so severely that she died from her injuries a day later. Both Hinton and Roffe claimed to be pregnant and were remanded until the next session of the assizes when they were examined by a jury of matrons, at which point Roffe was found to be pregnant and Hinton not. Hinton was hanged and Roffe was remanded further. There is no record of her having given birth. She died of natural causes in Horsham gaol in February 1593, fifteen months after her partner in crime was executed.

The use of benefit of clergy and the plea of pregnancy both clearly show that Tudor and Stuart justice was capable of a degree of nuance when determining the severity of a crime and therefore the appropriate punishment that should be meted out. And further legal latitude was introduced over the course of the first half of the sixteenth century by the increasing distinction that was made between the charge of manslaughter and that of murder.[3] In Anglo-Saxon times, 'slaying by stealth' (for example, poisoning or killing by ambush), an offence that clearly presaged the later notion of killing with malice aforethought, was regarded as a 'botless' crime, that is, one that could not be compensated for by payment to the victim's kin; compensation, however, was deemed appropriate for offences such as manslaughter (as we would call it today) and causing a death accidentally.

After the Norman Conquest, and particularly as a result of legal reform in the twelfth century, the situation changed dramatically. Now most felonies became capital offences, in part, no doubt, because England's Angevin rulers wished to introduce a greater degree of deterrence into the legal process; in part, too, because they stood to gain from a stricter interpretation of the law, since in theory the goods of executed criminals passed to the Crown. There were exceptions to the capital rule. If royal servants killed someone while carrying out a royal order, this was deemed justifiable homicide, just as killing thieves caught red-handed and outlaws who resisted arrest was regarded as permissible. But the situation for those who killed by accident or misadventure or in self-defence was more ambiguous. They would be convicted of homicide, and it was then for them to sue for a royal pardon (a system that, as the Sussex records show, survived well beyond medieval times). The assumption was that most killings would be capital offences, only the occasional exceptional case requiring royal intervention.

This inflexible legal framework clearly conflicted with community notions about degrees of culpability in homicide, and medieval juries – who would, after all, often have known the accused and the circumstances of the case at first hand – rapidly worked out ways in which they could bend the rules. The plea of self-defence proved particularly fertile ground. Theoretically, the rules here were very strict: the offender had to convince the court that he had no other means of escape from death than by attacking the person trying to kill him. In practice, though, coroners and trial juries applied a rather more liberal interpretation, often in the face of considerable scepticism on the part of the judge. Thus, for example, a plea of self-defence might well be accepted in a case where later a verdict of manslaughter would have been brought in. A verdict of accidental death was another way of sidestepping a conviction for homicide. Samples of court records show that by the mid fourteenth century only about 20 per cent of those accused of felonious homicide were actually convicted of the charge. Of the remainder, around a third were found to have killed in self-defence, and the balance to have slain accidentally.

This informal situation was clarified and codified in the early Tudor period. Perpetrators of premeditated homicide, or homicide carried out during the course of a robbery or similar offence, were now no longer able to claim benefit of clergy, though those accused of other, less reprehensible, forms of homicide could still make use of this potential escape route. At the same time legal texts started to establish a distinction between murder and manslaughter, the former being deemed to involve malice aforethought, the latter to have been unpremeditated: 'chance medley' as the legal treatises termed it.

Just how quickly the plea of manslaughter was adopted is demonstrated very clearly in those findings from Sussex coroners' inquests between 1485 and 1688 that still survive.[4] Between 1485 and 1558, out of a total of 244 surviving coroners' inquests, 65 resulted in verdicts of murder, 7 in manslaughter verdicts, and 14 in verdicts of killing in self-defence. From the period of Elizabeth I's reign (1558–1603), records of 582 Sussex coroners' inquests survive, of which 53 resulted in a verdict of murder, the same number in a verdict of manslaughter, and 12 in a verdict of self-defence. And for the period 1603–88, from a total of 521 inquests, 96 resulted in a verdict of murder, 69 in one of manslaughter, and a mere 4 in one of in self-defence (see Appendix, Table 2). Manslaughter, in other words, swiftly became a very common verdict in those cases where death was the unplanned consequence of a brawl. These findings also suggest that manslaughter constituted a slightly smaller proportion of felonious killing in the seventeenth century than it did in the second half of the sixteenth, evidence perhaps of the beginning of a withdrawal from the habit of casual violence between men, which was such a feature of medieval and early modern homicide.

The evidence of the Sussex records also suggests that high social status might on occasion help ensure a lighter punishment for a killer. When John Palmer, described as 'esquire' and so clearly a fairly wealthy gentleman, was convicted of manslaughter in 1604 for killing a 'very unruly' man in an East Grinstead tavern, he was excused the ignominy and pain of being branded. Of course, this might equally have been down to the level of provocation he had experienced. The Sussex records also show interesting vestiges of old patterns of justice. In two cases, for example, the medieval mechanism whereby a royal pardon was sought after a verdict of self-defence had been delivered is apparent (general pardons were also occasionally issued).

Where the fatal weapon is recorded in the Sussex record, it tends to be a knife (36 cases), a sword (13) or a cudgel (8) – scarcely surprising in an era when men would have commonly carried such weapons and so have drawn them when arguments flared. Staffs (recorded in 23 cases) were likewise commonly carried or kept at home ready for use, and given the prevalence of agriculture it is scarcely surprising to find that other implements employed in killing included a horse whip, driving goad, scythe, pitchfork, hedging beetle, shovel and 'spadestaff'. Nineteen victims were simply beaten or kicked to death, 6 were suffocated or strangled, and 4 were poisoned (see Appendix, Table 3).

There are also 9 cases recorded involving the discharge of firearms, but it's clear that this was almost always accidental. Tudor and Stuart Englishmen seem to have been incapable of following even the most basic rules of gun safety. A typical example comes from 1573, when William Bunne was accused of killing John Burton with a handgun loaded with hailshot. The coroner's inquest describes how Bunne had been standing hidden from view on a large beam in the barn of his employer, Thomas Palmer, gentleman, intending to kill harmful birds in the barn, and that Burton had been killed when he ran into 'le levell' of the gun when it was discharged.

II

As a rule (and bearing in mind that not all the Sussex assize records survive), the homicide rate that can be extrapolated from the records over the six decades from 1560 seems to be broadly in line with that of other areas of England in the same period. Assuming a population of just under 90,000 in the late sixteenth century, and making an allowance for missing assize records, we can estimate a minimum of 3–4 homicides per 100,000 of population annually in the 1560s, 1570s and 1580s, 5–6 per 100,000 in the 1590s, and then around 4 per 100,000 in the early decades of the seventeenth century.[5] The apparent sharp rise in the 1590s is striking, but it reflects a pattern to be found elsewhere. The fact is that this was a difficult decade, culminating in bad harvests around 1596 and official fears, some of them realised, of widespread public disorder. It is possible that a combination both of a harsher economic climate for the poor and greater attempts made by officialdom to control the population may have helped push up levels of reported homicide.

III

The apparent upsurge in violence in the 1590s was something of an isolated occurrence, and life seems to have returned to normal in the next few decades. But in 1642 the English Civil War broke out, lasting until 1646, and a second outbreak of fighting followed in 1648–9. Warfare also broke out in other parts of the British Isles, English troops seeing service in Scotland and Ireland. Richard Gough, who in his sixties completed a historical account of his home village, Myddle in Shropshire, has left us with a very vivid record of the appalling impact the war had on just one small community. He noted that of the 20 men from Myddle and the neighbouring townships of Marton and Newton who had joined the King's army, 13 never returned. These included Thomas Formeston, 'a very hopeful young man, but at what place he was killed I cannot say', and Richard Challenor, an illegitimate child who grew into 'a big lad', who went off to fight at Edgehill, the first major engagement of the war, and was never heard of again. Then there was Nathaniel Owen, whose father had been hanged and who was himself a ne'er do well;

he was badly injured in an alehouse brawl at Bridgenorth, his injuries leaving him unable to escape when a little later Parliamentary troops set fire to the town. Reece Vaughan, a member of the garrison at Hopton Castle, was cut to pieces when Parliamentarians stormed it. During the fighting there, another local man, John Arthurs, sometime servant to Richard Gough's father, also perished. Completing the list of the dead were Thomas Hayward, 'killed in the wars, but I cannot say where'; Thomas Taylor, 'killed, I think, at Oswestry'; the brothers William and Francis Preece (Gough noted that a third brother was hanged for horse theft); and four men who went to join the Royalist garrison at Shrewsbury, and were never heard of again. To Gough's knowledge, none of the smaller number of local men who fought for Parliament were killed in the wars, although one, John Mould, 'a pretty little fellow', was wounded in the leg by a musket ball which killed the horse that he was riding, so that 'his leg was healed but was very crooked as long as he lived'. 'And if so many died in these three towns', Gough reflected, 'we may reasonably guess that many thousands died in England in that war'.

Recent research has demonstrated the accuracy of this 'reasonable guess'.[6] The historian Charles Carlton has estimated that there were, in fact, 84,830 deaths in battle in England and Wales (34,130 Parliamentarian, 50,700 Royalist) over the course of the war, representing a level of fatalities proportionately equivalent to those suffered in the admittedly shorter period of the First World War. The 4,500–5,500 who died at the bloodiest battle of the Civil War, Marston Moor, fought in 1644, were, in proportional terms, twice as many as the casualties suffered on the first day of the Battle of the Somme. In Scotland, Carlton estimated that 27,245 people died – given the country's tiny population, a much higher proportional loss than England suffered.[7] And in Ireland, the death toll was even higher.

First there were those who died during the Irish Rebellion of 1641, then those who succumbed as a result of the continuous warfare of the 1640s, and finally those who perished during Cromwell's Irish campaigns in the early 1650s, not to mention those who died of famine or disease or as a consequence of the appropriation of Irish land for English and Scottish settlers. The late-seventeenth-century 'political arithmetician' (or, as we would put it today, economist) William Petty, at certain points an administrator in Ireland, put the overall death toll there at 600,000. As a rule one has to treat statistics from this period with considerable scepticism, but recent research suggests that Petty may not actually have been too far wrong.[8] The old Irish Gaelic culture was shattered.

Just how many men actually saw military service is unclear. Charles Carlton has suggested that it may have been as many as a quarter of those of fighting age. This could well be an over-estimate, but it reveals an essential truth: that tens of thousands of men with no previous experience of violence found themselves sent into combat. And the combat in question was normally at close quarters, frequently involving hand-to-hand fighting: even when musketeers fought musketeers, Civil War soldiers could see the men they were trying to kill and who were trying to kill them. A vast swathe of the population thus experienced conditions that would at best harden them and that might at worst brutalise them.

We have very few first-hand accounts of the experience of combat from the Civil War period but one that has survived is contained in the memoirs of Richard Atkyns, a Royalist who raised a troop of cavalry (about eighty men) at his own expense, which was allocated to the regiment of Prince Maurice, King Charles I's nephew. Atkyns was in more or less continuous action from March 1643, taking part in the small-scale, local actions that were so characteristic of the English Civil War. He himself declared that his regiment was more regularly deployed than any other in the Royalist army, 'which gave me more proficiency as a soldier, in half a year's time, than generally in the Low Countries [the great school for soldiering of the period] in 4 or 5 years; for there did hardly one week pass in the summer half year, in which there was not a battle or skirmish fought, or a beating up of quarters'.

Atkyns's memoirs include a couple of accounts of minor

engagements which capture the confusion of the battlefield, and the difficulties of trying to keep sometimes not very enthusiastic troops committed to combat. He also provides us with one of the few Civil War accounts we have of prolonged hand-to-hand fighting in his description of the Battle of Roundway Down on 13 July 1643, when he came very close to capturing the Parliamentarian general of horse, Sir Arthur Haselrig (whose name appears in various spellings). Atkyns was involved in a charge that took him straight towards the enemy general, who fired a carbine and two pistols at Atkyns without hitting him, and who then turned and fled when Atkyns struck him with his sword. Atkyns now fired a pistol at him, but because the bullet struck his sturdily constructed helmet it did not injure him. Atkyns therefore continued on the offensive, and the two men exchanged sword blows, Haselrig again being saved by his armour: 'I . . . stuck by him a good while, and tried him from head to saddle, and could not penetrate him, nor do him any hurt'. For his part, though, Haselrig was able to give Atkyns 'such a blow on the inside of my arm amongst the veins that I could hardly hold my sword'. Atkyns now tried to kill Haselrig's horse, and succeeded in harming it, while two of his officers tried – unsuccessfully – to shoot Haselrig through the head. When the general's horse faltered, 'his headpiece opened behind, and I gave him a prick on the neck, and had [i.e. would have] run him through the head had his horse not stumbled at the same place'. Haselrig, his horse foundering beneath him and surrounded by hostile troops, asked Atkyns 'what good will it do to kill a poor man', and on offer of quarter surrendered. However, in a demonstration of the vicissitudes of the Civil War (and indeed any) battlefield, an isolated unit of Parliamentarian cavalry ('a runaway troop of theirs') appeared, and charged to their general's rescue, Atkyns sustaining a slight wound from a pistol bullet 'which only took off the skin upon the blade bone of my shoulder'.[9]

Such accounts aside, we have very little evidence of how it felt to suffer or inflict violence on the battlefield of that era. We do not have the personal recollections which might tell us how musketeers felt as they tried to maintain their disciplined ranks and files as they loaded and fired their muskets at the same time as another group of men a hundred paces away were firing muskets into them, or what it was like when the two lines closed and they tried to beat out their opponents' brains with the butts of their weapons. We do not know how pikemen felt when they levelled their pikes as Prince Rupert's or Lieutenant-General Cromwell's cavalry swept towards them. We do not know how many Civil War soldiers enjoyed killing, although one seventeenth-century source records that the Royalist commander George Goring reached sexual climax as he rode and cut down fleeing enemies.[10]

We do know, however, that soldiers were not the only people to experience violence at that time. Civilians, too, were affected. Seventeenth-century warfare was not a hermetically sealed affair, confined to isolated military engagements. During the Thirty Years War, for example, which devastated central Europe between 1618 and 1648, ordinary people living in Germany, western France and Bohemia suffered and died on a vast scale. Contemporary English observers commented on this with a sense of both superiority and concern, and in the summer of 1642, as England lurched towards civil conflict, they experienced for themselves just what war could mean for civilians. The tone was set by the sequence of violent events that occurred in the small Northamptonshire village of Kilsby on 9 August 1642, around two weeks before Charles I in effect declared war on Parliament by raising his standard at Nottingham.

On that day about eighty Royalist cavalry rode into the village searching for weapons. According to an admittedly pro-Parliamentary pamphlet about the affair, they asked one of the villagers which side he supported, and on hearing that he favoured Parliament, promptly shot him. When another villager remonstrated with them, telling them that they had killed a faithful subject of the King, a trooper struck him three or four times with his sword, and as he ran away he was fired on. The troopers then proceeded to kill another man, named Henry Barfoote, and wounded others, one soldier inflicting injuries with a pitchfork.

In their hunt for the weapons they were convinced were concealed somewhere in the village, they held cocked pistols to William Bowkley's breast, threatening him with death if he did not cooperate, and also threatened Peter Meades in the same way. Meades fled, only to encounter three other soldiers who set about him with their swords. As he was being maltreated, further troopers arrived and said: 'What do you with that rogue? Come, we will fire the town.'[11] A later Royalist account of the incident was to claim that the soldiers had been fired on by the villagers, which might explain why they acted in such a brutal manner, but, whatever the precise rights and wrongs of the matter, the fact remains that blood was shed. And this was not an isolated incident.

Over the next few years, innumerable English towns and villages were to suffer comparable, or worse, experiences. The Nonconformist minister Richard Baxter was surely correct when he commented that as the war spread, 'I think there were few parishes where at one time or other blood had not been shed'.[12]

Dealing with the presence of troops in the short term was bad enough, but the fragmented nature of the conflict also created many local war zones in which the life of the civilian population was permanently insecure. Richard Gough recorded one incident that occurred at Myddle when he was a young boy. There was a Royalist garrison at nearby Sharwardine Castle, and one of the soldiers there, an Irish junior cavalry officer named Collins, habitually raided the parish, 'and took away cattle, provision, and bedding, and what he pleased'. One day he arrived with seven of his men to take away bedding. Margaret Challener, wife of a local blacksmith, dutifully showed him her best mattress, but he scornfully rejected it as being too coarse, threw it into a pond, and rode his horse over it in derision. Evidently a man of little sensitivity, Collins then stopped to have his horse shoed by Margaret's husband.

By chance Richard Manning, a soldier at the nearby

Parliamentarian garrison at Morton Corbett, happened to enter the village at that moment with a group of his comrades. He shot Collins with his carbine, his men captured two of the Royalists, and Manning went in pursuit of the others, but was thwarted when his horse was killed under him. As for the injured Collins, he was taken into the Challeners' house and laid on the floor. He asked for a mattress to be put under him, but was reminded that he had thrown the only one they had in the pond: 'he prayed her to forgive him', Richard Gough wrote, 'and lay that under him, which she did'. Collins died shortly afterwards.[13]

The Civil War was, then, clearly traumatic for combatant and civilian alike. But it is difficult to find much evidence of post-war trauma, even though so many hundreds of thousands of people were directly affected. Disabled soldiers detailed their wounds when they petitioned the authorities for pensions (Parliamentarian veterans in the 1650s, Royalist after 1660), but these petitions, like other sources, provide little upon which we can build an impression of the psychological impact of their experiences. Modern sensibilities would suggest that men engaged in hand-to-hand fighting, or in the massacre or maltreatment of prisoners of war or of civilians, would have been scarred by the experience. If so, the evidence has yet to be forthcoming.

That said, Richard Gough's reminiscences about Myddle do contain a tantalising anecdote about the long-term effects of war on one particular individual, a man called Peirce. He had served with a force sent by the Cromwellian regime to Flanders in the late 1650s to fight against Spain, and had then become a member of the garrison at Dunkirk. He subsequently returned to England, and when he was discharged, returned to Myddle and became the servant of a local gentleman. But, Gough recalled, 'Peirce was grown such a sad drunken fellow, and so accustomed to fighting', that his master dismissed him. He re-enlisted in the standing army set up after the Restoration, served in the English garrison at Tangiers (a very tough posting), and, being 'expert in arms', eventually became a captain. He ultimately died far from home, still serving in Tangiers.[14]

IV

How typical Peirce was it is impossible to know. He can scarcely have been unique. Yet the fact is that in the decades after the Civil War, levels of violence, far from increasing, actually started to decline. In the middle ages, as previously outlined, the rural homicide rate averaged about 20 per 100,000 of population. Estimates for the early modern period are more difficult to determine, and evidence from some counties, notably Cheshire, suggest very high levels of homicide prosecutions in the early seventeenth century.[15] The national average, according to a number of historians, seems to have been around 10 per 100,000 in the decades around 1600,[16] and these numbers (or, at least, the numbers based on levels of prosecution for homicide) fell markedly after the Civil War and into the eighteenth century.

In Sussex, for example, homicide rates fell from an estimated 2.6 per 100,000 in 1660–79 to 1.2 per 100,000 in 1700–19 to a mere 0.6 per 100,000 in the last two decades of the eighteenth century. Rural Surrey experienced a similar fall in the same periods from 4.3 per 100,000 to 3.5 and 0.9, a striking contrast to the rates estimated for the Elizabethan and Jacobean periods. For urban Surrey, which included the burgeoning urban and industrial borough of Southwark, the figures are, respectively, 8.1, 3.9 and 0.9 per 100,000, suggesting that the shift in behaviour was an urban as well as a rural phenomenon.[17] J. S. Cockburn's work on homicide in Kent between 1560 and the late twentieth century shows a similar pattern, albeit at higher overall levels.[18] He identifies a peak between 1580 and 1611 (with a rate of 6 per 100,000 of population in the 1590s), and a further minor peak of 5.1 per 100,000 in the 1670s, but then a decline – if not as steep as in Surrey and Sussex – to 2 per 100,000 over the late eighteenth century, and a further decline to below 1 per 100,000 after the 1820s.

Cockburn's painstaking work also shows shifts in the ways in which fatal assaults were carried out, at least in Kent.[19] The use of firearms increased, as might be expected given their increased availability and reliability, though it then declined in the course of the nineteenth century (as in the early days of firearm use, accidental discharge of weapons remained a problem; however, guns also increasingly came to be used to see off thieves and burglars – not infrequently with fatal consequences). But what is more significant is that over the same period the use of knives, swords, cudgels and staffs started to decrease. Sharp instruments accounted for nearly a third of the 231 homicides recorded in Kent between 1560 and 1599, but only 13 per cent of the 215 recorded between 1750 and 1799. The same pattern of decline can be detected in cases involving the use of blunt instruments. Poisoning remained a very rare event – only 22 cases are recorded in Kent for the whole of the period 1560–1799 – though, of course, here we can't be sure whether it really was virtually never employed or was used but escaped detection. The one form of fatal violence that saw a proportional rise over this long sweep of history was hitting and kicking (which rose from 6 per cent of cases recorded in the late sixteenth century to 30 per cent by the early nineteenth). References to strangulation and asphyxiation in the records examined by Cockburn tend to be confined to cases of infanticide.

That there is a close link between the changing nature of weapons employed in fights and assaults and the overall decline in homicide rates seems indisputable – and not just in Kent. Quite simply, right across England, the sort of weapons that would once have been readily to hand when an altercation arose (swords, knives, cudgels and the like) came to be less widely carried over the course of the late seventeenth and eighteenth centuries, and so when fights did break out they were far less likely to have fatal consequences than had once been the case.

We know that from the second quarter of the eighteenth century gentlemen became increasingly less likely to carry swords, and that those of their social inferiors anxious to ape them started to follow suit after about 1750. From around 1725, men from more humble stations in society no longer carried the formidable staffs, sometimes iron-tipped, that had been regarded as essential implements of self-defence in the sixteenth and seventeenth centuries. True, gun ownership became more widespread, but guns were rarely employed in the kind of quarrels that had once claimed lives. And while a large number of men continued to carry knives (which, one should remember, were essential work tools for many), they were less inclined to draw them in anger than their ancestors had been. Now it was far more likely that a quarrel would end in a fist fight rather than a stabbing (see Appendix, Table 4).

It's perhaps worth adding that this retreat from the use of weapons and the rise, particularly among the more well-to-do in society, of greater degrees of self-control, was not a uniquely English phenomenon. Although it's very difficult to make direct comparisons between England and its continental neighbours, not least because legal systems differed so markedly from country to country, it does appear to be the case that much of Germany, France, the Netherlands and Scandinavia – like England – moved from high levels of homicide in the middle ages to progressively lower ones over the eighteenth and early nineteenth centuries. (Southern Europe, conversely, was to retain high homicide rates until the late nineteenth century.)[20] From now on fatal attacks arising from what one might describe as casual male violence became less common, particularly among the better off in society. Instead, it was violence among family members or people who were otherwise involved emotionally that was to mark and to mar society – hardly a new phenomenon, of course, but more noticeable now that other forms of lethal violence were in decline. One sure indication of the shift from the casual to the domestic is the proportional rise in the number of female victims in late-Georgian and Victorian homicide cases.

That people's behaviour was changing is very apparent in eighteenth-century depositions dealing with violent deaths. Take, for example, a fight that took place during a drinking session at the Red Lion alehouse at High Leigh in Cheshire in March 1799. Conversation had apparently turned to the topic of fighting, and a certain John Mills, who according to one witness was 'much in liquor', then allegedly challenged a fellow drinker John Latham to fight. Latham declined ('he never had any quarrel with him in his life'), but another of those present, George Whiteleg, suggested first that Mills should fight another man the next morning for a guinea, and then that Mills should spar with him. Mills accepted the challenge, so the two men proceeded to strip off in the parlour of the alehouse and then stepped outside.

Mills struck the first blow, causing Whiteleg to reel a little, but then Whiteleg managed to knock his opponent to the ground. At this point Latham tried to interpose, saying, 'I think the battle is over,' but Mills declared, 'Thou shalt see whether it is or not,' and began to fight again. Whiteleg eventually knocked him down, and he died more or less instantly. (It comes as no great surprise to learn that drink was a not infrequent factor in fatal assaults: a sample of depositions relating to 64 homicides in northern England in the second half of the seventeenth century reveals that a third of them occurred following a drinking session in an alehouse.)[21]

What is interesting about this fatal encounter is not so much Mills's alcohol-induced aggression, as the relative formality of the fight. Far from setting about each other straightaway, Mills and Whiteleg first observed certain conventions: they stripped for the combat, and they then stepped outside. Once in the open, according to the various depositions made later, an onlooker named John Pownall told Whiteleg to watch where he hit Mills, and also told John Latham to ensure that it was a fair fight. As for Latham, not only did he try to stop the fight when Mills was knocked down the first time, but he testified that the fight got underway only when both parties had declared themselves ready. Mills himself was aware that a fight involved certain rules, and at one point he questioned whether Whiteleg was fighting fair, asking the onlookers, 'Do you allow rising blows?' In other words, while this may have been an alehouse brawl that got out of control, both participants and onlookers had a sense of 'fair play' – of what was allowed, and what should be avoided. This was not casual aggression.[22]

Other Cheshire depositions from the seventeenth and eighteenth centuries show that John Latham was not unique in his assumed role of peacemaker. In 1673, for example, when Richard Downes and Richard Davenport encountered each other in a Wilmslow alehouse and proceeded to quarrel about the price to be paid for loading turves, the landlord (according to his wife Margery Peirson) intervened, 'desired them not to fight in the house', and 'laid hold on Davenport & wished him to be quiet.' Davenport responded 'I will be quiet if he [Downes] will let me', and stayed behind with Margery in the alehouse when Downes suggested they should go outside to fight. Unfortunately, although Downes left briefly, he then returned and called Davenport out to fight ('I have beaten thee 20 times & I will beat thee again'). His confidence proved sadly misplaced. In the ensuing fight, Davenport inflicted fatal injuries on him.[23]

A not dissimilar pattern of events occurred in 1755 when an altercation over payment for a cow broke out in another Cheshire alehouse, this time at Butley. On this occasion a certain Thomas Bann threatened violence against John Hollingworth, but Hollingworth 'got hold of him and pulled him down and bid him sit still and said to him Thomas we have been neighbours a great while and I am not come here to fall out with thee. Let us part friends as we met.' Hannah Hudson (probably the wife of the owner of the alehouse) was later unable to confirm Hollingworth's account (she couldn't recall 'whether [which] of them got up first or whether [which of them] threatened'), but she, too, claimed that she tried to act the peacemaker, telling both men that she 'desired 'em to drop their argument and be quiet and endeavoured to stop them quarrelling'.

Whether or not it was, in fact, John Hollingworth or Hannah Hudson who tried to stop the situation getting out of control, his or her pleas fell on deaf ears. The two men ended up brawling.

Ultimately Hollingworth succeeded in knocking Bann to the ground. John Hudson, the owner of the alehouse, managed to pull the combatants apart, but it was too late: Bann had already suffered fatal injuries.[24]

A few years later, in 1798, a man named Samuel Fisher was killed by a blow to the temple at the Red Lion in Chistleton. He felt he had been cheated during a game involving pitching coins at a pin fixed to a table, had threatened to fight any person in the room and was ultimately worsted by a man named Lloyd. But before this happened, another man, Richard Edwards, who had offered to take up Fisher's challenge, 'was prevented by his friends persuading him to the contrary' (interestingly, according to one deposition, 'from the ill behaviour of Fisher [Edwards] began to pull off his clothes in order to accept the challenge' – further evidence that fighting was becoming more formalised). And Lloyd himself had been anxious to avoid a confrontation, saying to Fisher: 'do be quiet, nobody wishes to fight you and shake hands with me'.[25]

V

If the Cheshire depositions show that the 'chance medley' of early-sixteenth-century legal texts was becoming both rarer and less random, they also catalogue cases of the type that were now to become more significant – at least in relative statistical terms: cases involving not casual male violence, but premeditated assault. The death of Mary Statham alias Malone is a case in point. Her body was found in a mill pond at Lymm in 1798. At the inquest, the coroner's jury gave a verdict of murder by persons unknown, but local suspicions focussed firmly on a young man she was known to have been seeing: John Thornhill, butler in the household of the local rector, Archdeacon Egerton Leigh. Statham had been found to be pregnant when her body was examined, and the inevitable assumption was that Thornhill was the father. That was certainly the view of Phoebe Daniel, a friend of Statham's who lodged in the same house as her, a key witness both at the coroner's inquest and at Thornhill's subsequent trial at Chester. It was also the view of several of Leigh's servants, who testified that they had seen him on the night of Statham's disappearance holding bloodied clothes, which he had then attempted to wash, claiming that the blood had come from a cut finger. Thornhill was tried, convicted and executed.

This has all the hallmarks of a case we would expect to encounter today – violence within a relationship, a murderer seeking to be free of someone they regarded as an encumbrance. The tone of the depositions, and of a contemporary pamphlet describing the case, similarly have quite a modern tone to them. God was invoked, both by Egerton Leigh's wife and by one of Thornhill's fellow servants, who reminded him, when he was planning to run away, that he could not escape divine law. But the evidence about his alleged liaison with Statham and his attempts to wash and explain away his bloodied clothes is given in measured and factual terms. And, in what was increasingly to become a feature of criminal cases, members of the medical profession were also called as witnesses.[26]

VI

If there is one person of this period who exemplifies the general retreat from violence and at the same time the willingness to use it, someone who could at one moment accept that there should be rules that governed behaviour and at the next be quite prepared to disregard them, it is the prolific autobiographer John Cannon. He is of particular interest because, far from being a typical upper-class memoirist of the period, he came very much from the middle rank of society – from precisely that class whose slow relinquishment of violence can be traced in the declining homicide figures of the period.

Born of farming stock at West Lydford, Somerset, in 1684, Cannon showed considerable early academic promise at various parish schools. Unfortunately, though, any ambition he might have entertained towards further formal education had to be abandoned when his family fell on hard times and he was forced to enter the world of work as a 'servant in husbandry' – in effect, an agricultural labourer – at the age of only thirteen. He subsequently worked in the Excise service, then set up briefly as a maltster in Bridgewater before going bankrupt, and after that, apart from a spell as an exciseman again in 1729–30, earned his living as a schoolmaster and scrivener, among various other jobs. Latterly he lived at Glastonbury, where he extended his activities as a scrivener into conveyancing and accountancy, and also served as town schoolmaster and clerk to both the town's parishes. He married in 1714, fathered four surviving children and finally died in 1743.

Although Cannon's education had been cut short when he was very young, he was a formidable autodidact, an avid collector and reader of books – and an obsessive recorder of his own life. Over the years he kept voluminous records, and then in 1740–1, towards the end of his life, he turned these into the *Chronicles* of his life – roughly 700 closely written manuscript pages containing some 600,000 words – after which he destroyed all the earlier material he had compiled and drawn upon. These detailed *Chronicles* offer a fascinating insight into everyday behaviour of the period – and into Cannon's own outlook and attitudes.

Like most people before and since he took a keen interest in local crime and punishment, and his autobiography records a number of homicides and suicides. He describes, for example, a particularly brutal murder case from 1730 involving a local man named William White and a Shaftesbury shoemaker called Anthony Sutton. The two apparently met at an inn, where Sutton happened to mention that he had a letter to deliver but was not sure of the way. White offered to show him, the two men set out together, and as they walked they encountered two women whom White attempted to kiss and to molest. Sutton reproved him for his conduct, the two men quarrelled and the quarrel turned nasty. Ultimately, White felled Sutton with a hedge stake which killed him, and inserted the stake into his victim's mouth with such violence that both cheeks were torn out. He then hid the body in a ditch.

White was soon arrested and committed by the coroner to Ilchester gaol, where he was apparently tricked by other prisoners into confessing his crime. If that wasn't evidence enough, it was also noted that Sutton's corpse bled when White touched it – a sure indication of guilt. White was convicted at the assizes and hanged in chains near the place where he had committed the murder.

A more everyday killing that Cannon noted was another of those pub brawls that got out of control that seem to be such a hallmark of the period. Here, John Parsons, 'a very quiet honest man', had gone into the Cornish Chough ('a very bad house') where he had got into a quarrel with Charles Parker, 'a vile young man'. Parker wrestled Parsons to the ground, '& with his knees kneaded him on the bowels & members in such a violent & barbarous manner that the poor man languished & died in great torture & anguish.' Parsons left behind a widow and two children. Parker was found guilty of manslaughter.

But where Cannon's recollections are perhaps most revealing is in their chronicling of the sort of violence that never made its way into court records – the minor quarrels that can be so revealing of the tenor of everyday life. He records, for instance, a parish vestry meeting in 1737 when one of the vestry men, John Applin, arrived drunk, got into an argument with one of his colleagues, and threw a candlestick in his face. He describes how two men who had been drinking at his house (which he occasionally ran as an alehouse), 'stripped themselves & fought a fair battle' one evening. He tells how two women disputing their rights to a pew in one of Glastonbury's churches nearly came to blows in 1740; and how earlier that same year an infantry lieutenant horse-whipped a Glastonbury man who refused to fight a duel with him. Cannon also recalled an incident from earlier in his life when he had been asked by a certain William Parfet to draw up a will for his mother, then on her deathbed. He turned up at the house, only to be confronted and challenged by

Parfet's brother (apparently his mother had threatened to cut him out of the will), who was promptly felled by a blow from behind by a club-wielding William. Cannon thought the whole family to be mentally disturbed.

And John Cannon himself – respectable, literate and well-read as he was – was perfectly capable of violence when he thought the occasion demanded it. In 1710, while he was still a young man, he received 'a cursed rascally affront' from a drunken butcher named Anthony Atherton, who accosted him while he was carrying out his duties as an exciseman, 'cursing, swearing, & calling me rogue, rascal, dog & eavesdropping fellow, & struck at me with his whip'. Cannon pushed him and his horse 'down a precipice into a hollow way', and when Atherton rallied and he and his manservant went back on the offensive, 'I banged them both soundly'. Such was the level of the subsequent verbal abuse that Cannon reported the matter to a justice of the peace. In 1737 Jacob Meaker insulted Cannon's daughter while drinking at his house, whereupon Cannon struck him 'a smart blow on the face with my fist which fetched the blood away and he bled like a pig'. When Meaker's brother intervened, Cannon flattened him – 'my other guests commended me in this act,' he noted.

On another occasion, the wife of a man Cannon had knocked down after an altercation 'hauled him away but commended my act for he was so drunk he knew not what he said or did', adding that he had just spent half a guinea thinking it was sixpence. In 1742, by now in his fifties, Cannon knocked down a 'very drunk' man who had insulted and struck him at an alehouse. He also recorded two occasions when he struck his wife, incidents which clearly troubled him but for which he claimed extreme provocation.

Cannon, in other words, inhabited a world where affrays and more serious forms of violence, often accompanied by drunkenness and frequently preceded by abusive language, were a regular, if not necessarily sought after, occurrence. Yet he also lived in a society that could reject violent behaviour, and that was prepared to invoke the forces of law and order to avoid it. He recalls in his autobiography an incident that occurred when he was a young man visiting a local fair, in which a recruiting sergeant slipped a guinea into his hand and claimed to have enlisted him. Cannon resisted and a mob immediately assembled, which 'soundly thrashed' the sergeant. But what is interesting is that Cannon then led his defenders to a nearby inn where he knew a justice of the peace was drinking and got the justice to issue a reprimand to the recruiting sergeant. In other words, although he could have left the matter to mob rule, he chose not to. He got the justices involved on another occasion when violence broke out between some of his neighbours, and he records moments of restraint: when he 'managed' rather than fought a man who had threatened him, and when onlookers restrained a man named Peter Hunt when it looked as though he and Cannon were about to brawl.

He also records an incident that took place in 1738 involving two women who were due to appear at the quarter sessions for fighting but who agreed to a reconciliation, and another reconciliation that took place later that year after a scuffle between William Nicholls and Charles Parker at one of Glastonbury's pubs, following the intervention of Parker's mother and sister. Violence may have been part of the fabric of Cannon's everyday life, but so were restraining forces, both official and private.[27] Interestingly, there are even records that survive from Cannon's era of reconciliations taking place after the most appalling of assaults. When, for example, John Venables was seriously beaten up by Thomas Richards during a brawl in Cheshire in 1686, Richards 'went to see how the said Venables did & asked him for forgiveness who said he would forgive him with all his hart'.[28] Venables died shortly afterwards.

VII

Violence, then – and certainly fatal violence – was in retreat. By 1800 strangers or neighbours were far less likely to attack each other than they would have been two centuries before. By 1800, if a fight did break out it was less likely to have a fatal outcome: swords and clubs had given way to feet and fists. And by 1800 it was quite likely that a bystander would seek to intervene to stop a brawl or that, if it did go ahead, some sort of moderating, if rough, code of conduct would be invoked. The question is: why?

There is, of course, no single or easy answer. But it's tempting to turn to Elias and his civilising process for clues. As relative prosperity spread to a greater number of people, as commerce became more complex and more ubiquitous, so a widening circle of society came to have a vested interest in peace and stability and to become averse to too great a degree of risk-taking, impulsivity or instant gratification. As that great champion of trade Adam Smith put it: 'commerce and manufactures gradually introduced order and good government, and with them, the liberty and security of individuals, among the inhabitants of the country, who had before lived in a continual state of war with their neighbours'.[29] People became less violent because it was in their interests to do so: they felt that they had acquired a stake in society and were therefore less likely to behave in a way that might undermine its stability. And as those who had most to gain from such a society modified their behaviour, so those a little further down the pecking order started to imitate them and likewise turned their back on violent behaviour.

It's also tempting to suggest – admittedly, very speculatively – that the events of the 1640s might have played a part in this retreat from violence. Such was the bloodshed of the English Civil War that it seems to have resulted in a certain revulsion against brutality, or at least reduced the nation's capacity for it. Additionally, in causing the deaths of 100,000 or so young men it removed at a stroke many of that sector of society traditionally most prone to acts of civil aggression. More generally, the carnage of the Civil War, along with new strains of disease, notably an especially virulent form of smallpox, and mass emigration later in the century (particularly to England's American colonies), helped reduce the population in an era when agriculture had still not made the necessary strides to fully support it. The social and community pressures which had been such a dominant, if unrecognised, feature of English life in the century before 1640 were therefore alleviated to a certain extent, and it is arguable that this led to a diminution in interpersonal tensions and so, perhaps, in interpersonal violence.

One of the most striking features of life in the eighteenth century is the change that took place in attitudes to masculinity. The Elizabethan gentleman, quick to rise to a perceived insult (think, for example, of the warring Capulets and Montagues in *Romeo and Juliet*), gave way to a gentleman who might possibly be goaded to fight a duel (see Chapter 8) but who also valued the qualities of self-control and forbearance. Manliness was now felt to go hand in hand with what the new era termed 'politeness'. This was a malleable and somewhat ill-defined concept, but in rough terms it could be said to have encompassed such social qualities as polished manners, good taste, genteel comportment and a sense of moral responsibility. At first it was an exclusive social code for the elite. Over the decades, though, it increasingly came to be copied by people further down the social scale. Even among artisans and, to an extent, unskilled workers, the traditional rough culture in which casual violence was generally accepted started to change. One foreign visitor to London in 1765 compared the capital's streets to the 'state of nature' described by the seventeenth-century political thinker Thomas Hobbes, in which life was 'solitary, poor, nasty, brutish and short'. But by the end of the century other visitors were remarking on the general orderliness and civility of London's common people. By 1800, the English, if not exactly what the great legalist Sir William Blackstone described as 'a polite and commercial people', were on their way to becoming at least a rather gentler people, embracing what the Georgians called 'politeness' and what the Victorians would describe as 'respectability'.[30]

The Spanish Tragedie:

OR,

Hieronimo is mad againe.

Containing the lamentable end of *Don Horatio*, and
Belimperia; with the pittifull death of *Hieronimo*.

Newly corrected, amended, and enlarged with new
Additions of the *Painters* part, and others, as
it hath of late been diuers times acted.

LONDON,
Printed by W. White, for I. White and T. Langley,
and are to be fold at their Shop ouer againſt the
Sarazens head without New-gate. 1615.

The public's ravenous appetite for descriptions of violence was suggested by
the popularity of *The Spanish Tragedie* (1587), a wildly successful play which culminates
in the gory death of all its main characters. As theatres became more widespread
during the sixteenth and seventeenth centuries, sensationalist stories about
violence became ever more common.

CHAPTER 4

VIOLENCE IN PRINT: FROM MURDER PAMPHLETS TO REVENGE TRAGEDIES

I

In 1573 George Saunders, a respectable London merchant-tailor, fell victim to a murderous conspiracy involving his wife Ann, a 'gallant' named George Browne, and a widow, Anne Drury, who dabbled in fortune-telling and quack medicine. The motive for the crime was a straightforward one – Browne was infatuated with Ann Saunders and wanted to marry her. To that extent, then, this was scarcely an unprecedented case. But it achieved a measure of immediate fame by becoming the subject of a printed pamphlet. And in so doing it also achieved lasting fame as the first of a genre that was to prove hugely popular over the next two and a half centuries. In a matter of decades, murder pamphlets became a staple of the nascent publishing industry, eagerly snapped up by a fascinated and increasingly literate population. Indeed by the time Henry Goodcole came to write his 1635 pamphlet *The Adultresses Funerall Day*, which dealt with the case of Alice Clarke, burned at the stake for poisoning her husband,[1] he could draw parallels with a whole series of widely publicised murders that had made their way into print.

These stretched back to a killing made famous by a play – that of Thomas Arden (or Ardern) of Faversham in Kent in 1551 (another husband dying as a result of his wife's plotting)[2] – and forward to murders that had been committed 'within the compasse of foureteene moneths or there abouts': for example, the case of Enoch ap Evans, who had beheaded both his brother and his mother, and had been executed at Shrewsbury;[3] 'Country Tom and Canbery Besse' (subjects of another pamphlet by Goodcole), who had murdered several gentlemen in the London area;[4] and Mistress Page of Plymouth, who had murdered her husband.[5] Goodcole enjoyed a certain professional advantage in finding material for his pamphlets. Born in London's Clerkenwell in 1586, he became chaplain to the prisoners in Newgate gaol in 1620 where one of his major tasks was the spiritual preparation of capitally convicted felons for death, a duty that often included ministering to them as they stood on the scaffold. He therefore had first-hand knowledge of London's criminal underbelly. But as the range of parallel cases he describes shows, he could reach beyond the walls of Newgate to draw on a wealth of published literature.[6]

Goodcole's pamphlets, like the Saunders pamphlet they followed, were pretty typical of the genre in that they dealt not with everyday killings but sensational murders that either involved an extreme degree of cruelty or had an 'unnatural' element to them, notably the murder of one spouse by the other. Like the Saunders pamphlet, too, they had a strongly religious overtone. Goodcole was a parish clergyman for many years, as well as a Newgate chaplain. The possible author of the Saunders pamphlet, Arthur Golding, was not only the translator of Ovid's *Metamorphoses* (on which Shakespeare drew in a number of his plays) but of a number of religious tracts too. Both men viewed murder through the prism of human depravity, and as a manifestation of the divine purpose. As for the discovery of a murder and the identification of those responsible for it, this, too, was frequently viewed as the outcome of divine intervention.

An anonymous pamphlet from 1658 entitled *A True Relation of the Most Horrid and Barbarous Murders Committed by Abigail Hill* shows the extent to which a belief in divine retribution commingled with what was effectively popular superstition. Abigail Hill was convicted of murdering a number of pauper children who had been entrusted to her care, and the author of the pamphlet is at pains to place her crimes in a biblical context, reminding us that murder stretches back to the time of Cain and Abel and that 'we shall ever find God so tender in shedding of blood, that his Commandments are always and altogether expresse against it'. But he also points out that throughout history 'the murderer hath seldom escaped undiscovered or unpunished' and that proof of guilt can emerge in many different ways: whether through the subsequent behaviour of the murderer or the reaction of birds and beasts or the appearance of ghostly apparitions:

> For besides the checks [reprimands] of the conscience which showeth forth terror, and flew in the face of the murders, we shall find that it hath pleased God oftentimes in a miraculous manner to make discoveries of murders committed, sometimes by birds, sometimes by beasts, and sometimes by the apparition of the person murdered, of which histories can furnish us with abundant examples and no ages have been exempted from giving many remarkable demonstrations of it.

To support this assertion the author tells us of a 'cruell and covetous young man' who murdered his step-brother in the hope of gaining possession of his inheritance, and then attempted to cover his tracks by claiming that his step-brother had travelled abroad and died 'beyond the seas'. However, murder will out. While walking one day, the murderer was plagued by two ravens. Unable to scare or to shoot 'these two dreadfull and blackwinged summoners,' the pamphleteer tells us, 'his heart and his hope fainted and raving with dispaire he confessed the murder he committed'.[7]

Ghosts presented godly Protestants with something of a theological conundrum. On the one hand, their intervention in the detection of murder clearly illustrated divine providence at work. On the other hand, it was difficult to square the idea that troubled souls might populate some sort of gap between this world and the next with the

Reformation's rejection of the notion of purgatory. Authors of popular pamphlets were not so bothered by such intellectual niceties, and ghosts make a fairly frequent appearance in the literature of the age, for the most part as spectral presences who haunt their killer and bring his or her crimes to light. Thus a seventeenth-century report tells of a North Yorkshire man, murdered by his wife's lover, who returns from the grave to haunt him and, ultimately, to cause him to break down and confess to his crime.[8] Rather more bizarre is a late-seventeenth-century pamphlet that describes how a Northamptonshire man named William Clarke was accosted by a ghost who informed him, with admirable precision, that he had been beheaded 'two hundred and sixty and seven years, nine weeks, and two days ago' by people who had wanted to lay hands on his fortune, which was buried far away in Southwark. The ghost offered to show Clarke where the fortune was buried if he would meet him on London Bridge; and Clarke, having consulted the minister of his parish and various other godly men, duly travelled to London, met the ghost, and went on to unearth a considerable quantity of gold.[9]

Ghosts even intruded on the legal process on occasion. In 1728, for example, it was reported that a number of people claimed to have seen the ghost of a boy who had recently died. Up until the sightings, it had been assumed that he had died of natural causes, and so he had been buried without an inquest being conducted. But now, on the strength of the stories he was hearing, the coroner ordered that the body be exhumed. An inquest was held, and it was concluded that the boy had been strangled. A verdict of murder was therefore returned, although no one was ever convicted of the crime.[10]

The religious tone of these murder pamphlets is particularly noticeable in a very important early collection of murder accounts by Anthony Munday, *A View of Sundry Examples, reporting many straunge Murthers, sundry Persons periured, Signes and Tokens of God's Anger towards us*. Munday (1560?–1633) was a prolific author whose oeuvre comprised translations of French, Italian and Spanish romances and anti-Catholic tracts (since he had flirted with Catholicism in his youth, this was presumably an attempt to distance himself from his earlier indiscretions). In *A View of Sundry Examples* Munday briefly notes five suicides, an infanticide, a killing categorised as misadventure, and twelve murders. Like Goodcole and Golding, he is particularly interested in crimes involving family members, and his murder victims include two mothers, a brother, a brother-in-law, and two children who had their brains dashed out by their mother. And what, according to the title-page, links these cases together (along with an account of 'what straunge and monstrous children have of late beene borne', and a 'short discourse' about a recent earthquake) is that they are all manifestations of sin – or to quote the title-page again, of 'signes and tokens of God's anger towards us'. According to Munday, the human race is rife with sinfulness, and the Almighty is more than prepared to punish people for it:

> Beholde, howe the world is given to wickednesse, for one disdayneth that his neighbour shall thrive by him, another coveteth his neybour's goods uniustly, some one is bent to this vice, some to that . . . who goeth to wracke, whome they murder, whome they spoyle, the proofe whereof is current.[11]

This obsession with human weakness and sinfulness tends to mean that pamphleteers of the period are rarely interested in the niceties of motivation. Provocations offered by drunken and brutal husbands and unfaithful wives figure prominently, but little or no attempt is made to delve more deeply into what prompted the breakdown of a particular relationship or to explain why people might have behaved the way they did.

Consider, for example, the tragic events described in *The Unnaturall Grand-Mother*, a pamphlet published in 1659. The daughter of Elizabeth Hazard, 'a woman, that sold oranges and lemons neer Soper-lane end in Cheap-side', had left her child in the care of a trusted maidservant, but Elizabeth had decided to send the servant away and take the child to bed with her. The next morning, Elizabeth took her sleeping grandchild from her bed. Her initial intention, apparently, was to dash its brains out. Then, 'spying a great tub of water', she plunged the child's head underwater, holding it there until the child drowned. After that she dressed herself in her best clothes – something her neighbours commented on as she left the house – and, on encountering a maidservant, invited her back to 'see what I have done this morning'. The horrified maid, seeing the drowned child lying in the tub, immediately opened a window and cried out: 'Murder!' Of course, to a modern reader, Elizabeth immediately comes across as a severely mentally disturbed woman – someone to be pitied as much as her actions can be condemned. To the pamphleteer, however, she was an agent of the devil. And the fact that the murder was discovered so easily was simply an instance of God's unwillingness to 'suffer the murderer to go unpunished'. Interestingly, the pamphleteer is aware that Elizabeth had been unstable for quite a period: 'for this many years, she hath been tempted to kill the mother of this child before she was married, and had hid knives at severall times to that intent'. His conclusion as to why nothing had come of this before: 'God did prevent it'.[12]

Where blame is apportioned at a more human level in these pamphlets, it tends to be according to conventional notions of the mutual rights and responsibilities of wives and husbands. Take, for example, the very black-and-white treatment of a marriage gone sour in a tract of 1641 that describes how Anne Hamton of Westminster murdered her husband. The husband, 'a loving man indeed' who 'delighted in nothing more but to see his wife pleasant', worked hard on his and her behalf. Ann, by contrast, was always 'gossiping' with 'one young fellow or other', or with 'such women as were like to her selfe; never more joyfull than when she was out of her good husbands company', so that 'what her husband got by taking pains, she spent by taking her pleasure'. When he tried to remonstrate with her, she scolded him, and stormed off to complain about his conduct to her landlady, a close confidante. The landlady's proposed solution was the rather extreme one of poisoning him, which Anne duly did, giving him 'five drams of poison, enough to have destroyed ten men'. A surgeon was sent for, who 'ripped up his body' and found poison lying around his heart. Constables were called in immediately and arrested the two women, who were awaiting trial when the pamphlet was published. 'Harken to me you that be wives,' the pamphlet orders, 'and give attendance you which as yet be unmarried, regard the words of Saint Paul which commands [sic] that every wife should love her own husband as Christ the church'. A conventional message, conveyed within a very conventional account of a husband's murder.[13]

Such an obsession with sin and divine displeasure is typical of the obsessive desire for godliness that English Protestants – and, particularly, English Puritans – pursued throughout the first half of the seventeenth century. It is perhaps most noticeable in a murder pamphlet that was published in 1653, just four years after Charles 1's execution and at the height of the new Republic's power. It describes two murders carried out by a gentleman named Adam Sprackling, who lived on the Isle of Thanet in Kent, one of which was the exceptionally brutal slaughter of his wife ('a woman of precious report for many vertues'). Sprackling was clearly deranged, and determined, if unsuccessful, efforts were made to ensure his avoidance of the death penalty on grounds of insanity. But the author's interest in the case is motivated by purely religious considerations:

Against this sin of murther, the wrath of God hath been revealed from heaven, by his just and daily revengings of innocent blood upon murtherers. Treasures of examples of judgments in this kind, both old and new, ly [lie] before us. From the time of bloody Cain, to the blood thirsty popish rebels in Ireland, to which slaughter men of the scarlet whore of Rome, God hath given plenty of blood to drink. We see bloody men daily cut off by the sword of justice in all places . . . and the late murthers in the Isle of Thanet in the county of Kent, and the judgement of God of the murtherers, call for a book, wherein they may be written for examples to the generations present and to come.

At the end of the pamphlet the author (unusually for this genre) itemises nine lessons that should be learned from this tragedy, ranging from a warning to withstand temptations of all sorts, and especially those stimulated by malice and wrath, to a desire that central government should ensure the better government of the Isle of Thanet, and that a godly minister should be appointed there, since 'the dark corners of the earth are full of the habitations of cruelty'.[14]

If murder was all part of a divine plan, so could its detection be, and many pamphlets record the seemingly miraculous ways in which criminals were unmasked. In Hertfordshire in 1606, for example, a brother and sister who witnessed Annis [Agnes] Dell and her son George committing a robbery, were kidnapped by the duo, and taken to their house where young Anthony James was murdered and his sister had her tongue cut out. A little later, however, the girl miraculously regained the power of speech and was thus able to name her assailants, so that (as a contemporary pamphleteer wrote) 'by her the wonderfull workes of God might be glorified, and the murtherers discovered'.[15] The Dells were both hanged.

Divine intervention might also on occasion even lead to remorse on the part of the criminal. In the mid-1630s Thomas Shearwood and Elizabeth Evans embarked on a murderous crime spree in London, Elizabeth pretending to be a prostitute who led gullible gentlemen to suitable secluded places, Shearwood then killing them and rifling their corpses. One day, however, as Shearwood passed the place where one of their victims was laid out for public view, he experienced a severe nosebleed, which prompted him to advise his partner that 'wee must of necessity, leave of[f] this course of life'.[16]

II

If a Christian worldview lay at the heart of these murder pamphlets, it was one that had undergone a subtle change since medieval times. In the middle ages, notions of wrong-doing were viewed through the prism of the Seven Deadly Sins – a readily comprehensible list of human failings that ranged from wrath to lust, sloth to gluttony. With the Reformation, however, the emphasis moved from the Seven Deadly Sins to the Ten Commandments – and when it came to violence the Sixth Commandment in particular: 'Thou shalt not kill' (*Exodus*, 20:13).[17] That doesn't mean the Ten Commandments were wholly unfamiliar to late-medieval church-goers – various prose and verse paraphrases were in circulation – but the very fact that they were paraphrases reflects the Church's suspicion of direct lay access to the scriptures (hence its persecution of the Lollards and their English translation of the Bible).

With the Reformation, however, all this changed. Henry VIII's Injunctions of 1536, the Protestant Prayer Books of 1549 and 1552, and the Elizabethan religious settlement of 1559, all acknowledged that the Ten Commandments, the Creed and the Lord's Prayer were central to religious instruction. By the late sixteenth century children were, in theory at least, being regularly versed in the Catechism, that is taught the basics of Christianity every Sunday, and this involved not just learning about the Ten Commandments but memorising them, too. In parish churches, the wall paintings that had so vividly depicted Bible stories and the perils of sin, hell and purgatory were whitewashed over, and (usually on the basis of instructions from the local bishop) the Ten Commandments were either inscribed in their stead or written on boards that were prominently displayed.

In the high middle ages people were not allowed to read the Bible in English. Now they were being actively encouraged to do so, and increased levels of literacy meant that many were in a position to read it as well as the numerous devotional works that rolled off the printing presses in the later sixteenth and seventeenth centuries. In the high middle ages people were told to avoid the sin of wrath. Now they read or knew by heart the injunction contained in *Exodus*, 20:12. Christianity had become, at a popular level, a more intellectualised faith, its adherents expected to be more disciplined, more godly people who would be theologically aware and socially responsible, not to mention hard-working, sober, chaste, honest in their dealings with those around them – and non-violent. If the reality proved rather less than the vision, a minority at least of English men and women heeded the message, and tried to adapt their everyday conduct to its prescriptions, seeking to persuade their less virtuous neighbours to follow suit.

III

Commentaries on the Ten Commandments – of which many were produced in the later sixteenth and seventeenth centuries – reflect this Protestant worldview, while also showing a certain continuity with medieval ideas. John Dod's *A Plaine and Familiar Exposition of the Ten Commandments*, first published in 1604, is a case in point. Born in Cheshire in 1550, the youngest of seventeen children, Dod went to Cambridge before being ordained a priest in 1580. His Puritan views got him into trouble with the ecclesiastical authorities, and late in life (he died in 1645) he became associated with the growing opposition to Charles I that was to result in civil warfare in 1642; but he was nevertheless allowed to publish a number of works promoting godliness (in collaboration with the less well-documented Robert Cleaver), of which *A Plaine and Familiar Exposition of the Ten Commandments* proved the most popular. By 1635 it had gone through nineteen editions, and Dod had been given the nickname 'Decalogue Dod'.

Dod and Cleaver's objective was the creation of a godly – Puritan – England, but their analysis of the anger that leads to violence would not have jarred too much with a medieval Catholic audience. They urged their readers to avoid 'this foolish passion of rash anger' and to 'avoyde the occasions that will provoke us to it'. 'As men will keepe gun-powder, and towe and such dry stuffe from the fire,' they wrote, 'let us be as wise to preserve our soules from those sparkes, that would fire them with anger'. In a very familiar trope, they argued that anger led the individual to abandon the self-control which both the classical and the Christian traditions saw as desirable in human beings: a man that 'cannot rule himselfe' enough to avoid 'this unruly passion' showed those around him that he had 'no true knowledge of God, no knowledge of himselfe, no sound discretion, no settled order in his heart'. Readers should avoid ill-advised and scornful speeches that might provoke anger, and they should avoid the company of 'swaggerers and ruffians . . . the scumm and froth of all the earth', and 'riotousnesse, and drunkennesse'. Such trials and tribulations as they might experience should be viewed as instances of divine providence and not as human provocations. The good Christian lived on peaceable terms with his or her fellows.

Where Dod and Cleaver go beyond medieval notions of wrath, though, is in their extension of the Sixth Commandment to include all 'oppression and cruelty'. Thus the person who 'gave not meat to the hungry, and drinke to the thirsty, and cloathed not the naked, and visited not the sicke and imprisoned, and such like' would be guilty of murder. 'The charge of cruelty, and want of mercy', the authors continue, 'lyes heavy upon such: for he that turnes his eare, from the cry of the poore, shall cry himselfe and not be heard'. The same applies to those who did not pay their workmen fair wages. The two authors don't have much to say about gradations of violence, though they do comment that murder 'is so much more vile, by how much they be nearer bounde in any linke or bond to him that doth this wrong, as a brother the brother, a childe, the father, the wife, the husband, and such like'. But they do make a particular point of criticising those who commit suicide, the only form of criminal violence (as, we must remind ourselves, it then was) they actually discuss at any length:

> . . . most monstrous and unnaturall of all is it, for one to laie violent handes upon himselfe, to whom hee is bound by all bondes. For though one be neere to father and mother, &c., yet himselfe is most nere to himselfe, and hee ought to have most care of himselfe; therefore for one rend his owne soule and bodie asunder is moste horrible, and breakes most bondes of God and nature. And this no beast will doe.

Dod and Cleaver's exposition of the Sixth Commandment, then, is not just an injunction against violence and murder. It also promotes the broader values of the godly Christian Commonwealth.[18]

A more detailed, if less widely read, study of the Sixth Commandment was made later in the seventeenth century by Ezekiel Hopkins, born the son of a curate in Devon in 1634, and ultimately Bishop of Derry in Ireland (where he died in 1690). Hopkins may not have had the following that Dod enjoyed, but his works remained in print for a considerable period after his death, and his *An Exposition on the Ten Commandments* went through several impressions. Much of what he has to say chimes closely with Dod's thoughts. The Sixth Commandment, Hopkins argues, covers not only 'the perpetration of murther, and the actual imbruing of our hands in the blood of our brother', but also 'all causes and occasions leading to it'; 'cruelty and oppression' are also a breach of the commandment. Good Christians, then, should always seek to avoid envy and anger, though they may on occasion give in to 'vertuous anger': 'Religion doth not utterly root out and destroy the natural passions; but only moderate, and regulate them . . . Christianity does not make men stocks [i.e. senseless or stupid], but keeps them from being furies'.

Unlike Dod and Cleaver, Hopkins's strictures even extend to cruelty to animals. Some 'old hereticks', he notes, thought that the injunction not to kill extended to the killing of animals, and this was a wrong-headed view to his way of thinking: brute creatures could be killed 'for the use and service of our life'. But 'unmercifulness even towards them, and a cruel tormenting of them, not to satisfy our occasions [i.e. needs], and necessities, but our unreasonable passions, may be reducible as a sin against this commandment (for all acts of cruelty are so)'. Such sentiments may not have been new but, as we seek for the workings of a 'civilising process' from medieval times through to the present, it is interesting to see them stated at this time and in this context.[19]

Hopkins (unlike Dod and Cleaver) also considers the whole question of what constitutes justifiable killing. Capital punishment can be justified, he argues, because civil authorities are the agents of God: 'to speak properly, it is only God, and not man, that sheds the blood of wicked persons. The magistrate receives his commission from God, and doth it as his minister and servant'. Indeed 'in the execution of justice, magistrates, and such who have lawful power and authority, may and ought to put capital offenders to death', and 'if they do not, God will charge it upon them as their sin'.

Killing in war is also legitimate: 'there are some who decry this assertion,' Hopkins writes, 'and think it contrary to the temper of a Christian', but it is permitted 'in a public war to right ourselves upon injurious enemies' so long as 'the cause is just, the manner in which we prosecute it is warrantable, the authority which engageth us, being rightly constituted over us'. In the private arena, 'a man may shed blood in the necessary defence of his person, without being guilty of murder' (and Hopkins extends this to the use of violence to defend goods). Manslaughter, too, is defensible but only if it involves accidental death: 'and whatsoever is not this, is murther, and ought as such to be punish'd'. As for murder proper, it is a 'crying sin', and those guilty of it, those who abet or encourage a murderer or conceal the deed, and judges who fail to convict and punish murderers, are themselves complicit in the murder and so also deserving of death.

IV

So far I have explored Renaissance literary attitudes to violence and murder purely in the context of Christian teaching, but there is one genre – hugely popular at the time – in which Christian doctrine is far less overt: the revenge tragedy. In this murky theatrical world of corrupt courtiers, vicious murderers and victims turned killers, there is little room for theological subtlety. Behind the melodrama, though, we do get more than a glimpse of the moral values of the age that inspired it.

The first revenge tragedy proper was Thomas Kyd's *The Spanish*

Tragedy, which dates from around 1587. We know comparatively little about Kyd himself, except that he was born in London in 1558, the son of a scrivener, that he was educated at Merchant Taylors' School under one of the Elizabethan period's most noteworthy teachers and educational theorists, Richard Mulcaster, and that he earned his living as a London playwright and translator, dying in 1594. *The Spanish Tragedy* (first performed in the 1580s) was his great triumph: Philip Henslowe, holder of the rights to the work, recorded twenty-nine performances between its publication in 1592 and 1597, more than for any other dramatic work he held the rights to, while eleven editions were published between 1592 and 1633, a total which surpasses that of any work by Shakespeare within the same period. Adaptations of the play exist in Dutch and German, and we know that it was performed at Frankfurt in 1601, Dresden in 1626, and Prague in 1651. It concerns a Spanish bureaucrat, Hieronimo, his quest for justice and, when that fails, his revenge on those who have killed his son Horatio. The play's success spawned a genre that would flourish for some four decades.[20]

Extreme violence and brutality characterise revenge tragedies. Consider, for example, the fate of the Duchess of Malfi in the eponymous drama by John Webster. She has married below her station, secretly forming a union with Antonio, steward to her household, and having three children by him. Her brothers, the Cardinal, and Ferdinand, Duke of Calabria (her twin, who nurses an incestuous passion for her), holding that she has dishonoured the family name, therefore dispatch the villainous Bosola to arrange her murder. She is shown waxwork effigies of Antonio and her eldest son, which she is assured are their bodies, and is then strangled, along with her servant, Cariola, on stage, while executioners are sent to murder her children. Ferdinand then feels extreme remorse, and indeed shows early signs of insanity – he disowns Bosola's actions and refuses to pay his reward for the murders. After Ferdinand leaves him alone with the body, Bosola realises that the Duchess is still alive. He speaks to her in her dying moments, and is overcome with guilt.

Bosola switches sides, and attempts to save Antonio – but in the process accidentally kills him. In the end, Bosola kills both the Cardinal and Ferdinand, but is himself mortally injured in the process. He dies bemoaning the 'deep pit of darkness' in which 'fearful mankind live'. Webster's *The White Devil* is similarly blood-soaked. Here the Duke of Brachiano's lust for Vittoria Corombona incites him to arrange the murder of her husband Camillo and of his own wife Isabella, who dies when she kisses a portrait of the duke that has been coated with poison. As the genre demands, the two spouse killers are then suitably punished, Brachiano killed by a poisoned helmet he dons while jousting, Vittoria Corombona killed by Ludovico, an admirer of the deceased Isabella, and his friend Gasparo.

The denouement of revenge tragedies is famously extreme, invariably involving a stage strewn with bodies – think, for example, of the final scene of *Hamlet*. But even that pales in comparison with the last moments of *The Revenger's Tragedy* (usually attributed to Thomas Middleton, but possibly written by Cyril Tourneur). Here the man seeking revenge is Vindice, whose betrothed was poisoned nine years earlier by the evil duke whose sexual advances she rejected and who was also responsible for the death of Vindice's father. A disguised Vindice becomes a servant to the duke's son, Lussurioso, only to find that his first task is to persuade his own sister to become Lussurosio's lover. He kills the duke, and Lussurioso succeeds to the dukedom. In the final scene, where a court entertainment has been arranged to celebrate Lussurioso's elevation, a disguised Vindice and three accomplices (one of whom is his brother Hippolito) perform a masque and then stab Lussurioso and three of his noblemen. Two of the duke's other sons, Ambitioso and Supervacuo, along with the duke's illegitimate son Spurio and a fourth man, now enter, and Supervacuo, discovering that Lussurioso has been murdered, proclaims himself duke. Ambitioso stabs him to death, only to be stabbed in his turn by Spurio, whereupon the unnamed fourth man stabs Spurio for killing his lord.

The extraordinary number of deaths in such plays inevitably raises questions of the extent to which they might have reflected the worst of contemporary society, as well as the extent to which they might actually have promoted the violence they depicted – issues that still concern critics of violence on television and film today. But, in fact, it's fairly apparent that the audiences who watched and enjoyed revenge tragedies were fully aware that the moral universe of the revenger was not one they were being encouraged to enter.

In the first place, the plays were very clearly set in an exotic, fantasy world – most often Italy, sometimes Spain or another foreign land – countries that for an Elizabethan or Jacobean audience created the sort of gap between reality and imagination familiar to twentieth-century fans of the Wild West. Setting a play in Italy, in particular, sent a message that normal rules did not apply: popular prejudice had it that Italian public life was notoriously morally lax – something seemingly confirmed by the writings of Machiavelli, who to English readers appeared a proponent of amorality, and whose name quickly became a term of reproach, signifying the lower depths of villainy. Further distance was created by setting the plays at court (a place popularly associated with wickedness), populated by noblemen, noblewomen, kings and princes – people of a status that most audience members would rarely encounter in real life. This, as it happens, was also the world of the Italian novella, short stories which, either in the original or in translation, presented their readers with accounts similar to what a later reading public was to identify as the gothic, and which were very popular with Elizabethan readers.[21]

The extraordinary is also emphasised by the appearance of ghosts – symbols of a disordered cosmos. *The Spanish Tragedy* opens with the ghost of Andrea, a deceased Spanish courtier, lover of Bel Imperia, who also reappears later in the play, acting as a commentator on the plot along with a personified Revenge. In *The White Devil* Francisco's resolution to seek revenge is hardened by the appearance of the spectre of Isabella, his murdered sister, while in a less well-known play, *Antonio's Revenge*, the eponymous hero is, like Hamlet, urged by the ghost of his murdered father to do his filial duty by taking revenge on the father's killer. Madness is similarly invoked to show a world out of joint – a sign of social as well as personal disorder. Some of the revengers become so obsessed by their desire for vengeance as to become deranged themselves, while in other revenge plays, notably *The Duchess of Malfi* and a late arrival to the genre, Middleton and Rowley's *The Changeling* of 1622, mad men and women are introduced to act as a satire on an evidently deranged but theoretically sane society.

Nevertheless, the plays explore themes that would certainly have struck a chord with contemporary audiences, and approach from a secular point of view many of the issues with which religious writers of the period engaged. One of the most powerful is the connection between lust and violence. 'Duke – royal lecher. Go, grey-haired adultery', says Vindice in the opening line of *The Revenger's Tragedy*, as he clutches the skull of his deceased fiancée, Gloriana, sparking off a cycle of lust and revenge that reaches its climax when he poisons the skull of his dead sister, places it in the costume of a woman dressed for a masque, and encourages the duke to kiss it. Rape and incest also make an appearance in the play, each time sparking off a further cycle of death and revenge.

Ambition, too, is shown to be morally dangerous and a spur to villainy. It may be clothed in dissimulation, that 'Machiavellian' take on the world which early modern Englishmen found so reprehensible – Vindice in disguise worming his way into Lussurioso's trust, or Bosola pretending to be a faithful servant to the Duchess of Malfi while feeding intelligence about her to her brothers. There are also a number of very conventional comments about the court, that home of fawning flattery, dissimulation, and Machiavellian power-politics.

But above all, the plays display very powerfully the disapproval – or, at the very least, the moral ambiguity – that marked the Elizabethan and Jacobean view of revenge. Feuds, which had been part and parcel of European culture for centuries, were by the early seventeenth century increasingly discouraged by authorities that now wielded greater power and operated a more sophisticated legal system. Where they did occur, they were becoming more formalised. As I shall describe later, the duel – a form of very tightly controlled feud – made its first appearance in England in the 1570s. Revenge in general was something which both legal and religious authorities strongly criticised. In an essay of 1625, the legalist Francis Bacon wrote:

> Revenge is a kind of wild justice; which for the more man's nature runs to, the more ought law to weed it out. For as for the first wrong, it doth but offend the law; but the revenge of that wrong putteth the law out of office. Certainly, in taking revenge, a man is but even with his enemy; but in passing it over, he is superior . . . This is certain, that a man that studieth revenge keeps his own wounds green, which otherwise would heal and do well. Public revenges are for the most part fortunate . . . But in private revenges it is not so. Nay, rather, vindictive persons live the life of witches; who, as they are mischievous, so end they unfortunate.[22]

For religious writers such as Dod and Cleaver only God or those authorities he had appointed could exact revenge: 'we who have no authority, no commission,' they wrote, 'ought not to take life for life, nor eye for eye, nor tooth for tooth'.[23]

And this is what makes revenge tragedies so fascinating. On the one hand, we are invited to feel sympathy for its victim protagonists and the paths they feel compelled to tread. They exist in a universe riddled with corruption, where justice is denied to them. When they seek punishment of wrongdoers through legitimate means, they invariably fail. '[Y]ou have ravished justice, forced her to do your pleasure', says Vittoria Corombona in *The White Devil*, when she is wrongly accused of adultery by her judge, Cardinal Monticelso (III. ii.273–4). In Kyd's *Spanish Tragedy*, Hieronimo, whose son has been murdered, at first hopes for divine justice and then turns to the King of Spain, who proves too busy with high politics to hear his pleas. It is not surprising, then, that such characters should take the law into their own hands, to seek that 'rough justice' that Bacon describes. But the problem is that revenge ultimately destroys the revenger. Hieronimo becomes consumed by his obsession. In *The White Devil* Francisco's determination to wreak vengeance effectively destroys his humanity: 'what have I to do with tombs, or death – beds, funerals, or tears,' he asks when his sister is murdered, 'that have to meditate upon revenge' (IV.i.12–15).

So at the end of revenge plays, while the guilty may be punished, the once innocent invariably pay for what they have felt impelled to do. At the close of *The Duchess of Malfi*, Bosola, revenging himself and in so doing redeeming himself to an extent for his past wickedness, is fatally wounded. At the end of *The White Devil* Ludovico is arrested by a body of guards led, reassuringly, by the English Ambassador. When Vindice and Hippolito boast that they are responsible for the corpses that litter the stage at the denouement of *The Revenger's Tragedy* ('Twas somewhat witty carried' V.iii.100), they also seal their own fate. And *The Spanish Tragedy* closes with Hieronimo, who has bitten out his tongue, being given a knife to sharpen a quill pen to make a written confession, but rather using it to kill the Duke of Castile and then commit suicide. Evidently, the revenger could not be permitted to achieve his ends without fatal punishment befalling him, and to any earthly punishment was added the near certainty that the revenger had also forfeited his very soul. Audiences might sympathise with the revenger, much as modern cinema audiences might sympathise with the Charles Bronson character in the *Death Wish* series, or Clint Eastwood as Dirty Harry. But sympathy need not go so far as accepting the complete moral framework of the revenger. And as perhaps with the cinema anti-heroes of today, sympathy erodes as the revenger becomes more obsessive, as he destroys his own humanity in his quest for vengeance.

Social commentators, then as now, were concerned that the

violence to be found in popular literature and in plays might encourage similar behaviour in real life. But the moralising of revenge tragedies seems to be at one with the argument put forward in the early 1620s by John Reynolds, an Exeter merchant and writer, whose publications included a number of accounts of murders eventually collected together as *The Triumph of God's Revenge against the crying and execrable Sinne of Murther*:

> As well for the extirpating of that execrable sin of murder (which cries so loud to heaven for vengeance) as also to shew thee God's sacred justice, and righteous judgements in the vindication of the inhuman authors thereof, to the end, that (by the knowledge and reading of them) thou maiest become more charitable, and more hate cruelty, by these wretched and lamentable examples; having herein endeavoured (as much as in me lies) to make my reader a spectator, first of these foul and bloody crimes, and then of their condign and exemplary punishment, which (as a dismal storm and terrible tempest from heaven) fell on them on earth when they least dreamt or thought thereof.[24]

Reynolds's collection went into eleven editions by 1660, and continued to be published subsequently under a variety of titles and with additional stories added by subsequent authors. It is a tribute to the durability of the moral universe he describes. It also reflects, of course, the perennial appeal of the sensational murder story.

V

Over the next couple of centuries, the tone of popular and theological debate about violence in general, and the Sixth Commandment in particular, gradually changed. But the substance of the debate remained much the same. When, for example, Edward Nares, Rector of Biddenden in Kent (and from 1813 also Regius Professor of Modern History at the University of Oxford), in 1799 published a sermon he had preached on the Sixth Commandment, he, like his predecessors, took 'Thou shalt do no murder' to extend far beyond a prohibition on killing: 'if we think, a mere murder, is all that is inculcated in it [i.e. the Sixth Commandment],' he argues, 'we run the risk of falling into numberless errors'. His view was that 'the mere act of murder, is by no means all that is forbidden in the commandment under our consideration', and that it extends to 'every action, that may, in the most remote degree tend to the destruction of his neighbours'. There may be – 'and especially in these days' – 'numberless sad victims of violence', but they are vastly outnumbered by those 'lingering under the slower torments of mental anguish', anguish that has been inflicted upon them by the actions of their fellow human beings:

> Have I as a Christian, in all my dealings with the world, acted with that universal good will, love, and benevolence, which the gospel requires, and so practised all its moral doctrines, as to have 'turned many away from their wickedness, that they might live?' Or have I not rather seduced others by ill example into sinful courses to the ruin of the health of their bodies, and the reason of their minds? Have I not broken in on their peace by headstrong passions, and unreasonable violence?

This, then, is not a narrowly legal view of violence; it is one infused with Christian values. So far as Nares is concerned, the Sixth Commandment 'does absolutely extend to the prohibition of every unnecessary violence, every avoidable injury, affecting the existence, the peace, the ease, and comfort of every creature into which God hath breathed the breath of life.' Like Hopkins before him, he accepts the principle of killing in self-defence, and he supports what one might term official violence – the execution of 'some malefactors . . . their offences being incompatible with the security of the lives of others'. But the main thrust of his argument is to uphold Christian principles of charity and kindness.[25] The good Christian avoids 'causeless anger', 'intemperate expressions', and 'all wrath,

malice, strife, contentiousness, and hatred towards our fellow creatures'. And he or she behaves in the same way to those who are not
our 'fellow creatures', but rather those 'other creatures' which 'are
in our power, and in still greater degree subjected to us'. 'The anatomy of animals of all kinds', he declares, 'gives us every reason to
suppose them capable of all bodily pains like ourselves'. Killing for
food is permissible, but

> It argues an unaccountable perversion of man's principles, to
> see him seeking pleasure in a wanton abuse of the brute
> creation . . . I know not what mercy those have to expect at the
> hands of God, who can wilfully sport with the feelings not only
> of a harmless uncomplaining animal, but of a creature from
> whom perhaps he has derived some of the greatest (and cer-
> tainly the most disinterested) services.

Nevertheless, as the Puritanism of the sixteenth and seventeenth
centuries gave way to the more rational form of Christianity that
marked the Enlightenment of the later eighteenth and early nineteenth centuries, so the way in which the discussion of violence was
framed changed radically.

To the seventeenth-century mind, as we've seen, murder was evidence of God's anger with his sinful people, just as the revelation of
a murderer could be interpreted as the working out of divine providence. To the eighteenth-century mind, however, while murder
remained a transgression of God's commandments, it was viewed
not as a manifestation of collective wickedness, but the result of individual wrong-doing, individual cases deserving to attract attention
not because they were evidence of divine displeasure in general, but
of one person's failings in particular.

The break with the past was not, of course, an absolute one.
Ghosts, for example, continued to feature in murder pamphlets up
to the end of the eighteenth century and beyond, and for every progressive thinker advancing new ideas, there were plenty of ordinary
people holding to traditional ones. Nevertheless, little by little, the

old Puritan view of an angry God of the Old Testament consigning wrongdoers to eternal hellfire started to lapse. And the belief held by so many Christians in the early seventeenth century that they were living in the chaotic last days before the end of the world was one that by the late eighteenth century had only a few adherents. The devil, once viewed as a very real entity, became an increasingly marginalised figure, regarded by some writers as merely a metaphor for evil. Fear of witches disappeared almost altogether. Few denied the workings of divine providence, but the notion that God might regularly intervene in individual cases came to be one that only those in the more humble stations of life genuinely held to. Instead Anglican writers started to suggest that while to deny the possibility of miracles was the act of an atheist, the existence of an established Church made them unnecessary. In his 'Of Miracles' of 1748 David Hume went a sceptical step further, suggesting that the historical evidence supporting miracles was insufficient of itself to justify belief.

We can see this intellectual process at work very clearly in the shift in attitudes that took place by the end of the eighteenth century to the old notion that the body of a murdered person would bleed if touched by his or her killer, or even if the killer was merely present. The belief can be constantly found in murder pamphlets, legal texts and other commentaries on homicide between the late sixteenth and late eighteenth centuries. No less a figure than James I argued in his 1597 tract on witchcraft:

> In a secret murder, if the dead carcass be at any time hereafter handled by the murderer, it will gush out of blood, as if the blood were crying to the heavens for revenge of the murderer, God having appointed that secret supernatural sign for the trial of that secret unnatural crime.

The clergyman turned doctor John Webster, writing a few decades later in 1677, was rather more sceptical about the witchcraft in which the King so firmly believed, but cited various 'examples of those that have bled when the murtherers have been brought into the presence of the body murthered or caused to touch it'.

For instance, he tells of a case from County Durham in 1661, described to him by one of those who witnessed it, in which, when the suspected murderer was brought to touch the corpse, 'the lips and nostrils of the dead body wrought and opened as he touched (which made him afraid to touch the second time), then presently the corpse bled abundantly at the nostrils'. (The suspect, a glover named John How, was subsequently found guilty and executed.) By the end of the following century, however, such a belief had been firmly rejected by both mainstream religion and mainstream science. In 1827 that supreme representative of early-nineteenth-century utilitarianism, Jeremy Bentham, noted curtly of such magical proofs that 'Judges are no where prepared to credence them; and, this being understood, suitors are little prepared to hazard [risk] them.'[26]

Bentham apart, Christianity retained its central role in people's lives but, arguably, it no longer had the same influence that it had once enjoyed. The Newtonian cosmos had redefined God as the Great Clockmaker, and to the increasing number of people who accepted such a view, this more distanced creator of the universe was unlikely to spend his time sending ghosts, birds or beasts to unmask murderers. The old providential ideas survived, but in religious tracts and sermons, even in murder pamphlets and commentaries on the Decalogue, they were being increasingly challenged by the more 'rational' Christianity of the age of Enlightenment.

This – to our mind, secular rather than theological – attitude is apparent in the tone of murder pamphlets of the period. They tend to invoke God less frequently than their predecessors, and while they may offer moral lessons they tend to be most interested in the precise details of individual cases. Thus, for example, when John Wingrove wrote an account of one of the most notorious murder cases of the eighteenth century – that involving Elizabeth Brownrigg, who killed an apprentice named Mary Clifford in 1767 – he devoted some thirty-five pages of print to a very detailed description of all aspects of the case.

Brownrigg was clearly a monster. Wife of a London painter and decorator named James Brownrigg, she took in a number of pauper children whom she proceeded to subject to the most appalling brutality and abuse. One of her victims, Mary Jones, had come from London's Foundling Hospital and managed to escape and find her way back, but although the Hospital agreed to break her indenture with Brownrigg, they merely requested that James Brownrigg keep his wife in check. It was ultimately left to neighbours to raise the alarm, at which point the authorities visited the house and took away two more girls, Mary Mitchell and Mary Clifford. Clifford had suffered such terrible injuries that she died within days of her rescue. Mitchell, however, survived, and was able to give vivid testimony against her tormentor:

> Her mistress had frequently tied them up, both naked, with their arms across, to a staple which she had caused to be fixed in the cellar for that purpose, and whipped them in the most cruel manner for trifling offences; that on the Friday before, Mary Clifford was tied up in the manner above described and whipped six times, and she herself twice; that on the Sunday before, they were locked up in a dark place under the cellar stairs, where they had frequently been put before, and each had a piece of bread given to her, but nothing to drink, not even water.[27]

The case became a cause célèbre and the subject of four publications (including Wingrave's).

As for Brownrigg, she became an object of such hatred that the authorities feared mob violence. Indeed Wingrave, who was the constable involved in investigating the case, states that part of the reason he decided to go into print about the case was to dispel some of the wilder rumours that were floating around. Like Henry

Goodcole a century and a half before him, he had direct access to the accused. Unlike Goodcole, however, he was only really interested in the facts of the case, not the religious lessons that might be drawn from it (God is invoked on only a handful of occasions in the pamphlet). Brownrigg, incidentally, was hanged at Tyburn.

A similar tone permeates one of the other pamphlets on the Brownrigg case, the anonymous *An Appeal to Humanity in an Account of the Life and Cruel Actions of Elizabeth Brownrigg*. The tract begins by noting the 'horror and detestation of the public', which was stirred up by 'the shocking cruelties on the two unfortunate parish girls', and then continues:

> Other crimes, from the very nature of their motives, may admit of powerful alleviations: cruelty alone admits of no alleviation; as its motive can only be found in the confirmed depravity of the human heart. The peace and happiness of society, without doubt, require that the rights of property should be strictly guarded; yet will any man pretend to affirm that he, who steals my purse, who transfers to himself the property of another, is as culpable against nature, as the man, who without cause or remorse, exercises the most unremitting relentless cruelties towards his fellow-creatures? Does he not from the moment cease to be a man, when, disregarding the sacred ties of humanity, he indulges in all the wantonness of oppression? Has he not broke the great bond between him and nature? And can any punishment be deemed adequate to the enormity of his crime?[28]

This is the world of an Enlightenment civil society rather than that of a post-Reformation Christian Commonwealth. It is underpinned by Christian ideals, but the pamphleteer does not feel the compulsion his forebears felt to make constant references to God or the scriptures. Instead he talks of reason, of humanity, and of what contemporaries conceived of as 'nature'.

When necessary, though, Christian teachings could be invoked more directly. Take, for example, a contemporary account of the 1740 trial of a wealthy widow named Elizabeth Branch and her daughter Mary, accused at the Somerset assizes of murdering their maid-servant Jane Buttersworth. Elizabeth Branch had a bad local reputation – indeed her neighbours believed that her 'perverse dis-position', and in particular her treatment of the household's servants, had hastened her husband's death. She and her daughter certainly seem to have been tyrants. A former servant, Henry Butler, testified how on one occasion, when he dropped a plate while serving dinner, 'what with the fright and blows together, my lord, craving your lord-ship's pardon, I beshit myself', upon which the two Branch women 'took up my turd, thrust it into my mouth, and made me eat it'. Jane Buttersworth died, according to a Welsh dairymaid named Anne Somers, because, having taken too long to complete an errand and having then made the mistake of trying to cover it up with a lie, she was beaten with twigs about her bare bottom until she bled, and then with broom handles when she tried to escape.

For the most part, this litany of crimes is recorded in everyday language, but the reported speech of one of the three King's Coun-sels involved in the case strikes a very different note:

> My lord, and gentlemen of the jury, the heinousness and obliquity of the sin of murder, calls immediately to heaven for vengeance; for it is observable, gentlemen, and so it will appear by the evidence we shall produce on behalf of the king, that . . . providence, who will not suffer a crime of so black a die to go unpunished, regardful of the Almighty decree, 'Whoso shed-deth man's blood, by man shall his blood be shed', stirred up a stranger to the deceased (for, gentlemen, the deceased had no friends or relations) to make inquisition for her blood.

Such words weighed rather more heavily with the jury than those of the eight defence lawyers Branch lavished her money on. She and her daughter were convicted and hanged. It is surely significant that at a moment of high solemnity the King's Counsel should speak in such elevated religious language.[29]

Even so, by the nineteenth century the shift in the pamphleteer's tone from religious to secular was virtually complete. An 1822 broadsheet from Yorkshire, describing a case of infanticide in which the baby was thrown on a fire, adopts the language of melodrama: 'the blood curdles in our veins while we relate it; even credulity itself is staggered on hearing the tale . . . and in order to avoid the shame which an exposure of her situation might have drawn upon her, barbarously murdered the innocent infant in a manner at which human nature shudders'. But it doesn't talk about Christian doctrine.

Another Yorkshire broadsheet from the following year, which describes the attempted robbery and then murder of twenty-three-year-old Richard Walker (who 'bore an estimable character'), talks of exciting 'the utmost horror and sympathy', but makes no mention of the inscrutable workings of divine providence. Nor does that dealing with the very peculiar case of Mary M'Intosh, a young woman from the Edinburgh region, who was betrothed to be married to a Yorkshireman. She had gone to visit him, and he had left her mounted on his horse near Bowes while he went to transact some business. As she waited, three 'ruffians' appeared, who subjected her to verbal insults, pulled her from the horse, stripped her naked, 'performed outrages upon her person, which decency will not permit us to relate', and threatened to murder her. They then disembowelled her horse, and in the place of its entrails 'put the unfortunate young woman, sewed in the horse's skin'. Her fiancé eventually returned and freed her, but although she was able to identify her assailants to a constable who was called, 'the unfortunate woman could not survive the outrages committed, but expired some hours afterwards'. Again, there was no Christian moralising.

Lastly, we have the case of James Cheeseborough, aged twenty-seven and 'a person of weak intellect', living with his mother and an uncle near Leeds, both of whom he killed when his mother refused to give him any of the tobacco ('a thing of which he was passionately fond') she had bought. 'In this shocking instance', the author of the report muses, 'an insignificant ouse [ounce] of tobacco will probably cost the lives of three individuals'. He adds 'what an awful warning here is held up against the effects of sudden passion', but when he decides to cite a text decrying the effects of 'sudden passion', he does not turn to the Bible but to a line or two from Alexander Pope.[30] The transition from the Christian to the secular was complete.

A fifteenth-century manuscript depicts a man beating his wife, while onlookers watch from the doorway. Until the eighteenth century, it was widely accepted that men – as the heads of their families – had a right to hit their wives, children and servants. Even so, many writers cautioned husbands against the use of excessive force.

CHAPTER 5

DOMESTIC VIOLENCE: WIVES, HUSBANDS AND SERVANTS

I

Domestic violence today is a disturbingly common phenomenon. At the turn of the twenty-first century, an average of 2 women a week were killed by a male partner or former partner. Of the 3,249 women murdered between 1995 and 2009 in England and Wales, some 47 per cent were killed by someone with whom they were or had been in a relationship (the corresponding figure for men is 12 per cent of 6,808 victims). During the same period some 226,000 women and 67,000 men reported that they had been the victims of domestic abuse, while a staggering 2 million people – two-thirds of them women – claimed to have experienced domestic abuse at some point in their lives. The figures may not be quite as high as they were in the mid twentieth century, but the fact remains that for a significant minority of women, the most dangerous person they will ever know is the man with whom they have once been close.[1]

The picture before 1800 is a hazy one. Cases of domestic homicide are certainly recorded, though, as pointed out earlier, they are dwarfed statistically by homicides (frequently categorised at trial as manslaughter) arising from violence between unrelated males: a survey of crime in three south-eastern counties, for example, suggests that in the period 1558 to 1625 only about 13 per cent of homicide cases reaching the assizes involved the killing of a family member by another family member, or with another family member as accessory. But systematic evidence for non-fatal domestic violence is extremely hard to come by. Even today it is an undoubtedly under-reported crime. In the pre-Victorian era, the tendency not to report abuse seems to have been even more marked, and as a result levels of indictment for domestic violence were astonishingly low. Surviving records for the Essex assizes and quarter sessions between 1620 and 1680 reveal that of the 665 people (611 men and 54 women) indicted for assault, only 2 were charged with domestic violence: a gentleman accused of assaulting his wife, and a yeoman's wife accused of assaulting her husband.[2] Then as now, women locked in violent and abusive marriages (and, unlike today, unable to escape them via divorce) were either too scared or too ashamed to take official action. And then as now, men suffering at the hands of violent wives all too often felt too embarrassed to do anything about it.

Historically, there was also the issue of the extent to which a modicum of physical chastisement within a marriage was felt to be justified. Political, social and theological theorists (the categories overlapped) viewed the family as the fundamental building block of political authority, society and godliness, or, as the London clergyman William Gouge put it in a work of 1622, *Of domesticall duties*: 'necessary it is that good order be first set in families: for as they were before other polities, so they are somewhat the more necessary: and good members of a family are like to make good members of church and common-wealth'.[3] In such a godly Commonwealth, where the family was the microcosm of political authority, the head of the family was the monarch of his own little world, empowered to chastise those who failed in their religious or social duties.

Some later commentators have taken a rather bleak view of this set-up.[4] They view the families of earlier times as comparatively impersonal groups, characterised by low-key relationships between family members, a subjection of the interests of the individual to those of the wider kin group, and, of course, enforced deference to the male head of household. As for children, they simply had to accommodate themselves to the kinship group to which they belonged: the notion of 'childhood', it has been argued, did not really exist in Western Europe much before the eighteenth century.[5] It was only as feudalism finally succumbed to capitalism, and a traditional, community-based, kinship-dominated society started to give way to one in which individuals began to come to the fore, that the 'family' as we understand it today emerged.

Needless to say, many historians regard this portrait of the 'pre-modern' family as a caricature of the truth, and take a much more optimistic view. But the caricature of widespread brutality has proved difficult to erase, and there is still a widely held popular view that English society in the past was dominated by peasants and artisans who did little between leaving the fields or the workshop and going to bed than beating the assorted members of their households.

II

However extreme this view may be, it is certainly the case that the pre-twentieth-century 'family' was a very different animal from its present-day incarnation. Indeed even referring to it as a 'family' is somewhat problematic: it would probably be more accurate to talk of it as a 'household' since the chances are that even the only moderately well-to-do would have employed at least one domestic servant or apprentice. It has been estimated that perhaps 80 per cent of the labouring population during the seventeenth and eighteenth centuries spent at least part of their lives as live-in servants; while perhaps 40 per cent of the population under the age of twenty (mostly boys aged fourteen or above) served away from home as apprentices.[6] Thus into the complicated mix of family relationships was added that between the family and servants and apprentices and, indeed, between individual servants and apprentices. Families themselves were constantly shifting entities. Today, divorce unmakes and remakes families. Between the sixteenth and eighteenth centuries, the same function was performed by death, which was likely to end marriages after an average of only ten years. Many people therefore had the experience, then as now, of creating and maintaining relationships with step-children and step-parents. And then as now, this could lead to tensions. The recurring motif of the wicked step-mother in traditional fairy stories is not exactly reassuring.

The comparatively open nature of households meant that people lived their lives in a far more public way than we do today. Servants and apprentices gossiped. Close relatives, who in the early modern period were very likely to live nearby, observed and gossiped. Family matters were therefore open to the gaze of outsiders to an extent we are not familiar with today. It's not surprising, then, that while domestic abuse and violence may not often have come to the ears of court officials, there is quite an extensive anecdotal record. Violence within marriage, and within the household more generally, was a matter of interest to numerous people beyond those directly involved in it.[7] The better-documented cases of marital breakdown frequently report observations made by neighbours or show parents or sisters and brothers of spouses intervening, or trying to intervene.

And what is clear from the records that survive is not just that many families regularly experienced low-level violence, but that this violence was generally deemed acceptable. As already stated, husbands and fathers, as rulers of their little kingdoms, were allowed and expected to chastise erring wives and children. The same principle extended more generally to those in a position of authority – whether masters of apprentices, or employers of servants, or school-teachers. The sixteenth-century theologian and religious writer William Perkins, in a book of advice on how to run a household, felt he had to remind employers that they do not have power of life and death over their servants, but he regarded 'moderate correction' as permissible.

Of course, different people had different views of what 'moderate' meant. Those (usually men) who did find themselves brought before a court frequently defended themselves on the grounds that they were only offering a reasonable and justified level of correction. One such was Simon White, responding in 1588 before the London Church courts to allegations that he had been cruel to Elizabeth his wife:

> he hath sondrie tymes . . . being thereto much provoked by the said Elizabeth given her a blow upon the cheeke with his hand . . . and about 4 yeeres now last past . . . he did upon juste occasion chastise and correcte the said Elizabeth with a small beechen wand for her misusage and intolerable misbe-haviours towards him which he did in honest reasonable and moderate sorte.[8]

Witnesses in such cases generally offered their own opinion as to whether or not an individual had acted excessively. But whatever they felt about the particular circumstances that had brought people to court, they clearly accepted the principle of corrective violence.

John Cannon's *Chronicles* (see page 132) give a very good idea of the kinds of everyday events that could result in a beating. He recalls, for example, an occasion in 1703, when, at the age of seventeen, he fell foul of his father. He had stayed out late gambling with one of the family's servants ('a clownish fellow') and other 'sharpers', had lost all his money and arrived home to discover that the doors had been locked and that his father had left strict instructions that he should not be let in. When his father eventually relented and allowed him to be readmitted, he confronted Cannon, 'expostulated' with him, and struck him twice with his belt, at which the young man fell on his knees 'and begged pardon & forgiveness'.

On another occasion Cannon's father struck the 'clownish' servant, who responded by asking for the wages owed him and leaving. Both Cannon and his father were glad to see the back of him. And a few years after that, when Cannon was working as a farm servant for his uncle, he himself was placed in a position where he was allowed to mete out punishment. He had been given authority over two more junior servants, 'two very bad, loose & debauched boys', one of whom, 'a loose & profligate & a profane swearer & vain boaster' named James Billing, had a tendency to expose himself to a maidservant named Mary: he would show her 'his privities', and 'with his hand holding it up to her would brag what he could or would do if she would consent'. Cannon beat and reproved him for these 'base actions'. Billing seems to have felt that the punishment he received was fair enough; certainly it would have been preferable to being reported to his master.[9]

III

Although the law was unclear on such matters, it is apparent that a degree of physical correction of the various members of the household was regarded as permissible. And the same applied to wife-beating, which was only finally outlawed in 1891, despite earlier rulings that criticised the practice. Up until then the popular perception of the law was that Judge Sir Francis Buller had ruled in 1782 that a man was allowed to beat his wife, provided that he used a stick no thicker than his thumb (hence, according to some, the popularising of the expression 'rule of thumb'). In point of fact, recent research has suggested that Buller made no such ruling, but the principle of limited punishment that was enshrined here seems to have been the one that those in the legal profession would have accepted (interestingly, in 1836 a magistrate at the Marylebone police court actually asked a witness about the thickness of a stick with which a man was alleged to have struck his wife). In other words, 'moderate correction' was acceptable. Sir William Blackstone, arguably the eighteenth century's most important legal commentator, reasoned that since a husband was responsible for his wife's good behaviour, the law allowed him to chastise her, provided that 'this power of correction was confined within reasonable bounds'. Matthew Bacon, author of an abridgement of the law which was first published in 1736 and which was to reach its seventh edition by 1832, took a similar line:

The husband hath, by law, power and dominion over his wife, and may keep her by force within the bounds of duty, and may beat her, but not in violent or cruel manner; for, in such case, or if he but threaten to beat her outrageously, or use her barbarously, she may bind him to the peace.

Of course, such views do fail to define what 'reasonable', 'cruel', 'outrageously', 'barbarously' or even 'violent' meant in practice.[10]

Among clergymen and authors of moral tracts touching on the issue, views differed – and, indeed, sometimes vacillated. Thus, for example, when in 1617 the Puritan minister William Whately published the first edition of his *A Bride-Bush*, a handbook on how a successful marriage should be ordered, he argued that husbands should not correct their wives by violence, but rather by 'mild, gentle and wise proceeding'. But when he published a second edition two years later (the work was to be reprinted regularly through the seventeenth century) his views had changed. Now he suggested that blows with the hand or fist could be offered by husbands to wives who used 'extremities of unwifelike carriage'.[11] William Gouge, by contrast, from whose 1622 work *Of domesticall duties: eight treatises* I have already quoted, sought to tread a difficult line between the traditional, authoritarian view of marriage and physical gentleness. His book rejects any idea that husband and wife might be equal as 'a fond conceit', arguing instead that the man was 'the highest in the family, and hath both authoritie over all, and the charge of all is committed to his charge: he is as a king in his owne house'. This holds true even if the husband is his wife's social inferior or 'a man of lewd and beastly conditions, as a drunkard, a glutton, a prophane swaggerer, an impious swearer, and blasphemer'.

Yet Gouge stresses that husband and wife should be 'a mutuall help one to another' in bringing up children and in 'well governing' their family. And to his mind 'mutuall help' means the avoidance of physical violence. Those husbands who try to maintain their authority 'by violence and tyranny' are wrong to do so because while 'force may indeed cause feare', it is 'a slavish feare, such a feare as breedeth more hatred than love, more inward contempt, than outward respect'. Moreover – and this is a critical point for a seventeenth-century Protestant minister – Gouge says he can find no scriptural justification for wife-beating. His answer therefore, when he asks himself the direct question 'Can a husband beat his wife?' is 'With submission to better judgement, I think he may not':

> Can it be thought reasonable that she who is the man's perpetu-all bed-fellow, who hath power over his body, who is a joint parent of the children, a joint governour of the family, should be beaten by his hands? . . . the neere coniunction [conjunction] and very union that is betwixt man and wife suffreth not such dealing to passe betwixt them . . . man and wife are one flesh, and no sane man will beat himself . . . there is no hope of any good to proceed from a husband's beating his wife.[12]

Gouge's views can scarcely have been unique. But they do not appear to have been general.

IV

As mentioned, the head of the household's power to chastise extended beyond his immediate family to any servants and apprentices he might employ, and by virtue of their subordinate position, this could make life pretty grim for them. Of course, a younger son of the gentry apprenticed to a rich merchant in London or a major provincial town was likely to have a fairly easy ride (and a promising future). But the average boy or girl apprenticed to a small-town craftsman could find things tough, particularly if (as allowed in Poor Law legislation) they were imposed on a reluctant household by parish officials anxious to keep them off the poor rates.

Many cases are recorded of the children of the poor being appallingly treated by their masters and mistresses and, in extreme cases, being sadistically murdered by them. In Essex between 1620 and 1680 eleven indictments for the homicide of a servant or apprentice are recorded (as against thirty-one cases involving relatives). To make matters worse, parish apprentices, certainly those who were living at some distance from their home, or were orphaned, were likely to have few friends in the community who would be prepared to intervene on their behalf or otherwise help them, and judging from the Essex statistics the chances of convicting a master or mistress were quite slim (there was only once conviction out of the eleven cases, and even then the verdict was manslaughter and the sentence merely branding).

A case in point of just how isolated people in a subservient position could be is that of Joseph Green, an apprentice who died in 1799 after suffering prolonged and horrific abuse and starvation at the hands of his master, Charles Squire. Unnoticed by the wider community, he received kindness only at the hands of one person: a workhouse boy, who cut him down when he had been suspended for two hours by his ankles from a beam, and gave him 'a pork pie (which was for his own meal) and a halfpenny, which was all the money he had'. Charles Squire was executed at Stafford on 29 April 1799, his corpse being delivered to surgeons for dissection (a common outcome for murderers).[13]

One of the most appalling examples of a servant effectively tortured to death is that of Anne Nailor, 'a poor parish girl' who suffered a long period of systematic abuse by her employer Sarah Metyard, and her employer's daughter, Sarah Morgan Metyard. Anne Nailor died in 1762, but witnesses at the trial testified to a history of abuse stretching back to 1758. The girl was habitually beaten, tied up in a garret and left there for up to three days at a time. Finally, an extended period of imprisonment without 'victuals and other necessaries' resulted in her starving to death. The Metyards kept her body in a box 'till it was too offensive to be borne', and then dismembered it, burning a hand that had a distinguishing mark on it, and throwing the rest of the remains into a 'gully hole'. After a trial that lasted just seven hours, Metyard and her daughter were convicted both of Anne

Nailor's murder and that of her sister Mary (about whose death very little detail is given in the trial pamphlet), and were executed at Tyburn. Their crimes and punishment were commemorated in an eight-verse ballad.[14]

Elizabeth Rainbow's death in 1775 at the hands of her employer John Bolton illustrates another danger inherent in servants and apprentices living with the household. Bolton, a former army officer, had settled at Bulmer near Castle Howard in Yorkshire after marrying a gentlewoman who owned a small estate there. The couple had five or six children. In the late 1760s, Bolton took on parish apprentices from Ackworth, and one of them, Elizabeth Rainbow, 'grew up to woman's estate, and had the misfortune to be handsome', as the crown prosecutors at Bolton's trial delicately put it. One day Bolton and Rainbow were alone in the house, and when, some time later, Bolton's boy apprentice, Emmanuel Bowes, returned from an errand he had been sent on, his master told him that Rainbow had run away (she had apparently done so on previous occasions), but that he had taken her clothes and other possessions from her. The next day Bowes was told to fill in a cellar that had been dug under the house, Bolton explaining that it was too damp to be of use.

As Bowes laboured away, rumours started to circulate as to Elizabeth Rainbow's likely fate and Bolton's involvement in it. John Hall, the parish constable, informed a local justice of the peace that he was suspicious about her disappearance, recalling at the trial 'that it had been reported in the neighbourhood, that she had been missing for about a fortnight; it was supposed that she had been with child before that; it did not appear that Mr. Bolton had made any enquiry after her. The people were suspicious that some accident had happened'.[15] The justice accordingly issued a warrant for Bolton's arrest. At almost the same time Bolton arrived at the justice's house, bent on demanding of the JP that those who were spreading rumours about his connection with the death of Elizabeth Rainbow should be served with warrants for defamation. When the justice told Bolton of the constable's concerns, Bolton briefly returned home. He then rode off very rapidly towards York.

In his absence, the house was searched, and, sure enough, Rainbow's body was unearthed in the cellar, her hands tied behind her back and a garrotte around her neck. The surgeon who examined the body confirmed that she had been strangled, and also established that she had been four or five months pregnant at the time of her death. Local rumour had it that Bolton had bought some kind of abortifacient in York a few weeks earlier. Bolton was duly arrested in York, tried and found guilty. Protesting his innocence to the end, and shocking the court in so doing, he also rejected the admonition of two clergymen who attempted to bring him to an appropriate state of repentance. He was sentenced to death, but evaded execution by committing suicide by strangulation in his prison cell. The coroner's jury brought in a verdict of *felo de se*, and his body was sent to York County Hospital to be dissected.

This was, of course, an unusual case in terms of its extraordinary level of sadism, but administrative records contain plenty of references to less extreme forms of physical abuse. In 1637, for example, the Wiltshire assizes ordered that Edward Starkye, who had been bound over for abusing his apprentice John Dracott (a parish apprentice), should pay the overseers of the poor in Purton the sum of £6 13s 4d to place Dracott with another master, preferably 'an honest man'. At the 1654 Essex quarter sessions a carpenter named Thomas White was ordered to pay William Prentice's father the sum of £6 13s 4d plus twenty shillings for clothing William had been furnished with when the articles of apprenticeship were signed, and to release the boy, who had left him after suffering 'misusage and hardshipp'.

In 1659 John Waters and Mary his wife had their case referred for consideration by two justices after being bound over to answer for misusing their apprentice Susan Savage and assaulting Anne Nash (possibly a servant, but otherwise unidentified). James Almond, found guilty of 'much abusing' his apprentice Samuel Everitt, was ordered to discharge him and repay the boy's grandmother part of the £4 he had received when Everitt entered his service, as well as giving back all his 'linnen, wearing apparel & cloathes'.

As with wife-beating, the issue at stake in any dispute over alleged mistreatment was whether the punishment meted out was 'moderate correction'. In a Somerset case, an apprentice named Christopher Partridge was discharged from his apprenticeship because of the 'immoderate correccion' he had received from his master, William Holloway. However , when the Essex Quarter Sessions reviewed the alleged ill treatment of apprentice Benjamin Taylor at the hands of his master Daniel Dore in 1653, the conclusion was that Dore 'hath only corrected his apprentice in a moderate manner as by lawe hee may', and proceedings against him were dropped.[16]

V

On 11 August 1741 Phoebe Wood, aged about forty and from Woodford in Cheshire, was sitting by her door when she heard 'the noise of a quarrell' between two of her neighbours, Mary and David Simpson. Getting up to see what was going on, she saw Simpson strike his wife three times with a stick over the back and shoulders. Mary Simpson, she recalled later, 'buckled' under the blows. The following day Phoebe visited Mary, and found her in bed complaining of pains in her belly. Three days later Mary was dead. The coroner, Alexander Elcock, directed a woman named Lydia Royle to examine the body and report its condition, and it was also shown to the coroner's jury. All saw marks of violence on various parts of Mary's body, notably on her throat, breast and belly. Two neighbours, Elizabeth Leah and Mary Woodworth, both women in their forties, who had gone to confront Simpson when they heard of his wife's death, said that he admitted to striking her twice with a stick, but denied that he had hurt her much. However, Woodworth clearly didn't believe him. She had examined Mary Simpson's body as it lay in the house, she said, and could clearly see marks on her throat as well; her conclusion was 'that a hand or hands had been busy there as if it had been done to prevent shrieking'.[17] Nevertheless Simpson was acquitted.

Judging from the testimony given at the inquest, it's clear that Mary had been subjected to the most appalling violence for some time. A twenty-six-year-old neighbour, Hannah Royle, stated she had 'but all too frequently heard of their quarrels and difference', and that five months earlier Mary had confided to her that her husband beat her, and that he had struck her in the belly when she was pregnant, apparently intending to kill her unborn child. But as so often in cases of wife-beating, it's also clear that Mary hid the worst of her sufferings from most of the people around her. She may have told Hannah of the earlier beating, but when, the day after the assault that proved fatal, she went to ask her for change for a shilling and complained of feeling unwell and Hannah asked if her husband had been beating her again, 'the said Mary fetched up a sigh, and as this examinant understood, said nay, and went away'. Phoebe Wood, who had actually witnessed the assault, told the inquest that Mary had (as presumably on previous occasions) 'said nothing of suffering by her husband's blows'. Stuck in an abusive relationship, she clearly felt she had no choice but to endure it.

Even if Mary had decided that she could no longer bear to be with her husband, the courses of action open to her were very limited. She could, of course, have chosen simply to leave him, but this would have been a major step and possibly not a practicable one. Alternatively a woman of her station might have agreed to a wife sale, whereby she would be sold to another man, probably in the local marketplace, as Susan Henchard is sold by her husband Michael at the beginning of Thomas Hardy's *The Mayor of Casterbridge* (in reality, pace Hardy, most 'sales' were pre-arranged, conducted with the assent and to the satisfaction of all three parties).[18] But this was a popular, not a legally accepted solution. In formal terms all that English law offered to people who were unhappily married was separation *a mensa et thoro*, from bed and board. And separation did not mean that the marriage had come to an end: those who agreed to live apart were not allowed to remarry while their partner was alive, and were also legally expected to remain sexually inactive, preserving the veneer of marital fidelity.

As for divorce, this simply wasn't an option for most people.[19] Unlike the majority of other Protestant states, post-Reformation England maintained the Roman Catholic principle that marriage was indissoluble, and that a validly contracted or celebrated marriage could only be terminated by the death of one of the spouses. Marriages (as the marital misfortunes of Henry VIII so famously remind us) could be ended by annulment, but annulment was not the same as divorce: it was based on the principle that the marriage had never been valid in the first place (because, for example, one partner was already married when the marriage took place), and this left very little room for manoeuvre for those in an unhappy relationship. Divorce was finally made possible by Act of Parliament in the late seventeenth century, but it was both complicated and expensive. Only sixteen (for the most part aristocratic) marriages are recorded as having been terminated by divorce before 1750. There will have been many couples who, as an essay on marriage published by the *Newcastle Chronicle* on 3 September 1768 put it: 'after being married a twelvemonth, have nothing in common, but their name, their quality, their peevishness and their misery'. Unfortunately there was very little that such couples could do legally to engineer an end to their unhappy situation.

Wives were at a particular disadvantage because they had no legal existence as separate entities from their husbands under English common law, could not initiate litigation, and could not own property. Women regularly brought what was termed 'a portion' to their marriage, which might vary from a few shillings saved by a domestic servant to the hefty dowry brought by a daughter of the upper gentry or aristocracy. This passed directly to their husbands, who also took possession of any leasehold land their wives might have, along with the right to dispose of it and enjoy the profits of such freehold and copyhold land (i.e. land held from the manor) as their wives owned, although they could not dispose of it without consent. Attempts were sometimes made in particular cases to protect a woman's rights over her property; a contract, say, might be drawn up to limit what a husband could do with it. But property often became a bone of contention. So far as most men were concerned, their role was to be the breadwinner, and that entailed control of the family's finances; women were there to run the household and supervise the upbringing of children. In Victorian discussions of marriage this was part and parcel of their 'separate spheres' responsibilities. The fact that many women came to marriage with considerable experience of the economic world – whether as widows or former servants or workers – counted for little. In reality, of course, many couples seem to have been content with the division of labour prescribed in a traditional marriage, while for commentators on marriage, it suggested a contract that created a degree of reciprocity: the wife who failed to run the household properly deserved physical chastisement, but then the husband who failed to provide for his wife did not deserve her obedience.

Women's property – or rather, their lack of full legal control of it – not only rendered it difficult for them to make a clean break from a violent husband, it could also be a cause of marital dissension in itself. One of the ecclesiastical cause papers held in the archives of the Archbishop of York, which concerns a case brought for separation *a mensa et thoro*, demonstrates this particularly graphically. It involves a couple who married in middle age – Catherine and Robert Warburton – and it reads a bit like a Brontë novel. Catherine was forty, a spinster and a woman of property, when in 1792 she married Robert, a widower in his fifties. At first all went well but tensions mounted when the couple moved from the house they'd lived in when they first married – one owned by Catherine at Moor Monkton in Yorkshire – to a farm owned by her at Thorp Arch (also in Yorkshire).

The court documents tell us, without going into any detail, that Robert was suffering from 'family concerns', presumably financial, and it seems likely that Catherine had granted him property to help him out. Thereafter, as far as we can tell, Robert became fixated on acquiring as much of his wife's property as possible. To punish her for her resistance to his demands, he effectively imprisoned her in houses at Thorp Arch and Pontefract, and stopped her communicating with her friends. He refused to sleep with her. For a period of five weeks, he even refused to talk to her. After that, he had her locked in an attic, though he did at least instruct the servants to pass food to her. In desperation, she knocked a hole through the wall of the attic into an adjoining house, and managed to make contact with a servant there. The servant got a message to her friends and they rescued her.[20] It would be comforting to know that after that traumatic experience Catherine got the justice she so clearly deserved. Unfortunately, our sources dry up at the cliff-hanging moment of her rescue.

Property plays a part in another case described in the York archives, though here the ill treatment meted out was as much physical as mental. John Pighill, Rector of Patrington in the East Riding of Yorkshire, appears to have been a man capable of extraordinary acts of violence. His wife Elizabeth claimed that he had 'informed her in a serious and thoughtful manner [that] there was something on his spirits that he could not possibly drive away or get quit of without having her heart's blood', and that on one occasion he punched her in the face so hard that she nearly lost an eye. She also recalled that after she had decided to sleep apart from him, he came into her chamber, slashed her bedclothes with a knife, and then picked up a chair and began striking her with it so violently that, again, he almost blinded her. His 'chideing and brawling', she said, made her 'uneasy and uncomfortable' and rendered her 'the most miserable woman in the world'. John Pighill for his part claimed that Elizabeth would 'seldome . . . demeane herself as a good wife ought to do towards her husband', but that she 'studyed as she still does all possible meanes to disoblige, vex and trouble him'.

Be that as it may, what seems to have vexed him in particular was

Elizabeth's demand that of the £500 her father had provided her with by way of a dowry, lands worth £30 a year should be settled upon her to support her in the event of John's death. (On marriage, the wife's dowry became her husband's property, but it was not uncommon for a husband to agree to this type of arrangement as a sort of insurance policy for their spouse, especially if they hadn't made a will.) She alleged that John tried to wriggle out of this commitment, and she had even gone to the lengths of presenting a bill against him at the Court of Chancery at Westminster to force him to pay up. Elizabeth requested that the Archbishop of York should not license her husband to be non-resident at Patrington, as she feared that this was a ploy he was attempting to allow him to abscond and evade the Chancery suit. Whether or not she was successful, we do not know.

Between persistent mental abuse and all-out physical violence there were, of course, many gradations: as Charles Arthur, a Yorkshire clergyman giving evidence in a marital separation case in 1721, put it: 'there were several ways of using a wife ill without beating her'.[21] And some quarrels between husbands and wives seem to have taken very bizarre courses. In 1670, for example, Lady Grace Chatsworth complained that when she had been lying in bed, heavily pregnant, ill and suffering from a fever, her husband had deliberately brought 'a company of musicians' into the chamber next to hers, and 'caused them to strike and play very loudly to the danger of her health'. She had asked her husband to send them away, she said, but he had refused to do so, and they sat 'drinking & making a grievous noyse and caused the music to play until twelve o'clock at night'. In the interests of balance, it should be noted that in a similar case a few years later, it was the wife rather than the husband who stood accused of inflicting noise. In 1709 William Idelle complained that when he was ill his wife Elizabeth 'instead of keeping him company and comforting him . . . endeavoured to disturb him and make him uneasie by playing on her violin and other musical instruments making a great noise on purpose he believes to disquiet him'.[22]

The reaction of neighbours to familial discord tells us much about what was deemed socially acceptable and unacceptable. Of course, neighbours did not always know precisely what was going on: Phoebe Wood seems not to have been aware just how appallingly David Simpson treated his wife. And some would either have felt that what went on behind closed doors was none of their business, or that they ran the risk of bringing down the wrath of the wife-beater on themselves if they sought to intervene. But there are plenty of instances on record where people attempted to intervene, or relatives, neighbours or friends of abused or battered wives offered them at least temporary places of refuge. Sometimes friends and family would give as good as the wife got: in 1791 Alexander George Sinclair, a doctor, went to his wife's parents' house at Stroud in Kent, where she had gone to escape the abuse he had subjected her to, in the hope of persuading her to return to him. Her parents assaulted and beat him, and organised a ducking for him in the River Medway.[23] An indication that some wife-beaters, at least, thought that what they were doing might be wrong is contained in this diary entry for 19 December 1664 by Samuel Pepys:

> Going to bed betimes last night we waked betimes, and from our people's being forced to take the key to go out to light a candle, I was very angry and begun to find fault with my wife for not commanding her servants as she ought. Thereupon she giving me some cross answer I did strike her over her left eye such a blow as the poor wretch did cry out and was in great pain, but yet her spirit was such as to endeavour to bite and scratch me. But I coying [stroking] with her made her leave crying, and sent for butter and parsley, and friends presently one with another, and I up, vexed at my heart to think what I had done, for she was forced to lay a poultice or something to her eye all day, and is black, and the people of the house observed it.

Pepys was clearly ashamed of himself. He was also clearly worried about what others might think.[24]

VI

By the mid eighteenth century, Pepys's inner conviction that to lash out at a spouse was wrong seems to have become more prevalent in society as a whole. Although, as I have already mentioned, analysis of at least one county's quarter session and assize records suggests that husbands who beat their wives were rarely indicted for assault, the records of a number of counties show that even so the number of indictments rose as the century progressed. Likewise, it became not uncommon for wives to bind violent husbands over to keep the peace. During the Mary Simpson case, her neighbour Phoebe Wood mentioned that Mary had warned David Simpson that she would swear the peace against him. In the seventeenth century, husbands who failed to control their wives, or whose wives beat them, were occasionally subjected to a form of community mockery known as the charivari. By the nineteenth century, however, they were being replaced as objects of community satire by wife-beaters. A Surrey case from the 1840s, for example, records how a crowd gathered outside the home of a local wife-beater, subjected him to 'rough music' – a cacophony of whistles, horns, cowbells, rattles and beaten pans – and then fell silent to allow for a spokesman to deliver a verse admonition:

> *There is a man in this place.*
> *Has beat his wife!* [loudly, followed by a pause]
> *Has beat his wife!* [very loudly]
> *It is a great shame and disgrace*
> *To all who in this place*
> *It is indeed upon my life!!*

In Kent, twenty or so years later, a mob of villagers attempted to duck a wife-beater who had locked his wife out of their house after a violent altercation. The police were called and stopped the charivari. They did not, however, arrest any of the participants.[25] An article in the *Newcastle Courant* of 2 February 1799 reflects the growing sense of disapproval people felt towards those husbands who hit their wives. It related a (possibly apocryphal) incident in Derbyshire where a wife who had suffered numerous beatings from her husband tied him up in the bed-clothes while he was sleeping and 'thrashed him so soundly that he entered into a treaty of amity, which it is probable, a feeling recollection of his late sufferings will deter him from infringing'. The *Courant's* view was clear-cut: 'when a fellow's heart is so dead to sensibility as to warrant him striking a woman, it is to his shoulders that the remedy should be applied'.

Some, notably the historian Elizabeth Foyster, have suggested that this new 'sensibility' did not extend equally throughout all sectors of society, and certainly there does seem to be evidence from the late eighteenth century onwards that disapproval of wife-beating was more common among middle- and upper-class people than it was among the working class. Increasing levels of education and new concepts of refinement, noticeably of 'politeness', created a stratum of society that viewed such violence with distaste.[26] If you were a polite person of taste and refinement, the argument ran, you did not beat your wife. By the same token, if you did beat your wife, you were doing something that placed you beyond the norms of polite society. This in turn promoted the idea that wife-beating was essentially the preserve of the lower orders.

In 1786 a certain William White was committed to Bedford gaol after his wife Mary, a 'pauper', complained that he had beaten her. The presiding justice of the peace recorded that White had 'a savage stupid idea that he may beat his wife as much as he pleases, provided he does not kill her', and concluded that 'a little confinement will show him his error'. In other words, so far, at least, as the justice of the peace was concerned, there was a clear distinction to be made between the 'savage stupid idea' that might exist within the head of a man such as William White, and the notions that would govern the actions of, say, a justice of the peace.[27] The view that there was now a profound gulf between middle- and working-class standards in marital violence was neatly summed up by the lawyer and politician Sir John Nicholl, giving his opinions on an upper-class divorce case in 1827:

> A blow between parties in the lower conditions and in the higher stations of life bears a very different aspect. Among the lower classes blows sometimes pass between a married couple who, in the main, are very happy and have no desire to part; amidst very coarse habits such incidents occur almost as frequently as rude or reproachful words; a word and a blow go together. Still, even among the very lowest classes, there is generally a feeling of something unmanly in striking a woman; but if a gentleman, a person of education . . . uses personal violence to his wife, his equal in rank . . . such conduct in such a person carries with it something so degrading to the husband, and so insulting and mortifying to the wife, as to render the injury itself far more severe and insupportable.

Or, as another commentator, J. W. Kaye, put it in 1856: 'men of education and refinement do not strike women; neither do they strike each other'. The clear inference was that men who did not possess education or refinement tended to do both.[28]

VII

Kaye's comments, which he made in an essay on 'Outrages on Women', came at a critical moment in the history of English matrimony for by the 1840s not only was there a consensus among the upper echelons of society that wife-beating was wrong, there was also an increasingly vociferous body of opinion that held that those trapped in a miserable, violent marriage should be able to escape it.

One of the leading campaigners for divorce reform, Caroline Norton, had first-hand experience of what she condemned: her husband, the Tory MP George Norton, would appear to have been one of those human beings of whom nothing positive can be said: unable to forgive his wife for being cleverer and quicker than he was, he subjected her to a barrage of physical and mental abuse, accused her of adultery with the then Prime Minister, William Melbourne, refused to allow her to see her children, and tried to defraud her.

Others, such as the Whig MP Howard Elphinstone, who tried to introduce a Marriages and Divorces Bill in 1843, pointed out that even in those rare cases where divorce under existing laws was possible, its expense was almost prohibitive: a recent one had cost the wife involved the then enormous sum of £1,500, even though it was her adulterous (and insolvent) husband who was at fault. Reform, it was clear, was not only essential, it had growing public support.

The outcome was the Matrimonial Causes Act of 1857, which finally made civil divorce in England a legal option, albeit one which people were slow to take in large numbers. Curiously, though – at least so far as the modern observer is concerned – the legislation did not establish physical cruelty as grounds for divorce. It may be that legislation of 1828 (Offences against the Person Act) and more importantly 1853 (Act for the Better Prevention and Punishment of Aggravated Assaults upon Women and Children), which extended the right of justices to try violent offenders on summary conviction, was sufficient guarantee against violent husbands. More important, perhaps, was the feeling among Members of Parliament and judges that defining cruelty within marriage was either too difficult (unlike adultery, the most important of the accepted grounds for divorce), or would generally be extended to include too wide a range of abuses, many of which were perceived as petty.

The traditional objections to divorce on the grounds of cruelty were stated by Sir William Scott, Lord Stowell, in his summing up in the case of Evans vs Evans of 1790, when a Mrs Evans petitioned for divorce on the grounds of her husband's cruelty. He stressed that 'the general happiness of the married life is secured by its indissolubility', and continued:

When people understand that they must live together, except for a very few reasons known to the law, they learn to soften by mutual accommodation that yoke which they know that they cannot shake off; they become good husbands and wives, from the necessity of remaining husbands and wives . . . In this case, as in many others, the happiness of some individuals must be sacrificed for the greater and general good.

Interestingly, this view was deemed worth citing by the Royal Commission set up to investigate the law of divorce in 1853, and the findings of the 1853 Commission in turn proved very influential when the 1857 legislation was being debated. The 'greater and general good' meant, of course, the continued beating and murder of wives, the continuation of unhappy and abusive marriages, and the continued ruining or distorting of the lives of children daily confronted by domestic violence.[29] Divorce reform may have offered an escape route for those whose marriages had irretrievably broken down, but it could not address the broader issue of domestic violence. It remains a major social issue even today.

VIII

So far I've focussed on women as victims in the home – and, of course, statistically that emphasis is justified. But the historical record shows that they could on occasion be assailants. The Essex records I have already touched on reveal that a high proportion of women accused of homicide were accused of killing family members (24 from a total of 49, as opposed to 33 from 261 men). This pattern seems to be confirmed by a survey of homicide cases in Surrey between 1660 and 1800, though precise statistics are not given.[30] And again, although statistics are not offered, the authors of a study of crime in north-eastern England in the eighteenth century conclude that most women accused of non-infanticidal murder allegedly killed either family members, or neighbours or others known to them – in other words, that, unlike men, women were unlikely to pick a fight with a random stranger, but that the breakdown of domestic or other close relationships could lead to a fatal assault.[31] And when that happened, women were capable of being just as violent and brutal as men.

The case that most graphically illustrates this is one I touched on in the previous chapter: the murder of Jane Buttersworth at Hemington in Somerset in 1740. Her employer and principal assailant was Elizabeth Branch, widow of a lawyer (local gossip had it that she had poisoned him) and widely suspected of other earlier crimes: she was supposed to have killed her mother, disguising the murder as a suicide, and when some bones were found near her farm the assumption was that they were those of a servant that 'once lived with 'em, but the world never knew what was become of her'. Mean and avaricious, 'her common method was, to treat the servants with the utmost severity, in order to force 'em to desert their service, and thereby, to forfeit their wages'. Those who stayed were fed on bread, cheese and water, 'and hard usage and disquietude were their other comforts'. 'Madam Branch', according to one pamphlet, 'was a great reader; and her favourite pieces were said to be those that treated of tyranny and inhumanity; particularly that of Nero, who ript up his mother's belly to see how he was born.' These 'barbarous notions' were picked up by her daughter: 'she would often cut open mice and birds, torturing them for three hours together, before they expir'd.'[32]

Jane Buttersworth's death followed a period of sustained persecution. Thought guilty of a minor infraction, she was laid out on the floor, her skirts were pulled up, and she was beaten about her lower body and legs with rods or twigs until they broke, then beaten from room to room with (according to some accounts) broomsticks. A fellow servant named Anne James (who may, or may not, be the same person as the Anne Summers referred to in other pamphlets dealing with the case) eventually found her crouched down in a corner in the farm's brewhouse chamber, 'her head hanging on one shoulder, the blood streaming down both sides of her face, and groaning very much'.

Her employers wanted to send her on an errand, but she was not physically up it, telling James she could not see clearly. This provoked a further beating and kicking from Elizabeth Branch while her daughter looked on. Then Jane Buttersworth was ordered to do some dusting, and when that proved too much for her she was again beaten from room to room, and had a pail of water thrown over her (it was February, so the water would have been freezing). When she was then ordered to wash dishes, James intervened, pointing out that Buttersworth had not been fed that day, and adding that 'she has had beating enough'. But further mistreatment followed: Jane's hands were forced into the scalding water that had been prepared to wash the dishes in. She collapsed, and was put to bed. Her bloody clothes were hidden. Shortly afterwards, she died. The death was passed off as natural, the body buried and the coffinbearers treated to beer and 'a gammon of bacon'.

However, thanks in part to Anne James, a 'muttering' arose locally that Branch had murdered Buttersworth. Neighbours were understandably wary of Branch: her threatening nature and taste for litigation made them 'very cautious how they acted'. But when a supernatural light was seen hovering over the girl's grave, and then traversing the graveyard before returning to hover over the grave again, 'the testimony of the hand of God' was detected, and a group of neighbours opened the grave. Seeing the 'dismal condition' of Buttersworth's corpse, they had the Branches arrested and imprisoned pending a trial after a coroner's inquest. On their way to court, the women were pelted and attacked by a hostile crowd. Finally, on the morning of 3 May 1740, mother and daughter were hanged, to the evident satisfaction of the small crowd that had gathered to watch (the execution apparently took place early in the morning to ensure that there be no time for a larger mob to assemble).[33]

This was, of course, an extreme case, so it is not surprising that the Branches should have been so widely castigated in contemporary literature. However, as a rule, pamphlet writers reserved their most heavy moralising for wives who killed their husbands. Husband-killing, it will be remembered, was classified as petty treason until 1828, and until 1790 the penalty for a woman convicted of petty treason was not to be hanged but to be burned at the stake. An early example is provided by the case of Sarah Elestone, burned in 1678 after being tried at the Surrey assizes for killing her husband Thomas, a felt-maker and 'a man very laborious in his calling'.

He was aged about forty, his wife a few years older, and they had lived together 'very contentedly' for many years. But Sarah fell in with a set of 'lewd women', and turned to drunkenness, swearing and profaning the Lord's Day. Her husband, warned of her conduct by friends, tried to reclaim her, and when she refused to respond to his admonitions, he tried keeping her short of money, to which she responded by running up debts in his name and selling the furniture. This led in turn to her husband deciding 'to beat her out of this wicked course, but when he gave her blows, she proved herself ready to repay them', so that 'their neighbours hath been forced to part them at all hours of the night'. She returned home drunk after drinking with her 'gossips', and after another altercation killed her husband with a stab in the chest from a pair of shears. She was apprehended after a hue and cry was raised (a convention whereby local constables were permitted to pursue suspects across parishes and call on bystanders for help). She was then imprisoned, tried and convicted.

The pamphlet describing the incident ended with a brief account of her execution. Several ministers had brought her to a proper sense of repentance, and she died accepting her fate, and apparently making an appropriate speech warning her hearers against sin. The crime and the execution, so the author of the pamphlet assured his readers, 'must needs draw tears from our eyes if we have any room for pity or piety'. The story also reminded the readers, and those who come across such pamphlets today, of the tragic consequences of domestic relationships that go wrong.[34]

Natures
Cruell Step-Dames:

OR,

Matchlesse Monsters of the Female

Sex; *Elizabeth Barnes*, and *Anne Willis*.

Who were executed the 26. day of *April*,

1637. at Tyburne, for the unnaturall murthering of their owne Children,

Also, herein is contained their severall Confessions,
and the Courts just proceedings against other notorious
Malefactors, with their severall offences
this Sessions.

Further, a Relation of the wicked Life and

impenitent Death of *Iohn Flood*, who raped
his own Childe.

Printed at London for *Francis Coules*, dwelling in
the Old-Baily. 1637.

This 1637 pamphlet told the story of Anne Willis, who killed her illegitimate child and hid the body in a vault in Rosemary Hill, London. From the sixteenth century growing numbers of women were prosecuted for the murder of newborn children – leading some historians to suggest that Europe experienced an 'infanticide craze'.

CHAPTER 6

MOTHERS AND INFANTICIDE

I

Men may on the whole be more deadly than women, but historically there was one category of homicide that was an almost exclusively female preserve: infanticide, or to be more technically precise, neonaticide ('newborn child murder' was how people in the eighteenth century described it).[1] Known if not widely prosecuted in the middle ages, it began to figure regularly in court proceedings in England, and in other parts of Europe, as the sixteenth century progressed, and then became a constant feature.

In some modern cultures, the killing of baby girls is a not uncommon practice (often, at least in part, for economic reasons), but analysis of the Home Circuit records in the sixteenth and seventeenth centuries shows that in Elizabethan and Stuart times, newborn boys were as or more likely to be killed as girls: in the 139 cases between 1560 and 1624 where the sex of the dead child is known, 77 were male as opposed to 62 female. As for their mothers, these were almost invariably described as spinsters. Occasionally we encounter cases where married women fell under suspicion – for example, in December 1633 a coroner's inquest sought to establish whether Marion Eridge, wife of William Eridge of Appledore in Kent, had killed her newborn child in her husband's home the previous August (she was acquitted, and it is interesting to note how long it took for the baby's corpse to be discovered – perhaps there were more hiding places to hand for a married householder). But such cases are the exception rather than the rule.

Overall, then, infanticide involved unmarried women dealing with the consequences of unplanned pregnancies, and it's clear from the surviving records that it was a common and increasingly widely punished phenomenon, not just in England but in continental Europe, too. One historian of the legal system in France has even gone so far as to suggest that the early modern period experienced an 'infanticide craze', as a result of which more women were executed than those who met their deaths as a consequence of the European witch hunts.[2]

Surviving records from the Elizabethan and Jacobean Home Circuit of the assizes (covering Essex, Hertfordshire, Kent, Surrey and Sussex) show that between 1560 and 1624 some 160 women were accused of infanticide, of whom 53 were executed and 70 acquitted (see Appendix, Table 5). There were also a number of other cases where a guilty verdict was brought in but no clear record of punishment is given (for example, a married couple and a spinster were convicted of killing the spinster's newborn child; the man successfully pleaded benefit of clergy and was convicted of manslaughter, but we don't know what happened to the two women). And in a few cases the death of the child was either declared accidental or attributed to divine visitation (a verdict that roughly corresponds to the modern concept of death by natural causes). In some of those cases that ended in acquittal, the jurors followed the usual contemporary legal fiction of ascribing the death to 'John a Style', 'One at Noke' or even (in three cases) 'John Death'. This may sometimes have been because the facts of the case were impossible to establish with certainty, and sometimes because the jury wanted to extend clemency to the accused.

Issues of clemency also underlay a number of those cases (eighteen in total) where a plea of pregnancy on the part of the convicted woman was accepted and so the death penalty was either delayed or not carried out at all. Margaret Judge, for example, was convicted of infanticide at the Maidstone assizes in July 1560, and remanded on grounds of pregnancy. Her condition was, apparently, not formally investigated until July 1561, when she was examined by a 'jury of matrons' who found her to be pregnant. She was held in gaol, declared again to be pregnant in July 1563, returned to gaol, and finally pardoned in 1565.[3] Other women who pleaded pregnancy successfully were kept in gaol for a year or two, and then simply disappear from the records of the assizes; one suspects that in many cases they were released. That said, of course, the plea of pregnancy did occasionally fail, and the convicted woman was executed.[4]

As the sixteenth century wore on, though, it's clear that attitudes harshened and religion lay at the heart of this shift in thinking. The Reformation, and the subsequent Catholic Counter-Reformation, laid great stress on social discipline and instilling godliness into believers. Accordingly, in the more puritanical world of post-Reformation England, sexual immorality, along with all other areas of human sinfulness, came to be viewed more censoriously than it had once been. And since infanticide generally involved two sins – fornication and murder – it inevitably attracted particular moral opprobrium. Commentators made constant use of the two words 'cruel' and 'unnatural' when describing mothers who killed their children. The pamphleteer Henry Goodcole went further. Describing, in 1637, the trial and execution in Middlesex of a woman called Anne Willis, who had given birth to an illegitimate child, killed it, and concealed its body in a vault in Rosemary Lane near Tower Hill, he wrote:

> Oh cruell monsters of that tender sex . . . heaven's infinite compassion is compared unto the mother and infant, the neere tye between them, and the intire care of mothers over their children! When I lift up mine eyes towards the heavens, & again call them downe to the earth; birds and beasts, me thinks, do rise up in judgement against these unnaturall cruell beastes

in women's shapes. The swallow flieth high, and in the towring trees, churches and houses build their nestes, to preserve their yong ones out of danger; the sparrow watcheth alone on the house top, as careful what it had hatched and brought foorth. Beasts, such as lyons, wolves, tigers and foxes, have secret caves and woods where they hide their young, to preserve & foster them alive; but these bloody dogs degenerate from them. O let therefore the memorial of them perish.[5]

When the celebrated Non-conformist minister Matthew Henry, some decades later in 1701, preached in Chester gaol to a group of prisoners who included three women awaiting execution for infanticide, he took as his text *James*, 1:15: 'Then when lust hath conceived, it brought forth sin, and sin when it is finished bringeth forth death'. The sermon, Henry's biographer informs us, was 'a very aweful and awakening discourse'.[6]

If, though, the new spirit of condemnation had a religious basis, it also had a practical economic component to it. As the population increased in the late sixteenth century, so did levels of poverty and so, therefore, did calls on parish funds. In such an environment illegitimate children and their mothers were unlikely to find much official sympathy. Legislation of 1576 (the first to bring the issue of bastardy within the remit of secular government) acknowledged both the moral and economic facets of the issue. It stated that the bearing of bastards (and by implication the illicit sexual acts that caused them) constituted 'an offence against god's law and man's law' and that these bastards went on to be 'left to the charges of the parish where they were born, to the great burden of the same parish'. A few decades later, in 1610, a further statute talked of bastards being both 'the great dishonour of almighty God' and a financial drain. Their mothers, it concluded, were 'very lewd women' who should be sent to a house of correction for twelve months.[7] In the same year, a bill specifically prescribing the death penalty for those who killed their newborn bastard children went through two readings in Parliament, but pressure of other business meant that it did not reach the statute book.[8]

And then in 1624 came a landmark statute that was to shape how infanticide would be dealt with for the next 175 years.[9] Its preamble both set the moral tone and defined the problem:

> Whereas many lewd women that have been delivered of bastard children, to avoid their shame, and to escape punishment, do secretly bury or conceal their children, and after, if the child be found dead, the said women do allege, that the said child was born dead, whereas it falleth out sometimes (although hardly it is to be proved) that the said child or children were murthered by the said women, their lewd mothers, or by their assent or procurement.

There then followed the main provision of the act:

> If any woman after one month next ensuing the end of this session of parliament be delivered of any issue of her body, male or female, which being born alive, should by the laws of this realm be a bastard, and that she endeavour privately, either by drowning or secret burying thereof, or any other way, either by herself or the procuring of others, so to conceal the death thereof, as that it may not come to light, whether it were born alive or not, but be concealed: in every such case, the said mother so offending shall suffer death as in case of murder, except such mother can make proof by one witness at the least, that the child (whose death was by her so intended to be concealed) was born dead.

The act, then, not only confirmed the death penalty for infanticide but removed a traditional line of defence: that the child had been born dead. Thus when at an Old Bailey trial in 1674 two young women accused of killing their newborn children claimed that they had been stillborn, the court turned to the statute ('whereby it is provided that unless the same be proved by at least one credible witness, it shall be reputed and punished as murder') and condemned both of them to death.[10] Thus the 1624 statute created a new offence: the concealment of an infant death.

Through analysis of published assize calendars summed up in Table 6 (see Appendix) we can get some impression of the impact of the new statute by looking at prosecutions for infanticide at the Kent assizes between 1625 and 1689 (though there is a hiatus during the Commonwealth years of the 1650s). These certainly seem to suggest that a harsher approach was taken. Of the 86 accused in this period, some 40 were acquitted while 32 were sentenced to be hanged – a much bleaker outcome than that recorded for the Home Circuit between 1560 and 1624.[11] Figures for Essex between 1620 and 1680 show that out of 84 accused, 31 were hanged and 35 acquitted, with 11 of the hangings occurring in the 1630s. Here women were far more likely to suffer the death penalty for infanticide than for other forms of homicide (6 out of 41); and the seriousness with which the offence was treated is underlined when we compare it with the 5 (of 401 accused) women hanged for larceny in Essex in the same period, and the 24 (of 119 suspects) hanged for burglary or housebreaking, or, indeed, with the 20 Essex women hanged between 1620 and 1680 for witchcraft.[12]

A couple of qualifications do need to be made, though. The Kent results certainly display a punitive approach in the middle decades of the century, but guilty verdicts seem to become less likely after about 1660, while there were none after 1680. And tempting though it is to conclude that attitudes harshened after the 1624 Act, in the previous decades the figures are slightly distorted by the fact that so many women who were actually convicted were then able successfully to plead pregnancy and so escape execution: grouping together those sentenced to death, those found guilty but for whom no punishment is recorded, those pardoned after conviction, and those successfully pleading pregnancy after conviction, we find that a total of 79 women were convicted, as opposed to 70 acquitted. The ban on executing pregnant women remained in place throughout the seventeenth and eighteenth centuries and beyond, but as procedures tightened in the course of the late seventeenth and early eighteenth centuries, the use of a spurious plea of pregnancy as a first step towards a reprieve became less likely to succeed. But the fact remains that tough legal attitudes preceded the 1624 watershed.

The legal convention of the time was to say that the victims of infanticide had been strangled at birth. In fact, the methods of disposal were various. Agnes Barnes, a servant girl from Kent, gave birth to a bastard in her master's house in August 1559, and left it in a swine yard to be eaten by the pigs. In another Kentish case, dating from 1679, Elizabeth Courthopp was accused of drowning her child in a 'hog-tub' outside the house where she gave birth. In 1562 a Kentish servant girl threw her newborn child into a fire in her master's house, and some thirty years later another of the Kentish accused allegedly threw her newborn child into a 'seething furnace'. Other newborn children were drowned or suffocated in privies, thrown out of windows, or simply choked or strangled. Obviously capital convictions were most likely where it could be demonstrated that the deceased child had been severely injured, as with an Essex case where a newborn child had its throat cut and was subsequently thrown into a stream weighted with stones, or that of Elizabeth Browne, hanged in Kent in 1593 for killing her newborn child with a knife and tearing out its entrails, or that of Margaret Chandler of Richmond in Surrey who in 1591 allegedly tried to choke her newborn child with earth and a bone from a goose's leg, and left it 'grovelling' in a ditch where it died the following day.[13] Chandler died in prison while awaiting trial.

Most infanticidal mothers killed their children on their own, in secret. But sometimes they had accomplices – usually family members. In earlier cases, little detail is given, but there's usually enough to give us a sense of the terrible dilemmas and fractured relationships that led people to kill. Alice, wife of Robert Hilley, for example, who came from Gillingham in Kent, was acquitted in 1588 of the murder of an infant who was the product of her adulterous relationship with one Thomas Freemason. We are left wondering what effect all this had on her marriage. In 1565 Sibyl Ellyot of Kirdford in

Sussex was accused of murdering a child, with her husband, a clergyman named William Ellyot, acting as accessory, and burying the corpse in the vicarage garden. The Lewes assizes, however, concluded that the child had in fact been murdered by a spinster named Christine Grantham and that the Ellyots had acted as accessories. A year later, a fresh indictment was drawn up and all three were found guilty. Was William Ellyot the father of the child and Christine Grantham his servant and mistress? Did Sibyl Ellyot become involved because she wanted to hide her husband's shame? We can only speculate.[14]

When it comes to later cases, we sometimes have rather more to draw on. Take, for example, one investigated by Surrey Justice of the Peace Richard Wyatt in October 1774, which involved Mary Bailey, servant to an Egham gentleman named John Harcourt. Wyatt had already had dealings with the household just three weeks before, when he'd received complaints about Harcourt himself: probably 'disordered in his senses', Harcourt had threatened to kill his wife Margaret and servants and send them to hell, and had beaten and kicked his wife and threatened to stab a servant, Thomas Goldfinch, who had tried to intervene. Now Wyatt was being asked to establish whether Mary Bailey, a 'singlewoman', who had been hired as a cook by Harcourt's wife when she was already '2 months gone with child', had killed her newborn baby. According to Mary's own testimony, she had gone into labour on 3 September, and at around 8 a.m. the following morning had given birth to a child, which, she stated, was born dead (in support of this she claimed that a few days after she entered the Harcourts' employ she had 'plainly felt the motion' of the child within her as she lifted a tub of water, but that she had not felt it move since). Mary had then wrapped the body up in her shift, dressed herself, gone downstairs to get a pail of water and washed the blood from the floor where she had given birth. Next she had put the body of the child into the pail, and taken it to the privy, where she had deposited it. She produced some child's bedlinen and a child's cap, which she said she had acquired in preparation for the baby's arrival. (We don't know who found the corpse, nor what ultimately happened to Mary.)

As others gave their evidence, it became apparent that while some might have suspected that Mary had been pregnant, none had been absolutely sure of the fact. When Mrs Harcourt had commented that Mary had 'very much increase[d] in bulk', she had replied that it was her natural shape. And when a fellow servant, Elizabeth Stevens, had told Mary a number of times that she was convinced that Mary was pregnant, the girl had denied it every time. Even the father of the child, an apprentice to a Brentford apothecary, didn't seem to know, though he had noticed that Mary was looking 'round' when he had last seen her.

It was only after the birth that vague inklings turned to deep suspicions. Elizabeth Stevens, who shared a room with Mary, later reported that she had noticed how ill her fellow servant had been on 4 September; that she had walked around the room several times complaining of a cramp in her back. A few hours later Stevens had noticed that the floor had been washed, and that a chamber pot containing some bloody water was standing nearby. She had questioned Mary, who claimed that she had been vomiting, and that 'something had burst', which had brought a good deal of blood up from her stomach. Elizabeth had informed Margaret Harcourt, and it was she who speculated whether Mary might have given birth to a bastard child and destroyed it.[15]

Mary's tragic case was only too typical. Like so many others in her position, she was an unmarried servant living in a household with her employers and other servants. People may have suspected that she was pregnant, but they seem to have been prepared to go along with her alternative explanation – and presumably she was able to wear loose clothes that would conceal her condition. She gave birth alone, and (surprising, perhaps, for us today) without being immediately detected. After the birth, she disposed of the body of the child, cleaned up the area where she had given birth and tried to carry on as normal. Depending on your outlook, this could be viewed as extreme callousness on her part or a display of extraordinary psychological and physical resilience.

There were two principal reasons why a woman such as Mary Bailey would resort to such desperate measures. First, a bastard child would have been an enormous financial burden for her. In 1760 a Cheshire woman called Mary Cliff gave birth to a child she claimed was born dead. Asked if she would have killed the child had it been born alive, she wrung her hands, and declared that 'as God is my witness and I have a soul to be saved I would not have done such a thing for all the world but rather have gone begging from door to door with the child upon my back'. She may have said this for rhetorical effect, but this image of itinerant penury wasn't far removed from grim reality for women like her and Mary Bailey.[16]

But perhaps an even more potent consideration was shame. Bernard de Mandeville, a London-based Dutch physician and a sometimes acerbic commentator on the human condition, commented that whereas 'common whores' never killed their illegitimate children because 'they have lost their modesty to a greater degree, and the fear of shame makes hardly any impression upon them', this was not the case for 'the diligent, faithful and obliging' domestic servant with an 'abundance of modesty'. For such a young woman, 'the more modest she is now, and the more violently the dread of coming to shame hurries her away, the more wicked and more cruel her resolutions will be, against her self or what she bears'.[17] After all, her range of options was very narrow indeed. She could try to abort the foetus, but it was a criminal offence in this period, and the traditional herbal remedies, medicines and mild doses of poison that were commonly used were not necessarily effective and could prove fatal.

The modern alternative – adoption – scarcely existed in the seventeenth and eighteenth centuries. In London after 1739, the mothers of unwanted children could seek to leave their babies with the Foundling Hospital, but the institution was soon hopelessly overstretched, and in any case its reach did not extend beyond the capital. Abandoned babies might be taken to parish workhouses or even charitably minded individuals, but in general infanticide was the only real option for those women who did not feel able to keep their illegitimate children.

II

There must have been many deaths that went undetected, either because the mother successfully concealed the birth and murder of her child, or because others agreed to help her and then kept their silence. A case from Yorkshire illustrates this graphically – as well as showing the dangers of a subsequent falling out between those involved. In July 1665 a man simply identified as Henry Sole, apparently the master or employer of Sissilye Linscale, reported a story that Linscale had told him of the events surrounding the birth of a child to her cousin, Anne Linscale. Apparently Sissilye had been driving a cow home past the house of her aunt Jane Linscale, Anne's mother, when she heard Anne crying out 'very greviously', and went in to see what the matter was. Jane Linscale asked Sissilye to go and fetch help from a woman called Elizabeth Agarr, which she did.

Passing her aunt's house again a little later, she decided to go in and found a group of people gathered there: 'they did look strangely upon her, and did shut the door and kept her in'. Agarr took something from a paper wrapping she had with her, rolled it into a ball, and then made Anne Linscale swallow it, washing it down with the contents of a bottle she had brought. Shortly afterwards Anne gave birth to a child, presumably stillborn. Sissilye's aunt warned her: 'Good Sisse, do not speak of this, for if thou doest, we are all undone', while Elizabeth Agarr banged her hand on a table, and vowed to Sissilye that 'if ever she heard any word that she should speak of it, she would be the death of her'. Two of Sissilye's other cousins, Em and Pegg, took the baby out and buried it in a hole while Sissilye watched; she later said 'that she had many times been troubled about it [i.e. what she had witnessed], yet durst not speak of it for fear of getting some ill by them'. Indeed three days later, Jane and Em Linscale came to the house where she lived, 'and did revile her with very bad words'. The only reason the story came to light was because, according to Sissilye, Agarr had reviled her master (for reasons we don't know), and she felt she had to do something about it.[18] All those accused were ultimately acquitted.

A 1674 case from Kent shows the wider community becoming involved in a cover-up. Here at the Maidstone assizes on 7 April two women, Rebecca Hills of Tonge and Eve Sampson of Sutton, both spinsters, were tried for newborn child murder, Hills being acquitted, and Sampson being found guilty and hanged. Then at the next assizes on 28 July 1674, the parishioners of both Tonge and Sutton were indicted for burying the children of Hills and Sampson in their respective churchyards without informing the coroner, and two men from each of the parishes (one suspects they were the churchwardens) were fined a few shillings.[19] It's tempting to assume that local opinion was sympathetic to the plight of the two women, or perhaps the view was that the babies had been stillborn and no crime had therefore been committed.

In this context, it's perhaps worth mentioning a Cheshire case from 1728 in which a midwife named Hester Pixey, called to a house to examine two dead newborns, decided that they were the victims of a miscarriage, and so 'took the said children and buried them in the back side of the same house'. It was only the following day when, having discussed what she had done with someone else and 'being inform'd that she ought not to have done so', she decided to disinter them and report the matter.[20]

Other cases, though, quickly won both the attention and condemnation of the community. One such occurred in Backford in Cheshire in 1680, and it began when ten-year-old Thomas Dickson and his younger sister Elizabeth observed two swine 'rooting before Mary Stockton's door' and saw them unearth the body of a baby. As the two children discussed what to do, Mary Stockton emerged from her house, picked up the baby's body by its leg, and, telling Thomas that it was 'a piece of carrion', threw it behind the house.

Thomas and Elizabeth Dickson, however, were not so easily fooled. They told a young neighbour, Mary Hesketh, that they had seen 'a thing like a child on or against Mary Stockton's door for it had two feet & a round head', and Hesketh (almost certainly a domestic servant) told her employer, Elizabeth Denson. To begin with Denson told Hesketh to go to Stockton's to investigate, but Stockton claimed to be ill (although she did let slip the remark 'let all young women take warning by me & see what a burden I have carried').

Denson therefore co-opted another neighbour, Mary Larton, a yeoman's wife aged about forty, to go and confront Stockton. Under the two women's persistent questioning, Mary Stockton's initial denials crumbled. She admitted she had given birth, but claimed that the child was eight weeks premature (she didn't even have any clothing prepared for it, she said) and had been born 'in pieces' before being further damaged by the swine. The father was a seaman called John Leadbeater. According to William Denson (probably Elizabeth Denson's husband), when the women questioned Mary Stockton they told her to expose her breasts, and he saw Mary Larton 'draw milk forth of Mary Stockton's breast'. He then called in the parish constable to organise a search for the remains of the newborn. It was found with a cut in its thigh four inches long, a wound on its head so deep that it exposed the skull, and a number of other injuries. Mary Stockton was executed after her trial in 1681.

What is striking in this case is that it was women in a position of some authority in the community (Denson and Larton, both the wives of yeomen) who took it upon themselves to investigate. But this was not always the case. Those, for example, who denounced Elizabeth Holdinge, a spinster accused of killing her male bastard child at Great Saughall in Cheshire in 1686, were simply fellow workers and neighbours. It was Mary Foxe, a widow in her early thirties, who appears to have shared a bedchamber with Holdinge, who was the first to be suspicious. In the early hours of 31 October, she heard Elizabeth give a shriek. She asked what the matter was, and on being told that Elizabeth was 'sick at heart', felt her face and 'found her to be of a cold sweat'. She therefore called in two female neighbours. Holdinge, however, assured everyone she was better, denied Foxe's accusation that she had given birth (Foxe, incidentally, later testified that she had had no previous inkling that Holdinge might be pregnant), and went off to milk the cows. For her part Foxe, 'suspecting all might not be well', searched Holdinge's bed '& there found some tokens whereby this examinant believed she might have born a child'. Together with sixty-year-old labourer's wife Margaret Grindill, who had been one of the two women she had called in earlier, she searched Holdinge's bedding and became increasingly convinced that she had given birth. They and a third woman, Christian Helling, confronted Holdinge, who at last confessed and showed them the body of the baby, which she had kept locked in her box (many servant girls in her situation used their box to conceal things: it was the one private place they could call their own).

The coroner was called, and instructed Grindill to wash the child's body. As she did so, she saw some small marks on its head.[21] Holdinge was tried and executed. It's scarcely surprising that one recent historian has said: 'For unmarried women, the state of pregnancy was one in which other women – neighbours, friends and midwives – were not companions, but threats . . . pregnancy was an active problem for the household and the community, around which were built strategies of secrecy, exposure and confrontation.'[22]

Not all women were as discreet as Mary Bailey and Elizabeth Holdinge. In 1748 a certain Martha Roberts was taken on by Henry Ashcroft to 'work in needle work' at his house in Plumley in Cheshire. A 'pauper' according to one witness, she was, she said at her trial, the wife of a soldier in the 1st Regiment of Foot Guards (though she had not seen him for two years). She had an affair with a local man named John Grange, became pregnant by him, and, as with others in her predicament, tried to keep it secret, though it's hard to believe that this can have been particularly closely guarded: one witness at the coroner's inquest, Elizabeth Robertson, described how Roberts had come to borrow a pair of her stays in order to go to Over Knutsford fair on

Whitsun Tuesday, at which point the stays were 'a handful too wide for her', and then three weeks later asked if she could use them again, at which point they were too small. Robertson remarked on this, and Roberts at first denied there was anything untoward in her condition, but then admitted that she was pregnant and added that 'she had such stuff that would bring the child from her'. In her evidence to the coroner, Robertson could not remember precisely what this 'stuff' consisted of, but recalled Roberts telling her that 'what would kill the child would cure the pox'. Slightly inconsistently, she then reassured an anxious Robertson 'she would not commit any sin because the man and her were true to one another'.

If Roberts did in fact swallow the brew, it clearly had no effect whatsoever because in due course she gave birth at night in a 'boghouse' near her employer's house (she later said 'that the child had a long face like its father'), and then dropped the baby's body into a moat that ran beneath. She was later to claim that the child was born dead, but also to confide to her friend Robertson that she did not check whether this was in fact the case before she concealed the body. Certainly – and foolishly – she told Esther Price, another servant in the Ashcroft household, that 'she was very glad she got rid of it and desired this examinant would not tell any body of it'. Price also related that in the weeks that followed 'she saw the said Martha Roberts' milk run', but that Roberts – who seems to have been rather well versed in such matters – told her that 'she wore a piece of lead down her back to drive her suck away'. In her case lack of discretion was instrumental in uncovering her crime, though she was ultimately acquitted.[23]

III

As the eighteenth century progressed, ever fewer women were accused of murdering their newborn babies and convictions and executions for the crime became rare. In Cheshire, for example, the numbers dropped from 20 executed out of 63 accused in the years 1650–99, to 4 out of 31 in 1700–49 and 3 out of 18 in 1750–1800, the last execution – of a woman called Sarah Sant – coming in 1778. On the Northern Circuit of the assizes, some 200 cases were brought between 1720 and 1800, but only 6 women were convicted, and just 2 of these executed.[24]

Various factors account for this. First of all, there was a growing feeling that, whatever the 1624 Act might have to say on the matter, a stillbirth defence was legitimate. It was therefore invoked with increasing frequency and decreasing opposition as the nineteenth century loomed. At the same time, the circumstantial evidence that had traditionally featured so frequently in infanticide prosecutions started to hold less sway, and as judges discounted it more, so they were less likely to impose a capital verdict on the strength of it. And whereas the 1624 Act had rather assumed guilt until innocence could be proved, the spirit of the new age urged precisely the opposite. As the legal reformer and statesman William Eden put it in 1771:

> The modern exposition of this statute is a good instance, that cruel laws have a natural tendency to their own dissolution in the abhorrence of mankind. It is now a constant practice of the courts to require, that the body of the child shall be found before any conviction can take place; and if it should happen, that the mother had any child-bed linen, or other preparatives in her possession, prior to her delivery, it is generally admitted as a proof, that no concealment was intended. Moreover, it is not unusual to require some degree of evidence that the child was actually born alive, before the ungenerous presumption, that the mother was the wilful author of the death of her new-born infant, is permitted to affect her. These humane deviations from the harsh injunctions of the statute have nearly amounted to a tacit abrogation of it.[25]

The contrast between present-day 'humane deviations' and the 'harsh injunctions' of the past is striking here.

Scientific attempts to establish whether or not a baby had actually been murdered by its mother remained crude affairs right up to

Victorian times. In the sixteenth and seventeenth centuries, and for some time after, witnesses, especially midwives, often felt that they possessed sufficient expertise to offer a view (indeed coroners or justices of the peace quite often asked midwives to undertake a rudimentary investigation) but their opinion tended to be shaped by whether or not they had found wounds on the corpse.

In one typical case from Shocklach in Cheshire in February 1734, a local midwife, Elizabeth Jackson, was asked to examine the circumstances surrounding the murder of a newborn child the previous December. The mother, a servant named Dorothy Maddock, was dead, apparently poisoned by her master and lover, Thomas Peers. Elizabeth Jackson first examined Maddock's body (she reported that 'she could not find that any violence had been offered to her'), and then asked to see the body of the baby. One Elizabeth Taylor, who lived in the Peers household, produced the corpse from a drawer where it had been stuffed. It was wrapped up in a coarse cloth.

Jackson's view was that the body of the baby was distorted 'in such a manner as it could not be possibly brought into the world in such a shape'. She therefore asked Taylor a series of questions. Why had the child not been 'laid out straight'? Taylor had had 'no help' was the response. Why had no neighbouring women been sent for when Maddock went into labour? Taylor replied that 'the deceased would never consent to it'. Who had cut the child's navel string? The deceased had done it (Jackson believed that that act 'might probably destroy the dead child'). What had become of the afterbirth? Taylor had burned it. Who had laid out Maddock's corpse? Taylor and Thomas Peers had done so, leading the midwife to ask 'if it was not indecent for a man to lay hands upon a woman in that condition'.[26] This was scarcely a sophisticated medical investigation of the facts.

As the decades passed, midwives continued to be called upon to give evidence, but ever-more reliance was placed on the testimony of medical practitioners (all of them male in this period). They tended to focus on whether the child had probably been stillborn, whether it had reached its full term before being born, and whether it had suffered deliberately inflicted fatal injuries after birth – in other words, exactly the same issues that midwives addressed. Some also attempted a more scientific diagnosis, but as Mark Jackson, the leading expert on the medico-legal history of this period, has argued, what often emerged was little more than better-informed confusion – ideal for courts unwilling to convict.

Take, for example, the 'lung test'. This was supposed to show whether the baby had survived long enough to draw breath, and consisted of removing its lungs and seeing if they floated on water. If they did, then the baby must have inflated them, and so must have been born alive. It sounds superficially plausible and the method was increasingly commonly used in the late eighteenth century, but there was little consensus about it. At an Old Bailey trial in 1737 a doctor, relating how a coroner had asked him to carry out the lung test, said that 'without some other circumstances to corroborate this experiment, I should be loth to determine thereby positively' [i.e. be unequivocal that the child had been born alive], adding, 'I think the experiment (where a person's life is at stake) too slight to be built upon'. Similarly, in 1774 a correspondent to that great eighteenth-century clearing house of information and opinion, the *Gentleman's Magazine*, commented that the lung test 'may sometimes prove true', but that 'upon the whole it should be regarded no other way than as a very uncertain and precarious proof of the fact in question'. This inability to arrive at clear-cut medical opinions further aided the drift towards acquittals in newborn child murder cases.[27]

It's also apparent that – as William Eden's reference to 'humane deviations' from 'harsh injunctions' hints – social attitudes were starting to change. In the seventeenth century women accused of infanticide were 'murderous mothers' (to use Daniel Defoe's memorable term). By the middle decades of the following century, though, some commentators were regarding them rather more sympathetically: as unfortunates betrayed by their seducers – not just perpetrators but victims, too. Erasmus Darwin (1731–1802) was one such progressive thinker. He was a medical practitioner in

Lichfield whose range of interests included botany, agriculture and the education of women, and whose views on evolution were to presage (and, it has been claimed, influence) those of his more famous grandson, Charles. Called upon in 1767 to offer his opinion in a case of infanticide, he first addressed the medical issues (including a disquisition on the 'lung test'), and then made a wider, moral point:

> The women that have committed this most unnatural crime, are real objects of our greatest pity; their education has produced in them so much modesty, or sense of shame, that this artificial passion overturns the very instincts of nature! – what struggles there must be in their minds, what agonies! – and, at a time when, after the pains of parturition, nature has designed them in the sweet consolation of giving suck to a little helpless babe, that depends upon them for its hourly existence!

His conclusion was that 'the cause of this most horrid crime' was 'an excess of what is really a virtue, the sense of shame, or modesty. Such is the condition of human nature!'[28] This was a very far cry from the censorious Puritan view of a century before, and it has to be admitted that Darwin's argument was not a universally accepted one. Fallen women in the later eighteenth century were still widely regarded as tainted – they could, after all, have exercised their 'sense of shame, or modesty' at a rather earlier point in proceedings – while fallen women who killed were still generally felt to have transgressed society's and nature's laws. But his sympathetic views can nevertheless be found echoed elsewhere – and in some very highly respectable and influential quarters.

The physician extraordinary to Queen Caroline, William Hunter (1718–83), for example, followed the Darwin line very closely in his posthumously published essay 'On the uncertainty in the signs of murder, in the case of bastard children' (1784). A Lanarkshire physician, anatomist and male midwife who set up a very successful practice in London, he presided over a royal birth in 1762 (hence the awarding of the title 'physician extraordinary'), and was so trusted in upper-class circles that it was said that he helped a gentlewoman deliver two illegitimate children, who were then secreted in London's Foundling Hospital. He was a man of some status, then, and so when he wrote in his essay that infanticidal mothers were 'commonly objects of the greatest compassion; and generally are less criminal than the world imagines', his words would have carried weight.[29]

How far such sentiments actually affected the day-to-day workings of the courts is impossible to establish, but it is interesting to note that when Margaret Hedley was acquitted of child murder in 1773 it was because 'the pains and agony of her labour were so sudden and great at the time, that she knows not nor does she now recollect whether the child was born alive or dead'.[30] In other words, her own emotional state was being taken into account. By the second half of the eighteenth century the defence that the death of the infant occurred because the mothers were incapacitated by the distress caused by labour was becoming increasingly accepted.

IV

Given these various sea changes, it seems scarcely surprising that a number of attempts were made in the 1770s to repeal the 1624 statute and replace it with new legislation, even if the proposed new bills were lost due to the prorogation of Parliament, and the one that did get as far as the Lords then became mired down in debate. But the picture is not quite as straightforward as it seems. Much of the debate about the 1624 statute – and indeed much of the discussion of other long-standing laws at this time – had more to do with creating greater efficiency than with offering more clemency. The MP Thomas Lockhart, for example, pointed out to the Commons in 1773 that the problem with the law as it stood was that it rarely led to a conviction. He therefore supported a Bill that he thought would act as a greater deterrent to women thinking of killing their illegitimate children and concealing their deaths.

Paradoxically, those who opposed reform often did so because they felt the very anomalies that the current law enshrined offered a flexibility that made justice in individual cases more likely and reform therefore unnecessary. The subsequent outbreak of the American War of Independence in 1776 and war with the French over a decade later in 1789 further lessened the appetite for reform at home.

When repeal did finally come in 1803 it was guided through Parliament by the unlikeliest of reformers: Lord Chief Justice William Law, 1st Baron Ellenborough (1750–1818), and, according to one contemporary 'the worst tempered man living'. A man who rebuked barristers whom he thought were wasting his time, took the pleading of their cases into his own hands, humiliated and browbeat witnesses he thought untruthful, and constantly deployed a sharp and ironic wit in court, he was to boot an arch conservative, champion of the Church of England and the rights of the Crown, enemy of Catholic emancipation, and an outspoken opponent of legal reform. But it was precisely because he was such an arch conservative that he pushed repeal through. As Mark Jackson has convincingly argued, Ellenborough, like his immediate predecessors, was aware that the 1624 statute simply wasn't working. What he wanted to do was replace it with a law that would punish, and ideally deter, infanticidal mothers by being more certain in its operation.[31] The 1803 statute, which justified repealing the 1624 Act and an identical Irish Act passed in 1707 on the grounds that 'they have been in sundry cases difficult and inconvenient to put in practice', enacted that:

> The trials . . . of women charged with the issue of their bodies, male or female, which being born alive would by law be bastard, shall proceed and be governed by such and the like rules of evidence and presumption as are by law used and allowed to take place in respect to other trials for murder, and as if the two several Acts [i.e. of 1624 and 1707] had never been made.

The Act also set out what should be done to those who were acquitted of killing their children, but whose immorality was felt to deserve punishment: they were to be committed to prison or a house of correction for up to two years.[32] Within a couple of years of its passing, two women had been executed for infanticide on the Northern Circuit of the assizes, the first for nearly fifty years.

Yet, harsh in spirit though it might have been, the 1803 Act does symbolise the end of an era. From now on infanticide was increasingly to be viewed within a wider pattern of criminal behaviour, and not as a uniquely unnatural crime carried out by unnatural women. Newborn children, though, continued to be murdered. *The Times* of 15 August 1861 reported that 278 babies had been killed in the capital over the previous five years, their bodies turning up in the Thames, in canals, under railway arches, in doorways, in cellars and the like. For 1895 the London figure was 231. Direct comparisons with previous eras are tricky because criminal statistics from 1803 grouped the killing of newborns within the larger category of all children under the age of twelve months, but even so the official numbers are alarming: of the 5,722 homicides known to have taken place between 1878 and 1892 (of which about two-thirds led to prosecutions) around 20 per cent involved victims aged twelve months or less. By that measure young children were the most vulnerable of all groups in Victorian England.[33] And they were particularly vulnerable because in an era when many children succumbed in any case to poverty or disease in the early months of life, it was not too difficult to kill a child without arousing suspicion.[34] Child mortality among infants aged under one year may have been falling – from around 24 per cent in the 1790s, to 20 per cent in the early nineteenth century, to 15 per cent in the last two-thirds of the nineteenth century – but even that last figure was a high one behind which to hide (by 1930 child mortality had fallen to 6.5 per cent; in 2013 to 0.38 per cent of live births recorded in England and Wales).

There were many ways in which unwanted children might be done away with, but two peculiarly Victorian ones should perhaps be mentioned here. One was 'baby farming', a type of informal adoption (often initiated through newspaper advertisements) by which individuals agreed to take children off their parents' hands and put them out for adoption in return for a cash payment. Sometimes the children did indeed end up with childless couples who genuinely wanted to adopt a child, but as a number of high-profile cases over the second half of the nineteenth century demonstrated, it was not uncommon for baby-farmers to murder their charges or let them die through neglect (see page 457). There is also evidence to suggest that the widespread custom among working-class people of taking out funeral insurance led sometimes to the murder of infants for gain. Quite how common this was is impossible to tell – some middle-class commentators were convinced it was a regular occurrence – but that it did happen is unquestionable. Certainly insurance fraud is what seems to have motivated Robert and Ann Sandys to have poisoned two of their young daughters in the 1840s (Robert was convicted, but the trial jury acquitted Ann because they felt that she'd been acting under her husband's direction; see page 456).

Nineteenth-century attitudes to small children could be somewhat ambivalent. We read Dickens's description of the death of Little Nell in *The Old Curiosity Shop* or that of Jo the crossing sweeper in *Bleak House* and assume it was a sentimental age. But the belief we have today that the life of a newborn baby is sacrosanct was not so absolute then. The poet Arthur Hugh Clough's cynical observation 'Thou shalt not kill, but needst not strive, officiously to keep alive' had contemporary resonances. Even the radical Francis Place, rather earlier in the century, argued that life at all costs was not necessarily a praiseworthy goal. As he put it in his *Principles of Population* of 1822:

Neither do I regard the new-born child with any superstitious reverence. If the alternative were complete I should rather such a child should perish in the first hour of its existence than that it should spend seventy years of life in a state of misery and vice.[35]

Social reformers constantly struggled to improve the lot of children, their efforts culminating in the important Children and Young Persons Act of 1908. But it was an uphill battle.

As in the later Georgian period, attitudes to women who killed their offspring could be surprisingly sympathetic. The last mother to be executed for murdering a child aged under twelve months was Rebecca Smith, a depressive poverty-stricken woman married to a drunkard, who in 1849 confessed to having killed six of her previous children. After that, women convicted of killing their children were routinely sentenced to death, but then just as routinely reprieved and sent to prison. They might have sinned, the thinking ran, but they had suffered, too. As a judge summing up at an infanticide trial at the Warwickshire assizes in 1865 put it:

> Human nature revolts against pronouncing the doom of death against some ruined creature seduced into vice, perhaps by someone far more guilty than herself, and then hurried into crime at the last moment by the bewildering, maddening influences of agony, shame, and terror.[36]

Practical considerations, too, had an impact on verdicts in cases of suspected infanticide. According to the terminology of the time, a murder could only be deemed to have occurred if the child had been 'a reasonable being in the Queen's peace' – that is, had had a complete and separate existence from its mother. In other words, for a conviction to be secured the prosecution had to prove that the child had been killed after it had completed its exit from the womb. This was not easy to do. Besides, many doctors were clearly uneasy about giving a definitive ruling on something that might be instrumental in sending a fallen woman to her death. As for sympathetic juries, they had their own legal loophole. Early nineteenth-century legislation made concealment of a dead child a non-capital offence punishable by imprisonment. To the occasional irritation of judges, juries therefore had at their disposal a much softer option than a verdict of infanticide.[37]

Just how forgiving a court could be is shown by the outcome of a 1904 prosecution at the Central Criminal Court of Louisa Lunn, a twenty-year-old servant who had strangled a newborn baby and hidden its body up a chimney in the house in Wandsworth where she was employed. The jury found her guilty of manslaughter and recommended mercy, and the judge, to spontaneous applause from spectators, gave her a conditional discharge on a £10 recognisance. This was not an isolated case.[38]

But perhaps the most striking aspect of nineteenth-century cases of infanticide is the growing focus not on general issues of morality, nor specific questions of medical proof, but on the mother's mental state. By the end of Victoria's reign a common defence claim was that her actions had been influenced by the onset of puerperal fever and it proved a very effective one.[39] It's not hard to understand why. A diagnosis of puerperal fever provided a neat explanation of how a woman could reject her maternal instincts so utterly as to kill her newborn or infant child: clearly, the fever had rendered her confused, depressed, even homicidal. And this in turn seemed to fit nicely with the stereotype of the Victorian woman: a creature of irrational instincts who was far more likely to be sad or mad than to be calculatedly bad. It was much easier to think of her as guilty of temporary insanity than cold-blooded murder.

The final separation of infanticide from murder came with the passing of the 1922 Infanticide Act, which made infanticide a non-capital offence. For a verdict of infanticide to be returned, the victim had to have been newly born (an idea which was soon stretched), and been killed by the mother when 'she had not fully recovered from the effect of giving birth . . . and by reason thereof the balance of her mind was then disturbed'.[40] In 1624 the legislation that made concealment of a stillbirth a capital offence was couched in terms that emphasised human sinfulness and our natural inclination to immorality. Almost exactly three centuries later the new legislation talked of infanticide in terms of human psychology. There was no mention of sin.

An eighteenth-century engraving of a ducking stool, a common form of punishment whereby the victim was submerged in a river or pond. It was a common punishment for 'scolds' – women who caused a public nuisance – because the cold water was thought to cool their angry temperaments. Before the Industrial Revolution, slander and 'scolding' were considered almost as harmful as physical violence.

CHAPTER 7

VERBAL VIOLENCE:
SCOLDING, SLANDER AND LIBEL

I

In 1674 there appeared the first edition of a book that was to prove hugely popular over the next few decades: *The Government of the Tongue*. It was probably written by Richard Allestree, Regius Professor of Divinity at Oxford University and Provost of Eton College, who was also probably the author of *The Whole Duty of Man*, a book first published in 1658 during the Commonwealth period when its high Anglican tone was not appreciated, but that then went through over a hundred editions between 1663 and 1800. *The Whole Duty of Man* is a guide to correct Christian conduct. *The Government of the Tongue* addresses a narrower topic: the use and abuse of speech. Its scope is nevertheless ambitious. It's perhaps not surprising to find a chapter on 'atheistical discource' in a book written by a professor of divinity, but the author also addresses a whole, finely sub-divided range of other vices.

He talks about 'detraction': 'as it is applied to the reputation, it implies the impairing or lessening of a man in point of fame, rendering him less valued and esteemed by others'. He examines those opposite poles of gossip, 'lying defamation' and 'uncharitable truth'. He discusses 'scoffing and derision' and its corollary flattery ('a collective and cumulative baseness, it being in its elements a compound and a complex of the most sordid, hateful qualities incident to mankind'). Boasting, querulousness ('murmuring and complaining'), 'positiveness' ('being over confidant and peremptory') and 'obscene talk' (a short, two-page section) are similarly put under the microscope. And even then the author does not feel that he has covered everything there is to say on the subject, declaring in the Preface that 'should I have enlarged to the utmost compass of this theme, I should have made the volume of so affrighting a bulk, that few would have attempted it'.

What unites all these failings, in the author's view, is that they threaten the peace and stability of society. Attacking a person's reputation, for example, is

> . . . one of the grand incendiaries which disturbs the peace of the world, and has a great share of most of its quarrels. For could we examine all the feuds which harass persons, families, nay sometimes nations too, we should find the greater part from injurious, reproachful words, and that for one which is commenced upon the intuition of a real considerable interest [i.e. founded upon reality], there are many which owe their being to the licentiousness of the tongue.

As for scoffing and derision:

> . . . the world wants [lacks] not experiments [i.e. examples] of the mischiefs which have happened by too severe railleries; such fencing jest has proved earnest, and florets have oft turned to swords, and not only the friendship, but the men have fallen a sacrifice to a jest.

It is not surprising, the author concludes, that scripture reminds us that 'Death and life are in the power of the tongue' (*Proverbs*, 18:21).[1] All verbal abuses should therefore be shunned, or as the author of another tract on the need to govern the tongue, the eminent Elizabethan theologian William Perkins, puts it, people should 'avoyde all imprecations and cursings either against men or other creatures'.[2]

At one level there's nothing much here that would come as a surprise to readers today: most of us would agree with the fundamental point that bad words can be the prelude to bad acts. But the very fact that an entire – and influential – book could be written on the subject suggests that there was rather more to it than that to the seventeenth-century way of thinking. It's no coincidence that the proverb 'Sticks and stones may break my bones, but words will never harm me' is a very late one (the first reference to it comes in 1894). For people living in Tudor, Stuart or Georgian England, such a notion would have been entirely alien. Verbal abuse to people from Elizabethan to Georgian times was not merely unpleasant but positively dangerous. According to the late-seventeenth-century naturalist and antiquary Robert Plot it could even be fatal – in one incident, he records, two women actually appear to have scolded each other to death.[3] Speech at that time had an inherent power to damage and destroy far beyond what we would recognise today.

In particular, speech could destroy reputation, and as anyone familiar with *Othello* will know, reputation was everything: 'Reputation, reputation, reputation,' Michael Cassio says to Iago, 'O! I have lost my reputation. I have lost the immortal part of myself, and what remains is bestial.'[4] One's 'good name and fame' and credit were vital, whether in everyday conduct or the successful pursuit of a legal dispute. To be regarded as a person of 'no credit' meant that you were morally tarnished and had no standing in the community: people described as being of 'no credit' by witnesses in court cases were drunkards or thieves; they were sexually immoral or unreliable in their business transactions. Slanderous words could therefore have a devastating effect, and the definition of slander was accordingly a broad one, as the barrister John March explained in a treatise on the subject published in 1647:

> . . . all scandalous words which touch or concerne a man in his life, liberty or member, or any corporall punishment; or which scandal a man in his office or place of trust, or in his

calling or function by which he gains his living, or which tend to the slandering of his title or his disinheritance; or to the loss of his advancement or preferment, or any other particular damage; or lastly which charge a man to have any dangerous infectious disease.[5]

March was a common lawyer writing about issues that affected men. Slander cases heard in ecclesiastical courts introduce us to a rich seam of court records dealing with defamation of (and indeed by) women. And here the focus is almost invariably on sexual reputation. Case after case shows women (and occasionally men) calling other women whores or impugning their sexual probity (their husbands, of course, also had a stake in such matters – a man's reputation would suffer if it was suggested that he could not keep his wife faithful). Thus in 1696 Elizabeth Baxter, a country girl from Long Cliffe in Yorkshire, dismayed by gossip circulating about a supposedly pregnant unmarried woman, told the gossipers 'that they might as well take her life as her good name from her'.[6] Just before Christmas 1586 a service in a London church was disrupted when Ann Symes declared before the congregation that the minister, Mr Lisbye, had 'most shamefully committed carnal copulation with me and hast occupied me divers and sundry times', going on to explain precisely where these couplings had taken place. A very uncomfortable Lisbye 'before the whole assembly denied it and wishe[d] the ground might open under him if the accusation of Ann Symes were true'.[7]

Even more potentially damaging than slander was the curse, for while slander could destroy reputation, the curse could destroy life itself. In the Isle of Man, for example, where belief in the power of a curse seems to have held sway for longer and more strongly than in most parts of England, it lay at the heart of a number of cases heard by the island's ecclesiastical courts throughout the seventeenth and eighteenth centuries, and the fear it aroused was still being noted by folklorists in the nineteenth century. In 1695 a Manx man landed himself in trouble for wishing God's curse on two other individuals, and also 'for cursing in common, and saying God's curse upon them that took the top off his ling [peat] stack, and that they may both lose their hands and their feet, and the devil put out their eyes that did the same'.

A generation earlier a woman named Catherine Cottier alias Kneall is recorded as having cursed John Casement, wishing that 'he might have neither son or daughter about his fire or hearth to the third or fourth generation and that his house might be ruinated'.

Folklorists in the latter years of the nineteenth century noted a ritual of seven bitter curses, of which the most potent was that of the *Skeab Lome*, a Manx term which translates literally as 'the naked besom or broom', but which is more often rendered in this context as 'the besom of destruction'. This was a curse of annihilation, accompanied by an elaborate ritual. The curser, normally a woman, would face the door of the house of the object of her hatred, and with her hair uncovered would make a motion of sweeping with a besom, while uttering powerful maledictions. The intention was to harm or even kill through the power of the spoken word. And the threat was taken seriously. In Catherine Cottier's case, for example, the Church court ordered her to perform public penance in five of the Isle of Man's churches, to be whipped, to be fined six-pence, and to be put in the stocks at Ramsey for an hour.[8] The severity of her punishment matched the severity of her perceived crime.

The notion that a curse can harm has a history that stretches far back in time. In the middle ages its power was frequently invoked by the Church. Papal letters sometimes contained anathemas that cursed any who might have the temerity to disregard their contents. Even routine parish matters might lead to an ecclesiastical curse. When Thomas Perne, a fifteenth-century Cambridgeshire man, dis-covered that he had been robbed, he reported the matter to his vicar who made a public declaration in church that he would curse the thieves if the goods were not restored to their rightful owner. In Catholic countries the practice persisted into the seventeenth century. In 1628 the Bishop of Barcelona, infuriated by the theft of church plate and silver, put God's curse on the surrounding countryside – so successfully, apparently, that the crops were miraculously ruined. And even in Protestant countries the memory of the ecclesiastical curse lasted long after the Reformation. One Manx Church court record describes how in 1695 William Lacey of Andreas parish, seeing widow Jony Cowle out in the fields early on May Day morning and concluding that she was practising witchcraft, expressed the wish that she might be given 'the curse of the church which had been our old obsolete custom in this island in cases of yt [i.e. that] nature'.[9]

Strictly speaking, there was no place for such a belief in Protestant theology: for any human or human institution to invoke God's curse was, to the post-Reformation way of thinking, a blasphemous usurpation of the Almighty's powers. Thus the old practice of performing quarterly excommunications of thieves, murderers and enemies of the Church by the ritual of bell, book and candle (a ritual that deployed the full panoply of ecclesiastical weapons) was discontinued, and theologians and preachers urged their audiences not to pray for the downfall of those with whom they were in enmity. The Church of England did retain the Service of Commintation, by which the minister would read out to the congregation declarations of God's curse against a variety of sinners, but this was felt to be an act of petition, not one of usurpation of divine power. The shift in attitude is nicely demonstrated by the conversation that the Protestant martyr Julius Palmer, a former Fellow of Magdalen College, Oxford, had with his mother when, realising that the authorities were closing in on him, he visited her to collect some legacies due to him, and knelt to ask her blessing. She invoked Christ's curse on him as a heretic. He calmly pointed out to her that she had no power to control divine judgement. He was burned at Newbury in 1556 during the reign of Mary Tudor.[10]

But if Protestant doctrine banished the curse, it still retained a toehold in popular belief, and while it may have been most marked in places like the Isle of Man, references to it can nevertheless be found scattered among English records. Two early-seventeenth-century cases that were heard in the Archbishop of York's consistory court illustrate the point. In one John Wood of Wetherby complained that the widow Helen Hiley had come to him 'and kneeled upon her knees and said a vengeance of God light upon thee Wood . . . and all thy children, and I shall truly pray this praier for the[e] so long as I live'. In the other John Metcalfe of Leeds reported that Anne Dixon

> . . . did sit her downe upon her knees and cursed and banned him, and his wife, and bad a vengeance light upon the wife of the said John Metcalfe and upon that whoremaster and whoremonger harlot her husbande . . . and prayed God that they might never thrive.

The practice of the curser going down on their knees as though they were praying seems to have been widespread. A case from Chester in 1593 describes how Mary Weston was seen to 'fall down upon her knees, openly on the row, many being lookers on' before she cursed a man 'in railing & cursing manner in anger'. Five years later, according to ecclesiastical court records for the see of Hereford, a man called John Smyth, who had fallen out with one William Walton of Yarpole, was seen 'kneeling on his knees in the churchyard there, and praying unto God a heavy vengeance and a heavy plague might light upon him and all his cattle'.[11]

Whatever Protestant theologians might have said, there were many who argued that if the curser had indeed suffered a real wrong, divine providence might rightly bring misfortune to the person being cursed (of course, following the same logic, an unjustified curse might bring misfortune to its utterer). By the same token, a number of contemporaries suggested that the curses of the poor might be justified – the only weapon available to the weak and disadvantaged in a profoundly unequal society. There certainly seems to have been a view that curses could be effective. At best the person cursed must have felt psychologically profoundly uncomfortable; at worst they might suffer some misfortune that they attributed to the words spoken to or about them. William Perkins in his tract on the governance of the tongue concluded: 'in our contrey men often wish the plague, the poxe, the pestilence to their children, their servants, their cattle: and often it falls out accordingly'.[12]

II

The belief in a link between cursing and retribution was even more marked when it was not God being invoked but the power of evil. Throughout the late sixteenth century and the first decades of the seventeenth, people were convinced that witches could cause real harm to their victims by cursing them. William Perkins's *Discourse of the Damned Art of Witchcraft* (published in 1608 after his death) argued that 'witches are wont to practice their mischievous fact by cursing and banning' and that one sure way to detect witchcraft was 'if after cursing there followeth death, or at least some mischief'. Perkins's near contemporary the writer Thomas Cooper described a witch in the act of cursing, 'invocating, upon her bare knees (for so the manner is) the vengeance of God upon them. And if she can conveniently to their faces, breathing out these fearfull curses and direfull execrations against them'. It was, he said, 'an apish and blasphemous imitation of divine justice'.[13]

Witches might have had a whole armoury of evil weapons to draw on, not least creating and then damaging or destroying a model of their victim, but harsh words were among the most potent. The archives of the Archdeacon of Essex record a typical case from 1564 of an argument leading to a curse leading to an accusation of witchcraft. Elizabeth Lowys, wife of John Lowys of Great Waltham, had apparently been employed by Elizabeth Gale to spin wool for her, but the two women 'fell at variations for taking in of work' and Lowys had decided not to work for Gale any more. Trouble ensued when the two women next met:

Thereupon at their next meeting they fell out. And this deponent [i.e. Gale] told her that she lied and had told a wrong tale. And, among other talk, this deponent saith that she said, 'If it be as folk say, thou art a witch'. To whom the said Lowys wife answered, 'If I be a witch then the devil thee twitch'. And immediately upon that this deponent fell on a great quivering and quakering. And this was done about Saturday about five years past. And so after that [she] went home, continuing so until Wednesday, at which day she fell down . . . and was sick fourteen days that nobody thought she would have lived. And after then her neighbours sent for priests, to whom she uttered all. And then she sent for the said Lowys' wife, threatening her that if this deponent died she would be burned, and after her coming this deponent mended.[14]

Even slightly ambivalent or kind words could be suspect if they came from a supposed witch. In the pamphlet describing another Essex case, this time involving a local witch panic of 1582 centred on St Osyth's parish, William Bonner described the circumstances under which his wife was bewitched by Elizabeth Bennett:

The said Elizabeth Bennett and his wife were lovers [i.e. close friends] and familiar friends, and did accompany much together: and said that since Candlemas last his wife hath complained of a lameness in her knee, and that since also she hath been much troubled. And saith also that not ten days past the said Elizabeth Bennett being with his wife, she being sickly and sore troubled, the said Elizabeth used speeches to her, saying 'ah good woman how art thou laden', & then clasped her in her arms, and kissed her: whereupon presently after her upper lip swelled & was very big, and her eyes much sunked [sic] into her head, and she hath lain since in a very strange case.[15]

There's no suggestion here that Elizabeth Bennett uttered anything in the way of a formal curse, yet during the period of the witch hunts any words, however innocently intended, could be recalled and then endlessly picked over later, particularly if there had been a subsequent falling out. For the wretched Alice Samuel, caught up in the landmark Witches of Warboys case, just two words were sufficient. During a visit to the household of the Throckmortons, a local gentry family, Lady Cromwell, Oliver Cromwell's step-grandmother, cut off a lock of Alice Samuel's hair and threw it, together with her hair-cover, in the fire, presumably as a counter-magic measure. Alice Samuel, 'perceiving her selfe thus dealt with', asked Lady Cromwell, 'Madam, why do you use me thus? I never did you any harm as yet.' When Lady Cromwell later fell ill and died, those words 'as yet' were to be recalled, and led to the execution of the elder Samuels and their daughter.[16] Formal prosecution of witches slackened in England in the later seventeenth century, but among the population at large fear of the witch and her words was to persist well into Victorian times.

III

Cursing was the most extreme – and for the victim the most frightening – form of verbal attack. And because of its connection with witchcraft, it had a particular association with women (who made up perhaps 90 per cent of those accused of witchcraft in England in the sixteenth and seventeenth centuries). But the same is also largely true of some other forms of verbal attack. As a general rule, if contemporaries viewed physical violence as a predominantly male trait, they also regarded verbal violence as something of a female preserve. Indeed for many it seemed a truism, hence endless ballads satirising marriage that bore titles such as 'The Patient Husband and the Scoulding Wife'; 'The Scoulding Wife'; 'The New German Doctor: or, an Infallible Cure for a Scolding Wife'. Behind many of these there was a humorous point – or at least a love of perpetuating the stereotype of the nagging woman. But for contemporaries there was also a more serious consideration.

A harmonious household, peace between neighbours and an ordered community were all felt to be essential elements of a godly Commonwealth. Those who threatened any aspects of this – scolding wives included – undermined peace and good order. As the 'Homily against Strife and Contention' (which many post-Reformation Englishmen and women would have heard preached) put it, Christian folk should 'with all submission and meekness, with lenity and softness of mind, bearing one another by charity' work 'to keep the unity of spirit by the bond of peace' and pay careful regard to what they said:

> He that hath an evil tongue, troubleth all the town where he dwelleth, and sometime the whole country. And a railing tongue is a pestilence so full of contagiousness, that Saint Paul willeth Christian men to forbear the company of such ... he forbiddeth us to eat or drink with a scolder, or quarrel picker.[17]

In 1486 verbal abuse was even the subject of a lengthy order issued by the borough authorities at Hereford:

> It was decided concerning scolds that such mischief arose in the city through such persons, to wit, quarrelling, blows, defamation, disturbances of night's rest, and strife between neighbours often thence arising, as well as resistance to bailiffs, officers, and others, who were abused in their very presence, and often also the raising of hues and cries in breach of the king's peace, and to the disturbance of the city's quiet; wherefore, whenever scolds shall be taken and convicted, they shall have the judgment of the cucking stool ... And if they will not submit to be punished by such judgement, they shall be cast out of the city, and this by the king's bailiff and the city posse, if need be, on account of the divers ills and dangers which often may arise through such persons and their abettors; and if abettors there be, they shall be treated as perjurers and disturbers of the city's peace and quiet.

The *Homily* makes extensive use of the word 'he', which in this context includes, of course, both men and women. The Hereford order, on the other hand, which was written in Latin, uses the feminine form of the Latin for 'scolds' (*objurgatricibus*).[18] And by the late sixteenth century, the word 'scold' itself had shifted from being a term sometimes applied to a man, to one largely applied to a woman – a person who disturbed the peace of her neighbours, perhaps in consort with others, through verbal abuse, or one who deliberately spread malicious or false gossip (also frequently referred to as 'back-biting'), or – usually in the form 'scolding wife' – one who severely criticised her husband.[19] A tract written in 1650 by the otherwise obscure Moses à Vauts illustrates this latter usage. The author (who disparaged wife-beating but upheld a traditional view of husbandly authority) describes how women sometimes use 'fiery, piercing and poisonous' words of reproach against their husbands, and comments that it is 'unseemly and sordid for a man to vie words, or scold it out with a woman, referring the victory to the last and loudest syllable'. He continues:

Customary scolding and clamour (which we account but the lowest classis [category] and form of corrigible offences) is no argument of weakness, but of a stubborn and sinful strength; and by how much it resisteth admonition, it is so much the more rebellious and abominable. Shall any dare think that the holy spirit intended a woman to be tongue free? To rail, rail, rage, swear, blaspheme and defy heaven and her husband.[20]

So seriously was scolding regarded that it actually constituted a criminal offence, and accounts survive (admittedly, not a huge number) of scolding women being prosecuted in ecclesiastical, borough and local manorial courts. Records from the manor of Acomb (a settlement just outside York), for example, note fines levied on George Gill and two other men in 1582 because their wives scolded with their neighbours (clearly, husbands were expected to exercise control over their spouses): Margaret Gill being prosecuted in 1584 for scolding with Mrs Newarke, a member of one of the higher-status families in the village; the wife of Thomas Laburn being accused in 1619 of being a common scold; and Anne Akers being prosecuted in 1624 for scolding with her neighbours in the street.

The villager in Acomb appointed to impound stray animals – the pinder – came under fire from hostile women on a number of occasions, first in 1622 when he was scolded and cursed by a group of six, and then again several times in 1620. In the same year he was assaulted by John Jackson, while Jackson's wife Mabel scolded with another manorial official, the fence-viewer (that is, the official responsible for ensuring that fences were correctly located and properly maintained). The Jacksons were clearly trouble, since the following year John Jackson, by that time the manor's ale taster, is mentioned as having been involved in a number of assaults. Not all scolds referred to in the Acomb records were women: in 1584 two jurors, Robert Spacye and George Gill, were presented (that is, formerly prosecuted in an ecclesiastical or manorial court) 'for scolding in court'. But most scolds were female. As a rule, those named in the presentments were fined a shilling. However, Thomas Laburn's wife, regarded as a 'common scold' and hence a more persistent disrupter of her neighbours, was fined 20d.[21]

The fact that by the later sixteenth and seventeenth centuries the vast majority of those accused were women has led some to suggest that the Elizabethan and Stuart periods witnessed some kind of crisis in relations between the sexes, part of a broader crisis in law and order that marked the period. A male witness who commented in a 1622 Wiltshire case brought against an alleged scold that she 'will talk when she is angry as other women do and no otherwise' clearly reflected a contemporary view that scolding was an integral part of the female psyche.[22] His view seems to be at one with the flurry of misogynistic publications that appeared in Jacobean times (Joseph Swetnam's *Arraignment of Lewd, Idle, Froward and Unconstant Women* went through ten editions between 1615 and 1637). Yet overall the claim is a hard one to substantiate – after all, women were regularly being presented as scolds as far back as the late fourteenth century; it wasn't a peculiarly Elizabethan or Jacobean phenomenon. Nor is another suggestion that is sometimes made – that scolds were victims of patriarchal oppression – particularly convincing. Many scolds were prosecuted for what they said not to men but to other women. It would therefore be simplistic to claim that they were simply victims of male tyranny. Certainly, where details of their lives are known, some of the accused women seem worthy of our sympathy. Mary Stracke of Hempnall in Norfolk, for example, who was prosecuted in 1597 for being a common drunkard and a sower of discord among her neighbours and a source of community disruption in general ('a breaker of the Christian charity'), claimed plaintively that 'she have [sic] three children and is very poor, and when she spoke for her relief [i.e. asked for alms] they say she scoldeth'.[23] But among their number were some who appear simply to have been disruptive and aggressive.

One such figures prominently in the fourteenth-century records of the borough of Macclesfield in Cheshire. Her name was Amice Fletcher, the wife of the butcher and town burgess John Oldefield, and therefore a woman of some substance by the standards of her time. Her problems with authority began early on, for in 1355, while she was still a young woman, she was presented for illegally leaving her employment as a maidservant. Over the next few years she launched a number of civil actions at the town court, but as an alewife, or pub landlady, also found herself constantly at odds with the local authorities. She was continually accused of breaking the assize of ale (the contemporary equivalent of the licensing laws), and was prosecuted for receiving stolen goods and for theft, notably of turf and furzes essential for fuel. In 1372 she had her goods distrained for sheltering her maidservant after she had committed a felony. She was also prosecuted for over a dozen assaults, her victims including both men and women, and on several occasions she was presented as a common scold. Another disruptive woman in Macclesfield at the same time was Marion Pevere, who between 1351 and 1378 was presented five times for quarrelling, eight times for affray, five times for breaking the assize of ale (she was a brewer), and three times for theft, as well as being involved four times in debt litigation. Both women clearly lived up to William Sheppard's legal definition of a scold as 'a troublesome and angry woman'.[24]

As the evidence from Acomb suggests (and it is borne out by evidence from other jurisdictions), the commonest way to punish scolds was to fine them. But scolding is also associated with two rather more esoteric forms of punishment: the ducking stool (more often referred to as the 'cucking stool' in contemporary documents) and the scold's bridle, or branks – officially sanctioned corporal punishments in retaliation for the verbal violence of the scold. The first of these was, typically, a chair attached to a long pole set over a fulcrum that allowed the victim to be dipped (or 'ducked') into a stream or river – a punishment designed to shame the scold and curb her angry temperament. (Other offenders, notably prostitutes or other sexually incontinent women, might also find themselves in the ducking stool; the popular belief that witches were ducked, though, is a fiction.)

That the ducking stool was actually used in this way is indisputable – we know, for example, that the townships of Gillingham in Dorset and Henley-in-Arden in Warwickshire routinely immersed scolds in the 1620s and 1630s, as did the authorities at Nottingham.[25] But as the antiquarian J. W. Spargo pointed out in 1944 in his charmingly entitled book *Juridical Folklore in England, Illustrated by the Cucking Stool*, when it is mentioned in manorial records, it tends to be because it has actually been out of use for some time and needs to be repaired. A case from Nettleton in Wiltshire illustrates his point nicely. In 1612 two women were presented at the local manorial court for scolding. Following what was probably a not uncommon practice, the parish minister was asked to intervene, talk to the women and induce them to mend their ways. He did so. Two years later, however, the two women were again presented as scolds, and so this time it was decided that they should be punished by the ducking stool. There was a problem, though: the village did not actually possess one. Something suitable therefore had to be hastily improvised, but it soon fell into a state of disrepair.[26] The combination of expense and sporadic usage meant that although ducking stools figure large in popular history they were only really in operation in the comparatively few decades between 1560 and 1640.

The branks or scold's bridle has achieved a similarly mythic status, not least because for many it symbolises the perceived brutality of past ages. It was a metal cage fitted over the head, and usually contained a prong that was placed in the mouth to stop the victim speaking.[27] Today we regard such an implement as nothing less than barbarous. The late-seventeenth-century antiquary Robert Plot, however, reached a different conclusion when he examined a scold's bridle that he had found at Newcastle-under-Lyme:

> I look upon it as much to be preferred to the cucking stool, which not only endangers the health of the party, but also gives the tongue liberty 'twixt every dip, to neither of which is this at all liable: it being such a bridle for the tongue, as not only quite deprives them of speech, but brings shame for the transgression, and humility thereupon, before 'tis taken off ... nor is it taken off, till after the party begins to show all external signs imaginable of humiliation and amendment.[28]

Plot possibly had a point about the threat to health offered by the ducking stool – particularly if it was employed, as it sometimes certainly was, in the depths of winter. On the other hand, we know that scolds were sometimes put in the ducking stool without being ducked, in other words that they were shamed rather than physically punished. The 1486 order from Hereford I mentioned earlier, having stated that scolds should be placed in the cucking-stool, goes on to dictate 'there they shall stand with bare feet and their hair down, during such time as they may be seen by all passers-by on the road'. There was no suggestion here of physical punishment. Even so, it's hard to agree with Plot that the bridle was the humane option.

In mid-Victorian times T. N. Brushfield, medical superintendent of the Cheshire Lunatic Asylum, delivered a lecture on 'Obsolete Punishments' to the Chester Archaeological and Historic Society, in which he mentioned that he had either collected or come across some fifteen scold's bridles in Cheshire: from Macclesfield, Congleton, Carrington, Knutsford, and Acton (near Nantwich), Stockport and Chester (where he found four). How genuine these all were is a moot point, and Brushfield himself (along with later researchers) said that he had come across few references to a bridle actually being used (Robert Plot described the one he found in Newcastle-under-Lyme as 'an instrument scarce heard of, much less seen'.) There is no doubt, however, that it was fairly widely known in the north of England and in Scotland, where it seems to have been more commonly used (it may actually have started out as a Scottish form of punishment). In a critique of local government in Newcastle upon Tyne in 1655, Ralph Gardiner mentions the use of the branks (in a way that clearly suggests he disapproved of it), describing it as 'a crown, it being of iron, which was musled [muzzled] over the head and face, with a great gap of iron forced into the mouth, which forced the blood out'. This, he said, 'is the punishment which the magistrates do inflict on chiding, and scolding women'.[29]

Remarkably, we do actually have a victim's account of the use of the branks. Dorothy Waugh was a Quaker who in the autumn of 1655 took it upon herself to go to the marketplace in Carlisle to 'speak against all deceit and ungodly practices'. The authorities were less than impressed, and had Dorothy pulled from her pitch by the market cross and thrown into prison. When subsequently questioned by the mayor, she gave a series of disrespectful answers. In exasperation he called for the bridle. Dorothy Waugh's hat was then torn off, and the bridle 'as they called it' was put on her:

Which was a stone weight of iron by the relation of their own generation, & three bars of iron to come over my face, and a piece of it was put in my mouth, which was so unreasonable a big thing for that place as cannot be well related, which was locked to my head . . . and the bit in my mouth to keep me from speaking. And the mayor said he would make me an example to all that should ever come in that name [probably meaning Quakers]. And the people to see me so violently abused were broken into tears, but he cried out on them and said, for foolish pity, one might spoil a whole city. And the man that kept the prison door demanded two-pence of every one that came to see me while their bridle remained upon me.

Waugh was given a brief respite after three hours, but the bridle was then placed on her again and she was whipped out of Carlisle while wearing it. The mayor, she noted, had still not done with her: as she left the town, he insulted her with 'very vile and unsavoury words, which were not fit to proceed out of any man's mouth'.[30]

IV

If scolding was regarded as a predominantly female failing, slander observed no such gender barrier, even if, inevitably, there was a certain overlap between the two offences. But in terms of the law, scolding and slander were dealt with rather differently. Those accused of scolding usually went before church or manorial courts. Those accused of slander (or defamation) might be tried either in ecclesiastical or secular courts, the rough distinction (not invariably observed) being that where the misconduct alleged in a case of defamation would itself normally be heard before a Church court, then the defamation suit should be, too, while defamation that involved alleged misconduct that might lead to prosecution at a secular court should be tried by a secular court. Thus, for example, cases of slander involving allegations of sexual immorality generally ended up being heard in ecclesiastical courts, while slander involving an allegation of, say, theft would be felt to be a matter for the secular court.

In practice, of course, things were rather more complicated. If, for example, it was felt that a particular slander was so severe that it might lead to a breach of the peace, the person responsible for it might well be indicted in a secular court, regardless of the nature of their allegation. There they might be fined and forced to pay damages. If, on the other hand, they ended up in a Church court they might simply have to apologise. Church courts began to decline in importance in the course of the later seventeenth century, but they continued to hear defamation cases up to the end of that century and into the eighteenth. Most of them concerned women – usually married women – whose sexual reputation had become either the subject for local gossip or direct verbal attack (which, of course, in some circumstances might have been judged to be scolding).

A few cases from Tudor and Stuart Yorkshire Church courts give a flavour of the sort of insults involved. In one, a woman allegedly called a neighbour:

> Tinker whore, tinker's bitch, whore, quean [prostitute], drab [prostitute] and scold, drunkard, drunken whore, drunken quean, drunken harlot, drunken drab, and drunken scold, and said she was naughty [a word bearing much weightier connotations than it does at present] an evil and bad and a lewd woman.

In another case, Anne, wife of Thomas Griffith of Rowth, claimed that the local rector had called her a 'scurvy scabbed lousy filthy quean', and told her 'to put on her husband's breeches for he said she had worne them long enough'. A witness in a different case described how they overheard a man calling a woman 'a whore, a common whore, and an ugly whore and that she had a child two months or six weeks before her time and that he would prove her a whore with divers other such like most scandalous & defamatory words'. A similarly direct attack was alleged against another Ann, wife of John Milner, accused of defaming Isobel Clough in 1691. According to Clough's daughter, Milner came up to her in the street at Aberford '& pulled up her coats [i.e. skirts] and bid this examinate look and see that she hath not a burned arse, as that burn'd arse whore her mother had'. ('Burned' was a common euphemism for someone infected with gonorrhoea; and just in case that wasn't clear enough to Isobel Clough's daughter, Ann Milner was said to have added that her mother 'had got a clap and that one Christopher Burrell gave it her'.)

Verbal attacks on men tended to take a rather different form. A dispute over customs dues in a Hull church court case led to Martin Jeffraies calling Robert Williamson, a customs employee, 'lying fellow & drunken fellow & drunkard'; he added 'that if the farmers of his majesty's customs at Hull kept such drunken fellows as he the said Robert Williamson was, men should never be at quietness'. In another Hull case, an alderman called John Lister was described by Robert Walton as 'usurer, rank usurer'; 'the said John Lister', he claimed, 'had committed the crime of usury, and that above the rate of ten pounds for the hundred of one year [i.e. a 10 per cent interest rate]'. Clergymen, too, were frequently on the receiving end of abuse. In 1610 Leonard Marshall of Tadcaster allegedly called a minister named Henry Green 'a foolish drunkard and a foolish drunken lad', as well as 'a knave and a scurvy lying Knave'. In another case, this time not involving a clergyman, one man called another: 'rascal, drunken rascal, villain and scurvy scab & scurvy scabbed villain'. In some circumstances, such angry words might, of course, lead to actual violence, but for some victims launching an action for defamation was clearly preferable to launching a physical attack.

Although insults pepper legal records and other accounts, there is little evidence, outside the realms of literature, for 'flyting', a form of ritualised verbal duel in which (typically) two men attempted to use their wit to out-insult each other. Such duels were common in Norse and Anglo-Saxon literature (the term is of Norse origin), while in early-sixteenth-century Scotland the poets William Dunbar and Walter Kennedy famously competed in a flyting contest at the royal court, organised for the entertainment of James IV. The Shakespearian scholar Margaret Galway, who describes flyting as 'the oldest of all laughter-provoking devices in native English drama', identifies thirteen major flytings and seventeen minor ones in Shakespeare's comedies, arguing that the real turning point in Shakespeare's use of this device came with *The Taming of the Shrew* and its vituperative dialogue between Petruchio and various other characters. Lovers of Shakespeare might also call to mind the 'merry war' between Beatrice and Benedick in *Much Ado About Nothing*, a sustained verbal duel between two characters who, as gentleman and gentlewoman, almost by definition could not engage in physical violence. For Shakespeare, Galway argues, flyting was useful because it was both a familiar and popular comic device, and because it was also compatible with comic satire. Legal and other documents leave the distinct impression that although sophisticated verbal combat of the Beatrice and Benedick variety was rare in England's villages and small towns, wit and the ability to deliver, or contest, a verbal put-down, were valued skills.[31]

From the court's point of view, what was at stake here was not merely personal but communal. One often gets the impression in these slander cases that, just as women accused of scolding were felt to threaten the general well-being of all those around them, so those accused of defamation (who were often men) were felt to endanger the stability of a whole community. In one defamation case from the 1590s, for example, the Minister of Beverley, Brian Bywater, told one William Ramsden that he was 'a sower of discord and dissension amongst thy neighbourhood and hast left thy wife . . . there was nev[er] quietness in this town so long as thou tarriest here'; 'thou art a sower of dissension amongst thy neighbours', a witness recalled him saying, 'and suffrest thy wife and children to go begging'.[32] Given the number of times the same names crop up again and again in court records, it's not difficult to understand why in a small community a single individual could be felt to be capable of wreaking real havoc.

Roger Cowper, a churchwarden at Goldhanger in Essex in the 1590s, was clearly one such persistent nuisance. In 1591 he was accused of slandering Mr Knight, the parish's minister, slandering the parish sexton, slandering William Godfrey's wife, brawling with and railing at various of his neighbours, being a drunkard, disrupting sermons, and frequently swearing by the name of God. David Tarver of Great Oakley in Essex was brought before the courts in 1601 for 'being a most troublesome, disquiet and slanderous fellow among his honest neighbours, for calling the wife of James Bean witch, and for brawling with Philippa the wife of Robert Palmer'.[33]

If both men and women were capable of slander, it was men who were most likely to be accused of libel. Throughout the early modern period, of course, most people were illiterate, and possibly for this reason the modern distinction that slander is defamation that is spoken and libel is defamation that is written was a long way from being established. But written libels, often in verse (which meant they could be spread more widely through being sung or recited), were far from unknown and, like verbal defamation, could injure an individual's reputation or disrupt the community in which they were published. A particularly colourful example comes from Evesham in Worcestershire. Here at the Swan Inn in December 1605, a group of men sat drinking and discussing rumours that George Hawkins, a local squire and official, had fathered a bastard child. Convinced that he had, they decided to reward his 'lewdness' by composing a ballad about him, complete with illustrations. Unfortunately all of them were illiterate, but they managed to persuade Lancelot Ratsey, a tradesman from Coventry who was staying at the inn, to write out some verse at their dictation. It was, it has to be said, pretty dismal stuff. Part of it ran:

> I can no more
> This is the whore
> Of cowardly George Hawkins.
> He got with child,
> In a place most wild . . .
> It was in a privy,
> A place most filthy.

As the ballad grinds to a close it wishes 'an everlasting scorn' on the child's behalf to 'the whore thy mother/And the knave thy father'. A number of copies were made, so that as well as being sung 'in divers and sundry open and public places' the ballad cropped up on various walls, doors and posts around Evesham and was sent to other alehouses in the area. Hawkins obviously took all this very seriously. He decided to prosecute his tormentors in the Star Chamber at Westminster (Star Chamber was, as previously mentioned, effectively the Privy Council sitting as a court; it was a tribunal that had a wide and flexible jurisdiction over non-felonious offences and was much used by gentlemen like Hawkins as an arena for settling disputes).

The records of Star Chamber contain a scattering of other similar prosecutions, sometimes involving one unhappy individual such as George Hawkins, and sometimes involving the inhabitants of a whole town or village that had been satirised. Sexual immorality was a consistent if not universal theme. Often, as in the George Hawkins case, copies of a libel would be made and posted in various public locations – in one instance a libel was attached to a coffin at a funeral; in another, a libel written by labourers in Southwark in 1613 and fixed to the porch of the house of the person it was directed at attracted a 'great company' which 'resorted thither for the hearing and reading thereof'. Many might appear ridiculous to us today, but the fact that someone like George Hawkins could bring a prosecution over what to us seems nothing more than a derisory lampoon serves to show just how seriously people took issues of social standing and reputation right across all levels of English society.[34]

V

One other form of public taunting – which I have already touched on in Chapter 5 – should also be mentioned here: the charivari or 'riding' or (especially in the West Country) 'skimmington'. Whereas scolding or slander was handled by the courts, the whole point of the charivari was that it was community justice. From its inception in the sixteenth century up until the eighteenth it tended to be directed at a wife who beat her husband, or who was generally insubordinate, or who had cuckolded her husband (the categories were, of course, not mutually exclusive). From about the mid eighteenth century, as mentioned earlier, the focus shifted to husbands who beat their wives. The custom started to fade in the nineteenth century, but one tradition associated with it – the use of raucous noise or 'rough music' – attached itself to the staging of industrial disputes. Those involved were usually men, although women sometimes participated or provided encouragement or refreshments, and while local officials or people from higher social groups were sometimes implicated, charivaris tended to be the preserve of the poorer – often less reputable – part of the community. Typically, a large crowd would form, led by a mounted man, and process to their victim's house while making a loud noise with bells and drums. Once there the unfortunate object of their attention would be called or dragged out and be ridiculed or attacked. It must have been a terrifying experience, as Thomas Hardy makes only too clear in his description of an (admittedly fictional) skimmington in *The Mayor of Casterbridge*.

One particularly well-recorded skimmington occurred at the hamlet of Quemerford, outside the Wiltshire market town of Calne, in 1618. The victims were Thomas Mills and his wife Agnes; the local charge was that Agnes was insufficiently subordinate to her husband. Later in court, the couple described how their first inkling that something was about to happen was when they met a young man from Calne carrying a drum and accompanied by three or four men and ten or twelve boys. Asked by the Millses' landlord what they were doing there, they replied that they were coming to Quemerford because 'there was a skimmington there, and they came for him [i.e. Mills]'. They were persuaded to go away, but about midday there came from Calne:

Thomas, Earl of Lancaster, is beheaded for his role in the Despenser War of the 1320s – one of the periodic baronial revolts of the middle ages. As usual, a medieval chronicle does not shy away from the gruesome details.

Medieval executions were grisly and public affairs. This thirteenth-century manuscript shows the traitor William de Marisco being dragged behind a horse, on the way to receive the goriest punishment possible – hanging, drawing and quartering. De Marisco was among the first men to suffer this penalty.

Legal proceedings at the Court of King's Bench, as depicted
in a manuscript from around 1460. Late-medieval England had
what was, by the standards of the time, a very effective and
centralised system of royal justice.

Domestic violence has been a constant in English society over the centuries. This misericord in Carlisle Cathedral shows a wife beating her husband.

Ritualised fighting – in the form of tournaments – became increasingly popular during the middle ages. Here Richard II observes knights jousting.

The Battle of Barnet, 1471. Edward IV, distinguished by a gold circlet (representing a crown), kills an opponent, probably meant to represent the leader of the forces opposing him, the Earl of Warwick. In fact the battle was fought in thick fog, and Warwick was killed by Edward's soldiers, not by the king himself.

Crime and punishment in the early modern era: in this seventeenth-century woodcut a beggar is being whipped through the streets. The same punishment was used for petty thieves.

Burning at the stake was one of the most frightful of early modern punishments, here being inflicted on three Protestants burnt as heretics at Windsor in 1543. The last burnings for heresy came in 1612, although the sentence was retained for petty treason by women (which included husband murder) until 1790.

The execution of witches at Newcastle, where fifteen women were hanged in a witch hunt in 1650. Scotland experienced a mass witch panic in 1649-50, and the Newcastle authorities enlisted a Scottish witch-finder to help detect them. He is being paid for his services on the left of the picture.

Swordsmanship was a greatly valued skill not only in battle but in duelling, introduced to England from Italy in Tudor times as a means for gentlemen to settle disputes in a civilised way. This illustration also shows men using the old-fashioned broadsword, and wrestling.

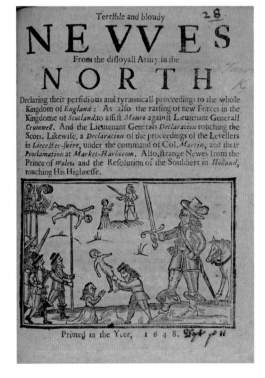

Warfare was brutal and chaotic, and this news pamphlet of 1648 – propaganda against Scottish soldiers who had fought for the king that year – would have seemed all too plausible.

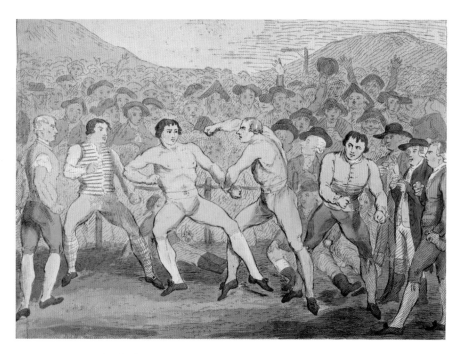

Boxing, 1788: the hitherto undefeated Birmingham boxer William Futrell is bested by 'Gentleman' John Jackson. Futrell was the author of a tract on the sport, and Jackson went on to teach boxing to the sons of the aristocracy.

'Skimmington rides' – demonstrations against unpopular local figures – were first recorded in the sixteenth century. This early-nineteenth-century sketch shows villagers ridiculing a married couple because the man had been beaten by his wife.

Mr Galley and Mr Chater put by ye Smugglers on one Horfe near Rowland Caftle.
A. Steele who was Admitted a Kings Evidence. B. Little Harry. C. Iackson D Carter.
E. Donner. F. Richards. 1. Mr Galley. 2. Mr Chater.

In February 1748 the Hawkhurst Gang seized customs collector William Galley and his acquaintance Daniel Chater and murdered them. Smuggling was a lucrative activity in the eighteenth century, perpetrated by highly organised and often violent gangs.

Highwaymen were among the most feared criminals in eighteenth-century England. Thomas Rowlandson's 1790 sketch 'The Chase of the Highwayman' shows a thief trying to escape a gang of men on horseback. Despite the romantic image it acquired, highway robbery always involved the use or threat of violence.

Organised crime and its consequences: Jonathan Wild, London's first real criminal entrepreneur, is pelted on his way to be hanged in 1725.

Elizabeth Brownrigg, executed in 1767 for beating a servant girl to death, was one of the most notorious killers of the eighteenth century – four pamphlets were published about the case.

The memoirs of excise officer John Cannon (c.1684–c.1743) offer a rare insight into everyday life – and violence – in the Georgian era.

Another drummer, named William Wiatt, and with him three or four hundred men, some like soldiers armed with pieces and other weapons, and a man riding upon a horse, having a night cap upon his head, two shoeing horns hanging by his ears, a counterfeit beard upon his chin made of a deer's tail, a smock upon the top of his garments, and he rode upon a red horse with a pair of pots under him, and in them some quantity of brewing grains, which he used to cast upon the press of people, rushing over thick upon him in the way as he passed; and he and all his company made a stand when they came just against this examinate's house, and then the gunners shot off their pieces, pipes and horns were sounded, together with lowbells and other smaller bells which the company had amongst them, and rams' horns and bucks' horns, carried upon forks were then and there lifted up and shown.

Stones were thrown at the windows of Thomas and Agnes's house, members of the crowd forced their way in, and Agnes was dragged out of the house, thrown into a wet hole, beaten, and had mud and filth plastered over her. The crowd had planned to take her and put her in the ducking stool at Calne, but were prevented (by whom we don't know) from so doing.

Whatever offence Agnes might actually have committed, it's clear that some of the couple's accusers were not exactly paragons of virtue themselves. One of the leaders, William Brooke, for example, was an excommunicate who had been charged with adultery and various offences against his neighbours, while his wife had been presented as a common scold. With people like those involved, it's not surprising that skimmingtons were so often sordidly vindictive affairs.[35] At Burton on Trent in 1618 a crowd chose to ignore the protestations of a couple they had found in bed together that they were actually married, and with the active participation of the town's constable, paraded them through the streets to the sound of rough music, manhandled them and put them in the stocks.[36] Sometimes the worm turned. In 1667 a Leeds man fired a shotgun into a crowd performing a riding outside his house, killing two of them.[37]

And sometimes the elements of public mockery were brought to bear on a vendetta that was largely private. A particularly bizarre example of this occurred in Cheshire in 1648 at the tail end of the Civil War. A Caernarvonshire gentleman named John Griffiths had struck up a friendship with a local man, Sir Hugh Calverley, and was spending quite a lot of time at his house – sometimes when Calverley was actually out. For some reason, he fell out badly with Calverley's clerk, a man named William Dodd (Dodd seems to have felt that Griffiths was abusing his master's hospitality), and suggested that Calverley should get rid of the man, both because he was a 'rank papist' and because he and another servant in the Calverley household were, so Griffiths claimed, plotting against him and trying to turn their master against him. Calverley replied, not unreasonably, that he was surprised that Griffiths should take such an interest in his servants, and added (possibly a little abruptly) that he would 'keep what servants I please in spite of your teeth'.

From that moment, the relationship between the men seems to have gone rapidly downhill. Some time later Griffiths was out hunting when he met by chance one of his own servants who warned him that Dodd was in the area, and had procured a warrant from the Parliamentarian general Sir Thomas Fairfax to disarm him (presumably Dodd had managed to convince the powers-that-be that Griffiths was likely to commit a breach of the peace). The servant also reported that there were 'above twenty lusty young fellows' gathered in nearby Sayton, where Calverley was landlord and where Griffiths had arranged to meet some friends, who had gathered to do him mischief. The course of action Griffiths now took suggests a certain, if somewhat twisted, sense of humour:

> Rather than that it should be said that I promised gentlemen to meet them, and afterwards that I durst not come; so I took my horse and I rid up into the middle of the town, but no man

durst offer to disarm me, or to meddle with me ... and I understanding the malitious plot which they intended against me, I purposefully to vex Sir Hugh and his champion Dodd, sent for a fiddler, and during the time my fellow coursers were drinking a cup of ale, we having run our match: I and my fiddler rid up to Sayton, and from one end of the town to the other, I made the fiddler play a rant named Roger of Calverley [presumably a deliberate pun on his enemy's name]; this I did to show, that I did not fear to be disarmed by them, and they may thank themselves for it, for if they had not first endeavoured to mischief me, I should not trouble myself to have vext them.

Sadly, the story does not have a suitably humorous ending. Several days after the mocking ride up and down Sayton, Griffiths chanced upon Dodd outside Calverley's house and started brawling with him. Dodd proved the better fighter, managing to get hold of Griffiths firmly by the hair. It also looked as though some of Calverley's tenants might be coming to intervene on Dodd's behalf. One of the two men accompanying Griffiths therefore fired a pistol loaded with hailshot into Dodd's buttocks. This had the desired effect of making Dodd let go of Griffiths's hair. Unfortunately, though, the wounds proved fatal. A coroner's jury – packed with Calverley's tenants, according to Griffiths – brought in a verdict of wilful murder.[38] The case serves as a useful reminder that the constant lack of restraint we find in quarrels before the eighteenth century was not the sole preserve of the rougher or poorer members of society.

VI

By the second half of the eighteenth century, defamation, scolding and the mocking rhyme were in retreat. The historian Robert B. Shoemaker has shown that defamation cases brought before London's ecclesiastical courts reached a peak of 198 in 1633, remained a regular feature of the courts' business in the late seventeenth and eighteenth centuries, but collapsed after 1750, until only one such suit was being heard a year in the late 1820s (the ecclesiastical courts' jurisdiction over defamation was abolished nationally in 1855).[39] Bindings-over at the Middlesex Quarter Sessions for slanderous or opprobrious words similarly declined massively after the mid eighteenth century. Since there's no evidence to suggest that other courts were picking up cases that the ecclesiastical courts and quarter sessions were no longer trying, one has to conclude that the apparent decline in litigation accurately reflects what was going on in society at the time.

Shoemaker's explanation for this is both simple and convincing. Quite clearly, community values had changed. Once, it mattered very much what your neighbours thought of you. You lived cheek by jowl with them, and so mocking rhymes, the charivari, gossip and slander could severely damage your standing. But by the late eighteenth century, as London burgeoned, community ties loosened. Shoemaker cites a late-eighteenth-century Church court case in which a witness deposed that 'she never troubles herself with the character or concerns of her neighbours'. In another a woman upbraided someone who was circulating gossip about an adulterous affair by saying: 'I wonder you are not ashamed of yourself to trouble your head so about your neighbours'.[40]

Reputation was no longer a community concern. It mattered only in relation to your social equals, your occupational or professional colleagues, your co-religionists, or your personal conscience. To an extent it was becoming internalised. Now, therefore, litigation for slander was no longer something which respectable people needed to concern themselves with, unless it happened to be that their professional reputation was in jeopardy (something that, of course, removed most contemporary women from the equation). Legal texts of the period also suggest that scolding was no longer taken seriously as a criminal offence, while other sources suggest that it was seen as something that was old fashioned, quaint and rustic.

London, as the nation's capital and its largest city, may have led this development, but the new ethos and the spread of 'polite' values went well beyond its perimeters.

The curse, too, was losing its earlier force. There were inevitably still those who believed in its power, just as they continued to believe in witches. But among the better off and the better educated, the old-fashioned curse must have seemed just that – old fashioned. It's intriguing therefore to find it at the heart of one of the poems in Wordsworth and Coleridge's *Lyrical Ballads* of 1798: Wordsworth's 'Goody Blake and Harry Gill'. Goody Blake is a poor but honest elderly woman who lives alone in a badly heated cottage. One night in winter she goes out to gather sticks from hedges in the area, including some belonging to the 'lusty drover' Harry Gill. Gill has long suspected the old woman of stealing from him in this way, and is lying in wait for her. When she appears he jumps out from his hiding place and seizes her by the arm. The old woman falls to her knees and calls on God 'who art never out of hearing' to ensure that Harry Gill will never be warm again. The curse works, and from that moment Gill never ceases to feel cold.

Wordsworth's mildly politically progressive moral is: 'Now think, ye farmers, all, I pray/Of Goody Blake and Harry Gill'. His source for the story, though, sheds an interestingly contemporary light on what to all intents and purposes seems an old-fashioned folktale. In 1794 and 1796 respectively, the doctor, botanist, polymath and grandfather of Charles Darwin, Erasmus Darwin, published the two volumes of one of his major works, *Zoonomia, or the Laws of Organic Life*; in the second volume he recorded the story on which Wordsworth based his poem (although the names in the poem are Wordsworth's invention). Darwin claimed that he had 'received good information of the truth of the following case, which was published a few years ago in the newspapers', but his view was that the farmer's ultimate infirmity was entirely imaginary: 'from this one insane idea [i.e. the efficacy of the curse],' Darwin wrote, 'he kept to his bed above twenty years for fear of the cold air, till at length he died'. Far from being a tale of superstition, then, the story in Darwin's hands became an illustration of a type of mental disorder: 'Where the patients are liable to mistake ideas of sensation for those of irritation, that is, imagination for realities . . . it is the voluntary actions exerted in consequence of this mistaken idea, which constitute insanity.' In other words, the farmer's infirmity is actually what a modern observer would call a psychosomatic illness.[41] A century before this, such a diagnosis would have been unthinkable.

Darwin, of course, stood on the cusp of a new world, which for many of his poorer contemporaries would have been terra incognita. For them the scold, the slanderer, the curser, might indeed be in retreat but words still held power beyond what the Enlightenment rationalist might claim. And they would doubtless have agreed with that familiar biblical text, 'Death and life are in the power of the tongue'.[42]

The frontispiece to Mr J. Olivier's *Fencing Familiarised, or a New Treatise on the Art of Sword Play* (1771). From the late 1500s, fencing grew in popularity among English noblemen who wanted to emulate their Italian upper-class contemporaries. Sword duels soon became a common way for gentlemen to defend their honour, if they felt they had been insulted.

CHAPTER 8

THE RISE AND FALL
OF THE DUEL

I

Sir John Reresby was fairly typical of the type of young Royalist gentleman who returned to England when Stuart rule was restored in 1660. Born in 1634 into the Yorkshire gentry (his family lived at Thrybergh Hall), he received a good education, studied at Cambridge and then spent some time at Gray's Inn. His father died in 1646, and a few years later the young Reresby, like so many who had backed the losing side in the Civil War, went abroad. There he eventually attached himself to the exiled Stuart court in Paris where he made such a good impression on Charles I's widow Henrietta Maria that when he returned to England at the Restoration of Charles II in 1660, she gave him the patronage he needed to secure a smooth entry into politics. He restored the fortunes of his family estates, which had suffered during the Commonwealth period, and then made his way up the local administrative hierarchy, becoming High Sheriff of Yorkshire in 1665 and a justice of the peace a few years later, before in 1673 becoming an MP at Westminster, where he soon won the favour of the Lord Treasurer, Thomas Osborne, Earl of Danby. His career continued to flourish. He was made justice of the peace for Westminster and Middlesex, and from 1682 served as Governor of York. He died in 1689.

Reresby was a staunch supporter of Charles II, an intelligent and – by the lights of his class and time – cultured man. He loved literature and could speak French well enough to be mistaken for a Frenchman. He was also fluent in Italian, had a working knowledge of German and Dutch, and some Greek and Latin. Like many gentlemen and women of the period, he was an accomplished musician as well as an amateur poet. He was also a diligent public servant, with a level of polish and attainment worthy of a diplomat – indeed on several occasions it was thought he might serve as an English envoy to a foreign court.[1]

But he appears to have been addicted to violence. In his *Memoirs* he notes that he has always been quick to take offence, and that he seems to have a knack for being drawn into 'quarrels', many of them almost extravagantly trivial. On one occasion, when he would have been about nineteen, he quarrelled with a Mr Spencer who had objected to Reresby drawing his sword to show another gentleman. The argument soon turned into a brawl that only came to an end when three others intervened, took Reresby's sword from him and broke it. Even then Reresby challenged Spencer to a duel, though he eventually agreed to a compromise whereby Spencer apologised and paid the cost of entertainment for Reresby and a group of his friends. Later, when Reresby was in France, he quarrelled with a Dutch gentleman and was advised by the local governor – who clearly judged Reresby's nature very swiftly – to move somewhere else. At Saumur he was at the receiving end of a challenge from a jealous gentleman servant of a young gentlewoman who had shown an interest in Reresby, and later delivered a challenge of his own to another French gentleman whom he had overheard making disrespectful comments about a married woman with whom Reresby was friendly. The gentleman refused the challenge, so when Reresby sought him out the following day he struck him several times with a cudgel – the standard, and degrading, way to deal with men who refused to fight a duel. The Frenchman did not draw his sword on that occasion, but the next night he and a dozen or so associates set upon Reresby and three of his friends, who had to seek refuge in a nearby house.[2]

Reresby does not appear to have mellowed with age. Within a few weeks of arriving back in England in 1660 he argued with a Yorkshire gentleman about the man's fiancée and threw a glass of wine in his face. This might well have led to a duel, he later recalled, but although the other gentleman was, strictly speaking, the injured party, he 'submitted' and the two made their peace. The following year, while in London, he quarrelled with and then cudgelled a Yorkshire gentleman named Calverley, and in April 1663 got into a fight with a complete stranger who had gratuitously suggested that the house Reresby had just emerged from was a house of ill-repute. Reresby went on the offensive – and found himself taking on more than he had bargained for:

> It should seem he had been shooting with a great cross-bow, which he had under his cloak, with which he struck at me before I could get out my sword, but missed me. By this time my cozen Tindall comes up to him, who he also struck at, and hitting on the head knockt him down. By this time I came up, and making a pass he wounded me with the end of the bow-last in my sword hand, that I had much to do to hold my sword till, recovering myself a little, I ran upon him and wounded him in the belly.

Now 'the rabble' stepped in, seized Reresby and Tindall and took them before a justice of the peace. The two men were bound over and bailed, and absconded when it looked as though their victim might actually die. Fortunately, in the end, the man recovered.

It was a few months after this incident, in the summer of 1663, that Reresby became involved in a full-scale duel. Invited to dinner at the Bear Inn 'at the bridge-foot' in London by Sir Henry Bellasis (or Belasyse), another gentleman with Yorkshire connections and a Member of Parliament, he ended up having a heated argument with an Irish gentleman called Macdemar who, earlier in the proceedings, had apparently presented Sir Henry with a venison pasty, one of the favoured delicacies of the period. Reresby so infuriated Macdemar that he demanded satisfaction: either, he said, Reresby should deny that he meant any harm by his words and beg Macdemar's pardon, or he should fight. Reresby – perhaps unsurprisingly, given his form to date – chose the latter option, and the two men agreed to fight in Hyde Park. On the way there Macdemar encountered another Irish gentleman who agreed to act as his second, while Bellasis offered to serve Reresby in the same way. And so the duel began:

> At the first pass I hurt him slightly on the sword hand, and at the same time he closing with me we both fell on the ground (he having hold of my sword and I of his). Sir Henry and his man were fighting at the same time close by [the French practice of seconds duelling alongside principals had entered England by now], and Sir Henry had got the better, wounded the other in the belly and disarmed him, and was coming in to us as we were both risen and I got his sword out of his hand, which I took home with me, but sent it to him the next day.

Macdemar's second was so seriously injured that for some weeks it looked as though he might actually die. Reresby and Bellasis therefore absconded, eventually taking refuge at the residence of Bellasis's patron, George Villiers, 2nd Duke of Buckingham – a man who, as we shall see, was similarly given to duelling. The wounded second eventually recovered.

Neither encroaching middle age nor high office seem to have stemmed Reresby's taste for violence and quarrelling, for as late as 1682, just a few years before his death, he managed to get himself embroiled in a quarrel with a fellow justice of the peace, Francis Jessop of Broomhall. The two men had been attending the West Riding Quarter Sessions at Rotherham, and had accepted an invitation from the Duke of Norfolk to dine with him that evening. The sessions had been somewhat dominated by prosecutions of religious Non-conformists, and Jessop, whose family had fought for Parliament in the Civil War and who, according to Reresby, was a 'known favourer of dissenters', had clearly been unhappy about the stiffer sentences now being handed down. He withdrew to consider his position, and then joined the company again:

> After a long debate in a private room to satisfy his doubts in that point, he cast some reflections on the justices in their former sessions, as well as on those there present, declaring that their proceedings and warrants were illegal: to which I replied that it was something saucy to arraign so many gentlemen of quality concerned in the commission of the peace for his single opinion. He stood up and retorted with great insolence, 'You are very impudent.' At which words I took up a leaden Standish [a receptacle for writing materials, or a large inkwell] (He sitting at a table some distance from me) and threw it in his face, where the edge lighting upon his cheek cut it quite through. We after drew our swords and I went into the middle of the chamber, but the company prevented his following me and afterwards reconciled us.

On the one hand, it's praiseworthy that two violently opposed men could agree to set aside their differences, have a drink together and end up expressing regret for what had happened. On the other hand, we have to remind ourselves that these were justices of the peace, that they drew swords on each other during a meeting of the quarter sessions, that Reresby was in his late forties by this point, and that 1682 was the year he became Governor of York.

Nor was that the end of his displays of temper. One Sunday in 1683 he entered York Minster to take Communion and discovered that the cushion he normally sat on had been removed and placed on Sir John Brooke's seat. Brooke was a man whose loyalty to the Stuarts was suspect, and whose weapons had been confiscated on Reresby's orders. There can have been little love lost between the two men, and Reresby clearly interpreted what had happened as a slight. Consequently, when Brooke, having taken his place in the Minster, stood up at a certain point in the service, Reresby grabbed the cushion and put it on his own seat. Afterwards Brooke asked Reresby if he had the same commission to take his cushion as he had to take his weapons. Reresby gave a suitably sharp retort, and waited for the inevitable challenge. When it didn't arrive, he sent a captain of the guard to inform Brooke that he was waiting to hear from him. Brooke in return sent a conciliatory message.

Most of Reresby's quarrels were with his equals, and he was also witness to many other duels among the gentry, but he was not beyond the occasional confrontation with those who were inferior to him in rank. In September 1660, for example, he was planning to take a ferry across the River Ouse at Selby during a journey from Thrybergh to York, when a dispute arose between his people and a number of locals about who should board the ferry boat first. In the ensuing fracas, Reresby was beaten with a cudgel and retaliated by wounding two of his opponents with his sword. A mob formed and Reresby was pulled from his horse. Fortunately he was rescued by his black servant and given shelter at the house of 'an honest man', emerging only when the crowd had dispersed.

Two years earlier, in 1658, he had a similar experience during a brief visit to London from the continent. England then, of course, was still a Commonwealth, and according to Reresby, the citizens of the capital 'had then so far imbued the custom and manners of a commonwealth that they could scarce endure the sight of a gentleman, so that the common salutation to a man well dressed was "French dog" or the like'. As a young Royalist gentleman Reresby could have been a target, but on this occasion it was in fact his valet, having made the mistake of wearing a feather in his hat, who attracted abuse from some workmen and had sand thrown at his clothes. The valet drew his sword, 'thinking to follow the custom of France in the like cases'. The 'rabble' attacked. Reresby and his valet were forced to seek refuge in a nearby house.

II

By the time Reresby drew his sword in anger for the first time, duelling had been part of English life for several decades. It was not, however, a home-grown fad, nor one that had evolved naturally from medieval codes of behaviour – though, of course, the idea that personal honour should, if necessary, be defended by force had a long history, stretching back to Homeric times. Rather, the formal duel was an import from Italy, and one that had its origins in the Tudor fascination with – and often admiration for – all things Italian. William Thomas's *The Historie of Italie* (1549) – among the first books in English to mention duelling – gives a very clear sense of this admiration.

Thomas was clerk of the council to the young Edward VI, who had spent five years in Italy, and clearly liked what he saw there. He praised Italian gentlemen. He applauded their conversation and (with a few exceptions) their manners: 'so honourable, so courtesie [i.e. courteous], so prudent, and so grave withal, that it should seem each one of them to have had a princely bringing up'. They knew how to bear themselves, he felt, they dressed well, and they were kind to strangers. At the same time, he noted, these Italian gentlemen were quick to anger if they felt they had been slandered, and if anyone spoke ill of them they 'shall die for it, if the party slandered may know it, and find time and place to doe it'. For this reason, the Italian gentry always went around armed (the English gentry, aping the Italians, were likewise to sport rapiers by the late sixteenth century). Their disputes, he observed, followed an agreed ritual: 'if one gentleman happens to defame an other, many times the defamed maketh his defiance by a writ called a cartello, and openly challengeth the defamer to fight in camp: so that there are seen sometime worthy trials between them'.[3]

In 1576 an Italian named Rocco Bonetti set up a fencing school in Blackfriars in London, and was soon able to boast the coats of arms of a number of important patrons on his walls. In the 1590s another fencing school was opened by two brothers, Jeronimo and Vincentio Saviolo. Jeronimo was killed in a duel with an Englishman named Cheese. Vincentio published a book on duelling techniques, *Vincentio Saviolo, His Practise*. Another Italian fencing-master, Giacomo di

Grassi, had his *True Art of Defence* published in English in 1594, while William Segar, portrait painter, officer of arms to the court of Elizabeth I and Garter King of Arms under James I, produced *The Booke of Honor and Armes* in 1589.[4]

That epitome of the Elizabethan gentlemen Philip Sidney (1554–86) – the poet and soldier who was to die so chivalrously at the Battle of Zutphen – was among the first Englishmen to be drawn into the world of duelling when in 1579 he became involved in a quarrel with the Earl of Oxford. The cause seems to have been political: at the time Elizabeth I was involved in marriage negotiations with the Duc d'Anjou, who was supported by Oxford and opposed by a faction to which Sidney was connected. But the actual occasion for the quarrel was a trivial one. Sidney was playing tennis at Greenwich Palace when Oxford appeared and demanded the use of the tennis court. Sidney refused, adding that a more polite request from Oxford would have prompted a more favourable response. Oxford then called Sidney a puppy, and repeated this slur to members of the French Embassy who were accompanying him. Sidney, according to one account, 'gave my lord a lie impossible . . . in respect all the world knows puppies are gotten by dogs and children by men'. Verbally bested, Oxford and his cohorts left, but a few days later a duel was agreed. It was only Elizabeth's intervention at this point that stopped things getting out of hand. Turning duelling conventions to her advantage, she pointed out that Sidney, although of impeccable lineage, was socially inferior to an earl, that duels could only occur between equals, and that she as monarch needed to ensure that correct social protocol was preserved. The duel did not take place.[5]

Duelling remained popular during James I's reign, seems to have died down under Charles I and during the Interregnum, but then came back in force after the Restoration of Charles II in 1660. It had been endemic among Royalist army officers and courtiers, many of them also soldiers, who had – like Sir John Reresby – attended the Stuart court in exile in France or the Low Countries, and it seems to have returned with them.[6] As for the reason why it should have proved so attractive to noblemen and gentry, this is stated again and again in Sir John Reresby's *Memoirs*. Quite simply, it became the approved means by which a gentleman of standing maintained his reputation and honour. After the brawl with his fellow JP Francis Jessop at the Rotherham sessions, Reresby reflected: 'I was sorry for the accident, it happening at a sessions of the peace, but the provocation could not be passed over' (admittedly, no duel ensued on this occasion). Following his argument with Sir John Brooke over the cushion in York Minster he reflected: 'I could have been very well content that no occasion of such disputes had offered themselves, but when they do I have found the best way to prevent them for the future is not to seem backward in seeking reparation.' He was similarly quick to react if he felt a member of his family had been insulted or the family honour impugned – as, for example, when his forty-year-old sister, apparently despairing of a better opportunity ('she was not handsome'), decided to marry a penniless lieutenant in the Irish army.[7] The marriage did not go ahead.

But if the duel reflected an age-old obsession with defending honour, it does also seem to reflect a peculiar touchiness among upper-class men in Western Europe from the mid sixteenth century onwards. Reresby, after all, was not alone among his contemporaries in being outraged by incidents and perceived slights that seem astonishingly petty to us. What may seem trivial to a later generation, however, was far from being so in a world where honour was very highly valued indeed. Medieval knights, of course, had also had a strongly developed sense of dignity, and one can detect a certain continuity between the old ideas of chivalry and the new sense of honour of the Renaissance gentleman, and between medieval single combats and the Renaissance duel. But there's no doubt (in my mind, at least) that overall the Renaissance gentleman was a different animal from his medieval ancestors: he was a courtier, not a knight, and as such he embraced a more complex social code than his predecessors. The physical courage of the soldier continued to matter, of course, but now it was overlaid by the etiquette and codes of civility of the courtier. As one historian of the duel has put it, 'As soon as the Italianate ideology of courtesy and civility began to be adopted in England, the duel of honour immediately followed suit.'[8] Those early Italianate influences did not last, but the duel of honour, and the extreme touchiness which prompted it, persisted into the nineteenth century.

Thus well into the late-Georgian era the very slightest of perceived slights could cause a reaction that strikes us as being out of all proportion. Take, for example, the quarrel that broke out in April 1803 between Lieutenant-Colonel Montgomery of the 9th Foot and a Royal Navy captain named James Macnamara. The two men were riding in Hyde Park, each with a Newfoundland dog trotting behind. When the two dogs began to fight Montgomery stepped in to separate them, demanded to know who the owner of the other dog was, and declared that he intended to knock the animal down. Macnamara overheard him, and responded that anybody who wanted to deal with his dog in that way would have to reckon with him first. An altercation followed, then an exchange of cards, and that evening the two men met on Primrose Hill. Each was a good shot and managed to wound the other, but Montgomery's injuries proved fatal. He was taken away to Chalk Farm where he died a few minutes later.

Being accused of lying was considered particularly offensive, and in duelling handbooks and the more formally conducted quarrels 'giving the lie' was, in effect, the point of no return on the pathway to a duel. To call a gentleman a liar was to savage his honour, reputation and social credit. Vincentio Saviolo, more of an expert in these matters than most, was unequivocal on the importance of this issue: 'hee unto whome the lie is wrongfullie given', he wrote, 'ought to challenge him that offreth that dishonour, and by the swoorde to prove himselfe no lyer'.[9] Joseph Addison, writing in the *Spectator* in 1711, took a more cynical view:

> The great violation of the point of honour from man to man, is giving the lie. One may tell a man he whores, drinks,

blasphemes, and it may pass unresented; but to say he lies, though but in jest, is an affront that nothing but blood can expiate. The reason perhaps may be, because no other vice implies a want [lack] of courage so much as making of a lie; and therefore telling a man he lies, is touching him in the most sensible part of his honour, and indirectly calling him a coward.[10]

Paradoxically, then, the duel, good manners and fine ideals were seen as going hand in hand. If you know that any deviation from the very highest of standards might cost you your life, apologists for the duel argued, you soon learn that it is best to curb your speech and your conduct in polite company. As Bernard de Mandeville put it – rather chillingly – in a work first published in 1704, 'It is strange that a nation should grudge seeing half a dozen men sacrific'd in a twelvemonth to obtain so valuable a blessing as the politeness of manners, the pleasures of conversation and the happiness of company, in general.'[11] To the Reresbys and Macnamaras of this world, what some might interpret simply as petulance and overreaction was nothing of the kind.

'I must not', Macnamara said at his trial, 'be supposed to be a man who sought safety by submitting to what custom has taught others to consider as a disgrace.' As a naval officer, he added, he often had to lead men into dangerous situations, and this was only possible if they respected him; if gentlemanly standards were not upheld the very security of the nation would be imperilled. Macnamara's views would have been readily endorsed by Lord Nelson, Lord Hood and other senior naval commanders who all came forward to give him character references. The jury were clearly swayed by his line of defence. When it came to the judge's summing up, Mr Justice Heath urged a verdict of manslaughter (murder sentences were not passed on duellists). The jury, however, found Macnamara not guilty.[12]

Up to about the middle of the sixteenth century gentry fighting on foot tended to do so with broadswords. These could inflict terrible wounds, though even a man not wearing armour stood a fair chance of avoiding fatal injury. But from about the mid sixteenth century gentlemen started carrying rapiers, which had sharp, pointed blades, and which, when thrust with sufficient force, were very likely to kill (using a broadsword, by contrast, involved slashing rather than thrusting). As pistols became popular, however, the rapier went into decline, and by the 1730s was rarely if ever worn in public. Surprisingly, perhaps, given the damage we know Macnamara's pistol was able to inflict on Montgomery, the number of fatalities in duels actually fell. Historian Robert B. Shoemaker's researches into 206 duels fought in London and the metropolitan area between 1660 and 1800 show that just under a quarter of those involving swords resulted in a fatality, while another quarter led to serious injury, but only 6.5 per cent of those who fought with pistols were killed, while over 70 per cent escaped without injury of any type.[13]

Obviously the inaccuracy of the eighteenth-century pistol may have played a part in this, though Shoemaker points out that from the 1770s the duelling pistols proper that were being introduced were lighter, better designed and more precise than earlier ones. But the main factor seems to have been that whereas in a sword duel, drawing blood was what gave satisfaction or proved honour, in a pistol duel it was discharging the weapon and standing immobile while one's opponent discharged his weapon in turn that counted. Inflicting injury was less of a consideration. Indeed, the evidence seems to suggest that it was considered bad form to aim too carefully. As Samuel Stanton put it in his treatise on how to conduct a duel written in 1790, 'it is highly improper for any person to put the pistol across his arm, or to be longer in taking aim than necessary: a moment or two is full sufficient to view your object, and fire'.[14] Some gentlemen were inevitably better shots than others. It was therefore important that a contest should be fought in a way that minimised their advantage (some had once worried that duelling with a sword was inherently unfair for the less experienced fighter). So, for example, by the early nineteenth century duellists were given a signal to fire (for example, a dropped handkerchief) so that neither would be able to take too long over aiming. During the same period it became accepted that a duel could be ended when one of the participants refused to fire, or fired his pistol in the air. Fatalities still occurred, of course, but as time went by it became accepted that honour could be satisfied without inflicting serious injury or death on one's adversary.

Duelling continued among those at the very top of society – the monarch excepted – into the 1820s and beyond. The Duke of Wellington, for example, fought a notorious duel with George Finch-Hatton, 10th Earl of Winchilsea, in 1829 over a political difference. Wellington, who had, for practical and political reasons, initially been ambivalent about Catholic emancipation, had come to accept that it was essential if civil war in Ireland was to be avoided. Winchilsea, a vigorous anti-Catholic, responded by withdrawing his support for the foundation of King's College, London (a Protestant foundation), which Wellington had earlier joined him in championing, and in a letter to the *Standard* newspaper accused Wellington of planning to use it as a vehicle for advancing Catholicism and undermining the Church of England. A furious exchange of letters followed, and then Wellington (who had never fought a duel before) challenged Winchilsea, quite possibly to discredit him politically and rally moderate opinion.

The duel was set for the morning of 21 March in Battersea Fields, then a soggy marshland. Wellington had as his second a veteran of the Peninsular War, Henry Hardinge, while Winchilsea had Viscount Falmouth. A doctor, John Hume, was also in attendance. The first attempt to complete proceedings was interrupted by a group of workmen, so the protagonists had to leap across drainage dykes to find a more secluded spot. Once there, Falmouth was so nervous that he was unable to load Winchilsea's pistols, and had to ask Hardinge to help, leaving Hume to help Wellington. Wellington fired first, missing Winchilsea (some accounts say that the bullet went through his lapel), at which point Winchilsea simply fired into the air.

Falmouth then presented Wellington and Hardinge with a written apology from his principal (evidence perhaps that the outcome of the duel had been pre-arranged), which Wellington found unsatisfactory, so it had to be amended and witnessed by Hume. Wellington emerged with his reputation enhanced and with stronger public support for emancipation.

Despite the etiquette that governed duels, not all of them went so smoothly. Perhaps the most shambolic was that fought between MPs John Wilkes and Samuel Martin in 1763 over a remark made by Martin in the House of Commons that seemed to imply Wilkes was a coward. In response, Wilkes sent a letter to Martin saying that he was the coward. Martin issued a challenge, and the two men met in Hyde Park, at The Circle, a place where people of fashion came to meet and to be seen. They found a secluded place to fight but there were no seconds, and the two men realised they had not established any rules for their combat. Martin suggested that they should stand back to back, take six paces, turn and fire. A nervous Wilkes asked when they would know to fire. He also insisted that they exchange one of their two pistols, so that neither had an advantage in weaponry. Once that had been settled the two men stood back to back. Martin walked six paces and turned to fire, but found that Wilkes was fiddling with one of his pistols, declaring he was not ready. This minor hiccup resolved, the two men fired, apparently without result. Wilkes then attempted to fire his second pistol but it failed to go off (ironically it was the one he had insisted Martin exchange with him – Martin was later to write that he thought Wilkes might have spilled powder out of the gun when checking to see if it was primed). Rather than fire his own second pistol, Martin walked up to Wilkes to see what the problem was, and discovered that although his first shot had been deflected by one of Wilkes's coat buttons, it had still managed to cause his opponent a severe injury. Martin immediately fled to France; Wilkes recovered.[15]

Incidents such as this did little to enhance the status of duelling in public opinion. Nor did the occasional story of women fighting each other.[16] We know that women on the continent were duelling as early as the seventeenth century. From eighteenth-century England a few accounts survive of women either seriously contemplating a duel or actually going ahead with one. In a London case from 1790, for example, one woman, declaring that 'she cannot exist under the public insults she has received from the Hon. Miss—', sent a challenge via an ensign, or junior officer, from the Coldstream Guards that stated: 'Honourable Men demand and receive satisfaction for similar injuries. And why are Maids of Honour so proscribed on such occasions?' The response was a damning put-down: since she was not a woman of honour, came the reply, there was no challenge to be met.

In the same year, two married women got into an argument over a gentleman for whose favours they were competing. One challenged the other, the challenge was accepted, and a duel was fixed for the following morning. When the two would-be combatants arrived at the venue, however, and one of them produced a pair of duelling pistols, a constable alerted by the maid of one of the women intervened and the duel had to be called off. And in 1792 the *Carlton House Magazine* published an account of a duel between Lady Almeria Braddock and a Mrs Elphinstone, complete with an illustration of the two women holding pistols.

The occasion for the quarrel was a somewhat tactless remark by Mrs Elphinstone. Apparently, while the two ladies were taking tea, she told Lady Braddock: 'You have been a very beautiful woman.' Picking up on the use of the past tense, Lady Braddock bristled, whereupon Mrs Elphinstone compounded the gaffe by telling her, 'You have a very good Autumn face, even now . . . The lilies and the roses are somewhat faded. Forty years ago I am told a young fellow could hardly gaze on you with impunity.' To make matters worse, she added that she understood Lady Braddock to be sixty. Lady Braddock countered that she was actually thirty. Mrs Elphinstone told her she lied ('That's false, my lady'), and Lady Braddock, in the approved fashion, responded, 'This is not to be borne, you have given me the lie direct . . . I must be under the necessity of calling you out.' The two women then withdrew to Hyde Park with pistols and swords, and honour was satisfied without, fortunately, any shedding of blood.

It's an amusing story. Unfortunately, it's almost certainly a work of fiction. No shred of substantiating evidence has ever been found and no Lady Almeria Braddock has ever been traced. Clearly it's a lampoon aimed at women obsessed with preserving their youth. At the same time, though, it's hard not to see in the tale of Lady Braddock and Mrs Elphinstone a satire on the absurdity of duelling.[17]

III

As previously mentioned, proponents of duelling felt that it promoted gentlemanly and polite behaviour. Another line of defence that might be advanced is that by ritualising aggression it helped to control it. It's noticeable, for example, that while the 'lower orders' were not permitted to duel, they nevertheless adopted some of the ethics of duelling (as I have touched on in Chapter 3), introducing rules of combat into fights that had once been random free-for-alls. In 1727 the French visitor César de Saussure noted of lower-class London men that when they had.

> . . . a disagreement which they cannot end up amicably, they retire into some quiet place and strip from their waist upwards . . . the two champions shake hands before commencing, and then attack each other courageously with their fists, and sometimes also with their heads, which they use like rams.[18]

Evidence is scanty, but it seems to be the case that such fights might well have occurred when men in the same trade accused each other of lying or cheating – in other words, that what might spark a duel among the gentry might also do so among poorer members of society. As the eighteenth century progressed, a set of conventions arose governing fights (for example, that a man should not strike his opponent while he was down), and these were vigorously enforced by onlookers (who would sometimes place bets on the outcome). De Saussure noted that it was customary for the combatants to shake hands before fighting, and that if they were in a fit condition to do so at the end, they would shake hands again when honour had been satisfied.

But for those who disapproved of duelling, no excuses would serve. Nor was disapproval slow in showing itself. First to pronounce was Lodowick Bryskett (c.1546–?1612) in his *A Discourse of Civill Life* of 1606. Bryskett was probably born in Hackney (at that time a village safely removed from the London sprawl), the son of an Italian merchant who had moved to England. His *Discourse* suggests that he had picked up his father's native tongue, as it was a translation of an earlier work by an Italian author, Giovanni Battista Giraldi Cinthio, and was typical of the many guides to gentlemanly behaviour published in the period. What makes it unusual is the lengthy passage dealing with and criticising duelling:

> There can be nothing more contrary to good discipline in a well-ordered commonwealth, than this wicked and unjust kind of fight, which destroyeth, so far forth as it beareth sway, all civil society. For it breedeth the contempt of God and his commandments, of religion, of laws, constitutions and civil government, of princes, of magistrates, and finally of country, parents, friends and kindred; to all which men are bound by reason natural and civil.

For Bryskett duels were disruptive, ungodly and brought out the worst in men. They were certainly no way to defend honour: 'he that taketh to revenge a private wrong, is so far from getting honour thereby, as he rather loseth whatsoever honour and reputation he had before'.[19]

A few years later, no less a figure than James I voiced his opposition. His *A Proclamation against Private Challenges and Combats*, no doubt provoked by some recent high-profile duels, was issued on 14 February 1614. It noted 'the slaughter which we find to have been strangely multiplied and increased of late' and argued that this resulted from his subjects' tendency 'to challenge any man into the field, towards whom they carry either grudge or malice in their minds, under the pretext or satisfaction of pretended wrongs'. Like many later commentators (and in fact like Bryskett) James's proclamation argued that to seek private revenge was to undermine civil society:

> For to speak truth, to what purpose serves the laws of God, the provisional institutions of man, and the course of ordinary justice in the commonwealth ... if it be free to subjects out of the distemper of their own distempered conceits, either to rate the quality of the wrong supposed, as is the satisfaction that belongs to it.

The proclamation also attacked what it conceived to be a faulty definition of honour – the tendency 'to think that any grain of worth of reputation or true honour, can be drawn out of any act that is absolutely repugnant to all such laws (as divine as human) as sway both religion and policies'. Claiming that continental monarchs who ruled territories where duelling was commonplace had already taken harsh measures against it, James promised that the utmost severity of the law would be brought to bear against challenges and duels, while the arguments of the proclamation were supported by a long treatise against 'combats and combatants' written by the Earl of Northampton. Interestingly, this proclamation had been preceded by an earlier one of 15 October 1613, *A Proclamation prohibiting the Publishing of any Reports or Writings of Duels*. Duels were evidently newsworthy, and the proclamation took the line that publications about them further encouraged them. Those guilty of writing about them were to be punished at the discretion of the Star Chamber, and, if considered necessary, could be banished from the royal court for seven years.

For Samuel Pepys – whose relatively unexalted position in society made him a potential observer of duels rather than a likely participant – such feuds between noblemen were pointless and embarrassing. In a diary entry for 17 January 1667/8 he records how the Duke of Buckingham, one of the most powerful men in the realm though given to quarrelling and dissolute living, had fought a duel with the Earl of Shrewsbury over an affair that Buckingham was having with Shrewsbury's wife. The duel was fought in the French style – so the two seconds on each side also participated – and it proved to be something of a bloodbath: one of the seconds was killed, Shrewsbury was badly wounded, and the others were injured to a greater or lesser extent. 'This will make the world think the king has good councillors about him', grumbled Pepys, 'when the Duke of Buckingham, the greatest man about him, is a fellow of no more sobriety than to fight about a whore.' A duel in July 1667 between Thomas Porter and Sir Henry Belasyse (whom we have already encountered in connection with Sir John Reresby) – 'the greatest friends in the world' – prompted Pepys to write: 'It is worth remembering the silliness of the quarrel, and is a kind of emblem of the general complexion of the whole kingdom at present.' When Belasyse died of his injuries a few days later, Pepys made a further note: 'it is pretty to see how the world talk of them as a couple of fools, that killed one another out of love'.[20]

While duelling had its defenders in the eighteenth century, the voices of its opponents became ever louder.[21] The anonymous author of *An Essay on Duelling* (1792), in a passage typical of the age, evoked both reason and sentiment in his condemnation:

> Let me address myself to cold, unimpassioned reason, and let me ask, where is the man, who, in the solemn hours of meditation, ever approved the practice of duelling? The mind shudders at the contemplation; our feelings revolt at the thought; the heart is appalled and trembles. Let him, I say, reflect on its horrors; let him enumerate its deviations; let him imagine a sword planted

in the bosom of a friend; let him conceive a dagger, just drawn from the wound, and reeking with the warm blood of one, who, perhaps, has been his benefactor. Can any future conduct make atonement for a crime so inhuman, for resentment so ungenerous?

The writer dismissed the old argument that fear of a challenge helped to preserve good manners, suggesting that these were just an empty show: 'the outward forms of politeness, which are chiefly composed of ridiculous grimace, ostentatious parade, and unmeaning gesticulation'.[22]

There were growing religious objections, too. When, for example, Edmund Chishull, a controversial writer, a strong Whig supporter and chaplain to Queen Anne, preached a sermon before the Queen at Windsor Chapel in 1712, arguing against duelling, he looked to scriptural authority to support his argument, taking as his text *Romans*, 12:19, 'Avenge not your selves', and attacking those

... who by their own unauthoris'd sentence, for every petty difference in word or deed, immediately condemn their adversary to capital punishment: nor this only, this is a pernicious practice, which by perverting an institution once intended for a justifiable and noble end [the judicial combat] is now fully known by the name of duel. This is that wild decision of the private sword: that effort of mistaken courage; exerted always against true honour which it boasts so much, as well as against true religion which it so little minds.

To Chishull duelling was both inconsistent with true honour and 'absolutely inconsistent with true religion'. Not only was vengeance God's prerogative, he argued, but for men willingly to engage in such a potentially fatal activity was tantamount to suicide – a sin and a felony. Chishull also reminded his audience of another biblical precept, that 'the bloodthirsty and deceitful man shall not live out half his days'.[23] These were views that were taken up and reinforced later in the century as a new force of Christian evangelicalism swept the nation.

There was legal unease, too. Although the custom was not to pass murder convictions on those who killed their opponents, there were some who felt that it was a custom that had little or no basis in law. A tract of 1773 written by Granville Sharp questioned how the plea of sudden anger could 'remove the imputation and guilt of murder, when a mortal wound is willfully given with a weapon'. He argued that 'the indulgence allowed by the courts to voluntary manslaughter in reencounters [confrontations], and in sudden affrays and duels, is indiscriminate, and without foundation in law', and that 'no man can give, or accept, a challenge, without his being guilty of wilful murder, if he kills his antagonist'. He also made a practical point: the unjustifiable leniency of the courts helped support the unjustifiable practices of the duellist.[24] By the nineteenth century, the legal argument was being evoked with increasing frequency by those opposed to duelling.

And by the mid nineteenth century the duel, having peaked briefly in the 1790s, had all but disappeared. An anti-duelling association was set up in 1843 (an earlier one in 1810 had failed to get off the ground) which recruited men of influence, many of them senior army and navy officers, to act as arbiters when quarrels arose. That same year new libel laws were passed that offered a powerful legal alternative to settling disputes on the duelling ground. The next year, the British army – the home of so many would-be duellists – made the acts of offering a challenge and of duelling offences for which both principals and seconds could be cashiered. The Prime Minister Sir Robert Peel legislated to deny the standard army pension to widows of officers who were killed in duels. The last duel in England was fought in 1852 between George Smyth and Colonel Romilly over an election dispute. In other European countries, notably Germany, it was to persist for rather longer.

Long before that even the proponents of duelling had sought to rein it in. When, for example, Lieutenant Samuel Stanton of the 37th

Regiment published his *The Principles of Duelling; with Rules to be observed in every Particular of It* in 1790, he was at pains to distinguish between duels that could be justified and those that were absurd overreactions. For him 'laudable and just purposes' included demanding satisfaction for a personal affront, or when 'unjust and false allegations are made against your honour and character'. However, 'evils and abuses' arose on those occasions when 'young men are vain and silly enough to imagine they shall never be respected or esteemed as persons of honour and courage, till they have signalised those qualities in a duel':

> What can be more ridiculous than to hear of gentlemen's opposing life to life, in consequence of mere trifle, not seriously worth a thought; and the more so, as it sometimes happens that one or both of them pay the forfeit; fatal consequences being no doubt as much to be apprehended in former as in the latter instance. What can be a greater proof of depravity of disposition and want of sense, than, exclusive of your own risk, then obliging another to hazard his life and family, merely because you choose to quarrel over a straw?

For Stanton, the duel was an institution worth preserving (in any case, he thought it was impossible to prohibit it) but it was essentially a last resort. It would, he said, 'redound much more to the honour and credit of gentlemen in general, if they were to compromise, or in any manner settle disputes, without proceeding to extremities, or flying upon every altercation, to duelling'. He was also at pains to say, of course, that only a gentleman could duel with a gentleman.[25]

Duels fought in the last few decades of the practice's existence show some of the restraining principles Stanton stood for in operation. The old French fashion tradition whereby seconds joined principals in the fighting fell away. Instead, it became an accepted part of the seconds' role to try to dissuade the principals from fighting. In an infamous duel in 1798 Prime Minister William Pitt the Younger and opposition MP George Tierney, who had quarrelled in the House of Commons, fired twice, but then as *The Times* recorded on 28 May, their seconds 'jointly interfered, and insisted that the matter should go no further, it being their decided opinion that sufficient satisfaction had been given, and that the business was ended with perfect honour to both parties'. Seconds might even seek to prevent injury altogether by loading pistols with insufficient powder – or, in an incident recorded in 1771, replacing the charges with parboiled potatoes.

Ultimately, though, it was changing public opinion that did for duelling. Gradually, many of the intellectual arguments made against the practice gained ground. A popular view also grew up that duelling was somehow that very worst of things: un-English; that what in the sixteenth century had been a fashionable Italian import was really a deplorable foreign vice – and a French one at that. Thus John Bennett, preaching a sermon against duelling at Manchester in 1783, informed his congregation that:

> I believe the prevalence of duelling, in this kingdom, is, considerably, owing to the fondness for even the fopperies and vices of our neighbours on the continent, among whom it is esteemed honourable, and where to have killed in this inhuman manner, a number of his fellow creatures, is, generally, admitted as a sovereign claim to honour and caresses. France, indeed, hath, of late, been a fruitful and a convenient nursery of every fashionable absurdity, and threatens to annihilate those sterling virtues, which, once, characterised the English as a people, and made their name admired and revered to the extremities of the globe.

Until Britain rejected the customs of 'so frivolous a nation', he concluded, 'her sun, I am persuaded, will gradually be setting, and her empire drawing to a close'.[26]

But a more significant factor than this popular Protestantism was both more deep-rooted and perhaps harder to pin down precisely. From the mid eighteenth century onwards the Industrial Revolution started to throw up a new, powerful middle class – a class whose final recognition as a force to be reckoned with came with the passing of the 1832 Reform Act. And this new middle class evolved a set of values that were often at variance with those of the upper classes, who had traditionally held sway. Many were evangelical Christians or religious Non-conformists. Many felt held back by or excluded from aristocratic society. For those who despised them, they were people who lacked breeding and were obsessed with money. Lieutenant Stanton's pro-duelling tract of 1790 has a side-swipe at them when discussing the principle that gentlemen should only fight other gentlemen:

> It is in England, money overbalances every thing; where the very scum of the earth bids defiance to rank, merit, abilities, and every laudable and good quality. In most other countries it weighs but its standard here it turns the balance, and carries everything before it, right or wrong.[27]

Conversely, those of the new middle class who regarded the nobility critically (if perhaps sometimes enviously) also looked askance at those aspects of behaviour that could be said to define them, duelling included. It's interesting to note in this context that John Bennett's Manchester sermon condemning duelling associates the habit with London – the home of polite society (it fears, though, that the nuisance is spreading: 'a spirit of duelling,' Bennett says, 'once immediately confined to the metropolis, hath, of late, displayed its malignant influence even in the northern part of the kingdom').[28]

In this new progressive and rational world, duelling seemed also hopelessly old fashioned. It belonged to an era when law and proper government scarcely existed. It hardly belonged to the modern world of commerce and industry. The barbarians might have indulged in it (some early critics traced it back to the fall of the Roman Empire), but the ancient classical world that eighteenth- and nineteenth-century people of education so admired had managed to promote a keen sense of honour without having to resort to the duel.

Besides, violence was not a masculine attribute that should be admired; self-restraint was more impressive in the modern world. A comment in *The Times* of 7 July 1843 summed up the middle-class position neatly:

> I have as much respect as any man for eminent rank and station but who can resist a feeling of deep regret for weakness such as the usage of duelling by the gentry this country exhibits . . . If the higher classes do really consider that an affront justifies a break of laws divine and human, a violation of right principle and feeling, in what esteem can their opinions be held?

Bourgeois sensibilities were certainly ruffled by a number of high-profile cases in the 1840s in which upper-class duellists who had been involved in duels that had proved fatal were either only very mildly sanctioned or escaped punishment altogether. The notion that the law should treat all equally was felt to have been undermined. That said, by this time the gentry and the men of 'eminent rank and station' were changing, too, influenced both by the self-control the middle classes prided themselves on and, in some cases, by the rise of evangelical Christianity. Even the army officer – once among the most active of duellists – was adapting to a new worldview. Perhaps the rise of organised mass warfare that started to develop during the wars against Revolutionary and Napoleonic France had its impact on those traditional virtues of military officers: individual honour and courage – though this is not a point that can be pushed too hard. What is undoubtedly true is that as the nineteenth century advanced, army officers came to think of themselves as part of a disciplined machine rather than as individual men of honour. They also knew that in the new world of Victorian respectability, they might well be court-martialled for fighting a duel, and that their careers would suffer as a result.[29]

Newspaper coverage of duels during these decades tended to be critical. Wellington may have emerged from his encounter with Winchilsea with his reputation enhanced, but there were those who said the challenge should never have been accepted in the first place. A couple of decades earlier, in September 1809, two cabinet ministers, Lord Castlereagh, at that time Secretary of State for War and Colonies, and George Canning, Foreign Secretary and a future Prime Minister, fought a similarly politically motivated duel on Putney Heath, during which Castlereagh, reckoned to be one of the best shots of the period, wounded his opponent in the thigh. The general reaction was dismay that two such highly placed politicians should attempt to settle their differences in this fashion. And when William Pitt fought George Tierney in 1798, there were those who felt that it was quite wrong for a prime minister to be putting his life at risk when the country was involved in a life-or-death struggle with Revolutionary France. It was an opinion shared by George III.[30] In the 1820s a flurry of duelling was matched by a flurry of hostile caricatures of duellists: mockery was, by now, becoming as effective a weapon against duelling as reasoned debate.

Over the next few years, other Members of Parliament would fight duels over words spoken in the house; pistol shots were even exchanged between rival candidates in the run-up to elections. But the duel had had its day. Two hundred and fifty years before, people could have argued that it was more civilised than random violence. The Victorians, however, would have argued that it was a bloodthirsty and antiquated form of settling disputes.

FOOT BALL AT RUGBY.

A sketch of a football match at Rugby School, 1845. According to legend, rugby football
was invented when a student at the school picked up the ball during a game in 1823.
During the nineteenth century, English public schools helped turn football from a
dangerous mob sport into a respectable gentleman's game.

CHAPTER 9

SPORT AND THE DECLINE
OF CASUAL VIOLENCE

I

They preserve an interesting old custom at Ashbourne in Derby-shire. Every Shrove Tuesday and Ash Wednesday, between 2 and 10 p.m., two local teams compete in the Royal Shrovetide Football Match. The Up'Ards (drawn from those who live north of Ash-bourne's Henmore Brook) try to reach the goal at Sturston Mill, while the Down'Ards (who live south of Henmore Brook) aim for Clifton Mill, three miles away. The mills themselves were demol-ished many years ago, but millstones positioned near where they formerly stood serve as goals. The game starts in Shaw Croft, once a field just outside the centre of the town, now a car park, where the ball is thrown ('turned up') to the players after everybody present has sung 'Auld Lang Syne' and 'God Save the Queen'; and to score (or 'goal the ball' in local terminology) a player (who has usually been selected beforehand) has to hit the millstones three times, while standing in the brook (the ball – which is larger than a normal football – is filled with cork so that it can float on water). Otherwise there are very few rules. Both sides can field as many participants as they wish, who tend to come together in a series of 'hugs' – akin to giant rugby scrums – until the ball comes free and a hug runner is able to seize it and run with it. Players are not allowed to hide the ball in a bag or in their clothing, and certainly cannot convey it by any sort of motor vehicle. Nor are they encouraged to indulge in any form of unnecessary violence (murder and manslaughter are, of course, strongly frowned upon). Even so, on the days the game is played, shops are boarded up and wise car-owners park far away.

Back in 1860 when attempts were made to abolish the match, its defenders claimed that it dated back to AD 217 when locals who had driven the Romans out of Derby (if only temporarily) celebrated their victory with a football match. That was wishful thinking: in fact it is first recorded around 1667, and acquired the 'Royal' element of its title as late as 1928 when the Prince of Wales (soon to be Edward VIII) took part – and received a bloodied nose for his troubles. But the tradition on which it is founded is certainly old. 'Folk football' can be traced back as far as the twelfth century.[1] Generally played on Shrove Tuesday or at other festivals, it involved large numbers of players (between 500 and 1,000 a side at Derby, just down the road from Ashbourne), and was staged, or at least started, in town centres.[2]

It was part and parcel of the often boisterous celebrations that accompanied key points in the Christian calendar, such as Christmas, Shrovetide, Easter, Whitsun, Midsummer, Michaelmas and All Souls Day, and that gentry and commoners alike enjoyed. Whitsun, for example, was the occasion for 'Whit Ales', which can be traced back to the middle ages, and which, picturesquely, often involved maypoles and Whit kings and queens and dancing, and, less picturesquely, were also an excuse for heavy drinking, illicit sex, bare-knuckle fighting, bull or badger baiting, cockfighting and throwing at cocks (i.e. throwing sticks at a tethered cock, the winner being he or she who threw the stick which killed it) – and Morris dancing (then often a less than genteel activity). When Morris dancers from Ascott-under-Wychwood had finished performing at nearby Pudlicote House in Pudlicote in the 1860s, they were persuaded by the gentlemen present to box for money, the first man to draw blood being given two shillings and sixpence and the second two shillings. They earned fourteen shillings overall, and had as much beer as they could drink.

But even as the Pudlicote House Morris dancers staggered home, they must have seemed something of an anachronism. For by mid-Victorian times, attitudes to popular festivals and sports had changed significantly. Once wholeheartedly enjoyed by all, they were now actively opposed by a significant portion of the community. At Ashbourne, for example, locals who loved the game and allies who loved the folklore behind it found themselves facing opposition from those who regarded it as a brutal and redundant custom. Prosecutions under the 1835 Highways Act were brought against a number of players on the grounds that they were blocking the highway. In 1879 the police were called in to stop the game, and the following year they fought a pitched battle with locals.

Fortunately, in Ashbourne's case, the football aficionados had some useful allies. Derbyshire's Chief Constable, Captain Parry, who seems to have been a man of infinite common sense, helped ensure that the match was re-routed just far enough from the town centre to make it acceptable to local shopkeepers. Others invoked notions of natural justice, tradition and patriotism, waving Union Flags and chanting anti-slavery slogans when prosecutions were brought in 1860. One supporter, in a letter to a local newspaper in 1891, suggested that the game mobilised that same English spirit that had guaranteed victory at Waterloo. As the local song has it, 'It's a glorious game, deny it who can/that tries the pluck of an Englishman'. The Ashbourne tradition survived.

Elsewhere, though, local popular football matches were gradually suppressed. At Derby in 1845, the mayor accepted a petition to ban the game, and arranged for alternative entertainment to be provided; this had to be called off when a group of dissidents kicked a football through the town centre. The following year the forces of opposition notched things up a gear, swearing in several hundred local people as special constables, and bringing over two troops of dragoons from Nottingham, to ensure the match was suppressed.

Again the footballers resisted, overwhelming the police and specials and injuring the mayor with a brickbat (the man who threw it was arrested but then rescued by the mob). Eventually the Riot Act had to be read, at which point the crowd decamped with the ball beyond the borough boundaries, and proceeded to fight a series of battles with the police, specials and the dragoons during which the authorities desperately tried to gain possession of the ball. But 1846 nevertheless marked the end of the Derby football match. For the next three years as Shrove Tuesday approached (at Derby the local men played on Shrove Tuesday, the local boys on Ash Wednesday) the authorities nervously prepared for disorder, but none came. Those who had argued that what might have been acceptable in the Derby of the past was inappropriate in a modern town of 40,000 inhabitants, had won.[3]

It wasn't just popular football that got stamped on. The same happened with such traditional celebrations as Bonfire Night.[4] Parliamentary legislation passed in the immediate aftermath of the discovery of the Gunpowder Plot in 1605 had enacted that there should be an annual service of thanksgiving for divine deliverance in every parish church in England, and over the years the celebrations had become more elaborate and often more raucous, ordinary citizens and local gentry alike participating. But by the early nineteenth century the forces of opposition were starting to mass. Shopkeepers in town centres feared the damage that bonfires and tumultuous crowds might inflict. Others deplored the growing tendency to burn unpopular figures in effigy – the Bishop of Exeter, an opponent of parliamentary reform, went up in flames in 1831, and a police spy at Bethnal Green was similarly treated two years later. (These burnings in effigy often assumed aspects of the charivari: the Bethnal Green police spy's effigy, for example, was not just burned but beaten, and a song especially written for the occasion was sung as it was taken in procession to the bonfire.)

By the mid-century mark, local authorities were regularly stepping in to suppress the occasion, though they often faced stiff opposition. In Brighton in 1834 the High Constable who tried to stop the traditional celebrations had the windows of the hotel he was staying in beaten in by bludgeon-wielding men who informed him that one of his predecessors had been happy to join in the fun – and had also given them money for drink. In Exeter, despite a ban, crowds gathered to celebrate Bonfire Night in the Cathedral Close in 1867 and again in 1879, and had to be cleared out at bayonet point by troops called upon by the civil authority. In 1852 in Guildford, where the 'Guildford Guys' took over the streets on Bonfire Night, a clergyman who dared to complain to the local authorities had fifty yards of palings taken from outside his house for the bonfire and the servant who was guarding his house was threatened with murder.

It took the arrival of a determined new mayor in 1863, backed by members of the country police, 150 special constables, 150 infantry, 50 dragoons and two companies of rifle volunteers (the Victorian equivalent of the territorial army), to stop disturbances on that year's Bonfire Night – and even then, two days after the troops finally left on 19 November, the Guys emerged to beat up a policeman, besiege the police station, attack the homes of those they knew to be hostile to their celebrations and wreck the front of the mayor's house. There were further incidents in 1865. In 1867 a municipal fireworks display was inaugurated at Guildford to help channel enthusiasm for Bonfire Night in a more acceptable direction.

Chelmsford's fight with 'Guys' lasted even longer. After local gentry and militia officers, who had previously patronised the celebrations, withdrew their support around 1860 and declared they were no longer prepared to provide wood, fireworks and a site away from the town centre for the bonfire and attendant celebrations, the mob took over, and for the next thirty years or so the Fifth was marked by the theft of anything that could be burned, drunkenness in the town centre, violence, and burnings in effigy. In 1866 the authorities had to call in the dragoons. It wasn't until 1888 that a new-style celebration was successfully launched, involving a grand torch-lit procession, civic bonfire and town carnival on

9 November – four days after, and so well away from, the traditional date. At the end of the proceedings the mayor asked the crowds to disperse quickly to prove that 'Chelmsford is orderly to the backbone'. It now was.

Various allied forces had come together to achieve this. In the countryside, the drive for more efficient, increasingly mechanised agriculture went hand in hand with a demand for a more orderly and disciplined workforce. Thus, whereas some Oxfordshire villages at the turn of the nineteenth century regarded Whitsun as a thirteen-day bacchanalia, by the mid-century it had become a far more restricted and restrained affair, and in the 1870s the thirteen days of excess were replaced by a one-day bank holiday. In other counties Whitsun celebrations, along with other traditional local customs – Plough Monday celebrations in Derbyshire, or mumming plays in Northamptonshire – came under similar attack, the heavy drinking, the sometimes forceful soliciting of money, food and beer, and the general unruliness all now increasingly regarded as socially unacceptable. In towns and cities, too, commerce and industry were, by the mid-century, increasingly insisting on a more tightly regulated workforce, owners and managers forming part of a new middle class that was keen to stress its distance from those further down the social scale: sometimes dismissive and fearful of them, always anxious to emphasise its own hard-won respectability.

That doesn't mean that pro- and anti-traditional pastimes lobbies divided cleanly along class lines. Things are rarely as tidy as that. In Derby, for example, those who sought to abolish the old football match included, as one would expect, clergymen, lawyers and owners of silk- and lace-making establishments. But their numbers were swelled by working-class men, including local trades unionists, who disliked the game's lack of discipline. On the other side of the divide, defenders of the game included not just those who wanted to play it but those members of the local gentry and assorted members of the middle class who regarded the traditional football match as a symbol of the old, paternalistic set of relations that had formerly bound society together. But overall, the nay-sayers were winning the day. So while the gentry at Pudlicote House might have been happy to celebrate in the traditional, inclusive, rough way, by the mid century most of their peers preferred to provide villagers with more 'rational' leisure activities at Whitsun, supporting the friendly societies and benefit clubs which many of the rural workforce were now joining, rather than paying for drinks.

Religion, too, played its part. Non-conformists, largely drawn from the lower middle class and skilled working class, had always been opposed to the way in which Christian festivals had been sub-verted by popular custom. They also valued self-discipline and self-help: it's scarcely surprising that the Temperance Movement, which got underway in the 1830s, should have included amongst its champions so many Non-conformists. At the same time, the arrival of evangelical Anglicanism, championed from the 1840s by the newly appointed Bishop of Oxford Samuel Wilberforce, son of William Wilberforce of anti-slavery fame, gave the Church of England a new moral force and earnestness. Now rural clergymen were dissuaded from such traditional pursuits as fox-hunting. They were also encouraged to pay more attention to their parishioners' leisure activ-ities and ensure that they were suitably restrained.[5]

Consequently when preparations for Whitsun celebrations at Cranfield in 1875 were being put in place by a local friendly society, the plans for the day were very different indeed from what might have been expected thirty or forty years earlier. Those involved now resolved

> That a feast shall be held on Whit Tuesday in every year, when the Society shall meet together by nine o'clock in the forenoon, on the feast day, to go to church in a decent manner, walking two and two and returning in the same order, and if any mem-ber neglects going to church he shall pay sixpence to the funds of the Society. Every member shall, on feast day, pay down three shillings and sixpence towards providing the feast . . . The feast

to close the same night at 9.30 o'clock, and no part of the expenses to come out of the funds.

II

Perhaps the best way to trace and to understand this seismic shift in attitudes is to look at the transformation that took place in the nineteenth century in that bastion of the middle and upper classes, the public school, and in that key attribute of Victorian public-school life, organised sport.

At the turn of the century, it has to be said, most public schools were pretty brutal institutions.[6] Because teachers were regarded as socially inferior to their pupils, discipline was hard to maintain, and those who did seek to uphold it often appear to have had a worryingly sadistic streak: the headmaster of Eton, John Keate, for example, flogged eighty boys a day in 1832. More often than not, control was delegated to senior boys, which was not only hardly the best way to run a school but also served to encourage the bullying of their juniors. Disorder was rife. Even full-scale riots are recorded, the last great public-school rebellion coming as late as 1851 at the recently established Marlborough College. It was precipitated by a fairly minor incident: a school porter, thought to be over-zealous in reporting misdemeanours, had stones thrown at him. When the headmaster, Reverend Matthew Wilkinson, heard about this, he sought first to identify the stone-throwers and, when this proved impossible, elected to punish the whole upper school. Demonstrations against the headmaster and his staff followed. Desks were broken up. Fireworks were thrown. Eventually 77 boys, most of them aged about thirteen, were hauled up before Wilkinson, who flogged or reprimanded 40 and expelled 5.

It's scarcely surprising that learning does not always seem to have been at much of a premium (the wealthier boys did not in any case need qualifications), nor that many were left pretty much to their own devices. Harrow's historian, describing the school as it was in Lord Byron's day, gives the following pen portrait:

> In such a crowded and relaxed school, with unbridled physicality and naked boys sharing beds, it is extremely unlikely that there was no homosexuality, but the evidence is meagre and often ambiguous . . . Equally, opportunities for relations with the opposite sex, especially servants, were much greater, in term and during the holidays, than in later more rigid and morally tense times. As Palmerston noticed, swearing was rife, as was alcohol. One memory of Byron is of his singing rowdy choruses at one of the Hill's outlets for liquor, Mother Barnard's. In short, Harrow prepared its pupils in almost every respect for their adult futures.

Local tradespeople did quite well out of the school, but in return had to accept snobbery, bad manners, occasional theft and assault. Poaching was not unknown either.[7]

This anarchic culture extended to sport. Cricket apart, discipline and prowess in sport were little regarded in early-nineteenth-century public schools. Football was played, but it owed more to the old folk-football traditions than anything else, not least in that every school had its own rules. At Charterhouse, then located in an old Carthusian monastery, it was played in the cloisters, rendering long passes impossible. The main skill was dribbling, although the game might be punctuated by scrums of fifty or sixty boys when the ball got lodged behind a buttress, and when it was kicked free, younger boys – fags – from the opposing team would rush to knock over the boy who had possession. The whole game, in fact, was accompanied by wild scrimmaging and 'hacking' (the deliberate kicking of shins). Space to play football at Westminster was similarly limited, and boys would apparently do anything short of murder to get the ball from an opponent. At Harrow, football was played on a large, but badly drained, field, which encouraged a more mobile game, while at Winchester a pitch of eighty by twenty-five yards encouraged accurate kicking punctuated by scrimmaging. At Shrewsbury a dribbling game was played (the rules there were among the first to enshrine the offside rule). Rugby School also had its own rules, and its own forms of violence. Fags were put in relatively dangerous defensive positions, while hacking was made both effective and painful by the wearing of heavy boots, known as 'navvies'.[8]

In the 1820s and 1830s, though, things began to change. And that they did so was very much down to the influence of the man who once described public schools as 'the very seat and nurseries of vice'.[9] Thomas Arnold (1795–1842) was a reforming zealot motivated by a determination to turn the boys in his care into 'Christian men' (as he put it in a famous letter of 1828). During his time as headmaster of Rugby he was a tireless innovator: he improved the status and pay of masters, emphasised their pastoral role, reformed the prefect system, ruthlessly expelled pupils who were disruptive or broke school rules, and widened the curriculum. His acolytes spread his message across the country, and over the next few decades as the middle-class appetite for education boomed, so did public schools, their numbers expanding from just 9 long-established foundations in 1860 to anywhere between 64 and 104 (depending on how a public school is defined) in 1902.

We get a very good sense of the zeal of Arnold's proselytism from perhaps the most famous of all school stories, *Tom Brown's School Days*. Its author, Thomas Hughes (1822–96), had been at Rugby during Arnold's time, before going on to become a barrister, county court judge and MP, and a Christian Socialist active in promoting working men's organisations and the emerging trades union movement.[10] And he had no doubts about the transforming power of Rugby's reforming headmaster and his ability to instil awe and admiration. He describes, for example, how Tom, sitting in chapel, observes 'the tall gallant form, the kindling eye, the voice, now soft as the low notes of a flute, now clear and stirring as the call of the light infantry bugle, of him who stood there Sunday after Sunday, witnessing and pleading for his Lord, the King of righteousness and love and glory, with whose spirit he was filled, and in whose power he spoke'; and, thinking back to his own time at Rugby, he recalls how 'we listened, as all boys in their better moods will listen (ay, and men too for the matter of that), to a man whom we felt to be, with all his heart and soul and strength, striving against whatever was mean and unmanly and unrighteous in our little world.'[11]

Hughes's initial impetus to write the book may simply have been to give his son an impression of public-school life. However, its moral message clearly struck a chord with Victorian readers and it proved both influential and massively popular, giving rise to a whole genre of public-school novels that would later include Rudyard Kipling's *Stalky & Co.* (1899) and H. A. Vachell's now largely forgotten *The Hill* (1905), and such magazines as *Boy's Own Paper* (first published in 1879) and – in the twentieth century – the *Gem* and *Magnet* (the latter featuring Billy Bunter stories), all of which proved hugely popular with children who themselves had no direct experience of public schools. Charles Kingsley, the reform-minded clergyman now principally remembered for his children's book *The Water Babies*, wrote to Hughes to tell him that he had come across a group of soldiers reading the book, and that one of them, 'some very fast fellow', had declared, 'If I had such a book in my childhood, I should have been a better man now!'

As Hughes himself acknowledged, the transformation Arnold wrought was not total (he describes Rugby as 'a very rough, not to say brutal place when I went there'). Bullying, in particular, remained an entrenched fact of everyday life, not least because the 'fagging' system that public schools adopted allowed senior boys to exploit juniors, and because prefects were permitted to inflict corporal punishment. Thus in *Tom Brown's School Days* the sadistic Flashman is free to pick on Tom at will. Shortly after Tom arrives at Rugby, he is tossed in a blanket until he hits the ceiling. On another occasion he is roasted over a fire until he faints. Significantly, when Flashman does finally receive his comeuppance it is not for bullying, but for getting drunk at a local pub. A contemporary reader picked up on what appeared to him to be an avoidance of outright condemnation on Hughes's part:

> I blame myself for not having earlier suggested whether you could not, in another edition of *Tom Brown*, or another story, denounce more decidedly the evil of *bullying* schools. You have indeed done so, and in the best way, by making Flashman the bully the most contemptible character; but in the scene of the *tossing*, and similar passages, you hardly suggest that such things should be stopped – and do not suggest any means of putting an end to them. This subject has been on my mind for years. It fills me with grief and misery to think what weak and nervous children go through at school – how their health and character for life are destroyed by rough and brutal treatment.

The correspondent went on to criticise what was clearly a deep-rooted contemporary belief that the cure for timidity and nervousness might be a bit of rough treatment. Nervous horses, he pointed out, are not cured by harshness, and 'a man who would regulate his watch with a crowbar would be considered an ass'. [12]

If bullying was not ended by Arnold's reforms, neither was violence on the part of teachers. Long after his time, masters continued to hand out corporal punishment with little in the way of checks on excess. Arnold himself is known to have beaten pupils on occasion, once so severely that the story made the newspapers.[13] In the 1880s M. C. Kemp, a sports-mad teacher at Harrow who had a reputation for eccentricity, encouraged his pet spaniel to bite boys who were unruly in class.[14] And in 1860, in what became something of a cause célèbre, Thomas Hopley, who ran a private school at Eastbourne and who enjoyed a reputation as a humanitarian and an enlightened educational theorist, actually beat one of his pupils to death.

Reginald Cancellor, aged thirteen or fourteen (some sources suggest fifteen) and suffering from hydrocephalus, had struggled to do some arithmetic, and Hopley had punished him by beating him for two hours with a stick and a skipping rope. He had then carried the boy up to bed, and wiped his blood from the staircase. Next morning, Cancellor was found to have died (Hopley claimed that he had still been alive when he was put to bed, and must have succumbed to a heart attack). When the case came to court, the teacher's defence was that Reginald had been a difficult pupil, and that his father had given Hopley written permission to beat him. This spared him from a murder charge (the judge's view was that parents and schoolmasters were allowed to use 'reasonable and moderate' chastisement), though he was sentenced to four years in prison for manslaughter.[15] His lack of repentance in court, however, and his publication of a series of self-justifying pamphlets, guaranteed him a flood of hate mail.

Nevertheless, though bullying and beating stubbornly remained part of the public-school ethos, the worst excesses of the pre-Arnold era were certainly toned down. The authors of *The Report of the Public Schools Commission* (frequently called the Clarendon Commission) noted in 1864 that the level of flogging in schools had declined, that relations between masters and pupils had become friendlier, and that religious and moral instruction had increased.

In few areas of school life was this general improvement more apparent than in the sports arena. As mentioned earlier, sport in the early-nineteenth-century public school had quite a lot in common with medieval football: it was often little more than a free-for-all. But by the time Hughes's Tom Brown reached school, things had started to change: Tom begins his time at Rugby by being introduced to the intricacies of rugby football (first played just a few years before)[16] and ends by captaining the cricket eleven through a very tricky match (though it's interesting to note that teachers are not much in evidence when Tom is playing either sport). And after Tom's time at school, not only did sport become ever-more rule-bound, it also came to be viewed as a valuable, if not essential, element of the curriculum.

Obviously, there was a strongly pragmatic aspect to this: games kept boys fit, and also helped keep them out of mischief, or at least occupied much of their time when they weren't either in class or in bed. But there was also a view, increasingly widely held, that sport built character. The correspondent who complained that Hughes did not take a sufficiently tough line with bullying in *Tom Brown's School Days*, suggested that a timid boy could not be transformed through persecution but he 'can be made bold by *healthy exercise and games* and *sports*'.[17] Others argued that sport instilled moral values – of self-control, of loyalty to team, house and school – the very values, in fact, that Tom, now captain of Rugby's cricket eleven, discusses with a teacher, towards the end of the novel:

> 'The discipline and reliance on one another which it teaches is so valuable, think,' went on the Master, 'it ought to be such an unselfish game. It merges the individual in the eleven; he doesn't play that he may win, but that his side may.'
>
> 'That's very true,' said Tom, 'and that's why football and cricket, now one comes to think of it, are such much better games than fives or hare-and-hounds, or any others where the object is to come in first or win for oneself, and not that one's side may win.'[18]

In his reforms at Rugby, Arnold had cultivated an ethos of Christian 'manliness'. As sport became ever-more important to the public-school timetable, that 'manliness' gradually joined with, and to a large extent was taken over by, a cult of athleticism. In the words of one historian, 'manliness' started to move 'from the chapel to the changing room'.[19] What emerged has often been described as 'muscular Christianity' – an attitude of mind that certainly had its roots in the Protestantism of Arnold's time but whose emphasis on sport, team participation, and a sense of fairness – 'playing the game' – gave it a secular spin.[20] It was muscular Christianity that provided Imperial Britain with its governing class – the former public schoolboys who went out to govern India or South Africa or Singapore according to the principles that they had learned at Rugby or Eton or Harrow. It could be a pretty philistine affair: in the early years of the twentieth century the headmaster J. H. Simpson, formerly a house-master at Rugby, and by now running a non-fee-paying boarding school for poor boys, suggested that 'many people think of the public schools, if they think of them at all, as being primarily places where boys learn to play games'[21]; while the future Prime Minister of India, Jawaharlal Nehru, who attended Harrow between 1905 and 1907, bemoaned 'how dull most of the English boys were as they could talk about nothing but games' (he also said that another contemporary from the sub-continent enjoyed considerable popularity at school because he happened to be good at cricket).

A generation later a Harrow housemaster claimed that 'to many parents, a good bowling action wipes out any blots on their son's reports'.[22] Nevertheless, it became a powerful educational ideology, for boys, masters and parents alike, in the decades before the Great War. What had, a hundred years before, been an unruly, often very violent adjunct to the school curriculum, had become central to it, and in the process had acquired both rules and a set of social values.

III

This gradual transformation of sport from popular medieval rough and tumble to Victorian regulated and 'civilising' activity even extended to bare-knuckle fighting.[23] I've already described how from around the mid-eighteenth century disputes that had once been settled by free-for-all fist fights started to acquire rules of conduct not dissimilar to those of the upper-class duel. Foreign and domestic observers noted that, in Georgian London at least, two men seeking to resolve a dispute by fighting might well opt to repair to an open space, strip to the waist, and then fight according to a rough and ready set of rules in front of a crowd of passers-by, who might well comment adversely if they felt those rules were being broken. At around the same time, if not earlier, professional boxing started to emerge, its first major star being James Figg (1684–1734), from Thame in Oxfordshire, who won virtually every match he fought. After him came Jack Broughton (*c*.1703–1789), a Thames waterman whose boxing talents were first noticed when he floored another waterman following a disagreement. Broughton was a big man – five foot eleven inches tall and well built – whose success in the ring was followed by a stint as a boxing entrepreneur. He also opened a boxing academy, published the first set of rules giving guidance to boxers (1743), and was ultimately buried in Westminster Abbey.

The next generation was dominated by Jewish prize fighter Daniel Mendoza (1764–1836), who achieved celebrity after fighting his first significant match, at Barnet in 1787, before the Prince of Wales (the future George IV). And at the beginning of the following century there was Tom Cribb (1781–1848), from Gloucestershire, who fought his first public contest, a seventy-six-round affair that lasted for more than two hours, in 1805. In time he became a publican, but was allowed to retain his champion's title until his death.

What made these men's careers possible was the growing commercialisation of the sport. In the early 1700s, bare-knuckle fighters would have made their living from country fairs and such like. As the eighteenth century advanced, however, fights were increasingly staged in specially built arenas (normally called amphitheatres). James Figg opened one on Oxford Road (as London's Oxford Street was then known), where he hosted the first known international boxing match in which John Whitacre bested an Italian challenger, the 'Venetian Gondolier'; Jack Broughton also opened a very successful amphitheatre in the 1740s. There the upper classes would flock to watch, to support – and to bet heavily. Some even became patrons: the Duke of Cumberland, for example, was Jack Broughton's patron until Broughton unfortunately lost a bout against John Slack, and equally unfortunately lost the duke his £10,000 bet.

So popular was boxing with the upper classes indeed that they would invite its leading practitioners to fight or give sparring demonstrations (a popular entertainment by the late eighteenth century) in front of distinguished foreign visitors. Tom Cribb was hauled out of retirement for a demonstration match before the Tsar of Russia in 1814. He was also one of a number of prize-fighters who, attired as pages, were given the honour of guarding the entrance to Westminster Hall on George IV's coronation day. Over time, learning to box even became fashionable among those members of the nobility and gentry who had once simply been happy to be spectators. By the 1780s Broughton was charging his well-to-do patrons five shillings a lesson, or a pound if he was required to stand and spar with a pupil. The retired Daniel Mendoza not only ran his pub but opened an academy – he was reckoned by many to be the best boxing instructor of his day. By 1800 the journey from street fight to 'the noble art of self-defence' was complete.

In the process, boxing – like public-school sport later in the century – became an expression of something larger than itself, an expression almost of national identity. It was felt to be quintessentially British – an honest, sturdy way of settling grievances, very different from the underhand despicable practices resorted to by foreigners. A ballad of around 1800 saw Britain's ongoing war with France as a boxing match between 'that ancient British boxer John Bull' and 'the elf, Bonaparte' and his second, the devil. A couple of decades or so later, one of boxing's greatest fans, Pierce Egan, was even more explicit in his *Boxiana: or, Sketches of Ancient & Modern Pugilism* (1829) in contrasting honest John Bull with the dastardly foreigner:

> Never let Britons be ashamed of science – yes, A SCIENCE that not only adds generosity to their disposition – humanity to their conduct – but courage to their national character. A country where the stiletto is not known – where trifling quarrels do not produce assassination, and where revenge is not finished by murder. Boxing removes these dreadful calamities; a contest is soon decided, and scarcely ever the frame sustains any material injury . . . the manly art of boxing has infused that true heroic courage, blended with humanity, into the hearts of Britons,

which have made them so renowned, terrific, and triumphant, in all parts of the world.[24]

And just as boxing – like public-school sport – became an expression of national identity, so – like public-school sport – it acquired rules and regulations. Broughton, anxious that his well-heeled patrons should not sustain facial injuries, introduced 'mufflers' (a form of boxing gloves). His rules of 1743 survived for over a century, until they were supplanted by the London Prize Ring Rules of 1853. And then a few years later, in 1865, a new code was devised. Largely the work of sports organiser, journalist and lightweight boxing champion John Graham Chambers,[25] it codified such matters as the size of the boxing ring, the division of a match into three-minute rounds with a minute's rest between each round, the use of boxing gloves, the banning of wrestling and hugging, and the banning of seconds or other persons from the ring while fighting was in progress.

Chambers had started to codify the rules during a visit to the United States in 1866, in the company of the Duke of Manchester and the Marquess of Queensberry, when the three men had sought to promote a sport that, at the time, enjoyed a less than enviable reputation on the other side of the Atlantic. To lend a touch of aristocratic lustre to the new code, it was agreed that it should be known as the Queensberry Rules. There was more than a touch of irony here. John Sholto Douglas, 9th Marquess of Queensberry, may in his time have been a keen runner, cricketer and steeplechaser (in which latter pursuit he broke both his arms and legs, fractured his collarbone twice and suffered concussion on several occasions), but he was also a brute, or as his obituary in *The Times* described him, a member of 'a type of aristocracy which is less common in our time than it was a century ago – a type which is associated in the public mind with a life of idleness and indulgence' (the obituary did not mention that his death was almost certainly hastened by syphilis). Foul and abusive to his family, the nemesis of his son Alfred Douglas's lover Oscar Wilde, Queensberry seems an unlikely champion of controlled violence, but the fact remains that thanks to the rules that bear his name, the sort of bloody, seventy-six-round match that Tom Cribb had once had to fight was consigned to the past.

IV

Meanwhile, the football played in public schools was also gaining a rule book. Practical considerations were at stake here. It was all very well for each public school to have its own set of rules on a day-to-day basis, but problems swiftly arose when inter-school matches were arranged or when keen footballers went on to Oxford or Cambridge and wanted to play each other. As football teams began to emerge in the 1850s and early 1860s, championed by ex-public schoolboys and Oxbridge graduates, it rapidly became apparent that a proper formalisation of rules was needed.[26]

The lead was taken by J. C. Thring, who had been involved in early, and unsuccessful, attempts to devise generally applicable rules while at Cambridge in 1846. In 1862, now a master at Uppingham, he issued a set of rules for the school's footballers, which later that year were to be closely paralleled by the rules agreed for a game between eleven Etonians and eleven Harrovians at Cambridge. A year later nine Cambridge students, representing six of the major public schools, got together and drafted what became known as the Cambridge Rules. And just a few days later, on 26 October 1863, the Football Association was formed following a meeting at the Freemasons' Tavern at Lincoln Inn's Fields in London dominated by ex-public schoolboys from the London area and the South East. All, apart from those representing Blackheath, were devoted to the 'dribbling game', which duly became known as 'association football'. A national set of rules was established; pitches after 1863 started to be demarcated, with halfway lines, centre circles and penalty areas worked out. Blackheath were less than impressed and left the Association in December 1863.

The formation of rugby union in 1871, and the controversy that surrounded its early days, offers a useful reminder of what association football was leaving behind.[27] Like the games from which it was descended, it was astonishingly violent. Association football players favoured dribbling. Rugby players indulged in hacking, kicking opponents on their shins or trying to trip them up. Some even kicked players not in possession of the ball. By the 1870s, of course, there were many who looked askance at such a throwback to the old-style school football, not least the professional men who were coming into the game and who were not too keen to be injured. But there were also those who felt that hacking was absolutely essential to the game.

Matters came to a head in 1869 when a young man named Lomax was trampled underfoot during a 'severe scrimmage' and suffered injuries so grave that according to a contemporary *Times* report: 'If he survives (which is still doubtful), it is feared he will be a cripple for life.' A year later a correspondent, who signed his letter 'A Surgeon', wrote to *The Times* to say that over the previous few weeks he had had to treat a boy with a broken collarbone, another with severe groin injuries, one with a severely injured ankle, one with a severely injured knee, and two who had then had to go home on crutches – all injured during rugby matches. 'Football is a manly game', he wrote in a subsequent letter as the debate continued in *The Times* correspondence columns, 'and accidents will occur even when played fairly, but "hacking" forms no part of the game, and is to my mind a brutal and unnecessary addition.' Traditionalists were unconvinced, and were as one with F. W. Campbell of Blackheath who had earlier declared that the abolition of hacking would emasculate the game: 'if you do away with it you will do away with all the courage and pluck of the game, and I will be bound to bring over a lot of Frenchmen who will beat you with a week's practice'. Despite the appeal to such Francophobia, hacking was banned. Yet rugby remained a violent sport. Between 1891 and 1893 there were 71 deaths, 121 broken legs, 33 broken arms, 54 broken collarbones, and 158 other injuries – and that was just in Yorkshire. In the years immediately before the First World War at least one insurance company is known to have refused to insure players in the recently formed Rugby League.[28]

As for association football, it remained a public-school preserve for the first years of its existence, and indeed for a decade after the inauguration of an annual competition for a Football Association Cup in 1871. But the cup final of 1882 marked a watershed. Not only did the Old Etonians team find itself opposed by the decidedly non-public-school Blackburn Rovers, but that year also marked the last victory for an amateur team of former public schoolboys. The 1883 competition was won by another Blackburn team, Blackburn Olympic, and from then until 1915 (when professional football was suspended for the duration of the First World War), it was regularly won by teams from the North and the Midlands. Some of these upstart teams had an indirect public-school pedigree: a quarter of those in Birmingham and a slightly smaller proportion in Liverpool, for example, were set up by clergy who had been educated at public schools and wished to bring the game's ethos to their flocks (Aston Villa had its origins in Villa Cross Wesleyan Chapel; Everton began as a Sunday School team, as did Blackpool and such southern clubs as Swindon, Southampton and Fulham). Elsewhere, ex-pupils of local grammar schools, emulating their public-school equivalents, gave rise to teams including Leicester City, while former pupils of a state school, Droop Street School, London, formed the team from which Queen's Park Rangers was to arise. Picking up on the muscular Christianity ethos that organised sport was a force for good, employers encouraged the formation of factory and workplace teams that would keep their workers away from pubs and trades unionism. And workers themselves set up teams: it was railwaymen who were the founding fathers at Crewe Alexandra and Manchester United (at Stoke an interesting variation occurred when Charterhouse Old Boys, who were working in managerial capacities for the railways, formed a football club), while men employed at Singers cycle factory at Coventry formed the team that was to become

Coventry City. A few cricket clubs also got in on the act, keen to find a sport that could occupy their players during the winter months.

In the early days of the Football Association the overwhelming presence of ex-public schoolboys meant that the amateur player dominated. But soon the professional footballer started to make his presence felt. By 1910 6,800 were registered with the Football Association, the more talented of them picking up £4 a week during the season and £3 a week in the summer (good money by the standards of the time). Simultaneously crowds at football matches were growing. By the 1890s league matches were regularly attracting 40,000 spectators, while the 1897 Cup Final attracted more than 60,000. Football was on its way to becoming big business. The more successful clubs found themselves having to invest in grandstands and terraces. Some turned themselves into limited liability companies, complete with share offers.

And the reason for this boom was that Association football came just as the pattern of working-class life was changing – and it happened to suit this change perfectly. Played in two forty-five-minute halves with a fifteen-minute half-time break, it was just the right leisure activity for workers who, from the 1860s, were widely (though not universally) being allowed to take Saturday afternoons off. It could be played in winter, too. Moreover, it could be enjoyed on the only weekend day when commercial sport could take place without arousing the ire of the Church and strict Sabbatarians (it was, in any case, illegal to take entrance money for sporting events on a Sunday at this time). People were therefore free to attend matches at will, to experience that sense of identity that supporting a football team gives, to chat about matches at work and in the pub, and (at a time of rising literacy) to read about them in their local paper. The rise of cheap public transport – particularly trams – made match attendance easy even for those who lived some way away. So when Blackburn Rovers won the FA Cup in 1884 crowds of people gathered to cheer them as they processed through the streets of their home town, preceded by a band in a horse-drawn vehicle. The team were then given a civic reception.

Football had come full circle. It had started out as a working-class sport, and by the later Victorian era had returned to the working class. But it had been transformed in the process. In 1845 the respectable inhabitants of Derby petitioned the mayor to ban the 500 or so a side teams playing traditional football in the town. In 1908 41,467 people, most of them working class, were let in to St James' Park, Newcastle United's ground, to watch a football match between Newcastle United and Nottingham Forest. That such a vast crowd should have been allowed to gather, even in what was essentially a private space, would have been unthinkable a few decades earlier when the only mass entertainment likely to be permitted was a public execution.[29] Inevitably, crowd trouble was sometimes a problem, and what we would call football hooliganism not unknown (see pages 544–5), but by and large Victorian and Edwardian spectators were a peaceful lot. As one of the leading sports journals of the period, the *Athletic News*, commented in 1899: 'it is striking proof of the peacefulness of football crowds that, as a rule, half a dozen flat-footed Robertos [bobbies, i.e. policemen] serve to keep both the members and ticket-holders and the casual sixpenny gentlemen as well in order'.[30] Similar self-restraint operated on the pitch, too. In 1863 individual players had tended to hog the ball, and the emphasis was on constant attack. By and by, though, the emphasis shifted to teamwork and tactics, with what was to become a standard pattern emerging of five forwards attacking and six defenders nearer the goal. The crowds were now in the stands rather than on the pitch. As the historian Jim Walvin put it, 'Crudely stated, football had been rendered safe by the wider disciplines of industrial society.'[31]

V

Johan Huizinga's classic *Homo Ludens* of 1938 argues that play is the central component of culture.[32] That may be somewhat exaggerated, but it is certainly the case that sport holds up a mirror to society. And the way in which English sport developed in the pre-First World

War era tells us much about the 'civilising' of society that we have seen elsewhere. Activities that were aggressive by design – like fist- and sword-fighting – gradually became the rule-bound sports of boxing and fencing. Popular, rough pastimes like football became 'character-building' team activities. Participators and spectators alike, it could be argued, were able to channel their violent urges and achieve catharsis. In fact, it has been argued that the levels of violence a society is willing to accept in its pastimes and sports provides a rough guide to the levels of violence it finds more generally acceptable. Changes in the one therefore can be indicative of changes in the other.[33] Of course, even the most apparently innocuous of games can lead to violence: a pioneering study of medieval homicide tells of a case from 1254 in which William of Wenden quarrelled with a knight identified as Robert, son of Bernard, over a game of chess; one of Robert's servants attacked William when he saw that his master was in danger, and William killed him with a knife and fled.[34] Nevertheless the overall pattern of growing control and restraint is unmistakable. As the father of the idea of the 'civilising process', Norbert Elias, asked, 'What kind of societies are they, one may ask, where people in great numbers and almost world-wide enjoy, as actors or spectators, physical contests between individual people or teams of people, and the tensions, the excitement engendered by these contests under conditions where no blood flows, no serious harm is done to each other by the contestants.'[35]

TURPIN'S RIDE TO YORK.

An illustration from William Harrison Ainsworth's 1834 novel *Rookwood*, which popularised the story of the eighteenth-century highwayman Dick Turpin. Ainsworth's Turpin was a hero; the historical Turpin was a thug who was a member of a brutal criminal gang.

CHAPTER 10

VIOLENCE AND ORGANISED CRIME: HIGHWAYMEN AND SMUGGLERS

I

For many who appropriate things that are very definitely not their own, violence is at best an avoidable and at worst a necessary evil. The average burglar would presumably rather leave their victim's home unnoticed than have to confront the angry householder. But when it comes to organised crime, violence – whether implicit or actual – is almost always present. That most notorious and emblematic of twentieth-century English criminal gangs, the Krays, drew their power from a climate of fear punctuated by brutal punishment. Victims of their extortion rackets knew precisely what would happen to them if they failed to pay up. Their foot soldiers likewise knew that if they stepped out of line they might be beaten up or murdered; Jack 'The Hat' McVitie, for example, a relatively unimportant acquaintance of the gang, was stabbed to death for failing to carry out a contract killing. Paradoxically, that sanction of retribution also had a restraining effect: by shaping gang hierarchies and member status it also helped impose order and prevent internal anarchy. It was an operation founded on regulated intimidation, and it made the Krays very powerful.

Such relatively high levels of organisation that the Krays, or their near neighbours the Richardsons, displayed are hard to find among earlier criminal groups. I've already talked about some of the gangs of robbers who periodically sprang up in medieval records, but they seem to have been fairly loose confederations. In Elizabethan England, similarly, while evidence certainly exists of street gangs in London, their organisation and personnel appear to have been quite fluid – and also quite small-scale. A letter of 1585, for example, from William Fleetwood, Recorder of London, to Lord Burghley, Elizabeth I's chief minister, talks of the arrest of a former gentleman and merchant named Wotton, who had kept an alehouse that was then closed for 'some misdemeanour' committed there, and who subsequently 'reared up a new trade of life'. In what had once been his alehouse

> There was a school house set up to learn [i.e. teach] young boys to cut purses. There were hung up two devices, one was a pocket, the other was a purse. The pocket had in it certain counters and was hung about with hawk's bells, and over the top having a little sacring bell [traditionally, a small bell rung at the elevation of the Host and the chalice in a Roman Catholic Mass]; and he that could out a counter without any noise, was allowed to be a *Public Foyster* [pickpocket]; and he that could take a piece of silver out of the purse without any noise of the bells, he was adjudged a *Judicial Nipper* [cutpurse].[1]

This is scarcely criminal conspiracy on the scale of the Krays.

In fact, it was not until the eighteenth century that England could really boast its first criminal entrepreneur. Jonathan Wild (1683–1725), born and raised in Wolverhampton, was an honest tradesman, at least to start with. In around 1707, however, he left his wife, children and trade and moved to London, where he set about establishing a criminal empire.[2] His great claim was that he could trace stolen goods and so return them to their owners. His great secret was that he was able to do this because he had an intimate knowledge of, and a willingness to work with, London's professional thieves. Occasionally, he might turn a less than co-operative accomplice over to the authorities, not only to punish him and to warn others of what might happen to them if they stepped out of line, but to improve his own standing and public reputation.

There is little direct evidence that Wild or his associates used violence to discipline or intimidate those with whom he had dealings, but at the same time it's hard to believe that someone whose empire included protection rackets would have been able to operate successfully if the threat of retribution had not been there. He was eventually exposed and executed, and seems to have had no direct successors, or, at least, no successor who achieved a similar level of notoriety. That said, at the end of the century, Patrick Colquhoun, who would in time head the Thames River Police, estimated that there were fifty or sixty large-scale receivers of stolen goods in London in 1795, and that ten of these had the resources to fund the purchase of really valuable articles.

Jonathan Wild apart, such evidence as we have of gangs during the eighteenth century (mainly in the London area) suggests relatively low levels of criminal organisation.[3] There were certainly 'flash houses' – alehouses or similar establishments whose owners were willing or happy to entertain or lodge criminals and receivers of stolen goods, and who might also be linked with prostitution and other underworld activities. But the criminal gangs themselves tended to be loosely organised and impermanent, with a shifting membership and, in many cases, no determined hierarchy. Even the largest rarely exceeded fifteen or sixteen members; four or five was the usual number. If the occasion arose, of course, they might make use of their network of contacts, who might take on work for other gangs, too. But that no evidence survives to suggest that physical intimidation was regularly used to keep gang members in line seems to confirm just how loose their affiliations were: the loyalty through fear we find in later times does not seem to have existed.

In fact, what these eighteenth-century gangs actually tended to have in common was that they were frequently brought down by disloyalty, as a member turned king's evidence in the hopes of winning a pardon or a reward (in the absence of a professional police force, the authorities relied heavily on both to bring criminals to book). To try to forestall this, gang members or individual criminals often swore oaths of friendship or loyalty to each other – an oath sworn by a gang in 1780, for example, states that 'who ever should prosecute, or appear as evidence against any of the gang, should be marked for vengeance, and these rules every member binds himself by the most infernal oaths to observe, and never to *peach* [i.e. impeach, turn King's evidence], but to die *mute'*.

How effective this was in practice, however, is highly questionable. Ralph Wilson, a Yorkshireman who joined a gang of highwaymen in London to finance his gambling habit, swore an oath of silence, but when later arrested for robbing a mail coach he swiftly went back on his promise. His excuse (included in a self-justifying pamphlet that he later wrote) was that he had heard that one of his associates was planning to turn King's evidence, and had decided he had no option other than to secure a pardon by getting in first. He can scarcely have been untypical.

II

Perhaps the most infamous of eighteenth-century criminals were highwaymen. They also happen to be a group we know a fair amount about, since they were often the subject of contemporary pamphlets, and featured heavily in the popular compendia of criminal activities pioneered by Captain Alexander Smith's *The History of the Lives of the Most Noted Highway-Men, Foot-Pads, Housebreakers, Shop-Lifts, and Cheats of both Sexes* (1714). Smith's book, which itself owed much to the earlier traditions of rogue literature (fictionalised accounts of the doings of petty criminals and others), is for the most part a collection of unconnected stories, which tend to portray highwaymen as tricksters or pranksters rather than as career criminals (though most of them, he tells us, ended on the gallows). Indeed the focus on anecdotes and colourful incidents to be found in all such accounts can make it quite difficult to work out the precise details of how highwaymen operated and what networks, if any, they belonged to. Nevertheless, the wealth of such snippets allows us to arrive at a reasonably accurate picture of their activities.[4]

In the popular imagination, however, contemporary testimony has been displaced by an account that was written just at the time when better policing, better roads and the gradual replacement of traditional haunts by urban sprawl were seeing an end to the highwayman and his way of life. William Harrison Ainsworth's *Rookwood*, first published in 1834, is a sprawling, loosely plotted novel, combining what by then were rather unfashionable Gothic elements with the taste for the historical introduced and popularised by Sir Walter Scott.[5] He's largely forgotten today but Ainsworth was a major figure in his time, and in his fictional portrayal of the real-life Dick Turpin, who was executed in 1739 at York for horse-theft, he created the lasting image of the highwayman as folk hero: gallant and dashing, brave and devil-may-care. Ainsworth even goes so far as to compare his Turpin to Nelson; he is, we are told, 'the last of a race, which (we were almost about to say we regret) is now altogether extinct'; he and his like display 'the chivalrous spirit which animated successively the bosoms of so many knights of the road . . . that passionate love of enterprise, that high spirit of devotion to the fair sex'. Ainsworth's Turpin is the proud possessor of a noble horse called Black Bess. His exploits include a heroic ride from London to York and he is steadfast in his defence of the noble calling of the highwayman:

> Look at a highwayman mounted on his flying steed, with his pistols in his holsters, and his mask upon his face. What can be a more gallant sight? . . . England, sir, has every reason to be proud of her highwaymen. They are peculiar to her clime, and are as much before the brigand of Italy, or the contrabandist of Spain, or the cut-purse of France – as her sailors are, before all the rest of the world.

A handful of highwaymen were indeed the noble, brave people

Ainsworth portrays. Jack Ovet, hanged at Leicester in 1708, apparently fell in love with the young lady he robbed when he held up a stagecoach, and wrote her a flowery letter promising to mend his ways if she would marry him (she sent him a polite but firm refusal). A generation or so earlier, Claude Duval had established a similar reputation for gallantry. A young man from Normandy who had made the acquaintance of Royalist émigrés in Paris in the 1650s and had returned to England with them at the Restoration, Duval was portrayed after his death in 1670 as a silk-clad daredevil and ladies' man, who behaved impeccably while robbing women or their husbands. But in general, it has to be said, highwaymen were thugs.

A young confederate of the highway robber William Udall, named Thomas Raby, cut off a woman's finger to obtain the ring she refused to give him. A short time later, Udall is recorded as having robbed a young woman he came across in Fenchurch Street, taking her cloak, handkerchief and a purse with a few halfpence in it. Both men were hanged at Tyburn in 1739. Jack Blewitt was hanged at Hertford in 1713 for robbing a farmer's daughter and shooting her through the head. Tim Buckley, who had been pressed into the army in Flanders by a constable at St Giles in the Fields, deserted, returned to England, raped the constable's wife at pistol-point, and robbed her. Buckley was captured after a shoot-out with three gentlemen and two of their servants in which he discharged eight pistols and killed two of his adversaries. He was hanged for highway robbery in 1701. A year later the highwayman Tom Jones was executed at Launceston for robbing a farmer's wife whom he also raped.

Buckley's military career is not untypical of that of a number of highwaymen executed in the late seventeenth and eighteenth centuries. Richard Dudley followed a similar path. Scion of a Northamptonshire family whose loyalty to the Royalist cause in the Civil War had been their ruin, Dudley was rewarded by Charles II at the Restoration with a commission, became a captain in the army and was posted to Tangiers. Even by the military standards of the time, he seems to have been a violent man, on one occasion ordering his sergeant to knock a man down for standing out of line when on parade, and then seizing the sergeant's halberd from his hand and cleaving the skull of the unfortunate soldier in two. The man died instantly, but Dudley went unpunished; indeed the incident is recorded by the compiler of the *Complete Newgate Calendar* without comment. On his return to England he became a highwayman, notching up eighty indictments for robbery in Middlesex alone before he was executed at Tyburn.

The real Dick Turpin may not have had a military background, but he too displayed the savagery typical of his fellow criminals. Trained as a butcher in his native Essex, his first foray into crime seems to have been as a fence for a very well-organised gang of deer-thieves, headed by the Gregory brothers. When the local authorities managed to curb their deer-stealing activities, the gang, of which Turpin had now become a fully-fledged member, embarked on a series of house robberies, at first in Essex, then wider afield around London. Armed and masked, they would burst into their victims' houses, terrorise them into revealing the whereabouts of their money and jewellery, and beat them up if they failed to supply the relevant information quickly enough.

The climax of their brutality came with their attack on Earlsbury Farm in Edgware (then nothing more than a village) on the evening of 4 February 1735. The gang broke into the house and tied up the servants. They seized the owner, Joseph Lawrence, a man in his seventies, pulled his breeches down, and dragged him around the house by his nose and hair while demanding to know where his money and valuables were. At one point Turpin beat him across his bare buttocks with a pistol. Lawrence also had a kettle of hot water emptied over his head, and was tortured, still bare-buttocked, over a fire. While all this was going on a servant girl named Dorothy Street was taken upstairs by one of the Gregory brothers and raped at pistol point.[6]

Nothing could be further removed from the noble exploits of Ainsworth's highwayman than this sadistic affair. And the

Earlsbury Farm attack also reveals something else. We tend to think of highwaymen as lone wolves who were forced to take to the road for any of a whole range of more or less tragic reasons: perhaps they were down on their luck, or had perpetrated some error that forced them to flee from the society of law-abiding people. But Turpin's involvement with the Gregory Gang shows that – as in other areas of eighteenth-century crime – highwaymen were not necessarily loners, and that they frequently formed loose and temporary associations with others.

Irishman Patrick O'Bryan is a case in point. He served with the Coldstream Guards for some years, then turned petty fraudster, graduated to being a footpad and later became a highwayman, gathering a gang of confederates around him as he did so. His victims, according to the accounts we have of him, included the royal mistress Nell Gwyn. One by one his accomplices were arrested. Indeed his own career should have come to an end when he was hanged for highway robbery at Gloucester. However, when his body was handed over to his friends for burial he was found still to be breathing.

For some, such a miraculous escape from death might have served as a wake-up call. But O'Bryan was soon back to his bad old ways. A year later, he happened to come across the man who had betrayed him, shot him through the head and dismembered the corpse. Then, with a group of four associates, he broke in to a house near Trowbridge belonging to a Wiltshire gentleman named Lancelot Wilmot and proceeded first to tie up Wilmot, his wife and daughter and their three servants, and then to murder the couple and gang-rape their daughter before stabbing her to death. After that, they set the house on fire, left the servants to their fate in the flames, and escaped with goods and money estimated at £2,500. Even after this appalling crime O'Bryan might have evaded justice yet again, had it not been for the fact that one of his associates was later captured and convicted for an offence committed at Bedford and made a gallows confession that implicated the former guardsman. O'Bryan was arrested, tried at Salisbury assizes in April 1689, convicted and executed. His body was hanged in chains at the site of Wilmot's house.

The gang element to the highwayman's life seems to have increased his propensity for savage violence – one gets the impression that members egged each other on to acts of quite unnecessary cruelty. The brothers Isaac and Thomas Hallam, who robbed and killed a youth named William Wright, leaving his body in a post-chaise near Market Rasen in Lincolnshire, almost severed his head from his body in the attack. On another occasion they told a post boy whom they were robbing to blow his horn, and then, telling him he had sounded his own death knell, cut his throat and that of his horse. After their capture and conviction, they confessed to a further murder and sixty-three robberies. They were hanged in 1733.

Just occasionally, though, a highwayman would go beyond the bounds of what even his fellow criminals regarded as an acceptable level of violence. Jocelin Harwood, a young man with a good background, had been a highway robber for about two years when he heard that quantities of money and plate were to be found at the house of Sir Nehemiah Burroughs in Shropshire, and decided to burgle him. Harwood and two associates duly broke into the house and proceeded to tie up Burroughs, his wife and his servants. Harwood then went to the couple's daughters' chamber. There, one of the girls, begging to be treated civilly, pointed out that it was in the highwaymen's interest to treat her well as she would be able to identify them if they were ever arrested. It was a mistake. Harwood promptly drew his sword, killed the two girls and then went back and murdered their parents. After that he and his fellow robbers left the house. So horrified were his companions by what Harwood had done, however, that they then overpowered him, shot his horse, and left him tied up and with a piece of the plate they had stolen. He was soon found and arrested. At his trial he spat in the faces of the judge and jury. He was condemned to death and his corpse was hanged in chains. He was just twenty-three.

There was clearly a level of organisation within such criminal gangs, however rudimentary it might have been, and however easily it may have broken down. It would be interesting to know how Harwood learned about Burroughs's wealth. Was it a matter of common knowledge or did Harwood have some sort of inside information? We certainly know that some highwaymen prepared carefully before they carried out a crime. William Page rode around the outskirts of London in a two-horse trap, making a detailed map of the roads within a twenty-mile radius of the capital. Richard Ferguson ('Galloping Dick') had worked as a postilion, had a good knowledge of the gentry who employed such servants, and, indeed, could pass himself off as a gentleman. So when he became associated with a gang it was decided that he should gather information about the movements of gentry – for example, at what times post-chaises were being hired by them – so that they could be targeted as they travelled through London's outskirts. His inside knowledge gave him a unique role, and it seems fair to assume that other gangs made use of specialists, too.

Gangs also needed networks of contacts to provide them with accommodation, to hide them if necessary and to help them dispose of their hauls. The 'gentleman highwayman' James MacLaine (the name appears in several variant spellings) made the mistake of trying to pass on clothing seized from one of his victims to an honest dealer, who recognised the items as being stolen and alerted a constable. Others were far more careful. It's hard to imagine that William Davis, the 'Golden Farmer', hanged in 1689 at the age of sixty-four after shooting a butcher who tried to apprehend him, could have operated successfully as a highway robber for forty years had he not had intelligence networks, friendly alehouses where he could stay, and receivers for the watches he stole or the three rings he once wrested from the fingers of the Duchess of Albemarle. The autobiography of Ralph Wilson, the Yorkshireman who joined a gang of highwaymen in London when he needed to finance his gambling habit, confirms as much in his description of the flash house he used as a base and the members of the criminal underworld with whom he was in regular contact.[7] That was, however, about as far as organised crime went in the Georgian era.[8]

III

The criminal London underworld of William Harrison Ainsworth's time, just a handful of decades later, operated via a similar web of informal networks and small-scale gangs. And the most famous of these is, like Ainsworth's Dick Turpin, fictional. Charles Dickens's *Oliver Twist*, written in part as a polemic condemning the 1834 Poor Law Amendment Act, presents the reader with a London teeming with slums and rookeries, in the depths of which Fagin operates a gang of youngsters schooled in the arts of pickpocketing.[9] The key roles are clearly defined: Fagin is the mastermind, the Artful Dodger and his friends are the gang's foot soldiers (interestingly we get a sense of a distinction being made between adult and child criminals here – it's the period when, according to one historian, the notion of juvenile delinquency is invented).[10]

Nevertheless, the gang operates at a pretty low and traditional level. Fagin deals in stolen pocket handkerchiefs and small items of jewellery, and while he trains his young charges to steal, they are not sent out with specific assignments in mind. Fagin's associate Bill Sikes is a violent figure, but he's certainly no twentieth-century-style enforcer: indeed it is unclear what he actually does on most days. When he takes young Oliver out to burgle a house at Chertsey, we are looking at a type of criminal organisation redolent of that of the Gregory Gang a century earlier. We even have in the character of Noah Claypole that terror of eighteenth-century gangs – the insider who testifies against his former comrades in order to win a pardon.

Dickens's probable model for Fagin was Isaac ('Ikey') Solomon, a Jewish receiver of stolen goods who was eventually transported to Australia; and while Solomon's career was certainly more colourful than Fagin's, its essentials weren't very different.[11] Born near

Petticoat Lane in 1787, he was selling fruit in the streets at the age of eight, but then, to boost his earnings, began to pass counterfeit coin, got to know some of the thieves in his area, and by the time he was fourteen had graduated to picking pockets. From there he moved on to become a receiver of stolen goods, but, as with many London criminals of the time, this was not an immutable progression, and before long he was back thieving again. Caught and sentenced at the Old Bailey to transportation in 1807, he was held in a hulk at Chatham pending deportation to Australia, but was never actually sent. He was pardoned after spending six years in the hulk, possibly helped by an uncle who lived at Chatham, and for whom Solomon went to live and work as a salesman after his release.

Solomon earned £150 while working for his uncle, but was soon back at his old game: fencing small objects like jewellery or plate (he flirted briefly with the extremely risky trade of dealing in forged banknotes, which would have earned him the death sentence, but soon thought better of it). Former Bow Street Runner Henry Goddard later recorded in his memoirs a typical Solomon transaction. Two men posing as sweeps had stolen seven large candlesticks from the Travellers Club in London, two of which were subsequently discovered at Solomon's establishment in White Lion Street, in Seven Dials. Solomon was arrested, but was let off after turning King's evidence.[12]

His business subsequently grew so large that he acquired a second house, in Islington, where he kept stolen goods and also lodged a newly acquired mistress. Eventually arrested again for receiving stolen goods, he managed to escape from custody and disappeared to New York, leaving his wife to help keep the London business going. Unfortunately, she was arrested (according to Solomon she was set up by his rivals), and was then convicted and sent to Van Diemen's Land (today's Tasmania) for fourteen years. Solomon decided to go and join her, and set up shop in Hobart, only to be identified, arrested, sent back to England, and – rather bizarrely given where he'd just been sent back from – sentenced to seven years' transportation in 1831. His petition to be sent to Hobart, where his son was managing the shop he had established, was accepted, and Solomon was to become an overseer of convicts on the basis of his good behaviour. He was declared a free man in 1844, and died in 1850. Throughout his criminal career he relied on good contacts and an efficient network for disposing of stolen goods. The report in the *Newgate Calendar* that at one point he had goods worth £20,000 in his possession is almost certainly an exaggeration, but there is no doubting his business acumen. There is also little evidence that he employed violence. He was a crook with contacts, not a Moriarty-style master criminal.

In 1815, when the young Solomon was embarking on his career in crime, the authorities in London compiled 'A List of Houses of Resort for Thieves of every Description', which now sits among the Home Office papers in the National Archives.[13] It describes sixty-seven 'flash houses' scattered across the capital, and, when fleshed out with other contemporary documents, gives us a very good idea of the mechanics of the London underworld in the Regency period. As mentioned before, flash houses generally offered drink, accommodation, rooms for gambling, and, in some cases, a 'close room' for 'night gambling and debauchery'. They averaged fifty to seventy regular patrons, and there seems to have been a certain hierarchy to them, ranging from those that attracted established and experienced criminals to those frequented by petty thieves. Many regular visitors were no more than children – often under thirteen and as young as eight – and many of the girls among them were clearly destined for a life of prostitution. The landlords of these flash houses would take a share of their clients' proceeds in return for the hospitality on offer. They also dealt in stolen goods, advanced credit on the security of goods yet to be stolen, and connived at the robbery of unfortunate members of the public who made the mistake of entering the premises by chance or were lured there by one of their female patrons.

In many ways these flash houses were not dissimilar from their

Georgian predecessors – useful refuges that offered the basics and didn't ask any awkward questions. There were some signs, though, that they were beginning to change. In many early houses of ill-repute, the criminal element was an adjunct. By the 1810s, though, some were being patronised by criminals so brutal as to make them unsafe for anyone else: their whole purpose was a criminal one. And in some, the police had become something of a fixture, accepting drinks on the house – often so many that they became dead drunk and thus oblivious to the criminal activities that were being resumed around them – and gambling with other patrons. Many were quite happy to accept bribes, too – perhaps a bottle of spirits or a silk hand-kerchief to persuade them to forget to pursue a particular line of enquiry. A corrupt, or at least compliant, police force – so essential to the development and survival of sophisticated criminal gangs – was emerging. It's not clear, though, how much violent intimidation went on in these flash houses. We do know that at one in Clerkenwell in the 1810s a sailor was robbed and murdered and his body thrown through a 'convenient aperture' in the wall into the River Fleet, and, of course, many of the crimes planned in such establishments were by their very nature violent affairs.

A couple of generations after the list was compiled, and a gener-ation after Solomon was transported, the criminal underbelly of London was revisited by the writer and journalist Henry Mayhew (1812–87). His *London Labour and the London Poor*, first published in 1851 and based on extensive interviews, was the forerunner of the massive social surveys that were to come later in Victoria's reign, and provides us with an astonishingly vivid picture of mid-Victorian destitution and criminality. But it is essentially the small-scale crim-inality that had characterised the London poor for at least two centuries. There is little evidence of organised crime in Mayhew's account, nor of gang violence or coercion. Perhaps Mayhew's inform-ants came from a different stratum of the criminal class. Certainly, while he refers to 'opulent Jews of Hounsditch and its vicinity, whose coffers are said to be overflowing with gold' when talking about receivers of stolen goods, the ones he actually describes in detail are decidedly not opulent: they trade in the miserable pickings of the petty thieves, handling cheap clothing, workmen's tools, and other items of small value. Some of the pawnbrokers Mayhew came across were definitely less than scrupulous; we know that some kept pots permanently on a fire so that they could melt down stolen silver-ware the moment it was brought in. But he does not seem to have had an entrée into the world of high crime, and the evidence suggests that that world was in any case still a relatively small one.[14]

Even prostitution seems to have been a fairly haphazard business in Mayhew's London.[15] Though estimates vary wildly, there were certainly a vast number of prostitutes around – anywhere between 5,000 and 220,000 in London at the mid-century point, and between 30,000 (the official police estimate) and 500,000 nationally (this at a time when the population of England and Wales was 18 million). (A little later in the century, in 1881, 5,942 women were tried for prostitution-related offences in London, 4,615 in Liverpool and 2,091 in Manchester. And we know that in the fifty years between 1837 and 1887 some 1,400 prostitutes or brothel keepers were living in York, a town with a population of only 50,000.) They covered the whole gamut from the full-time prostitute to the woman (often married) who desperately needed to find money quickly to deal with an immediate financial problem – and, of course, their very different levels of involvement in the trade helps to explain in part why estimates of their numbers differ so radically.

For their part brothels encompassed everything from upmarket establishments to small terraced houses where a middle-aged woman, possibly an ex-prostitute, might rent out two or three rooms to working girls. But for the most part we are talking about street prostitutes. Few had pimps (or 'bullies' as they were known), and while some might inhabit the upper-class brothel of the popular imagination, most ended up taking their clients to cheap rooms in cheap lodging houses.

Although pimps seem to have been comparatively rare, many

prostitutes worked in an atmosphere of coercion. Typical of the sort of lives they led was that of the young prostitute of about twenty-three whom Mayhew persuaded (after a glass or two of wine) to speak to him in a respectable-looking brothel off Langham Place. She told him how she had met a woman (presumably the brothel owner or an associate) in the street, and, having chatted to her, accepted an invitation to go home and have tea. She was then taken to what Mayhew described as a 'branch establishment' of the brothel south of the Thames where she was 'conquered and her spirit broken': she was plied with alcohol, and made to sign papers which, she believed, gave the brothel owner great power over her. After that, 'they clothed her and fed her well, and gradually inured her to that sort of life.'[16] However, that was not an end to the constraints they placed on her:

Her life was a life of perfect slavery; she was seldom if ever allowed to go out, and then not without being watched. Why was this? Because she would 'cut it' if she got a chance, they knew that very well and took very good care she shouldn't have much opportunity. Their house was rather popular, and they had lots of visitors; she had some particular friends who always came to see her. They paid her well, but she hardly got any of the money. What was the point? She couldn't go out and spend it.

One senses an undercurrent of suppressed violence here, though there is little evidence of brothel owners (who tended, in any case, to be women) attacking or beating those who worked for them. Overt violence came from clients who abused the prostitutes or, more often, it seems, prostitutes and their associates who robbed their clients.

This is where the 'bully' seems to have come into his own. Mayhew, in the course of his discussion of bullies, writes that if a well-dressed man went into an 'immoral house' in the East End, he would certainly be robbed, though he adds reassuringly 'but not maltreated to any greater extent than was absolutely necessary to obtain his money, and other valuables he might chance to have about him'.[17] That seems to have been about the level of complexity that Victorian prostitution reached. Of course, it's always possible that there were criminal organisations that operated in a more sophisticated way, but if so they certainly evaded the attention of the contemporary forces of order and guardians of public morality, whose main focus of attention was, in any case, the poor, street-walking prostitutes who fell within the provisions of the notorious Contagious Diseases Acts 1864–9 (a series of acts that enabled close policing and medical supervision of prostitutes to protect the armed forces in particular and the male sex in general from venereal disease). So while prostitution may have been widely prevalent, it operated at the level of petty crime.

IV

Our fullest picture of a fully-fledged London gang in the pre-First World War era comes from the memoirs of Arthur Harding,[18] who was born in the East End in 1886 and lived in the area formerly known as the 'Old Nichol' (immortalised in a book by Arthur Morrison as 'The Jago').[19] He was a bright child, but left school early and drifted through various manual jobs before turning to his crime: he and his friends had taken to socialising at a coffee shop that was also used by local petty criminals, and gradually began to emulate and to assist them, notably in stealing goods off the back of carts (an activity which led to his first brush with the police). Harding then graduated to pickpocketing in the company of a gang of mainly Jewish boys, while also gaining a reputation as a hard man, or 'terror' in the jargon of the day.

He and a group of other youths who were good at and enjoyed fighting gradually gained a local reputation, the focus of their criminal attention being Jewish 'spielers' – illegal gambling houses – from which they extorted money. Soon, however, they came into conflict with another gang headed by a swarthy Jewish man known as Darky the Coon, and in 1911 a dispute over prostitutes descended first into an assault by Darky on one of Harding's associates, Tommy Taylor, and then a fully-fledged fight in a Bishopsgate pub, the Blue Coat Boy, conducted with fists and broken glasses, and (on the part of Taylor) a knife. Harding's gang were arrested and tried, and Harding, who had previous convictions to his name, was sentenced to twenty-one months in Wormwood Scrubs for possessing a firearm, and three years in Portland for causing a dangerous affray. He was, in fact, to spend most of the next decade in prison.

Harding's memoirs are dominated by violence. The 'terrors' hand out punishment to those who offend or cross them. 'Spielers' are raided or, along with turf accountants, forced to pay protection money. Policemen receive savage beatings, though they can also hand them out (Harding has much to say about police corruption). Harding's gang all carry revolvers; he himself is particularly fond of his Royal Ulster Constabulary revolver, which he bought for half a crown and which fires very heavy bullets. True, the guns are there more for show than for use, but they are part and parcel of the nakedly aggressive front the gang presents to outsiders. This regularly spills over into violence, not only in the course of everyday 'business' but whenever personal or group honour is threatened.

Harding's arrest in 1911 was a case in point. He actually had little respect for Tommy Taylor who, like Darky the Coon, lived off immoral earnings, but on balance felt that Taylor was 'one of our lot', and that was sufficient. When Harding was eventually released from prison, he met Darky by chance near Aldgate, and the two men went for a drink together. This was the sort of loose association to be expected among criminals of the time. Affiliations were often casual. Like-minded people might form gangs but membership was generally fluid. All the hallmarks of organised crime were there, but in London, at least, it was still embryonic.

As for Harding (whose real name was Tresalean), he ultimately married, went straight, bought a house in suburban Chingford, and finally died in Whipps Cross Hospital in August 1981.[20]

V

There was one type of underworld activity that did operate in a very tight-knit way, and ironically, perhaps, it involved a group who, like highwaymen, have acquired a strongly romantic veneer with the passage of time: smugglers.

Smuggling is one of those activities that goes back many centuries – it has presumably existed ever since governments decided that one way to raise money was to place duties on imported or exported goods. In Britain, though, it really took off over the course of the eighteenth century.[21] Constant warfare with other European countries (in particular, France) required vast levels of expenditure, which growing international trade promised to help pay for. Customs duties therefore climbed sky high.[22] Tea, for example, which was probably the most frequently smuggled commodity, cost on average five shillings a pound in the early eighteenth century when bought legitimately via the East India Company, but as little as sixpence a pound when bought illegally via Amsterdam. Smuggling of tea therefore became rife. An official inquiry by the Board of Customs in 1783 estimated that more than 20 million pounds of tea was being illicitly imported each year. This was borne out the following year, when, in order to undermine smuggling and re-establish the East India Company's monopoly, the duty on imported tea was slashed from 119 to 12.5 per cent and a huge rise of reported legal imports (from less than 5 million pounds to over 13 million) was reported. When war against Revolutionary France broke out in 1793, the duty went up again, and so did the quantity of smuggled tea.[23]

Smuggling on such an industrial scale – and it extended beyond tea to brandy, tobacco, wine, gin and other goods – clearly required the complicity of a great many people, and there is plenty of evidence to suggest that otherwise perfectly law-abiding folk were quite happy to buy from smugglers. People of taste and fashion happily drank contraband tea at polite tea parties in London; squires quaffed smuggled brandy after a day's hunting; ladies wore gowns made from contraband silk (Lady Holderness's closet contained 114 contraband silk gowns from Paris).[24] The highly respectable clergyman and diarist James Woodforde had no qualms about buying goods direct from his local smuggler.

At the same time, smuggling required high levels of organisation. When in October 1747 the smuggler John Diamond, leader of a group known as the Hawkhurst Gang, arranged a raid on the customs house at Poole in Dorset to 'liberate' between thirteen and fourteen hundredweight of illegal confiscated tea, he was able to call on the services of sixty men, all of them armed, all of them highly experienced. And it's clear that he had good contacts abroad, since the tea he seized back had been en route from Guernsey when it was intercepted by the authorities. We know from other accounts that often a hundred men or more would gather on beaches waiting for smuggling vessels to arrive. They would then load the contraband onto pack-horses for onward distribution to private individuals or dealers. Perhaps half of all smuggled goods ended up in London.

There was good money to be made. The agronomist Arthur Young, reflecting on the wages of rural workers in Sussex half a century after the Poole raid, calculated that a labourer helping load packhorses with smuggled goods and then conducting them away from the shoreline might earn ten shillings and sixpence a time – comfortably more than he might expect to earn in a week from regular employment.[25] Leaders of smuggling gangs were reputed to have amassed large fortunes. Precisely what sort of people they were remains a little obscure. Most seem to have been men of reasonable means, or at least possessed of sufficient capital to raise the investment required for their first foray into smuggling. Richard Perrin, a key member of the notorious Hawkhurst Gang, for example, was a carpenter by trade. He was doing well until a 'palsy' affected his right hand, at which point he decided to pursue a very different path.

The combination of high stakes and large gangs ensured often frightening levels of violence and intimidation. The aftermath of Diamond's raid at Poole demonstrates this graphically. At the time it seemed that the smugglers had got away with it. They successfully recovered the tea that had been confiscated from them and took it away. However, as some of them were passing through Fordingbridge in Hampshire, John Diamond happened to come across an old acquaintance, an elderly shoemaker called Daniel Chater, and foolishly gave him a bag of tea. Chater gossiped, the gossip spread, and within a few weeks had reached the ears of Mr Shearer, collector of customs at Southampton. He spoke to Chater and persuaded him to tell a justice of the peace what he knew. In February 1748, therefore, Chater, accompanied by a revenue officer named William Galley, set off to make an official deposition.

Unfortunately, en route the two men decided to stop at the White Hart pub at Rowlands Castle. It was run by a widow named Elizabeth Paine, who was a confederate of the local smugglers. Discovering that 'these two strangers had come to do the smugglers harm', she sent one of her sons to alert the gang. William Jackson and William Carter soon arrived, assaulted Chater and verbally abused Galley, and then, pretending to be remorseful, drank rum with them until the shoemaker and the revenue official were inebriated. As the two men slept, the smugglers searched them and found a letter that confirmed that Chater was to give evidence against Diamond. More smugglers arrived, and the decision was taken to kill the two men.

Jackson woke them up by raking their foreheads with his spurs and then using a horse whip on them. They were tied on to a horse and whipped as the party of men moved away from the inn, Jackson covering Chater and Galley with a pistol and threatening to blow their brains out if they made any noise. One of the group, Samuel Downer ('Little Sam'), then put his hand into Galley's breeches and squeezed his genitals so tightly that Galley fell off the horse. Thinking that he had broken his neck, the smugglers buried him. Later, when his corpse was unearthed, it was found that he had covered his face with his hands. He had clearly been buried alive.

Now, as the group stopped at another pub, Chater was led away to the house of the father of one of the gang, Richard Mills, and chained up, while the smugglers sent for reinforcements from among their associates. Soon fourteen men had gathered to discuss what should be done with their captive. While they did so they shouted at him and physically abused him. They cut him across the eyes with a knife, virtually blinding him, and sliced through the top of his nose. Richard Mills Junior suggested that they should rig up a gun with a string that all would hold, so that each smuggler would be implicated in shooting Chater and none would therefore be tempted to turn King's evidence. This was rejected on the grounds that it would put Chater out of his misery too quickly. Instead, he was whipped until he was bloody, hanged over a well with a rope, and then thrown in. Hearing him groan, the smugglers lugged over a couple of gateposts and some large stones and hurled them in. Chater fell silent. His horse had escaped earlier in the proceedings, but the gang killed Galley's horse, flayed it and cut it into pieces.[26]

The murders only came to light when an anonymous letter, revealing where Galley had been buried, was received by a justice of the peace. Chater's body was found a little later. A special assizes was called, and seven men were arrested and charged with the murders. All were found guilty. Richard Mills and his two sons, who were convicted as accessories, were sentenced to be hanged. The other four were sentenced to be hanged in chains. William Jackson, who had been in on the murderous assault from the start, was very ill during the trial and died before he could be executed. It was believed his demise had been hastened by the thought of the fate in store for him.

The raid on the customs house at Poole had a particularly bloody aftermath, but it was certainly not a unique event. At Gorleston in Norfolk a former Royal Navy man was beaten up in an alehouse where he had gone for a drink because he was suspected of being an informer. Henry Nursey, hiding in Beccles after giving information against fifteen smugglers, was pulled from his bed one night, whipped, put on a horse wearing only his shirt, and then kidnapped and taken to Flushing for three months, presumably to prevent him from giving any more away. Arthur Gray, a 'master smuggler', and his mistress were reported to have been full of glee when an informer was brought to their house to be beaten and tortured.[27] In 1746, a group of smugglers who had seized contraband wine from a local custom store rode through Lewes at noon, intimidating the locals with drawn pistols and blunderbusses.

A similar show of force was displayed by smugglers at Rye the following year: twenty-four of them rode through the town carrying contraband goods, stopping at one of the town's inns to drink, and firing their pistols to intimidate the locals. A young man called James Marshall showed too much interest in what they were up to; they seized him and he had still not been heard of again some time later when a report of the incident surfaced in the *Gentleman's Magazine*.[28] And a year after that, a party of smugglers at Wrangle in Norfolk, who had been refused lodgings by the landlady of an alehouse and who had witnessed one of their number being arrested there, fired through the windows, forced their way in, and then proceeded to wreck the place systematically, breaking chairs, tables and glasses and throwing them into the road outside, and letting the beer and ale run into the cellars. They also beat up the four or five people they held responsible for their colleague's arrest.

Smugglers knew that if they were caught and convicted, they might be transported to the colonies, fined so heavily that they spent the rest of their lives in gaol, pressed into service with the Royal Navy, or, in extreme cases, executed. The stakes were therefore very high; fighting to avoid capture and violence against informers were both inevitable. As early as 1662 a statute against smuggling described the risks faced by those who fought against it, commenting that customs officers were regularly

... hindered, affronted, abused, beaten and wounded to the hazard of their lives in the due execution of their several trusts and services in their respective places by armed companies and multitudes of men and goods prohibited and uncustomed have by force and violence . . . been forcibly carried and conveyed away.[29]

A House of Commons Committee on smuggling convened in 1733 concluded that smugglers 'not only in the country and remote parts of the kingdom, but in London itself', comprising gangs of forty or fifty people 'armed with swords, pistols and other weapons', were proving so powerful that neither revenue officers, nor justices of the peace, nor even the military could 'put a stop to these pernicious practices'.[30] And at times virtual guerrilla warfare broke out between smugglers and the authorities in counties such as Sussex.[31] The 'Gentleman in Chichester' to whom we owe the account of the deaths of Galley and Chater summed up the situation in the following words:

The smugglers had reigned a long time uncontrolled; the officers of the customs were too few to encounter them; they rode in troops to fetch their goods, and carried them off in triumph in daylight; nay, so audacious had they grown, that they were not afraid of the regular troops that were sent into the county to keep them in awe, of which we have several instances. If any of them happened to be taken, and the proof was ever so clear against him, no magistrate in the country durst commit him to gaol; if he did he was sure to have his house or his barns set on fire, or some other mischief done him, if he was so happy to escape with his life.[32]

Matters grew so bad in Goudhurst in the 1740s, where local smugglers had actually threatened to burn the town and kill its inhabitants, that a local militia had to be organised to combat them. Even then, it took a fire fight in April 1747 during which two of the smugglers were killed to bring things under control. In Wingham in the same year, the Hawkhurst Gang and smugglers from Folkestone, who had fallen out over a division of the spoils from their smuggling, fought a running battle through the streets.[33]

The forces of law and order were generally hopelessly outnumbered and outgunned. Revenue officers tended to work in pairs, and so were no match for gangs wielding carbines, pistols, cutlasses and horse whips loaded with weights. Thus while the two customs officers at Lydd in Kent noted 145 occasions between April 1743 and March 1744 when they knew smugglers to be active in their area, they could do little to intervene. Later in the eighteenth century it was not unknown for smugglers to have cannon mounted on shore, ready to give covering fire if needed as contraband was unloaded. At Prussia Cove in Cornwall smugglers installed a battery of cannon for this purpose at the time of the American War of Independence, under the pretence that it was for defence against foreign invasion.

Intercepting smugglers at sea was likewise problematic. The vessels operated by the smugglers were frequently larger than the Revenue cruisers sent against them, and carried more numerous crews and a heavier armament, usually including carriage guns (naval cannon) and swivel guns. Faced with a Revenue cutter, the smugglers' response was therefore usually to fight. A fairly typical incident took place in 1741 when a Revenue cruiser tried to take the *Jolly Boys*, an armed smuggling cutter with twenty-two men on board. The cutter's crew opened fire with swivel guns and small arms, severely wounding two of the Revenue cruiser's crew and disabling their ship. By the later eighteenth century smugglers were using boats of 200–300 tons displacement, which could carry around twenty carriage guns and a crew of perhaps a hundred. The commanders of these vessels were even willing to take on the Royal Navy ships that were sometimes sent against them.

Nor was calling in the army always helpful. Military commanders liked to use their units in a concentrated way, both to ensure internal discipline and to outmatch the numbers of smugglers they were likely to face. The civilian authorities, however, preferred to deploy small groups of soldiers, sometimes numbering no more than two or three, whom they would billet in alehouses in readiness. It was an approach that offered the twin advantages of flexibility and swiftness of response, but, of course, two or three soldiers against a mob were scarcely favourable odds, and billeting them in local inns offered all sorts of opportunities for bribery and corruption. In any case, the military never particularly liked giving assistance to the civil authorities, particularly if it involved opening fire on civilians. The smugglers had no such scruples. The list of customs officers intimidated or killed in the line of duty is a depressing one.

By the middle of the nineteenth century the old style of smuggling, based on gangs and violence, had largely passed away. With the Napoleonic Wars came the building of Martello towers and the placing of large garrisons of troops around the south-eastern coast, which, while intended to forestall invasion, had the indirect effect of discouraging illegal activity. In 1809 a Preventive Waterguard, which in 1822 was to become the Coastguard, was established – a more effective anti-smuggling force than anything that had gone before. And the year after Napoleon was defeated at Waterloo, Royal Navy sailors established a blockade along sections of the Kent and Sussex coast. But what finally put paid to smuggling was the adoption of free trade in the 1840s. As customs duties plummeted, so the incentive to smuggle simply vanished.

Not until Prohibition in 1920s America was another decision taken by government – in the US to ban alcohol; in eighteenth-century Britain, to raise excise duties – to have such unforeseen criminal consequences. In both cases, legislation not only led to law-breaking on a breathtaking scale, but also the rise in highly organised gangs. There is a certain irony in all this. As I suggest in Chapter 13, the capitalism that started to shape British life in the nineteenth century – and that underpinned American society in the

1920s – undoubtedly contributed to a general decline in violence. The raw capitalism that underpinned smuggling, however, and the huge profits at stake, led to organised crime at a level never before seen in Britain, and of a sophistication not matched for perhaps 150 years.

The Burning & Plundering of NEWGATE & Setting the Felons at Liberty by the Mob.

This engraving of 1780 depicts rioters setting fire to Newgate Prison during the Gordon Riots, the most destructive bout of disorder in the history of London. In Georgian England 'the mob' was notorious for the almost casual way in which it seemed to resort to rioting, but while disturbances may often have seemed like random outbursts of violence, rioters often had very clear aims and goals.

CHAPTER 11

THE GEORGIAN MOB

I

Between the sixteenth and nineteenth centuries English Roman Catholics were subject to constant discrimination. In Elizabeth I's reign, recusants – those who remained true to the Church of Rome – could be heavily fined. Roman Catholic priests faced the death penalty if caught, and the lay folk who either sheltered them or distributed papal propaganda could well pay for their actions with their lives. As time passed, the more draconian legislation against Catholics lapsed, but they remained barred from voting and from public office, their rights to own land and to inherit it were severely curtailed, and they were saddled with special taxes.

At a popular level, Roman Catholics became the bogeymen of English society. They were regarded as potential traitors, as the people who had martyred 300 victims during Mary Tudor's reign, and who had masterminded the Spanish Armada, the Gunpowder Plot, the Irish Rebellion of 1641, the (mainly imaginary) 'Popish Plot' of the 1670s, and the Jacobite risings of 1715 and 1745. Their superpower allies – first Spain, later France – were viewed as arbitrary and tyrannical regimes infused by popery whose values were diametrically opposed to those of freedom-loving, parliamentary, Protestant England.

In 1778, however, Parliament passed an Act to relieve George III's Roman Catholic subjects 'from certain penalties and disabilities': now, if called upon to swear the oath of allegiance to the king, they no longer also had to condemn the Roman Catholic Church, and certain restrictions on preaching, publishing and land ownership were removed. Given the generally anti-Catholic mood of the nation, it comes as no surprise to learn that this was a pragmatic rather than an enlightened move. For the previous two years Britain had been locked in a war with her American colonists, and it was going badly. The First Catholic Relief Act (known at the time as The Papist Act), it was hoped, would make it easier to recruit soldiers from the Scottish Highlands, home to many Catholics. It might also placate the Irish Catholics, tenants of Protestant landlords who could otherwise be tempted to emigrate to America, which was gaining the upper hand in the fight for independence and was likely to establish religious tolerance if it became a republic. The bill was introduced in the House of Commons by Sir George Savile, and supported in the Lords by Lord Rockingham, who owned land in Ireland. It was passed largely unopposed.

Trouble started when, as was constitutionally necessary, a separate bill was introduced in the Commons to extend the legislation to Scotland. Almost immediately, rioting broke out north of the border, particularly in Edinburgh where local Catholics had to seek shelter in Edinburgh Castle. At the same time a somewhat unlikely 'anti-popery' leader arose: Lord George Gordon (1751–1793), Scottish aristocrat and Member of Parliament for the English pocket borough of Ludgershall, member of a family of eccentrics (as teenagers, Lord George's mother and her sister were given to riding through central Edinburgh on a pig), a man with strong humanitarian impulses (his time with the Royal Navy had made him sympathetic to the plight of the common seaman), but also an individual viewed by one recent biographer as 'unbalanced, irresponsible and dangerous'.[1] Interestingly, Gordon had not voted against the First Catholic Relief Act. But he made the Scottish Bill a cause célèbre and helped whip up such opposition to it that it had to be abandoned.

With Protestantism in Scotland duly reinforced, popular opposition to the liberalisation of anti-Catholic legislation started to grow on the English side of the border, too. In 1779 a Protestant Association was established to work for the repeal of the Relief Act. A little later, in November, Gordon became its president. He threw himself into action, lobbying George III personally and making wild speeches in Parliament in which he claimed that armed men would be called out in Scotland and Ireland to oppose the Act. He also decried George III and his ruling ministry as popish and encouraged the Association to organise local petitions across the country. The London petition proved particularly successful, gaining some 44,000 signatures, and at a meeting of the Association on 29 May 1780 it was decided that it should be presented to Parliament. On Friday, 2 June 1780, therefore, Gordon entered the Commons, petition in hand. At the same time, a crowd of supporters, some 60,000 strong, which had gathered at St George's Fields in Southwark (a traditional place for mass demonstrations, now the site of Waterloo Station), marched on Westminster. Described in contemporary accounts as a mixture of respectable-looking tradesmen and honest Protestant householders, many of them sported blue cockades emblazoned with the words 'No Popery'.

Matters started to get out of hand almost straightaway. A number of peers, notably those identified as pro-Catholic, were attacked and roughed up. The Duke of Northumberland was pulled from his coach along with his secretary and beaten; when he arrived at the House of Lords he discovered that his pocket had been picked. Lord Mansfield, Lord Chief Justice, had the windows of his coach smashed and his wig torn from his head. Members of the Commons escaped more lightly, although Sir George Savile, who had introduced the Relief Act, had his coach broken up. Troops were eventually summoned and managed to disperse the crowd, though not without having to endure verbal and physical abuse – a detachment of foot guards in Union Street and St Margaret's Street had their hats knocked off and sticks poked into their buttocks. In Parliament, meanwhile, the petition was rejected by 192 to 6 votes.

A lull followed, but then around midnight trouble broke out again. A crowd of men carrying spades, pickaxes, hammers and crowbars, gathered outside a well-known Catholic place of worship, the Sardinian Ambassador's chapel, in Duke Street off Lincoln's Inn Fields, smashed its doors and windows, emptied it of furniture and other contents, burned these on a bonfire and consigned the building to the flames. The Bavarian Ambassador's chapel met the same fate. Rioters went largely unchallenged. Few justices of the peace were in evidence, and without their guiding hand troops were unwilling to take action. A rare exception was Samson Rainforth, the King's tallow chandler and a former constable who, assisted by a Mr Maberley, directed troops to arrest thirteen men he perceived to be trouble-makers. In revenge for this militarily assisted citizen's arrest, the mob were to destroy his house, and that of Mr Maberley, too, a couple of days later.[2]

Saturday, 3 June was a quiet day, the only large crowd reported being that which gathered to see the thirteen arrested men being conducted to Bow Street by soldiers. As on the Friday, the mob hurled verbal abuse, stones and general filth from the streets at the troops. It soon emerged that most of the men who had been apprehended were guilty merely of being bystanders (some of them were Catholics, one a Russian army officer). Most were therefore discharged.

By Saturday evening it must have seemed as though the unrest had run its course, but on Sunday, 4 June crowds gathered outside a Catholic chapel in Moorfields (the area was home to prosperous Catholic merchants and poor Irish immigrants; the latter were unpopular with other locals both for their religion and their willingness to work for low wages). The mob was persuaded to disperse, but reappeared the next day to pull down the chapel and several houses, including one belonging to a wealthy Irish silk merchant named James Malo. A desperate Malo attempted to enlist the help of the Lord Mayor of London, Brackley Kennett, but to no avail: throughout the riots Kennett was to prove more or less supine.

There then followed forty-eight hours of intense rioting in Moorfields, during which many houses were systematically wrecked.

By Tuesday the rioting was spreading. Simultaneously, the range of its targets was broadening. Catholic chapels and the residences of prominent Catholics continued to be attacked and destroyed (two chapels in Spitalfields were burned down), but the mob now also started to vent its fury on the homes of unpopular politicians. This was the day when the houses of Samson Rainforth and Mr Maberley were wrecked, while a military guard had to be stationed at the residences of Sir George Savile and the politician Edmund Burke (who was known to be an advocate of Catholic toleration). The Lord Mayor, though, remained frozen into inaction. When a young Coldstream Guards ensign named Gascoyne asked for instructions to deal with rioters who had rifled a house and were burning its furniture in the street, Kennett told the officer not to bother him and, pressed further, simply walked away. Gascoyne formed his detachment in a circle around the bonfire, only to have the rioters, undeterred, throw furniture over the troops' heads into the blaze. A justice of the peace, William Hyde, read the Riot Act to crowds trying to stop Members of Parliament entering Westminster. They responded by burning down his house that night. They also destroyed the home of Sir John Fielding, London's most notable magistrate.

The mob grew more ambitious. Descending on Newgate, London's oldest and largest prison, they first made what was more or less a formal request for its surrender, and then, when the prison's keeper refused, forced their way in and proceeded to gut the place: furniture was seized and thrown into the street; it was soon joined by doors, panelling and floorboards. By eight o'clock that evening Newgate was in flames, and its 300 or so prisoners had been released. Their enthusiasm for prison wrecking now well and truly aroused, the mob turned their attention to Bridewell and the nearby New Prison in Clerkenwell. For good measure, they also attacked the

Bloomsbury Square houses of Lord Chief Justice Mansfield and his neighbour the Archbishop of York, the former because he held the leading legal office in what was regarded by the rioters as a pro-Catholic government, the latter because he was a friend of the former and so deemed guilty by association.

Here a justice of the peace, Mr Burden, ordered troops under Lieutenant-colonel John Woodford (ironically Lord George Gordon's brother-in-law) to open fire on the rioters. The troops fired a single volley, most of them aiming over the heads of the crowd. Nevertheless four were killed and seven others wounded. Woodford then marched his men away, apparently with Justice Burden's blessing.

By Wednesday ('Black Wednesday' to the politician Horace Walpole) the level and extent of rioting had become such that there was a very real possibility that the authorities could lose control of the capital. Leading Catholics and politicians alike were fearful of what might happen to them. Prisons continued to be looted and emptied of their inmates. There were even rumours that the Bank of England would be attacked. It was this latter alarming prospect that finally goaded Kennett into taking something resembling action. He ordered troops to assemble around the Bank and position cannon in its courtyard, while Royal Navy sailors were instructed to bring thick ropes up from Deptford that could be tied across nearby streets to impede any attack. That evening further troops were drafted in from Holborn, where they had been guarding a large distillery belonging to a Catholic named Langdale, and the Bank was rendered secure, at least for the time being.

The unfortunate Langdale, however, found his distillery left to the tender mercies of the mob. True to form, they duly ran amok. They broke down doors, smashed windows, looted furniture and papers, and then piled everything together in a vast street bonfire. Some went in search of the secret Catholic chapel they were convinced was situated somewhere in the distillery. And then they set fire to the distillery itself, which exploded into flames as the gin stored there caught fire. Rivulets of gin and rum spread into the gutters of the surrounding streets. Hundreds of people risked their lives to rush into the cellars of the burning building in order to seize as much drink as they could. They even scooped it up from the floor, gulping it until they collapsed. By the time the militia arrived, at least twenty people had drunk themselves to death. Many more were overcome by flames and alcoholic fumes. So intense was the fire that it spread to over twenty neighbouring houses. There were also outbreaks of trouble on the fringes of the city and as far north as Highgate, and some rioting in Southwark and Bermondsey.

It was left to George III to wrest back control of the city from the mob. Calling together a meeting of his Privy Council, he demanded to know whether troops had to wait until an official such as a justice of the peace gave them explicit instructions, or whether they could fire on rioting mobs at their own discretion. The view of most of the councillors – soon to be supported by Attorney-General Alexander Wedderburn, later created 1st Earl of Rosslyn, who was late to the meeting – was that the military should be given their head. A Royal Proclamation was therefore issued, followed swiftly by a General Order from the Adjutant General's office to all army officers in London. At this point, there were probably 10,000 soldiers – regulars and militia – gathered in and around the capital. And now they acted decisively. They rapidly took control of the bridges over the Thames, effectively splitting the rioters apart from each other. At 4 a.m. when rioters, some of them armed with muskets, finally made a determined attack on the Bank of England, they were halted by a volley of shots from the soldiers, followed up by charges by detachments of the Horse Guards and light infantry. As the rioters retreated they were fired at by troops stationed along the way.

By the next morning, it was clear that order had at last been reimposed on the capital. But it had come at a high price. We will never know for sure just how many people perished during the Gordon Riots, but a recent estimate has suggested that 210 were killed by troops, and that 75 later died of their wounds (a further 173 are known to have been wounded by gunshot). If one adds to those the people who were crushed to death or died in burning buildings (one thinks, for example, of the incident at Langdale's distillery), a contemporary estimate of 700 doesn't seem unreasonable. Some 450 people were arrested during and after the disturbances, of whom 160 were tried for various offences – over 100 of them at the Old Bailey, about 50 by a special commission in Southwark, and 3 at the Surrey assizes at Guildford. Sixty-two were sentenced to death, of whom 25 were actually executed; 85 were acquitted; the others were imprisoned for between a month and five years.

According to the historian George Rudé, 22 of those tried were small-scale employers, shopkeepers, pedlars and independent crafts-men; 6 were sailors and 4 soldiers; 76 were wage-earners – journeymen and apprentices, waiters and domestic servants – while 20 were women. This rather gives the lie to the assumption made by later generations – notably by Charles Dickens in *Barnaby Rudge* – that the Gordon Rioters were no more than a gin-sodden, criminal mob of social dregs, out for mischief and plunder. In fact, although things clearly got badly out of control, their targets were quite precise – initially well-to-do Catholics for the most part, and then, as the riots developed, the well-to-do more generally.

One of the householders whose property was threatened during the disturbances in Bermondsey tried to turn away the mob by pointing out that he was Protestant. One of their number, however, a bargemaker, retorted that 'Protestant or not, no gentleman need be possessed of more than £1,000 a year; that is enough for any gentleman to live upon'. This, as Rudé put it, suggests that 'there lay a deeper social purpose: a groping desire to settle accounts with the rich, if only for a day, and to achieve some rough kind of social just-ice', an attitude that gave the disturbances 'a social complexion which its original promoters had not intended and with which they had little sympathy'.[3]

As for Lord George Gordon, he was tried for high treason in February 1781 but was acquitted, thanks largely to the brilliant defence mounted by his defence council, Thomas Erskine, then a young and relatively inexperienced barrister, later to become Lord Chancellor. It must have helped his case that none of the 44,000 people who had signed the Protestant Association's London petitions were among those tried for involvement in the rioting. Most people would probably then have chosen to fade into the background. Gordon, however, did not. True to his fiery and eccentric nature, he continued to champion causes close to his heart, and simultaneously to rub those in authority up the wrong way. Finally, in 1787 he was convicted both for attacking the administration of justice in a pamphlet and for libelling the French queen, Marie Antoinette, and was dispatched – with a degree of poetic justice – to a refurbished and repaired Newgate prison. In the meantime he had converted to Judaism, adopting the name Israel Abraham George Gordon, and embracing his new religion with the fervour he had once reserved for Protestantism. He also learned the bagpipes. He died – still in prison – in 1793.

II

To contemporary observers, the events of those few days in June 1780 were exceptional ('the history of the last week would fill you with amazement: it is without any modern example,' Dr Johnson wrote to his friend, Hester Thrale). They were not, however, unique. Outbreaks of civil unrest punctuated the eighteenth century; the 'mob' was a regular fixture. For the historian Max Beloff, writing in the 1930s, 'the London mob was always ready to swell at every disturbance, whether or not its own interests were being directly affected'. For the prolific historian of Georgian England J. H. Plumb, 'burning, looting and destruction by the mob was a commonplace of life'. In his view,

No nation rioted more easily or more savagely – from 1714 to 1830 angry mobs, burning and looting, were as prevalent as disease, and as frequent in the countryside as in the great towns . . . mobs and destruction, they were a part of life, and expressions of those sharp conflicts in society were what helped to foster the spirit of the nation.[4]

Almost anything, it seemed, could prompt the English mob to riot.[5] They rioted over the availability and price of food, above all of grain. They rioted against their employers. They rioted at elections. They rioted (as events in London in 1780 amply demonstrate) over religion. They rioted when Royal Navy press gangs entered their communities in search of recruits. They rioted at the introduction of tollgates and turnpikes, and destroyed them rather than paying to use the roads they controlled. They rioted in 1757 when the government attempted to rationalise recruitment into the militia. They rioted when a Bill was put forward to allow Jews to become naturalised citizens. They rioted in support of the radical politician John Wilkes. Male apprentices were frequently involved in rioting. Pinpointing precisely when discontent becomes a fully-fledged riot is tricky, but it would be fair to say that between 1790 and 1810 the nation witnessed some thousand popular disturbances.

It is not surprising, then, that one of the most famous (if most frequently misunderstood) of English statutes dealing with civil control should date from this period. Statute 1 George I, stat 2, cap 5 was passed in 1714, took effect from 1 August 1715 and remained in force until the early twentieth century. Its preamble describes it as 'An Act for Preventing Tumults and Riotous Assemblies, and for the more Speedy and Effectual Punishing the Rioters'. Its interpretation played a vital role in the ultimate course that the Gordon Riots took, and concerns about the best or most practical way to implement it shaped the way in which many riots unfolded well into the nineteenth century. The circumstances that led to the passing of the Riot Act were very particular ones, but they were also not untypical of many of the flashpoints for discontent that were to recur throughout the century.[6] The Glorious Revolution of 1688 had been a bloodless affair (though not in Ireland or, to a lesser extent, in Scotland), but it had left a country divided between the small minority who opposed the new regime outright and favoured a restoration of the Stuarts, those who were out and out supporters of the new King, William III, and those who, if not exactly opposed to the new regime in principle, resented its toleration of Protestant dissenters, and its support of the moneyed interest groups and the high taxes that helped finance William's wars against Louis XIV of France. Political, religious and economic discontents thus intermingled, creating factions and conflicting interest groups.

The death of Queen Anne in 1714 and arrival on the scene of her successor, George I, Elector of Hanover, brought these divisions to the fore and provoked one of the worst – if sporadic – bouts of civil disorder eighteenth-century provincial England was to experience. Although the Tory-dominated Parliament had unanimously supported the King's accession, George I from the outset favoured the Whigs, who had been such loyal supporters of William III and the Glorious Revolution and such outspoken enemies of the Stuarts. Tories and Tory-supporting High Churchmen soon found themselves eased from office. Whigs took their place. Party conflict had expressed itself along religious lines in the previous reign, notably in the attacks on London dissenting houses that had come in the wake of the impeachment for sedition of Dr Henry Sacheverell, a Tory and high-church clergyman who had preached a sermon on 5 November 1709 implicitly criticising the 1688 Revolution and the current Whig government. Now tensions surfaced again. In August 1714 a High Church mob attacked a dissenting chapel at Congleton in Cheshire. Two months later, on 20 October, celebrations to mark George I's coronation were disrupted by mobs in over twenty places in southern England. Some rioters were even heard to voice their support for the Stuart pretender to the throne, James Stuart. Discontent continued to smoulder thereafter, and then burst out anew in May and June 1715.

George I's birthday on 28 May was marked in London by a

number of hostile demonstrations, and in Oxford celebrations of the royal occasion were attacked by a crowd of students and townsfolk who then went on to sack a Presbyterian chapel, making a bonfire of its pews, pulpit and window-frames, upon which they burned an effigy of the chapel's minister. The following day they turned their attention to Quaker and Baptist meeting-houses. In Manchester, where a mob had proclaimed James Stuart as King James III earlier that month, a Presbyterian chapel was sacked and loyalists roughed up. The political persuasion of local magistrates became clear when indictments were handed out, not to the demonstrators, but to those loyalists who had had the temerity to light a bonfire celebrating George's birthday. James Francis Edward Stuart's birthday on 10 June was the occasion for more demonstrations, and over the next few weeks there was a wave of attacks on Non-conformist chapels and meeting houses throughout much of northern and midland England. As in Manchester, the political sympathies of those in authority often meant that disturbances were not stopped and that rioters were not subsequently prosecuted.

It was against this background that the Riot Act was passed – just a few months before James Stuart arrived back in Scotland from exile to stage his ill-fated bid for the crown. Condemning the 'many rebellious riots and tumults' which had recently occurred 'to the disturbance of the public peace and endangering of his majesty's person and government', the Act sought both to achieve 'the preventing and suppressing of such riots and tumults' and 'the more speedy and effectual punishing thereof' (among its more detailed clauses was one which specifically sought to protect chapels and other places of religious worship). Up until 1715, the common law position was that if three or more persons came together with the intent to commit an illegal act they constituted an illegal assembly, and hence were guilty of a misdemeanour; but that if three or more persons gathered to commit an illegal act through force or violence, they were guilty of riot and could be charged as felons. Those guilty only of illegal assembly could be dispersed by the authorities (though what that meant in practice was not clear). Those who rioted opened themselves up to the risk of injury or death – even private individuals could legally take up arms against them.

The 1715 Act did not supersede the common law position, but it did give it sharper teeth. Now a justice of the peace or equivalent officer seeking to deal with any group of twelve or more people gathered together with the intention of acting unlawfully or causing a riot, was instructed to read out a Proclamation in the King's name ordering them to disperse within an hour. If they failed to do so, they were guilty not just of a felony but of a capital felony (making it much harder for sympathetic juries to acquit them), and those who took action against them were indemnified for any injury or deaths they might cause (making it much easier for local magistrates, and, by extension, central government, to control riots as they saw fit).

But if the Act seemed clear in principle, carrying out its provisions in practice proved to be problematic. It was predicated on a justice of the peace reading out a proclamation, but as the Gordon Riots showed, this required a degree of courage that not all justices possessed. To make matters worse, its enforcement relied on that most unpopular of seventeenth- and eighteenth-century bodies, the army. For many contemporaries, a standing army was a potential tool of tyranny, and the involvement of the military in the suppression of riots a matter for considerable disquiet. Indeed, as the Gordon Riots again show, the presence of soldiers could actually exacerbate an already volatile situation, particularly if they were not given clear instructions. They might become victims themselves, or be panicked into overreaction.

Just how badly wrong things could go is graphically demonstrated by the Porteous Riots, which shook Edinburgh in April 1736.[7] A local smuggler named Andrew Wilson had been condemned to be hanged in the Grassmarket. Fearful of his popularity with the mob, and of a possible rescue attempt, the city authorities ordered an armed guard, commanded by Captain John Porteous, to take position around the gallows. The hanging went ahead, but when a few minutes later the hangman attempted to remove the body, members of the crowd cut it down and made off with it, presumably in the hope of reviving Wilson. Porteous later claimed that at this point he tried to get his men to disengage peacefully from the mob, but that they were compelled to fire in self-defence. It seems more likely, though, that he instigated the massacre that followed, grabbing a musket from one of his men (according to some accounts), firing it into the crowd at point-blank range, and then ordering his troops to do likewise. The general consensus is that three volleys were fired in all, killing six and injuring many others. Porteous was arrested that day, accused of murder, and sentenced to death. Political pressure from London resulted in a stay of execution and a petition for a formal appeal.

The Edinburgh mob, however, had other ideas. On 7 September, one day before the sentence originally handed down was due to be carried out, some 4,000 people besieged the Tolbooth prison where Porteous was being held. They finally managed to break in late that night, dragged Porteous away and lynched him where Wilson had met his end, stringing him up on a dyer's pole and beating him mercilessly. The local army commander, General Moyle, was alerted to what was going and might indeed have been able to save Porteous, but he refused to act without a written warrant. Porteous died shortly before midnight.

Even when the Riot Act was correctly invoked, trouble could still ensue. In 1768, for example, in the course of various demonstrations held in London in support of the radical politician John Wilkes, Justice Samuel Guillam read the Act to a crowd which had gathered at St George's Fields in Southwark, opposite the King's Bench prison where Wilkes was incarcerated, and the starting point just twelve years later for the Gordon Riots. As he was reading out the Act, he was struck on the head by a stone. An officer and three soldiers chased the young man who had thrown it, but succeeded only in bayoneting and shooting a man named William Allen, who had nothing to do with the stone throwing and who had not even been part of the demonstration. The mob grew increasingly hostile, and so about two hours later Guillam read the Riot Act again, and then ordered the soldiers to open fire. This they did, killing, according to different accounts, between six and eleven people, and wounding a number of others.

A coroner's jury found the soldiers who had killed William Allen guilty of murder; they were later acquitted by a grand jury heavily packed with pro-government jurors. Justice Guillam, too, was tried for murder – at his trial he was so terrified that he fainted twice – but was acquitted. The fact that legal proceedings went ahead at all showed that there was clearly a disparity between the letter of the law – which, after all, not only theoretically supported Justice Guillam but the soldiers who killed William Allen – and what others felt to be justice.[8]

And herein lay the problem for the military. As Lord Hervey put it in the 1730s:

> When . . . two or three hundred men are ordered by their officer to go against two or three thousand rioters, if they refuse to go it will be a mutiny, and they will be condemned by a court martial and shot; if they go and do not fire, they will probably be knocked on the head; and if they do fire and kill anybody, they will be tried by a jury and hanged – such are the absurdities of our laws at present.[9]

A century later General Sir Charles Napier (see pages 366–7), who had gained considerable experience of handling crowds during the Chartist disturbances in northern England, touched on the same problem from the soldier's point of view:

> Shall I be *shot* for my forebearance by a court martial, or *hanged* for over zeal by a jury? . . . When a riot has taken place and all is over; when everything is known; when fear, danger, confusion, hurry, all are passed, then comes forth the wise, the heroic, the patriotic, 'How undecided the officer was', exclaims

the first; 'he ought to have charged at once', cries the second; 'that redcoated butcher must be hanged', says the third.[10]

Justices were similarly subject to a number of competing pressures. Some, of course, as already pointed out, were not necessarily sympathetic to whatever it was that Westminster politicians might be trying to achieve. More generally, many felt that central government was becoming too strong in any case, that local problems should be left to local authorities, and that the military should only be called in in extremis. Not surprisingly, too, they worried about the effect soldiers might have on a crowd, they worried about how best to put the Riot Act into action, and they worried that, like Samuel Gilliam, they might face prosecution if it was later felt that they had authorised the use of excessive force.

John Evans, Mayor of Carmarthen, who was faced with a corn riot in 1757 (a year which saw widespread rioting throughout England and Wales), tried to do everything by the book. He had the Riot Act read. On several occasions he asked the rioters to disperse. He went so far as to offer to secure grain for them at a lower price. Only when all this had failed and the mob had attacked him and the troops he had called in with pickaxes and other weapons, did he order the soldiers to open fire (five rioters perished as a result). Even so, a private prosecution for murder was taken out against him, and although he was acquitted without the jury leaving the courtroom, the very fact that the legal process should have got this far again demonstrates how uncertain the interpretation of the Riot Act could be.[11]

There were practicalities to be considered, too. Calling in the troops could be a lengthy process, especially if all of what were considered to be the necessary formalities were observed. In fact, as the historian Tony Hayter has pointed out, it could take well over a week to deal with a riot, especially if it had broken out some way away from the capital. Towards the end of day one, faced with a situation that was clearly getting out of control, the local magistrates might decide to write to the Secretary of State at Westminster to request military assistance. Given the appalling condition of most eighteenth-century English roads, it could then take until the morning of the fifth day for a messenger on horseback from, say, Cornwall, to reach Westminster. After a brief consultation, the message would be sent to the War Office and the use of troops closest to the scene of the riot would be authorised. It would then take another four days or so to get this message back. The chances were that, aware of the disturbances and of the magistrates' message to the Secretary of State, troops stationed locally would already be ready to act; yet even then it might take the best part of another day to move infantry from their billets to the scene of rioting.

In other words, from the time magistrates decided to request military assistance from central government to the final arrival of the troops, eleven days might well have elapsed. It is little wonder that the magistrates attempted to defuse disturbances with whatever means of persuasion at their disposal, or largely let matters run their course until the troops arrived.

Sometimes, diplomacy worked. Nathaniel Cholmley, a Yorkshire justice, described in a letter to the Earl of Newcastle, how he had been able to defuse a tense situation during the especially riotous year of 1757:

> I got amongst them as soon as I could, and after some reasoning, and a little strong beer I got them to promise me to disperse, and go home without doing any further mischief. They did not quite keep their words, but went into the town of Whitby – made some people give them a little money for drink, but committed no damage: I was then in hopes we had done with such riotous proceedings.[12]

Other accounts tell of magistrates negotiating with the mob, discussing its grievances and trying, or at least promising, to do something about them. Their softly, softly approach might even extend to the moment of final justice. In 1761, for example, a serious riot broke out at Hexham, when a mob, which according to some estimates was 8–9,000 strong, decided to make clear their feelings about the recently introduced Militia Act. The Yorkshire militia was called in, and after considerable provocation and several readings of the Riot Act, opened fire, killing at least twenty-two people (in some accounts as many as sixty). During the scuffles a militia officer and two militiamen were also killed. Yet only two of the mob were ultimately tried, and while both were found guilty of treason only one was actually executed. One can't help wondering whether the authorities in most other European countries of the period would have been inclined to show such leniency. Perhaps embarrassment at a badly handled situation was the key factor here. Even if the lowest estimate of fatalities is accepted, the treatment of the Hexham rioters of 1761 remains the bloodiest example of military force against crowds in all the provincial riots of the period.[13]

III

Seemingly the most bizarre of eighteenth-century riots involved the introduction of the Gregorian Calendar in 1752. Two years earlier Parliament had finally bitten the bullet and decided that England should move away from the old Julian Calendar (named after Julius Caesar and promulgated in 45 BC) to the astronomically more precise calendar inaugurated by Pope Gregory XIII in 1582 and adopted elsewhere in Europe. To bring England in line with the Gregorian Calendar, however, there would have to be a recalibration, since by the mid-century mark England was out of step with Europe by eleven days. Accordingly, an adjustment was made in the autumn of 1752. George III's subjects went to bed on Wednesday, 2 September and arose the next day on Thursday, 14 September. And the result was pandemonium. People objected to the popish overtones of the new calendar. They worried about the impact of the 'missing' days on the timing of contracts and payment of rents and wages, and other very practical matters. They feared that, at a stroke, eleven days had been removed from their natural life spans . . . and rioted accordingly.

Except that they didn't. Although the 'Give us Our Eleven Days' riots swiftly entered popular consciousness, and although it is certainly the case that many were genuinely concerned about the practical implications of adopting the new calendar and that some did indeed worry that their lives might be shortened, there is absolutely no evidence that rioting ever took place. The story almost certainly had its origins in a Hogarth print depicting disorders at the 1754 Oxfordshire elections, in which he has one figure holding up a placard displaying the words 'give us our eleven days'. Within a few years, though, myth had achieved the authority of assumed historical fact.[14]

But myths can be revealing, and it is tempting to see in Hogarth's print and the rapid acceptance of the story that it seemed just about anything could stir the Georgian mob to violence, and that riots were frequently no more than outpourings of irrational anger. J. H. Plumb's remark that 'burning, looting and destruction by the mob was a commonplace of life', which I quoted earlier, seems of a piece with this.

The truth, though, is more subtle. Back in 1971, the redoubtable left-wing historian Edward Thompson, probably best remembered for his *The Making of the English Working Class* of 1963, wrote an essay entitled 'The Moral Economy of the English Crowd in the Eighteenth Century', in which he looked at the food riots common in the eighteenth century and at what he described as the 'spasmodic view of popular history' traditionally used to characterise them.[15] According to this view, Thompson argued:

> . . . the common people can scarcely be taken as historical agents before the French Revolution. Before this period they intrude occasionally and spasmodically upon the historical canvas in periods of sudden social disturbance. These intrusions are compulsive, rather than self-conscious or self-activating: they are simple responses to economic stimuli. It is sufficient to mention a bad harvest or a down-turn in

trade, and all requirements of historical explanation are satisfied.

In other words, the generally accepted view was that hunger prompted people to protest, as one would expect, but that they then behaved entirely impulsively and irrationally.

Thompson, however, was not persuaded. His examination of eighteenth-century food riots suggested that there was far more method than madness to the crowd. They had a strong sense of right and wrong, he suggested – their 'legitimising notions', as he put it, providing a moral basis for their actions. And they believed in what Thompson called a 'moral economy'. Increasingly, from the late seventeenth century onwards tension built up between the growing forces of market capitalism and the laissez-faire attitude to price setting that went with it, and older notions of an economy in which, if necessary, official interventions could be made. Regulating the free market in grain and other foodstuffs in favour of the consumer had been a central element in Tudor and early Stuart policy. Even as late as 1795 – a year of severe food riots – there were those in positions of authority who openly voiced their support for the old laws that sought to prevent manipulation of the grain market by speculators.

Labouring families might expect to spend half their income on bread in good times, and virtually all of it in bad. It seems scarcely surprising then that when grain prices increased, people invoked the old codes of intervention. In 1693 at Banbury and Chipping Norton the mob 'took away the corne by force out of the wagons, as it was carrying away by the ingrossers [those who had bought up most of the corn in the hope of selling it at a higher price], saying that they were resolved to put the law in execution, since the magistrates neglected it'. In 1795, when the Riot Act was read to a group of women who had boarded a grain ship at Bath, they replied that they were not rioting but merely preventing the unfair export of corn. To show their fundamental loyalty they broke into an extempore rendition of 'God Save the King'. Elsewhere, and on various occasions, rioters did not simply seize food but imposed what they considered to be a 'just price'. In Gloucestershire in 1766, for example, according to a report from the county's sheriff, rioters

> . . . visited farmers, millers, bakers and hucksters' shops, sell-
> ing corn, flour, bread, cheese, butter, and bacon, at their own
> prices. They returned in general the produce [i.e. the money] to
> the proprietors or in their absence left the money for them; and
> behaved with great regularity and decency where they were
> not opposed, with outrage and violence where they were: but
> pilfered very little, which to prevent, they will not now suffer
> women and boys to go with them.

I mentioned earlier how justices of the peace sometimes tried to negotiate with rioters. Their words did not necessarily fall on deaf ears.[16]

Another left-wing historian, Eric Hobsbawm, detected a similar demonstration of what might be considered rioting in his study of the machine-breaking that occurred during the early years of the Industrial Revolution. Between 1811 and 1816 textile workers in the East Midlands, South Lancashire and West Yorkshire, concerned about their future employment prospects, smashed the new machinery of mill-owners. The mill hands acted while allegedly under the direction of a mythical leader named Ned (or King) Ludd. These 'Luddites' were to become a byword for anyone bone-headedly opposed to technological change, or, indeed, innovation more generally. As Hobsbawm, characterising traditional views, put it:

> The early labour movement did not know what it was doing,
> but merely reacted, blindly and gropingly, to the pressure of
> misery, as animals in the laboratory react to electric currents.
> The conscious views of most students may be summed up as
> follows: the triumph of mechanisation was inevitable. We can
> understand, and sympathise with, the long rear-guard action
> which all but a minority of favoured workers fought against

the new system; but we must accept its pointlessness and its inevitable defeat.

But, in fact – certainly in Hobsbawm's view – the Luddites were not mindless wreckers. There were proto-trades unionists, though trades unionists who, when roused, did not resort to strike action but to 'collective bargaining by riot'. Hobsbawm's researches into Luddism in the East Midlands showed that the smashing of machinery was never an end in itself. It was an, admittedly violent, negotiating ploy designed to coerce employers to stop introducing machinery and return to the old employment practices.[17]

Food rioters and Luddites generally had one aim – or a narrow range of aims – in mind. But sometimes we can find evidence of quite tightly knit groups rioting about a whole range of issues that concerned them. One such was the textile workers of Colchester in Essex (a town of 10–12,000 people between 1650 and 1750). They had already developed a reputation for radicalism in the sixteenth and early seventeenth centuries (there had been talk of a general rising of weavers in the area in 1566, and another during the 1620s). As England slid towards Civil War in 1640–42 they rioted again, directing particular attention to the houses of Catholic aristocrats living in the area. They rioted against the imposition of the Hearth Tax in 1668, chasing two tax collectors out of the town in the process (a boy had been told to sound a horn the moment he saw the collectors arrive). In 1675 around 500 weavers, summoned again by the sounding of a horn, rioted against wage cuts, gave 'saucy' answers when threatened with the military, and then, encouraged by a group of townswomen, attacked the house of a Quaker corn-dealer (the riot was deemed serious enough to justify sending the supposed ringleaders to face the Privy Council in Westminster).

In 1715, after a long period of slow decline in the Essex/Suffolk cloth industry, there was a further major riot which again prompted the intervention of the Privy Council and resulted in a partial victory for the textile workers when an Act of Parliament addressing some of their grievances was passed the following year. Further minor disturbances continued in the 1720s, followed by a major one in 1740 (a year which saw widespread grain rioting in England), when a man named George Mallard, sword in hand, led a mob intent on preventing the departure of a boat laden with corn bound for London. Every generation between 1640 and 1740 in Colchester witnessed some disturbance or other. It might be to do with religion, or taxes, or grain shortages, or working conditions. But collectively what all these riots had in common was that they were instigated by a particular group of people and that they reflected that group's concerns and prejudices.[18] For the most part the rioters in Colchester – and elsewhere – were not drawn from the bottom of society but were men (and their womenfolk) with skills and with that sense of solidarity that comes from shared experience at the workplace. Such people enjoyed what might almost be called 'pre-class consciousness', shaped by a shared culture as much as by pure economics – the use of a horn in Colchester to summon people together even suggests that they might have had shared rituals as well.

These concerns and prejudices, it should be added, tended to be quite conservative in nature. Eighteenth-century rioters of the Colchester variety were rarely interested in achieving major political or social change. They were more interested in defending rights or customs, resisting innovations, or trying to get grievances remedied. As Edward Thompson put it when defining his concept of the 'legitimising notion':

> By the notion of legitimation I mean that the men and women in the crowd were informed by the belief that they were defending traditional rights or customs; and, in general, that they were supported by the wider consensus of the community.[19]

Groups certainly existed who were regarded by contemporaries as inherently dangerous: the colliers of Kingswood Forest near Bristol, for example, were described as 'a set of ungovernable people'.[20] But, despite occasional loose talk, there is little by way of sustained evidence to suggest that any group of eighteenth-century rioters contemplated a fundamental restructuring of the whole social or political order: for the most part, they operated strictly within the realms of the possible. That was of little consolation to those who were on the receiving end: it is terrifying to be threatened, jostled, beaten, or to have one's house or workshop torn down. But that doesn't mean that wholesale revolution is in the air.

Not that riots didn't often have a political dimension to them. England was, after all, a highly politicised nation. A strong two-party system had been created by the Glorious Revolution. Elections occurred regularly (ten between 1695 and 1715) and relatively high levels of literacy (by contemporary European standards) guaranteed constant engagement with political debate. Around a fifth of adult males were eligible to vote at the start of the eighteenth century. At election time, rioting sometimes played its part in manipulating the results. But, here as elsewhere, it could also be a clarion call for traditional rights and responsibilities. The mob were proud to be free-born Britons. They believed that their lives were protected by ancient laws, that they had rights. They also believed that their betters should remember this, and if they didn't there were ways to remind them. As for their betters, they were only too aware that they lacked the means to suppress the mob, that heavy-handedness – whether shooting down or stringing up too many of the mob's members – could be counter-productive, and that conciliation and compromise were usually the best means of dealing with popular disturbances. It is not for nothing that the political system of eighteenth-century England has been described as 'oligarchy tempered by riot'.

But the point is that oligarchy was tempered. It was never threatened. The mob could be vicious, as the fate of John Porteous reminds us, but its objectives were, on the whole, limited, and the worst that generally happened in the course of an eighteenth-century riot was the roughing up of the odd corn merchant or parish constable. Georgian rioters inhabited a very different world from that of their medieval forebears. In 1381 as in 1780, the rebels targeted property

(John of Gaunt's palace, for example) and they attacked and emptied prisons. But in 1381 the rebels were also happy to kill those they considered their enemies – high officers of state, foreign merchants – and they killed them brutally in broad daylight. In 1780, by contrast, some leading politicians might have been jostled or assaulted, but none was killed. Those who died during the Gordon Riots did not perish at the deliberate hands of the mob, but were victims of the chaos it caused and of the military clampdown that brought it to an end. When we think of 1381 we think of calculated assassination: of Simon Sudbury, Archbishop of Canterbury and Chancellor of England, beheaded by the rebels; of Wat Tyler stabbed by one of the King's men. When we think of 1780 we think of the wretches who burned to death in Langdale's distillery.

IV

As the nineteenth century dawned a new type of radical became apparent: more bookish, more considered – and more politically engaged. Samuel Bamford was a typical example. Born of lower-middle-class Protestant dissenting parentage at Middleton in Lancashire in 1788, he attended Manchester Grammar School and then worked in a variety of jobs, notably as a warehouseman. Looking back in his autobiography at the England he had known in his twenties, he recalled the wave of unrest that followed the end of the struggle against Napoleon in 1815, when 'the elements of convulsion were at work among the masses of our labouring population'. There were, he reminisced, riots in Westminster over proposed legislation designed to regulate the grain trade in London. There was machine-breaking by the unemployed at Bury. Luddites destroyed thirty weaving frames in Nottingham. There was rioting in Ely ('not suppressed without bloodshed'), Birmingham (led by the unemployed), Newcastle (colliers and others), Preston (unemployed weavers) and Merthyr Tydfil (workers resisting reduced wages), while north of the border the high price of grain led to the plundering of more than a hundred shops in Dundee alone. But, he also suggested, a sea change was taking place among those whose sense of social oppression and economic hardship was driving them to demonstrate:

At this time the writings of William Cobbett [1763–1835] suddenly became of great authority; they were read on nearly every cottage hearth in the manufacturing districts of South Lancashire, in those of Leicester, Derby and Nottingham; also in many of the Scottish manufacturing towns. Their influence was speedily visible; he directed his readers [particularly in his hugely popular weekly *Political Register*] to the true cause of their sufferings – misgovernment; and to its proper corrective – parliamentary reform. Riots soon became scarce, and from that time they have never obtained their ancient vogue, with the labourers of this country.[21]

One suspects that in suggesting that the writings of Cobbett were being eagerly discussed in every industrial worker's dwelling Bamford was exaggerating somewhat, and there were certainly still old-style riots enough to come. But he does touch on a fundamental truth. While his catalogue of riots shows that the former triggers for unrest – bad harvests and economic downturn – persisted in the years after Waterloo, a new sophistication in the response of those adversely affected was also becoming apparent. Sections of the working class now organised themselves into trades unions, utilising the weapon of the strike (often accompanied by disorder and the intimidation of employers and blacklegs) rather than the riot to show their discontent. At the same time men like Bamford took up the cudgels, not just for social but political change. The French Revolution, though never likely to be replicated on English soil, had had a huge impact on English political consciousness. Radicals associated events in France with liberty, equality and fraternity – a heady mix of ideals for a whole new generation of largely self-educated artisans and working men (of whom Samuel Bamford was one). English activists, therefore, came to believe that the solution to social ills

was political reform, not intermittent social protest, and that political reform could only be won if working men gained, via the ballot
box, a say in the running of the country.

Such radicalism, of course, terrified those in authority, who associated the French Revolution with regicide, anarchy and war. And
their sense of fear was exacerbated by the social upheavals wrought
by the industrialisation and urbanisation that even as early as 1815
was starting to reshape parts of England. As a result, while political
change was essential, so far as political radicals were concerned, the
very mention of the word sparked fears of revolution among those in
authority. And it was the exaggerated fears of this latter group that
sparked one of the most notorious tragedies in the history of popular
politics in England, which unfolded at St Peter's Fields at Manchester
on 16 August 1819.[22]

The occasion was a mass meeting organised by the recently formed
Manchester Patriotic Union. The members – a mixture of old-style artisans whose livelihood was being threatened by the onset of
industrialisation and workers who had acquired new jobs as a result of
it – saw parliamentary reform as a necessary first step to social reform.
The major draw was to be the famous agitator Henry Hunt, who had
acquired such a reputation for public speaking that he was known as
'Orator' Hunt. The day was a fine one, and some 60,000 people – among
them families and groups representing various local townships –
gathered at the fields. Press reports generally stressed the scruffiness of
those who assembled on that day, but in reality many in this crowd
were wearing their best clothes. To control them the local magistrates
had at their disposal what amounted to a small army: around 400 special
constables, 600 men of the 15th Hussars, several hundred men from two
infantry regiments, and a detachment of the Royal Artillery with two
cannon. Also on standby were 400 members of the Cheshire Yeomanry
(analogous to modern Territorials, but mounted) and 120 members of
the Manchester and Salford Yeomanry – all volunteers drawn from
local property owners (the Manchester and Salford Yeomanry were
essentially the local Tory Party on horseback) and all virtually untrained.

The senior magistrate present, William Hulton, was a prominent local landholder. The senior officer in the north, General Sir John Byng, felt that his presence was not necessary and opted instead to allow Lieutenant-Colonel Guy L'Estrange to take charge of any military intervention that might be necessary. It proved to be a tragic mistake. Byng was an experienced officer who understood crowd control. The previous year he had managed to control demonstrations in Lancashire without shedding blood. L'Estrange lacked his experience and finesse.

The Home Office had encouraged the magistrates to take a hard line, so the decision was taken early on in the proceedings to arrest Hunt and other speakers. At first it was hoped that the special constables could keep a corridor open through the crowd to allow the authorities to get to Hunt and his colleague, but they were overwhelmed by the sheer number of people. The Chief Constable of Manchester therefore asked the magistrates to authorise the deployment of the military. This was agreed, and instructions were sent to the 15th Hussars and the Manchester and Salford Yeomanry. Since the Yeomanry were closer to the demonstration they set off immediately, revealing in the process a dangerous mix of enthusiasm and belligerence (earlier that year the Cheshire Yeomanry had been famously humiliated in their attempt to take a French-style cap of liberty from demonstrators at Stockport; their Manchester and Salford brethren were determined not to be similarly embarrassed).

As they clattered through the streets, a local married woman, Ann Fildes, with her two-year-old son William in her arms, pressed herself against a wall to keep out of their way. When she thought the coast was clear, she stepped back into the street and was immediately ridden down by a straggler desperately trying to catch up with his comrades. She was injured; her son died. The first victim of the day was thus a two-year-old boy in the care of someone who was not even present at the mass meeting. The soldier responsible was never identified.

Precisely how events then unfolded was to prove a hugely

contentious issue in the aftermath, but most accounts seem to agree that the barely trained Yeomanry, who according to many witnesses were drunk and who were certainly riding horses unused to large bodies of people, panicked when they found their path blocked by the crowd, and began to lash out with their sabres. When the more disciplined 15th Hussars arrived a little later, they assumed that their Yeomanry comrades must be under attack, and rode into the crowd after them. Whether or not they wielded their sabres as freely as the Yeomanry is uncertain, but their arrival prompted the crowd to flee in panic and in the process many of them were injured or killed. Overall, that day, 15 people died or sustained fatal injuries, and upwards of 400 were injured. Among the dead were John Lees, a veteran of Waterloo, killed by sabre cuts; John Ashworth, a special constable, sabred and then trampled underfoot by cavalry horses; William Evans, also a special constable, trampled to death by cavalry horses; Sarah Jones, mother of seven children, killed by a blow from a special constable's truncheon; and Mary Heys, pregnant mother of six children, ridden over and severely injured, who died a little time later when she gave birth prematurely. The fact that two on-duty special constables perished in the massacre shows just how out of control the Yeomanry clearly were.

The response of those in authority was entirely predictable: a government crackdown on political dissidents, and a whitewash of the events of the day. The *Manchester Observer* which had long been critical of the government and refused to toe the official line on the demonstration, was harassed continually and forced to close in 1821 (its final editorial recommended that its readers should turn to a new publication, the *Manchester Guardian*). Before it vanished, though, its editor James Wroe coined the term by which the events of 16 August were to pass into history: 'Peterloo Massacre' combined a reminder of where the tragedy had unfolded – St Peter's Fields – with a memory of Europe's most recent battle – Waterloo – so turning what the government hoped would be viewed as a demonstration gone awry to a bloodbath for which the forces of law and order were responsible. Wroe also published a pamphlet that gave a 'faithful narrative' of those events. Its success carried the story to all corners of the country.

After Peterloo the authorities seem to have become understandably nervous about strong-arm tactics against demonstrators. Lord John Russell, during his time as Home Secretary in the 1830s, declared that 'for his part he would rather that any [military] force should be employed in case of local disturbance than the local corps of Yeomanry'.[23] So when another radical movement – Chartism – emerged in 1838 the general tendency was to deal with it temperately. The Chartists, like the members of the Manchester Patriotic Union and other similar organisations that came before them, were middle- and working-class radicals (typically artisans and upper-working-class skilled workers). Their contention was that the 1832 Reform Act – which had widened the franchise – had not gone far enough, and they therefore promulgated a People's Charter, demanding adult male suffrage, the secret ballot, an ending to property qualifications for Members of Parliament, the payment of Members of Parliament, equalisation of the size of parliamentary constituencies, and annual Parliaments.

Historians have tended to downplay Chartism's revolutionary potential, but that is not how it appeared at the time. Some Chartists openly believed in using force, and armed and drilled their supporters accordingly. Since they were active at a time of widespread general unrest – particularly in industrial areas – it is scarcely surprising that they should have been regarded fearfully. Yet Chartist demonstrations were rarely suppressed by force. An incident at Newport in November 1839 when at least twenty-two people were killed when troops fired into a crowd was appalling, but it was also exceptional.[24]

In the critical years 1839–41 military forces in the region of England that stretched between the Scottish border and Nottinghamshire and Leicestershire were under the command of a remarkable man: Major-General Sir Charles Napier. Something of a political radical himself, he had considerable sympathy for the Chartists: 'so far as it falls within my limited sphere', he wrote, 'all shall be done to assist the poor, for they are ill-used and suffering'. And he made it clear that he regarded the use of force against demonstrators very much as a last resort:

> Good God what a work! To send grape-shot from our guns into a helpless mass of fellow citizens; sweeping the streets with fire and charging with cavalry, destroying poor people whose only crime is that they have been ill-governed and reduced to such straits that they seek redress by arms.

There's no doubt that his light-touch approach certainly avoided much unnecessary bloodshed. Here, for example, is his description of the way he handled a riot in an unnamed village, when he had been called out by the local and elderly justice of the peace:

> ... [there] came a call for troops to disperse a mob in the country. I rode out, ordering dragoons to follow me. Mr N– [presumably a magistrate] and I found the mob, which would not notice us and marched on. Old N– put on his spectacles, pulled out the Riot Act, and read it in an audible voice – to who? Myself and about a dozen old women, looking out at their doors to see what we were at! We came back, found another mob, and ordered it to disperse. No. Mr N– told me to disperse it. I laughed, the dragoons laughed, the young women of the mob laughed, and then old N– laughed, and so the second act of folly passed.[25]

It was a far cry from the events of Peterloo.

V

When the final great Chartist demonstration came in 1848 the authorities were not only more prepared than they had ever been before, but they also displayed considerable wisdom in their handling of it. Such level-headedness was a considerable achievement given how genuinely fearful people were that the demonstration that took place on Kennington Common on 10 April 1848 might well lead to revolution.[26] The decade had been a harsh one for working people (it was later to be described as 'the Hungry Forties'). In 1846 the grain harvest had failed, and in both that year and the following one the potato harvest had been disastrous. There had been rioting in a number of English and Scottish cities, a revival in Chartist activity that in some areas had acquired a quasi-military aspect, and worrying reports of growing links between English radicals and Irish nationalists. Then on 22 February 1848 Paris had risen up against King Louis Philippe in the first of a wave of revolutions that swept across Europe over the next few months. It must have seemed that the Chartist decision to deliver a new petition to Parliament for political change was the precursor to something much more radical.

An indication of just how worried the authorities were is suggested by the extraordinary level of policing put in place. Eight thousand troops were drafted in to London for the day of the demonstration, along with over 1,200 enrolled pensioners (ex-soldiers taken on as auxiliaries), some 4,000 police, and a remarkable total of 85,000 special constables (eye-witnesses reckoned that there were more special constables than there were actual Chartists). The meeting was allowed to take place but the police refused to let the demonstrators march to Westminster, and the military were given control of the bridges across the Thames, which, of course, any procession from Kennington would have to cross. Thereafter tension swiftly turned to farce. When the great Chartist petition, stacked into three horse-drawn carriages, arrived at the Houses of Parliament, it was found to contain numerous false and forged signatures. There were even some obscene ones among them. The Chartists ceased to be a threat and became instead a laughing stock, recalled in embarrassment by Charles Kingsley's otherwise broadly sympathetic *Alton Locke* (1850):

Above all, the people would not rise. Whatever sympathy they had with us, they did not care to show it. And then futility after futility exposed itself. The meeting which was to have been counted by hundreds of thousands, numbered hardly its tens of thousands; and of them a frightful proportion were of those very rascal classes, against whom we ourselves had offered to be sworn in as special constables . . . the meeting broke up pitiably piecemeal, drenched and cowed, body and soul, by pouring rain on its way home—for the very heavens mercifully helped to quench our folly—while the monster-petition crawled ludicrously away in a hack cab, to be dragged to the floor of the House of Commons amid roars of laughter.

There were to be clashes with the police over the summer and mass arrests, but the failure of the Kennington meeting effectively marked the end of Chartism.

The 1848 demonstrations were a far cry from the riots of the eighteenth century. But they, too, marked the end of an era and the commencement of a new one. Chartism was a brief attempt to bring together various interest groups into a national organisation whose main aim was to exert pressure to promote further parliamentary reform that would extend the vote to working men (the 1832 Reform Act had been cruelly disappointing in that respect). The failure of Chartism, coupled with economic recovery in the 1850s, led working people to seek more local solutions to their grievances and to become involved in self-help organisations: trades unions, co-operative societies, friendly societies, churches and chapels. At the same time the social instability inherent in the early stages of the formation of Britain's industrial cities – an instability perhaps always more serious in the eyes of those in authority than in reality – was replaced by a new era of calm and an emerging 'respectable' working class. In the 1830s and 1840s the middle classes would have regarded the working class on the whole as criminally inclined and potentially revolutionary. By the 1860s, fear was focussed on a small subset of the working class: the 'residuum' or 'criminal class', something akin to Karl Marx's *lumpenproletariat*. England remained two nations, but the poorer nation now looked considerably less threatening.

The forces of law and order were changing, too. There was now a professional police force. Railways could move troops quickly to areas of unrest. The electric telegraph could relay information and requests for help in an instant. Rioting might still occur on occasion, but it could be much more swiftly contained. Besides, as the mass recruitment of special constables in 1848 showed – and they were to be found not just in London but also in provincial towns – an increasing proportion of the population was opposed to the notion of creating a public disturbance to achieve a particular goal. The 'possessing classes' – who now included everyone from the aristocracy to what at the time was termed the shopkeeping class – favoured the status quo over disruption. Those further down the pecking order were now more likely to join a trades union than a riot. The old world of paternalism and deference punctuated by plebeian unrest had gone, to be replaced by a new form of stability.

The laſt Dying Speech and Con-
feſſion, Parentage and Behaviour, of the
TWO UNFORTUNATE
MALEFACTORS,

Executed this Day before the Debtor's Door, Newgate.
To which is added, The Copy of a moſt excellent Prayer, written and
uſed by *Thomas Hunter*, during his Confinement, and is recommended
to the Uſe of every Perſon.

Printed and Sold in London.

The title page from a pamphlet of 1784 that describes the crimes and executions of two
men convicted of forgery and burglary. Public hangings traditionally attracted large
crowds but they also became increasingly controversial, and by the mid-nineteenth
century other forms of suitable punishment were being explored.

CHAPTER 12

STATE VIOLENCE AND THE END OF THE OLD PUNISHMENT REGIME

I

Anthony Babington played a very dangerous game, and lost. Born in Derbyshire in 1561, the son of a gentry family with Roman Catholic leanings, he became attracted to the cause of Mary, Queen of Scots while a pageboy in the household of the 6th Earl of Shrewsbury (at the time Mary's jailer), and then, in 1586, hatched a plot to assassinate Elizabeth I and replace her on the English throne with the Scottish queen. The hope was that not only English Catholics but Catholic Europe would come to his aid.

The conspiracy, however, was doomed almost from the start. Babington proved a poor, indecisive leader, and, in any case, his plans soon became known to Sir Francis Walsingham, Elizabeth's principal secretary and spy master. In August the ringleaders were apprehended; trial and conviction followed rapidly; and on 20 September Babington and six of his co-conspirators were dragged to a specially constructed gallows in St Giles's Fields – St Giles being the London parish where the plot was first hatched. Their execution followed the method approved for non-noble traitors: hanging, drawing and quartering. Two decades later, when sentencing the Gunpowder plotters in 1605, the Attorney General, Sir Edward Lord Coke, described the process thus:

[The traitor] shall be strangled, being hanged up by the neck between heaven and earth, as deemed unworthy of either: as likewise, the eyes of men may behold, and their hearts condemn him. Then he is to be cut down alive, and to have his privy parts cut off and burnt before his face as being unworthily begotten, and unfit to leave any generation after him. His bowels and inlaid parts taken out and burnt, who inwardly had harboured in his heart such horrible treason. After, to have his head cut off, which had imagined the mischief. And lastly his body to be quartered, and the quarters set up in some high and eminent place, to the view and detestation of men, and to become prey for the fowls of the air.

A further batch of seven Babington plotters was dispatched on 21 September, but, thanks to Elizabeth's intervention, they were spared the full agony of live mutilation that their brethren had been forced to endure the day before: they were hanged until they were dead, and only then were their bodies carved up. Despite the 'fearfull spectacle' of their execution, Babington and his friends won little sympathy from the thousands of spectators who gathered to watch. As a contemporary wrote:

Ye odiousness of their treason was so settled in every man's heart, as there appeared no sadness nor alteration among the people at the mangling and quartering of their bodies. Yea the whole multitude, without any signe of lamentation, greedylye beheld the spectacle from the first to the last.[1]

II

Such officially sanctioned violence came at a time when, as previously described, overall levels of violence in English society were markedly higher than they were to be two hundred or so years later. This inevitably raises the question of to what extent levels of crime and severity of punishment were linked. It's not an easy question to answer. To argue, for example, that the Elizabethans punished their malefactors more brutally than the Victorians because they felt it was the only way to control individuals who were themselves so violent and so numerous, is simplistic, and also fails to explain how the cycle of violence was gradually broken, or at least reduced in intensity between Tudor times and the early-Victorian period.

Rather, it seems that the nature of official punishment, like the crimes it punished, was a response to a whole range of forces. These involved the shifting nature of English society, which created a larger class of people with a stake in law and order (see Chapter 13); changing views both of the nature of the criminal and the purpose of punishment (see Chapter 12); changes in attitudes to pain and suffering; and changes in attitude to particular types of crime. Punishment, like crime, tells us about the nature of English society at particular moments in its development.

Perhaps the key distinguishing feature of punishment in medieval times and the early modern period was the use of public shaming. As explained in Chapter 7, personal reputation was held to be of such importance in medieval times and afterwards, that to attack it was frequently regarded as a criminal offence. It therefore seems entirely logical that one way to punish people was to humiliate them. It matched punishment to crime. It also served as an overt warning to others of what might happen to them too if they misbehaved. In 1529 five London women found guilty of prostitution were taken from prison and marched through the streets, wearing the striped hoods traditionally sported by prostitutes and carrying white rods (the symbolism of which is not entirely clear). Pans and basins were beaten before them in a demonstration of 'rough music' (see page 246). When they reached Newgate, they were publicly banned from ever returning to the capital.

In 1551 Edmund Ellis, convicted of cheating at cards, was put in the pillory with playing cards pinned or sewn to his clothes, and was then paraded sitting backwards on a horse (a common practice in punishments) across London Bridge to Southwark, before he was again set in the pillory, this time with his ear nailed to it. In Norwich in 1568 Robert Archer was convicted of behaving like a vagrant and deceiving people with rings that he had presumably used to perform conjuring tricks. He was put in the stocks with the rings attached to him, along with a piece of paper that explained his offence – a warning to the townsfolk to avoid people like him and any temptation they might feel to emulate him.[2] Perhaps the most elaborate visual punishment of all was that arranged for the Londoner William Campion when in 1478 he was found guilty of tapping a water conduit and transferring the water running through it into his own well. He was paraded on a horse, with a model of a water conduit on his head, which was constantly refilled.[3]

Another popular method of punishing wrongdoers through humiliation was to 'cart' them: in other words, to place them in a cart that would then be dragged through the streets. In the decades around 1600 Middlesex magistrates commonly resorted to this approach in their bid to control brothel keepers and other offenders against sexual morality. A madam named Elizabeth Hollande, for example, was put in a cart at Newgate, and paraded around urban Middlesex. She was forced to wear a paper that outlined her offence, and rough music was performed in front of the cart. She was then fined £40 and had to find sureties for her good behaviour.[4]

Punishments ordered by the ecclesiastical courts also had a pronounced element of shaming to them. Of course, in extreme cases, the clergy could opt for excommunication – exclusion of the offender from the community of the godly – but far more common was penance performed in public. In theory it could be inflicted for any infringement of ecclesiastical law, but it was most frequently imposed on those found guilty of fornication or adultery (a major concern of ecclesiastical tribunals, which serves to explain why they were so constantly referred to as 'the bawdy courts'). In pre-Reformation times, penances could be ornate affairs. When in 1532 John Cronkshay of Pendle in Lancashire was found guilty of adultery with Emma the wife of Richard Cronkshay (his cousin), he was ordered to process in front of Padiham chapel the next Sunday, bare-headed and bare-footed, wearing rags and carrying a lighted half-pound candle in each hand. He was then to go into the chapel, make a public apology to the man he had offended and beg his for-giveness, and kneel in front of the altar throughout Mass. This procedure was to be repeated on the two following Sundays at two other churches, and on the Feast of the Immaculate Conception at a third, Clitheroe.[5] Such elaborate ritual did not survive the Reforma-tion, but the essence of the penance remained. By the late sixteenth century it involved an offender appearing before the congregation of his or her parish, usually at Sunday service, normally wearing a white sheet and carrying a white wand, and sometimes wearing a paper describing their offence. There they would make a public con-fession of their fault, express their sorrow for it and their awareness of its sinful nature, and exhort their co-parishioners to avoid falling into a similar state of sinfulness.

None of these punishments involved physical retribution per se, though it needs to be stressed again how seriously people regarded assaults on personal reputation. But public shaming often had a vio-lent element to it.[6] Parading people through the street inevitably invited verbal and physical abuse from the crowd. If the victim was placed in a pillory, with his or her head and hands secured in holes in planks which ran across the top of the post at head height, then it was an open invitation to hurl more than words at them – they might well be pelted with stones, filth and rotting vegetables. A vic-tim to whom the crowd felt sympathetic might escape with no more than their dignity injured (usually they would just have a placard attached to them that outlined their offence, though occasionally one of their ears might be nailed to the woodwork). Daniel Defoe, placed in the pillory in 1703 for allegedly libelling the Church of Eng-land, was famously feted by the crowd, who in a demonstration of support probably organised by Defoe's political allies, covered the pillory with flowers, formed a guard around it and drank his health.[7] A victim of the pillory to whom the crowd felt hostile, however, might well die from the injuries he or she received while at their mercy. It has been estimated that over the course of the eighteenth century nine people died as a result of the treatment they received from the crowd while standing in the pillory, and another five were badly injured. Sodomites had an especially rough time.

In some cases, physical punishment was officially meted out. Vagrants, for example, were commonly whipped in public by parish constables. Those convicted of petty larceny (that is, theft of goods worth less than a shilling) could also suffer the same fate. Male or female, they would be stripped to the waist, and then whipped until their backs were, as contemporary documents frequently put it, 'bloody'. Special whipping posts were erected in town centres. Alternatively, the guilty party might be tied to the end of a cart and paraded through the town while being lashed across the back.

III

The ultimate sanction carried out before the public gaze was, of course, execution.[8] By 1700, eight times a year at London's Tyburn, and twice a year in county assize towns, condemned felons would be hanged before vast crowds. The number of those dispatched in this way was huge. It has been estimated that in the hundred years between 1530 and 1630 somewhere in the region of 75,000 people were executed in England. Between 1805 and 1832, towards the end of the period when public execution was the norm, 2,028 men and women were hanged for felony in England and Wales. The crimes of this later group were various. About a fifth – 395 – were executed for murder, and a further 107 for attempted murder. One hundred and two people were executed for rape, and 50 for 'sodomy' (defined as male penetrative homosexual sex). Burglary convictions claimed 419, robbery 276, animal theft 178, and larceny in a dwelling house 65. Forgery (mostly of bank notes and commercial documents) and related offences were responsible for the forfeiting of 282 lives.[9] Other victims were found guilty of crimes that ranged from arson to counterfeiting coins.

Execution could be messy and protracted. Beheading was reserved for upper-class male traitors, their female counterparts (Anne Boleyn; Mary, Queen of Scots) having the option of being executed by a swordsman. Hanging had become established as the standard punishment for felony by the late middle ages, and was regularly meted out to murderers, thieves, burglars, highway robbers, rapists, arsonists and, from 1563, those (usually women) convicted of witchcraft. Until the Victorians perfected the 'drop' – the process whereby a trapdoor was opened beneath the condemned man or woman, so ensuring that (assuming all went well) their neck was immediately broken – it was little more than death by strangulation. The condemned might be 'turned off' a ladder (a possible origin of the superstition that walking under one is unlucky) or have to stand, rope tied around their neck, on a cart that was then driven off. Death could take up to half an hour. During that time the faces of the condemned would contort uncontrollably (though they were normally covered by a nightcap or hood), their legs would kick out wildly and hopelessly to find some sort of purchase, and they would lose control of their bowels and bladders. Friends, relatives or even the hangman might pull on their legs in a desperate attempt to end their suffering. Even so, some were found to be still alive when cut down, resulting in clashes between the onlookers, who felt that anyone who survived a 'half hanging' should be spared, and the presiding official, who argued that the original sentence had to be carried out.

To make matters worse, executioners not infrequently botched the job. Perhaps the most famous of them all, Jack Ketch, who was hangman for London and Middlesex in the late seventeenth century and whose name was to become a generic term for this calling, made an appalling mess of the beheading of William, Lord Russell in 1683. Two years later, he handled the execution of the Duke of Monmouth with an equal lack of aplomb. Charles II's illegitimate son, who had led an unsuccessful Protestant rising against the Catholic James II, enjoyed considerable public sympathy. The authorities therefore badly needed a smoothly run execution. It took Ketch at least five blows with the axe, however, to make an end of his aristocratic victim. Indeed, he nearly gave up halfway through the process, and after the fifth blow had to resort to a knife to sever the head from the body. The diarist John Evelyn reckoned that if Ketch had not been escorted from the execution site under guard the crowd would have ripped him to pieces.[10]

Ketch, of course, was meant to be a professional. Many executioners, though, were not. The custom on the Northern assize circuit, for example, which was probably followed in many other regions, was to allow a capitally convicted felon to carry out an execution in return for a pardon. Thus in one of the minor ironies of the operation of the eighteenth-century criminal justice system, Dick Turpin's executioner at York in 1739 was a highwayman named Thomas Hadfield.[11] London and Middlesex did have an official hangman (the number of executions justified the post), but even so accounts of executions at Tyburn include stories of breaking ropes, of halters slipping off necks, of carts being driven away from under the condemned before nightcaps had been placed over their faces, even of gallows collapsing during executions and the condemned then having to wait until repairs had been carried out. Similar mishaps are recorded in provincial executions. Generally speaking, the crowd did not like an incompetent hangman. They were less than impressed, for example, with William (or John) Curry (also known as 'Mutton' Curry because he had twice been convicted of sheep-stealing) when he turned up drunk to officiate at the York scaffold in April 1821, waved a noose at the crowd and mockingly asked them if anyone would like to come up and try it on, and then, having managed to get the cap over the condemned man's head, failed to do likewise with the noose and proceeded to dislodge the cap each time he tried to put right his mistake. The condemned man, suddenly able to see his surroundings again, 'stared wildly around upon the spectators', according to a contemporary report in The Times. Cries of 'Hang Jack Ketch!' went up, and Curry was assaulted and roughed up on his way home.[12]

As with less lethal forms of public shaming, the point of an execution held in public was to attract a crowd. And the crowds that thronged to executions could – particularly in the eighteenth century – be vast. It has been estimated that up to 100,000 people might turn up to a London hanging. As for 'celebrity' criminals, they were a draw even before the main event. When Jack Sheppard, a house breaker who had attracted considerable notoriety for his escapes from prison, was awaiting execution in 1724, his gaolers at Newgate made a small fortune from the admittance fees they charged the crowds of people who came to see him.[13] When the highwayman James MacLaine (as mentioned previously, his name appears to have been spelled various ways), known as 'The Gentleman Highwayman', was awaiting the same fate in the same prison in 1750, an estimated 3,000 people visited.[14] And when, early in 1739, it became apparent that a certain John Palmer, held in the county gaol for Yorkshire at York Castle awaiting trial for horse theft, was in fact the notorious highwayman Richard Turpin, he became a major tourist attraction. 'Since he was suspected to be Turpin', a contemporary noted, 'the whole country have flock'd to see him, and have been very liberal to him, insomuch as he has wine constantly before him.' The same contemporary noted that the gaoler at York Castle had made £100 from selling liquor to Turpin and his visitors. A 'Letter from York', published in the *General Evening Post* of 8 March 1739, dwelt on his extraordinary celebrity:

> A great concourse of people flock to see him, and they all give him money. He seems very sure that nobody is alive that can hurt him, and told the gentlemen with whom he used to hunt, that he hoped to have another day's sport with them yet. And that if he had thought they would have made such a rout with him he would have owned it [i.e. his identity] before ... He is put every night in the condemned hold, which is a very strong place.[15]

An extreme case was that of the lead-up to the trial in 1790 of Renwick Williams, 'The Monster', accused of a series of violent assaults on women. According to one contemporary press account, he held a ball in Newgate to which twenty couples were invited, music for dancing being provided by two violins and a flute. A substantial cold buffet and selection of wines was provided.[16] It's not surprising that Bernard de Mandeville (1670–1733), an Anglo-Dutch physician cum political philosopher who had settled in London, and a somewhat sceptical observer of his fellow humans, complained in 1725 of the 'seas of beer' consumed by capitally convicted felons in prison.[17]

IV

To many contemporaries, the crowd at an execution was no better than the howling mob of a riot. De Mandeville, writing in 1725, for example, gave the following evocative description:

> It is incredible what a scene of confusion all this often makes, which yet grows worse near the gallows; and the violent efforts of the most sturdy and resolute of the mob on one side, and the potent efforts of the rugged gaolers, and others, to beat them off, on the other; the terrible blows that are struck, the heads that are broke, the pieces of swingeing sticks, and blood, that fly about, the men that are knock'd down and trampled upon, are beyond imagination, whilst the dissonance of voices, and the variety of outcries, for different reasons, that are heard there, together with the sound of more distant noises, make such a discord not to be paralleled.[18]

In reality, though, things were a little more complicated.[19] While any crowd could well contain elements that were bloodthirsty, drunk, semi-criminal and, if not wholly amoral, at least immoral, they had their own codes of behaviour. As already mentioned, they had no time for incompetent hangmen. When it came to these hangmen's victims, the crowd might, according to their view of the condemned criminal, howl abuse or weep in sympathy. After the execution, they might, again according to their view of the criminal, allow the body to be taken away for dissection (it was customary to use the bodies of executed felons for anatomy lessons in medical schools), or they might try to recover it to prevent what popular culture regarded as a violation of the corpse by the medical profession. The body of Dick Turpin, for example, secretly disinterred after burial by a local doctor, presumably with dissection in mind, was recovered by a mob, and reburied in quick lime to prevent any further attentions from the surgeons.[20] In extreme cases, if they thought that the executed person had been falsely accused, they might rescue the body from the authorities and lay it outside the house of the accuser.

Not that their response was always morally straightforward. As their sympathy for Turpin shows, the mob liked their folk heroes, even if those heroes were less than praiseworthy. Turpin was a brute. But he was also a larger than life figure who chose to 'die game'. His last few weeks in York Castle gaol were convivial ones. He sent away the clergyman who tried to prepare him spiritually for death. On the day set for his execution – Saturday, 7 April 1739 – he put on a new frock coat and pumps bought specially for the occasion (not an uncommon thing to do; condemned criminals were sometimes said to look like bridegrooms on the day of their execution). As he was taken (with his coffin) in a cart along the traditional death route from York Castle up Micklegate and thence through Micklegate Bar on to what is now Tadcaster Road to the place of execution, York Tyburn (adjacent to York racecourse), he 'behav'd himself with amazing assurance' and 'bow'd to the spectators as he passed'. He was accompanied not only by a strong guard appointed by the Sheriff of Yorkshire to forestall any rescue attempts, but by five men he had paid to follow the cart and ensure that his body was buried properly. At the execution site he gave way to a brief attack of nerves, which manifested themselves in a tremor in his left leg, but he managed to get them under control.

Like those at Tyburn, the York gallows took the form of a horizontal triangle supported by a post at each corner, and Turpin was placed on a ladder set leaning against one of the beams forming the triangle, with the halter around his neck and the rope attached to the beam. After a few words with the hangman, he 'threw himself off the ladder, and expired directly'. According to the pamphlet that described his death he 'went off this stage with as much intrepidity and unconcern, as if he had been taking his horse to go on a journey'. We don't actually know how the crowd reacted to this show of bravado, but given Turpin's notoriety and the esteem in which those who died game were held, we can assume that they admired him for it.[21]

Turpin, though, was something of an exception. As a rule, the crowd responded most sympathetically to those whose punishment – in the crowd's view – outweighed their crime, or those who showed proper remorse at the moment of execution. The 'last dying speech' seems to have had a long pedigree in the history of English capital punishment. Indeed it was discussed in some detail in a publication of 1697 by the clergyman John Kettlewell, who set out to give practical hints on how best to conduct yourself if ever you found yourself in the unfortunate position of having to give a last speech from the scaffold:

> When you are brought from prison to execution, own the justice of your sentence: profess your abhorrence and true repentance of the crime which you dye for, and all your other sins. Declare the satisfaction you have made, or would make, were you able, to all you have wronged. Beg all persons to forgive you, who have suffered by you in any kind, and all who have ever learnt any ill from your acquaintance and example. Declare that you do from your heart, forgive all persons, and that you bear not the least ill will against any of your prosecutors, or the judges and juries who were concerned with bringing you to justice . . . therefore take diligent care, not to show uneasie remembrance and resentment, of the evils or injuries you have suffer'd, but only of those that you your self have done.[22]

All the elements of a Christian repentance are here: an acknowledgement that the punishment is justified, a public apology, and a proper, forgiving state of mind. To that public act of confession might well be added an account of how the condemned man or woman came to his or her current parlous situation; how, perhaps, youthful disobedience and an early neglect of church attendance had been followed by drinking, gambling and consorting with loose women, and how those loose morals had in turn led to more serious criminal offences that had culminated in the crime for which the condemned person was about to pay with their life. Officiating clergymen were anxious that the condemned should not die in a state of despair, and also hoped that a heartfelt confession of sinfulness, even at this late point, would lead to the granting of divine mercy and the entry of the immortal soul of the executed felon into heaven rather than hell. For the most part, spectators at executions seem to have similarly hoped for displays of contrition.[23] Prisoners whose final words ran to expectation and who were seen to 'die penitent' could expect the sympathy of the crowd. Those who refused to do so invited its wrath or, at the very least, its indifference.

In 1682 the Leeds antiquary Ralph Thoresby described how he had witnessed the execution of a murderer who had confessed his guilt on the scaffold but refused to show repentance. His conduct, Thoresby wrote, 'struck tears into my eyes', but it also left the 'many thousand spectators' who were attending the execution 'exceedingly frustrated in their expectations'.[24] The crowd may have taken a ghoulish interest in the execution of a criminal but that does not mean that it simultaneously suspended any sense of morality. If a criminal publicly shamed and punished in this way showed contrition, then the public acknowledged that contrition.

V

Gradually official attitudes to the public shaming of criminals underwent a sea change. Ecclesiastical courts, revived after the Restoration in 1660, which had once required people to perform penance before the community as a whole, made ever less use of this sanction. In London, by the late eighteenth century, for example, those being punished for defamation generally had to make atonement, not in the main body of the church but in the parish vestry, and not before the whole congregation but only in the presence of their victim, the minister, and the churchwardens. By 1831, according to the Royal Commission set up to investigate the ecclesiastical courts, public penance was a very rare phenomenon indeed.[25]

The meting out of lesser public punishments by secular authorities also declined. Evidence from what in the seventeenth century was England's second city – Norwich – shows this very clearly. Between 1580 and 1645 the Norwich Mayor's Court imposed public whippings on 2,093 men and 1,086 women (at a time when the population of the city was around the 15,000 mark). But between 1660 and 1700 only 139 whippings were authorised. In the earlier period, some 433 offenders, most of them men, were put in the stocks. After 1660, though, only 6 were punished in this way, the last of them in 1687. In the earlier period 25 women were ducked in the river in the town's ducking stool. After 1660, only one was ducked (in 1670). The 'carting' of offenders seems to have ceased after 1660, while the cage, which in Norwich as elsewhere was located in the town square and in which petty criminals (usually women) were put on public show, accommodated 32 offenders between 1580 and 1645 but was not used at all after 1660. Even the pillory declined in popularity, though admittedly its use survived longer than some other forms of punishment. London secular court records show that it was used – on a regular, if infrequent, basis – throughout the eighteenth century and persisted into the nineteenth.

There seem to have been a number of practical reasons why the pillory should have fallen from use. In the first place, it's clear that the authorities became uneasy about the way in which the crowd could change a public shaming into a death sentence. Such was the fate, for example, of William Smith, one of two men pilloried for sodomy in London in April 1780. Sodomites were invariably the objects of mob hostility, and the two wretched men were pelted with missiles. According to one account, Smith died after being hit on the head by a brickbat. Other accounts reported, however, that because Smith was quite a short man, he was unable to touch the ground fully with his feet when his head had been locked in the pillory and so slowly strangled to death (he is said to have pointed this out to the officials who were on hand, but they were too afraid of the mob to do anything about it). Outraged that Smith's supposedly lesser punishment should have proved 'an instrument of death', Edmund Burke raised the issue in Parliament, blaming both the mob and the presiding authorities.[26]

Then there were concerns that the use of the pillory for political offenders could very easily backfire – as it did in Daniel Defoe's case, and as it did again in 1812 when somewhere between 12,000 and 20,000 people turned out to express their support for Daniel Eaton, who had been sentenced for publishing the third part of *The Age of Reason* by the notorious radical Tom Paine. And finally there was the issue of whether it was right to subject people of superior social standing to the tender mercies of the mob, even if they happened also to be criminals. Objections were made, for example, to the pillorying of Thomas, Lord Cochrane in 1814 for Stock Exchange fraud, the judge and legal writer Thomas Talfourd also pointing out that 'those whom you suffer to riot on the side of the laws may soon learn to oppose them with similar outrages . . . we educate them for revolution and carnage'.[27]

In response to these various pressures a new statute was passed in 1816, restricting the pillory to those found guilty of perjury ('the punishment of the pillory has in many cases been inexpedient and not fully to answer the purpose for which it was intended', the statute argued); and the pillory disappeared altogether from English life when the punishment for perjurers was amended by a further statute in 1837.

But if issues of crowd behaviour help explain why the pillory should ultimately have disappeared, they don't provide the full answer. And they certainly don't explain why there should have been a virtually simultaneous decline in, say, public whipping – after all, unlike the pillory, it was one of a number of punishments in the official armoury that was wholly in the control of those administering it; it was not left to the tender mercies of the crowd. Clearly other, less tangible factors were also at work: for reasons that even now are not entirely clear, the public shaming of criminals was, by the latter part of the eighteenth century, falling from favour. Just as the charivari and the ducking stool slowly disappeared, and scolding and lampooning ceased to be regarded as matters for the court, so the idea that people should be punished before the community as a whole started to lose favour. Thus when it was announced that a man convicted of theft was to be whipped 'in a medium state of nakedness' through the streets of Chester, the *Chester Chronicle* was less than impressed. In a report dated 20 April 1792 it complained: 'This mode of punishment (not less impolitic than it is indecent) is generally and justly hastening to its exit, and in a few years more is likely to be remembered only with astonishment.' The journalist had correctly captured the changing mood of the time.

That does not mean, of course, that legally sanctioned physical punishment and humiliation ceased, but they did move to a more private sphere. Humiliation in the open gave way to short terms of incarceration in the local house of correction. Chastisement of criminals before their fellow citizens gave way to chastisement behind bars.[28] In London private whipping started to gain ground in the eighteenth century. In the first decade of the nineteenth century 95 men in London were whipped at the cart's tail and 28 at whipping posts, but 471 men and 85 women were whipped in prisons or in houses of correction. That no women should have been whipped in public by this time is significant – and in fact public whipping of women was ended in 1817. The public whipping of men continued until 1862.

There is no evidence that the frequency of whipping immediately declined once it was taking place behind bars. Indeed, in the same year that public whipping of men was abolished, a panic about a supposed wave of garrotting in the capital actually led to whipping's increased use: street robbers convicted in the aftermath of the garrotting scare could find themselves subjected to between one and three flogging sessions, followed by a spell of penal servitude. Thereafter the use of flogging was extended, particularly to young offenders being tried at local summary courts: 3,400 of them were whipped after sentencing in 1900 alone. The number of lashes meted out varied. The Garrotting Act gave judges the discretionary power to sentence persons aged over sixteen convicted under the Act to three whippings, each of up to 50 strokes, in additional to penal servitude for life; offenders under sixteen were liable to up to three whippings, each of 25 strokes. Later the flogging of young offenders convicted before local summary courts seems to have been a much more arbitrary affair: twelve-year-old boys might receive 60 strokes of the birch; boys as young as ten might be given 48 lashes of a custom-made, smaller cat o' nine tails.[29] It was not until 1948 that the practice of whipping was finally abolished. Clearly, the principle of corporal punishment retained favour for many decades after it ceased to be a public spectacle – and long after 1948, too.[30]

When it comes to military floggings, though, what might be termed a 'civilising' process is very apparent. The nineteenth-century British army had a number of means of punishment at its disposal, ranging from execution to various lesser sanctions imposed at the discretion of regimental commanders: short periods of solitary imprisonment, confinement to barracks, docking pay, or extra fatigues. Flogging was regarded as key – the only way, according to diehard military opinion, of ensuring that discipline was maintained among soldiers, who unlike the rank and file of continental armies, were drawn from the 'dregs of society'. To civilian radicals (and a very few military figures), however, flogging was barbarous, not least because it could occasionally result in death: in the era of Waterloo an unspecified number of offences could result in an unspecified number of strokes from the cat o' nine tails, and it is chilling to note that it was regarded as a major concession when it was decided in 1807 that floggings should be restricted to a maximum of 1,000 lashes. Pressure on the military led, by the mid-century mark, to a further reduction in the number of lashes that could be inflicted, by which time flogging was becoming less frequent in any case, its place generally being taken by short terms of imprisonment (from 1844 military prisons were introduced at a number of major depots in Britain, Ireland and across the Empire). There were resurgences of flogging during the military emergencies of the Crimean War and the Indian Mutiny. It was finally abolished by the Army Act of 1881 (which, incidentally, defined twenty-seven capital offences under military law), but was retained as a punishment in military prisons. It also made a brief reappearance during the Second World War. A number of men convicted of military offences during the Chindit campaigns in Burma in 1943 apparently opted for brief floggings from senior NCOs in preference to more formal proceedings.[31]

VI

Nowhere is the retreat from public punishment more apparent than in the gradual abandonment, and ultimate abolition in 1868, of public execution. Its more extreme forms were already in decline in the eighteenth century. The last beheading of a nobleman for treason, for example, took place in 1747, when Simon Fraser, 11th Lord Lovatt, aged eighty or so, paid a deadly price for his belated participation in the Jacobite Rebellion (he was, apparently, amused when a wooden stand collapsed as he was making his way to the gallows, killing up to twenty spectators). Thereafter instances of treason among the upper echelons of society became ever rarer, and the need for salutary punishment correspondingly diminished.

Women convicted of killing their husbands and consequently found guilty of 'petty treason' (a crime that also included counterfeiting coin) were traditionally burned at the stake, but this, too, fell into disuse by the end of the century. Even before then, the way in which it was carried out had been moderated somewhat, in that whereas once the victim had had to suffer the agony of the flames, by the eighteenth century it had become the custom for the executioner to strangle the condemned before igniting the pyre. Things went badly wrong, however, in the case of Katherine Hayes, convicted in 1726 for killing and dismembering her husband with the assistance of two male accomplices: because the fire was lit prematurely, the executioner was unable to reach her in order to strangle her, and she was therefore burnt alive.

What partly seems to have prompted the final abolition in 1790 of burning – never common as a punishment in any case – was the controversy surrounding the burning at Newgate in 1788 of Margaret Sullivan, who had been found guilty of counterfeiting coin. As *The Times* pointed out it seemed extraordinary that Britain should be consigning a woman to the flames 'for putting a pennyworth of quicksilver on a half-penny worth of brass' when it was simultaneously denouncing slavery and the practice of widow-burning in India. Practical considerations were in play, too. The London sheriffs had reported concerns about crowd control at such executions, and the recent decision to relocate hangings from Tyburn to the area immediately outside Newgate prison meant that any burnings now decreed had to be carried out in a built-up area, something that was not exactly popular with local residents: when Phoebe Harris was burned for coining in 1786, *The Times* reported that several people living near Newgate had been made ill 'by the smoke which issued from the body of the unhappy female victim'. The fact that such pragmatic concerns should have been taken into account serves as a useful reminder not to assume too readily that every reform is an automatic indication of a liberalising or humanitarian instinct at work. Even so, it's interesting to note that *The Times* should have referred to Phoebe Harris as an 'unhappy female victim'.[32]

The most extreme of punishments – hanging, drawing and

quartering for high treason – was also in decline by the mid eighteenth century, and was unthinkable by the early nineteenth, although it remained on the statute books. As the fate of the Babington conspirators showed, it was an exercise in calculated cruelty. The convicted man would be dragged to the place of execution facedown on a hurdle. There he would be hanged for a short period, but be cut down before he was dead. He would then be castrated and disembowelled, his genitals and intestines being burned in a fire before him. After that he would be decapitated, his body would be cut into four quarters, which together with his head would be boiled in pitch, and his remains would be publicly displayed as a warning to others. That, at least, was the theory, though the grislier aspects of the practice were in effect discontinued after 1782. Thus when five men were sentenced to death in 1820 for the Cato Street conspiracy to murder the Prime Minister and his cabinet, their sentence was commuted to hanging and beheading. Even then the authorities were clearly worried about the possible reaction of the crowd, and ensured that soldiers from both the foot and horse guards were there on the day, along with 700 constables and their assistants and six light artillery pieces. In the event, the crowd caused no trouble. They did, however, boo and hiss while the decapitations were being carried out. Similar reactions had been noted three years earlier when three men were hanged and decapitated for treason at Derby.[33] Clearly even this modified form of execution was out of step with the times.

A number of men were sentenced to be hanged, drawn and quartered after the Newport Chartist rising of 1839, but their sentences were commuted to transportation. The Treason Felony Act of 1848 made penal servitude the standard penalty for all but the most heinous acts of treason; and hanging, drawing and quartering was finally abolished as a side effect of the Forfeiture Act of 1870. In legal theory, however, capital punishment for treason was not abolished until the Crime and Disorder Act of 1998 (perhaps best known for introducing Anti Social Behaviour Orders).

As for the public exhibition of the corpses of criminals executed for particularly heinous crimes, this ceased in the 1830s. The custom had been to gibbet them – to hang their bodies either in chains or in metal baskets at the scene of their crime – and leave them to rot. But by the 1830s, the view was increasingly expressed that this was a custom that belonged to the past. An attempt in 1827 to gibbet a murderer on the road near Brigg in Lincolnshire was blocked by a public outcry. Five years later, in 1832, the body of William Jobling, a Jarrow miner gibbeted for murdering a local magistrate, was simply taken from the gibbet by his workmates and given a proper burial.[34] In the same year – the year of the Great Reform Act – the final English gibbeting took place, when the body of James Cook, a young bookbinder convicted of murder, was brought from Leicester county gaol and displayed before a crowd estimated at 20,000 strong. The antiquarian William Kelly, who was there on the day, recalled half a century later that his father had taken him 'because he had no doubt that it would be the last time that such an event would ever take place in England', a view that nicely blended past and present: Kelly's father clearly thought both that gibbeting was a suitable spectacle for a young boy and that it had had its day.

Cook's corpse was soon brought down by order of the Home Secretary, and the practice of gibbeting was abolished in 1834. During the parliamentary debate that preceded abolition, Edward Harbord, 3rd Baron Suffield, who had, to the despair of his family, become a Whig after the Peterloo Massacre and a supporter of penal reform and the abolition of the slave trade, expressed the view that gibbeting was out of line with current public feeling, that it was fit only for scaring children and brutalising the minds of those who saw the rotting corpse, and that it served no moral purpose.

Public hanging, too, was in decline by this period, and had been since before 1700. As previously stated, around 75,000 people were executed in England between 1530 and 1630, yet the best estimate for the total between 1770 and 1830 is a relatively modest 7,000.[35] In the single year 1598, 74 people were capitally convicted in Devon, of whom perhaps 60 were actually executed (these deaths came towards the end of a period that had seen a series of bad harvests and so widespread distress and a corresponding increase in theft and prosecution for theft). By contrast, the figure for the whole of the Western assize (of which Devon was just one part) for the period 1805–14 is 82.[36]

Quite why the number of executions should have dropped so suddenly around the middle of the seventeenth century and stayed low over much of the eighteenth is one of the biggest puzzles of the history of punishment in England; it has to be admitted that no wholly satisfactory explanation has yet been found. But it is possible to offer some tentative suggestions. One is, of course, that the 'civilising' force described by Norbert Elias was starting to make its effect felt. Back in the early sixteenth century, in his *Utopia* of 1516, Thomas More had criticised the frequency with which thieves were executed, suggesting that hanging was an unduly harsh and also ineffective punishment. A century later the jurist Sir Edward Coke wrote in his *Institutes of the Laws of England* 'what a lamentable case it is to see so many Christian men and women strangled on the cursed tree of that gallows', adding that if it were somehow possible for a person to see all those who had been executed gathered together in one place: 'if there were any spark of charity or grace in him, it would make his heart bleed for pity and compassion'.

Addressing Parliament in 1656, Oliver Cromwell told MPs that 'there are abominable laws that will be in your power to alter', explaining that 'ill framing' of the laws made it possible 'to hang a man for sixpence, three pence, I know not what'.[37] Of course, there were plenty of dissenting voices, but it does seem – certainly by the mid eighteenth century – that those who expressed reservations about the wide application of the death penalty were in the ascendant.[38] Indeed a parliamentary committee reported in 1751 that it felt that the scope of capital punishment should be limited, although in the event its recommendations were not followed. The following decade saw Cesare Beccaria's landmark *Dei delitti e delle pene* (published in English in 1767), which among other things argued that milder but more certain, fixed and predictable punishments were preferable to the lottery of the *ancien régime* system of criminal justice.

There's no evidence of concerted demands for root and branch reform of the punishment system in England at this time. But judges and juries, prosecutors and defenders, as well as the public at large, were all aware of various loopholes, some of them little more than legal fictions, that allowed the exercise of restraint in potentially capital cases. This helps explain the apparent mismatch between the high number of convicted criminals who should have been executed under English law and the relatively small number who actually were.

Some of these loopholes had been around for a long time. Benefit of clergy, by which a literate man was able to escape capital conviction for many forms of felony (notably manslaughter and grand larceny) was, as described in Chapter 3, clearly being extended to the illiterate by the late sixteenth century. Benefit of the belly, according to which pregnant women could not be hanged until after the birth of their child, was by late-Elizabethan times being adapted into a legal fiction that worked to the advantage of various categories of female offender.

It also seems to be the case that in many trials for theft, the value of the goods stolen was deliberately undervalued to save the accused from a conviction for the capital crime of grand larceny (officially invoked when the goods were worth more than a shilling). Richard Gough records a story about one of his contemporaries in the Shropshire parish of Myddle, one John Aston, 'a sort of silly [i.e. simple-minded] fellow, very idle' who had a tendency to pilfer from his neighbours but only to be verbally reprimanded ('well cajoled') in return. Only reprimanded, that is, until the day he stole twenty-four cocks and hens from another villager and found himself being indicted at Shrewsbury assizes. The judge noted Aston's simple-mindedness, and in his summing up told the jury that the man was clearly guilty, but that they would 'doe well to consider the value' of the goods stolen. The jury took the hint, and found Aston guilty of a crime worth elevenpence, 'at which', Richard Gough writes, 'the judge laught heartily and said he was glad to heare that cocks and henns were so cheap in this country'.[39]

We have no way of telling precisely how often the legal process was manipulated in this way to remove a plaintiff from the danger of capital punishment, but it is worth noting that of 2,381 men known on the basis of surviving documentation to have been indicted for larceny at the Essex assizes and quarter sessions between 1620 and 1680, 105 were hanged, 485 were branded after supposedly passing the reading test, which qualified them for benefit of clergy, and 394 were whipped (the punishment for petty larceny).[40]

Here, then, was an anomaly. By the end of the eighteenth century there were approximately 200 offences under English law that carried the death penalty (they were known as the 'Bloody Code'). Yet, in practice, many people convicted of an offence that, according to the letter of the law, carried a death sentence, were able to avoid it. In the meantime, alternative forms of – non-lethal – punishment had sprung up, largely because it was felt that those convicted of non-capital felonies often merited more thoroughgoing punishment than merely being branded on the hand. In 1718, confronted with the crime wave that followed the demobilisation of soldiers and sailors after the War of the Spanish Succession, Parliament passed an Act permitting the transportation of convicted felons to the American colonies for a period of seven or, for more severe offences, fourteen years. Those who dared to return before their allotted time faced the death penalty. Over the next few decades, until transportation to America came to an end in 1776, around 30,000 convicts were transported from England, perhaps 13,000 from Ireland and in the region of 700 from Scotland, most of them being sent to Virginia and Maryland. This represented a significant investment, in terms of time, money and transport, in a radically new penal policy.[41] It was followed by a similar, and better-known, scheme in Australia. On 20 January 1788 the first fleet landed at Botany Bay in Australia, carrying 736 convicts, 188 of them women. By 1868, when transportation to Australia ended, some 160,000 British and Irish convicts had been sent there.[42]

The outbreak of the French Revolution in 1789, and the fear it triggered among other European governments, caused a temporary hardening of official views of capital punishment, but with Napoleon's final defeat in 1815 reform was once again in the air. In 1818, for example, Parliament debated whether to repeal the act that had made shoplifting a capital offence. Those in favour of changing the status quo made a two-fold argument: that it was wrong to execute someone for such a comparatively trivial crime and that the existing law was in any case ineffective – 655 people had been prosecuted for shoplifting between 1805 and 1817, but, of those, 177 had been acquitted, 365 had been found guilty of simple larceny, and the 113 who had been convicted had not actually then been executed.[43] Those opposed to reform invoked the argument of ultimate sanction: none might actually have been executed, they argued, but the fact that the death penalty was available to judges meant that they had the necessary tools to hand to deal with repeat or particularly hardened offenders. Besides, the death penalty was a deterrent, championed by no less a figure than Archdeacon William Paley, whose *Principles of Moral and Political Philosophy* of 1785 had argued that the objective of capital punishment was not so much justice as deterrence based on terror. (Rather chillingly Paley had answered the one unanswerable objection to capital punishment – that mistakes cannot be rectified – with the suggestion that an innocent man who was executed could be 'considered as falling for his country'.[44])

The era after the First Reform Act saw the final dismantling of the Bloody Code. By 1837 capital punishment was restricted to twelve offences: murder and attempted murder, rape and carnal abuse of girls aged under ten, 'unnatural' offences (bestiality and male homosexual intercourse), robbery involving cutting or wounding the victim, arson when lives were endangered, piracy when murder was attempted, riot and feloniously destroying buildings, embezzlement by servants of the Bank of England, and high treason. Rape and felonious riot were removed from the list in 1841, and by 1861 murder, treason, arson in the royal dockyards, and piracy were the only four remaining capital crimes.[45] From 1837 in practice only murderers were executed. Between that year and the ending of public execution in 1868 a total of 347 murderers were executed in England and Wales, along with three people found guilty of attempted murder.[46] An alternative form of punishment was taking hold.

VII

It would be wrong to see the rise of the prison as some inevitable and inexorable process. Its evolution was far too uneven for that claim to be sustained. But between Georgian and Victorian times it came to occupy a central role in the handling and treatment of convicted criminals. The first initiatives, dating from the 1730s, were very much ad hoc local efforts, where labour was often added to imprisonment to form a secondary punishment for offenders for whom hanging was seen as too severe a penalty. A number of new model county gaols were constructed, notably that at Horsham, built at the behest of the Sussex justices of the peace and to the designs of the Duke of Richmond's surveyor. Just a couple of years before it was completed in 1779 a landmark book on prison reform appeared: John Howard's *The State of the Prisons in England and Wales*. Meticulously researched, it gave a powerful boost to a developing notion that a network of improved and modernised prisons might be put at the centre of the criminal justice system. Nevertheless other routes continued to be explored.

When the revolt of Britain's American colonies put an end to transportation across the Atlantic, two old ships, the *Justitia* and the *Censor*, were anchored on the Thames off Woolwich in August 1776 to hold 300 convicts, who were sent ashore each day to carry out public works. By 1815 there were five of these 'hulks' holding 2,429 convicts. And, as already mentioned, from 1788 Australia became a dumping ground for unwanted prisoners (Greenland having been considered and rejected). John Howard and his supporters did in fact manage to get legislation for a national penitentiary pushed through in 1779, but with no practical consequences.

For the next decade or so little happened. Then, in 1792, Gloucestershire's sheriff, Sir George Onesiphorus Paul, pushed ahead with five new local houses of correction and a new county gaol, all based on the principle (inspired in part by experiments in the United States) that what a prison sentence should achieve was not just the punishment but the reform of the offender. The Gloucestershire experiment in turn helped to inform the deliberations of the influential Holford Committee, which made its report in 1811, and whose findings resulted in the building of Millbank Prison (completed in 1816 at considerable expense to the taxpayer) on the site now occupied by Tate Britain. And then in 1840 legislation was passed enabling the construction of what was to become regarded as the epitome of the reformatory prison, Pentonville, a building that symbolises the massive shift in attitudes to the punishment of prisoners that had taken place over a period of a century or so.

Hardened Elizabethan criminals shown Pentonville at work would have struggled to comprehend what sort of institution it represented, and how precisely its inhabitants were being punished. In their own time, they would have expected execution, or at the very least public humiliation. Now they would see their successors being confined in a building where they received, at public expense, bread and cocoa for breakfast, gruel for lunch and stew for supper. They were permitted to write one letter a week, and were given regular moral instruction. They were no longer punished in public, but spent most of the time in their cells with only a Bible and (it was hoped) their awakening conscience for company. Even at this early stage in the evolution of the modern prison the opinion was expressed that it was too soft on criminals.[47]

It's tempting to view the new restrictions placed on the use of the death penalty as evidence for a growing abolitionist movement. But the reality is rather more complicated than that. Arguably, the objective of many of the reformers was not to punish more mildly, but to punish more effectively:[48] they could see that a wide gap had opened up between capital convictions and executions and felt that the status quo was untenable, that they faced a stark choice between embracing reform or preserving an absurdity. Moreover popular opinion still favoured the death sentence. Commoners, not to mention a few aristocratic enthusiasts, continued to flock to public executions. In 1820 spectators were prepared to pay three guineas to secure good vantage points from which to view the hanging and beheading of the Cato Street conspirators.[49]

Hangmen could achieve celebrity status. William Marwood, for example, who took over as hangman for London and Middlesex in 1874, and who perfected the 'long drop' that ensured the prisoner's neck was broken instantly, acquired admiring fans to whom he would happily show off his favourite ropes, while newspaper reporters would join him to chat about executions over a drink in the pub. Within three weeks of his death in 1883, the authorities had received 1,400 letters applying for his old job. Applicants stressed their reliability, their physical strength and the durability of their nerves. One said he had practised hanging dummies and felt he could improve the existing system of execution. Another stated that he would be willing to execute ten people a day, underlining this point three times. Yet another staked his claim to the job on the basis of being a pig slaughterer; his profession, he said, had given him nerves of iron. Even today, of course, polls suggest that almost half of the British population are in favour of capital punishment. One wonders how many of them would willingly become executioners.[50]

Even so, there does seem to have been a growing uneasiness, certainly among many middle-class people, about the death penalty. Some clearly sympathised with those who had to suffer the gallows, and identified with them.[51] Some sensed a contradiction between the message of Christianity and the exaction of brutal punishment. And some, such as the prison reformer John Howard, felt both religious and personal qualms: a dissenter deeply concerned with establishing what God's purpose for him was, he had himself experienced the horrors of incarceration – in a dungeon at Brest – after the ship he was on was captured by a French privateer. In fact, dissenters – notably Quakers – were to play a crucial role in penal reform. Elizabeth Fry (1780–1845), for example, worked closely with women prisoners. In 1863 the Quaker William Tallack (1831–1908) became secretary of the recently formed Society for the Abolition of the Death Penalty (which in 1866 evolved into the Howard Association). Like his co-religionists he passionately believed that criminals and prisoners, whatever their faults, were fellow human beings, and that they could all too easily be the victims of their environment.

The abolitionists were, however, very much in a minority, and even then some within their ranks wavered in their loyalty to the cause. John Stuart Mill, for example, although an advocate of abolition at certain points earlier in his career, came out in opposition to it in an 1860 House of Commons debate on the issue, his argument being that it was not only the most appropriate but also the 'least cruel' punishment for murder.[52] Charles Dickens was similarly equivocal. At first he condemned death by hanging, notably in a series of letters to the Daily News written in 1846, recalling how horrified he had been by one of the most celebrated executions of the period, that in 1840 of the murderer François Courvoisier, a Swiss valet convicted of cutting the throat of his employer, Lord William Russell:

> . . . if any one among us could have saved the man (we said so, afterwards, with one accord), he would have done it. It [i.e. the execution] was so loathsome, pitiful, and vile a sight, that the law appeared to be as bad as he, or worse; being very much the stronger, and shedding around it a far more dismal contagion.

By the end of the following decade, however, Dickens had come out in support of the death penalty in the case of the falsely accused poisoner Dr Thomas Smethurst.

That said, Dickens was consistent in his loathing for public executions. Looking back at the hanging of Courvoisier, he recalled how he had recoiled at the behaviour of those who had gathered to watch a man die:

> I did not see one token in all the immense crowd; at the windows, in the streets, on the house-tops, anywhere; of any one emotion suitable to the occasion. No sorrow, no salutary terror, no abhorrence, no seriousness; nothing but ribaldry, debauchery, levity, drunkenness, and flaunting vice in fifty other shapes. I should have deemed it impossible that I could ever have felt any large assemblage of my fellow-creatures to be so odious.

Dickens was not alone. Concerns were persistently expressed in Victorian England about crowd behaviour and crowd control, just as they were voiced in Germany in the aftermath of the 1848 revolutions (there the abolition of public execution followed in various states between 1853 and 1861).[53] And one can sense, too – certainly in Dickens's observations – a strong class element to the disapproval: in a letter he wrote to *The Times* on 13 November 1849, following the execution of husband and wife Frederick and Maria Manning for murdering Maria's wealthy lover, he talked of the 'thieves, low prostitutes, ruffians and vagabonds of every kind' who gathered to watch the couple die.

An additional factor in the growing distaste for public executions was not just that they were sometimes botched but that on occasion it was hard to feel anything but sympathy for the victim. One wonders, for example, how onlookers must have felt as they watched the eighteen-year-old girl who in 1849 had to be dragged by six men to her execution in Bristol. We certainly know that they were outraged by the fiasco that attended the hanging of the murderer William Bousfield, who had tried to commit suicide by throwing himself onto a fire in his cell the night before his execution in 1856, and was brought to the scaffold at Newgate too weak to stand and with his face swathed in bandages. When the drop opened beneath him, he summoned up the strength to lodge his toes on the edge of the trap,

and was only finally dispatched when the executioner, William Calcraft, went underneath the scaffold to pull on his legs. By now the
crowd were openly hostile. They jeered Calcraft and called him a
murderer.[54]

After the narrowing of the death penalty in 1861 down to four
offences, a Royal Commission was set up in 1864 to consider whether
it should be abolished altogether. Four of the twelve commissioners
were abolitionists, but they only managed to win over one of the
others to their side. The commission, therefore, voted in favour of
the retention of the death penalty but, by a vote of seven to five, also
recommended the abolition of public execution (the abolitionists,
anxious to preserve execution in its most unpalatable form in hopes
of influencing public opinion in the future, actually voted in favour
of retaining public hangings). When the Commission's recommendations were debated in Parliament, some agreed with Lord
Malmesbury, who argued that the 'fear of disgrace' that went with
public execution acted as a deterrent. More, though, agreed with
Lord Shaftesbury that 'in the great class from which murderers
were taken the sense of shame was wholly extinct', and that the
advantages of removing executions from public sight far outweighed
the disadvantages.

On 26 May 1868, therefore, the Irish Fenian Michael Barrett
achieved the dubious fame of being the last man to be publicly executed in England. He had been found guilty of a (badly miscalculated)
bomb attack on Clerkenwell prison to rescue a number of Fenians
incarcerated there, where twelve people had died and over fifty
had been injured.[55] He died game, apparently gaining the sympathy
of the crowd (we do not know how many of them were Irish), who
booed and cat-called the hangman. Less than three months later,
on 12 August, the first person to be executed inside prison met his
fate at Maidstone gaol. He was an eighteen-year-old railway porter
named Thomas Wells, who had murdered his station master after
being reprimanded by him. The machinery of execution had to be
improvised in the prison, with a hole dug to accommodate Wells's

body as it dropped, and a scaffold erected above it. Following the tradition observed in public executions he dressed in his porter's uniform – presumably the smartest clothing available to him – and, rather poignantly, wore a flower in his buttonhole. He was offered consolation by the prison chaplain, drank a cup of tea, and then had a linen cover placed over his head and was positioned on the drop. He survived for two minutes after it fell. Inaugurating a new custom, a black flag was raised above the prison immediately after his death, viewed not by the throngs who would have gathered for a public execution but by a mere twenty people. Ironically, there were probably more witnesses on the inside than on the out: as well as the prison governor, the prison chaplain, the hangman and other officials who were present, there were also sixteen newspaper reporters.[56]

Thereafter, while the death penalty was to remain on the statute book until 1965 (if not finally abolished until 1998), it was carried out far away from public gaze. For many that was a significant advance. It didn't however mean the end of botched executions and unnecessary suffering. William Marwood's successor as London and Middlesex hangman, for example, one Bartholomew Binns, who had previously been employed as a platelayer on the Lancashire and Yorkshire railway, took ineptness to a new level. He bungled his second and fourth executions, and at the coroner's inquest following his third, the prison governor expressed the opinion that the hanging had been carried out clumsily and inefficiently. When it came to what would have been his fifth execution, Binns was too drunk to carry it out. Binns's career as a hangman lasted for about a year, by which time he had executed 9 men and 2 women.[57]

PART III

‘VIOLENCE IS ALWAYS
ON THE AGENDA’:
THE MODERN AGE

PITY THE POOR GAROTTERS!

JOE HUGGINS. "O, PLEASE, SIR, DON'T! MR. PETER TAYLOR SAYS AS I'M DELICATE, AND A COWARD, AND DIDN'T OUGHT TO BE FLOGGED!!"

MR. BULL. "AH, INDEED! YOUR FRIEND, MR. PETER TAYLOR, SHOULD HAVE REMINDED YOU OF THAT BEFORE YOU THROTTLED THE OLD GENTLEMAN. LET HIM HAVE IT SOUNDLY, WARDER."

In 1862 newspapers and magazines became obsessed with the notion that 'garrotters' were at large on the nation's streets – part of a general fear of urban violent crime. In fact, the Victorian era witnessed a remarkable decline in law-breaking. This *Punch* cartoon ridiculed the idea – proposed by some MPs – that garrotters should not face flogging in prison.

CHAPTER 13

AN ENGLISH MIRACLE?

I

If the seventeenth and eighteenth centuries saw a gradual withdrawal from the crime and violence of medieval and Tudor
times – fewer murders, fewer assaults, less brawling – the following
era witnessed a further decline so sharp that two modern criminologists, Sir Leon Radzinowicz and Roger Hood, have dubbed it 'The
English Miracle'.[1] It was a decline on which the Victorians prided
themselves: '[I]t may with little fear of contradiction be asserted that
there never was, in any nation of which we have a history, a time in
which life and property were so secure as they are at present in England', Luke Owen Pike boasted in his monumental and pioneering
two-volume *A History of Crime in England*, published in 1873 and 1876.
He went on:

> The sense of security is almost everywhere diffused . . . There
> are, of course, in most great cities some quarters of evil repute,
> in which assault and robbery are now and again committed.
> There is, perhaps, to be found a lingering and flickering of the
> old sanctuaries and similar resorts. But any man of average stat-
> ure and strength may wander about on foot and alone, at any
> hour of the day or night, through the greatest of all cities and its

suburbs, along the high roads, and through unfrequented country lanes, and never have so much as the thought of danger thrust upon him, unless he goes out of his way to court it.[2]

The figures – certainly for the later part of the century – seem to bear out this optimistic, not to say triumphalist, view.

Between 1861 and 1865, 59,394 indictable offences were recorded in England and Wales – equivalent to an offence rate of 287.9 per 100,000 of population. Around about the same number of offences were recorded for the next five-year period, but since the population was rising sharply at the time, the actual average per 100,000 dropped slightly – to 270.5. Thereafter, apart from a blip between 1881 and 1885 when 60,220 indictable offences were recorded, the rate fell steadily. The five years between 1896 and 1900, for example, show not only lower total numbers than a quarter of a century earlier (51,612 cases as against 59,394) but a massive reduction in the average per 100,000 people – down from the high two hundreds to 175.6.[3] True, statistics for sexual assaults seem to have remained pretty constant over this period; however – as later – this was not so much because sexual violence remained immune from the changes clearly sweeping the country as because there was a greater willingness to report and prosecute such cases. In fact, of all the various types of crime that fed into the statistics, only burglary and housebreaking seem to have resisted the general trend downwards, no doubt because they were the offences most likely to be committed by a hard core of 'professional' criminals.

Murder rates started to decline from the mid-century mark. There was a brief upward trend in the 1860s, but thereafter the number of homicide indictments declined from an average of 299.4 per annum in the 1860s to 215.1 per annum. Over the same period, the homicide rate per 100,000 of population similarly fell markedly. In 1851 it stood at 1.9 per 100,000, in 1861 at 1.3, in 1911 at 0.6. In other words, in the sixty years after 1851, cases of homicide dropped by nearly two-thirds.

Most killers now were unskilled workers, ranging from factory hands to farm servants; most were men (male murderers outnumbered female murderers by seven to one); and by the late nineteenth century at least half of all of them were found guilty of murdering their wife or their mistress. Upper-class murderers were few in number; professional criminals who killed in the commission of another crime similarly quite rare (hence the reason that both types of killer tended to draw a lot of newspaper coverage when they struck). Murder, in other words, was a largely domestic affair – often the outcome of a long period of violence and unhappiness. As Sir John Macdonell, a lawyer and legal reformer, noted in his commentary on the 1905 edition of *The Judicial Criminal Statistics*:

> I am inclined to think that this crime is not generally the crime of the so-called criminal classes, but is in most cases rather an incident in miserable lives in which disputes, quarrels, angry words and blows are common. The short history of a large number of cases which have been examined might be summed up thus: – domestic quarrels and brawls; much previous ill-treatment; drinking, fighting, blows; a long course of brutality and absence of self restraint. This crime is generally the last in a series of acts of violence.[4]

This was a very different pattern from the one that had prevailed three or so centuries before. Murder had retreated from being a general social problem to one that was most commonly the outcome of relationships gone wrong.

As with homicide rates, so with indictments for felonious and malicious wounding, which dropped from a high of 3.5 per 100,000 in 1871 to 2.7 in 1901 to 2.0 in 1911. And the decline in the figures for assault – by far the most frequent violent offence – are even more remarkable. Most assault cases were dealt with summarily by local magistrates at petty sessions, so it is difficult to make direct comparisons between indictable (in effect, 'serious') offences and assault prosecutions. But even so it would be hard to interpret the near halving of cases (from 383.8 per 100,000 in 1861 to 197.2 in 1901) as anything other than evidence of an extraordinary social shift (see Appendix, Table 7).

II

As the figures were falling, crime was also becoming an increasingly urban phenomenon. In the early days of the Industrial Revolution, in particular, there was widespread concern that England's burgeoning industrial towns and cities were becoming hotbeds of crime and disorder and the breeding ground for the next generation of hardened criminals. Early-nineteenth-century crime statistics suggest that this concern was not without grounds. As mentioned previously, recorded homicide rates were relatively low in the years around 1800: 0.9 per 100,000 people in Surrey, 0.6 in Sussex, 0.8 in Essex and 1.1 in London and Middlesex. But over the next few decades, homicide levels in those counties that were industrialising rose markedly – Lancashire, Cheshire, Staffordshire and Glamorgan reaching 2.51 and above for the period 1834–48, and Warwickshire and Nottinghamshire 2.01–2.5: over double the level to be found in London just a generation before or indeed thirty years later. Meanwhile rural areas proved to be bastions of relative calm. In that fourteen-year span between 1834 and 1848, homicide rates for Lincolnshire, Westmorland and Cumberland were a modest 1.01–1.50 per 100,000. In Cornwall, Sussex and Suffolk they were even lower.

Much of the reason for this early increase in urban crime levels is that those who flocked to the burgeoning towns and cities of the 1830s and 1840s in search of work included a large number of unattached young men – traditionally the social group most likely to cause trouble. (By the same token, the fact that potential troublemakers were leaving the countryside helped make rural areas more tranquil.[5]) Once there, the men found themselves forced into poorly paid jobs and squalid housing. In places such as Liverpool,

Manchester, Stockport and Merthyr their numbers were further swelled by desperately poor Irish immigrants – and these cities experienced particularly acute crime problems as a result. Matters were made worse by the economic woes of the 1840s, which led to high levels of unemployment. It's scarcely surprising that the Chartists should have flourished in this decade, nor that many cities should have become synonymous with grinding poverty, drunkenness and despair.

The poorest areas of those cities, the parts described by Luke Owen Pike as 'quarters of evil repute', tended therefore to be places where violence and violent crime became concentrated – home to the 'rookeries' that Dickens described so vividly in *Oliver Twist*, where criminal gangs would gather amid conditions of appalling squalor in warrens of slum tenements that only the most foolhardy of outsiders would dare to enter. Even when economic circumstances improved from the 1850s onwards the tough inner-city areas remained, though the worst of the rookeries were gradually swept away by urban improvements in later Victorian times. Meanwhile the landscape of England and Wales continue to change inexorably. In 1831 about a third of the population of England and Wales lived in towns of more than 20,000 people. By 1891 that proportion had grown to two-thirds.

Confronted by these rapid changes, and the social problems that had sprung up with them, many were convinced that they faced a deeply uncertain, if not downright worrying, future. They could see the old ways of life disappearing, and were nervous about the new ones that were coming to take their place. Something of that mood of anxiety is caught in a description of Manchester in 1835 by the French historian and political writer Alexis de Tocqueville:

Thirty or forty factories rise on top of the hills I have just described. Their six storeys tower up; their huge enclosures give notice from afar of the centralisation of industry. The wretched dwellings of the poor are scattered haphazard around them . . . From this foul drain the greatest stream of human industry flows out to fertilise the whole world. From this filthy sewer pure gold flows. Here humanity attains its most complete development and its most brutish; here civilisation works its miracles, and civilised man is turned back almost into a savage.[6]

De Tocqueville's observations nicely capture the mid-nineteenth-century mood of ambivalence. On the one hand, here was a new world that was bringing forth previously unimaginable material improvements and technological achievements. On the other, there seemed to be a heavy price to be paid for such advances: material progress was being offset by the dark, anarchic threat of the industrial slums. It was a theme to which Friedrich Engels would return a decade later in his *The Condition of the Working Class in England*.

For middle-class observers their poorer urban brethren seemed at once fascinating, intimidating and incomprehensible, while their worst element – habitual, in some cases professional, criminals – seemed worryingly prevalent. In 1838 it was estimated that there were 135,000 criminals at large, with a further 25,000 in prisons and reformatories. The 1851 census was even more alarming, not to say alarmist: it suggested that there might be as many as 304,000 criminals in England and Wales (at a time when the total population was around 18 million). These were a class apart, with different values and different aspirations from respectable citizens. In the eyes of middle-class commentators they even looked different.

In 1836 the author of a tract on 'Artisans and Machinery' described the 'inferior classes in the manufacturing towns and districts' in the following terms:

Judging them by the same rules which have been applied to mark the advancement of man from a savage state, they have made but few steps forward; and though their primitive nature is disguised and modified by the force of external circumstances, they differ but little in inherent qualities from the uncultivated child of nature, and shew their distinction rather in the mode rather than the reality of their debased condition.[7]

A few years later, in 1851, the social commentator Henry Mayhew went even further in his description of London's street people:

> There is a greater development of the animal than of the intellectual or moral nature of man ... they are more or less distinguished for their high cheek-bones and protruding jaws – for their use of slang language – for their lax ideas of property – for their general improvidence – their repugnance to continuous labour – their disregard of female honour – their love of cruelty – their pugnacity – and their utter want of religion.[8]

Mayhew's comments to some extent anticipate the views put forward a little later by one of the founding fathers of criminology, the Italian Cesare Lombroso (1835–1909). In 1876 Lombroso, a former doctor with the Italian army, then director of various insane asylums and finally Chair of Legal Medicine and Public Hygiene at the University of Turin, published his best-known work, *L'uomo delinquente* [*Criminal Man*] in which he argued for the existence of the 'born criminal': a physically, mentally and morally inferior, even atavistic, human type owing much to primates and early human forms. Such a creature, Lombroso argued, could be recognised by particular physical characteristics – a sloping forehead, large ears, or an asymmetrical face or cranium.[9] Lombrosos's views, although widely popularised, were to be much challenged in British criminological circles, notably in Charles Goring's *The English Convict* of 1913, which rejected, on scientific grounds, the idea of a distinctive criminal physiognomy. But the presumption that criminals were somehow a breed apart, whose secrets could be revealed not by moralists but by specialists, experts and professionals, took root. And so while physiognomy became a controversial area of study, the belief that proper scientific investigation of criminals could yield up their secrets gained ground.

It was a view espoused, for example, by Henry Maudsley, possibly the leading psychiatrist of the late nineteenth century, who wrote in 1874:

> It is certain . . . that lunatics and criminals are as much manufactured articles as are steam engines and calico-printing machines, only the processes of the organic manufactures are so complex that we are not able to follow them. They are neither accidents nor anomalies in the universe, but come by law and testify to causality; and it is the business of science to find out what the causes are and by what laws they work.[10]

Theories about the 'criminal class' thus evolved over the course of the century, but the idea that, whatever the causes, there was a definable 'criminal class' remained strongly rooted.[11]

So far as the middle class was concerned, therefore, criminals lived in a separate moral and physical universe. Moreover it was a universe that was markedly, indeed increasingly, at variance with their own. For while in the popular imagination the 'criminal' remained a fixed entity, his observers were changing. They were leaving behind such old-style rough entertainments as bull-baiting, cock-fighting and bare-knuckle fighting. They were starting to view duelling among the nobility as an uncivilised anachronism. They looked askance at casual violence. They craved law and order, respect and respectability. They were, in a sense, becoming 'civilised'.

This transition was particularly marked in the domestic arena, notably in changing attitudes to violence within marriage. What had once been pretty widely accepted, now came to be viewed as unseemly. 'Chastisement' of wives certainly remained legally permissible, if it had been provoked by verbal or physical abuse, or infidelity, or the neglect of domestic duties (particularly if this was due to habitual drunkenness). But at the same time it seems the better educated and more well-to-do increasingly frowned upon it. At the 1828 trial of a man accused of beating his supposedly unfaithful wife to death with a stick, the presiding judge declared that 'I shall certainly not lay it down as the law of England that a man may *at all* chastise his wife. I am rather of opinion that a man does not possess that power.' The accused was convicted of murder and executed. Three years later the clause suggesting that a man had the right to chastise his wife was excised from a standard legal handbook of the time, Burn's *Justice of the Peace*, and from then on the notion of the right of chastisement seems to have disappeared from assize trials.

Trials of wife-killers show a hardening of the official line. As the Victorian era progressed, there seems to have been an increasing tendency for guilty men to be convicted of murder rather than man-slaughter, even when death was inflicted by beating or kicking rather than by a weapon, and even in those fairly rare cases where the husband had been provoked to violence by his wife's infidelity. In America and a number of European countries a crime of passion might elicit the sympathy of judge and jury; not so in England. Reporting the acquittal of the killer of an adulterous wife in Paris, *The Times* of 27 September 1884 dismissed the trial as 'one of those cases in which French juries reduce the institution of trial by jury to the ridiculous'.[12]

Urban working-class culture, by contrast, seemed to be rooted in the more violent past. Or, as John Carter Wood, one of the most ori-ginal historians currently working on nineteenth-century violence, puts it:

> In nineteenth-century England I believe that the most import-ant dynamic (but certainly not the only one) was the interaction between two dominant mentalities of violence. One I label 'civilised' (representing an emergent culture of middle- and upper-class refinement that idealised rationality and self-restraint) and another I call 'customary' (originating in an older social context, legitimating direct physical confrontation, appealing to less restrained notions of propriety and becoming associated with the poor and the working-classes).[13]

It is easy to be morally judgemental here. Carter Wood's careful use of the word 'customary', however, emphasises that elements of the Victorian working class simply preserved a traditional acceptance of certain forms of 'legitimate', or at least culturally acceptable, violence. It wasn't that they were somehow becoming more brutal; it was that their attitudes now seemed out of step with those of their more prosperous neighbours, who were leaving behind the culture in which casual, everyday violence was part of normality. Those adhering to this 'customary' culture were not changing. It was the middle and upper classes, from mid-century joined by growing ranks of the respectable working class – the 'civilised' element of society – who were increasingly making a break from the past.

In the process the attitude of educated people to violence, and, in particular, to violent crime, underwent a seismic change. There had always been official condemnation of physical force that was felt to be excessive, and, of course, its extreme forms had long been punishable by law. At a popular level broadside ballads and murder pamphlets had for centuries decried 'unnatural' or 'horrible' acts, while clergymen had spoken out from their pulpits against sins committed against the Sixth Commandment. But in 1800 violence was not seen as a 'social problem' nor as something that was the hallmark of particular groups or classes of society. By 1870 it was. Discussion of the individual criminal had been joined by discussion of the criminal 'classes', of which the criminal 'types' I touched on a little earlier were members.

John Carter Wood has gone so far as to argue that the first half of the nineteenth century witnessed the 'invention of violence'.[14] For the first time in English history, a sizeable proportion of the population were not only turning their backs on 'customary' violence, but labelling and condemning those who weren't, and regarding them almost as a species apart. As for those guilty of criminal violence, they came to be viewed as a fundamental threat to civilised values. A leading article in *The Times* of 29 March 1870 declared that habitual criminals were 'more alien from the rest of the community than a hostile army . . . The civilised world is simply the carcase on which they prey, and London above all, is to them a place to sack.'

III

But if the Victorians condemned violence, they were also fascinated by it. Sensational cases were not only celebrated in pamphlets and broadside ballads but were turned into plays. Murderers and their victims were captured in wax effigies and displayed at Madame Tussaud's or rendered as Staffordshire pottery figures. After the serial killer William Palmer was executed in 1856, details of the case and of the trial proceedings were published in classical Greek.[15] Above all, the popular press, which developed swiftly after the abolition of the duty on newspapers in 1855, and which was enthusiastically taken up by an increasingly literate public, wallowed in violent crime in all its excess. If John Carter Wood is right to say that violence was invented in the nineteenth century, then the writer Judith Flanders is to some extent justified in asserting that murder was invented at the same time.[16]

With Victorian popular journalism we see for the first time the shaping of public views of crime through the medium of print. If a newspaper thought a particular crime worthy of note, it could become a popular obsession – as, for example, the Whitechapel murders of 1888 swiftly became. If it decided that an isolated event suggested a trend, then it could create mass panic on which other newspapers would then feed. The burgeoning legend of Spring-heeled Jack is a case in point. It seems to have had its origin in two apparently unconnected incidents that took place in 1837. In one a servant girl named Mary Stevens, walking back to her employers' house after visiting her parents, was sexually assaulted by what she described as a rather peculiar man on Clapham Common. In the other, which occurred the following day in a street near where Mary Stevens worked, a strange-looking man jumped in front of a coach, causing it to crash, and then leaped over a nine-foot-high wall.

Other sightings of this mysterious figure then followed: in Brixton, Stockwell, Vauxhall, Camberwell, Lewisham and Blackheath. The strange man was variously said to shine with a blue light or to spurt fire, to be clad in brass or steel armour, and to wear 'spring shoes and large claw gloves'. A play about him, *Spring-heeled Jack, the Terror of London*, appeared in 1840, and in 1863 a forty-part penny dreadful serial describing his exploits was published. His last alleged appearance was in Liverpool in 1904. That such a palpably ridiculous urban legend could not only arise in the first place but be sustained for such a long period demonstrates the extent to which fear of crime and popular journalism fed off each other throughout the nineteenth century and beyond.[17]

Adding to this very heady mix of information, surmise and misinformation were the annual, officially gathered crime statistics for England and Wales. The first set appeared in 1810 and covered indictable offences committed over the previous five years, the exercise being prompted by ongoing parliamentary wrangles over the possible need for reform of the criminal law. From 1834, thanks to the Criminal Registrar Samuel Redgrave, historian of art by inclination but civil servant by career, logical categorisation of the raw numbers was introduced – ranging at the criminal violence end of the spectrum from simple assault to homicide.[18] Then as now, those statistics still had to be interpreted, and interpretations could vary wildly, but a large segment of public opinion nevertheless accepted them at more or less face value, and politicians and newspaper editors seeking to influence or form public opinion were happy to do the same.

For the first few decades in which they were collated they certainly did little to reassure people. They suggested, for example, that whereas the population of England and Wales had increased by 35 per cent between 1810 and 1840, committals for trial had increased by 275 per cent. The number of committals was to go on increasing into the 1840s. Apparently ever-rising levels of crime did little to reassure those already concerned about the agitations of the Chartists. For many in the 1840s the whole of respectable society appeared to be under threat.

IV

Changes in society as a whole were shadowed by changes to the operation of law and order. It is possible, for example, to argue for a link between the gradual middle-class withdrawal from violence and a hardening of official attitudes to those found guilty of such offences as assault. Records of the Essex quarter sessions from the mid eighteenth century to the early 1820s certainly seem to suggest this (see Appendix, Table 8).

Assault was, of course, a broadly defined offence, and most complaints were dealt with informally by justices of the peace or else tried at petty sessions, hence rarely resulted in formal indictment. But it's interesting to note that of those who were formally indicted and convicted of the offence between 1748 and 1752, the vast majority were given a nominal fine, whereas for the period 1819–21 they tended to be imprisoned (if only for a month or so). In the earlier period, about three-quarters of those accused went on to confess, which suggests that they cannot have viewed the punishment they faced as particularly worrying or onerous. In the later period, most pleaded not guilty and were therefore tried formally, which suggests that they did not exactly relish the prospect of the punishment that possibly confronted them. In the earlier period, the pattern of confession followed by a nominal fine suggests a relatively informal settlement – perhaps compensatory payment was agreed between the accused and the victim. By the 1820s that informality had given way to formal sanctions. One is led to conclude that the eighteenth-century Essex magistrate was considerably more tolerant of low levels of violence than his nineteenth-century successor.

In 1828 came one of the great landmark pieces of criminal reform – the Offences Against the Person Act, steered through

Parliament by the then Home Secretary Robert Peel. It broadened and refined the definition of what a crime of violence was, its aim being both to facilitate the conduct of trials and to ensure greater efficiency in the gaining of convictions. It also gave judges a range of sentencing options that extended to transportation for life. Less than a decade later it was followed by the 1837 Offences Against the Person Act which, contrary to the general liberalising tendency of legislation at the time, extended the death penalty for certain categories of crimes of violence, although manslaughter remained almost invariably punishable by imprisonment. The old 'Bloody Code' had therefore given way to a legal instrument that was more precise and, where it was deemed necessary, more ruthlessly efficient. By the mid-century mark murder had become the only crime for which the death penalty was likely to be awarded.

In tandem with changing approaches to sentencing came a new attitude to imprisonment. Prisons had, of course, been in existence since medieval times, and had been used to incarcerate a few categories of criminals. But their main function in the criminal justice system (they had, of course, also contained persons imprisoned for debt) had been to hold suspected felons before trial. Now, not only was imprisonment becoming an ever-more common form of punishment, but its nature was, by the late 1830s, undergoing a fundamental transformation.

Championed by a small but active group of philanthropists – many of them deeply religious – and taken up by Parliament in 1839, a new form of prison, the penitentiary, was introduced, designed not just to punish but to reform. In essence, it offered a three-stage programme of rehabilitation. During the first, the prisoner was kept in solitary confinement for ten months, his only reading material a Bible, his only regular visitor the prison chaplain. The idea was that, confined in this way, the wrongdoer would contemplate his past misdemeanours and reach a suitable level of repentance. After that, he would serve at least two years' hard labour on public works in the company of other convicts – ideally in Australia. And only then, assuming he had behaved well, would he be given a ticket-of-leave and be released back into society, though it was made clear to him that if he reverted to crime or became the object of any kind of suspicion that ticket-of-leave would be revoked. All in all, it was an intimidating mix of middle-class high-mindedness and Victorian authoritarianism.

V

And then in 1862 came an event that caused a perfect storm in which middle-class fears about working-class criminals, whipped up by a hysterical press, collided with the new, 'enlightened' approach to crime and punishment. At around 1 a.m. on 17 July, Hugh Pilkington, a cotton merchant and manufacturer as well as Member of Parliament for Blackburn since 1847, set out for his lodgings in St James's from the House of Commons. As he crossed Pall Mall he was assaulted, knocked to the ground and robbed of his watch and chain, though his assailants, in their hurry, did not rifle his pockets and steal the money they contained.

Pilkington was quite badly hurt in the attack: when help arrived it was found that his head was covered in blood, and that his jaw had been severely gashed. It transpired that he had been held by the head and choked when initially attacked. The next day his plight was the subject of an animated debate in the House of Commons. Horror was expressed that a Member of Parliament could be assaulted – and in Pall Mall of all places. The sense of outrage was heightened by the news that another eminently respectable citizen, a naturalist named Hawkins, had been attacked in the same way and in a 'safe' part of central London that same night.

From the point of view of the champions of prison reform, the attacks could not have come at a worse time. There had never been much popular enthusiasm for their views in any case, and by the mid-century mark there was a widespread feeling that the changes they had set in motion were not really working, not least because of the growing reluctance of Australian colonies to accept more convicts (only sparsely populated Western Australia continued to take them after 1852). By the 1860s a large number of convicts were actually serving out their sentences in England, and, more worryingly, a fair number of ticket-of-leave recipients – to all intents and purposes serious offenders, who had not fully served their sentences – were at large. The police found it hard to keep tabs on released prisoners, and also felt that they were not being given a strong enough lead by those in authority. To the sceptics, prison reform was in tatters and had been proved a nonsense. *The Saturday Review* for 30 August 1862 commented acidly:

> It is clear that we have not yet found out what to do with our criminals. We neither reform them, nor hang them, nor keep them under lock and key, nor ship them to the Antipodes. Our moral sewage is neither deodorised nor floated out to sea but remains in the midst of us polluting and poisoning our own air.

To make matters worse, there had been recent disturbances in prisons, notably at Portland in 1858 and, more seriously, at Chatham in 1861. At Chatham, the prison authorities had completely lost control over the prisoners, and 500 soldiers had had to be called in to restore order.[19] Meanwhile, recently released crime statistics had shown a rise in indictments (due, no doubt in part, to a brief period of economic depression).

The *Spectator* was among the first to join the fray after the attack on Hugh Pilkington. Its 19 July edition claimed that 'highway robbery is becoming an institution in London, and roads like the Bayswater Road are as unsafe as Naples', and suggested that the only reason that the authorities were now taking any notice was because 'some ruffian with less brains than his fellows' had attacked an MP. The police also came in for a lot of criticism. But then the hostility of the press was redirected towards those it deemed to be soft on crime. The *Manchester Guardian* of 2 November 1862 put it thus:

Under the influence of our humanity mongers, we have nursed and fostered a race of hardened villains, who are perfectly well acquainted with the comforts of all the gaols in the kingdom, who have fully earned the liberality with which the penalties appointed by law and awarded by the judges are mitigated in practice, and who, for all we know, look upon their brief intervals in confinement as seasonable opportunities for renovating their health and strength. Well the public is now learning, in a rather startling fashion, what is the natural result of making pets of thieves and garrotters.

It's the classic argument that is still familiar to us today: 'humanity mongers' (or 'do-gooders' as we would call them) have made a nonsense of the penal system, punishments are insufficiently tough, and gaol is a soft option – we are all at threat because of these misplaced liberal instincts.[20] The assault on Hugh Pilkington proved this.

The choice of the word 'garrotters' by the *Guardian* writer to characterise some of the dangerous elements at loose in society was not a casual one. Technically, of course, garrotting in this context had a very precise meaning – the temporary asphyxiation of the victim through choking – and it was hardly one that characterised the average street robber, though it was certainly not new. There had, for example, been a similar panic in 1856, leading *The Times* to speak of 'the infamous garotte system' and to publish thirty-one letters on the subject between October of that year and February 1857. But with its overtones of calculated cruelty and life-threatening danger, and its nod to the Indian thuggee cult that was still fresh in the popular imagination (some correspondents referred to the phenomenon as 'thuggee'), 'garrotting' was the perfect word to invoke in the hysteria that followed the attack on Pilkington.

That hordes of garrotters really were at work in London in 1862 seems very unlikely, not least because accusations of garrotting only really seem to have become widespread after the publicity storm that followed the Pall Mall mugging. But once the word had lodged in the popular imagination, like mugging in the late twentieth century, it proved hard to shift. Accounts of garrotters multiplied. An anonymous correspondent even supplied the *Cornhill Magazine* with an introduction to 'the Science of Garrotting', claiming (on the basis of a conversation he had had with a prison convict) that garrotters were not lone wolves but organised groups who worked in threes, with two men keeping lookout and a third carrying out the actual attack:

> The third ruffian, coming swiftly up, flings his right arm around the victim, striking him smartly on the forehead. Instinctively he throws his head back, and in that moment loses every chance of escape. His throat is fully offered to his assailant, who instantly embraces it with his left arm, the bone just above the wrist being pressed against the 'apple' of the throat. At the same moment the garrotter, dropping his right hand, seizes the other's left wrist; and thus supplied with a powerful lever, draws his back upon his breast and there holds him. The 'nasty man's' part is done. His burden is helpless from the first moment, and speedily becomes insensible; all he has now to do is to be a little merciful.[21]

Such journalism drove the fears of the respectable to new heights. The 1856 panic had been stoked by newspaper expressions of concern about walking the streets at night, and had also engendered various suggestions for developing new means of self-defence, as well as satirical comment in the illustrated papers. But now widespread public concern led to the adoption of a number of counter measures, among them reinforced anti-garrotting collars. These measures, in turn, prompted new levels of satire in the popular illustrated journals, notably *Punch*, where ornate versions of anti-garrotting collars and other devices were imagined.

In the immediate aftermath of the attack on Pilkington the police arrested two ticket-of-leave men on suspicion of having carried out the assault, but the evidence against them was flimsy and the authorities had to content themselves with gaoling the pair for three months as suspicious persons. Soon London was awash with stories of garrotters at work. Thirty-two cases were reported by the press in November. In the same month twenty-three alleged garrotters were tried at the Old Bailey, of whom fifteen had previous criminal convictions and two were the ticket-of-leave men accused of assaulting and robbing Pilkington. Some garrotting stories were clearly fabricated by members of the public. At the trial of a woman who had been arrested trying to commit suicide by strangling herself with a handkerchief but who claimed in court that she had been garrotted, the chief clerk commented that 'it was another of those extraordinary stories that were now afloat, as to people being stopped in the street and garrotted . . . half the cases that were reported to the police were not true'. In December 1862 one of London's senior detectives, William Hamilton, went so far as to try publicly to refute press reports that three people had died as a result of garrotting attacks. Speaking at the Guildhall he announced that the authors of these reports would be prosecuted, and that 'those frequently concocted garrotting cases' had given the public a false sense of 'the insecurity of the metropolis'.

Not that the police themselves always avoided jumping on the bandwagon. When John 'Boney' Redwood, a consumptive former soldier with two minor convictions to his name, was arrested at the height of the panic for stealing £2 from a very drunk victim, the police claimed that they had seen him knock the man to the ground. Redwood, fearing a fit-up, declared: 'I know there have been a good many garrotte robberies about, and now you have me I suppose I must suffer for it.' He was right. Even though it emerged at the trial that the police had held the alleged victim in prison until he agreed to identify Redwood as the perpetrator, Redwood was sentenced to ten years' penal servitude. At any other time his offence would have been punished by a short spell in prison.[22] Others undoubtedly suffered as Redwood did.

Despite all the hysteria, not many cases made their way into court. The year before the panic, forty-five prosecutions for robbery with violence were brought before the Central Criminal Court. That number climbed by a relatively modest twenty in 1862, and even then it's by no means clear just how many of these extra cases actually involved garrotting. Indeed it's possible that the rise in arrests was simply down to a heavy police presence on the streets of London that followed in the wake of the 17 July attacks. Some suggested that what brought the garrotting crisis to an end was the heavy sentencing policy of Mr Justice Baron Bramwell, who put away those brought before him for periods ranging from three months to life. Others, though, argued convincingly that increased vigilance by the police in the autumn of 1862 had led to the apprehension of a small group of very active robbers. A few years later, in 1866, Mr Justice Lush was to argue that he had put an end to an outbreak of garrotting in Manchester by handing down stiff sentences. The following year the judge responsible for the Northern Circuit, Mr Justice Keating, said he could find no evidence to support Mr Justice Lush's optimism. It was a debate about cause and effect that still rages today.

The garrotting panic may have been little more than a media scare, but it had two important consequences. The first was the Security from Violence Bill, also known as the Garrotters' Act, which was introduced in Parliament on 24 February 1863 by Charles Adderley MP, later Baron Norton. Adderley, who was Conservative member for Staffordshire North, had published a tract on the ticket-of-leave system in 1857, and had a reputation for being progressive in matters of penal policy (he was particularly supportive of education and training for young offenders). But the Act he sponsored was a draconian one. Now judges could not only sentence convicted felons to spells in prison or to penal servitude but could recommend up to three floggings for them as well. It was therefore possible for a man convicted of robbery with violence to be sentenced to life imprisonment and 150 lashes. Some judges made the most of this new Act. Mr Justice Day, for example, ordered a total of 1,961 lashes of the cat or strokes of the birch at Liverpool in 1893 alone. He was credited with bringing down a local criminal team, the 'High Rip Gang'. Joseph Collinson of the Humanitarian League pointed out, however, that before Day had initiated his flogging campaign there had been an annual average of 56 robbery cases in Liverpool, and that when it came to an end the average was 79.

The more fundamental consequence of the garrotting scare, though, was an overhaul of the English prison system and the replacement of the optimistic reformatory regime introduced in the 1830s by something much more severe. Early in 1863 very public criticism was made of the liberal regime operating in Winchester gaol by Henry Howard Molyneux Herbert, 4th Earl of Carnarvon, member of the House of Lords and a justice of the peace in Hampshire.[23] His remarks were rapidly taken up by the press and subsequently debated in the Lords. At about the same time, and in response to mounting public pressure, a Royal Commission on the penal system was set up. Its final report did not entirely jettison the reformatory ideal, but it did leave the way open for a new Penal Servitude Act of 1864. Gradually more punitive attitudes, based on the notion that penal servitude was not 'sufficiently dreaded', took hold, and these were to bear fruit in the Prisons Act of 1877, which emphasised the notion of deterrence and also sought to ensure uniformity in the punishment of criminals by bringing England and Wales's 116 local prisons under central control.

The new, more unforgiving approach, and the legislation in which it was enshrined in 1877, was embodied in the person of Edmund Du Cane, from 1869 the chair of the Board of Directors of Convict Prisons and inspector general of military prisons. Aged thirty-nine when appointed to this office, Du Cane (1830–1903) was a Royal Engineers officer who had been involved in the prison system since 1863. Although he had some liberal attitudes (for example on the possibility of reforming young offenders) he was autocratic, intolerant of criticism, a disciplinarian and an admirer of order with a real gift for administration. The creation in 1877 of a national prison system based on the principle of deterrence was very much to his taste, and something he had worked towards since 1869.

VI

The great irony of all this is that the Garrotting Panic came just at the time when, as suggested earlier, figures for violent crime – even in the inner cities – were starting to fall. For the Mr Justice Lushes of this world this was no doubt a simple illustration of cause and effect: harsher punishments and more severe prison regimes, such men would have claimed, were deterring the criminal classes from their usual pursuits. The evidence, though, as already intimated, doesn't really support this. Others might have argued that by the mid-Victorian era more systematic policing was helping to drive down violent crime. Certainly, the replacement of the old ad hoc – and often hopelessly incompetent – bodies with the tightly organised Metropolitan Police by Sir Robert Peel in 1829 marked a watershed in the history of law and order. And while the police might not have been immediately popular and the London model not immediately adopted elsewhere (it wasn't until 1835 that the Municipal Corporations Act empowered towns to set up modern police forces and even then the 1839 Rural Constabulary Bill met with some resistance), by the second half of the nineteenth century a nationwide network of policing was both in place and widely accepted.[24]

That said, though, the existence of a more effective body of law enforcers didn't automatically guarantee their effectiveness in reducing crimes of violence. The police, then as now, were best suited to a role that involved detection rather than prevention. Their visible presence on the street almost certainly deterred certain crimes and criminals, but officers could not be everywhere all the time, and as the number of assaults on policemen shows, there were some tough urban pockets that they entered at their peril, unless in large numbers on exceptional occasions. Their champions viewed them as the 'domestic missionaries' who were helping to civilise the urban working class – and it's true that local 'police courts' helped to provide cheap, local justice. But as an engine of social change, the impact of the police was, at best, patchy.

Indeed it has been argued that the machinery of Victorian law and order, rather than driving down levels of violent crime, simply concealed them. That, at least, is the contention of a fascinating article, 'Rationing Crime', published by the historian Howard Taylor in 1998. Struck by the apparent stability in the level of criminal prosecutions brought in England between the mid nineteenth century and the 1920s, Taylor argued for what he termed a 'supply side' aspect to the workings of law and order: the levels of prosecution, he suggested, were determined not by how many crimes had actually been committed, but by what funds were available from the Treasury and local authorities to deal with them. Wilmot Seton, he pointed out, who in 1856 was appointed the Treasury Clerk responsible for funding criminal prosecutions, declared his intention to practise 'the strictest economy consistent with due administration of justice'. His successors followed suit.

At the same time local authorities unwilling to have the costs of prosecuting criminals passed on to them, and local police forces unwilling to see levels of prosecution increase, carefully selected which cases to prosecute and so were able to manage their budgets. All the statistical evidence from the period, as well as a mass of opinion, attests to a decline in crime in the late nineteenth and early twentieth century, but Taylor's thesis serves as a warning not to take this at absolute face value. As with other eras, Victorian crime statistics can be tricky to interpret.

This seems to have been the case even with the most serious of all crimes: murder. As previously mentioned, the murder rate in England and Wales stayed remarkably constant between 1851 and the 1920s, averaging around 150 cases per annum (with up to a 20 per cent variation either way in particular years). This may have been due, at least in part, to an unwillingness on the part of coroners to push the investigation of some suspicious deaths too far. The editor of *The Judicial Statistics* commented in 1899 that 'coroners' juries return as death by accident or misadventure or from natural causes many cases which are really homicide'.

A few years later the splendidly named Horatio Nelson Hardy, divisional surgeon to the Metropolitan Police at Dulwich, made a similar admission when giving evidence to a parliamentary select committee on death certification. Pressed about his contention that he had 'come across and reported over and over again, cases of children found dead under highly suspicious circumstances and that no action has been taken upon the police report', he replied that coroners were unwilling to incur the costs of having doctors perform autopsies: 'each coroner', he said, 'tries to make out that the expenses of his district are less than another; there is a sort of competition amongst coroners in that way not to exceed the other coroners in the amount they spend, because they think the County Council grudges it.'[25]

In fact (and even accepting that the crime statistics are not all that they appear), what seems to have lain behind the Victorian Miracle was not more effective law enforcement or tougher sentencing but something that is far harder to isolate and quantify: something like the 'civilising process' described by Norbert Elias that I have touched on several times before, and which from the mid nineteenth century was extending itself to sections of the English working class.

As we have seen in previous chapters, the working class, surely never as 'dangerous' in reality as early-nineteenth-century observers had imagined, was developing a 'respectable' stratum. Economics helped here: for many working-class men, especially skilled workers, wages were rising from the 1860s, and a growing number of working-class households were able to afford those consumer goods which might be classified as 'decencies'. From the 1870s basic education at least was available to all, and must have helped broaden the horizon of many working-class children. 'Respectability' now became both a possibility and a goal, and at this social level came to encompass sobriety, thrift, a maintenance of 'appearance' – and a diminished propensity to get into fights. To this was added the various influences of non-conformist religion, trades union activity, and, by the last two decades of the nineteenth century at least, participation in sports clubs and other social organisations. More adult men, and their families with them, felt they had achieved a stake in society, formalised by the extension of the franchise to at least a proportion of working-class males via the 1867 and 1884 Reform Acts. Accordingly, the traditional 'rough' culture of the past declined further, although there were, of course, many urban areas where it continued to flourish.

There is, wage levels apart, admittedly little hard statistical evidence for this social trend away from violence. But there is plenty of anecdotal evidence. It was, for example, something that social commentators frequently touched on. The economist Alfred Marshall wrote optimistically in one of his early essays, 'The Future of the Working Classes' (1873), that 'All ranks of society are rising', and concluded from this that 'on the whole they are better and more cultivated than their forefathers were . . . Even if we take the ruder labourers, we find something to set off against the accounts of their habits of indulging in drink and rough pastimes.'

A generation later, in 1901, the Criminal Registrar declared 'we have witnessed a great change in manners: the substitution of words without blows for blows with or without words; an approximation in the manners of different classes; a decline in the spirit of lawlessness'.[26] Late-Victorian newspapers, despite their tendency to indulge in scaremongering, also detected the wind of change. The *East London Advertiser*, for example, a Conservative-leaning newspaper covering what for contemporaries was one of the most crime-ridden areas of the country, suggested on 25 August 1888 (ironically, less than a week before the first of the Jack the Ripper murders) that even though a number of crimes had been recorded in the area over the previous few weeks

There is no cause for despair over the state of the people. Strike an average in this generation and in the last, and when they are compared together, there will be shown a happy improvement in our condition. East London is now on a moral and social 'down grade', for the lower strata of our population, in which most of these evils arise, is slowly but surely being reached by the influences of a better age and a truer charity.

Working-class memoirs similarly touch on this idea that working-class people were retreating from 'traditional' aggressive behaviour. A case in point is the autobiography of Joe Toole, who was born in Salford in 1887. It describes a childhood before the First World War in which a degree of violence, or at least of aggression, informed everyday life: 'You had to fight to survive . . . you had to periodic-ally defend your skin, which included your honour'; 'If you didn't swear vigorously, nobody believed what you said'. But it also describes how the young Toole, having started out as a street scaven-ger and newspaper vendor, decided to leave this life behind him. A gulf opened up between the ambitious Toole and 'the lads at the street corner' who 'now referred to me as a snob, who was learning more than was good for him'.

The crunch point came when a local gang asked him to join in a fight they were planning with another gang. He refused: 'a new world had opened up for me which was quite unknown for them', he recalls in his autobiography. Instead Toole opted for a lifetime of activism in the labour movement, becoming Labour MP for Salford South and then Lord Mayor of Manchester for 1936–7.[27]

The attraction for some of the life Toole left behind him is well described by William Bowen, who also grew up in working-class Salford, though in the 1880s rather than in the 1900s:

As a boy one Sunday afternoon, after closing time, a glorious summer afternoon, a crowd came out of a public house with two men stripped to their naked waists who began to fight and they fought until their naked bodies were streaming with blood. I thought, when I am a man I would like to be able to fight like that.[28]

Nevertheless, it was a way of life that was now in general decline.

One can see here how attitudes to violence could become one of the dividing lines between those working men who were attracted to the new ideas of 'respectability', and those who remained attached to more traditional forms of behaviour. For the latter group, the 'hard man' remained a masculine ideal. For the former, self-improvement, the pursuit of skilled employment, perhaps attachment to church or chapel or to political or trades union activity, were key. Joe Toole clearly felt he was crossing a social chasm in moving from one to the other.

Of course, aggression in itself does not denote criminal violence, but for many contemporaries there was ever less of a discernible gap between the two, and by the late nineteenth century, social observers were making clear distinctions between the growing numbers of the 'respectable' working class and a tougher, more violent, often criminal element. One of the best known by-products of Charles Booth's multi-volume *Inquiry into the Life and Labour of the People in London*, produced between 1886 and 1903, were 'Maps Descriptive of London Poverty', which depicted colour-coded zones distinguishing between those who were 'Poor', those who were 'Very poor, casual' (whom he characterised as being in 'chronic want') and those who belonged to the 'Lowest class', whom he described as 'vicious, semi-criminal'. Obviously crime, not least criminal violence, changes. Nevertheless, by the time Booth was conducting his researches most social commentators, along with law and order administrators and other officials, were distinguishing between what might be described as a 'respectable' working class and the 'residuum' – Booth's 'vicious, semi-criminal' groups and what these days might be described as a criminal underclass.

VII

One notable development in the otherwise comparatively peaceable late-Victorian city was the rise of the youth gang, precursor of the teenage gang that was to become such a mark of British urban life in the second half of the twentieth century. Active in Liverpool, Glasgow and Birmingham, it was to be found above all in the Manchester area. Historian Andrew Davies, who has painstakingly studied local Manchester newspapers for the period 1870–1900, has discovered they contain some 270 reports of gang violence, frequently involving what were known locally as 'scuttlers'. These were mostly working-class youths aged between fourteen and nineteen, the majority of whom were employed in unskilled manual trades. The gangs they belonged to fought over territory, over perceived slights to their honour, and over perceived slights to their members' girlfriends (there were, indeed, what one newspaper report described as 'scuttlerettes', who joined in the fighting).

At one point, the Salford police had to deal with an eighteen-month feud between the Hope Street and the Ordsall Lane gangs, during which a number of gang members were knifed (the general intention seems to have been to wound rather than kill, although Andrew Davies records that five people died as a result of gang violence during the thirty-five years the Manchester gangs were active). The typical scuttler – and this seems to be a Manchester variation on a much wider working-class youth practice – donned a white muffler, bell-bottomed trousers held up by a belt with a large, heavy metal buckle that doubled as a knuckle-duster, clogs with pointed toes capped with steel, and wore his hair over his forehead in a 'donkey fringe' with his cap pushed back to show it off. Like so many later gang members, the scuttlers seemed to be most active in the years between leaving school and getting married, after which they for the most part settled into normal working life.[29]

The Manchester scuttlers were in decline in the course of the 1890s, but towards the end of the century worries were expressed in newspapers about a new type of youth gang. The summer of 1898 was a particularly hot one, and this may help to explain why quite a few of the people who decided to make the most of the August Bank Holiday ended up being brought before the courts for drunkenness,

disorderly behaviour, fighting, assaults on the police and street robberies. But to the newspapers these were not random acts of senseless
violence but the actions of organised working-class thugs, and a new
word was coined to describe the perpetrators: hooligans (possibly
derived from 'Hooley's gang').

Hooligans were, so it was claimed, strongly territorial, and fought
battles with rivals. They wrecked pubs and coffee stalls and assaulted
the staff. They mugged old ladies, attacked French café owners and
Italian ice-cream vendors, and picked fights with the police. In South
London they sported iron-capped boots, 'calculated to kill easily'.
The fact that they carried knives and operated in 'cowardly' packs,
kicking men when they were down, made them that most reprehensible of all things: un-English. Fears at the turn of the century that
they were graduating from knives to pistols led to legislation in
1903 that prohibited the sale and carrying of such weapons. The
view of the press was that severe gaol sentences and flogging were
called for.[30]

As with the garrotters nearly four decades before, there is no evidence whatsoever that organised gangs of hooligans actually existed.
Thomas Holmes, a senior London policeman, said the whole thing
was 'press-manufactured'. Patrick McIntyre, an ex-Scotland Yard
detective turned publican and crime reporter, wrote that it was a
non-existent phenomenon seized upon by the press 'as a suitable and
sensational means of filling their columns' during the 'silly season'.
But it's interesting that the kind of violent, sometimes criminal activity that had commonly accompanied public holidays a century or so
before should now have become so firmly linked with the working
class. And it's noteworthy that this outbreak of lawlessness should,
by the late-Victorian era, have seemed so exceptional that newspapers could only explain it in terms of gangs. That such rowdiness
was generally perpetrated by a particular age group – people, in
other words, who later grew out of it – is also significant.

In fact, of course, mindless violence was far from being a working-
class monopoly. Upper-class young men were just as capable of

trouble-making on occasion, particularly in the aftermath of annual celebratory occasions. So, for example, each 5 November during the nineteenth century and well into the twentieth, undergraduates in Oxford almost invariably ended up brawling with city youths and the police. Particularly violent altercations occurred during Guy Fawkes Night in 1907, when, according to *Jackson's Oxford Journal* for 9 November 1907, 'a crowd of considerable proportions, in which town and gown were about equally represented' paraded up the High and then turned on each other. Thirty arrests were made on that occasion, and eight undergraduates and four townspeople were subsequently charged.

Sporting events could lead to trouble, too. On 13 July 1863 – just after the Oaks and Derby race meetings and ironically on the day on which the Garrotters' Act was passed – *The Times* reported that some upper-class young men had run amok in Cremorne Gardens, 'breaking windows and glasses by wholesale, hustling and insulting women, bonneting the bystanders, striking right and left with sticks and umbrellas, and assaulting the police in the execution of their duty'. Four of the rowdies were convicted of causing damage worth £300 and each was fined £50.

The attitude taken by the authorities and by newspapers towards upper-class hooligans, however, was very different from the one they adopted to their working-class brethren. *Jackson's Oxford Journal*, having reported the events of 5 November in some detail, added that 'as usual, the police took the hurly-burly in good part'. *The Times* report on the Cremorne Gardens incident suggested that it was no more than the result of 'boisterous spirits we are said to have inherited as a nation from our Northern ancestors' and recognised 'the licence claimed by young gentlemen' to behave boisterously on occasion. In the normal run of events, indeed, it would have been 'too ordinary an occurrence to deserve any comment'; it was only the extent of the damage caused that made the event worthy of record. The paper also reported the words of the judge passing sentence on the four rowdies: it was, he said, 'with feelings of great pain that I pass sentence upon you . . . and I can make great allowance for the youthful spirit which has been exhibited by you.'[31] Working-class violence, it seemed, was a criminal matter; upper-class violence simply an excess of high spirits.

VIII

If that attitude suggests a degree of crassness on the part of the judiciary, it's not a charge that can be levelled generally. Although the aftermath of the Garrotting Panic shows that law-makers and judges could react in a knee-jerk way, the usual hallmark of nineteenth-century legal processes was considered change and reform. It was, after all, the era when the 'Bloody Code' was disassembled. And these changes and reforms, as suggested in Chapter 12, can be viewed as useful windows on broader trends and transformations. Two in particular are worth noting here. The first was the clarification of what had previously been one of the most problematic of defences in murder trials, not guilty by reason of insanity – a development that shows how much more sophisticated and considered the law was becoming, particularly in its growing recourse to outside, non-legal experts. The second was an increasingly sympathetic legal attitude to rape victims.

Ironically, the occasion for the change to the insanity plea was precisely one of those causes célèbres that could so easily have resulted in hasty and poor policy-making. On 20 January 1843, Daniel McNaughtan (his surname seems to have been spelled in various ways) shot Sir Robert Peel's private secretary, Edward Drummond, believing Drummond to be the Prime Minister himself. Drummond died five days later, and in early March McNaughtan was put on trial for murder at the Old Bailey. The defence pleaded insanity, arguing that McNaughtan was 'the victim of a fierce and fearful delusion' that Peel's Tories were his enemies. The jury, swayed by evidence from a team of medical experts, agreed with the defence.

The decision was viewed as controversial in some quarters, not least by Queen Victoria who, just three years before, had faced an assassination attempt by a man named Edward Oxford, and had had to sit angrily by as the initial charge of treason gave way to an acquittal by reason of insanity (Oxford had then been confined to Bethlem Hospital). But when the issue was debated in the House of Lords in the immediate aftermath of McNaughtan's acquittal, Chief Justice Tindal gave the judges' reply to queries levelled at them by the House about the verdict, which laid out what became known as the M'Naghten (or more usually today McNaughton) Rules.

Previously, the notion of insanity had been interpreted in different ways by different courts: for example, some held that an individual was insane if he or she could not distinguish between good and evil; others that it came down to whether the defendant 'did not know what he did'. The M'Naghten Rules tightened the guidelines. From now on, an insanity verdict could be brought in if, having heard evidence from medical experts, the jury concluded that 'at the time of committing the act, the accused was labouring under such a defect of reason, from disease of the mind, as not to know the nature and quality of the act he was doing or, if he did know it, that he did not know what he was doing was wrong.' It was a ruling that was to be bitterly contested by some, but it became a hugely influential guideline throughout the English-speaking world well into the twentieth century.[32] As we have noted, the definition of insanity was now in the hands of mental-health experts, whose views were likely to veer in favour of the accused. And, in their actual application, the M'Naghten Rules had the effect, through their role in the final decision-making process, of retaining a degree of discretion for the judge and the jury.

The adoption of the M'Naghten Rules is symptomatic of the care with which trials of what was England's only real capital offence were generally conducted. The statistics bear this out. In the decades around 1900 approximately 40 per cent of those accused of murder were ultimately acquitted, and another 20 per cent found insane on arraignment or else found guilty but insane after trial. Of the 40 per cent who were convicted and sentenced to death, about half were saved by the royal prerogative, with such factors as diminished responsibility or other mental-health considerations short of clear insanity, a lack of intent, the youth of the offender, old age, or a crime committed by a man of usual good character while drunk, all being taken into account. Courts, then, didn't assume guilt, and they carefully weighed a number of factors when considering the fate of a defendant: the status and reputation of the accused, the status and reputation of the deceased, the exact circumstances of the offence, the level of force used, mitigating factors such as provocation or violence offered by the victim, medical evidence, and, increasingly, the mental state of the accused at the time of the trial.

Take, for instance, the fate of wife-murderers in England and Wales between 1841 and 1900. As murder rates generally declined, domestic homicide assumed greater relative prominence, and greater absolute prominence as more cases were taken to court (the number of men accused of murdering their wives doubled between the 1850s and the 1890s). In theory, defendants in such cases were also more likely to be found guilty and hanged than murderers in general. But of the 701 men who stood trial in that sixty-year period, just 225 – under a third – were ultimately executed, while 96 were found to be insane, and hence escaped punishment and in many cases trial.[33] It's a similar picture with the far less serious crime of assault, where, again, a fair proportion of those accused (35–40 per cent) were ultimately acquitted.

A degree of sensitivity is, as previously intimated, even apparent in an area of the criminal law where historians have traditionally taken a dim view of Victorian attitudes: rape. To our eyes, nineteenth-century attitudes to female victims frequently seem callous or uncomprehending. A woman generally stood a chance of bringing a successful rape charge only if she was of previously unbesmirched reputation and was of a higher social standing than the man she accused. She was unlikely to be successful if it could be shown that she was sexually promiscuous, or even sexually experienced. But this was not inevitably the case, and it became less so as the century advanced. As early as 1811, in the case of the alleged rape of a sixteen-year-old servant girl named Harriet Halliday, the judge, Baron Wood, blocked the defence counsel's attempts to open up lines of evidence aimed at impugning her sexual reputation. A capital conviction followed. A decade later Wood blocked attempts by the defence council in another rape trial to interrogate the complainant about her sexual history, and instructed the jury in his summing up to ignore that aspect of her life: 'that has nothing to do with the prisoner at the bar; she had no right to be ravished on that account'.

Wood was not alone. Justice Holroyd expressed similar sentiments during a rape trial in Birmingham in 1825. And in 1855, in what was probably the first legal decision of its kind, a young female prostitute secured the conviction of four men who had gang-raped her. Given the somewhat hypocritical Victorian attitude to prostitutes – widely used by men of all types and conditions, but also socially shunned – this was a considerable achievement.[34]

It's perhaps not surprising, therefore, that women in the second half of the century were more prepared to bring allegations of sexual assault than they had been in the first. In the five-year period between 1856 and 1860 498 incidents were brought to the attention of the police, of which 267 were then prosecuted. In the four-year period between 1911 and 1914, by contrast, 1,817 cases were known to the police, of which 1,246 were taken to trial – an increase in the committal rate of 1.37 to 3.42 per 100,000 of population over the relevant period.

Rape convictions nationally remained low in the early nineteenth century: just six in 1837 and seven in 1838 (the last execution for rape took place in 1836). But when in 1841 the death penalty for rape was abolished, and replaced by transportation for life, and when further legislation in 1845 removed this mandatory punishment, allowing judges to impose lesser sentences, the number of prosecutions rose, as did the conviction rate. In 1836–40, when a rapist could still be sentenced to death, the conviction rate stood at 10 per cent. It rose to 33 per cent in 1841–5, and to over 50 per cent thereafter. Martin Wiener, working on the records of hundreds of trials from the later nineteenth century, argues that the conviction rate by then stood at 60 per cent – far higher than the current conviction rate for rape cases in England and Wales. Victorian England may by our lights have been patriarchal and misogynistic, but the fact remains that sexual violence was being far more seriously addressed than it had ever been before, and rapists were being punished for their crimes.

In the following century such shifting attitudes were to prove crucial, for as society continued to move away from acts of aggression towards neighbours and strangers, so the problems of violence within relationships and families came ever-more to the fore. Over the next decades issues such as child abuse, displays of physical force within relationships, and rape (a crime in which the majority of victims know their assailant) were to assume far greater prominence than they had ever done previously. They were also to prove frustratingly intractable.

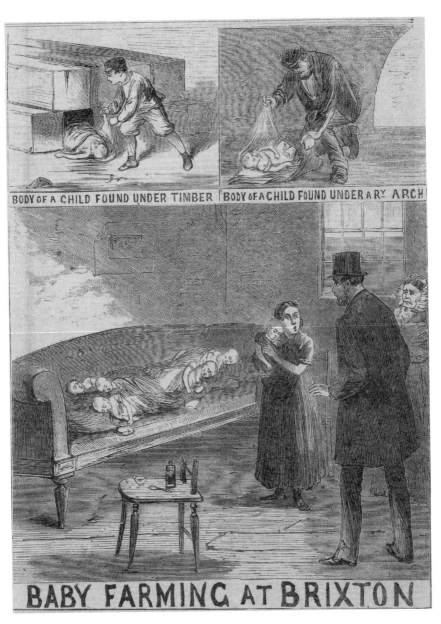

BABY FARMING AT BRIXTON

The 1870 Brixton 'baby-farming' case, in which Margaret Waters drugged and starved up to nineteen children left in her care, caused widespread revulsion. Over the past four centuries, as rates of violence between strangers have dropped, people have become far more aware of the danger potentially posed by those they know.

CHAPTER 14

PARTNERS AND CHILDREN, VICTIMS AND KILLERS

I

The popular perception today is that violence is the act of a stranger: the murderer in the shadows, the drunken brawler, the burglar surprised by the householder, the mugger attacking the passer-by. But as suggested in earlier chapters, while that may have been true once, it doesn't really hold up today. In the twenty-first century there is a high chance that assailant and victim will be known to each other, that when it comes to homicidal violence it is relations or acquaintances who are to be feared just as much as strangers, and that the most dangerous place for many of us is not the street but the home. Police statistics for the financial year 2011/12 suggest that of 172 women victims of homicide aged over 16, 51 per cent were killed by partners or ex-partners and 18 per cent by other family members (the corresponding figures for the 367 adult male victims are much lower: 5 per cent and 11 per cent respectively). Of the 47 victims aged between one year and sixteen, two-thirds were murdered by a parent, while over recent years parents have also routinely been responsible for 90 per cent of the deaths of children aged less than one year.

A House of Commons report of 24 December 2013, based on data from the Crime Survey for England and Wales for 2011/12 (the Crime

Survey is based on social survey techniques rather than police statistics), suggested that 1,200,000 women and 700,000 men experienced domestic abuse in a twelve-month period, while the Crown Prosecution Service prosecuted 79,268 people for domestic violence proper, of whom 58,138, or 73.3 per cent, were convicted.[1] The Home Office has estimated that perhaps one in four women in the United Kingdom has been physically attacked at some point or other by a partner, while an earlier Crime Survey, for 2001, showed that young women between the ages of sixteen and eighteen were especially vulnerable to attacks by boyfriends or partners and that just over half of the 237,000 estimated instances of rape and serious sexual assault suffered by women were inflicted by male partners or former partners. Violence is presumably also sometimes present in lesbian and gay relationships, though here the true facts are even harder to ascertain: groups that might regard themselves as estranged from officialdom have a tendency to under-report problems.

Domestic violence against women has a long history. Outright condemnation of it has a rather shorter one, yet it's salutary to realise that a form of behaviour that has been consistently highlighted and criticised since at least mid-Victorian times should still be so prevalent today. It has, after all, been well over 150 years since J. W. Kaye published his seminal article on 'Outrages on Women' (1856). There he described how 'in the criminal annals of England, outrages upon women have of late years held a distressingly prominent position', adding that 'scarcely a day passes that does not add one or more to the published cases of this description of offence'. And Kaye's was not a lone Victorian voice. Frances Power Cobbe wrote an article entitled 'Wife Torture in England' which appeared in the *Contemporary Review* in 1878.[2] In fiction, Anne Brontë's 1840s pioneering portrait of an abusive husband in *The Tenant of Wildfell Hall* was joined later in the century by such campaigning novels as Monica Caird's *The Wing of Azrael* (1889). Conan Doyle, too, took up the issue in one of the Sherlock Holmes short stories he wrote for the *Strand* magazine in 1904. The victim in 'The Adventure of the Abbey Grange' is the drunken, wife-beating Sir Eustace Brackenstall; his assailant, Captain Croker, is an admirer of Lady Brackenstall, who has been stirred to action by reports of Brackenstall's brutal conduct. Having solved the case, Holmes opts (not for the first time) to follow his conscience rather than the letter of the law. He asks Watson to act as informal jury, and when Watson brings in a verdict of not guilty, allows Croker to go free.[3] That a hugely popular character in a widely read magazine should follow this line is surely significant.

And yet, despite this groundswell of opinion, and despite legislation that sought to give women more rights in marriage (such as the Married Women's Property Acts of 1870, 1882 and 1893), wives continued to be victims. Of 480 murderers executed between 1837 and 1901, 127 – over a quarter – had been convicted of killing their wives, and a further 30 had murdered partners variously described as 'concubines', 'paramours', or 'sweethearts' (as against 5 women condemned for murdering their husbands, 25 parents sentenced to hang for killing their children, and 25 people sentenced for killing a close relative).[4] The Victorians increasingly associated wife-beating with the lower classes, but clearly this social group was not uniquely culpable. Moreover women, then as now, tended not to report abuse. Some clearly felt that the authorities would regard it as too trivial to investigate; others felt too embarrassed or ashamed to talk about it; others again feared that reporting an incident would only lead to further mistreatment.

In political terms, the first half of the twentieth century saw huge advances for women.[5] The pre-1914 fight for the vote, dominated by the militant Women's Social and Political Union, was won in 1918 with the passing of the Representation of the People Act, which extended the franchise to women over thirty (subject to certain property qualifications); while the Parliament (Qualification of Women) Act of the same year gave women the right to stand for Parliament (including, paradoxically, those aged between 21 and 30 who were as yet unable to vote); and in 1928 the Representation of the People (Equal Franchise) Act finally gave the vote to men and women on equal terms. Women were therefore now in a position to campaign for political and social change from within Westminster, even if few female MPs were actually returned to Parliament.

Simultaneously, the various political parties came to realise that it was now in their interests to pass legislation that would win women's votes, though it has to be admitted that their ambitions tended to be circumscribed and sometimes patronising: campaigning against the Labour Party, Nesta Webster, a British Union of Fascists activist, argued that it would 'promise the mill and factory girls silk stockings and an easy life to get their votes'.[6] Nevertheless, although the achievements of the inter-war period might in some ways be regarded as something of an anti-climax after the much-publicised achievement of winning the vote, one key piece of legislation was passed: the 1937 Matrimonial Causes Act, which extended grounds for divorce to cruelty, desertion for at least three years, and incurable insanity. Women's political groups, notably the National Union of Societies for Equal Citizenship, the successor to the non-militant National Union of Women's Suffrage Societies, played a key role in its promotion – a reminder that women continued to be active politically.

Other advances for women between 1918 and 1939 and in the years immediately after the Second World War tended to be more behind the scenes. At the level of local politics an increasing number served as local councillors or mayors, helping to oversee improvements in working-class housing, health (including maternal and child welfare clinics), education, and care for widows, orphans and the blind. Women also contributed to and benefited from the increasing level and coordination of help offered to individuals and families. This had its roots in Victorian times, in the formation by Helen Bosanquet and Octavia Hill in 1869 of the Charity Organisation Society, which sought to coordinate the work of the various philanthropic bodies then operating in London and that introduced the notion of casework and the caseworker.

Help for the family was given some legislative muscle by reforms brought in by the Liberal Party in the years immediately before the First World War (old age pensions, national insurance, and so on) and, far more substantially, by the foundation of the Welfare State after 1945. But arguably of more importance to the abused wife was the further development of that notion of caseworkers introduced by the Charity Organisation Society and their evolution into social workers. Key to this development was the work of Eileen Young-husband (1902–1981), who in 1945 was commissioned by the United Kingdom Carnegie Trust to undertake a survey of the needs of welfare recipients and who in her subsequent report (updated in 1951) recommended the provision of formal training for social workers. Subsequent work for the Ministry of Health led to the foundation of the Council for Education and Training in Social Work and the establishment of social-work training courses in Britain's poly-technics and universities.[7]

Nevertheless the issue of domestic abuse did not really achieve national prominence until the 1970s when a newly resurgent women's movement made it one of its core concerns. 'Wife-beating' had entered the lexicon in the 1830s. Now it was joined by 'wife-battering'. And the stories that emerged – often paralleling accounts from a century or more previously – showed just how frequently abuse went far beyond the occasional or isolated beating. Victims reported being verbally bullied and of living in a climate of constant fear. Their husbands, they said, would relentlessly tell them that they were worthless, and would lash out at the least perceived prov-ocation, even if they were pregnant or there were children present. Often battered wives found themselves virtual prisoners in their own homes, unable to see their friends or have any sort of a social life. It was a picture depressingly familiar to anyone who had ever read Frances Power Cobbe's 'Wife Torture in England'.

This time, though, the women's movement made it a public cause and a political issue. Activists such as Erin Pizzey, herself the child of violent and abusive parents, came to the fore. Pizzey was a leading light in the creation of the Chiswick Women's Aid Group in 1971: a self-help and social organisation for mothers, which, with the help of the local council, went on to set up a refuge for those seeking to escape domestic violence.[8] It proved to be the prototype for a large number of similar projects that were established nationally.[9]

What the writings of Pizzey and other commentators made clear was that in the early 1970s it was very difficult indeed to get official help for battered women. Just as women reporting rape were all too often treated as though they bore part of the guilt, so there was too often an assumption that a husband's violence was, to a lesser or greater degree, his wife's fault. Moreover, because what was often referred to as 'the sanctity of the family' was regarded as the very bedrock of society, official agencies were reluctant to get involved or to take sides in marital disputes. Women who reported violence to the authorities were often advised to try to seek a reconciliation with their abuser, even if they and their children were clearly being subjected to repeated physical abuse. Their doctors might well do no more than prescribe tranquillisers; their vicars would advise them to stay with their husbands for the good of their families; their local police would regard their accusations as unimportant.

The level of indifference generally displayed by those in positions of power – and by society as a whole – is depressingly clear in the harrowing testimonies of individual victims. Janine Turner's *Behind Closed Doors*, for example, describes the appalling sequence of events experienced by a woman she identifies simply as Mandy. (Turner herself, incidentally, had experienced a violent marriage.) Mandy and her four children had suffered constant violence from her husband, and she was eventually driven to seek a court order against him. When she got home, and he found out what she had done, he beat her up. She therefore called the police. Their advice was that she should talk to her solicitor, which she did the next morning, and he set about organising a further court hearing. Before that could take place her husband assaulted and raped her several times. At the hearing itself he appeared so contrite that the decision was taken to let him off with a warning. Once back at home, though, he immediately reverted to form. And so a recurring pattern was created: Mandy's husband would beat her up, she would call the police, they would refer her to her solicitor, a court hearing would be arranged, her husband would put on his remorseful act, the court would let him off, the unhappy couple would return home, and he would then assault her again. Eventually Mandy sought to get an exclusion order, which would have ensured the arrest of her husband if he offended again. The court decided, however, that there was insufficient evidence to grant one.[10]

Over time some progress was made. Thanks to continuing campaigns by the Women's Movement, the publicity that surrounded the setting up of women's refuges, and the resulting public awareness of an issue that had so long been ignored, Parliament passed the Domestic Violence and Matrimonial Proceedings Act in 1976, and two years later the Domestic Proceedings and Magistrates' Courts Act, which between them, among other things, provided more protection for victims, or potential victims, of violence through civil protection orders (injunctions) than was previously available under existing law. But, it has to be said, while they carried considerable symbolic importance, as later legislation demonstrated they left many issues imperfectly resolved and were in any case imperfectly enforced. Women's organisations continued to campaign.

Eventually, decades later, a raft of tighter and clearer legislation was passed. Part 4 of the Family Law Act of 1996, and the more thoroughgoing Domestic Violence, Crime and Victims Act of 2004, set out to create a simpler set of legal remedies for victims of domestic or relationship violence, and to deal with different types of relationship: from cohabiting and non-cohabiting heterosexual couples, married or otherwise, to gay and lesbian couples. The Protection from Harassment Act of 1997 is also worth mentioning, since it tackled a common, post-separation issue – harassment, threat or assault by a former partner – although it was a little vague about the actual definition of harassment beyond saying that in certain circumstances it might well include acts that in other contexts were perfectly legal, such as inappropriate texting or sitting in a parked car outside someone's home.

Enforcement, too, improved. The approach taken by the police in cases of domestic abuse is crucial. If they are supportive, they can help defuse situations or ensure that the legal process runs its full course. If they are indifferent, their tone can convince a victim that she stands no chance of securing justice – even that she may be in the wrong – while leaving the abuser confident that he can continue to get away with it or that what he is doing is not really a crime. Back in the 1970s, the police as a whole were indifferent. But mounting criticism from women's groups led in 1986 to a Home Office Circular that set out a code for police forces to follow in cases of domestic violence. A year later the Metropolitan Police set up specialist police domestic violence units, followed soon after by the West Yorkshire Police; and the success of these initiatives led to another Home Office Circular in 1990 that encouraged the establishment of specialist domestic violence officers, and stipulated that police officers should regard domestic violence as a serious offence likely to lead to arrest, and that, in liaison with other agencies, they should provide information and advice to victims. Obviously, this still left much to the discretion of individual forces and individual officers, but at least a framework had been created, if not an infallible system.

The struggle to make domestic violence socially unacceptable and subject to legal sanction has largely been won. Yet it stubbornly remains a feature of everyday life in some families and relationships, and it's hard to resist the suspicion that there is a gulf between the abuse that occurs and the abuse that is reported. The problem is socially pervasive. Its perpetrators can come from any social class and any ethnic group. Some can be shown to be mentally unwell, but many more are not. Some are alcoholics; others don't drink. Some are unemployed; others have full-time jobs. If abusers have anything in common, it is a view that they are the rulers of their own small kingdoms, that their wives, partners and children are essentially their property, and that the principles of restraint that govern their behaviour in society as a whole do not apply at a domestic level. Many men guilty of physical attacks on their partners have indeed expressed surprise that anyone should think that what they were doing was wrong. Consider Janine Turner's explanation of why her husband battered her:

> I believe it was the only way he could show how all-powerful he was. He was irresponsible and he knew it. So he felt he had to compensate. He took out all the anger he felt against the world, against his mother who had betrayed him as a boy to be brought up by his grandparents, out on me. I was his property, or so he thought. He could do what he liked in his own home without having any form of comeback. He seemed genuinely astonished when it was suggested that it wasn't the thing to do. Maybe he had been brought up on beatings and had had time to get used to the idea before I came along.[11]

Janine Turner's suggestion that, in her husband's case, brutal behaviour had been passed down the generations is not an isolated one: there is evidence to suggest that people who have been the victims of violence may themselves become violent, though this is far from being universal. Nor, of course, can it be treated as any kind of excuse for Janine Turner's 'long dark nights worrying about how I would face another day'.

Historically, and indeed until very recently, there were practical reasons why women who were systematically beaten nevertheless decided to stay with their abusers. They might not have felt able to take refuge with family or friends, and since they would have been regarded as having made themselves voluntarily homeless they were not eligible for official assistance until the mid-1990s (hence the reason why refuges for battered women became such a key priority in the 1970s).[12]

Yet it is noteworthy how often battered women have withdrawn charges of abuse, or have returned to their abusive partner after a spell away from him. This inevitably suggests that more than practical considerations are at stake when a woman contemplates leaving a violent partner. She may well feel conflicting emotions: she hates the abuse but still loves the abuser, to the extent of believing his protestations of regret or deluding herself that he will somehow improve. Alternatively, it quite often seems to be the case that women who have been subjected to long-term physical and psychological abuse become so demoralised that they cannot stir themselves to positive action – even that they start to convince themselves that they must somehow be to blame for the treatment that is being meted to them. Yet another possible explanation is posited by Erin Pizzey in her highly controversial book *Prone to Violence*, first published in 1982. According to her, some battered women are complicit in their own abuse because they find the experience exciting. Indeed they may actually seek out relationships in which they will be physically harmed. It's a view that led to Pizzey's final estrangement from mainstream feminism and won her much criticism, though she would have argued that her views stemmed from considerable first-hand experience working with battered women.[13]

All studies agree that it is male aggression that predominates in domestic violence, but it is not unknown for the husband or male partner in a heterosexual relationship to be the victim. Increasing awareness of the domestic abuse of men is challenging received wisdom on the subject, but in general, it seems to be that female violence within relationships differs from male violence in two important respects. Firstly, it tends, though certainly not in all cases, to be retaliatory: women fight, injure or kill to defend themselves or their children from their violent partner. Secondly, and partly for that reason, it does not generally amount to that long-term, systematic abuse that so often characterises male violence within intimate relationships. But in a minority of instances it is the man who has to endure an atmosphere of constant criticism and belittlement, fear of physical abuse and concern for the safety of his children. He may choose to endure the relationship for precisely the same reason that abused women do: because he wants to keep the family together, because he still loves his partner, because he hopes things will improve, or simply because he has nowhere else to go. And, as with many abused women, he may opt to keep quiet about his sufferings because he feels ashamed of them. Indeed, the chances are that he is more likely to keep quiet than a woman would be. That masculine fear of mockery, going right back to the satires about henpecked husbands that were so popular in the seventeenth century, still persists today. [14]

If abuse of partners remains a feature of contemporary life, abuse of older relatives threatens to become even more of an issue as life expectancy continues to increase and we become a society – as we soon will be – where the number of people aged over sixty-five exceeds those under sixteen.[15] We know little about levels of abuse of elderly people in earlier times but anecdotes survive to show that, even though it was regarded as contrary to the Fifth Commandment ('Honour thy father and thy mother'), it was certainly not unknown, particularly, one suspects, in workhouses and similar institutions. A pamphlet dating from around 1780 describes a young gentleman named Robert Davis, living near Exeter, who, having promised to look after his parents in their old age, wheedled their money out of them and then left them to die in poverty. A guilty conscience, made more guilty by an incident during which the coach in which he was travelling was struck by lightning, led to a breakdown and deathbed repentance. The fact that the pamphleteer should bemoan 'cruel, wicked and disobedient children' suggests that he could probably think of other cases, too.[16]

But if elder abuse existed in earlier periods, it is in the more recent past that it has become a matter of focussed concern. 'Granny bashing' or 'granny battering' first entered public consciousness in the 1970s (the two terms seem to have been coined around 1975). Care homes may be the settings for such abuse: staff lashing out at elderly, sometimes difficult patients is not unknown, and in extreme cases becomes systemic. But abuse also occurs within the family. In 2006 a United Kingdom Prevalence Study of Elder Mistreatment reported that of the 2,111 respondents, all aged sixty-six or older, and all living in private homes, 2.6 per cent reported some kind of abuse by family members, close friends or care workers. This most commonly took the form of neglect. Financial exploitation was the next most common problem reported. But a small minority – 0.4 per cent – reported physical abuse, the same percentage talked of psychological abuse, and 0.2 per cent alleged sexual abuse.

The experiences of 'Mrs E' were particularly distressing but not, it seems, particularly unusual. She was a woman of eighty-two, deaf and possibly suffering from dementia. Her daughter and son-in-law, who lived with her, were both alcoholics, and habitually stole money from her. Her daughter also hit her. She was forced to sleep on a settee, and when her daughter and son-in-law finally moved out they took nearly all her furniture, including the fridge. If another recent study is to be believed, it's more common for men to abuse the elderly than for woman to do so, but Mrs E's daughter is nevertheless far from being unique in her cruelty. Of the 70 abusers highlighted in the report, 40 were male family members, 20 female. It's a social problem that, if current demographic trends are anything to go by, is likely to get worse rather than better.

II

Even so, the type of violence within the family that – understandably, perhaps – receives the greatest scrutiny today is child abuse. It is, as discussed in Chapter 5, a form of extreme behaviour with a very long history. It has also, to some extent, changed in form over time. Up until the nineteenth century, the crime that most concerned society was the murder of unwanted babies. Isolated instances of cruelty and violence shown to children certainly came to public attention – one thinks, for example, of the wretched apprentice Joseph Green, starved and beaten to death by his master in 1799, or of the wicked Elizabeth Branch who murdered her servant Jane Buttersworth in 1740; but the concept of child abuse as a discrete form of violent behaviour did not really exist. Arguably, indeed, it was not until the late nineteenth century that violent abuse of children became an area of concern in its own right.[17]

That this change should have taken place is very much due to Victorian England's population explosion, to the vast increase in the number of children that inevitably accompanied it and the pressures within the family that this caused. Today some 17.5 per cent of the population of England and Wales is under fifteen years old. But in 1861 that proportion was 33 per cent, and was to remain at around that level for the next fifty years. By 1915 the average number of children per household stood at 2.5; in the 1860s it had stood at 6. Many of these children died young. The Registrar General's Annual Report for 1888, which recorded about 800,000 births, also recorded 511,000 deaths, of which 120,000 were the deaths of children aged less than one year. Given the perils of childbirth and the relatively primitive level of Victorian health care, it is not surprising to find that even in the relatively leafy and affluent suburb of Dulwich, some 19 per cent of children in the 1890s failed to reach their fifth birthday, but in slum areas the percentage figure was closer to 50. Poverty and disease proved to be remorseless killers. Parents frequently could not afford to feed their children properly, or were so ground down by the conditions in which they lived that they could not care for them adequately. Ignorance about hygiene also played its part.

But although official figures do not exist, it's also impossible to discount the theory that some of the child deaths recorded were the result of violent abuse. Children could, of course, be critical to the well-being of poor families because they could be put to work at a very early age, perhaps at home or else bringing in money via paid employment – one historian has described such young workers as children without a childhood. However, in the early years at least, they would inevitably be a drain on family finances and a potential cause of friction. It's not difficult to imagine circumstances in which desperate, brutalised or drunken parents would lash out.

There is also evidence of cruelty of a more calculated variety. One of the great growth industries in Victorian Britain was life insurance, and, of course, for the greedy of a murderous disposition, life insurance offers temptation. A number of women were to fall victim to serial wife-killers in the course of the century (see Chapter 16), as were people who were not actually related to those who insured their lives. For example, the 'Black Widows' of Liverpool – two sisters Catherine Flannagan and Margaret Higgins – were found guilty of poisoning Margaret's husband Thomas for the insurance money (for which crime they were tried and convicted in 1884), but were also suspected of causing a number of other deaths, including that of a lodger named Margaret Jennings.[18]

Children, similarly, could prove vulnerable. Because infant mortality was so high, and the cost of funerals significant, it was not uncommon to insure children's lives, particularly among the working classes for whom the cost of a funeral would have been a major drain on family finances. The Friendly Societies Act of 1793 sought to regulate bodies that offered various forms of insurance, and some of these came to specialise in life insurance or funeral benefits, but over time they were joined by unregulated, illegal funeral clubs, often run by a local publican, that could generally be guaranteed not to ask too many questions about a premature or unexpected death (those that did had a tendency not to gain but to lose custom). For some parents, the prospect of a guaranteed swift pay-out proved irresistible.

In an early case, dating from 1840, Robert and Ann Sandys, who lived in a cellar room in Stockport, were accused of administering arsenic to two of their young daughters whose lives they had previously insured with a local burial club, the Philanthropic. The two were put on trial, and Robert was found guilty.[19] Over the next few decades other parents were to be similarly accused. It's impossible to put a number on just how many children perished in this way, though it's worth noting that a number of contemporary observers were convinced that it was a common crime. It was a form of insurance that rapidly declined after the passing of the Children's Act of 1908, which, among other things, made it illegal for people paid to look after children to take out insurance on behalf of their charges. Thereafter there seems to have been a marked decline in the number of children murdered for insurance money.

Equally appalling was the practice of baby-farming, by which unwanted, often illegitimate young children were 'adopted' by others for a cash payment. They might then be sold on as cheap labour, but in many instances they simply died of neglect. It was, after all, in the baby-farmer's interest, once they had been paid for taking on a child, that the child should die before they had incurred too much expense on its behalf. In some cases, matters went far beyond neglect. In the Finchley baby-farming scandal of the early 1900s, for example, many – possibly dozens – of babies were poisoned and their corpses disposed of. In the Brixton baby-farming case of 1870, Margaret Waters was found to have systematically drugged and starved the infants in her care, and to have killed up to nineteen of them. An eye-witness later recalled of one of Waters's victims:

> There was scarcely a bit of flesh on the bones of Miss Cowen's child, and I could recognise it only by the hair. It did not cry at all, being much too weak for that, and was evidently dying. It was scarcely human. I mean that it looked more than a monkey than a child. It was a shadow. [20]

The child died shortly afterwards. Margaret Waters was tried, convicted and hanged. Given cruelty such as this, it's not hard to understand why the lot of illegitimate children in Victorian England was so often a hard one. There were contemporary estimates that in some parts of the country up to 90 per cent of them died before their first birthday.

The first concerted steps to counter the abuse of children were taken in the 1880s.[21] In 1883 the Liverpool merchant banker Thomas Agnew, who on a trip to America a couple of years earlier had been impressed by the work of the recently formed New York Society for the Prevention of Cruelty to Children, set up a charity in Liverpool to provide help for children who had been harmed or were at risk.

Similar societies in other parts of Britain soon followed, and in 1889 they came together as the National Society for the Prevention of Cruelty to Children (NSPCC). (Scotland retained a separate system, while the Liverpool Society was to remain independent until 1953.)

These various societies saw their role as threefold: to provide practical help for children at risk (the London Society, for example, set up a shelter in Harpur Street in 1884); to prosecute adults deemed to have abused children; and to lobby for more effective legislation to protect the young. It was a controversial programme in many quarters, involving a degree of outside involvement in family life that many contemporaries felt to be totally unwarranted (particularly controversial when, as in a famous case brought in Shrewsbury in 1886, the parents accused of abuse were well-to-do). Nevertheless, their campaigning bore legislative fruit. In 1889 an Act for the Prevention of Cruelty to, and Protection of, Children was passed, making it a criminal offence to treat a boy aged under fourteen or a girl under sixteen in a manner likely to cause 'unnecessary suffering or injury to health', and giving courts the power to take children away from convicted parents or guardians.

Further legislation of 1894 and 1899 reinforced and amended the 1889 Act, in particular giving Poor Law boards the right to act *in loco parentis* for deserted children in care, and children whose parents were in prison. And in 1904 the Prevention of Cruelty to Children Act consolidated previous legislation, extended the network of institutions involved, and transferred responsibility for the care of children from Poor Law guardians to the relevant local authority. Four years later came what has sometimes been described as the 'Children's Charter' (confusingly, the same title was given to the 1889 Act) – the Children Act 1908. Much of it was actually concerned with problems of juvenile delinquency: it laid open the way for the establishment of juvenile courts and stipulated that offenders under the age of fourteen should be dealt with separately from adults. But even here we see the enshrinement of a principle that children should not be treated in the same way as their elders. The increased powers given to the courts to act in cases of abuse, while partly designed with the practical intention of removing children from environments that might turn them into deviants and future criminals, also had a strongly humanitarian impulse.

There was further legislation in the following decades – for example, a Maternity and Child Welfare Act of 1918, which extended welfare provision to unmarried mothers, and a Children and Young Persons Act of 1933 that consolidated previous legislation. But it was the couple of decades after the Second World War that saw two really fundamental developments in child welfare. The first was the Children Act of 1948, which created a comprehensive system of child-care services to match the reforms the new welfare state was enacting in such areas as health and education. The second was a greater medical focus on the tell-tale physical signs of abuse (prompted, initially, by radiologists in 1950s America). In 1962 the paediatrician C. Henry Kempe and a group of his associates published a research paper in the *Journal of the American Medical Association* that suggested medical practitioners were not paying sufficient attention to the problem and advocated that doctors should report all suspected cases of child abuse to the police or child protection agencies.[22] (Kempe went on to found his own journal, *Child Abuse & Neglect: The International Journal*, and by the end of the twentieth century there were around a dozen scholarly journals dealing with aspects of family violence.) Such was the publicity that surrounded this and other subsequent US studies that before long forensic pathologists and paediatricians in the UK were conducting their own research.

In December 1963 two orthopaedic surgeons, D. L. Griffiths and F. J. Moynihan, published an article in the *British Medical Journal* on the 'Battered Baby Syndrome', which endorsed Kempe's argument that greater awareness of the issue was required and greater preparedness to report abuse.[23] Five years later, the NSPCC set up a Battered Child Research Unit, which liaised closely with Kempe. But while the unit quickly established itself as the main agency working on child abuse in the United Kingdom, and although one of its leaders, Joan Court, went on to join the Department of Health and Social Security (DHSS) and encouraged further initiatives via the nation's social work agencies, the level of public awareness of the issue remained relatively low.

It took the tragic death of seven-year-old Maria Colwell at the hands of her stepfather (he was found guilty of manslaughter) in January 1973, and the media storm that followed, to make child abuse a national issue. It also became part and parcel of a wider and intensely political debate about the country's moral welfare, a debate that had arguably been kick-started by Sir Keith Joseph, Secretary of State for Social Services 1970–4 in the Conservative Heath government, when he had expressed concerns about what he described as a 'cycle of deprivation' via which criminality, poverty, fecklessness and welfare dependency were passed from generation to generation.

Yet, as with wife-beating, greater awareness of the problem and the creation of networks of professionals to deal with it, was only successful to a degree. In 1977 a Parliamentary Select Committee on Violence in the Family suggested that around 300 children aged four or under died every year in England and Wales from abuse. A few years later the NSPCC gave a figure of 198, estimating that 154 of these deaths had come at the hands of parents or carers (in the interests of balance, however, it should be mentioned that the Registrar General in 1985 gave a figure of just 8 child deaths through abuse). It seems that there may have been an overall decline in abuse over the past few decades, though changes to the ways in which statistics are compiled makes that a difficult assertion to prove absolutely; but abuse nevertheless persists. Less extreme forms of violence also appear to be quite widely spread, though here reliable statistics are even harder to come by. Abuse that occurs behind closed doors can be astonishingly difficult to spot, let alone prove.

The 1993 study *Beyond Blame*, which examined a number of cases that had ultimately resulted in the death of the child victim, is depressingly revealing about the challenges of diagnosis – as well as about the levels of cruelty that child abuse can involve.[24] Victims, it showed, were often malnourished and left alone in squalid conditions for long periods of time. Babies went with their nappies unchanged. Many abuse victims 'failed to thrive': their physical development was poor and they were severely underweight. In one case three children living with their unmarried mother suffered from recurrent chest infections, weight loss, and a variety of injuries caused by accidents that occurred when they were unsupervised; they were often left alone in the house without food, they were infected with nits, and babies' nappies were only infrequently changed. One boy was severely maltreated over several years by his stepfather, a man who himself came from a severely deprived background and who had a track record of violence: he would burn the child's legs, lock him in a cupboard, and force him to drink lager; he would not allow the boy to play with toys in the flat he shared with the child's mother; and would tie up the child's penis and put a cork in his anus to prevent incontinence. Yet children admitted to hospital with fractures would often be returned to their parents with no comment made, and many parents would go out of their way to hide abuse: one couple – a mother and a stepfather – persistently concealed a child's broken leg from a visiting social worker.

I've already suggested that the abuse of spouses can occur at every social level. The same is true of child abuse – particularly of child sexual abuse. Yet it is difficult not to suspect that the physical maltreatment of children is more common among people who are themselves struggling: who have limited material resources, who have problems keeping a stable and loving relationship together, who have children when they themselves are young, vulnerable and financially insecure. There is also evidence to suggest that those who have themselves been neglected or abused as children, or have been brought up in homes where violence was the norm, are more likely to visit abuse on the next generation, although this is certainly not a foregone conclusion.

The fact is that parenting is difficult, so it follows that it will prove particularly hard for those who are emotionally less resilient. All too often, someone found guilty of child abuse is also found to have a previous record of violent behaviour. One abusive father had previously been imprisoned for killing his first child when she was just nine weeks old; a mother responsible for killing her child admitted that some time before, she had smothered her first baby; another victim's father had previously assaulted a child so violently that he had left it blind and mentally disabled; and another father had served time for attacking his three-week-old daughter by his first wife and for harming his second wife's daughter (from a previous marriage) when she was two and a half.

In at least half the cases where children died as a result of abuse there was evidence of violence within the adult relationship, and that violence sometimes extended to professionals involved in the child's case: police officers, social workers, nursing staff, visiting educational welfare officers.[25]

Perhaps the most shocking of all recent cases is that of Victoria Climbié, who died in 2000 at the age of just eight.[26] Climbié, by all accounts a naturally happy and enthusiastic child, had been born in Ivory Coast, taken under the wing of her great-aunt Marie-Therese Kouao, and had then accompanied her – with the agreement of Victoria's parents – first to Paris and afterwards to London. Once there Victoria was alternately neglected and physically abused by Kouao, the abuse escalating when Kouao's lover Carl John Manning moved in with them.

Victoria appears to have been beaten on an almost daily basis with implements that ranged from shoes and coat hangers to a bicycle chain. Eventually she was confined to an unheated bathroom, where her emaciated body was wrapped in a black plastic sack to prevent her from soiling the bath she was forced to sleep in. When she was admitted to the North Middlesex Hospital on 24 February 2000 she was unconscious and cold, her body extensively bruised. As her condition deteriorated, she was transferred to the paediatric intensive care unit at St Mary's Hospital, Paddington, where she died on 25 February. Dr Nathaniel Carey, the Home Office pathologist who carried out the subsequent post mortem, discovered that her heart, lungs and kidneys had all failed. He noted 128 separate injuries to her body: 'There is really not anywhere that is spared', he reported, 'there is scarring all over the body.' 'All non-accidental injuries to children are awful and difficult for everybody to deal with,' he went on to say, 'but in terms of the nature and extent of the injury, and the almost systematic nature of the inflicted injury, I certainly regard this as the worst I have ever dealt with, and it is just about the worst I have ever heard of.'

On 12 January 2001 Kouao and Manning were convicted of murder. The inquiry into Climbié's death, presided over by Lord Laming, revealed numerous failings in the various social work, health and police agencies involved in her case. His findings also showed just how far attitudes to child abuse had changed in little more than a century. In the 1890s, both blame and responsibility would have been placed fairly and squarely on the shoulders of the parents or carers. By 2001 the blame for Victoria's death might have attached to Kouao and Manning, but responsibility for the welfare of this vulnerable child was felt to lie with officials. 'In the end,' the Laming report said, as it painstakingly examined failings in the welfare system, 'she died a slow, lonely death – abandoned, unheard and unnoticed.'

III

On extremely rare occasions, young children can prove to be the aggressors rather than the victims. Various examples can be gleaned from historical records.[27] In 1748, for example, ten-year-old William York, who lived in a Suffolk workhouse, murdered a five-year-old girl with a knife and billhook after she fouled the bed the two of them shared. He was found guilty of murder and sentenced to death, but pardoned on condition he join the Royal Navy. In 1778 three girls aged eight, nine and ten were tried at the Huntington assizes for killing a three year old. They had thrust a stick to which three pins had been attached into the toddler's genitals, and she had died after her injuries became infected. The girls were acquitted after being found *doli incapax* (literally, being incapable of doing wrong, or, in legal terms, being incapable of understanding the seriousness of actions taken). In 1854 ten-year-old Ann Levick, who had been sent on an errand by her aunt and who had taken the aunt's baby with her, was found a little later in tears, holding the baby, who, it was swiftly established, had had its throat cut. She claimed that the fatal blow had been struck by a stranger but the coroner's inquest found her guilty of wilful murder, although she was acquitted at her subsequent trial. In 1855 nine small boys were playing at a brickfield in Liverpool when a dispute broke out between two of them, Alfred Fitz, aged nine, and a seven year old called James Fleeson. Fitz knocked the younger boy down with a brick, and then, with the assistance of John Breen, another nine year old, threw him into a nearby canal, where he died. Fitz and Breen were tried at Lancaster assizes, where the jury found them guilty of manslaughter, and put forward a strong plea for mercy. The presiding judge, Mr Justice Baron Platt, having ascertained that the boys would receive an education if incarcerated, told them:

> You did not mean to kill this little boy, I have no doubts. You must be confined for twelve months in the House of Correction, where you will have the advantage of instruction from the schoolmaster and the chaplain.

The attitude of the jury and the course taken by the judge stands in stark contrast to some similar more recent cases.[28]

So unusual is the murder of one young child by another, and so widely separated are such cases in time and place, that it is unwise to suggest common underlying motives. But it does seem arguable in some instances, at least, that the aggression that begets aggression in adult child-abusers is also a factor with young killers. Take, for example, the 1968 case of eleven-year-old Mary Bell. She and thirteen-year-old Norma Bell (no relation) were arrested for the murder of Martin Brown, aged four years and two months, and Brian Howe, aged three years and four months. Both boys had been strangled, but the pressure applied had been so light that it seemed highly unlikely that an adult could have been responsible (indeed the injuries on Martin Brown's body were so minor that initially an open verdict on his death was recorded). Howe had also suffered very minor stab wounds, including one on his scrotum, apparently inflicted by a small pair of scissors, and a letter 'N', possibly altered to 'M', had been cut with a razor blade.

At their trial in Newcastle Norma Bell was acquitted, while Mary Bell was found guilty of manslaughter on the grounds of diminished responsibility and sentenced to life imprisonment, although she was released twelve years later at the age of twenty-three (she now lives under an assumed name). For journalist and writer Gitta Sereny, author of two books about Bell, the key to understanding her was the appalling way in which her mother (who had welcomed her birth with the words 'take that thing away from me') had persistently treated her. Mary had been constantly beaten and, she later said, forced to have oral sex with men while a toddler. Her mother – who was a prostitute – had also frequently been absent from home, her place being taken by Bell's surrogate father. He was, by all accounts, a decent man but often in trouble with the police.[29]

Aggression at home also seems to have been a key factor in the attacks made by two brothers, aged ten and twelve, on an eleven-year-old boy and his nine-year-old brother at Edlington, South Yorkshire, in April 2009. Here the two victims were pelted with bricks and stones and stabbed with a knife; one was forced to strip naked and perform a sex act, a mobile phone was stolen, and both brothers then received burns when their assailants covered them with a sheet and set it on fire. Their attackers, who were sentenced to indefinite detention, came, it emerged, from a family with a history of violence.[30]

And difficulties within the family also played their part in the most widely publicised of all twentieth-century cases of child murder by children – that of toddler James Bulger by Jon Venables and Robert Thompson (both aged ten) in 1993 – although the details of the case also show the dangers inherent in too reductive an explanation of motive. The circumstances remain fresh in many people's minds.

On 12 February 1993 a security camera captured James Bulger, a month away from his third birthday and two hours away from death, trustingly holding Venables's hand, as Venables, with Thompson just a few steps ahead, led him from the New Strand Shopping Centre in Bootle.[31] James's mother Denise, who had taken her eye off her son for a split second, raised the alarm almost straightaway, but the two boys had already embarked on a meandering two-and-a-half mile walk to a section of little-used railway track off Walton Lane. At various points along the way they were challenged by passers-by, but always seemed to have a convincing reason why they should be in the company of a child showing signs of distress.

Once alone with James, they threw a tin of paint they had earlier shoplifted in his face, pelted him with bricks, and beat him over the head with a fishplate: a two-foot strip of steel used to attach railway plates to sleepers. When he was dead, they covered his body with rubble and laid it on the railway line, hoping that it would be hit by a passing train and that the death would therefore appear to have been an accident. There was also some evidence that there may have been a sexual element to the killing.

There is no doubt that both Venables and Thompson had their fair share of trouble at home. Venables's parents had split up when he was three, although his father continued to exercise a parental role, and it did seem at certain points that the couple might become reconciled. Jon Venables's older brother and younger sister both had learning difficulties, and were educated at special schools. He too struggled at primary school, could be anti-social and disruptive in class, and after a particularly serious incident was moved to another school where, because of his learning difficulties, he was placed in a class with younger pupils. It was here that he met Robert Thompson, who was also being held back a year. Thompson was not regarded as an especially disruptive pupil, although he was frequently involved in playground problems. His home life was not a particularly happy one. His mother Ann had been the victim of violent abuse at the hands of both her father and her husband, and her marriage had broken up in October 1988, just a matter of days before a fire at the family home. Ann found herself unable to cope, although the indications are that she was pulling herself together at the time of James Bulger's murder, while Robert's older brothers worked at keeping the family together.

At the time, much was made of Venables's and Thompson's family circumstances, and of the social problems that a post-industrial Merseyside faced, bedevilled as it was with high unemployment, social deprivation and crime. More vaguely, there was a sense that the murder and its aftermath demonstrated what was wrong with contemporary British society: family breakdown, loss of respect for authority, an overly liberal education system, soft policies on juvenile offenders and on crime generally, all contributing to the development of a vicious underclass. All this was of a piece with what was to be said after the Edlington case, when Prime Minister David Cameron would speak of a 'broken society' riddled with drug and alcohol abuse, violent videos and families in crisis.

None of this hand-wringing or finger-pointing explains why, at a time and in a city where no other even remotely comparable crimes were being committed, Venables and Thompson should have decided to abduct and kill a toddler. Some commentators simply wrote them off as evil, but – even if one believes in the concept of evil – that too seems simplistic. The view of the school staff was that while the two boys clearly had problems, and caused trouble for others, there was nothing really exceptional about their misbehaviour, and certainly nothing to suggest they were potential killers. That's not to say that there wasn't a degree of premeditation in what they did. Jon Venables's form teacher recalled that the worst behaved she had ever seen him was the day before James Bulger's death. And on the day itself, the two boys tried to entice another toddler away from its mother before they lighted on James Bulger (a witness also later recalled seeing two boys in late-January, one of whom he identified as Venables, tapping on the window of a store to draw a child away from its mother). A possible part-explanation of their actions is that they had decided in some vague way to 'get a kid', and that having successfully abducted James, and walked two and a half miles around the outskirts of Liverpool with him without being caught, they did not know what to do with him other than kill him and try to make his death look like an accident.

Alfred Fritz and John Breen, the two boys who killed James Fleeson in 1855, reportedly said, after assaulting their victim, 'let us throw him in the canal, or else we will be catched'. One can't help wondering whether Thompson and Venables weren't motivated by a similar concern. Murder, to their limited ten-year-old imaginations, seemed paradoxically the only way not to get into trouble for what they had done. And there is no doubt that Venables and Thompson (like, one suspects, Fritz and Breen a century before them) egged each other on. This doesn't begin to excuse what they did, but it may go a little way to help explain it.

The trial of Venables and Thompson was held at Preston Crown Court and ran from 1 to 24 November 1993. Trying ten year olds presented legal problems. In England and Wales the age of legal responsibility is ten, although offenders aged ten to seventeen are usually treated differently to adults. However, both the police questioning of Venables and Thompson (which was carried out in a very sensitive and professional manner) and the early stages of the trial established that each of the boys did have a clear sense that killing another child was wrong, and hence it was legally possible to bring a verdict of wilful murder against them as if they were adults.

The next problem was sentencing. Emotions about the case were running high on Merseyside. Early in the investigation the police had brought in a boy for questioning. His home had then been besieged by the media and angry locals, there had been a near riot outside the police station where it was thought, wrongly, that he was being held, and although the boy had then been cleared of any connection with the killing of James Bulger, he and his family subsequently had to move. Wreaths, bunches of flowers, teddy bears and other children's toys were left in profusion in the shopping centre where James had been abducted and in Cherry Lane, Walton, close to where his body was found. On the Saturday following the discovery of his body, with Liverpool playing a home match against Ipswich, a large banner reading 'R.I.P. James' was displayed at the Kop. When Venables and Thompson were committed in late-February, an angry mob gathered and six arrests were made.

The reaction in Merseyside was mirrored nationally. The petition launched by James Bulger's parents to secure full life sentences for Venables and Thompson was picked up by the *Sun* newspaper, which printed coupons that readers could send to the Home Secretary, Michael Howard. In an interview with the *Mail on Sunday* on 21 February Prime Minister John Major commented on the need for a crusade against crime, and a focus on the victim rather than the offender, declaring: 'Society needs to condemn a little more and understand a little less.' Michael Howard made a crowd-pleasing speech to the annual Conservative Party conference on 6 October 1993, three days after Venables and Thompson had been taken to Preston Crown Court for an initial visit to familiarise them with the place, and this was commented on favourably by the tabloids and the Conservative broadsheets. After passing sentence, the presiding judge, Sir Michael Morland, suggested a tariff (that is, a minimum sentence) of eight years for Venables and Thompson. The Lord Chief Justice agreed with the tenor of Morland's summing up at the end of the trial, but suggested a tariff of ten years. For his part – and acutely aware of public opinion – Michael Howard had been thinking in terms of twenty to twenty-five years, but he was also anxious not to diverge too far from the recommendations of the judge and the Lord Chief Justice, so the tariff that was finally set was fifteen years.

In fact both of James Bulger's killers were released after eight years. Venables, however, has since been imprisoned for a variety of offences, including child pornography.

IV

The horrified and uncomprehending reaction at the time of James Bulger's murder is entirely understandable. It must have seemed a uniquely terrible crime. Yet, strangely enough, records survive of an astonishingly similar incident that occurred in Stockport, just outside Manchester, 130 years earlier. In 1861 Stockport was a cotton-weaving and hat-making town, and on 11 April of that year, the son of a power-loom weaver named Ralph Burgess, two-year-old George Burgess, was reported missing by a woman named Sarah Ann Warren, employed to nurse him (that is, care for and breast-feed him as necessary) while his parents were at work. She last recalled seeing him at 2 p.m. Half an hour later, unable to find him, she reported the matter to the police. The following day, the little boy's body was found by John Buckley, a farm labourer. He was naked apart from a pair of clogs, and had been severely beaten. The actual cause of death was drowning – the toddler's head had been pushed down between two stones in a stream.

As in the Bulger case, it soon transpired that he had been abducted and killed by two boys – Peter Henry Barratt and James Bradley, both of them aged eight. And as in the Bulger case, passers-by had seen them with the little boy, had asked them what they were up to, and had been satisfied with their explanations. The first of two witnesses at the trial (both of them women, one accompanied at the time of her encounter with the boys by her teenage son) had noticed that the toddler was clearly in distress; the second had seen the trio at 4 p.m., by which time George had been undressed, but had decided not to intervene. When arrested neither of the boys seemed to have a real idea just how serious their crime was, and both confessed in a manner that can only be described as matter of fact. In the 1860s the age of legal responsibility was seven, although the notion of *doli inca-pax* went up to fourteen. However, while the coroner presiding over George Burgess's inquest explained this to the jury, he also made it clear that he felt that the boys had committed wilful murder. This was, accordingly, the jury's verdict. The case was therefore passed to be heard at the August assizes.

It attracted considerable press and public interest; 1861 had been a difficult year in general. Concerns had been expressed about levels of crime, and about misery and social deprivation among the labouring population. Moreover, a new element had been added to the fears of 'respectable' people: the juvenile delinquent. In the eighteenth century juveniles were rarely prosecuted before the courts, and the 'young offender' was not seen as a particular social problem. But by the 1840s this had changed: avid readers of the crime statistics of that decade would have discovered that 29 per cent of those indicted were juveniles. The eighteenth-century apprentice and live-in servant had been replaced – or at least supplemented – by the nineteenth-century industrial worker, less tightly controlled than his forebears (though apprentices could be pretty wild) and, so far as his more critical contemporaries were concerned, working in institutions that were little more than seminaries of crime: factories.[32] The killing of young George Burgess was thus a case that seemed to epitomise all that was wrong with contemporary society, not least the threat juvenile offenders posed to it. The press seized on the characters and social class of the two accused and proceeded to rip them apart. The *Macclesfield Courier and Herald* of 20 April 1861, for example, argued that

> ... the prisoners were in their way average specimens of the little street Arabs who infest all our great towns. Their crime alone renders them exceptional. But their habits and lives were those of that class.

The press also brought in their verdict long before the case reached court. *Reynold's Weekly*, a national paper, informed its readers on

22 April that 'there was no want [lack] of deliberation in the transaction: it was as deliberately contrived a proceeding as any murder in the records of the Old Bailey'.

At the assizes, however, the presiding judge, Sir Charles Compton, who had decided to hold back Barratt and Bradley's trial until last, made it very clear that he did not agree with the popular view. And it is here that the 1861 case parts company with the 1993 murder of James Bulger. In 1993 the judiciary were under enormous pressure to convict and to punish severely. In his 1861 summing up, by contrast, Sir Charles declared that what Burgess's killers had done was mere 'babyish mischief' and recommended a verdict of manslaughter. When that verdict was forthcoming, he stipulated that the boys should spend a month in prison and then five years in a reformatory. As he explained to them:

> I am going to send you to a place where you will have the opportunity of becoming good boys, for there you will have a chance of being brought up in a way you should be, and I doubt not that in time, when you come to understand the nature of the crime you have committed, you will repent of what you have done.

Public and press reaction to the verdict was generally favourable. And despite initial displays of hostility when the two boys appeared at the coroner's inquest on Burgess, the case was not conducted to the sound of mobs braying for vengeance. Even more remarkably, as far as we can tell, the families of the two killers continued to live peacefully in Stockport. No evidence has ever been found that either Peter Henry Barratt or James Bradley reoffended.[33]

It is salutary to think that in 1861 a judge could believe that two young child-killers could be reformed and rehabilitated (a view very much in line with progressive attitudes to the penal system at the time), while in 1993 the popularly held view was that it is possible for two young child-killers to be evil and incapable of redemption. But overall, we certainly have a better and more nuanced understanding

of what drives people to harm and to kill than our Victorian forebears had, and all the evidence about violence within and around
the family suggests that it is less prevalent than it was, say, fifty years
ago, even if it is very far from being eradicated. At the very least,
there is now a generally accepted view that physical aggression
towards spouses, partners and children is always wrong, that would
not have prevailed a few decades back.

Just how much things have changed even in very recent times is
demonstrated by the transformation that has taken place in our view
of bullying. Interestingly the negative connotations of the word are
relatively recent ('bully' was originally a term of endearment).
When Tom Brown went to Rugby it was a given that children pick
on each other (as, of course, do adults). It was also a given that low-
level bullying should be accepted as part of the rough and tumble of
everyday life – even that it could be character-building. That view
has changed, but only over the past couple of decades.

Research into the effects of bullying was pioneered as late as the
1970s in Scandinavia, notably by Dan Olweus, who, after holding
posts in his native Sweden, was Professor of Psychology at Norway's
Bergen University and whose bullying prevention programme has
been widely implemented internationally. In England the first
important studies appeared in the 1980s, and in 1989 bullying was
identified as a cause for concern in the Elton Report on school discipline, published under the auspices of the Department of Education
and Science. It was rapidly followed by the Gulbenkian Foundation
setting up a working party on bullying in schools. This survey supported a number of projects, one of the most fruitful of them being
a research project headed by Professor Peter K. Smith of the University of Sheffield into bullying in Sheffield schools. Smith's work
resulted in the Sheffield Anti-Bullying Project, an interventionist
project working along lines pioneered in Norway, which has proved
influential in the United Kingdom.

The conventional wisdom had been that bullying is something
we all experience, that it prepares us for the realities of adult life, and

that we tend to forget what we suffered as children as we get older. The new research, however, suggested that bullying not only lowers the victim's self-esteem but also their mental and physical health and motivation to study, and that, in extreme cases, it can mark them for life.[34]

The conventional wisdom had been that bullying should only be a concern when it was violently physical. The new research showed that just the threat of violence, not to mention name-calling and spreading malicious stories (more recently, cyber-bullying), can have devastating effects and that persistent bullying, even at a non-physical level, can lead to suicide.

It was indeed a much-publicised suicide by a teenage girl in 1992 that helped raise awareness of school bullying as an issue of major concern. Increasingly from the mid-1990s onwards it was joined by campaigns, notably by trades unions, to end bullying in the workplace.[35] In Victorian times bullying was accepted to the point where it could even be institutionalised as fagging in public schools. Today, bullying is regarded as socially unacceptable.

Domestic violence, child abuse and bullying are, sadly, still deeply embedded in our society to a greater or lesser extent. But at least the problems have been both identified and condemned – in other words, we know that they *are* problems and that something needs to be done about them. If society still has a long way to go, it has also travelled a long way over the past couple of centuries.

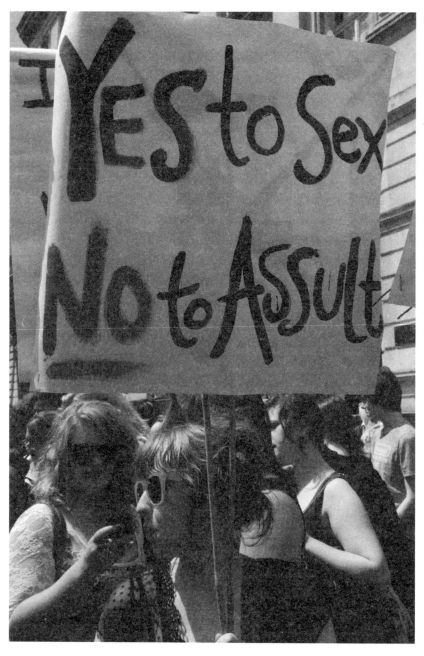

Rape has been a criminal offence in England for centuries, but remains common. This photo shows women at a 2012 London demonstration protesting against a 'culture of rape'.

CHAPTER 15

WOMEN AND SEXUAL VIOLENCE

I

In January 1971 Susan Brownmiller, a New York journalist and free-lance writer, attended a radical feminist 'speak-out' on rape and, later that year, a conference dedicated to the topic. Four years after that she published the seminal *Against Our Will: Men, Women and Rape*, a powerful work that offered a completely fresh perspective on rape and sexual violence and that also ambitiously attempted to chronicle them. 'My purpose in this book', Brownmiller declared in her final sentences, 'has been to give rape its history. Now we must deny it a future.'[1]

Against Our Will begins its history of rape by postulating a prehistoric society – living in a state of nature, as it were – in which rape was endemic and men regarded gang rape as an important form of male bonding. Marriage arose because women opted to give themselves to one rapist rather than many. As societies developed, rape became the main means by which men expressed their will and kept women subjugated. If it was punished, this was because men regarded their wives and daughters as property that needed to be protected: a daughter's value in the marriage market, for example, would diminish if she lost her virginity to sexual assault. 'From pre-historic times to the present', the book claims, 'rape has played a

critical function. It is nothing more or less than a conscious process of intimidation by which *all* men keep *all* women in a state
of fear.'

If there is one area of human experience that seems to bear out
Brownmiller's assertion that rape is a violent, not a sexual act, it is
war. Throughout history armies have not only fought but raped.[2]
Some 2 million German women are estimated to have been
raped – in numerous cases, gang-raped – as the Soviet army swept
into Germany in 1945. Many victims subsequently committed suicide. It has been suggested that there are particular reasons why the
Red Army should have proved so brutal. Ten million Russian civilians had perished during the German invasion: the desire to achieve
revenge, to bring the full horror of war home to the German people,
must have been overwhelming; against a more general background
of looting, destruction and murder, the systematic raping of a
defeated enemy's womenfolk must have been seen as an important
act of humiliation. Moreover, it may have been that troops were
being swept up in a barracks culture that was reacting against the
essentially puritanical nature of pre-war Soviet society. But it's worth
noting that it wasn't only the Russians who raped German women.
Attacks were also carried out by American, British, Canadian and
French armies in 1945 during the final weeks of warfare and the first
weeks of peace, though on nothing like the scale of their Russian
allies.[3] Particular circumstances, then, may dictate the extent of sexual assaults during war, but the underlying threat seems to be a
constant.

Rape was a horrifying feature of the Bosnian War of 1992–5: here
we know that some commanding officers not only gave their men
permission to attack women but carried out rapes themselves. It also
marked the Rwandan genocide of 1994.[4] In both conflicts many of
the victims were killed after they had been assaulted, but many
others were left alive so that their humiliation could be experienced
by what was left of their families.

Overall, though, Brownmiller's thesis has proved controversial and has been widely challenged. Its presupposition that all men wish to keep all women in a constant state of fear was as problematic in 1975 as it is today. Its rejection of a sexual motive for rape is equally questionable. We know from accounts of convicted rapists that, whatever precisely is going on in their minds at the time of an assault, it is not necessarily or solely a desire to dominate the female sex. It's also difficult to believe that the long literary and legal traditions that link rape with lust can be entirely wrong. As the American legal writer and feminist Catharine MacKinnon pithily put it: 'if it's violence not sex why didn't he just hit her?'[5] Rape is a multi-faceted crime that cannot be reduced to a simple universal explanation: some rapes are the result of lust, others of a need to express male domination over women, others of a desire for revenge or for a sense of superiority; many arise from a complex mixture of motives.[6]

Some evolutionary biologists have similarly criticised Brownmiller's rejection of a sexual motive in rape. They argue that nature has provided males with the ability to overcome resistance to sexual intercourse that will ensure the survival of the species, and that rape is an adaptation of a form of behaviour that helps males pass their genes on. The idea has been restated as recently as 2000 in Randy Thornhill and Craig Palmer's *A Natural History of Rape.* [7]

There is a certain irony here. Such views, it could be argued, in being as dogmatic about a sexual motive as Brownmiller was about physical domination, support her fundamental contention that rape is hard-wired in to the male psyche. And they are controversial in their own right. Experts disagree as to levels of coercive sex among other animals, notably primates, so it is very tricky to establish an evolutionary urge to rape in other species. It is also difficult to see how evolutionary biology explains the rape of women not of childbearing age. And, as I said in the Introduction, it fails to take account of the way in which different human cultures have developed differently over a historical time-span too short to have been moulded by biological evolution.[8]

In terms of creating a history of rape *Against Our Will* is similarly contentious, though never less than stimulating and thought-provoking. Take, for example, its discussion of the roots of the word 'rape'. As Brownmiller points out, throughout the middle ages, the Latin term for rape, *rapere* (literally, 'to take'), could signify both what a modern reader would consider rape and what would now be regarded as abduction. This would seem to confirm Brownmiller's fundamental contention that women have, throughout history, essentially been regarded as property. But the reality is rather more complicated. It is certainly the case that an indictment for *raptus* might well be brought to protect family interests in those instances where the daughters of property-owners, or heiresses, or widows in possession of lands had been abducted. But we know that although many of these abductions must have been forcible (a reminder that violence was an intrinsic part of medieval social relations), others were carried out with the full consent of the 'victim', who was essentially fleeing home in order to enter a marriage of which her family did not approve.

Moreover, although the word *rapere* might cover two activities that to our minds are wholly separate, medieval courts were perfectly capable of making the distinction: a charge of rape might well specifically state that the accused had had carnal knowledge of a woman against her will or had violated her body.[9] Although it was a distinction that became muddied over time, it can be seen in a 1576 statute that removed convicted rapists from benefit of clergy. The statute's reference to 'the most wicked and felonious rapes and ravishments of women, maids, wives and damosels', which is redolent of earlier phraseology, is admittedly ambiguous. But it is crystal clear in its statement 'that if any person shall carnally know and abuse any woman-child under the age of ten years, every such unlawful and carnal knowledge shall be felony, and the offender thereof being truly convicted shall suffer as a felon without allowance of clergy'.[10] Rape in this context is rape as we understand it today, and not abduction.

One of the earliest pronouncements on rape to have survived is that enshrined in Alfred the Great's legal code, composed towards the end of the ninth century, and, in many ways, strikingly 'enlightened' to our twenty-first-century eyes. It distinguishes between abduction, rape and lesser forms of sexual assault, and stresses that the seriousness of these offences is magnified by the fact that they have been committed without their victim's consent. The Anglo-Saxon criminal code was based on a system of compensation whose level varied according to the social status of the victim. Thus a man who seized a maiden of the 'ceorl' (roughly speaking, free peasant) class would have to pay her five shillings' compensation; if he threw her to the ground but did not rape her, he would pay ten shillings; if he actually raped her she would receive sixty shillings, or half that if she was not a virgin. If a ceorl's slave woman was raped, compensation was due, and a sixty-shilling fine. If a male slave raped a female one, he would be castrated. Raping an under-age girl incurred the same penalties as those for raping an adult woman; and raping higher-born women involved higher levels of compensation (as was the case with other crimes committed against upper-class people). Thus Alfred's code covered all social strata, including slaves; all women and not just virgins; and it involved payment of compensation to the victim direct, not to her family. To what extent this code was a policy statement rather than a reflection of actual practice is unclear. But it's nevertheless a sophisticated treatment of sexual assault against women, very probably reflecting the relatively high status that women enjoyed in Anglo-Saxon society.

The Norman Conquest in 1066 meant the end of the Anglo-Saxon laws and, according to some scholars, the status previously held by women. But early post-Conquest legal treatises, possibly influenced by their Anglo-Saxon predecessors, continued to maintain a distinction, albeit an increasingly uncertain one, between rape and abduction, and to regard rape (in the context of assault) as sexual intercourse inflicted by men on non-consenting women. A work widely attributed to Ranulf de Glanvill, Chief Justiciar of England during the reign of Henry II (1154–89), stated that a rape case would follow when 'a woman charges a man with violating her by force'; in the following century, Henry de Bracton described rape as a crime 'imputed by a woman to the man by whom she has been ravished against the king's peace'. Lust was viewed as the mainspring of rape. Bracton, possibly in line with wider opinion, argued that rape should be punished by blinding and castration, the first so that the perpetrator would 'lose his eyes which gave him sight of the maiden's beauty for which he coveted her', the second so that he would 'lose as well the testicles which excited his hot lust'.[11]

Initially, the onus of prosecution was placed on the victim through a process known as appeal of felony (or, more specifically, appeal of rape), which was, in effect, a form of private prosecution. The procedure, it has to be said, was not exactly sympathetic to her feelings or suffering. According to Glanvill, she had to go to the nearest township 'soon after the deed is done' and 'there show to trustworthy men the injury done to her, and any effusion of blood there may be and any tearing of her clothes'. She then had to repeat this process before local royal officials (typically the coroner), and presumably had to tell her story yet again in court before a judge and jury. As today, this was all daunting in the extreme, and as a rule it was highly unlikely to result in a conviction unless the accuser was a woman of high status. It's hardly surprising that many rape charges were dropped, possibly following an out of court settlement involving financial compensation. The few cases that did end in a guilty verdict were usually punished by a fine rather than mutilation or death. Surviving medieval records rarely go into much detail, but enough information is contained in early court rolls to hint at the nature of some of these instances of forced sexual intercourse and violence. In a Cornish case of 1201 Marina, daughter of Everwin, appealed Roger de Barid of rape, claiming that he had thrown her down and taken her virginity. Witnesses attested that they had seen her bleeding. In the same year and in the same county Lucy, sister of William Ballard, appealed Stephen Hoker, claiming that he had taken her into a booth and forced her to have intercourse with him.

The serjeant of the hundred, a local law officer, stated that she had been seen bleeding, though it's not clear whether this was caused by loss of virginity or injuries sustained during the attack. Violence accompanying a rape is far less ambiguous in a Yorkshire prosecution from about the same time: here Sibba, daughter of William, appealed William the son of Hugh of Bolton that he raped her near the village of Wheldrake, beat her and made her bloody.[12]

The two forms of 'raptus', rape and abduction, impinged on each other more rather than less as the middle ages progressed – in legal terms, at least – to the point where they became rather confused. For the Norman elite and their successors, obsessed as they were with issues of land tenure and inheritance, abduction of a female member of their family, whether consensual or not, was a matter of deep concern. Thus when the Statutes of Westminster (1275 and 1285) were enacted, the legal distinction between rape as coercive sex and as abduction was eroded. Simultaneously, the focus shifted from the rights of the female victim of forced sex to the interests of her family.

The Statute of Rapes (1382) that superseded these two pieces of legislation was actually occasioned by an abduction case: a knight named Sir Thomas West had petitioned John of Gaunt over the alleged abduction and rape of his daughter Eleanor (in fact, it transpired, young Eleanor had defied her father to marry a man of whom he did not approve, and Sir Thomas had brought the allegations of abduction and rape in the hope of dissolving the marriage). To add to the confusion, although the 1382 Statute placed an emphasis on abduction, it was couched in terms of rape as forced sex, and it also blurred the definitions of female consent in rape and abduction charges.

From then on it is astonishingly difficult for the historian to work out whether a late-medieval 'rape' charge involved non-consensual sexual intercourse, abduction of an unwilling girl (the situation was complicated further by the term 'ravishment' being used to cover the abduction of male heirs or wards), a consensual marriage entered into against the wishes of the family involved, a husband targeting an adulterous wife and her lover, or a husband confronted by a wife who was trying to escape a violent or abusive marriage (this last possibility might help explain odd cases where fathers were accused of abducting their daughters).[13] Legal remedies were extended by the second Statute of Westminster, by which the old system of appeal of rape was now joined by crown prosecution through indictment. Confusingly, moreover, compensation for those whose womenfolk had been abducted was also now sometimes sought by the families of those who had been sexually assaulted. This elision of rape and abduction was continued in legislation of 1487. It was not until the 1576 statute mentioned earlier that a demarcation line was properly drawn.

II

As in other areas of violent crime, our knowledge of rape in the middle ages is largely confined to surviving documentation about individual cases. But by the time we reach the second half of the sixteenth century, it is possible to put some statistical flesh on the anecdotal bones. Even for this later period, of course, the evidence is patchy, but surviving indictments from the five counties of the Home Circuit of the assizes – Essex, Hertfordshire, Kent, Surrey and Sussex – are revealing (with the proviso, of course, that this has always been an under-reported crime and that Tudor women would certainly have thought twice before taking rapists to court).[14] Extant indictments show a total of 88 men being indicted for rape in these five counties during the reign of Elizabeth I (1558–1603). Of these, 15 were hanged, by this point the standard punishment for convicted rapists. A further 4 were found guilty but escaped the noose by claiming benefit of clergy (this was before the 1576 legislation that closed this loophole); they, presumably, were branded. Another 4 were remanded after being found guilty (one died in gaol). Four were recorded as being 'at large' (in other words they had not been apprehended), one suffered *peine forte et dure* after refusing to plead (a process which involved heaping stones or other weights on the accused's chest until either a plea was entered or the accused died); in one case no verdict was recorded; and in another the verdict cannot be recovered due to damage to the document. In all, then, 23 of the accused, or just over a quarter, were found guilty and punished, while 62 were acquitted. Most came from the tradesmen class; four were clergymen; one was described as a gentleman.

These men's alleged victims were almost invariably unmarried – indeed 35 of them were aged eleven or younger. On the surface, this seems a truly shocking proportion of the whole, but it almost certainly reflects a tendency to take the rape of a child more seriously than that of an adolescent or adult. As for the other victims, several were described as servants, which suggests that they, too, may well have been young (some are described as 'daughter of'), while only 6 were married (one of them to the rector of Chelmsford in Essex), and one was a widow. Very little detail is given about any individual case, although occasionally we get tantalising incidental details, particularly about location: Henry Cherry, an Essex brewer of beer, was hanged after he raped Mathea Phippes in The Catherine Wheel at Shenfield; Richard Roulfe, a Greenwich waterman, allegedly raped Joan Kerby on a boat at Deptford; other rapes were said to have taken place in the fields or on the highway. There are references to the labourers John Edwards and David Fludde who were executed after being convicted separately for – it appears – raping the same woman in August 1567.

In two other cases one is left wondering whether the fact that the alleged rapists seem to have been outsiders counted against them. Adrian Edes or Couton, a miner ('collier'), who was executed for the rape of Agnes Walker in Sussex in 1569, may well have been one of the German mineworkers whose expertise was so key to the Sussex coal industry at this time (the clue here is that Adrian was not a common English forename then). William Davey, executed in the same county in 1577 for the rape of Alice Shotter, was not exactly a foreigner, but neither was he a local: he came from Chiddingfold in Surrey. No gang rapes are recorded in the surviving indictments, and few of the men were accused of attacking more than one woman, the exceptions being Ralph Smythe, a Sussex man charged with raping two servant girls; John Hardye, an Essex man accused in 1591 of raping two girls aged nine on several occasions and another aged seven; and John Henshaw of Deptford in Kent.

Henshaw's case is unusual in that when he was accused of raping six-year-old Alice Keeling and seven-year-old Agnes Keeling just a few days apart from one another in August 1584, he was also accused of raping eight-year-old Elizabeth Rowson in February 1583. One can only assume that when the Keeling affair became public, it revived suspicions of a likely earlier attack. Henshaw was nevertheless acquitted, as were Smythe and Hardye. It is interesting that those accused of raping children were no more likely to be convicted than anyone else.

In a handful of capital cases it seems likely that the accused were sentenced to death because their crimes extended beyond rape. One such was John Daye, who, accused of raping the widow Agnes Cole at Ardleigh in Essex, had apparently done so while he was burgling her house, and so faced an additional capital charge. Thomas Synderford from Kent, hanged for raping Bridget, the wife of John Howkins, in 1592, seems to have been something of a career criminal: he was also convicted of grand larceny that year, and had been whipped for theft four years previously. Edward Sharpe from Essex was charged with rape in 1590, but was actually hanged for very unwisely exploiting his position as a purveyance collector (purveyance was in effect a tax in kind levied to feed the royal household) in order to take for himself twelve chickens he had collected on the Queen's behalf. And then there were a couple of cases where the sentence was murder (which means that they are not included in the overall tally given above) but where rape was involved. Anthony Case was executed for murder in 1592 because, fearing she would report that he had raped her, he had broken the neck of a servant named Judith Smyth and had thrown her body into a pond. Richard ap Beavans, a petty chapman who raped six-year-old Agnes Newe in November 1599, similarly faced a murder charge when the girl died as a result of the attack four months later.

In all these cases, it's clear that by the Elizabethan era 'rape' was starting to lose its dual medieval meaning. By the time the Cambridgeshire barrister and justice of the peace Michael Dalton published his legal guide, *The Countrey Justice*, in 1618 the idea of rape as abduction was largely subsidiary to the concept of rape as enforced, non-consensual sexual intercourse. In the following passage from the 1643 edition a certain ambiguity is still apparent with the reference to taking away a maid by force, but rape in its modern sense is what emerges most clearly:

> For to ravish a woman where she doth neither consent before nor after; or to ravish any woman by force, though she do consent after, it is felony: and the offender shall have no benefit of clergy . . . If a man take away a maid by force, and ravish her, and after she giveth her consent, and marrieth him, yet it is rape. Now ravishment is here take in one and the same signification with rape, which is a violent deflowering of a woman, or carnal knowledge had of the body of a woman, against her will.

For Dalton, as for medieval commentators, a rape complaint had to be swiftly reported if it was to be viewed as valid (though he noted some differences in legal opinion as to just how swiftly): 'a woman that is ravished', he wrote, ought 'presently [i.e. at once] to levy open hue and cry, or to complain presently to some credible persons'. He pointed out that anyone aiding or procuring a rape was indictable as a principal – so, for example, a woman could be prosecuted for helping a man to rape another woman. He also repeated a strange legal and medical dictum – medieval in origin – that, since sexual intercourse without consent could not result in conception, an accusation of rape could not be sustained if the alleged victim subsequently became pregnant. He noted the opinion of an earlier writer that it would help a defendant if he could claim that the woman involved 'before the ravishment ... was his concubine'. He also noted – interestingly, given the period in which he was writing – that if a prostitute was forced to have sex against her will, that constituted rape.[15]

To an extent, the complexities and ambiguities that surrounded the issue of rape in the late sixteenth and seventeenth centuries are reflected in the culture in which Renaissance England became steeped: that of classical Greece and Rome. From Roman history, educated contemporaries would have learned the story of the Rape of the Sabine Women – here, of course, rape meant abduction. From Greek mythology they would have learned of Persephone, daughter of Zeus and Demeter, who was seized by Hades and taken to the underworld to be his wife – abduction again. From Greek mythology they would also have read of Zeus, the arch-rapist, who raped Europa, daughter of the Phoenician King Agenor, in the shape of a bull; Nemesis, goddess of retribution, in the shape of a swan when she had taken the form of a goose; Leda, daughter of the Aetolian King Thestius and wife of Tyndareus, King of Sparta, again in the shape of a swan (the result of this union being the egg from which Helen of Troy was hatched). And they would have learned how Zeus raped Danae, daughter of the King of Argos and Eurydice, in the shape of a shower of golden rain, how Peleus seized and then married the sea-nymph Thetis, and how the nymph Daphne escaped the god Apollo's attentions only by turning herself into a laurel tree. From all these stories they would have picked up a celebration of male sexual aggression: these are, after all, rapists who are divine beings, and they pursue their prey in ways that evoke the heroic worlds of warfare and hunting.[16]

It comes as no surprise then that when Ben Jonson's Volpone plots to have sexual intercourse with a not entirely willing Celia, he declares that she is 'like Europa now, and I like Jove' (III.vii.222).[17] Nor that Shakespeare should have drawn on classical rape stories in his poetry and plays. His *Rape of Lucretia*, which derives from Livy, presents rape at its most violent and horrific. It relates how Sextus Tarquinius, son of the corrupt monarch Lucius Tarquinius Superbus, who is staying at the home of Lucretia while her husband is at war, one night sneaks into her bedroom and tells her if she does not give in to his sexual advances and become his queen he will kill both her and a slave, put the slave's body in her bed and then claim that he had caught them in flagrante delicto. She submits to Sextus, but the next day informs her father, chief magistrate of Rome, of the rape and then stabs herself to death. In the revolt that follows, Lucius Tarquinius Superbus is deposed and the Roman Republic established.

Another Roman rape story, that of the rape of Philomel, lies behind Shakespeare's early play *Titus Andronicus*. In the original tale Philomel, daughter of Pandion, King of Athens, is raped by her brother-in-law, King Tereus of Thrace, husband of her sister Procne. She threatens to make the rape known, so he cuts out her tongue and keeps her in a cabin in the woods. Philomel, however, weaves the story of her fate into a tapestry which she sends to Procne, and Procne then wreaks revenge on Tereus by killing their son Itys (or Itylos), and serving his cooked remains to Tereus. Shakespeare's adaptation makes free use of the original story, though it draws heavily on Ovid's retelling of Greek and Roman myths in his *Metamorphoses*. Ovid himself wrote in approving terms of rape in his *Ars Amatoria*:

> *Force is all right to employ, and women like you to use it;*
> *What they enjoy they pretend they were unwilling to give.*
> *One who is overcome, and suddenly, forcefully taken,*
> *Welcomes the wanton assault, takes it as proof of her charm.*
> *But if you let her go untouched when you could have compelled her,*
> *Though she pretends to be glad, she will be gloomy at heart.*

Many from classical times onwards regarded the *Ars Amatoria* as an immoral work but it was also widely read. It expressed a view of forced sex to which some at least of its Elizabethan and Jacobean readers would, one suspects, have been sympathetic.[18]

III

On 14 November 1642 the daughter of Adam Fisher (we do not know her name, but we are told she was a 'younge virgine') went to visit friends at Totnes in Devon, about a mile from where she lived. She stayed longer than she had intended, and her friends urged her to stay the night. They had good reason. The English Civil War had now reached Devon in the shape of a Royalist army from Cornwall that was marching to besiege Exeter. The times were dangerous and uncertain. But the girl declined her friends' offer, saying that her father would be unhappy if she did not return that night; she was determined, she said, 'hap what might hap, to go home that night, trusting in God to protect her from deboyst [i.e. debauched] cavaliers'.

As she made her way home in the dark, she met a local gentleman, Ralph Ashley, whom she knew. He asked her why she was out so late, and, when she explained, offered to take her home, 'for the times are dangerous, and but a little before there are soldiers which I have cause to suspect would do thee some outrage'. Accepting his offer, she got on his horse behind him. A little way on, he announced that he was going to take a detour to avoid the danger of encountering any soldiers, but when they arrived at an isolated spot, he proceeded to dismount and persuaded the girl to do the same. Now he started to make sexual advances towards her, and when she resisted, 'he went about to ravish her, taking a grievous oath that no power on heaven or earth could save her from his lust'. She tried to fight him off, calling on God to help her, but Ashley continued his onslaught, telling her 'there was no power could redeem her'.

No sooner had he said this than 'a fearful comet burst out of the air, so that it was as light as high noon'. The girl swooned ('the poor virgin was intranced') and Ashley, seeing her lying on the ground before him, declared 'God damn him, alive or dead he would enjoy her'. It was a foolhardy mistake. A stream of fire came from the comet, 'in the perfect shape, and exact resemblance a flaming sword', and struck him. Some local shepherds came to see what was going on. Ashley confessed to them that he had intended to rape the girl ('that round-headed whore'), and then died 'raving and blaspheming to the terror and amazement of the beholders'. The shepherds carried the girl, whom they assumed to be dead, back to her father's house, where she lay in a trance until the next morning. When she came to, her first words were ones of gratitude to the Lord for her deliverance.

Clearly there was a moral to be drawn here, and the author of the pamphlet was not slow in coming up with one:

> Reader, here is a precedent for all those that are customary blasphemers, and live after the lusts of the flesh, especially all those cavaliers which esteem murder & rapine the chief principals of their religion, for doubtless this is but a beginning of God's vengeance for not only he, but they and we, and all of us, unless we repent we shall all likewise perish.

It was, of course, a crude piece of anti-cavalier propaganda: the wicked Ralph Ashley commits one of the most appalling of all crimes – moreover, one that involves the sin of lust – and, far from repenting, dies blaspheming.[19] His divine punishment is entirely in line with the capital punishment that would have awaited him had he had to face a terrestrial judge.

But, as with so many aspects of rape over its long history, the true position regarding judgement and punishment at this time is a very complicated one. According to the strict letter of the law, rape was among the most serious of offences, punishable by hanging until as late as 1841 and, as already mentioned, removed from benefit of clergy by a statute of 1576. Yet in practice, the law (then as now) neither deterred rapists, nor resulted in a high proportion of rapists being punished. Surviving records of cases from various courts in

Essex between 1620 and 1680 reveal that forty-one indictments resulted in only six executions. A similar picture emerges from the Surrey assizes in the eighteenth century – here it proved very difficult to obtain a capital conviction for rape. And all the evidence suggests that one key reason for this was that judges and juries (all of whom would, of course, have been male) felt that the crime was not sufficiently serious to merit the punishment that was supposed to go with it.

A case from 1784 illustrates this well. Elizabeth Tarrier, an orphan and a servant at the Fountain Inn in Monmouth Street, London, alleged that she had been raped by a neighbour to whom she had been sent with beer. Her aunt learned of the matter, and her uncle went to talk to her about what had happened ('I said, "Bet, what has happened: I insist on your telling the rights of it"'). He decided to prosecute. The landlord of the pub and his wife, however, felt that this was a wholly disproportionate response: 'Now see what you have done, Betty,' said the wife, to which the landlord added, 'Aye . . . now the man will be taken up and hanged.' Elizabeth's uncle stuck to his guns: he was, he said, 'determined to follow the law of him'; but ultimately the accused man was acquitted.

In another case, from Bedfordshire in 1817, the hanging of a man for rape so outraged local people that a crowd of 200 surrounded the rape victim's house, brandishing obscene effigies of her and her parents.[20] It's scarcely surprising that, faced with the ordeal of giving evidence and the unlikelihood of securing a conviction, many rape victims should have settled for the lesser charge of assault. Nor is it surprising that convictions for rape should have risen sharply in the years after the abolition of the death sentence: from 10 per cent between 1836 and 1840 (the year of abolition) to 33 per cent between 1841 and 1845.[21] It is interesting to note that the proportion of men standing trial who were convicted in this later period is roughly equivalent to that obtaining in England and Wales today.[22]

The other major reason why convictions were so difficult to secure was that, then as now, proving beyond all doubt precisely what had happened was extremely difficult. One of the leading English legal commentators of the seventeenth century, Sir Matthew Hale, put it this way: 'rape is a most detestable crime, and therefore ought severely and impartially to be punished with death; but it must be remembered, that it is an accusation easy to be made, hard to be proved, but harder to be defended by the party accused, though innocent.'[23] Given a degree of innate scepticism on the part of male juries and judges plus the understandable unwillingness of many victims to go through gruelling cross-examination, the low level of convictions is not hard to comprehend.

Those cases for which detailed accounts survive can prove harrowing reading. Consider the deposition of eleven-year-old Patience Ditchfield, employed as the feeder of a carding engine at a cotton works owned by a Mr Matthew Longsdale in Lymm in Cheshire in 1800. William Renshaw was her 'slubber' there, that is the operator of a slubbing machine which processed cotton yarn, and two boys also worked with him on the machine. On the day in question, he sent the two boys (one of whom was his son) out of the room, took hold of Patience's hand and led her to a pile of waste cotton, where 'he pulled down his breeches and took his cock out and opened her hand and put it in her hand and asked whether she thought she could take it'. He then took her 'between the engine and the billy', and once there he

> . . . heaved her petticoats up, unbuttoned his breeches and got between her legs, that she did what she could but she could not make him get off her for her life, that he kept holding her thighs wide and put his cock into her as far as he could but he could not get it in for that he continued on her till the feeder was run up about three minutes, that she perceived he had hurt her for she both ached and smarted when she made water, that she perceived something about her thighs like blood but she never looked, that the Monday following he asked her to go to the carding room but she refused, that she continues very ill.

Patience told some other workers at the mill of the rape, but was too afraid to tell her parents. She developed an infection, and died a few days afterwards. Before she died her father, a cotton spinner, complained to a justice of the peace ('he prays justice may be done') and two doctors were called in, both of whom subsequently gave evidence to the justice.[24] William Renshaw was prosecuted for murder but acquitted.

Another case from the period that, like the Patience Ditchfield one, was recorded in some detail, had a very different outcome. In 1797 John Briant was brought up before the Old Bailey accused of raping fourteen-year-old Jane Bell. Bell, whose employer worked in the milk trade, was raped in Hyde Park after her assailant had engaged her in conversation as she locked her employer's cows into Green Park. At the trial, she told how Briant took her to an isolated spot, threw her down on a depression in a slope, knelt, loosened his britches, grabbed her when she almost got away, threw her down again, 'and entered my body'. At this point, the judge asked for clarification: 'Though we all know what is meant, you must tell us what he entered your body with; was it with his hands or with his legs?' The girl responded 'from between his thighs' and, on being questioned further, said that it was Briant's penis and that he lay on top of her for a quarter of an hour. Eventually, she managed to cry out, and attracted the attention of a lady and gentleman who pulled Briant off her. The lady said 'she would not leave him until he was taken up [i.e. arrested]', and he was committed to Bow Street.

Having given her testimony, Bell was then remorselessly cross-examined. She was asked if she 'ever had any man in your body before'. She denied this, along with a follow-up question: 'Has any man had to do with you since?' She was also questioned very closely about whether she had known Briant before the incident. The cross-examination now changed tack as she was asked if she knew a tavern called the Duke of York's Arms in Clarges Street. When she denied that she did, she was told: 'I will tell you candidly, that I am instructed to call witnesses to prove the contrary of all this.' She was also asked if she had 'ever been in a public house, within a month or two before that [the evening before the rape] with any man'. Clearly, an attempt was being made to suggest that the young teenager was a loose woman. She was also subjected to further questioning about the actual rape, why she had not cried out earlier ('he stopped my mouth when he took hold of me first'), and why she had not succeeded in running away ('because I could not, he was too strong for me').

Jane Bell's employer, Sarah Pollard, was called as a witness. She described the girl's condition after the rape and also gave her view of Jane's character: 'she was a modest good girl, as ever came into a house,' Pollard maintained; ' . . . she never had any followers, nor kept any company . . . she was as clean and fair a girl as ever sun shone upon, for I had examined her about the course of human nature [i.e. sexual intercourse], and she did not know what I meant, she was so perfectly clear.'

Defence witnesses, on the other hand, testified that Jane Bell had been seen drinking with Briant on various occasions, and that there had been a professional dispute between Pollard and Briant's employer (both were in the milk trade).

Sarah Pollard gave further evidence, claiming that one of the defence witnesses, Hannah Cusack, had tried to bribe Bell not to appear in court, and furthermore deposed that she had come across Cusack and other of Briant's supporters 'rioting' (i.e. mistreating and threatening) the girl. Samuel Pollard, Sarah's husband, although unable to confirm the allegations of attempted bribery, said that Hannah Cusack had expressed the opinion that Bell should be imprisoned and pilloried (presumably for perjury) if she took Briant to court. Briant's supporters did not win the day: he was convicted and hanged.

Another Old Bailey trial, from the previous year, throws an interesting light on how a case might be conducted when it involved a child. Here the accused was fifty-two-year-old David Scott; his alleged victim an eleven-year-old girl named Mary Homewood. As the jury was reminded at the beginning of proceedings, the law

defined the age of consent in rape cases as ten, so since 'this unfortunate object is eleven, one year beyond the age of the act; therefore
the question of consent will be material for you to consider in the
present case'. Mary was the daughter of the landlord of the Golden
Harp in Lamb Street and worked as a pot-girl there. The rape was
supposed to have occurred when she took beer to Scott in the nearby
dye-house where he worked. The counsel for the prosecution, in his
statement to the jury, addressed the issue of the reliability of a child
witness:

> She is of the tender age of eleven; we shall be inclined, perhaps,
> to hope, that from those tender years, her heart had not received
> any taint or corruption; yet, we know, in this great metropolis,
> young as that person may be, it may pass into the heart of per-
> sons, so young, to forget the duty they owe to society, and
> sometimes have a very wicked intent at so tender an age. Gen-
> tlemen, that is the fact you will have to try; I desire, on the part
> of the prosecution, that you will watch her narrowly, and if you
> find, from the manner in which she tells her story, that she
> deserves credit ... if she should falter in any part of it, if you
> should find she does not tell her story in such a way as you
> think deserves credit, you will acquit him, and by so doing,
> you will do your duty.

Mary made a good start. When asked if she knew the nature of an
oath, she said she did. When she was then asked 'What would be the
consequences, if you should swear false?', she answered 'If I should
take a false oath, I should go to the devil'. She was then formally
sworn.

Her account of the rape was very clear. She described how Scott
had laid her down upon 'the large bench'; how he'd stopped her from
calling out by putting his hand over her mouth; and how he 'opened
his breeches, and put something into my body', at which she 'hol-
loaed out several times'. She was then subjected to detailed
questioning about the circumstances of the rape – for example,

'which hand did he use to open his breeches, and pull up your pet-
ticoats' (to which she answered 'I cannot rightly tell, I was so
frightened'). She was further asked: 'You tell us he put something
into your body; what did he put into your body? Was it any part
of your own body? – you must overcome all shame, and tell us
the truth.' Her response was that it was 'something that he pulled
out of his breeches', which he then put 'into my private parts'.
She was asked whether this gave her pain, how far he went into her
body, how long he stayed there, whether anything passed from
his body into hers, and whether any other man had ever entered
her body.

She was also cross-examined by the defence counsel who, more
gentle than many, began by telling her: 'Don't be frightened my
good girl, but answer the questions that I shall put to you, as did that
gentleman.' His questions were nevertheless very detailed, and
included some clearly designed to ascertain whether her parents had
put her up to the prosecution.

According to Mary, when Scott had finished raping her, he offered
her money, which she refused. She then went home where her
mother 'licked' her for having been away for so long. Over the next
few days Mary's private parts became so sore she could scarcely walk
(she had been infected with a venereal disease). But it was only when
the unabashed Scott turned up at the bar and sat drinking in the tap-
room that the truth came out. Told to serve him, Mary informed her
mother, 'I will carry Scott no more beer', and then described what
had happened. Her mother called her father, informed him what
Mary had told her, upon which 'my father called the prisoner out,
and said something to him'. Even then it took several more days
before Scott was officially reported, largely because Mary's mother
was concerned that were the business to become public 'it might
make an alarm in the neighbourhood, and disgrace the child's character', and because Mary's father had hoped that Scott would go to
Scotland and so vanish from the picture.

Scott, however, 'did not go out of the way'. So as the days passed with the guilty man still very much around, and gossip beginning to circulate (Mary's mother had told a neighbour what had happened), Mary's father decided to act and a prosecution was brought. In court Scott produced character witnesses. He also claimed that Homewood had offered to drop the charges against him in return for twenty guineas. To no avail. He was convicted and hanged.[25]

Such cases as that of the rapists Briant and Scott give us a very good sense of the circumstances that commonly surrounded a sexual assault. But, of course, we will never know just how many rapes that were equally serious were never reported. Rape indictments were rare in Georgian England: rapes and attempted rapes prosecuted at the Surrey assizes in the second half of the eighteenth century, for example, never numbered more than four a year. Indeed, one suspects that many cases tried as attempted rape were in fact rape cases where the victim was unwilling to admit publicly to having been raped. Moreover, given how rarely a rape prosecution ended in conviction, many victims may have decided to prosecute rape as attempted rape in the knowledge that conviction (normally resulting in fine or imprisonment) was more likely, and thus the chances of the perpetrator receiving at least some punishment were enhanced.

A survey of rape and attempted rape cases for Surrey between 1660 and 1800 demonstrates that whereas only one-fifth of rape charges resulted in a conviction, two-thirds of the men charged with attempted rape were found guilty.[26] And the penalties for attempted rape could be severe. Thomas Greenwood, found guilty at the Worcester assizes in 1726 of attempted rape, was forced to stand in the pillory. Within weeks of being set free he sexually assaulted two women. One managed to flee; but the other was held fast by Greenwood who tried 'to rip up her private parts' when she resisted him. This time, for what contemporary newspapers described as 'so inhuman an action', he was sentenced to be whipped from one end of Worcester to the other on three market days and to serve two years' hard labour at the local house of correction.[27]

Despite the existence of men such as Greenwood, and the difficulty of bringing successful prosecutions for rape, it would nevertheless be misleading to suggest that women between Tudor and Victorian times went in constant fear of sexual assault. There is no evidence to suggest that there was an overwhelming fear of rape, or that such concerns as women might have had inhibited them from going about their daily business, or indeed that the men of the period systematically 'used' rape to control women. It's worth bearing in mind that Adam Fisher's daughter did not think it foolhardy to set off home after dark, even though there was a royalist army in the vicinity. A century and a half later, Sarah Pollard, Jane Bell's employer, clearly did not worry for the safety of her servant girls when they were sent to look after the cows. When she was questioned about the matter at the Old Bailey she said that while she frequently sent out three or four of her servants together, she was not concerned about Bell's safety when she went out alone: 'It is very hard that I should be obliged to have one servant guard another for four hundred yards,' she answered testily to one question thrown at her.

And to return to one of Brownmiller's contentions, there is little to support the view that in the seventeenth and eighteenth centuries the main concerns of the parents of raped women were for their daughters' loss of value on the marriage market. When in 1750 Thomas Allen of Stretton in Cheshire discovered that his four-year-old daughter Margaret was being raped by Benjamin King ('and found her thighs and linen all very bloody and her body much torn and lacerated') it's hard to imagine that his emotions were any different from those of a modern parent.[28]

Over the following decades and centuries the law regarding rape was amended and refined. As I've already mentioned, it ceased to be a capital offence in 1841, when the Substitution of Punishments for Death Act determined that, rather than face the hangman's noose, convicted rapists should be transported for life. This legislation was in turn replaced by the Penal Servitude Act of 1857, which stipulated penal servitude for life for the convicted rapist, although this Act was largely overtaken by that enduringly important piece of legislation, the 1861 Offences against the Person Act. Penal servitude was finally abolished by the Criminal Justice Act of 1948, which substituted a term in prison that could extend to life, an approach continued by the 1956 Sexual Offences Act. The 1956 Act harked back to the old common law view of non-consensual sex, but it did also state that for a man to administer 'any drug, matter or thing' to a woman that might enable or facilitate intercourse was rape, and that he would be guilty of the crime if it could be demonstrated that he had been 'reckless' as to whether she had consented or not. Male rape was recognised by law in 1994, while the Sexual Offences Act 2003 made rape gender-neutral, and also broadened the definition of what constituted rape. The 1956 and 2003 legislation made sex with a girl (1956) or child of either sex (2003) rape, regardless of consent.

IV

Attitudes, both private and official, have changed since Jane Bell's time, and, in general, accusations of rape are taken far more seriously than they once were. But Brownmiller's hope, expressed at the end of *Against Our Will*, that rape would be denied a future is a long way from being fulfilled. Some prejudices are certainly on the wane: for example, the old view that it is impossible for most men to overcome a woman of normal physical strength and rape her. Others persist, notably the 'no means yes' attitude – the notion that women are less likely to admit to sexual desire than men, and that an initial refusal is really just an invitation to the man to persist, and to use force if necessary. Allied to this is the idea that women actually enjoy rape, a fundamental misconception that in recent times received a boost from the research carried out by Freud and his followers into rape fantasies among women: in a short paper, 'The Economic Problem of Masochism', published in 1924, Freud argued that women were masochistic in nature and had a lust for pain; his suggestion was developed by his followers, notably the psychoanalyst Helene

Deutsch, in her influential *Psychoanalysis of the Sexual Functions of Women* (1925) which, in Susan Brownmiller's opinion, demonstrates a belief 'in the fundamental rightness of rape as an archetypal female experience', which Deutsch more or less equated with sexual intercourse in general.[29]

There is also still a view that some forms of rape are not as serious as others – a view that puts 'real' rapes carried out by strangers at one end of the scale and those that involve 'date rape' or 'acquaintance rape' (or indeed marital rape, criminalised in England in 1991) right at the other end. And there is a lingering prejudice that most rape accusations are unfounded, that they are made by women who are fantasists or neurotic, or who have come to regret what had been a consensual sexual act, or who are angry with a man who has rejected them.

For all these reasons, rape remains a massively under-reported crime. Victims tend to be reluctant to report attacks, whether out of fear, or a sense of embarrassment or shame, or a belief that their complaint will not be taken seriously. They also know that they will face a tough time in court, as they are forensically cross-examined about facts and motive, and have to demonstrate that they resisted their assailant (rape is the one violent crime where victims have to prove this). If at the time of the assault they had been drinking, taking drugs, behaving flirtatiously, or been dressed in a manner which the defence council, judge or jury might construe as 'provocative', their case becomes that much harder to sustain. It's not surprising, then, that victims of rape often feel that it is they who are on trial, as their characters and lifestyles are put under the legal spotlight.

Statistics for England and Wales from January 2013 suggest that on average each year over the previous three years, 60–95,000 people living in England and Wales, the overwhelming majority of them women, were raped. Of these rapes, an annual average of 15,670 were recorded by the police. These offences led to court proceedings against 2,910 persons, of whom 1,070 were convicted. In other words, only between a quarter and a sixth of rapes were recorded by the police, and of these only one in fifteen cases resulted in a conviction. In the previous chapter I discussed how assault is commonest among people who are known to one another. The same is true of rape. Around 90 per cent of serious sexual offences (the category into which rape is subsumed in official statistics) are committed by partners or ex-partners (by far the largest category), family members, or other people known to the victim.[30]

Official attitudes to rape inevitably affect both the likelihood of its being reported and of a conviction being secured. And, it has to be said, official attitudes have been slow to change. When Brownmiller conducted her research in the 1970s she came across endless cases where police in the US had been unsympathetic and unwilling to act. Least likely to receive an open-minded hearing were prostitutes (often thought to be seeking vengeance for non-payment by a client), and those (usually married in the opinion of the police) who were suspected of having had consensual sex and then later regretting it.

The situation in Britain was much the same, as a 1982 BBC fly-on-the-wall documentary, *Police*, demonstrated only too clearly. Film makers Roger Graef and Charles Stewart had been given permission to film E Division of Thames Valley Police at work, and in Episode 3 of the series, 'A Complaint of Rape', they showed how the police dealt with a woman with a history of psychiatric problems who claimed that she had been raped by three strangers (her face was not shown; instead the camera adopted her viewpoint, so that those watching the programme got a sense of how it felt to be at the receiving end of what was, in effect, a police interrogation). And what the woman experienced made for shocking viewing. The officers bullied and belittled her. They dismissed her story out of hand. One of them declared, 'This is the biggest bollocks I've ever heard.' It was not the police's finest hour.[31]

Who, then, are the rapists?[32] In the nineteenth century, as social investigators exploring Victorian England's urban slums became interested in the idea of a 'criminal' class, the view was that the

Massacre at St Peters or "BRITONS STRIKE HOME"!!!

In 1819 local yeoman cavalry killed between eleven and fifteen people, and injured at least 400, when they charged a peaceful demonstration at St Peter's Fields, Manchester, in what became known as the 'Peterloo Massacre'. The cavalryman to the left is telling his comrades, 'Remember, the more you kill the less poor rates you'll have to pay.'

With some notable exceptions, political protest became more peaceful in the course of the nineteenth century. Here a Blackburn crowd gathers to support the passing of the 1832 Great Reform Act.

A hanging at Newgate Prison in 1824. The moving of the place of execution in London from Tyburn to Newgate did not prevent large crowds of spectators from forming. Public execution was ultimately abolished in 1868.

By the late nineteenth century, the state was more interested in trying to reform criminals than hurting or humiliating them – this 1880 painting by William Powell Frith shows inmates walking in silence in one of the courtyards of Millbank Prison.

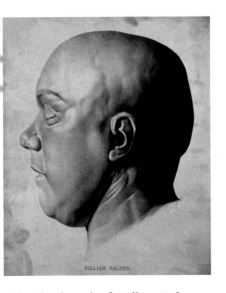

The deathmask of William Palmer, executed in 1856 – one of the first English serial killers to become a national celebrity.

The Whitechapel murders became an international media sensation. This illustration of the discovery of one of Jack the Ripper's victims appeared in a French magazine in 1891.

THE NEMESIS OF NEGLECT.

Many Victorians speculated whether crimes of violence reflected deeper social problems. This cartoon from *Punch* magazine, published during the Jack the Ripper killings, portrays murder as a ghostly figure rising from the poverty of East London's slums.

By the 1830s, the right of a man to chastise his wife was coming to be seen as legally questionable. Caroline Norton (1808–77) became a celebrated campaigner for divorce reform after suffering abuse at the hands of her husband, George Norton MP.

In 1874, the Prime Minister, Benjamin Disraeli, ignored calls to punish wife-beaters more harshly. This cartoon, which appeared in *Punch* magazine, speculates about the consequences. By this time wife-beating was clearly, if probably erroneously, regarded as a lower-class activity.

"WOMAN'S WRONGS."

BRUTAL HUSBAND. "AH! YOU'D BETTER GO SNIVELLIN' TO THE 'OUSE O' COMMONS, *YOU* HAD! MUCH THEY'RE LIKELY TO DO FOR YER! YAH! READ THAT!"

"MR. DISRAELI.—There can be but one feeling in the House on the subject of these dastardly attacks—not upon the weaker but the fairer sex. (*A laugh.*) I am sure the House shares the indignation of my hon. friend who will, I hope, consider he has secured the object he had in view by raising, | the question. * * * Assuring my hon. friend that Her Majesty's Government will not lose sight of the question, I must ask him not to press his Motion further on the present occasion.'—*Parliamentary Report, Monday, May* 18.

Ashbourne's annual 'Royal Shrovetide Football' preserves
a boisterous folk custom that dates back centuries. This
photograph is from the early 1900s.

In the nineteenth century, sports became ever more rule-
bound, ever more 'respectable' – and ever less violent. This
photograph shows gentlemen fencing, one assumes, rather
than duelling.

Twentieth-century public violence: police arrest a demonstrator during the 1926 General Strike.

Police take away a man at a football match in Birmingham in 1978. By the 1970s, football hooliganism had come to be seen as a major social problem.

An injured striker is carried to safety during the 'Battle of Orgreave', the most violent altercation of the 1984–5 Miners' Strike.

The Kray Twins, the most notorious gang leaders in the rough streets of 1960s London.

Peter Sutcliffe – better known as the 'Yorkshire Ripper' – is escorted into the courtroom on the first day of his trial in 1981.

Harold Shipman, the mild-mannered doctor who became the most prolific murderer ever recorded in England.

Violence in the twenty-first century: a campaign tries to stamp out verbal and physical bullying in British schools.

Burning buildings in Croydon, London, during the riots of summer 2011 – the latest of England's sporadic outbreaks of urban unrest.

An anti-rape poster created by West Yorkshire Police. Sexual abuse remains one of the most common forms of violence today.

lowest of the low were most likely to rape, just as they were more likely to commit assault. They were, it was argued, immersed in a culture where violence was an everyday occurrence, where overcrowding had eroded respect for women, where social restraint had broken down in the face of dysfunctional families and general rootlessness. They were also prone to drunkenness – and drunkenness dissolved the inhibitions that governed restraint. There were certainly upper-class rapists, the social commentators agreed, but their numbers were dwarfed by working-class sexual predators. This was a view that was to be picked up again in the second half of the twentieth century as criminologists examined what they referred to as 'subcultures of violence'.

All the evidence, though, suggests that this is a horribly oversimplified view. There is no doubt that Victorian slums witnessed a level of general violence not seen elsewhere, but sexual violence seems to be rooted in the male psyche in a way that goes beyond the rapist's immediate circumstances. Take, for example, the various studies that have been carried out among male college students in the United States. These are people who, one would hope, would have relatively enlightened attitudes, yet although different surveys have come up with results that vary slightly in terms of absolute numbers, overall what they reveal is that a high proportion of respondents admit to having been involved in rapes and attempted rapes, that between 25 and 30 per cent of respondents say they would commit rape if they were certain that they could get away with it, and that a large proportion feel that date rape is permissible under certain circumstances, and is a less serious offence than rape by a stranger.[33]

Is rape linked to pornography? The view of many feminist campaigners is that it certainly is, because it degrades women and encourages men to view them merely as sex objects. In violent pornography, the victims are almost always women, who are generally shown to have a secret desire for, and enjoyment of, the abuse being handed out, so perpetuating the 'no means yes' and 'they enjoy it really' rape myths. And since pornography is designed to arouse men sexually, it follows that men who view it will come to associate sexual violence with sexual pleasure. Libertarian feminists, on the other hand, tend to argue that a radical feminist position on rape, by supporting laws passed by the patriarchy to defend women, aligns it with conservative attitudes to pornography. They therefore argue that feminist involvement in the production and consumption of pornography will actually enhance female sexual liberation, a view that ties in with broader libertarian hostility to censorship, even if it also happens to serve the arguments of those who are involved in the porn industry. On balance, it's difficult not to view such hard-core pornography as, at the very least, something that trivialises rape.[34]

The link between the use of pornography and the perpetration of violence seems an entirely plausible intellectual argument, but research studies (most of them carried out in the US) do not confirm it unambiguously or uniformly. Indeed it has proved astonishingly difficult to establish a convincing link between them. Some have argued that this is because we are looking through the wrong end of the telescope. It is not that watching violent (or even non-violent) pornography encourages men to rape: it is that men who are more likely to rape are also more likely to use pornography. That said, one study of 193 female rape victims did find that in a quarter of cases the rapist said that his attitudes had been affected or reinforced by pornography – which suggests that while not all rapists use pornography, and that not all men who use it rape, there is some connection between the two.[35] (Perversely, some men have sought to blame rape on feminism, claiming that it has destabilised traditional male roles, causing a 'crisis of masculinity' and therefore a sexual backlash; Susan Brownmiller cites an extraordinary headline from an issue of *True Life Confessions* magazine: 'Gang raped by 7 boys – because I led their girls into a women's lib club'.[36])

Rape, like domestic abuse, remains a fact of contemporary life. But, as with domestic abuse, there is no doubt that it is now viewed in a different light. As Garthine Walker, reviewing England between the sixteenth and eighteenth centuries, puts it:

> Early modern people situated rape and other acts of sexual coercion on a spectrum that incorporated inhuman cruelty and wickedness at one end and 'unremarkable' acts of sexual aggression on the other ... The actual configurations of the rapist vary both within societies and across time.[37]

Newspaper headlines for 5 January 1981, the day Peter Sutcliffe first appeared in court charged with the murder of thirteen women. The 'Yorkshire Ripper' case attracted enormous press interest and involved massive mobilisation of police resources. Since the rise of the mass media and modern policing in the nineteenth century, serial killers have frequently grabbed the attention of the public.

CHAPTER 16

THE SERIAL KILLER: A VERY
MODERN MURDERER?

I

Murderers' names are remembered only comparatively rarely. The names of serial killers, on the other hand, swiftly become part of folk mythology: from Jack the Ripper to John Christie to the Yorkshire Ripper to Harold Shipman. And, in recent times, they have become a staple of popular culture, too, endlessly portrayed in crime novels and films. Some are depicted pursuing personal vendettas, as, for example, Honoria Waynflete does in Agatha Christie's *Murder is Easy* (1939) when she embarks on a killing spree designed to implicate the man who broke their engagement. Some kill for gain, as Louis Mazzini (played by Dennis Price) does in the classic black comedy *Kind Hearts and Coronets* (1949) when he seeks to murder those who stand between him and the D'Ascoyne inheritance. Many more have highly twisted motives, killing for the thrill of it or to fulfil some deep-rooted hedonistic or sexual need, as Mark Lewis (played by Carl Boehm) does in the 1960 film *Peeping Tom* when he films his female victims to preserve their dying expressions of terror.

The standard definition of a serial killer is a fairly broad one: someone who murders three or more people over a period of at least thirty days (as distinct from such mass or spree murderers as Michael

Ryan who shot and killed sixteen people at Hungerford on a single day in August 1987). It's that latter category of serial killer, though – the murderer who kills according to an often bizarre self-imposed pattern – that is the dominating popular perception today.

Such serial killers as we know of from earlier times, however, tend to fall into the Louis Mazzini category. Thomas Deloney (c.1543–1600) tells of a landlord of the Crane Inn at Colnbrook in Buckinghamshire who placed the bed in the best room over a trapdoor above the kitchen, so that he could pitch wealthy sleeping guests to their deaths into a boiling cauldron below and thus take their possessions for himself. It's very obviously a folktale, but it seems to have been an old one even when Deloney recorded it in his prose narrative *Thomas of Reading* (first published in 1602), and it clearly taps into the fear of a murderous stranger that many medieval and Tudor travellers must have experienced.

Its real-life counterpart is the 'bloody innkeeper' of Pultoe (on the Gloucester–Bristol road) whose crimes are recorded in a pamphlet of 1675. Apparently a smith had moved into the former inn that year, and while digging up the backyard to lay foundations for a new smithy, had come across human remains. He had alerted his neighbours and with their help proceeded to excavate more extensively, ultimately uncovering the corpses of seven people. The assumption was that they had all fallen victim to the previous innkeeper and his wife who, despite the relative isolation of the inn and its very occasional custom, seemed to have become unaccountably rich and had moved to a much grander property in Gloucester. Whether or not they were ever brought to justice is unknown. One assumes that their victims afterwards received a Christian burial.[1]

A similarly businesslike attitude to serial killing was taken by Thomas Sherwood and Elizabeth Evans, 'Country Tom and Canbery Besse', who were executed at Tyburn in 1635. Besse was a London prostitute who picked up customers and took them to fields on the edge of town where Tom would lie in wait to murder and rob them. The pair dispatched three men – a merchant, a gentleman named

THE SERIAL KILLER: A VERY MODERN MURDERER?

Thomas Clarke, and Michael Lowe, son of a former Lord Mayor of London – before they were caught. [2] A few decades later, Thomas Lancaster, who had signed a marriage contract that granted him his father-in-law's estate in return for supporting various relations on its profits, decided to evade his financial responsibilities by poisoning his wife, his father-in-law, three of his sisters, an aunt, a cousin and a young servant. He was, not surprisingly, caught and executed in 1672. [3]

Although nothing was ever proved against him, suspicions of poisoning for gain figure prominently in the career of the painter and writer on art Thomas Griffiths Wainewright (1794–1847) – a man who liked to live beyond his means and who was lucky enough to achieve this due to a series of convenient deaths. His uncle, George Edwards Griffiths, a bachelor, died shortly after Wainewright and his wife Ann moved in with him, enabling Wainewright, as next of kin, to claim his estate. Ann Wainewright's mother, Mrs Abercromby, died suddenly and in great pain in 1830, not long after expressing her objections to the Wainewrights' decision to insure the life of Ann's twenty-one-year-old half-sister Helen Abercromby. Helen herself died a few months later, in December. Her symptoms had proved remarkably similar to those exhibited by her mother and were not inconsistent with strychnine poisoning. But tests for such poisons were still uncertain, and an autopsy suggested instead that she had died of a gastric chill, aggravated by a supper of beer and oysters she had eaten a few days before. Wainewright was widely suspected of having had a hand in all these deaths, but nothing could be proved. When he was finally prosecuted in 1837 it was not for poisoning but for forgery. Convicted and transported to Tasmania, he ended his days as a moderately successful portrait painter. [4]

There is some – admittedly anecdotal rather than statistical – evidence to suggest that serial killings of this nature increased in the nineteenth century. Perhaps the authorities were just a little bit more effective in detecting such killers. Perhaps the rise of life insurance, previously mentioned in Chapter 14, was partly responsible, in that it put temptation readily in the way of the desperate or the naturally

scheming. Take, for example, one of the most dramatic and convo-
luted of all Victorian cases, that of Mary Ann Cotton, who was born
near Sunderland in 1832, for here the theme that runs through much
of her murderous life is the killing of those close to her for gain.[5]

We have only a vague impression of what Mary Ann was like: a
Times report described her as 'cold, reserved'. That, however, was
long after she was arrested and suggests wisdom after the event.
Other contemporary newspapers suggested that she was physically
very attractive. Judging from the speed and frequency with which
she was able to start new relationships, there was clearly more to her
than the 'cold, reserved' label suggests.[6]

Although there is much about Mary Ann that we don't know, the
basic facts of her life are fairly well chronicled. She was born in Low
Moorsley (Sunderland) in 1832, the daughter of a colliery worker. Her
childhood was marred by tragedy. When she was not yet ten, her
father fell to his death down a mine shaft. She spent the next few
years, first living at home with her (remarried) mother, then working as a nurse for a local family, and after that training to become a
dressmaker. Finally, in 1852, at the age of twenty she married a colliery labourer called William Mowbray, following him first to Devon
where he worked on the railway, and then back to the North of England where he was employed first at South Hetton Colliery and then
on board a steamship as a stoker. She had five children by him, all
but one of whom died young (even by Victorian standards, this represents a very high level of infant mortality). But Mary Ann seems to
have been permanently restless, and when William Mowbray died
in 1865, of what his death certificate described as typhus fever, his
widow, who had had the good sense to insure his life, claimed the
not inconsiderable sum of £35, and proceeded to move to Seaham
Harbour in County Durham. By that point she was in a relationship
with a local miner called Joseph Nattrass – sources differ as to
whether this liaison began before or after Mowbray's death.

She was, however, never to marry Nattrass, who soon became
engaged to, and then married, another woman. Mary Ann therefore

left Seaham Harbour and took up work as a nurse at the infirmary at Sunderland. It was here that she met and married her second husband: a former patient named George Ward, who was, like Mowbray, a stoker by trade. Ward did not last long. By November 1865 he was seriously ill and unable to work, and within a year he had succumbed to what his death certificate described as cholera and typhoid fever. Again, Mary Ann collected on the insurance.

With Ward dead, she moved on to become housekeeper to a recently widowed shipwright named James Robinson. Again, death and disaster followed in her wake. Robinson's youngest child died shortly after Mary Ann's arrival on the scene, and a few weeks after that her own mother, who had sent word that she was ill, died within days of Mary Ann turning up to look after her. Three more deaths followed in quick succession: those of two of Robinson's children and Mary Ann's daughter by William Mowbray. Robinson's sisters appear to have been suspicious but Robinson himself seems to have trusted Mary Ann wholeheartedly at this point. He had embarked on a relationship with her not long after she came to work for him; by the time the three children died, Mary Ann was pregnant by him, and in August 1867 he married her. Their baby was born in November. It died early the following year.

Within two years, however, the marriage was over. Over the course of 1869 Robinson learned that his wife had been taking money from his account, had appropriated cash she was supposed to have banked for him, and had even sent his son to pawn family possessions. Furious arguments followed, and Mary Ann antagonised her husband further by trying to persuade him to take out life insurance for himself and the three surviving children (two of Robinson's; one of Mary Ann's from a previous marriage). In the end Mary Ann walked out, taking their new baby with her but possibly hoping for a reconciliation. That was not forthcoming, and a little later the baby was returned to his father. The child was to be one of just two of Mary Ann's children to survive. Robinson for his part achieved the distinction of being the only one of Mary Ann's husbands to outlive her.

Very much down on her luck, Mary Ann may now have resorted to prostitution, or, as seems more likely, worked briefly in a laundry. But then things started to improve for her. Margaret Cotton, with whom she was very friendly, introduced Mary Ann to her recently widowed brother Frederick with whom Mary Ann soon struck up a relationship. Within a matter of weeks the thrifty Margaret, who had managed to put by some quite substantial savings, was dead. Shortly after that Mary Ann found herself pregnant by Frederick, and the couple married (bigamously) at Newcastle in September 1870. Unfortunately – and not for the first time – Mary Ann seems to have wearied of her husband remarkably quickly. Finding that her old lover Joseph Nattrass – now unattached – was living not far away, she soon rekindled her relationship with him, and shortly after Frederick died of gastric fever in September 1871 (his life, like that of his two children, was insured), she let Nattrass move in as her lodger.

If Mary Ann's reunion with her old lover suggests a natural conclusion to the story, the truth was very different, for now she embarked on yet another relationship, this time with an excise officer. Soon she was pregnant for the twelfth time. A further crop of deaths inevitably followed. In the spring of 1872 Joseph Nattrass died of gastric fever shortly after revising his will in Mary Ann's favour. At around the same time the child Mary Ann had had by Frederick Cotton, along with a child from Cotton's former marriage, also perished. That left just one child from Mary Ann's marriage to Frederick Cotton, Charles Edward Cotton. But his days, too, were numbered. On 6 July 1872, Thomas Riley, a local parish officer, asked Mary Ann if she would be prepared to nurse a local woman suffering from smallpox. She responded that her responsibilities towards Charles Edward made that impossible, but also intimated that he was frail and would probably end up going the way of the rest of the Cotton family (she also revealed the level of her attachment to the child in her care by asking if he could be admitted to the local workhouse). A week later Charles Edward was dead.

A deeply suspicious Riley told the police and a local doctor that he suspected foul play, and persisted with his accusation even when the coroner's jury returned a verdict of death by natural causes. Further forensic tests revealed traces of arsenic in Charles Edward's body, and press investigations soon unearthed the trail of bodies that Mary Ann seemed to have left in her wake, some of which, like those of Nattrass and two of Frederick Cotton's children, were found, when exhumed, to show traces of poison.

By this time Mary Ann was seven months pregnant with the excise officer's child, so her trial was delayed until March 1873. The verdict was something of a foregone conclusion. The press had endlessly raked over her past, there was strong local feeling against her, and her barrister, who was appointed very late on in the proceedings, was given only three days to prepare his case. Mary Ann was found guilty on the specimen charge of murdering Charles Edward and sentenced to death. She wrote desperate letters pleading for clemency – she even contacted James Robinson to ask for his help – but although a petition was organised by her former employers at the Sunderland Infirmary she was hanged at Durham Castle on 24 March, the first woman to be executed in County Durham since 1799. Her executioner was the famous William Calcraft. He employed his favoured short drop method: she died slowly of asphyxiation.

When the main events of her life are summarised like this, it seems extraordinary that it should have taken so long to bring Mary Ann's murderous spree to an end. She was, after all, a creature of habit, killing those close to her for financial gain or personal advancement, and generally employing the same weapon: arsenic. And we know that some people – James Robinson's sisters, for example – entertained suspicions of her. Yet it was not until she met Riley and made her foolishly blatant remark about the likely fate of Charles Edward – and then acted on it – that anyone thought to report her activities to the authorities. It makes one wonder how many other serial killers, both in Mary Ann's time and in the centuries before, went undetected.

Of course, the fact that she moved fairly frequently – to Cornwall and then to various towns and villages in the north – helped conceal her activities; so, too, did the fact that she was operating at a time when general levels of mortality, particularly among children, were high. One of the most striking features of her case is that we have no idea how many people she actually killed, nor, indeed, when she embarked on her career as a poisoner. It's possible that the final tally of her victims exceeded twenty, but we can't be sure: perhaps it would be best to accept the total of seventeen in the most recent analysis of her case.[7]

Mary Ann's downfall was very much due to a chance encounter with someone who then became suspicious, but two other factors were also involved, which were to become increasingly important in future cases: forensic science and the popular press. When the initial autopsy on Charles Edward was carried out, it was conducted by a local GP with little experience of post mortems and little in the way of suitable equipment. He found a white substance in the boy's intestines but was unable to tell whether this was poison or medicine – hence the reason the jury at the inquest decided that Charles Edward had died of natural causes. In an earlier era, one suspects, this is where the case would have ended. However, the doctor was clearly both more curious and more competent than many of his predecessors, for he decided to retain specimens from the boy's stomach, and when he conducted further tests after the inquest he was able to detect traces of arsenic – a finding then confirmed by Dr Thomas Scattergood, a toxicologist at the Leeds School of Medicine.

Not all murder cases in Victorian England were to receive this level of expert attention, but although some cases were to be badly botched, and some methods employed were highly dubious (one thinks, for example, of the photographing of Jack the Ripper's victims' eyes in the belief that they retained an image of the last person they saw), forensic science was nevertheless to make ever-more of a contribution.

The popular press, too, proved significant in Mary Ann's case. The *Newcastle Courant* followed the unfolding events avidly, even devoting an editorial to the final outcome on 28 March 1873 when it concluded that 'the West Auckland poisoner [Cotton had been living there when she poisoned her last victim] deserved to be spoken of in the same breath as the blackest murderers that have ever disgraced humanity'. The *Courant*'s local rival, the *Northern Echo*, similarly devoted many column inches to the affair. Many of the more lurid stories the papers ran were little other than wild speculation, but they did unearth much about Mary Ann's earlier life and helped ensure that the initial inquest's findings did not stand.[8]

Mary Ann Cotton achieved celebrity, her likeness exhibited at Madame Tussaud's and at least one local fair. A broadside ballad (by now a declining genre) was written about her. A popular melodrama about her life and crimes was staged, and in the year following her execution a greyhound was named after her. She also became part of popular folklore through a skipping song that was still being sung by children in the North East within living memory:

> Mary Ann Cotton,
> She's dead and she's rotten.
> She lies in her bed
> With her eyes wide open.
> Sing, sing, oh, what can I sing?
> Mary Ann Cotton is tied up with string.
> Where, where? Up in the air.
> Sellin' black puddens a penny a pair.

It's a strange epitaph for a woman who is now regarded as one of England's earliest serial killers.

II

Mary Ann's crimes were chronicled in the pages of *The Times*, but she remained a local rather than a national celebrity. William Palmer, 'The Rugeley Poisoner', on the other hand could claim to be the first serial killer whose life and crimes became familiar to all.[9] It's not difficult to see why. The cast of Mary Ann's story were struggling working-class people, the central villain the daughter of a miner. Those caught up in Palmer's crimes, by contrast, were professional middle-class people, the central villain the son of a successful timber merchant. Newspapers and their readers alike were fascinated by the gulf between Palmer's apparent respectability and the depravity of his crimes.

Palmer was born in 1824, trained as a doctor and by 1846 was practising medicine in his native town of Rugeley in Staffordshire. Like Mary Ann he appears to have turned to murder early in adult life, and, like her, to have done so for financial gain. Married in 1847 to a ward in chancery whose guardians had opposed the match, he openly begrudged the expense involved in raising children and, while we cannot be sure how many of his offspring he murdered and how many died of natural causes, the fact remains that four of his five children (the exception was his eldest, William) died in infancy, as did two of his illegitimate children. His mother-in-law died in 1849 within a fortnight of coming to live at his house. Palmer then laid claim to her property.

What finally brought him down, though, was not his murderous home life but his growing obsession with horse racing. A keen gambler, he then started to own and to breed his own horses, and from about 1852 more or less gave up practising medicine to concentrate on the turf. The first horse he owned, appropriately named Goldfinder, won the Tradesmen's Plate at Chester races in 1853, earning Palmer £2,770. Unfortunately, this early success was not sustained, and soon he had incurred huge debts. He insured his wife's life for £13,000 and when she died of 'bilious cholera' in 1854, he used most of the insurance money to pay off his debtors (almost exactly nine months after his wife's death, his maidservant bore a child). He then took out an insurance policy on his alcoholic brother Walter, who died shortly afterwards. Not surprisingly the insurers were suspicious and refused to pay out, but before the matter could be settled

Palmer had moved on to his next victim, a racing acquaintance named John Parsons Cook.

The two men attended Shrewsbury races on 13 November 1855, where Cook won heavily. Palmer managed falsely to claim the winnings, and then, to cover his tracks, attempted to poison Cook at the hotel in which they were both staying. Cook survived this attack, but although he accused Palmer of doctoring his drink, he then rather bizarrely agreed to accompany him back to Rugeley. Here Palmer tampered with his friend's food and drink, and is thought to have substituted poison for the pills Cook was taking to deal with his continuing illness. Cook died five days later. His stepfather raised the alarm when he arrived in Rugeley to find Palmer organising a hasty funeral and failed to find the papers relating to his stepson's racing and betting affairs.

Forensic science helped secure Palmer's conviction at the Old Bailey in May 1856 (it was felt that local opinion was too prejudiced for him to be tried in Staffordshire), but it has to be said that the medical experts called upon proved astonishingly inept. First it emerged that Palmer had actually been invited to attend Cook's post mortem, and, not surprisingly, had done his best to damage or steal the internal organs before they could be sent to London for analysis. Then it became clear that because strychnine was a fairly recent poison, not one of the nine experts mobilised by the prosecution had experience of observing its action on human beings (experiments had been carried out on rabbits, but these were not thought to throw conclusive light on a case involving humans). Defence medical witnesses gave equally uncertain and sometimes contradictory evidence. Nevertheless the circumstantial evidence seemed damning.

It emerged that a man named Leonard Bladen, to whom Palmer owed £800 in betting debts, had died in 1850 while staying with him. It was also pointed out that four of his children had died young, not to mention his wife and brother (both of whose bodies were exhumed). As with Mary Ann Cotton, nobody could be sure just how many deaths Palmer might have been responsible for. Conservative estimates suggested seven victims. More sensational accounts argued for sixteen. But judge and jury had no doubt that Palmer deserved to die. He was hanged outside Stafford gaol on 14 June 1856, before a crowd of 30,000. (Whether or not he would be convicted today on the strength of the evidence given at his trial is a moot point; some have argued that it was insufficiently conclusive. The poet and novelist Robert Graves even went so far as to argue, in his 1957 book *They Hanged My Saintly Billy* – the title comes from a remark Palmer's mother is supposed to have made – that he was innocent.) Ironically, Palmer's horse, The Chicken, on which he had lost so much money, went on to win the Cesarewitch under its new name, Vengeance.

Palmer's trial came just a year after the abolition of the newspaper tax ushered in a new era of popular journalism, and it proved a public sensation. A special edition of the *Illustrated Times* focussing on the sordid events of his life sold 400,000 copies. Other publications dedicated to the case ranged from traditional murder pamphlets to an account of the medical evidence offered at the trial by Alfred Swaine Taylor, the doctor who had headed the prosecution's team of expert witnesses. Figures of Palmer and a selection of his victims were exhibited at Madame Tussaud's, and he was also rendered as a Staffordshire pottery figurine. Railway excursions were laid on to allow the curious to visit the scene of the murder. Alternatively, they could, for four months after his execution, attend a re-staging of his hanging, featuring his executioner, twice every morning at Wilmslow racecourse in Cheshire. Charles Dickens and Wilkie Collins were both fascinated by the case – it has been suggested that Dickens's Inspector Bucket in *Bleak House* is based on the policeman who investigated one of Palmer's insurance frauds. It has also been suggested that the drinker's greeting 'What's your poison?' originated with the Palmer case, although it should be noted that its first recorded use was actually in the United States.[10]

III

Both the Mary Ann Cotton and William Palmer cases display 'modern' features in terms of the publicity that surrounded them and the – admittedly stumbling – part that forensic science played in their resolution. But in their essentials they were not dissimilar to those scattered earlier accounts of serial killers where the driving motive for murder was pure greed. True, in Mary Ann's case, more than a desire for money seems to have been at stake: even when she secured relative security with the shipwright James Robinson she seems to have been incapable of settling down, continuing obsessively to form new and murderous relationships. Yet even then the pursuit of money seems to have been at the forefront of her mind.

With the Whitechapel murders of 1888, on the other hand, we encounter a type of serial murderer that up until then had been so strikingly rare as to be virtually unheard of: the violently sadistic, possibly sexually motivated killer. The killing spree that began with the discovery of the body of Mary Ann (or 'Polly') Nichols at Buck's Row on the morning of 31 August 1888, and that appears to have ended with the slaughter of Mary Jane Kelly a little over two months later, has been so exhaustively chronicled that a detailed summary here seems scarcely necessary. What was common to all five 'canonical' victims (there is some disagreement as to how many times the serial killer actually struck) was that they were women who were down on their luck and who all lived within a short distance of one other in one of London's worst slum areas.

The life of middle-aged Mary Ann Nichols was fairly representative of those of her fellow victims. Born the daughter of a London locksmith named Edward Walker in 1845, she had married and had five children by a printer named William Nichols, but their marriage hit a turbulent phase and then finally broke up in 1880, possibly because Mary Ann had become a heavy drinker. After that her life went into a downward spiral and was spent sleeping in workhouses or else rough in Trafalgar Square, forming temporary liaisons with a couple of men, continuing to drink heavily, slipping in and out of prostitution. She was found work by the matron of a Lambeth workhouse, but stole clothing from her employer and absconded. On the last night of her life she was denied a bed at a common lodging house as she lacked the fourpence necessary to pay for it. She left after telling the house's deputy keeper laughingly: 'I'll soon get my doss money. See what a jolly bonnet I've got now.' Her body was discovered a few hours later by Charles Cross, an employee of Pickford's haulage company, on his way to work.

The next victim, Annie Chapman, a woman in her late forties, whose body was discovered on 8 September, had similarly experienced a failed marriage and subsequently drifted into heavy drinking and prostitution. Elizabeth Stride, murdered on 1 October, had been a prostitute in her home country Sweden, and in the years before her murder had been summonsed on a number of occasions for being drunk and disorderly. Catherine Eddowes, killed the same day, had gone from a failed relationship to drinking and casual prostitution, while Mary Jane Kelly, at twenty-five the youngest of the victims, whose body was found on 9 November, had worked in a brothel and was known to be a heavy drinker.[11]

The attacks were astonishingly brutal. Nichols, who was found with her skirt up around her waist, and the 'jolly bonnet' lying by her head, appears to have been grabbed from behind before her throat was cut. She also suffered severe cuts to the abdomen (the doctor who first saw her corpse suggested that it might have taken four or five minutes to inflict such injuries). Chapman was also mutilated by her assailant, and if the next victim, Stride, escaped being cut about after death, it's probably only because her killer was disturbed before he could inflict further harm. His other victim that night, Eddowes, suffered a far worse fate. Her throat was cut, her intestines pulled out and placed over her left shoulder, her left kidney and uterus removed, and her face mutilated. As for Mary Jane Kelly, Dr Thomas Bond, who carried out the initial post mortem, described her injuries as follows:

The whole of the surface of the abdomen & thighs were removed & the abdominal cavity emptied of its viscera. The breasts were cut off, the arms mutilated by several jagged wounds & the face hacked beyond recognition of features. The tissues of the neck were severed down to the bone. The viscera were found in various parts, viz; the uterus & kidneys with one breast under the head, the other breast by the right foot, the liver between the feet, the intestines by the right side & the spleen by the left side of the body.[12]

If the crimes of William Palmer were a national sensation, those of the Whitechapel killer were to become a national obsession. From a twenty-first-century vantage point this scarcely seems very surprising: a series of apparently connected, horrific murders and the inability of the forces of law and order to bring the culprit to book make for a compelling narrative. One can't help wondering, though, whether such a furore would have occurred in an earlier era. The victims, after all, were all lower-class – fallen – women. They lived beyond the knowledge and concern of 'civilised' society. The murder of prostitutes was, depressingly, nothing new, even if the 1888 attacks happened to be particularly brutal. But the Victorian popular press, supplemented by other forms of cheap print, notably old-style murder pamphlets, gave the Whitechapel murders a national prominence unthinkable just a few decades before.

Between 31 August and 16 November 1888 *The Times* devoted some 113,000 words to the murders, the evening *Pall Mall Gazette* about 81,500, and two Sunday publications, *Lloyds Weekly* and the *People*, 89,000 and 80,000 words respectively.[13] The day after Mary Jane Kelly's death the *Star* sold 300,000 copies. Journalists explored every avenue: the possible identity of the murderer (variously given as a butcher, a Jewish kosher butcher, a doctor, a surgeon, 'Asiatics', Greek gipsies, and, somewhat implausibly, three American cowboys who had decided to stay in London for a while after touring England as performers in Wild West shows);[14] the conduct of the police (widely criticised) was explored; and, more generally, the moral and physical state of the East End of London.[15] The letters pages were filled with theories, accusations and hand-wringing. It was all part and parcel of what contemporaries referred to as the 'New Journalism', championed by such figures as the editor of the *Pall Mall Gazette* W. T. Stead: a journalism which was avowedly populist, crusading and opinionated, and often sensationalist. It's scarcely surprising, given such coverage, that the day Mary Jane Kelly was buried at the Roman Catholic cemetery at Leytonstone, thousands of men and women should have turned out to line the route her cortège took along Hackney Road, Whitechapel Road and through Stratford.

It's even just possible that the very name 'Jack the Ripper', by which the killer swiftly became known, was the invention of a newspaperman. On 27 September 1888 a letter arrived at the Central News Office, addressed to 'The Boss'. Signed Jack the Ripper, it mocked the police for their inability to find the murderer and claimed: 'I am down on whores and I shant quit ripping them till I do get buckled.'[16] Its authenticity has been much debated. Some certainly believe it to be the work of the killer. But many years later, one of the officers involved in the case, the by then retired Chief Inspector John George Littlechild, claimed that at the time it was generally thought at Scotland Yard that the author was either the journalist 'Tom Bullen' (Thomas J. Bulling) or his boss John Moore.[17] If so, it marks the point where, both for good and for ill, journalism and murder inquiries became inextricably linked with one another.

IV

Towards the end of *From Hell*, that remarkable graphic novel interpretation of the Jack the Ripper murders, Sir William Gull, Queen Victoria's physician and (as represented therein) perpetrator of the murders, says to his associate, the coachman John Netley: 'It is beginning, Netley. Only just beginning. For better or worse, the twentieth century. I have delivered it.'[18] Apocalyptic words. But it certainly seems to be the case that serial killers proliferated in the years after the Whitechapel murders.

Some, as in previous centuries, still murdered largely from greed.

The thief, swindler and bigamist George Joseph Smith, for example, who was hanged in 1915, was convicted of killing three women for gain in what became known as the 'Brides in the Bath Murders'. The fraudster John George Haigh, who was hanged in 1949, was convicted of murdering six people (he claimed to have killed a further three), and then forging papers to lay claim to their possessions. After killing his victims he dissolved their bodies in acid (believing mistakenly that a murder charge could not be brought if no body could be found). Forensic evidence proved critical in both cases. The pathologist Bernard Spilsbury was able to demonstrate conclusively that Smith's last victim was murdered rather than having accidentally drowned; while the pathologist Keith Simpson, who was called in to examine the workshop where Haigh had dissolved his victims' bodies, was able to unearth three human gallstones and part of a denture that was later identified as having belonged to Mrs Durand-Deacon by her dentist. At the same time, coverage of the murders in the press ensured that these serial killers achieved a prominence in the national imagination that their pre-Victorian ancestors had never had.

Smith and Haigh in their greed had many antecedents. But the serial killers who have arguably achieved greatest notoriety in the hundred years or so since Jack the Ripper do not seem to have been motivated by the desire for material gain. Indeed, when Ronald M. Holmes and James De Burger compiled a typology of serial killers in the 1980s they ignored the Palmer-type case altogether, focussing instead on four very different types of killer: those driven by inner voices or visions; those who set themselves a mission to kill a certain type of person; hedonists, who revel in the excitement of killing; and those who seek gratification in gaining the power of life and death over their victims.[19] Inevitably these four categories often overlap with one another,[20] and in some cases greed and sadism seem to play their part also. This certainly appears to be the case, for example, with Thomas Neill Cream, the 'Lambeth Poisoner', who murdered a number of people (his British victims were all prostitutes) on both sides of the Atlantic before he was hanged at Newgate in 1892. He clearly killed for hope of personal gain in some instances, but also revelled in the infliction of suffering on his victims. And as the twentieth century progressed, it was this element of sadism that seems to have become predominant among serial killers.

Various names have achieved national infamy. There was Gordon Frederick Cummins, dubbed 'the Blackout Ripper', who murdered and mutilated four women and attacked two others in the early months of 1942 (and who may also have been responsible for a couple of murders the previous year). There were Ian Brady and Myra Hindley, the 'Moors Murderers', who tortured and murdered five children between July 1963 and October 1965. There were Bruce George Peter Lee, a pyromaniac responsible for eleven deaths in the 1960s, Dennis Nilsen, who murdered possibly as many as fifteen young men in London in the late 1970s and early 1980s, and Frederick and Rosemary West, who, before their arrest in 1994, tortured, raped and killed numerous young women, including members of their own family.

But of all recent English serial killers it is perhaps Peter Sutcliffe, the 'Yorkshire Ripper', who has left the deepest mark on the popular imagination.[21] There are various points of similarity between his case and that of the Whitechapel murderer. Like Jack the Ripper, Sutcliffe targeted prostitutes (though not unfailingly: his victims also included a building society clerk and a student). Like Jack the Ripper, Sutcliffe was brutal and sadistic: his first victim, Wilma McCann, a prostitute living in the Chapeltown area of Leeds, whom Sutcliffe killed in the early hours of 30 October 1975, suffered hammer blows to her head, and fifteen stab wounds; her body was found lying on its back with her trousers pulled down around her knees, her bra pushed up to reveal her breasts, and traces of semen on her clothing. Other victims were bludgeoned, stabbed and mutilated.[22] Like Jack the Ripper, too, Sutcliffe proved elusive.

Massive police resources were put into the hunt for the Yorkshire Ripper.[23] By the autumn of 1979 a team of around 250 were involved in an investigation that was ultimately to involve the questioning of 260,000 people, the taking of 32,000 statements, the recording of 5,400,000 car registrations, mainly in the red-light areas of Leeds, Bradford and Manchester, the accumulation of twenty-four tons of paper records, and the expenditure of £6,000,000. Yet, from the start, it was to be a deeply flawed investigation. The local police force had recently undergone a major reorganisation that had left in its wake administrative teething problems. It was, in any case, overwhelmed by the sheer quantity of information that it had to process – all hand-written on index cards. And it was wrong-footed early on by a group of hoax letters and an associated tape-recording purporting to come from the murderer.

Previous hoax letters had been dismissed, but these, signed 'Jack the Ripper', appeared to include details that had not been made public (particularly concerning the killing of Vera Millward in Man-chester), while the voice on the tape, with its strong Wearside accent, convinced the officer leading the investigation, George Oldfield, that he should focus his attentions there rather than in West Yorkshire where the real killer lived. Such was Oldfield's conviction he was on the right track that dissenting views were ignored, including that of DCI David Zachreson, one of the officers running the north-eastern operation, who, having gone back over newspaper reports about the Ripper killings, realised that the supposedly inside know-ledge that 'Wearside Jack' (as the owner of the voice on the tape became known) possessed about the killing of Vera Millward had in fact been widely reported in the press, and that the letters bore some resemblance to the Jack the Ripper letters some ninety years previously. It was not until 2005 that 'Wearside Jack' was finally unmasked, when a DNA sample from the gummed seal of one of the envelopes was matched to a Sunderland man. He was subse-quently sentenced to eight years in jail for perverting the course of justice.

Some of the mistakes made by the police seem, in retrospect, quite extraordinary. They had, for example, been given a good description of the Ripper by one of his few surviving victims: Marcella Claxton, assaulted by Sutcliffe in May 1976 so severely that her head required fifty-two stitches. She described him as a bearded white man with a Yorkshire accent. But Claxton's testimony was ignored, and the incident was not linked to the Ripper case until much later when Sutcliffe himself admitted the assault after his arrest.

The description offered by fourteen-year-old Tracy Browne, struck four times with a hammer by an assailant who then ran off when he saw a car approaching, was similarly rejected out of hand. Chief Constable Ronald Gregory later explained that the West Yorkshire Police made no connection between what had happened to her and the activities of the Yorkshire Ripper because she was not a prostitute and had been struck with a piece of wood rather than anything heavier (forensic and medical evidence, though, suggested otherwise), and because the assault had taken place in the countryside rather than in the urban areas the Ripper was known to favour. It is scarcely surprising that the report by Her Majesty's Inspector of Constabulary, Lawrence Byford, circulated in December 1981, should have taken a strongly critical view of the West Yorkshire force's handling of the case.

When Sutcliffe was finally arrested it emerged that he had been interviewed on nine separate occasions between November 1977 and February 1980 in connection with the Yorkshire Ripper investigations – he was, for example, one of some 5,000 men interviewed when police sought to trace who might have handed the new £5 note to the prostitute Jean Jordan that was found in her handbag after her murder in October 1977. But connections were never made, leads never followed up. In the course of one police interview, on 29 July 1979, the two officers questioning Sutcliffe noted that his face resembled that of a Photofit picture of the suspect that had been issued, and that his shoe size corresponded with that of footprints found near some of the murder sites. They were also unhappy with the account Sutcliffe gave of his whereabouts on key dates. But although they submitted a comprehensive report, the senior officer to whom it was sent had no recollection of receiving it, and it does not survive.

A friend of Sutcliffe's, Trevor Birdsall, became so suspicious that he wrote an anonymous letter to the police that not only gave Sutcliffe's name and address but described an incident in Halifax when Sutcliffe had attacked a woman (Birdsall and Sutcliffe had been out together that night in Birdsall's car). At his girlfriend's prompting, Birdsall then followed up the letter with a visit to police headquarters in Bradford where he told all he knew. But if his statement was written down, it, too, appears to have vanished, and his letter was not correctly filed. When the police did finally catch Sutcliffe it was more or less by chance.

I have dwelt on the police investigation of the Yorkshire Ripper case because it inevitably raises questions about serial killers in earlier times. If all the resources of a modern police force (working, admittedly, in the days before police records were computerised) could fail to identify a killer for over five years, one wonders how many murders from previous eras went unsolved. And if it was not until after Sutcliffe was arrested that the full extent of his crimes became clear, one wonders how many apparently disconnected cases in earlier times were in fact linked. It is quite conceivable that earlier Sutcliffes, travelling around the country in the course of their work, killed as often and as brutally as he did. But we will never know. After all, the Victorian police failed to make an arrest in the Jack the Ripper case, even though the murderer operated in a very small area of East London. It's something one has to bear in mind before too readily branding the modern era the age of the serial killer, even if we accept that his or her nature has changed or note the number of cases there have been since the Second World War.

When we read about early serial murderers, we often don't find out much about their motivation beyond what their actions suggest. We simply can't be sure, for example, what first prompted Mary Ann Cotton to kill. In Peter Sutcliffe's case, on the other hand, there is more to work with. We know that whereas his father was very much a man's man – an extrovert, who was good at sport and popular with women – Peter was a weak, shy and introverted child, who under-performed at school and was bullied. His brothers took after his larger-than-life father. He felt closest to his mother, and must have been devastated when he discovered in his early twenties that she had been having an affair. In an attempt to toughen himself up, he became an obsessive body-builder in his teenage years, and acquired an interest in motorbikes and cars (which he liked to drive very fast). He also found himself a girlfriend. The testimonies of friends and relatives suggest, however, that he was never wholly comfortable with the masculine persona he attempted to project. This early tension between two conflicting sides of his nature may well go part of the way to explaining his later actions.

According to the feminist academic Nicole Ward Jouve, Sutcliffe first turned to a prostitute when he discovered that his girlfriend (later to become his wife) had apparently become involved with another man. It proved a humiliating experience for him but an obsession was established. He would cruise the red-light districts of Leeds and Brad-ford. Soon, according to some accounts, he was visiting prostitutes on a regular basis, and may possibly have contracted sexually transmitted infections from a couple of them. It's tempting, in the light of Ward Jouve's careful examination of the interconnectedness of his personal life and his career of violence, to think there could have been a connection between his first murder and the news that his wife had suffered a miscarriage. Fatherhood – a basic element of masculinity – had been denied him. Sutcliffe was later to claim that God directed him to kill prostitutes, but none of his final three victims was engaged in the sex trade and neither were the two women whom he assaulted, but was unable to kill, during this last phase of his killing spree. Nor was one of his earliest victims, Tracy Browne, who was, as previously mentioned, just fourteen when she was attacked in rural Silsden in August 1975. One gets the impression that Sutcliffe simply wanted to kill women, and that if his victims frequently were prostitutes, this was only because they were easier targets than most other women.

Ronald M. Holmes and James De Burger talk of the serial killer with a self-appointed mission to murder, and in Sutcliffe's case one gets the impression that he saw himself as some sort of divinely ordained 'streetcleaner'. But there was clearly more to it than that. Many of the killings have strongly sexual overtones. Sutcliffe would partially strip and mutilate his victims. He would repeatedly stab their vaginas, and traces of semen were sometimes found on their bodies or clothing. In fact, Sutcliffe seems to have had many of the early experiences that are thought to characterise lust killers. He was also obsessed with the physicality of murder and possibly with the female body. We know that as his killing career gathered pace he liked to spend time at a wax-works museum in Morecambe whose exhibits included a room full of anatomical models, many of them displaying the internal organs of women.

Even so all this knowledge gets us only so far. Sutcliffe was a violent misogynist, but then he grew up in a culture that was not exactly free from either misogyny or casual violence towards women. Thus when Wearside Jack's tape was played at Leeds United's ground at Elland Road – and at other football grounds – the appeal for help that went with it was usually drowned out by choruses of 'There's Only One Yorkshire Ripper' and shouts of 'Eleven–Nil'. There were also T-shirts on sale carrying the 'II–0' slogan or lapel badges reading 'Leeds United – more feared than the Yorkshire Ripper'. Yet this was not a culture that produced other Yorkshire Rippers. Nor did other men who had equally difficult or traumatic childhoods or who went to see such violently pornographic films as *Violation of the Bitch* (the focus for a protest outside a Bradford cinema in 1979, during which eleven women were arrested) automatically become brutalised as a result. At first Peter Sutcliffe denied that he suffered from any mental instability and was able to describe his attacks calmly and dispassionately. Later he was to claim divine sanction for what he had done, saying that he had heard voices while working as a gravedigger in Bingley. Prosecution and defence psychiatrists who examined him before his trial were convinced that he suffered from paranoid schizophrenia, and that he should be charged with manslaughter on the grounds of diminished responsibility.

At first the Attorney General, Sir Michael Havers, QC, seemed sympathetic to this course of action. But in the event – one can't help suspecting out of fear of public opinion – Sutcliffe's diminished responsibility plea was rejected and he was sent for trial by jury. He was found guilty of murder on all counts, though interestingly only by a majority verdict of ten to two – one wonders whether those jurors who dissented questioned his mental state. Shortly after his arrival at Parkhurst Prison he was found to be suffering from schizophrenia. In March 1984 he was transferred to Broadmoor High Security Hospital Prison. We know so much about him, and yet still so little.

V

Have recent decades seen an increase in the number of serial killers and their victims? The evidence compiled by the criminologist and former prison governor Professor David Wilson seems to suggest that they may have.[24] He has identified seventeen serial killers or pairs of serial killers who were in operation between 1960 and 2006, and who together were responsible for the deaths of 326 people. This is a minimum figure: Wilson excludes deaths of people who were presumed to have been the victims of a serial killer but whose murderer was never caught (for example, those killed by 'Jack the Stripper', who was held responsible for the killing of eight prostitutes in London between 1959 and 1965), as well as foreigners who killed in Britain and Britons who killed abroad. His findings suggest a trend upwards, from an average of three victims a year in the early years of his survey to eleven towards the end. In most years, he reckons, an average of two serial killers were operating. The overall figures, it has to be said, are dwarfed by the overall murder rate in each year, and if the 215 murders ascribed to Dr Harold Shipman are omitted, the annual average is actually less than two a year. But the serial killer is nevertheless a feature of contemporary life.

530

Wilson is sceptical of the merits of trying to generalise about what motivates serial killers to murder. He argues that (as Peter Sutcliffe's life demonstrates) the traits that make one serial killer (genetic makeup, sexuality, relation to mother or father, harsh childhood experiences), in other circumstances and other families make law-abiding citizens. He also argues that we can learn very little from the killers themselves: they either produce self-serving stories that reveal little about their crimes (like the III-page 'autobiography' Fred West wrote before he committed suicide in gaol) or else, like Harold Shipman, say nothing. But, he suggests, we do learn a lot about the nature of our society by studying the victims of serial killers. These tend in his view to belong to groups best characterised as the vulnerable: the elderly (as with Shipman), women involved in prostitution (as with Peter Sutcliffe), gay men (as with Dennis Nilsen), rootless young people, described by Wilson as 'runaways and throwaways' (as with Fred and Rosemary West), and children (as with the nurse Beverly Allitt, convicted in 1993 of four murders).

Seen through this victim lens, serial killing 'becomes a useful guide that reveals the limits of our current social arrangements and the inadequacy of our provision for the social and economic protection of the poor and vulnerable'. Wilson is anxious to make it clear that he is not seeking here to excuse the killer or simply 'blame society'. He is, however,

> . . . trying to demonstrate that those who want to kill repeatedly can only achieve this objective when the social structure in which they operate allows them to do so by placing value on one group to the detriment of others. For when this happens and when communities are fractures and anxious, when people feel isolated and cut off from each other, and when the bonds of mutual support have been all but eradicated as each individual believes they have to struggle simply to survive, those who want to kill large numbers of their fellow human beings achieve their purpose.[25]

Wilson thus creates a picture of a post-1960s Britain which, as it moves away from the social cohesion that industry once gave it towards one based on more individualistic, neo-liberal social and economic policies, is becoming 'exclusive' rather than 'inclusive'. And it is in an 'exclusive' society that the serial killer thrives – a society in which, one should note, only one of Dennis Nilsen's fifteen victims, a Canadian visiting England named Ken Ockenden, was the object of an exhaustive search on the part of his relatives.

How persuasive is this theory? We are, of course, hampered by the lack of consistent hard evidence for earlier periods, which makes any kind of statistical comparisons virtually impossible. But even so, such anecdotal evidence as survives suggests that if there were fewer serial killers in the past (which does, on balance, seem to be the case), that is not because the right social conditions for them did not exist. One thinks of late-Tudor England, when so many vagrants of the 'runaways and throwaways' type Wilson describes were at large. One thinks, too, of the waifs, strays and prostitutes of Hogarth's London, or the rootless poor of Victorian times. Wilson's 'marginal' theory certainly helps to explain many of the victims of past serial killers, from the children killed by Mary Ann Cotton to the prostitutes murdered by Jack the Ripper. But it doesn't explain why the twentieth century witnessed an increase in their number.

Nor does it explain why the nature of the serial killer has changed. As I've already suggested, before the Whitechapel murders, and indeed for some decades after, most serial killers seem to have been motivated, at least in part, by greed. In recent times, most serial killers seem to be driven by a desire for sexual gratification or by a love of killing for its own sake. It's possible to theorise about the decline of the former type of serial killer: better policing, better links between different agencies and authorities, and tighter legal and insurance rules arguably make it much more difficult for a Mary Ann Cotton to flourish today. But it's harder to theorise about the rise of the modern serial killer. Perhaps their actions are in part encouraged by the level of popular and media attention they receive.

Perhaps, as some recent US studies have suggested, a culture which, through movies, comics and computer games, to a certain extent appears to glorify violence, persuades some people, especially men, to cross the line from fantasy cruelty to real-life depravity. Clearly, there is some quality in a tiny handful of people that stimulates a desire to control others, to enjoy the exercise of the power of life and death over those they deem to be less valuable than themselves.[26]

VI

The fact is that there is something intangible and incomprehensible about the modern serial killer. We can understand why a debt-ridden William Palmer might resort to murder, even if we also condemn him. But it is virtually impossible fully to enter the mind of a Peter Sutcliffe or a Dennis Nilsen or a Fred West. And when it comes to England's most prolific serial killer we face an even more enigmatic figure. He was not a maladjusted loner, like Dennis Nilsen, nor a socially awkward individual, like Peter Sutcliffe, nor a man with clearly psychotic tendencies, like Fred West. He was a married, middle-aged doctor.[27] And if we expect a mass murderer to look the part, Harold Frederick Shipman very definitely did not: he was a mild-looking man, bespectacled and bearded, of whom the most incisive description would be that he resembled a birdwatcher or a somewhat eccentric vicar. Yet on 31 January 2000 at Preston Crown Court Shipman was convicted of killing 15 people, all aged between forty-nine and eighty-two, 11 of them over sixty-five. Most had died at home, in the afternoon, some in his presence. All had been poisoned through injection of drugs. Further investigations indicated that Shipman might well have been killing his patients as far back as 1975, in which case he might have been responsible for over 215 deaths.

There's little if anything in his life story to help explain why he should have taken the path he did. Born on 14 January 1946 in Nottingham he seems to have had a normal childhood, attending the local grammar school, where he proved a good if undistinguished pupil. Those teachers who could recall him years later, remembered a serious and quiet boy, who was good at rugby. He studied at the Leeds School of Medicine, and graduated in 1970 with an MBChB degree (Bachelor of Medicine and Surgery). He then became a junior hospital registrar at Pontefract General Infirmary, and after a year there, in August 1971, a fully licensed physician. By this time he was married, and he and his wife were to have four children together.

It was only after Shipman left Pontefract Infirmary in March 1974 and joined a medical practice in Todmorden in West Yorkshire that the first intimation of anything untoward about him was noticed. In July 1975 a receptionist at the practice expressed a concern that Shipman seemed to be over-prescribing pethidine (also widely known as Meperidine or Demerol), a synthetic opioid widely used as a painkiller and, when first introduced in the 1930s, regarded as a more useful, and less addictive, drug than morphine. When Shipman was confronted with the accusation, he claimed that he was injecting himself with up to 700 mg of the drug daily (a standard dose as a painkiller would be 100 mg). Not surprisingly, his partners insisted that he seek treatment for his addiction. Shipman objected violently, and six weeks later was thrown out of the partnership. Tried at Halifax Magistrates Court he pleaded guilty to various charges of obtaining and possessing pethidine and forging prescriptions, and was fined £600. Following a closed hearing by the General Medical Council, he was banned from practising medicine for just under two years, and was forbidden to have controlled substances in his office. This last provision, it seems, was not enforced.

An apparently reformed Dr Shipman resumed practising in 1977 at the Donneybrook House practice at Hyde, near Manchester, and was to work there for another fifteen years, prior to starting his own practice in 1993. Throughout this period he cemented the reputation he had started to gain in Todmorden, as a dedicated doctor of the old school, a little arrogant, perhaps, but well liked and respected by his patients, on whose behalf he proved unusually willing to make home visits. Nevertheless some people in Hyde were beginning to suspect that all was not well with Shipman's practice. A local taxi driver, John Shaw, who often drove elderly women to doctor's or hospital appointments, noticed not just that an abnormal number of his customers were dying, but that many of them seemed to be Shipman's patients. In 1996 Shaw and his wife began to keep a record of these deaths, although at this stage he did not feel able to voice his suspicions to the police (quite simply, and probably correctly, he wondered whether he would be believed). His tally of suspicious deaths relating to Shipman had risen to about twenty.

Others, too, had become suspicious, notably Deborah Bambroffe, who worked at the local funeral directors, Frank Massey and Sons. She was married to David Bambroffe, also employed by the firm, which was run by her father Alan Massey. She too had noticed that a seemingly disproportionate number of Shipman's patients were dying, and that their deaths seemed to follow an established and uncertain pattern. Most were elderly women; they frequently died sitting in a chair fully clothed, rather than lying in bed in their night-clothes, as one would expect with seriously ill people; some had their sleeves rolled up as though in preparation for an injection; and they were often found dead shortly after a visit by Shipman. She discussed her concerns with her husband, who came to share them, and Alan Massey, who was more sceptical, but all three felt an understandable reticence about turning a sense of unease into a formal accusation. In any case, Shipman was the Masseys' family doctor and had proved assiduous and caring.

An official whistle was finally blown by a doctor at a neighbouring surgery in the spring of 1998. Dr Linda Reynolds had noted the high level of deaths at Shipman's practice. She was also aware of Deborah Bambroffe's concerns. On 24 March, therefore, she shared her concerns with Manchester South's coroner, John Pollard. What followed, however, was a light-touch – and, as it turned out, entirely inadequate – police investigation. Evidence was insufficiently weighed, interviews with witnesses cursory. One gets the impression

from the subsequent inquiry headed by Dame Janet Smith that key
figures simply could not bring themselves to countenance the idea
that a popular local doctor could also be a murderer. It's not therefore very surprising that the investigation was closed less than a
month later, on 17 April. The police conclusion was that Shipman
had no case to answer. Their actions were subsequently to be much
criticised.[28]

Finally Shipman over-reached himself. On 24 June 1998, the body
of eighty-one-year-old Kathleen Grundy was found at her home.
The well-to-do widow of a former mayor of Hyde, she had taken a
very active part in the life of the community, and indeed had been
expected that day at a centre for the elderly where she helped out.
The police called Mrs Grundy's daughter, Angela Woodruff, a solicitor, to inform her of her mother's death, and Woodruff proceeded to
make contact with Shipman, who had seen her mother shortly
before she died. He informed her that no post mortem was necessary: he had signed a death certificate that gave the cause of death,
very unusually, as 'old age'. Woodruff was confident that her mother
had been in good health at the time of her death.

Even so she did not actually become suspicious until a few days
later when much to her surprise she heard from her mother's solici-
tors that they had received a new (and very badly typed) will that not
only made Shipman Kathleen Grundy's beneficiary but stipulated
that, contrary to her long-expressed desire to be buried, she should
be cremated. Woodruff raised the alarm, her mother's body was
exhumed and found to contain traces of morphine, and Shipman
was duly arrested and charged with Kathleen Grundy's murder,
attempted theft by deception, and three counts of forgery. Further
exhumations of victims followed, and additional murder charges
were brought.

The public inquiry established early in 2001 estimated that Shipman might have killed 250 people in a murderous career that might
well have stretched back to his time at Pontefract General Infirmary
in 1971. The list of confirmed victims, the first of whom died in March

1975, numbers 215, many of them aged over eighty but some in their forties and fifties. Most were women, but perhaps a fifth were men, including the youngest victim of all, forty-two-year-old Peter Lewis, who was murdered in January 1985. The frequency with which Shipman killed seems to have increased as he got older: there are a scattering of cases in the 1970s and 1980s (of course, it's possible that not all were recorded), but 30 people perished in 1996, 37 in 1997, and 18 over the first six months of 1998. In March 1998 alone, he killed seven times. Why, when it came to his final victim, Shipman should have departed from his usual modus operandi and forged a will is unknown. Some have suggested that the sloppiness of the forgery actually betrayed his desire – whether conscious or unconscious – to be caught.

Shipman never sought to explain his actions, and, unfortunately, Dame Janet Smith in her report on the case declared that although she had attempted to uncover Shipman's motivations, it had proved impossible to do so. Transcripts of his police interviews suggest a confident, not to say arrogant, personality, though one of the officers who interviewed him recalled that he broke down on one or two occasions when confronted with evidence that he could not explain away. Some have suggested that he killed simply because he enjoyed killing, that he revelled in the power of life and death he held over his patients. Some have argued that there was an obsessive-compulsive side to his nature that made it impossible for him to break his killing cycle once he had embarked on it. He may have gone on killing purely because, having done it, he realised he could get away with it. Some have theorised that Shipman's mother's death from lung cancer when he was seventeen gave him an experience both of pain and the relief of pain through morphine injections that triggered his murderous killing spree. And there might also be something lurking in this notion to explain that other great puzzle: why so many of his victims were elderly women. But we will never know.

Sentenced to life imprisonment, Shipman committed suicide in prison on 13 January 2004, the eve of his fifty-eighth birthday. In the 'Foreword' to the audit on Shipman's clinical practice, Professor Liam Donaldson, the Chief Medical Officer, reassured his readers that 'Everything points to the fact that a doctor with the sinister and macabre motivation of Harold Shipman is a once in a lifetime occurrence.'

VII

If David Wilson is right, the peak year for the British serial killer was 1986, when four such murderers were known to be operating. Their activities were dwarfed by those of other types of killer (there were 506 convictions that year for homicide), yet, as I have already shown, their crimes loomed disproportionately large in the popular imagination. This was, after all, the decade when the very term 'serial killer' (probably first coined in the mid-1970s) became common currency, given a particular boost by its inclusion in a *Newsweek* article early in 1984.[29]

Once, the idea of the human monster who killed again and again had been the stuff of folklore – one thinks of the fairytale figure Bluebeard, or the Colnbrook innkeeper, or of Peter Grimes, the Aldeburgh fisherman who, according to the early nineteenth-century poet George Crabbe, took on a series of apprentices from London, all of whom then died in suspicious circumstances (Crabbe's son was later to claim that the story was based on a real-life incident). Now it had become a barometer against which to measure society as a whole. Was the serial killer a freakish, unpredictable phenomenon or a reflection of a society from which some felt so alienated that they turned to killing? *American Psycho*, the 1991 novel by Bret Easton Ellis, set in Manhattan during the Wall Street boom years of the 1980s, offers an interesting twist on this, in that its protagonist, the serial killer Patrick Bateman, is not an outcast from contemporary capitalism but one of its flag bearers. Today, certainly judging from the way in which serial killers are regularly characterised in films, police procedural dramas, and novels, and from real-life accounts of such murderers as Levi Bellfield, who killed Milly Dowler, they have perhaps become something else: a dark mirror that we hold up to ourselves, to remind us of the worst actions of which human beings are capable.

A young football fan is arrested by police after England is knocked out of the 2006
World Cup. From the 1960s onwards, football hooliganism was viewed as a major
social problem – but there has been a relative lull in levels of
violence in sport over the last decade.

CHAPTER 17

PUBLIC VIOLENCE: FROM
FOOTBALL HOOLIGANISM
TO INNER-CITY RIOTS

I

The point at which rowdy behaviour becomes dangerous disorder has, historically, been a finely balanced one – and, in England at least, frequently bound up with issues of social class. As previously pointed out in Chapter 13, behaviour held to be 'boisterous spirits' among young upper-class Victorian men running amok in Cremorne Gardens, was interpreted as terrifying acts of senseless violence when those involved were the lower-class 'hooligans' who blighted London's August 1898 bank holiday.

This more critical, more fearful view of young men from poorer backgrounds continued into the twentieth century and, arguably, persists today. Thus the teddy boys who emerged in the post-war years (initially in working-class areas in South and East London) swiftly became popular bogeymen, even though most were content simply to don the Edwardian-inspired fashions that gave them their nickname. That some teddy boys were violent is unquestionable: in 1956 groups of them wrecked cinemas showing *Blackboard Jungle*; two years later, numbers of them were involved in ugly race riots in London's Notting Hill and in Nottingham.[1] That does not mean, though, that they were an inherently violent social phenomenon.

In the following decade, mods and rockers commanded national headlines when they engaged in violent clashes in such seaside towns as Margate and Brighton – the Brighton fracas lasted two days. But again, while there was certainly a violent undertone to aspects of their behaviour (many, for example, carried flick knives and coshes), fear of what they represented and what they might do seems to have been out of all proportion to the crimes that they actually committed.

In reality, the mods and rockers caused little damage to property, and most of those brought before the courts were charged, not with violence, but with threatening behaviour or obstructing the police. Media attention, though, was constant and, it has to be said, verged on the hysterical. According to an inventory of press cuttings for the period 15 May–12 June 1964 prepared for Margate Corporation, the disturbances received 724 mentions in the media, comprising 270 accounts of what actually happened – or was deemed to have happened – 223 editorials and comment pieces by columnists, 110 articles that either took the form of summaries of concerned speeches by public figures on events that Whitsun or interviews with them, and 121 letters from readers.

Analysing the mods and rockers phenomenon, the sociologist Stanley Cohen suggested that the disproportionate worry it caused was clear evidence that society had given way to one of its periodic moods of 'moral panic'.[2] In other words, as with garrotters in Victorian times, skinheads in the 1960s and 1970s, and hoodies more recently, a definable group had created a level of public fear out of all proportion to the danger that it actually posed.[3] In Cohen's words a moral panic is when

A condition, episode, person or group of persons emerges to become defined as a threat to societal values and interests; its nature is presented in a stylised and stereotypical fashion by the mass media; the moral barricades are manned by editors, bishops, politicians and other right-thinking people; socially accredited experts pronounce their diagnoses and solutions; ways of coping are evolved or (more often) resorted to; the condition then disappears, submerges or deteriorates and becomes more visible. Sometimes the object of the panic is quite novel and at other times it is something which has been in existence long enough, but suddenly appears in the limelight. Sometimes the panic passes over and is forgotten, except in folklore and collective memory; at other times it has more serious and long lasting repercussions and might produce such changes as those in legal and social policy or even in the way society conceives itself.

The mods and rockers conflict was one of those phenomena soon passed over and largely forgotten.

II

Another group of potential trouble-makers – again typically assumed to be young, white and working-class – made a rather deeper and more lasting dent on public consciousness in the post-war years: football hooligans.[4] They were certainly not a new phenomenon. Crowd problems at football matches go back virtually to the birth of the sport. Between 1895 and 1914 misbehaviour by spectators led the Football Association to close grounds on 46 occasions, and to issue formal warnings to clubs on a further 64. The *Leicester Daily Mercury* for the same period recorded 59 incidents in Leicestershire and a further 100 elsewhere in the UK, where fans had been guilty of threatening or abusive behaviour, drunkenness, pitch invasions, or missile-throwing at or assaults on rival fans, players or match officials (referees had an especially hard time).[5] In the inter-war period Millwall's grounds were closed twice for two weeks at a time in the 1920s and 1930s following crowd trouble, and 43 incidents were reported at Leicester City between 1921 and 1939. That said, most trouble-making was on a pretty minor scale. Only 6 of those 43 inter-war incidents at Leicester, for example, went much beyond what at the time would have been described as 'barracking' or 'unsporting' behaviour (4 led to individual charges of being drunk and disorderly, and 2 involved several fans acting together – an assault on a railway passenger; vandalism on a train).

It's therefore not too surprising that an editorial in the *Leicester Mercury*, commenting on the orderly crowd behaviour at the 1928 Cup Final, should have taken an upbeat view of the average football fan:

> Students of people in the mass will probably tell us that we are better behaved, and that we make merry nowadays without the discreditable manifestations that were at one time thought to be inseparable from these public rejoicings. Rejoicing and sobriety go hand in hand and great crowds distinguish themselves with a sense of discipline that is creditable all round. May we infer that we are an improving people?[6]

The popularity of football boomed after 1945, with a record 77 million attendances at League and Cup matches in the 1949–50 season. And, gradually, crowd behaviour began to worsen. By the late 1950s reports of football-related disorder were becoming quite regular: Liverpool and Everton supporters, for example, not infrequently faced accusations of vandalising the trains that took them to and from away matches. By the 1966–7 season (in the aftermath of England's World Cup victory) reports of fighting between rival groups of fans, both inside and outside football stadia, had become both more common and more widespread. A ritual evolved whereby youths and young men formed regular if informal groupings, one of whose primary functions was to defend their 'end' – in other words, what they deemed to be 'their' stretch of terracing. Such aggressively territorial behaviour culminated in the Heysel stadium disaster of 1985 when, after some initial missile-throwing and skirmishing between Liverpool and Juventus supporters at the European Cup Final, a group of Liverpool fans stormed a fence separating them from their Italian rivals, leading to panic and the collapse of a perimeter wall. Thirty-nine people were killed and around 600 were injured.

That football hooliganism was a genuine social problem in the England of the 1960s, 1970s and 1980s is undeniable. It's hard to disagree with the Football Association's assessment that fear of violence at football matches contributed to a post-war slump in attendance (from that peak of 77 million during the 1949–50 season, to between 25–9 million in the 1960s, and with a further decline in the 1970s, though, of course, the televising of football matches played a very significant role, too, in dwindling match attendance).

There can also be little doubt that a shift in the way the issue was perceived exaggerated its nature and extent. In early-twentieth-century reports of problems at football matches the emphasis tended to be on youthful high spirits or over-zealous behaviour by those in authority. Well into the 1960s newspapers tended to argue that football violence was far more common abroad than it was at home. But from about 1967 the tone and language changed. That post-war sense of unease about the new type of British youth – the teddy boy, the mod and the rocker, the student activist, the skinhead – began to extend to the overly boisterous football fan. Troublemakers on and off the terraces ceased to be guilty merely of youthful high spirits and became 'thugs', 'mindless morons', 'animals' and 'savages'. Those seeking to curb them were engaged in a 'war' against hooliganism (the group that advised Margaret Thatcher on football policy after the Heysel disaster was dubbed her 'War Cabinet').

From the mid-1970s, a number of newspapers started to publish league tables that ranked clubs by the number of violent incidents their supporters were responsible for or by the number of their supporters arrested. Press demonisation of football fans reached its nadir in 1989 when the Hillsborough disaster, in which ninety-six people were crushed to death at an inadequately policed match, was characterised by the *Sun* in its 19 April edition as a display of hooliganism at its most appalling. Liverpool supporters, so the paper falsely claimed, had been guilty of picking the pockets of the injured and dying, attacking emergency service workers, urinating on the injured and beating up a police constable giving the kiss of life to a victim. By this time, one could argue, football hooligans had become so demonised that they were felt to be symbolic of everything that was wrong with British society.

And it was perhaps because of this that they also became the stuff of popular drama: a prism through which current social ills could be seen refracted. The 1989 made-for-television film *The Firm*, for example, which is based loosely on West Ham's hooligan firm – the Inter City Firm (ICF) – portrays the relatively well-to-do 'Bex' whose life revolves around football violence, and who even envisages a national hooligan network. Like his fellow hooligans, he believes that his actions confer prestige and status (a view with which his wife firmly disagrees) and when he is shot and killed by the leader of a rival firm he becomes a hero to his followers.

The 1995 film *I.D.* centres on an undercover policeman sent to infiltrate 'Shadwell Town's' firm of hooligans only to become, gradually, just like them: hard-drinking, macho and aggressive. The team's name seems to be an allusion to Millwall, which at that time had a reputation for violence, and which was itself the focus of a 1977 BBC *Panorama* Special which looked at its hard-core hooligan 'F-Troop' and at 'Harry the Dog', a 'nutter' (a status roughly equivalent to that of a berserker in Norse culture), who had, apparently, attempted single-handedly to take Bristol Rovers' 'end' at one particular match.

As I have said, there is no doubt that levels of football hooliganism *did* rise in the course of the 1960s and 1970s, though the woolliness of the statistics available makes it very difficult to judge by how much. As to why they should have done so, that much-debated question remains mired in controversy.[7] The radical criminologist Ian Taylor put forward a left-wing analysis, suggesting that violence at football matches was a working-class response to a game that had largely been taken over by wealthy businessmen, that was populated by players who had ever-more tenuous connections with the communities from which their fans were drawn, and that was in any case becoming ever-more of a bourgeois pursuit.[8]

Academics at the Centre for Contemporary Cultural Studies at Birmingham University, by contrast, and, I think, rather more convincingly, argued that football hooliganism was part and parcel of a post-war youth sub-culture that was, on the whole, less deferential to authority than previous generations had been and simultaneously thrived on a sense of shared identity and community – that 'being' a football hooligan with a group of like-minded people gave individuals a sense of belonging and excitement. The Birmingham team also stressed the close relationship that fans felt with their chosen clubs, while simultaneously, like Taylor, exploring the alienation many also suffered from an increasingly commercialised game. And it made the important point that much of the 'violence' associated with football hooligans was essentially ritualistic or symbolic – aggressive without actually being physically violent.

Members of the University of Leicester's Sociology Department, notably Eric Dunning, have also published their views on the roots of football hooliganism, Dunning viewing it from the perspective of Norbert Elias's 'civilising process' (Elias had taught at Leicester until his retirement) and so proposing that among the lower, or 'rough', working class the process had yet to become fully established. The Leicester group's work, funded by the Football Trust, has come in for criticism from other social scientists, but it has carried out and helped facilitate an impressive body of research that leaves one suspecting British football hooligans have been more studied by academics than any other deviant group in history: indeed, there was a joke current in the 1970s that half of those attending any given football match would be sociologists undertaking participant observation. During the 1980s the Sir Norman Chester Centre for Football Research, a body that publishes regular reports on football-related matters, became part of the Leicester University sociology department.[9]

Those outside the realms of academe have their own theories.

Some attribute football hooliganism to alcohol consumption (27 per cent of arrests at League matches in 2000–1 were for alcohol-related offences), others to the breakdown of traditional family life, others to poor education, and others still to the end of National Service and the loss of the discipline it imposed.[10] For their part, the police have highlighted the fear that football hooliganism is an organised activity, possibly on occasion orchestrated by extreme right-wing organisations that have insinuated their way into the fan base. There may be an element of truth in any or all of these suggestions, but one senses that they tend more towards popular prejudice than fact-based interpretation: people see what they want to see.

To make matters even more problematic, it's not entirely clear what precisely constitutes hooliganism. From a legal point of view, it can be anything from throwing an empty crisp packet to murder. The anthropologist Gary Armstrong noted an occasion on which a youth running away from an Indian restaurant without paying the bill one Saturday evening was charged with breach of the peace and the offence added to that match day's crime figures – suggesting that not paying for onion bhajis can be viewed as an act of hooliganism.[11] It's also difficult to pinpoint precisely when behaviour at a football match tips over from being boisterous to aggressive and from aggressive to intimidating and dangerous: so much is in the eye of the beholder.

But thanks to studies of individual clubs, we are able to get a strong sense of the nature and modus operandi of the die-hard football hooligan. One such is Gary Armstrong's brilliant *Football Hooligans*, which explores the world of Sheffield United's hooligan 'Blades' from the point of view of someone who was himself raised in Sheffield and is a lifelong United supporter. The Blades consisted of a core of perhaps 60, an outer core of around 40, and 'peripherals' who numbered 200 or so. There was no fixed membership or structure and the group's personnel was constantly shifting, though those who had gained experience or the respect of others might well take the lead on specific occasions. Of the 190 who attended one particular away match in April 1987, most had jobs (for the most part in an unskilled or semi-skilled capacity), most were in their early twenties, around two-thirds had criminal convictions (mostly for offences against the person or property), but only a handful were school drop-outs. Armstrong could be quite scathing about other scholars working in this field (he gave the Leicester group an especially tough time), but his overall conclusions were not too dissimilar from the findings of others: those labelled football hooligans tended to be young working-class males from a city that had experienced major economic change; they were fanatical supporters of their club; and they found that being a Blade gave them a sense of belonging, what anthropologists have described as *communitas*.

Their attitude to violence was, according to Armstrong, strongly ritualised. They certainly believed that fighting was morally acceptable – indeed, on occasion, desirable – but it was not the inevitable end result of their activities. In fact, it was as much symbolic as physical, generally taking the form of stand-offs with rival groups of supporters that only infrequently led to actual violence. 'Nutters', who ignored accepted conventions and wanted to push things much further, were not generally regarded as desirable role models. There was, in other words, a theatrical quality to the Blades' behaviour. 'Blades', Armstrong argued, 'play to various audiences and, like thespians worldwide, they and their fellow performers need to adhere to the boundaries of the plot and understand the script' – not, of course, that that precluded the occasional fluffing of lines, missed cues and the need for improvisation. Armstrong's estimate was that between 1980 and 1995 no more than 25 Sheffield United and Sheffield Wednesday supporters needed hospital treatment in the wake of football-related violence, and that in the same period 5 supporters of rival clubs who had run foul of the Blades, along with 3 police officers, ended up there. Those figures might be of little consolation to those bystanders caught up in frightening confrontations between battling fans, or those innocent fans who got swept up in the melee, but they do serve as a corrective to a widespread popular view that all football hooligans want to do is beat their rivals senseless. Armstrong viewed them as 'consenting adults involved in hooligan rituals'.[12]

At heart the modern football hooligan is, of course, motivated by much the same instincts as governed the duelling seventeenth-century aristocrat or the eighteenth-century pub brawler: a desire to be seen as tough, a concern with reputation, a determination to react decisively to perceived insults or slights: here as elsewhere, violence is connected to notions of masculinity and male honour. And it's not hard to see why football should be the arena for this. It may be a game of skill and tactics, but it is also one that involves toughness, stamina, courage and loyalty. In looking at the hardened fan one is reminded of that emphasis on a link between manliness and games-playing that was such a part of the Victorian public-school ethos and that was then refashioned by working-class football aficionados towards the end of that century. One can't help but wonder also whether the undoubted upsurge in football hooliganism that took place from the late 1960s onwards didn't have something to do with the erosion of traditional manual work, especially jobs that up until then had been a staple of working-class male employment and that had previously helped cement a sense of individual status and worth. For some young men at least, the gaining and maintaining of a reputation for hardness and the sense of identity provided by membership of the local football club's 'firm', offered a measure of compensation for what they had lost as the old patterns of work and employment shifted.

Football itself has changed markedly in recent years. The Bradford City fire of 1985 and the Hillsborough disaster of 1989 revealed enormous shortcomings in stadium design and crowd control. At Bradford, fifty-six people perished during a match with Lincoln City when a dropped match or cigarette ignited rubbish that had accumulated under the antiquated wooden stand. At Hillsborough, as already mentioned, poor police management resulted in overcrowding in the pens (the animal terminology is interesting) reserved for Liverpool fans and one of the worst fatal crushes of the modern era.[13] The Taylor Report into the Hillsborough tragedy recommended that stadia in the Football League should become all-seater venues, and this move, along with other changes to crowd control, has undoubtedly restricted the scope for misbehaving and hooliganism.[14] In recent years CCTV cameras have sprung up everywhere, carefully monitoring those arriving at or leaving matches.

And the law has become tougher, too. Entering a stadium when drunk or in possession of alcohol is now an offence, as is taking alcohol on to trains or coaches when travelling to a football match; throwing any object at or towards the pitch or spectator areas, going on to the pitch without lawful excuse, and indecent or racist chanting. Breaches of any of these rules can now result in a Football Banning Order that prohibits the person convicted from attending a football match anywhere in the world for three years, makes an infringement of this order a criminal offence, and requires those served with a banning order to report to a police station whenever the England team plays abroad. As of 30 January 2012 some 3,058 people were listed on the register of those formally banned.[15]

Even Millwall has changed. In 1993 the Old Den was demolished and the club moved to a new ground nearby. It was the end of an era, almost of a way of life. As one Millwall fan put it in *The Lion Roars*, Millwall's fanzine:

> I always thought of the Den as being different from other grounds, a seething cauldron of passion that made the Den such an unpopular place for visiting teams . . . Here's one supporter that doesn't want to move, the new ground will be too expensive for me, I doubt I'll be a regular anymore. I suppose I'm a victim of change.

Millwall's uniqueness was captured in a remarkable study by Garry Robson, a book so heavily theoretical in the manner of the late French sociologist Pierre Bourdieu that one can't help wondering whether it should have been entitled not *No One Likes Us, We Don't Care*, but *Pierre Bourdieu Meets Harry the Dog*. It is nevertheless a fascinating survey that captures the fanatical devotion that Millwall supporters feel for a club that, to be blunt, is unlikely ever to make it to the top (and I write as a supportive ex-local). One senses the strong sense of local pride, the almost carnivalesque rituals that accompany home fixtures, and the powerful working-class spirit that together create 'Millwallness'.

It was hardly surprising that when the Old Den finally closed, supporters virtually dismantled it in their frenzy to seize part of its structure or a section of turf by way of a souvenir. Attempts by the police to clear the ground led to a full-scale confrontation. The new-style, all-seater stadium with its expensive tickets is a very different place and so it seems somehow symbolically appropriate that two years after the demise of the Old Den it was reported that Harry the Dog had died.[16] Not that that is any indication of an end to football hooliganism: there were, after all, 1,599 arrests at League matches in the course of the 2013–14 season (though that has to be set in the context of an overall attendance figure of 29 million).[17] As Gary Armstrong says, 'there will always be young men who, when honour has been felt to be transgressed, take a punch and give two in return'.[18]

III

Levels of football hooliganism have not persistently declined over the past century. Instead, there have been peaks and troughs, culminating in the current relative lull. The same is true of another area of violence traditionally associated with the working class: that which has on occasion accompanied industrial disputes. Here, peaks in the 1910s and again in the late 1970s and early 1980s can be set against periods of relative quiet in, for example, the 1930s, suggesting that the last hundred years have not witnessed a single, inexorable downward trend in physical aggression in industrial disputes but a jagged line shaped by very particular – and often highly political – circumstances.

For those who recall news footage of the worst of the miners' strike of 1984/5 it may come as some surprise to learn that the industrial strife in the years immediately before the First World War was far more violent and bloody.[19] Increased competition from abroad and a partly related decline in some industries in Britain had led to a squeeze on wages at a period when the cost of living overall was rising. At the same time, trades unions had become more radical, in part because the 1880s and 1890s had seen a vast rise in recruitment among unskilled workers who were less inclined to toe the traditional trades union line, in part because some trades union leaders, notably the charismatic Tom Mann, had become disillusioned with reform by parliamentary process and had turned instead to syndicalism – a movement that espoused direct action by workers and that had already been taken up by activists on the Continent, notably in France and Belgium.

The first of the Edwardian era's large-scale strikes took place in the Rhondda in Wales in 1910–11. Precipitated by a management lock-out at the Ely Pit on 1 September 1910 where workers had refused to accept reduced pay and conditions, it rapidly escalated to draw in some 13,000 miners. Large numbers of outside police were called in to help the local constabulary. Magistrates put the army on standby. By August 1911, when the strike finally collapsed, some 2,985,000 working days had been lost. And while it lasted the strike proved both acrimonious and brutal. In the town square of Tonypandy, for example, on 7–8 November 1910 – in what was probably the most violent of all the confrontations – police and miners fought a virtual pitched battle in which around 80 police and 500 locals were injured, and one striker killed.[20]

In 1911 it was the turn of shipping, docks, railway and road haulage workers. A strike among seamen at Southampton in June rapidly spread to other ports, and swiftly drew in dockers and carters. In most of the affected ports there was violence on the picket lines, riots and looting. Hull was particularly badly affected. Sir George Askwith, the government negotiator called in to help arbitrate between the employers and 15,000 angry Hull dockers (some of whom were heard crying 'burn the docks'), later recalled a local councillor saying that he had been in Paris at the time of the Commune in 1871, but had seen nothing then that compared with the scenes he was witnessing now: 'women with hair streaming and half nude, reeling through the streets smashing and destroying'.[21] Other docks struck, with dockers at London, the last major port to come out, starting an unofficial strike on 29 July. The following month a transport strike, in large measure orchestrated by Tom Mann, broke out in Liverpool and swiftly developed into a national railway strike. Over the course of 1911, there were, in fact, 872 separate strikes and 10,155,000 working days were lost. The following year, with a million miners on strike and a large-scale dock dispute in London, a staggering 40,890,000 working days were lost. This dropped to 9,804,000 days in 1913, but there were nevertheless 1,459 separate disputes that year, a figure not surpassed until 1920.

Industrial violence is not, of course, a self-contained affair shaped only by those on strike. Much depends on the way in which the authorities react to it, and the stance taken by the Liberal government of the time was a firm one. Rattled in any case by a militant suffragette campaign and – far more serious – facing the prospect of all-out civil war in Ireland, as Home Rulers and Nationalists squared up against Ulster Loyalists, they opted for heavy police presences, and decisive action, at industrial flashpoints. During the Liverpool strikes of 1911, for example, police were called in to protect blackleg workers being brought in to replace the striking, largely female, workforce of 2,000 at Wilson Brothers Bobbin Works at Garston.[22] When protesters cat-called and threw stones at the strike-breakers making their way, under police protection, to the trams that would take them home at the end of their shift, the police responded with baton charges that left a number of women and, according to some accounts, children, injured.

On 13 August of that year there was fighting on an even larger scale between police and strikers at a mass meeting addressed by Tom Mann. A policeman was killed while the riots went on into the night, exacerbated by Catholic and Protestant tensions in the city.

Two days later rioters went on to attack police vans carrying strikers to prison. On this occasion it was troops, who had been patrolling the streets since 13 August, who took action, opening fire and killing two men, one a striker, the other a bystander hit by a stray bullet as he attempted to put up the shutters on his windows.

The police bore the brunt of enforcement against strikers. The military, who barely a century before had perpetrated the Peterloo Massacre, were certainly in evidence (troops were sent to around thirty trouble spots in 1911), but were far more circumspect than their predecessors had been, thanks largely to the officer in charge, Major-General C. F. N. Macready, an experienced and level-headed soldier who ensured that troops were deployed under instruction from the Home Office rather than potentially overreacting local magistrates. His overall approach was demonstrated when, having taken troops into the South Wales Coalfields in 1910, he concluded that the problems there had been greatly exaggerated, and decided to withdraw when he realised that the military were more likely to provoke than to discourage disorder. Other officers followed his lead. In the following year, for example, Chesterfield railway station was wrecked by rioting transport workers; the Riot Act had been read to a stone-throwing crowd without effect. The mayor, sheltering from a hail of missiles, requested the officer in charge of a detachment of the West Yorkshire Regiment to open fire, but was met with a blank refusal. A tragic exception to military restraint occurred at Llanelli in the same year, 1911. Here, troops fired on stone-throwing strikers who were attempting to stop a train from passing. Two were killed.[23]

Individual strikes were ultimately defeated. But overall the trades unions won considerable concessions, not least – for miners – the Coal Mines (Minimum Wage) Act of 1912. Buoyed by their sense of new-found power, the transport workers, railwaymen and miners' unions came together in a 'Triple Alliance' in 1914, promising mutual support and a continuation of the sympathetic strikes that had been such a feature of industrial action over the previous few years.

Unrest among Scottish miners early that year might well have led to a General Strike by the autumn. As it was, the outbreak of war in August brought a temporary halt to domestic hostilities.

Industrial relations remained tense after 1918. After a short-lived boom, a post-war economic slump, which between mid-1920 and mid-1921 led to a 20 per cent decline in industrial production, raised both unemployment levels and friction between workers and bosses. Matters came to a head in 1926. In the course of the General Strike of that year, 1.7 million workers came out in support of 1.25 million miners, who were facing cuts to their pay. Nine days of negotiating stalemate ensued followed by defeat for the strikers, brought down by a government that had planned for the confrontation (for example, troops were kept on hand to move food supplies from the docks by lorries, and the lorries were protected by armoured cars) and could therefore afford to be intransigent.[24]

The mythology that has grown up around the General Strike has created an image of good-humoured strike-breaking by middle-class volunteers and restraint on the part of those taking industrial action, symbolised by the football match that was famously played between strikers and the police at Plymouth. The truth, though, is that while violence was never as extreme nor as pervasive as it had been in the pre-war years, an undercurrent of physical conflict was nevertheless frequently apparent. In the North East, police fought battles with pickets attempting to stop motor transport on the Durham–Newcastle road, there were riots in Newcastle itself, and the 'Flying Scotsman' was derailed by angry strikers near the mining community of Cramlington (eight men were subsequently imprisoned for this). There were riots and clashes between police and strikers in Southsea, Swansea, Nottingham and Plymouth (notwithstanding the football match), while at Preston a crowd of 5,000 people tried to storm a police station to rescue a striker who had been arrested. London witnessed numerous clashes, notably in and around the docks. At New Cross, pickets tried to stop trams leaving their depot and had to be scattered by a police baton charge (the volunteer drivers felt too intimidated subsequently to take their trams out). At nearby Deptford Broadway a political meeting degenerated into a clash between strikers and the police: injuries were sustained on both sides, several mounted policemen being unhorsed and roughed up.

The defeat of the General Strike, and the brief period of economic prosperity that followed, marked the end of an era of trades union militancy. And although the economy was to collapse again in 1929 in the aftermath of the Wall Street Crash of that year, militancy did not return. In part, this was because the unemployment that swept areas of the North of England and Wales in the early 1930s was so severe that strike action in the communities worst affected seemed scarcely an adequate or practical response (there was a wave of strikes between 1929 and 1932, but far fewer working days were lost than had been the case in, say, 1913 or 1921).

In part, the retreat from militancy can be explained by the fact that those not thrown out of work by the economic downturn, and those able to find employment again once the economy began to revive, began to find themselves better off than they had ever previously been. North-eastern England, Western Scotland, West Lancashire and South Wales might have been badly hit by the 'Great Slump', but in Greater London, the South generally, and the Midlands, new, relatively high-tech industries (for example, car manufacturing) sprang up in the 1930s, bringing with them a modest level of prosperity. By 1939 those in work were both enjoying wages that were double those of 1914, and, thanks to falling prices, seeing their money go further than ever before. Thus while trades union membership began to recover in the years before the Second World War, to the point in 1939 where there were 6,298,000 members, more than there had been in 1926 and the highest number since 1921, the number of days lost through industrial disputes totalled only 1,356,000.

Terrible slums still existed in many parts of the country, but the inter-war period saw the construction of 4 million new houses (the housing industry thus became a major employer), among which were 1.5 million council homes – sufficient for 10 per cent of working-class households. By the time war broke out, two-thirds of homes were wired for electricity, many had a radio set and an electric iron, 11 million people had annual paid holidays, and a few skilled workers had joined the nation's 2 million car owners. Appalling social deprivation remained, but those fortunate enough to have a job were also fortunate enough to be better fed, better clothed, better housed and healthier than their parents, let alone their grandparents, had been.

The lot of working people improved again, after a decade of war and austerity, in the early 1950s. But as progress started to stall from the late 1960s, so industrial tensions grew once again, notably in early 1974 when the coalminers' strike obliged Edward Heath's government to bring in a three-day week to conserve energy supplies, and again from the end of 1978 to early 1979 when nearly 30 million days were lost during the wave of interrelated strikes that formed the 'Winter of Discontent'. As a rule, though, while disputes were bitterly contested, the levels of violence involved were comparatively low. The relative power of the trades unions, and the unwillingness of the governments of the time to face them down, meant that strikes became almost ritualised affairs, with their pickets, rules to work and lock-outs operating according to accepted conventions – conventions that made recourse to violence largely unnecessary.

Not that physical confrontation suddenly became a thing of the past. As the press was eager to report, there were a number of occasions when pickets offered low-level violence to blacklegs or the police. In particular, during the bitterly contested Grunwick Dispute (1976–8), fought by a predominantly female, Asian workforce over the issue of union recognition, clashes were frequent and brutal, particularly when the Metropolitan Police drafted in its Special Patrol Group to enforce public order.

What Grunwick demonstrated was that even in an era far

removed from that of the industrial conflict of Edwardian times, protest could very easily and quickly tip over into violence, and that violence could feed upon itself and escalate once it became a feature of a dispute. Here, a workforce that felt marginalised came up against an intransigent management; each side then called upon allies (trades unionists, the media, politicians) who drew the battle lines ever more aggressively; and an often heavy-handed police force, drafted in to ensure peaceful protest, ended up making things worse.

A similar sense of escalating confrontation between immovable camps emerges from the dispute that defined industrial relations in the first half of the 1980s: the coalminers' strike. Here on the one hand was a hard-line left-wing miners' leader, Arthur Scargill, and on the other a hard-line Conservative Prime Minister, Margaret Thatcher. Scargill had tried to engineer a confrontation in 1981, but the government, as yet unready to take on the NUM, had not risen to the bait. But it had subsequently started to prepare for a show-down, and, echoing the preparations made by the powers-that-be in the run-up to the 1926 General Strike, had begun gradually to build up its coal stocks (also ensuring that supplies from abroad could be acquired if needed). It continued to push a policy whereby oil rather than coal was favoured for electricity generation, and reactivated the police National Reporting Centre (NRC) which was to prove so instrumental in coordinating police action during the strike that was to follow. It also appointed the tough Ian MacGregor as Chairman of the National Coal Board in September 1983, a Scots-American with a reputation for an anti-union stance in the US, where he had settled during the Second World War, and a man who had earlier been simultaneously hailed for turning round the ailing British steel industry and criticised for shedding half its workforce to achieve this.

There's no doubt that the British coal industry of the time faced real challenges. It had been in steady decline for most of the post-war period: the number of collieries had fallen from 698 in 1960 to 292 in

1971; on average 25,000 men had left the industry annually during the 1960s. To an extent what MacGregor now proposed – lowering the annual target for coal production and the closure of non-economic pits – made sense (complete sense to a governing generation that was busy rejecting Keynesian economics). But the personalities involved, and the savageness of the cuts proposed at a time when unemployment levels already stood at over 3 million, guaranteed bitter confrontation. The move to strike action was finally precipitated by the announcement of the closure of the Cortonwood colliery in South Yorkshire, whose 839 miners had only recently been given assurances that the pit would remain open for at least another five years. The miners voted to fight the closure, and the Yorkshire NUM called out the region's 56,000 miners on 9 March 1984.

Two factors served to make the miners' strike particularly violent. The first was the division within the miners' own camp. Not everyone had favoured industrial action so many felt alienated when Scargill went over their heads and, rather than call a national ballot of NUM members, made a unilateral (and so technically illegal) decision to bring the union out on strike. The result was that while picketing in areas where the strike was solid for the most part involved little more than shoving and name-calling, it often acquired a violent edge where striking miners confronted those who had elected to carry on working.[25] It was, for example, felt necessary to send a thousand police to Gascoigne Wood drift mine on one occasion in August 1984 to protect the one Yorkshire miner who had decided to return to work there. Elsewhere, intimidation by flying pickets of moderate Nottinghamshire miners helped precipitate the formation of a break-away union: here miners who had opted to keep working were pelted with stones and paint, and their families threatened. A campaign launched by the National Coal Board in November to get miners back to work caused a hardening of the line: increased picket-line violence and a petrol bomb attack on a police station in South Yorkshire. That month also witnessed the death of taxi driver David Wilkie, who was killed by a concrete slab dropped from a bridge by two striking miners as he drove another miner to work at the Merthyr Vale Colliery in South Wales.

There's also no doubt that the tough line promoted by the government and upheld by its servants, notably the police, made a bad situation infinitely worse. Some police action was legally distinctly dubious: for example, setting up roadblocks and turning back men who might be pickets (at one point the Kent police would not allow anyone they suspected to be travelling to support the miners' strike to use the northbound lane of the Dartford tunnel). But far more serious was the provocation and violence that the police themselves perpetrated, particularly those bussed in from outside the strike areas to oversee picket lines. The Metropolitan Police seem to have behaved particularly badly, stoking the flames by taunting strikers with waved £10 notes, and using brute force to manage crowds. Even their own colleagues took a dim view of them: George Moores, chairman of the South Yorkshire Police Authority, for example, when discussing payments due to the Met for their 'assistance', commented:

> It'd take a hundred years to investigate all the complaints against that bunch of yobbos . . . I don't see why I should pay people to come here to knock around the people that I represent.[26]

It was an outside force – in this instance the Manchester Police – who were responsible for a debacle at the South Yorkshire village of Armthorpe that bore all the appearances of a police riot. Here on 22 August 1984, after several days of tension, a column of fifty-two police vehicles disgorged officers in full riot gear who proceeded to attack pickets and chase them through the village, even breaking into private houses to remove pickets who had been given shelter there. Afterwards, one woman described how eight police officers had pursued two pickets through her house, beaten them viciously, and then shouted verbal abuse at her. Previously lukewarm in her support of the strike, she now joined a local miners' support group and went on the picket line.[27]

The worst of the violence centred on the Orgreave coke depot, near Sheffield. Trouble began there on 25 May 1984 when the British Steel Corporation sent in convoys of trucks to move coke from supply steelworks around Scunthorpe. It reached a climax on 18 June. On that day between 5,000 and 8,000 miners were confronted by around 6,000 police drawn from ten counties, many in riot gear, among them some 40 or so mounted officers. Pushing and stone-throwing escalated as lorries came in to collect the coke. Pickets were then pushed back by mounted police and squads of riot police. A brief lull ensued, followed by missile-throwing and battles between such pickets as were left (many had already dispersed) and the police. Fifty-one miners and 72 policemen were injured. At the time, blame for the 'Battle of Orgreave' was overwhelmingly attached to the miners, 93 of whom were arrested, with a total of 95 being subsequently charged for offences committed that day. It is surely significant, though, that proceedings against them were dropped when they were brought to trial in 1987, and that the South Yorkshire police in addition agreed to pay £425,000 compensation and £100,000 legal costs to 39 of them in an out of court settlement.[28]

Industrial violence tends to stem from a position of weakness rather than strength. In the 1960s and early 1970s, when confidence in the British economy was high and unions powerful, disputes may have been numerous, but their resolution was generally peaceful. The miners' strike, however, took place against a background of high inflation, high unemployment and ever tougher trades union regulation (the 1982 Employment Act restricted the closed shop, reduced dismissal compensation and allowed employers to sack striking workers; the 1984 Trade Union Act compelled unions to hold secret ballots of individual members before calling on them to take strike action). In retrospect the strike can be viewed more as a last gasp of union power than a confident flexing of union muscle.

The same is true of the last great industrial dispute of the Thatcher years: that fought between the Times group of newspapers under their new owner, Australian media entrepreneur Rupert Murdoch, and the print unions who up until then had controlled the day-to-day running of Fleet Street. The ingredients were not dissimilar to those that stoked the miners' dispute: a hard-line management that seems to have been more or less determined to provoke a dispute, a heavily unionised workforce that feared what effect proposed changes to work practices (here, the introduction of new technology) would have on jobs and salaries, and a government prepared to co-opt the police to help defeat the unions. Murdoch's plan was to move production of his newspapers to a new site in Wapping that would be equipped with the latest technology installed by the American computer firm Atex, and thereby cut back on what was widely perceived by observers of the newspaper industry as over-manning. At a meeting early in 1986 he informed representatives of the relevant unions that the current workforce would be laid off, that they would receive only the minimum legal redundancy payment, and that no member of the existing workforce would be employed at Wapping. Strike action was inevitably called, and followed, equally inevitably, by mass sackings.[29]

As in the miners' strike, the print unions' chief weapon was the picket and the employer's weapon of choice the police. Over 1,000 per day of the latter were deployed to protect lorries carrying Murdoch's papers leaving steel-fenced, razor-wire-protected 'Fortress Wapping'. In the first ten months of the dispute their overtime payments amounted to £4.6 million. Clashes were commonplace, 400 people being injured and about 1,000 arrested before the strike finally collapsed in February 1987. The failure of the Wapping strike, coming so soon after the defeat of the miners, marked the end of old-style trades unionism. In 1979, trades union membership peaked at 13 million. By 2000 it had fallen to 8 million and by 2014 to 6.4 million – just 1 in 4 of the working population. Union weakness was compounded by ever-increasing government curbs on union freedom of action.

Strikes in the twenty-first century have been far smaller and more limited affairs than their twentieth-century predecessors.

IV

If there's been a decline in the violence that has sometimes gone hand in hand with people on strike or – in the form of football hooliganism – at leisure, another form of popular violence has proved far more intractable: the violence of urban unrest. It is, of course, nothing new. As I have pointed out in earlier chapters the street mob has been a fixture of English life for centuries, whether in the terrifyingly violent form of the crowds that rampaged through London in 1381, killing and lynching, or the destructive form of the Gordon Rioters who attacked and burned property over the course of six days in 1780. The frequency with which it erupts may differ from era to era, but there has never been a period in English history entirely free from riot or civil disturbance of some sort.

One particular constant has been the political protest that spills over into violence. In the nineteenth century popular demonstrations that escalated into scuffles had been a hallmark of the debate over the Reform Bill in 1831. A generation later, in 1866, a public gathering organised by the Reform League to push for further parliamentary reform degenerated into violent demonstrations in Hyde Park, in the course of which railings were ripped up and stones thrown at the police. In both cases, though, physical aggression tended to be a side effect rather than an aim. Every crowd might have had its sprinkling of trouble-makers, but for the vast majority of demonstrators what mattered was having their voices heard rather than their fists felt.

The same was true a century later of the many rallies held to protest against the Vietnam War: among the throngs there were undoubtedly knots of anarchists and other individuals hell-bent on mischief, but most people were there simply to protest peacefully. When trouble did occur, it tended not to break out immediately but

in response to perceived heavy-handedness on the part of the authorities. Thus, for example, the big anti-war gathering that took place in
Trafalgar Square on 17 March 1968 was described by most observers
as good-humoured; it was only when mounted police were sent in
to push back the crowds that were making their way to the US
Embassy in Grosvenor Square that the situation deteriorated, culminating in 200 arrests and 86 injuries.

To that extent, it's perhaps valid to make a distinction between
the political protest that brings together a diverse group of people in
a single cause, where altercations may possibly occur, and the political protest (rare in England) made by a unified group intent on
intimidation, which will almost certainly end in violence. The anti-
Iraq War demonstrations of 2003 are examples of the former (only
three arrests were made in the course of the huge London gathering
on 15 February); the rallies held by the British Union of Fascists in the
1930s all too often an example of the latter.

The Poll Tax Riots of 1990 constitute an extreme example of the
classic English political demonstration. Margaret Thatcher's decision to reform the way in which local government was financed
might have seemed a slightly abstruse issue in itself, but her proposed solution was deeply controversial and thus polarised society
in a way that the Vietnam War had done a generation earlier. At a
stroke, she intended to replace the somewhat ramshackle old system
of rates, which fell on homeowners, to a flat charge that would be
levied on all those aged over eighteen (with some exemptions and
qualifications); 19 million rate-payers were therefore to be replaced
by 25 million payers of the new charge, many in rented accommodation, many struggling financially, many likely to be Labour
supporters (for example, affluent Tory-voting Outer London stood
to gain £168.7 million from the reforms, while Inner London would
lose just over £340 million).[30] Given her known suspicion of local,
often Labour-dominated government (she had already abolished the
Greater London Council and six regional councils), her reforms
appeared to many to be ideologically motivated and socially highly

divisive. A tax and funding reform thus took on a highly charged political force, encouraging a black-and-white response: you were either for it or against it. Those against it, in a nod to history, opted to rename what was formally known as the Community Charge, the Poll Tax.

The Community Charge was first trialled in Scotland in 1989, and met with immediate opposition there: some 16 per cent of those liable to pay refused to do so. Early 1990 saw a rash of anti-Poll Tax protests in England. In the socially deprived London borough of Hackney, 5,000 people battled the police outside the town hall. There were skirmishes between police and demonstrators in Haringey at a demonstration during which local councillors were attacked. In Nottingham demonstrators dressed as Robin Hood and his Merry Men attempted to throw custard pies at councillors, including, somewhat serendipitously, the Sheriff of Nottingham. There were even demonstrations in Tunbridge Wells. Matters came to a head in London on 31 March. Estimates of the size of the crowd involved, as always, vary, but possibly 200,000 people gathered in an initially peaceful protest which turned first to confusion when it converged on Trafalgar Square, which has a capacity of about 60,000 (the demonstration's organisers' request to redirect their march to Hyde Park was refused), and then to violence as police, fearful of an attack on Downing Street, tried to block marchers heading through Whitehall.

There's no doubt that, as usual on these occasions, some demonstrators were bent on mischief, and chose to interpret the deployment of mounted riot police as a deliberate act of provocation, but there's also no doubt that a bad situation was made worse by the sheer crush of the numbers involved. As the demonstration broke up, some groups made their way to the West End. Shop windows were broken, shops looted, cars were overturned, and wine bars, shops and other premises wrecked. Skirmishing between police and rioters continued until 3 a.m. By midnight 113 people had been injured, and 339 arrests made. Months later Margaret Thatcher's successor, John

Major, announced that the Poll Tax would be scrapped, and legislation was passed shortly before the 1992 general election, replacing the Community Charge with the Council Tax.

V

Political demonstrations tend to follow a straightforward, easily comprehensible pattern: people come together with a common, usually peaceful purpose; and trouble, when it does occur, generally stems from issues of crowd control or small groups of trouble-makers (the presence of agents provocateurs has been alleged ever since the time of the Gordon Riots). Social or community demonstrations, on the other hand, are – inevitably – far more complex, with a myriad of potential causes and outcomes. There will be deep underlying causes, often national in scope, but what precipitates trouble will be local and may, to outsiders at least, seem relatively minor. Moreover, the progress of social riots is unpredictable. Some remain localised – as, for example, the Notting Hill race riots of 1958, or the rioting in the St Paul's area of Bristol in April 1980. Others spread rapidly well beyond the area of the initial flashpoint, and may well spark imitators many miles away.

The complexity of modern mob violence is well demonstrated by the Brixton riots of 1981. That there should have been social unrest in England at the time is unsurprising. Margaret Thatcher's determination after 1979 to tackle an inflation rate that stood at 11 per cent, and to put in place monetarist restraints on fiscal policy, had precipitated a massive contraction in manufacturing (25 per cent between 1979 and 1981) and a short-term hike in unemployment.[31] By the end of 1981, 2.7 million people were out of work, double the level that Thatcher had inherited. But that fact doesn't begin to explain the events that unfolded in April in South London. True, Brixton had been hit by recession, but it had not been as badly affected as, say, the industrial heartlands of the Midlands and the North. And yet industrial England did not riot: Brixton did.

So while the economic downturn was almost certainly a factor in the outbreak of violence and lawlessness that began on 11 April, it was not the determining reason. For that, we have to look to reasons closer to home and to the sense of anger and frustration that had been building among Brixton's black community (who accounted for about 25 per cent of the area's population). Many of them second-generation, born to parents who had come from the Caribbean in the late 1940s and 1950s, they struggled with high levels of unemployment – 1 in every 2 of young black men locally had no job – and poor housing, and felt discriminated against by the police, arguing that they used their powers of stop and search (the so-called 'sus' laws) disproportionately against the black community. Tensions had already been heightened in January when the police had refused to treat an arson attack in New Cross, in which thirteen black youngsters had died, as possibly racially motivated. They were made worse by a decision in early April to step up the level of stop and search operations in an area codenamed 'Swamp 81' – a choice later to be described as an 'unfortunate' one by Lord Scarman, who conducted an inquiry into the riots.

But the immediate trigger – one that reflects just how bad relations between the police and the black community were at the time – was the outcome of a misunderstanding. On 10 April a uniformed police officer patrolling Atlantic Road saw a black youth, Michael Bailey, apparently running away from three others. The officer stopped him and realised that the young man had been stabbed in the back. Bailey broke free but was stopped again, at which point the policeman attempted not only to give him immediate first aid but to get him to hospital. The crowd that had by now gathered, however, were convinced that Bailey was being arrested, intervened to 'rescue' him and made their own arrangements to get him medical care. That night the police increased the number of patrols in the area. The following day, as rumours and counter-rumours spread through the community, many took to the streets, police cars were pelted with bricks and shops looted. By early evening a full-scale riot was taking place that was to suck in 7,300 police officers and result in 450 injuries, 354 arrests, widespread fire-bombing and damage variously estimated at between £6.5 and £7.5 million.

The Brixton riots were followed three months later by widespread rioting in other inner-city areas in England, many of which had a sizeable non-white population: in Southall in West London rioting began after the borough's Asian population reacted sharply against skinhead violence; at Wood Green in North London a mob of 300–400 youths smashed and looted a shopping centre; at Moss Side in Manchester shops were attacked and looted, and the local police station attacked; there was renewed rioting in Brixton, and serious disturbances in other parts of London; and on Friday 10 July rioting was reported in nine English towns, between Reading and Hull.[32] By far the most publicised, and possibly the most serious of the July disturbances, came in the Toxteth area of Liverpool, part of Liverpool 8 where most of the city's then 30,000 black community was concentrated.

There on 3 July a black youth fell off his motorbike while being chased by the police, and was rescued by about 40 other black youths. The next night police were apparently lured into a trap where they were attacked by about 150 youths, both white and black; shops were looted and burned, cars were overturned or burned, police were attacked with fire bombs, and a BBC television camera was smashed by a masked gang and its crew threatened. The next day, Sunday 5 July, police were overwhelmed by large numbers of youths, both black and white, who, *inter alia*, drove stolen milk floats, a purloined concrete mixer, and a commandeered fire engine into the police lines. They also hurled missiles at the police, who were forced to retreat and leave the streets to the rioters' mercy. Shops were looted, buildings set on fire, and some 282 police officers were injured, of whom 229 needed hospital treatment. At 2.15 a.m. the Chief Constable of Merseyside, ignoring Home Office guidelines, ordered that CS gas be used against the rioters. Rioting continued into 6 July, when the police, reinforced by contingents from Lancashire, Cheshire and Greater Manchester, finally regained control. By then 781 officers had been injured, 1,070 crimes recorded, and 705 arrests made.

When Lord Scarman issued his report on the Brixton riots in November 1981 he dismissed many of the popular explanations that were circulating: the breakdown of respect for traditional social values in society, left-wing education policies or the failings of schools more generally, politically motivated agitators from outside, and simple human wickedness. Instead, he looked at local socio-economic issues, the lack of hope among Brixton's black youth, and the tensions engendered by heavy-handed policing. Interestingly, he also suggested tentatively that media coverage might have fanned the flames both in Brixton and in what some felt to be the 'copy-cat' July riots. But above all he picked up on a mood of antagonised frustration: 'the riots', he wrote, 'were essentially an outburst of anger and resentment by young black people against the police'. For her part the Chair of the Merseyside Police Committee, Margaret Simey, was to comment of the Toxteth rioters that, given social deprivation and local police heavy-handedness, the rioters 'would be apathetic fools . . . if they didn't protest'. And a petrol-bomber in Brixton told an Indian journalist: 'They don't want to know till we do something. Got to tell them we're here.' The disenfranchised, in other words, felt that rioting was the only way they could get their voices heard.[33] Such a mind-set meant that it took only relatively minor incidents to spark off major disturbances.

VI

In some ways the wave of rioting that engulfed England between 6 and 10 August 2011 seemed like a re-run of the 1981 riots.[34] Again, there was a single, local flashpoint – this time Tottenham in North-east London which erupted on the evening of Saturday 6 August. Again, rioting spread elsewhere – though much more swiftly this time. On

Sunday 7 August Enfield, Lambeth and Waltham Forest were witnessing disorder and looting. By Monday 8 August rioting was widespread across the London area, and was also occurring, with varying degrees of intensity, in a number of other cities. In all, sixty-six locations were affected.

It was later estimated by the panel appointed by the government to investigate the causes of the riots and suggest future approaches, that between 13,000 and 15,000 people nationally had taken to the streets, of whom 4,000 were arrested; and that 5,000 crimes had been committed, including 5 homicides, 366 incidents of violence against the person, 1,860 incidents of arson or criminal damage, and 1,649 burglaries. The total cost of putting right the damage caused by the riots was estimated at half a billion pounds. There seems little doubt that constant media coverage encouraged copy-cat riots and that – in true twenty-first-century fashion – social media had not only spread the word but helped those bent on trouble co-ordinate their efforts. Some commentators suggested that the rioters had more idea of what was going on than the police sent to contain them.

As in 1981 there was a background of local discontent underlying the riots. They tended to occur in pockets of deprivation (often with a significant non-white population), suffering from poor housing and high levels of unemployment. Ninety per cent of those brought to justice were male; most of them had previous criminal convictions (over 80 had committed 50 or more offences); three-quarters of them were aged under twenty-four. As in 1981, rioting was triggered by a particular incident: armed police officers involved in Operation Trident, targeting gun crime within London's black community, had pursued a suspect, Mark Duggan, on 4 August, stopped the minicab in which he was travelling and opened fire, killing Duggan outright.

As in 1981 controversy and rumour quickly spread, many people believing that Duggan had effectively been executed or, at least, that the police were not telling the truth. And as in 1981, public demonstration soon tipped over into confrontations with the police (made worse by rumours that they had maltreated a teenage black demonstrator) and then into arson and looting. Many of the remarks made by demonstrators in 2011 chime closely with those made by rioters in 1981. A North London rioter was quoted as saying: 'When no one cares about you you're gonna eventually make them care, you're gonna cause a disturbance.' And an unemployed man from Salford, in his early twenties, stated: 'I became involved in the riots in Salford because it was a chance to tell the police, tell the government, and tell everyone else for that matter that we get fucking hacked off around here and we won't stand for it.'[35] Eighty-one per cent of a sample of 270 rioters interviewed in a survey conducted jointly by the *Guardian* and the London School of Economics thought that riots would happen again.

But the events of the summer of 2011 also bring to the fore another, perhaps previously under-reported, feature of the appeal of the English riot to those involved: the momentary love of disorder, the sense of cocking a snook at those in authority, the feeling that – if only for a few hours or days – the world has been turned upside down and those at the bottom of the heap are suddenly on top. 'We had total control of the precinct', the unemployed Salford man quoted above reminisced: 'There's a massive police station there, and they couldn't do anything, it was ours for a day. Salford was more like a party atmosphere.' 'What I really noticed that day was that we had control,' said a sixteen-year-old boy who became swept up in riots in Birmingham and who was later convicted of theft. 'It felt great. We could do what we wanted to do. We could do as much damage as we can, and we could not be stopped.'

Collective violence has declined in certain areas of life – at football matches or when industrial action is being taken. But all the evidence suggests that the periodic urban riot is here to stay. Shifts in social attitudes, a changing economy and preventive legislation have all borne down on the football hooligan and the violent striker; the urban rioter is far harder to deal with. It's been suggested that we now live in a 40/30/30 society, where (leaving aside the super-rich)

40 per cent of the population are doing reasonably well, 30 per cent are coping, and the 30 per cent who are unemployed or are in badly paid or casual work are struggling. And it's from the ranks of the struggling that so many of today's rioters spring. Of those – overwhelmingly male and overwhelmingly young – suspects facing trial in the aftermath of the 2011 rioting, some 35 per cent were claiming out-of-work benefits (as against a national average of 12 per cent). Over a quarter were aged between ten and seventeen, of whom 44 per cent came from homes in the lowest 10 per cent income bracket, 42 per cent received free school meals, 66 per cent were classified as having some form of educational special need, and 30 per cent were persistent absentees from school. Three-quarters of all those tried had a previous criminal conviction or caution. One wonders what stake such people feel they have in society and to what extent they feel bound by its rules. And one therefore speculates not so much whether they will riot again, but when.

The iconic front cover of *A Clockwork Orange*, designed for the book's 1972 re-issue. In the early 1970s Stanley Kubrick's film adaptation was widely criticised for its graphic depiction of rape, murder and torture. It thus became part of a wider debate about the role that some believe fictional violence plays in promoting real-life acts of aggression.

CHAPTER 18

A CULTURE OF VIOLENCE?
FILM AND TELEVISION

I

In October 1944 George Orwell published an article about detective
fiction entitled 'Raffles and Miss Blandish'. It was a classic Orwellian
production: a mixture of strongly moral socialism and somewhat
nostalgic patriotism that emphasised the basic decency of pre-war
Britain. And it sought to make a comparison. On the one hand,
Orwell argued, there was the old type of genteel English detective
fiction, typified by E. W. Hornung's stories about Raffles, the
'amateur cracksman', burglar and keen cricket player bent on making
his way in polite society. On the other hand, there was the newly
popular and very violent American-style detective fiction, typified
by *No Orchids for Miss Blandish* (actually written by an English author,
James Hadley Chase). On the one hand, Orwell suggested, there
was the untroubling moral universe of Raffles:

> It is important to note that by modern standards Raffles' crimes
> are very petty ones . . . And though the stories are convincing in
> their physical detail, they contain very little sensationalism – very
> few corpses, hardly any blood, no sex crimes, no sadism, no per-
> versions of any kind . . . They belong to a time when people had
> standards, though they happened to be very foolish standards.

On the other hand, there was the deeply unpleasant world of *No Orchids for Miss Blandish*, whose basic plot (a young heiress is kidnapped and ultimately appears to fall for her abductor) belied an almost pornographic violence:

> . . . the subject-matter is much more sordid and brutal than this suggests. The book contains eight full-dress murders, an unassessable number of casual killings and woundings, an exhumation (with a careful reminder of the stench), the flogging of Miss Blandish, the torture of another women with redhot cigarette ends, a strip-tease act, a third-degree scene of unheard-of cruelty, and much else of the same kind . . . it takes for granted the most complete corruption and self-seeking as the norm of human behaviour.[1]

Little more than a year later, in February 1946, Orwell revisited the world of killing in 'The Decline of the English Murder', though this time contrasting not fictional but real murders of earlier eras with those of today. His essential point was much the same: that the modern murderer was a far more depraved beast than his or her predecessors. The article opens with the cosy image of a man settling down with his pipe and cup of tea after his Sunday lunch to read a nice juicy murder story in the *News of the World*. Having considered various Victorian and early-twentieth-century murders (and suggesting that there was a Golden Age of English murder that extended from 1850 to 1925), it offers the following formula for the 'perfect' murder (at least, from a *News of the World* reader's point of view):

> The murderer should be a little man of the professional class – a dentist or a solicitor, say – living an intensely respectable life somewhere in the suburbs, and preferably in a semi-detached house, which will allow neighbours to hear suspicious sounds through the wall . . . He should go astray through cherishing a passion for his secretary or the wife of a rival professional man, and should bring himself to the point of murder after

long and terrible wrestles with his conscience. Having decided on murder, he should plan it all with the utmost cunning, and only slip up over some tiny, unforeseeable detail. The means chosen should, of course, be poison.

The article then introduces a modern, real-life murder of extreme brutality: the 'Cleft Chin Murder' of October 1944. The two killers involved – Elizabeth Jones, an ex-waitress with ambitions to be a stripper or a gangster's moll, and Karl Hulten, an American army deserter who claimed to be an officer and to have formerly been a gangster – could not have been more different from the 'little man of the professional class' who (according to Orwell) had once garnered the headlines. They had only just met and so barely knew one another when they embarked on a spree of astonishingly random violence, stealing a lorry and running down a nurse cycling along a country road in order to rob her; picking up a hitchhiker, assaulting her, robbing her and then throwing her into a river; and finally murdering a cleft-chinned taxi driver, George Edward Heath, taking the £8 they found on him, and then spending the money at the greyhound races. Hulten was hanged in March 1945; Jones was sentenced to death, but reprieved, and released from prison in 1954.

In Orwell's eyes, Hulten's background was noteworthy. 'Perhaps it is significant', he wrote, 'that the most talked-of English murder of recent years should have been committed by an American and an English [Jones was in fact Welsh] girl who had become partly Americanised.'[2] America, in other words, was the source of a corrosive new culture that was making its impact felt even in the rarefied arenas of fictional and real-life murders. More than that, the Cleft Chin Murder demonstrated how killing that had once at least involved a degree of emotion had become casual and unconcerned. In 'Raffles and Miss Blandish' Orwell complains that the old distinctions between right and wrong that one can sense 'even in a book like Raffles' have been lost, and that No Orchids for Miss Blandish represents a new amoral world of 'cruelty and sexual perversion', a world in which fascism thrives.

The idea that the 'quality' of English murder was somehow in jeopardy was not a new one. In 1869 Leslie (later Sir Leslie) Stephen, former mountaineer, sometime fellow of Trinity Hall, Cambridge, writer and critic, first editor of the *Dictionary of National Biography* – and father of Virginia Woolf – had published an essay entitled 'The Decay of Murder'. Overtly satirical in tone, it argued that standards of murder were dropping and earlier sophistication was giving way to mundane acts of uninspired savagery:

> Murders are not only immoral – an objection to which they have long been liable – but they are becoming simply gross, stupid, and brutal. They are in the style of novelists and painters who are incapable of reproducing the beautiful, and try to stun us by sheer undiluted horrors.

The reason for this, in Stephen's view, was not that British life was becoming infected by the American influence (à la Orwell) but that it was becoming boringly uniform:

> The Utopia of modern reformers would be a country in which every man should be dressed in a regulation suit of the same dingy colour, and his character, like his cloth, be cut to one uniform pattern . . . under these circumstances it is hardly likely to be expected that we should get up good murders.[3]

There is, of course, a very large element of facetiousness here, which harks back to earlier essayists who had written satirical pieces in praise of 'good murders'. Thomas de Quincey was one such. His piece 'On Murder Considered as One of the Fine Arts', published in 1827 in the fashionable *Blackwood's Magazine*, envisioned the existence of 'The Society of Connoisseurs in Murder' who 'profess to be curious as to homicide: amateurs and dilettanti in the various modes of bloodshed; and, in short, Murder-Fanciers'. De Quincey, in this deeply ironic piece of writing, wanted to see murder refashioned in such a way as to appeal to people of sensibility, not just to newspaper readers avidly reading the latest account of a bloody killing. Thus de

Quincey argued that murder should be regarded as an aesthetic, not a moral issue, conceptualised along the lines by which Aristotle conceptualised tragedy.[4] Stephen's point was perhaps more barbed: society was becoming trivial and coarse. But both these authors posit a distinction between the actuality of murder and some more complex, satirically idealised, version of it.

De Quincey's and Stephen's essays, then, suggest a certain literary lineage for Orwell's two offerings. But Orwell sounded a sharper note. He clearly felt that modern murder – and more particularly the modern depiction of murder – was damaging society, that it was corrosive: he describes reading *No Orchids for Miss Blandish* as the equivalent of taking 'a header into the cesspool'.[5] One could argue that his two contributions mark the point at which concerns about the depiction of violence became a more or less constant feature of debates about the state of English society and its future direction.

II

People had, of course, long written about – and revelled in – murder, from the authors of broadside ballads to the hack writers of murder pamphlets to the dramatists who transformed real-life crimes into popular plays. At the more literary end of things, murders were a staple of the journals that were so much a part of cultural life over the first two-thirds of the nineteenth century, and such a common feature of mid-Victorian novels that they became something of a target for satire. Thus in *Thornycroft Hall*, a now largely forgotten novel by Emma Jane Worboise, published in 1864, Miss Arabella Ward gleefully records the mounting body count of the novel she is currently reading:

'There are no less than five murders in this book,' said Arabella, taking up the volume before her. 'Five murders, very interesting cases of slow poisoning, and two elopements, and several faithless wives; and everybody gets into a predicament – into the most awful situations you can conceive; but the hero and the heroine – they are both of them poisoned, only they get well again somehow – are married at last, and have a castle left them, and ever so much a year. Oh, it is so exciting and beautifully written!'[6]

Cousin Ellen is not impressed ('. . . such stories are unfit for our reading. What has a young girl to do with such shameful wickedness?') but her real-life novel-reading contemporaries would not have agreed. And, of course, by the time *Thornycroft Hall* was published they would also have been able to indulge themselves in reading the endless sequence of murder cases, trials and executions described in Victorian England's burgeoning popular press.

From time to time, worries were expressed about the possible social impact of a diet of fictional violence. In the 1830s, for example, at the peak of the craze for 'Newgate Novels' – fictionalised accounts of notorious crimes and criminals – some argued that they were having a pernicious effect on their readers, and encouraging what today would be called copy-cat crimes.[7] But violence nevertheless continued to be depicted between the covers of books, while on-stage it could be remarkably graphic: one thinks, for example, of the blinding of Gloucester, or the severing of Alonzo's finger in Middleton and Rowley's *The Changeling,* or the use of bags full of sheep's guts to lend authenticity to on-stage disembowelments, or the stage re-enactments of one of the most notorious of all nineteenth-century killings, that of Maria Marten murdered by her lover, William Corder, who then buried Maria's corpse in the 'Red Barn' in Polstead, Suffolk, in 1827. (Corder was later hanged; it's been suggested that the anonymously written *Maria Marten, or the Murder in the Red Barn* was the most regularly performed of all Victorian dramas.)

As a rule, the authorities let such gruesome representations of violent and criminal acts go unchecked – the Lord Chamberlain had the power after 1737 to ban plays at will, but rarely exercised his authority to stop performances on the grounds of violence. That said, there were exceptions. In the wake of the murder of Lord William Russell by his valet in 1840, for example (see page 401), and newspaper reports that his killer had been influenced by a visit to see a play about the notorious Georgian criminal Jack Sheppard (based on William Harrison Ainsworth's eponymous Newgate Novel), further performances were banned.[8] It was a foreshadowing of the media-fed moral panics that were to become so prevalent a century later, and not for the first or last time the authorities took firm action on the basis of weak evidence (the valet denied that the play had had any impact on him).

Once cinema arrived, though, attitudes hardened. Perhaps its very novelty served to invite closer inspection and criticism. Perhaps its immediacy, even in its comparatively crude early form, served to disturb some of its first viewers. At any rate, concerns about the new medium started to be expressed almost from the start. Short films from the 1890s that depicted prize fights drew disapproving comments from contemporary moralists. *The Times* complained in a piece entitled 'Cinematography and the Child', published on 12 April 1913, that on-screen violence could adversely affect younger viewers:

> Before these children's greedy eyes with heartless indiscrimination horrors unimaginable are . . . presented night after night . . . terrific massacres, horrible catastrophes, motor-car smashes, public hangings, lynchings . . . All who care for the moral well-being and education of the child will set their faces like flint against this form of excitement.

Concern was followed, in time, by censorship. The Cinematograph Act of 1909, whose original intention was to tighten up safety in cinemas (notoriously prone to fire thanks to the industry's use of cellulose nitrate for its film stock), was the first stepping stone along the way, because it gave local authorities the power to grant cinema licences: once they had established via the 1911 case of the London County Council v. the Bermondsey Bioscope Co. that it was legal to refuse a licence on grounds other than those of safety (in this case, the issue was Sunday opening), the path was left clear for local disapproval of a particular film to turn into a ban. And soon a suitably controversial test case came along. The 1912 American film *From the Manger to the Cross*, a retelling of Christ's life filmed in the Holy Land and much praised by Christian and Jewish leaders, might have seemed inoffensive to most but the *Daily Mail* rounded on it, denounced it as blasphemous, and so stirred up a media storm.

The film industry's response to the furore was to set up a self-policing organisation: the British Board of Film Censors. Established in the same year as *From the Manger to the Cross*, to the general approval of government and local authorities alike, its early focus was not so much on blasphemy as on issues of general morality (the depiction of sex, prostitution, drunkenness) and politically sensitive issues (during the First World War, for instance, there was a ban on the realistic depiction of battle, on showing anything that might hold the 'King's uniform' up to ridicule, and on material that might prove helpful to the enemy. Concerns about violence were secondary, though gruesome murders, executions, strangulations and the effects of vitriol-throwing were all listed as things to be avoided.[9] The board had two weapons at its disposal: it could determine at what age someone should be allowed to see a film (initially there were two certificates: U and A), and it could also insist on cuts being made as a condition for a certificate being granted: when, for example, *Frankenstein* (1931) was shown in Britain for the first time, a scene showing the monster drowning a small girl was excised (this was not sufficient for the London County Council or the Manchester City Council, who banned children from seeing the film at all; the result was the introduction in 1932 of an H (horror) certificate).[10]

Frankenstein apart, fears about on-screen violence were not common before the Second World War. After 1945, however, they became ever-more frequent. General warnings about screen violence were being made to film-makers by the Board by the late 1940s, and by the middle of the following decade worries about the supposed lawlessness of contemporary youth were resulting in cuts and an X-certificate rating (introduced in 1951) for two 1955 films: *Rebel Without a Cause*, a James Dean vehicle about a troubled adolescent, and *Blackboard Jungle*, which was set in a tough inner-city school. When it came to László Benedek's 1953 film *The Wild One* ('a spectacle of unbridled hooliganism'), the BBFC couldn't even bring itself to grant the film a rating, a state of affairs that persisted for thirteen years, although some local councils did allow screenings to take place. In the first seven months of 1955, in fact, 44 per cent of cuts made at the behest of the Board involved the removal of violent sequences.[11] Defending their actions, those in authority pointed to the riots that accompanied some showings of *Rock Around the Clock* and the disruption caused by gangs of teddy boys during screenings of *Blackboard Jungle* as evidence of a clear causal link between on-screen and off-screen violence.

Of course, as official and media worries of the time suggest, the concerns voiced about film violence were as much, if not more, to do with wider concerns about the state of society and the perceived shortcomings of contemporary youth as they were with what was actually up on the screen. Certainly today most cinema goers would regard a film such as *Rebel Without a Cause* as pretty tame stuff. The same is not true, though, of the more graphic films that started to be made in the 1960s, as film-makers began to push at the boundaries of what could and could not be shown. The scene in *Bonnie and Clyde* (1967) where Depression-era outlaw Bonnie, played by Faye Dunaway, jerks in spasms as bullets tear into her, retains its power to shock. Sam Peckinpah's *The Wild Bunch* (1969) took violence in Westerns to a new level, with its lingering slow-motion sequences and final incredibly bloody shoot-out. Realistic violence had come to stay at the movies, culminating in what the film scholars describe as 'The New Violence' of the 1990s and, in particular, of such Quentin Tarantino films as *Reservoir Dogs* (1992) and *Pulp Fiction* (1994). By now, exploding heads, maimings, severed limbs and bloody injuries were part of the stock-in-trade of the film-maker. Violence had become the territory of the special effects department.

III

The film that perhaps best exemplifies the suggestive power of on-screen violence, and that also points up the sensory gulf that exists between the experience of reading about brutality and seeing it portrayed in a film, is Stanley Kubrick's highly controversial *A Clockwork Orange* (1971). Based on Anthony Burgess's dystopic novel of 1962, set in the London of the (then) near future, it centres on Alex, a psychopathic but intelligent young delinquent who is head of a gang of 'droogs': Pete, Georgie and Dim.[12] The opening scene shows them drinking drug-laced milk in the Korova Milk Bar. They then embark on a night of violence: savagely beating an elderly vagrant they come across, battling with a rival gang, headed by Billyboy, who are about to gang-rape a young woman they have stripped, and driving out into the country in a stolen car where they break into the house of a writer named Frank Alexander, beat him and leave him permanently crippled after forcing him to watch while they rape his wife.

The next day Alex confronts a rebellious mood among his droogs, who feel that their criminal activities are insufficiently remunerative; at first he adopts a diplomatic approach, then he beats them up. That night they attack the house of the artistically inclined owner of a health farm. Alex, who enters the house alone, inflicts what prove to be fatal injuries on the woman with one of her phallic sculptures. Hearing police sirens, he tries to escape, but is knocked unconscious by a milk bottle wielded by Dim, and left to be captured by the police. He is sentenced to fourteen years' imprisonment, but agrees to undergo the Ludovico Technique, a type of drug-laden aversion therapy aimed at 'curing' violent criminals by subjecting them to an endless diet of violent films. Alex is declared 'cured' after a demonstration staged by the Minister of the Interior in which he proves incapable of retaliating when struck and assaulted by a man, is released, undergoes various vicissitudes, and as the film closes imagines himself having sex with a woman in front of a crowd, a voice-over commenting ironically: 'I was cured, all right!'

The film differs in various ways from the novel (not least in the fact that it ignores Burgess's final, optimistic chapter – which was included in the UK edition but omitted in the US – and that it under-plays the lapsed Catholic Burgess's examination of free will; Burgess was to fall out with Kubrick and become one of the film's sternest critics). It is also, arguably, softer in some ways. In the novel the girl who is about to be raped by Billyboy's gang is ten; in the film she is rather older. In the novel, Alex slays a defenceless eighty-year-old woman; in the film his victim is middle-aged, played by Miriam Kar-lin, then in her late-forties. In the novel, Alex drugs and then rapes two ten-year-old girls he picks up in a record store. In the film they are teenagers, and the sex (which is speeded up and performed to the William Tell Overture) appears to be consensual.

Yet novel and film had very different critical receptions. The reviews for the novel were generally respectful, praising the inven-tiveness of the language (the Droogs speak their own form of Russian-influenced English) even if some criticised the demands the book made on the reader and expressed uneasiness about its violent nature. The film, by contrast, was widely condemned – by the Con-ference of Catholic Bishops' Office for Film and Broadcasting in the United States, for example, and by many commentators in the UK (where it was released with an X-certificate). An article in the *Sun* dated 1 June 1972 argued that it was 'unparalleled in its concentrated parade of violence, viciousness and cruelty'.

Perhaps the scene that best exemplifies the visceral power film can have is the one in which Alex beats up Mr Alexander and then proceeds to attack Mrs Alexander while singing the Gene Kelly hit 'Singin' in the Rain'. The song is not mentioned in the original text, but somehow its employment in the film adds a sense of chill to a moment of ultra-violence. It is perhaps this power that serves to explain how, while the novel went largely ignored by the wider public, the film swiftly became mired in controversy. People objected to the fact that it appeared to revel in its use of violence, even to promote it. Media hysteria reached boiling point when it emerged that a sixteen-year-old youth from Oxfordshire named James Palmer had beaten a tramp to death after his friends had described the film to him (it should be emphasised that Palmer had not himself seen it). Then in November 1973 it was reported that a Dutch tourist had been raped by a gang singing 'Singin' in the Rain'. By then Kubrick, disenchanted by the controversy and hostility the film had aroused in Britain, had withdrawn it.

IV

Television in the 1960s and 1970s followed a far more cautious path.[13] The idea of a 9 p.m. watershed, separating programmes suitable for all from those appropriate only for adults, was introduced in 1964, and, of course, was not dissimilar in intention to the system of film classification that had been operating (with modification) for decades, but a watershed that applied in the home was inevitably a far more porous affair than a rating that applied in a cinema and therefore easily open to both abuse and criticism. The 1979 BBC booklet *The Portrayal of Violence in Television Programmes*, which covered drama, documentaries, news broadcasts and programmes for children and teenagers (thought to be especially vulnerable to the corrupting influence of the media), understandably adopted a careful middle path when suggesting guidelines for the presentation of violence. Pointing out that aggression is a part of life, and that any television service that attempts to reflect and interpret reality (whether through a dramatic work or through a news broadcast) cannot therefore exclude it altogether from its programmes, it nevertheless urged caution, arguing that an overly permissive approach could bring accusations that television was contributing to society's violence, not merely recording it. One recent, blood-thirsty broadcast it was particularly concerned about, in terms of correct scheduling, was John Webster's 1612 play *The Duchess of Malfi* – an unlikely vehicle, one would have thought, for encouraging twentieth-century television viewers to violence.

Yet even though films and television were regulated and self-censoring, there were many people, from the 1960s onwards, who felt that the goalposts were moving too far and too fast; that what was now perceived as 'acceptable' was out of kilter with what was right. Some, from traditional Anglican or evangelical backgrounds, argued that greater explicitness in sex and violence flew in the face of Christian teaching. Others – generally on the political right – felt uneasy about the more relaxed social values they were starting to witness, particularly among the young. And some – notably the campaigner Mary Whitehouse – combined religious and political-cum-social concerns.[14] In the 1940s Whitehouse (1910–2001) and her husband Ernest were members of the Oxford Group, an evangelical movement, which in 1938 renamed itself Moral Re-Armament (MRA). But MRA also had a strongly politically conservative aspect to it: its founder Frank Buchman was known to have made admiring remarks about Hitler, whom he regarded as a bulwark against the communist Anti-Christ.[15]

While working as a teacher, Whitehouse was disturbed to discover that some of the girls in her class had seen a BBC current affairs programme, *Meeting Point*, in which pre-marital sex had been discussed in largely non-judgemental terms. To her mind, such a stance not only symbolised Britain's moral decline but contributed to it. Her worries about the effects of what she regarded as the corrupting influence of television – and, more generally, of contemporary society – seem to have coalesced in 1963, and she began badgering highly placed staff in the BBC and ITV with her concerns. When, in January 1964, she learned that the BBC's charter was to be renewed unaltered by Parliament, she launched the 'Clean-Up TV' campaign, which led directly to the foundation of the National Viewers' and Listeners' Association (NVLA) in 1965.

Whitehouse's – and the NVLA's – campaigns were conducted on

a pretty broad front. They condemned the discussion or portrayal of sex. They disapproved of swearing. They were uneasy about depictions of war and suffering. In a speech she made at the height of the Vietnam War in 1970, Whitehouse, rather bizarrely and certainly paradoxically, argued that the screening of war footage would create, not nations of warmongers, as the logic of her usual line of argument would have suggested, but nations of pacifists who would leave the democracies in which they lived at risk. And yet Mary Whitehouse and her supporters hated violence. Her 1970 speech (given at a Royal College of Nursing-hosted conference on 'The Violent Society') set out their objections:

> When the movement which I represent was founded in 1963, we said quite simply that the constant presentation of violence on our television screens would significantly promote and help to create a violent society. We were ridiculed for our pains, called cranks and accused of being squeamish. We sensed then, and believe strongly now, that the screening of violence, horror, shock and obscenity into the home, where the viewer sits comfortably, detached, in his easy chair, where he can switch off mentally or physically whenever he wishes, can have nothing but a destructive effect upon our sensitivities and our society. So do the real horrors of war, death, and poverty become no more than conversation pieces, fantasy worlds, increasingly accepted as no more than entertainment.[16]

Television, then, to Whitehouse's way of seeing things, was not only corrupting people, it was also de-sensitising them (though her speech contains a tacit acceptance that people could switch off their televisions if they didn't like what they were seeing). Even a fairly mild children's programme like *Doctor Who* could pose a risk to its viewers (Whitehouse described the 1975 serial *Genesis of the Daleks* as 'teatime brutality for tots'). And as for 'video nasties' (it's been suggested that she coined the term in 1982), these were wholly beyond the pale: films such as *Death Trap* and *Driller Killer*, she argued, offered not only appalling levels of gratuitous violence, but, because children could very easily get hold of any copies that happened to be lying about the house, were a danger even to the audience for whom they were very definitely not intended. (The distributors of both films were subsequently prosecuted.)[17]

A measure of just how strongly those sympathetic to Mary Whitehouse's views felt is demonstrated by a *Daily Mail* editorial of 30 June 1983 entitled 'Rape of Our Children's Minds'.[18] Taking the connection between video nasties and moral corruption as read, it argued that unless the government took adequate steps to prevent it, the nation would be submerged in a 'sea of filth'. Children would 'buy sadism from the video-pusher as easily – and almost as cheaply – as they can buy fruit gums from the sweetie shop'. The result? Women would be 'savaged and defiled by youths weaned on a diet of rape videos'. It contrasted 'these perverted horrors' and 'a creed so perverted that it spawned such horrors in awful truth' with a Golden Age when 'children went off with their Saturday sixpence to see Roy Rogers and Trigger'. And looking back two centuries and more to the filth and squalor of Hogarth's London, it asked, 'Are the video shops of today any less squalid or corrupting than the gin alleys of two centuries ago?'

Others stepped in, too. The devoutly Christian Chief Constable of the Greater Manchester Police, James Anderton, for example, increased the number of raids on video shops. (On one occasion his men confiscated the Dolly Parton musical *The Best Little Whorehouse in Texas*, under the misapprehension that it was pornographic.) It became one of those issues to which the media and moral commentators endlessly returned, long after there was anything new to say. Perhaps one shouldn't be too surprised therefore that in 1982 the distributors of the Italian-made *Cannibal Holocaust* should have written anonymously to Mary Whitehouse to complain about the film, in the hopes of winning some publicity and so boosting sales.

Just how much influence Whitehouse and her supporters had on film and television programme-making in general is debatable. Most people working in the two industries professed to regard her as an irrelevant nuisance, though one detects a degree of anxiety in some of their reactions, and there were certainly cases where television programmes were re-edited following one of her interventions. But the attacks that she and those sympathetic to her views made on video nasties came at a politically opportune moment. In 1983 there was an election; the Conservatives were keen to portray themselves as the party of law, order and decency, and their manifesto accordingly contained a proposal to deal with violent and obscene videos. There was therefore, for once, a legislative outcome to a media and public scare: the Video Recordings Act 1984. This renamed the British Board of Film Censors as the British Board of Film Classification, and made the Board responsible for the vetting of videos. Supplying unclassified videos became a criminal offence, as did supplying videos with a 15- or 18-certificate to under-aged persons. A number of low-budget sex and violence flicks were denied certificates, as were such mainstream films as *The Exorcist* and *Straw Dogs* – all therefore had to be removed from video-store shelves. As the video nasty scare subsided, though, so did censorship, and an attempt to pass further legislation to tighten the Board's guidelines failed.

V

Those who supported the Video Recordings Act certainly and passionately believed that the depiction of violence served to promote it.[19] Jerry Hayes, then the newly elected MP for Harlow as well as a barrister, took a pretty robust view on the BBC Radio 4 programme *You, the Jury*. Dismissing the idea of a 'cosy intellectual argument' on the subject, he suggested that the theories of 'academics' who light-heartedly referred to 'various conflicts as to the evidence' were rather less convincing than the critical views of a Salvation Army representative, who 'didn't give you fanciful intellectual argument. He gave you hard evidence of what is happening on the streets and in the homes'.[20] In other words, Hayes – like many others – argued that inconclusive or ambiguous studies by researchers counted for nothing when set against the unequivocal testimony of those on the front line of social care, who certainly feared that fictional violence inspired real-life violence. Or as a correspondent to *The Times* of 18 April 1969 put it: 'Frankly I am a little tired of being told we must put up with all shows of violence till the sociologists or psychiatrists can measure the effects.'

The problem, though, was that the evidence *was* ambiguous. Take, for example, the findings of the Parliamentary Group Video Enquiry, published as *Video Violence and Children* (Part 1, based solely on an analysis of the data collected by the Enquiry, was released just in time to have a bearing on the Video Recordings Act; Part 2 followed in March 1984). At one level – and on one key issue – the report seemed absolutely clear: a significant proportion of 6–16 year olds surveyed, it concluded, had seen at least one video nasty (the figure recorded in Part 1 of the report was just over 40 per cent of children and teenagers; Part 2 suggested that it was 45.5 per cent). It was a shockingly high figure, and one that viewed in isolation seemed fully to justify parliamentary legislation. The idea that, as the press reported it, 'half' (admittedly a slight exaggeration of the report's figure) of all British children were sitting down and watching films that were wholly inappropriate for them, was deeply disturbing.

There was, however, a problem with this much-reported figure, as Graham Murdock, a research fellow at the University of Leicester and author of a book on mass media and secondary schoolchildren, pointed out. The methodology was questionable. The figures had been based on a questionnaire handed out in schools to randomly selected classes (monitored by teachers) that asked a series of introductory questions – i.e. what were the children's favourite pop stars, films and videos? Did they have a video at home? Had they seen a video at somebody else's house? – and then asked them to look at a list of 113 video titles, among them 34 'nasties' (none of which was highlighted on the questionnaire). Children were instructed to grade any video they had seen as 'great', 'just all right', or 'awful'. So far, so good. But as Murdock points out (and as a few moments' reflection makes obvious) total accuracy is impossible in any self-completion study of this type. People forget things, they get bored, they misunderstand what they are meant to do, they fill in the form carelessly or even randomly. This is especially true of children, who also have a tendency to want to live up to what they perceive to be adults' expectations of them. And when it came to video nasties, while children would certainly remember characters and incidents, they might, after the event, have problems in distinguishing between, say, *Cannibal Apocalypse, Cannibal Holocaust, Cannibal Terror, Cannibal Ferox* and *Cannibal Man* (all titles that were included in the questionnaire).

What was more, Murdock discovered, none of the usual controls or methods of cross-checking had been built into the analysis of the questionnaires. He cited an exercise carried out by two other academics, Guy Cumberbatch and Paul Bates, who handed out the same questionnaire to five classes of 11 year olds, but with a number of fake titles sprinkled among the genuine ones: *Vampire Holocaust, Zombies from Beyond Space,* and so on. Sixty-eight per cent of the respondents claimed to have seen these non-existent videos. One of the members of the enquiry, Brian Brown, then Head of a Television Research Unit at Oxford Polytechnic, worried that it had been carried out in too much of a rush and with too few controls. He later recalled that after the first part of the report was released, he happened to bump into Raymond Johnston, Parliamentary Research Director of Christian Action Research and Education (CARE), a right-wing Christian organisation that had evolved from the Festival of Light. Brown had queried what he felt to be Johnston's rather simplistic and unsupported views on the video nasty issue at an initial meeting of the enquiry. Now he found himself being shaken by the hand and congratulated on the report: 'This is exactly what *we* wanted,' Johnston informed him.[21]

If researchers couldn't even be sure which films a group of 11 year olds had seen, what chance was there, one wonders, of answering the deeper questions that prompted the enquiry?

VI

The fears of those who opposed video nasties then – and who are concerned about the effects of the internet, violent films, television, and videos now – fall into various categories.[22] First of all, there is the worry that fictional violence inspires imitation: that if we watch violence on the screen, we will ourselves become more violent. This occurs on a spectrum that ranges from aggressive behaviour at one end to copy-cat crimes at the other. Secondly, there is the argument that watching violent material de-sensitises us; we become inured to violence in real life, both individually and collectively as a society. Thirdly, there is the suggestion that if we view violence we will become more fearful, less willing to venture out of our homes, and, in extreme cases, prey to panic attacks or mental problems. A more neutral theory – that watching violence purges us of our violent impulses in a moment of catharsis – can be immediately dismissed, since there is absolutely no evidence to support it. If there were, then presumably hungry people would feel less so after watching a film like *Babette's Feast*.

Of all these lines of argument it is perhaps the first – that fictional violence inspires real-life violence – that has proved to be both the most powerfully emotive and the most controversial. Various attempts have been made to test it. One of the earliest and most interesting was that conducted by Albert Bandura, a Canadian psychologist who has spent his professional career at Stanford University, and who developed social learning theory, which argues that the foundation of the learning process is to imitate behaviour witnessed in others. In 1961 he constructed an experiment with three groups of 3–6 year olds (all of whom had already been tested for innate violent tendencies, to ensure that each group contained a balanced sample). The first group was shown a film of an adult behaving aggressively to a toy known as a Bobo doll. The second group was also shown a film of the Bobo doll, but this time the adult involved did not act in an aggressive manner. And the third, control group were not shown a Bobo doll at all.

The children were then led into a playroom that contained a number of toys that included a Bobo doll and their behaviour was monitored. What very quickly became clear was that children who had seen the violent Bobo doll film tended to be far more aggressive to others than those who hadn't – a finding confirmed by other experiments that have exposed children from various age groups to violent cartoons or children's TV programmes. (Boys, incidentally, tended to be more physically aggressive than girls, but when it came to verbal aggression the two sexes behaved in more or less the same way.) The Bobo doll experiment certainly suggests that witnessing violence encourages imitation, though, of course, it doesn't show whether this tendency to imitate is a long-term result (and, of course, it is predicated on the challengeable assumption that the behaviour of nursery-school-age children is the same as that of the population at large).

Other experiments have taken the form of correlation exercises whereby respondents have been asked to list their favourite TV programmes, which have then been analysed for violent content, and correlated with the respondents' self-reported checklist of graded aggressive or violent activities, ranging from fighting at school to being arrested for violent offences. As with Bandura's experiment it is possible to trace a link in the findings of these exercises between watching violence on TV and behaving violently. But as with Bandura's experiment, the results are not unambiguously clear. Leaving aside the question of how truthful or accurate individual respondents might be, there is the problem of establishing causality: do those who enjoy watching violence on television become more prone to acting aggressively in real life, or are those who act aggressively in real life more likely to enjoy watching violence on television?

A similar question about causality arises among those longer-term surveys known as longitudinal studies. A US study that looked at the same group of people when they were aged 8, 19 and 30, for example, certainly showed that those men who had a taste for violent TV at the age of 8 were about twice as likely to have a serious criminal conviction at the age of 30 than those who as children had preferred more gentle television. But it's hard to know whether they were innately violent and thus drawn to violent television (and so later to crime), or whether it was the violent television that sparked their later behaviour. The same researchers extended their field of enquiry to Australia, Finland, Poland and Israel, and discovered, with local variations of course, a fundamentally similar pattern which showed no, or at best very little, connection between watching TV violence and violent behaviour in children. Even those studies which do posit mild connections have had their findings challenged, with critics pointing out that the levels of aggressive behaviour connected to television are invariably very low in absolute terms. More recent research has indicated, possibly because of an acceptance of greater female assertiveness in society, that patterns of behaviour among girls and women are starting to resemble those among boys and men.[23]

To add an extra level of complexity to the whole debate, we have to ask ourselves what precisely constitutes TV violence and whether there is a qualitative difference between its different manifestations. Surely, for example, the experience of seeing a news broadcast that includes footage of war, or of the aftermath of a battle or a massacre, or reports of a murder, is different from that of watching a drama in which any aggression may, at one level, be less troubling because it's fictional, but at another level has all the uncomfortably personal impact that goes with story-telling? And what about children's cartoons such as *Tom and Jerry*, which are, from start to finish, astonishingly violent? Then there's the issue of us, the viewers. Too many of the public pronouncements made about the effects of violence seem to assume that we are an undifferentiated mass who lack critical discernment. The reality is, of course, very different. Viewers are divided one from another by class, sex, age and race, and all of these variables come into play when we watch violence on the TV, at the cinema, or on a video or DVD, while all of us also draw on our personal experiences and attitudes, including those pertaining to violence, as we watch.

The study *Women Viewing Violence* illustrates the point compellingly. Drawing on a study of fourteen viewing groups of English and Scottish women, that included middle- and working-class women, black and Asian women as well as white, and women who had and who had not experienced violence, its findings showed just how much responses to particular programmes were shaped by individual circumstances.[24] Thus, for example, the drama *Closing Ranks*, whose central character was a corrupt and violent policeman who abused his wife, was regarded as being principally about domestic violence by 45 per cent of the women who had themselves experienced domestic violence, and as being about police corruption by 80 per cent of those who had not. A number of middle-class viewers expressed dismay that the police could be portrayed so negatively. There were different reactions, too, to a screening of *The Accused*.

This much-acclaimed 1988 Hollywood film explores the aftermath of an appalling gang rape of a young woman in a bar crowded with men, and considers the extent to which the victim (played by Jodie Foster), who was wearing a short skirt, dancing sexily, indulging in sexual banter and drinking quite heavily before she was attacked, could be said to have 'asked for it'. Virtually all the women who saw it thought it was a realistic treatment of rape and were sympathetic to the victim. But they disagreed about whether it should have been shown on television. One of their number, a rape counsellor, went so far as to argue that it should not have been given a general cinematic release, though she did feel that it would have made a good training film for her unit.

The debate about screened violence continues to rumble on, and has been given new impetus in recent years by the rise of computer games. Many of these are, it has to be admitted, very graphic and brutal indeed. The *Grand Theft Auto* series, for example, allows players to kill opponents at will, to torture a suspected terrorist, have sex with prostitutes (offscreen), rob them (onscreen) and grope lap dancers. It also makes constant use of obscene language.[25] It's not surprising therefore that media pundits have rushed to print with the same objections as their predecessors twenty or thirty years earlier. Boris Johnson, for example, complained in a *Daily Telegraph* comment piece in 2006:

> We get on with our hedonistic 21st-century lives while in some other room the nippers are bleeping and zapping in speechless rapture, their passive faces washed in explosions and gore. They sit for so long that their souls seem to have been sucked down the cathode ray tube.
>
> They become like blinking lizards, motionless, absorbed, only the twitching of their hands showing they are still conscious. These machines teach them nothing. They stimulate no ratiocination, discovery or feat of memory – though some of them may cunningly pretend to be educational.[26]

Media hyperbole has, inevitably, been accompanied from time to time by media panic. In 2004 it was widely reported that a 17-year-old youth, Warren Leblanc, had killed 14-year-old Stefan Pakeerah with a claw hammer in a Leicester car park in apparent imitation of a killing technique used in the violent computer game *Manhunt* (a game that had, incidentally, been banned in New Zealand). What followed was a media rerun of the fury and editorialising that accompanied the aftermath of the release of *A Clockwork Orange*. It was only later it emerged that it was the victim, not the murderer, who was the *Manhunt* fan, and that the motive for the killing was actually robbery.[27]

As with film and television, the jury is out on the question of whether violent video and computer games affect everyday behaviour. Exhaustive research in the US, some of it harking back to Banduras's approach, has proved inconclusive. The one unequivocal finding – which confirms classic gender stereotypes – is that boys are fonder of the games than girls. British and Scandinavian research, which has tended to focus on interviews with gaming fans, has been similarly unrevelatory. The lack of a smoking gun (as it were) does suggest, however, that, while we should be cautious about what we allow young children to watch, we should also not worry overmuch about the popularity of virtual violence.[28] One is left concluding that the vast majority of children and adolescents have a clear sense of the difference between fantasy and real life: they enjoy all a computer game can offer them, but once they switch it off they know they are back in the real world where everyday rules of conduct apply. They are not passive receptacles waiting to be filled with thoughts of violence, but rather active participants, discerning about what precisely it is that they see in front of them. They are in control of the media; the media does not control them. One can understand and sympathise with parental concerns about the possible effects of computer games on their children. One suspects, though, that computer games are more harmful to the family budget than to the family's mental welfare.

Looking at the wider world of children's games, the 'Lion and Lamb' Project, based in the United States, has argued that violent toys promote violence and aggression as a means of settling disputes, that they make violence seem fun or 'cool', that they encourage aggressive competition, and that they create a world in which there are 'enemies' who must be destroyed.[29] It's an entirely understandable line of argument, and it's not therefore surprising that many parents refuse to buy such toys for their children, and that they are banned from many playgroups, nurseries and infant schools. Yet once again academic investigation has failed to find a causal link. Research conducted among British, Italian and German children has demonstrated that, as with computer games, children normally have a very clear concept of the boundaries that exist between play and real life: one researcher pointed out that children themselves, when asked, were adamant that playing with war toys did not make them aggressive, and understandably concluded: 'and aren't they the ones who should know?'[30]

Peter K. Smith, author of another survey, concluded that, 'while respecting their right to do so, I find little to support the extreme anti-war-toy position of some parents who ban any kind of war play in their home'.[31] To add a practical note to that caveat: since even the distinctly unwarlike Lego can be fashioned into a passable model of a gun, it's questionable in any case whether banning war-themed toys automatically means the end of war-themed games and activities.

One counter-argument to concerns about fictional and play violence is perhaps worth citing, not least because it dates back well over a century and a half to the time of the moral panic that surrounded the publication of the Newgate Novels. Seeking to rebut critics of the genre, one of its leading practitioners, Edward George Earle Bulwer-Lytton, 1st Baron Lytton (author of a number of forgotten novels that include *Eugene Aram* and *The Last Days of Pompeii*, and originator of the phrase 'the pen is mightier than the sword'), came up with an intriguing argument. In his 1833 work *England and the English* he wrote:

> The superficial jest against our partiality to a newspaper tale of murder, or our passion for the *spectacle* of the gibbet, proves exactly the reverse of what it asserts. It is the tender who are the most susceptible to the excitation of terror. It is the women who hang with the deepest interest over a tale or a play of gloomy or tragic interest ... If you observe a ballad-vender [*sic*] hawking his wares, it is the bloodiest murders that the women purchase. It is exactly from our unacquaintedness with crime, viz., from the restless and mysterious curiosity it excites, that we feel a dread pleasure in marvelling at its details. This principle will suffice to prove that the avidity with which we purchase accounts of atrocity, is the reverse of a proof of our own cruelty of disposition.[32]

Some would argue this is a not unpersuasive view. At the very least, it's prompted by precisely the same kind of generalised assumption about human behaviour that governs the argument that the depiction of violence leads to violence in real life.

VII

One final cautionary tale is perhaps worth mentioning.

On 19 August 1987 Michael Ryan embarked on a killing spree that left sixteen dead and fifteen injured in the small Berkshire town of Hungerford. His first victim was a woman, whom he gunned down at a local beauty spot. He then got back in his car, stopped at a petrol station (where he unsuccessfully tried to shoot the cashier), went back home, donned military-style gear, packed a bag of survivalist kit, pumped bullets into his car because it wouldn't start, set fire to his house with petrol he had bought for the purpose (three adjacent houses burned down along with his own), shot his pet Labrador, and then went on the rampage. Victims were shot at random; they included his mother who had tried to intercede with him. Finally, he took refuge in his old secondary school. The police tried to persuade him to surrender, but at 6.52 p.m. he committed suicide by shooting himself in the head.[33]

Ryan loved guns. His mother had bought him an air rifle when he was an adolescent, and he had occasionally used it to harass his neighbours' children. Once he was of an age to own guns legally, he acquired a shotgun and licence, and joined two gun clubs. At the time of the killings he owned two shotguns, three pistols, a .30 Underwood M1 carbine and a 7.62 Kalashnikov assault rifle, and his neighbours recalled him endlessly cleaning, stripping and fussing over them. Nobody at the gun clubs seems to have regarded him as in any way odd or unusual. Police checks revealed nothing untoward. It might seem a little surprising to us now that a Berkshire man should feel the need to own a Kalashnikov, but then lots of people in the county at that time owned weapons. Ryan's arsenal didn't mark him out in any way (though as the journalist Julie Burchill commented, it was difficult to imagine the Brixton police of 1987 taking a similarly relaxed view of a young black man in possession of a licensed Kalashnikov).

Michael Ryan was a loner. The general view was that he had been spoiled by his mother, and had become something of a mummy's boy. He was bullied at school, where he did badly, and left without gaining any qualifications. He went on to the Newbury College of Further Education but did badly there as well, eventually dropping out and drifting his way through various unskilled jobs. He made few friends, and so as far as is known had minimal contact with women. Perhaps to offset this he indulged in a complex fantasy life, claiming to have been a paratrooper and to have a fiancée whom circumstances never quite permitted him to marry. He was also a keen reader of survivalist magazines and collected survivalist kit and militaria. The uncharitable would have characterised him in the summer of 1987 as a twenty-seven-year-old loser, five foot six inches tall, possessed of thinning hair, an incipient beer gut and few prospects.

We have no idea why he killed when he did. However, the media swiftly came up with their own theory. Some of the witnesses and survivors of the Hungerford massacre had described Ryan as a 'Rambo'-like figure (although it is difficult to discern any close resemblance between Michael Ryan and Sylvester Stallone). One witness to the killings thought – incorrectly, as it turned out – that Ryan was wearing a Rambo-style bandana on the day he ran amok. Since the Rambo film *First Blood* had been released only a few years before and so was fresh in people's minds, it seemed superficially plausible that he had in some way been influenced by the film. The facts that it wasn't clear whether Ryan had actually been to see it, and that none of the scenes in the film bore any resemblance to his shooting spree, were ignored. The transition from seemingly motiveless killer to clearly film-influenced killer was swiftly achieved.

In the aftermath of a terrible tragedy it is understandable that people should seek an easily comprehensible explanation. That someone should kill simply because they want to seems irrational to most people. But to allow simplistic explanations to hold sway instead is dangerous. Mike Purdy, who was working at the Old Bailey in the era of *A Clockwork Orange*, later recalled how the film's notoriety soon worked its way into the legal process:

> At the Old Bailey we kept seeing people on assault charges who had seen the film and been impelled to go and beat someone up. Most of us who worked in the court thought this was a load of rubbish but unfortunately such cases got a lot of publicity and many judges would impose lesser sentences in these cases. It got to the stage when we referred to these cases as 'Clockwork Orange Defences', and it became almost boring as one after another tried using this excuse.[34]

More worrying than that is the thought that by focussing on at best unproved theories about the connections between fictional and real-life violence, we are distracted from identifying the more direct causes of aggression and brutality.

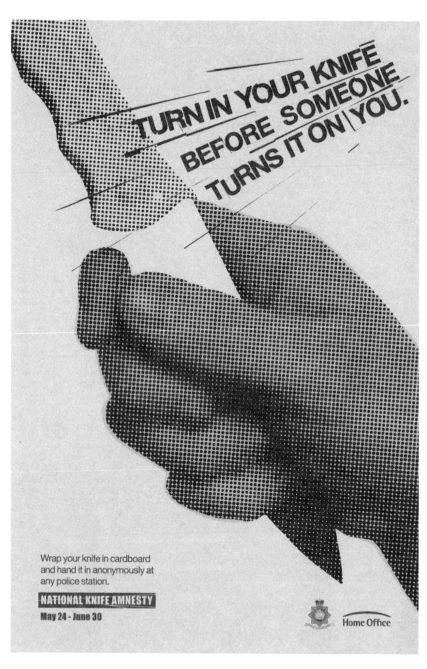

A 2006 poster promoting a knife amnesty. Are levels of violence
falling in contemporary England?

CHAPTER 19

PEAKS AND TROUGHS:
PATTERNS OF VIOLENCE TODAY

———◄►———

I

I've written this book amid daily reminders of violence and violent crime – in newspapers, on radio and television, and in film. Some cases that have impinged on my consciousness earned barely more than a paragraph on a back page of a regional paper. Others briefly became media sensations, their details minutely picked over. A few achieved the status of national scandal, inviting anguished debates about the nature of Britain today and the threats to law and order.

At a local level, for example, I recall how on Sunday, 7 July 2013 in York, the city in which I work, Scott Apps, a 42-year-old homeless man on bail for two unprovoked assaults, created a disturbance during Morning Service in York Minster, and then attacked a steward and a member of the Archbishop of York's staff who tried to restrain him. It was one of those incidents with which history is littered, and might have received little public attention had it not taken place during a Church of England Synod when the proposed ordination of female bishops was being debated (spokesmen were at pains to point out that the incident had no connection with this contentious issue). A few months before this, a 17-year-old girl was attacked outside a McDonald's in central York on a Friday night, and suffered a black eye and facial bruising. Again, the case would probably have attracted little notice but for a singular detail: her attacker, a woman in her early twenties, who was caught on CCTV, had dyed red hair and was covered in green body paint, earning her the moniker 'The Incredible Hulk'.

Other minor incidents in York came and went: a Friday-evening assault by three teenagers on a 19 year old outside a takeaway in Rougier Street; a dispute over a taxi, two days later and in the same area, that culminated in a woman being spat at and hit in the face; an attack a month later on a woman out cycling near York racecourse by a 23-year-old man who, it was alleged, had committed a burglary earlier on the day in question and had to be tasered by the arresting officers when he knocked one of them to the ground; the violent shaking and hospitalisation of a baby; a scattering of sexual assaults; one or two shooting incidents.[1]

Then there were the more serious Yorkshire cases. In May 2013 John Sowden, of no fixed address, was sentenced to a minimum of fifteen years' imprisonment for killing Christopher Rooney in his Mexborough flat. He had apparently befriended Rooney, but had then started to take advantage of him, and had finally broken into his home and subjected him to a brutal assault. Three months later, at Wath-upon-Dearne in South Yorkshire, Peter Redfern, aged 70, strangled his 67-year-old wife, and inflicted fatal head injuries on their 33-year-old daughter. Neighbours were shocked and uncomprehending. Other cases included the killing of a 4 year old in Keighley in January; a fatal domestic confrontation in Whitby in February; the murder in December of a Sheffield factory worker by a colleague who lay in wait for him as he returned home, the two having earlier quarrelled at work.

And then there was a case that made national headlines. On Christmas Eve 2012, 68-year-old Alan Greaves was murdered as he made his way to the parish church of St Saviour's in the High Green area of Sheffield, where he was due to play the organ at Midnight Communion. Greaves was a devoted family man, father of four and grandfather, a pillar of the local community, organist at his church for forty years, and a former social worker. His killers, who had been drinking heavily, were two step-brothers in their early twenties, Jonathan Bowling and Ashley Foster. They had no motive for their actions beyond a desire to pick on someone: apparently they had been stalking the streets looking for a victim, and when they came across Alan Greaves, Jonathan Bowling attacked him with a pickaxe handle. Greaves died in hospital three days later. Bowling was subsequently found guilty of murder and was jailed for life (with a twenty-five-year tariff); Foster, who had turned himself in shortly after the attack and claimed that he had tried to restrain Bowling (who had previous convictions for aggressive and violent behaviour), received a nine-year sentence for manslaughter.

It's not hard to understand why this particular case should have received so much media attention. The murder took place on Christmas Eve. The victim was on his way to church. He was clearly a remarkable and kind individual – the polar opposite of the men who attacked him (according to some witnesses, Bowling and Foster were later heard laughing about what they had done). Both at his funeral service (which was packed with well-wishers) and in later interviews, his wife acted with an extraordinary, quiet dignity and expressed her willingness to forgive her husband's killers. That stark contrast between civilised and barbarous behaviour on the evening before Christmas clearly struck a chord with many.

It's also not hard to comprehend why the murder in London of Drummer Lee Rigby of the Royal Regiment of Fusiliers a few months later on 22 May 2013 should have been one of those cases that not only drew national attention but also provoked national debate. Twenty-five-year-old Rigby, married (though separated) and with a young child, was off duty when he was attacked near the Royal Artillery Barracks by Michael Adebolajo and Michael Adebowale, both in their twenties, both British of Nigerian descent, and both converts to Islam. The two men drove a car at Rigby, knocked him to the ground, and attacked him with knives and a cleaver, apparently trying to behead their victim. In the commission of the murder and subsequently, the men claimed that their actions were a response to the British army's involvement in Iraq and Afghanistan. The brutality of the attack and its very public nature would in itself have drawn public attention, but the two attackers' stated motivation, coming at a time when disquiet about extremism within Islam was already very much a national concern, inevitably triggered off a debate about the 'enemy within': a fear that society was increasingly under threat from a minority of radicalised British Muslims.[2]

II

This brief overview of some of the violent crime that afflicted England in the six-month period from late 2012 to mid 2013 shows what a complex and multi-faceted phenomenon it remains. Many of the crimes committed sit firmly within the domestic sphere, one that, as suggested in earlier chapters, remains a potent breeding ground for violence of all types: child abuse; sexual assault; the battering – even murder – of family members, close relatives and partners. But then there are those crimes – the murder of Alan Greaves being a particularly extreme example – that remind us that although assaults on passers-by and strangers are far, far less common than they were in, say, medieval or Elizabethan times, they nevertheless remain a feature of everyday life. And there are those crimes, such as the murder of Lee Rigby, that have a particularly 'modern' flavour to them, feeding as they do into a broader contemporary debate. Terrorism in England is, of course, nothing new, whether perpetrated by Fenians in the 1880s or by the Angry Brigade and the IRA in the 1970s. But Islamic terrorism carried out on home soil is a recent phenomenon.

Taken altogether this bundle of very different types and levels of violent crime inspires two questions. Is there a core of violence within English society that can never be eliminated? And is it possible that the decline in violence that can be traced, however unevenly, over hundreds of years has now halted? Might it even go into reverse?

III

The overall pattern of crime statistics in the twentieth century was, it has to be said, not particularly encouraging (see Appendix, Table 9).[3] Far from showing a decline, however small or uncertain, the number of crimes reported to the police actually rose at a steady rate over the course of the 1920s, increased more rapidly between the 1930s and the 1950s, and then spiralled upwards during the 1960s. Just over 80,000 were reported in 1901. Six decades later that figure had multiplied tenfold. Of course, the overall population of England and Wales had risen in that period too, but the escalation was nevertheless remarkable. For every crime committed in 1901, 14 were being carried out in the mid-1960s and the crime rate per 100,000 of population had increased ninefold.

When it comes to *violent* crime, however, the figures are rather less alarming. Homicides (murders, manslaughters and infanticides) known to the police stayed low right up until the 1930s, then rose during the war years, but returned to 1930s levels in the 1950s. There was then quite a sharp climb in the 1960s, at least in percentage terms, but the overall numbers involved nevertheless remained quite low – 348 a year on average between 1961 and 1970 compared with annual averages of 310 and 316 for 1951–60 and 1931–40 respectively. (A complicating factor here is the continuing advances made in medical care: by the 1950s victims of violent assault were less likely to succumb to their injuries than had been the case even half a century earlier.)

The numbers of cases of felonious and malicious wounding showed a far steeper rise in the post-war period, but, as with rape, this may well be because people felt more inclined to report such crimes than had once been the case. It could therefore be argued that an increase in the crime figures quite possibly signifies a decrease in the population's tolerance of such behaviour, rather than an increasing propensity to indulge in it.

Evidence from magistrates' courts (see Appendix, Table 10) for the forty-year period following the First World War seems to support the general thesis (though with the usual caveats applied to over-literal interpretation of any set of crime statistics). It can be seen that cases of common assault in England and Wales reached a peak of 25,089 on average per year between 1925 and 1929, but then declined to just over 12,000 a year between 1955 and 1959 – suggesting cases that in the 1920s were regarded as sufficiently minor to be dealt with in the magistrates' court were by the 1950s being regarded as serious enough to be taken before the criminal bench. During the same period, crimes of violence brought before the criminal bench rose from an annual average of 2,954 in 1920–4 to 20,532 in 1955–9 – precisely the sort of mirror image one would expect to see. Of course, one cannot dismiss the more straightforward explanation that more cases were being brought before the criminal bench because a greater number of serious offences were actually being committed. But it seems unlikely. In the same way, it is tempting to view the increasing number of reported assaults on the police (the numbers are fairly static for the first decades of the twentieth century but show a marked rise in the 1950s) as evidence not that more police were being attacked in the post-war years, but that by the 1950s officers were more prepared to launch a prosecution when attacked than their forebears had been.

The overall pattern of murders committed in the twentieth century confirms that general decline in the danger posed by strangers referred to earlier. Of the 741 people murdered in England and Wales between 1957 and 1962, for example, less than a fifth (147) fell victim to someone unknown to them; whereas 396 were killed by relatives or other intimates and 201 were killed by acquaintances (the nature of the relationships in the other 7 cases is unknown). These figures include 132 cases where husbands killed wives, 24 where wives killed husbands, 52 where fathers killed a child, 56 where mothers killed a child, and 47 where men killed a lover. Perhaps because killings by a stranger had become a comparatively rare event by this time, they not only tended to attract considerable public attention when they did happen, but were also liable to be punished more heavily.

Under the terms of the 1957 Homicide Act, which redrew the line between capital and non-capital homicide, killing a relative became a crime that, statistically, was highly likely to attract a non-capital sentence, while killing a stranger was highly likely to result in the death penalty: the 1957–1962 murder statistics I have just touched on show that 53 per cent of the murders over that period involved relatives, but that murders by relatives accounted for 59.5 per cent of 616 non-capital cases and only 22.5 per cent of the 125 capital ones. Interestingly, most of those convicted in capital cases – some 84 per cent of the total – had a history of criminal behaviour (for non-capital cases the figure was 55 per cent).[4] This was a society, then, where not only were murderer and victim likely to be known to each other, but where, if the murderer was a stranger, it was more than likely he or she already had a criminal record.

One other finding, both intriguing and tragic, emerges from this mass of statistics. During that 1957–1962 period some 229 of the 700 people accused of murder went on to commit suicide. It's a phenomenon that's not unknown in earlier generations, but in statistical terms it became more striking during the mid twentieth century – so striking, in fact, that it prompted a detailed study by the psychiatrist D. J. West. He was careful not to over-simplify or generalise. There was nevertheless a discernible pattern to the murder-suicides he reviewed: a disproportionate number involved people who had turned their aggression against members of their own family, especially children, before turning it against themselves. In the year West published his findings, 1965, a third of all murders (as opposed to homicides) in England and Wales ended in the suicide of the killer, an astonishingly high proportion that offers indirect confirmation of the extent to which modern murder in England and Wales is so often a domestic affair as well as offering a hint of the desperation that so often lies at the heart of killing within the family.[5]

It is worth noting that murder followed by suicide is, in statistical terms, far less significant in a country such as the USA, where the murder of strangers is proportionately more common. Of the 741 homicides in England and Wales between 1957 and 1962, 386, or 52 per cent, involved the killing of people related by blood or marriage. In the United States, for the slightly later period 1976–2005, the equivalent figure was 15 per cent. It is not surprising therefore that in the year that a third of English murderers went on to commit suicide – 1967 – just 4 per cent of American murderers did likewise.[6]

IV

As in previous periods, all the statistical evidence suggests that, whatever the broader general trends may have been, levels of violent crime in the twentieth century and first years of the twenty-first fluctuated from decade to decade. The later 1920s and 1930s, for example, seem to have been relatively tranquil. Despite the labour unrest of the 1920s, and the appalling economic impact of the Great Depression, family life seems to have remained relatively stable (not that that precluded violence) and communities relatively cohesive. It would be wrong to describe the period as a golden age, but there were no obvious spikes in violent crime.

The 1960s and 1970s, by contrast, mark the beginning of quite a long period of rising levels of violence. The annual homicide rate rose consistently and continuously. Increases in non-homicidal violence, admittedly more subject to changes in attitude to reporting, were even more marked. Prosecutions of offences that fell into the category of serious wounding or other acts endangering life rose from an annual average of 2,285 in the 1960s to 4,110 in the 1970s, 6,623 in the 1980s, and 13,962 in the 1990s. There was also a measurable increase in the number of violent street robberies from the later 1960s, leading to the popularisation of a term previously more common in the US – mugging – and a general fear that England's cities were no longer safe.[7] The fatal stabbing of 68-year-old Graham Hills near Waterloo Station in 1972 in the course of what the police described as a 'mugging gone wrong', widely reported at the time, was regarded as emblematic of a new threat to civil society.

Specific events contributed to this sense of a society facing an upsurge in violence. The revival of sectarian conflict in Northern Ireland had, by the early 1970s, spilled over to the British mainland. In February 1972, a month after the 'Bloody Sunday' shootings in Londonderry, when British soldiers had opened fire on a civil rights demonstration, killing 13 protesters outright, the IRA bombed an officers' mess in Aldershot, killing 7 people. Two years later, in November 1974, the IRA left bombs in two Birmingham pubs, killing 21 and injuring 182. It was the bloodiest of seven attacks that year, and the IRA campaign was to continue intermittently into the 1990s and beyond.[8]

This was also the period of the Angry Brigade, a group of shadowy extremists who (rather like the far more murderous Baader-Meinhof gang in West Germany) seem to have had their roots in the student unrest of the 1960s – their ideological position, judging from their communiqués, was a mix of anarchism and Marxism. Between 1970 and 1972 they carried out perhaps twenty-five bombings, targeting everything from banks and embassies to the Miss World competition of 1970 (or, more correctly, a BBC outside broadcast van involved in the event), taking in, on the way, the Ford factory at Ilford, a Biba boutique, an army recruiting office on London's Holloway Road, the Post Office Tower, and the headquarters of the Royal Tank Regiment. The group achieved particular notoriety in January 1971 when it bombed the home of Robert Carr, Secretary of State for Employment, following the introduction of new Industrial Relations legislation.[9] The arrest of the core members of the group in August 1971, and the conviction of four of them the following year, largely put an end to the Brigade's significant activity, although there were later incidents.

The previous few years had also seen a rise in violent organised crime. From the late 1950s the Kray twins operated their protection and extortion rackets in London's East End, diversifying into illegal gambling and then taking advantage of the legalisation of gambling in 1961 to move in on casinos and gambling clubs. From their South London base in the early 1960s Charlie and Eddie Richardson ran a criminal syndicate that rivalled that of the Krays. Both gangs were characterised by the astonishing levels of brutality and viciousness they showed to rival gang members and associates deemed to have overstepped the mark. The Richardsons would burn their victims with cigarettes, whip them, pull their teeth out with pliers, remove their toes with bolt cutters, administer electric shocks to their genitalia and nipples – even nail them to the floor. The Krays' reputation for savage violence (Ronnie Kray was a paranoid schizophrenic) had the desired effect of ensuring that few were prepared to stand up to them, let alone testify against them. Only the Richardson gang posed any kind of challenge.

Tension soon arose between the two gangs, culminating in the shooting of an associate of the Krays, Richard Hart, in a club in Catford, and the murder of an associate of the Richardsons, George Cornell, who had described Ronnie Kray, a known homosexual, as 'that fat poof'.[10] The Richardsons were tried and convicted at the Old Bailey in April 1967. Retribution came to the Krays a year later. Nevertheless other lesser-known gangsters continued to operate in London and elsewhere. The period also witnessed a rise in another type of crime – armed robbery – which similarly operated on a gang principle, even if the gangs involved were rather more temporary and fluid in membership than those operating protection rackets.

And then there were those specific violent crimes that sparked public soul-searching. Within months of the abolition of the death penalty in 1965, two high-profile murder cases reawakened the debate about capital punishment: the shooting dead of three policemen in Shepherd's Bush by career criminal Harry Roberts in August 1966, and the murder of five (initially thought to be three) children by Ian Brady and Myra Hindley between July 1963 and October 1965. The latter case – popularly known as the Moors Murders because the corpses of two victims were unearthed on Saddleworth Moor in the South Pennines – understandably also raised more fundamental fears: the fact that all the victims were children, that some had been tortured before being killed (the court was played a tape either Brady or Hindley had made of 10-year-old Lesley Ann Downey screaming), that Brady and Hindley showed no signs of contrition when confronted with irrefutable evidence of what they had done, perhaps especially that a woman should be involved in the murder of children, evoked not only widespread revulsion, but public agonising over what such sadistic killings might say about a possible deep-rooted moral malaise.[11]

It's scarcely surprising, then, given all these high-profile cases, that contemporaries should have been alarmed by the direction in which society seemed to be heading. In December 1965 the *Sun* worried that 'Britain's big cities are being taken over by . . . an engulfing wave of crime.' At the end of 1972 the *Sunday Times* went so far as to say that this had been Britain's 'year' of violence. Many felt that Britain was becoming a 'violent society' – that each new beating or stabbing or shooting that made the headlines indicated a country that had lost its way and was on the slide.[12] In an article for the *New Statesman* in February 1974, the Lord Chancellor, Lord Hailsham, cast his net even wider and suggested that such apparently disparate phenomena as 'the war in Bangladesh, Cyprus, the Middle East . . . the Angry Brigade, the Kennedy murders, Northern Ireland, bombs in Whitehall and the Old Bailey . . . the mugging in the tube . . .' might be 'different parts of the same slippery slope'.[13]

But, of course, it's a very big step from identifying a cluster of particularly appalling individual acts or specific types of crime to suggesting that there is a single or simple violent culture underpinning them all. The politically motivated IRA and Angry Brigade had nothing in common with the more traditionally 'criminal' Kray twins or Richardson brothers. Ian Brady had nothing in common with Harry Roberts. Each of the strands of violence that so dominated the headlines in this period had their own hinterland and complex chain of cause and effect.

Thus the Krays – to take just one example – did not appear from nowhere in response to some general social malaise. They were an extreme manifestation of a form of organised crime that certainly stretched back Arthur Harding in the 1900s (see Chapter 10), and their direct antecedents included such figures as William Kimber, who led the loosely affiliated 'Birmingham Boys' (which also had South London connections); Edward Emmanuel, who is reputed to have controlled the Jewish underworld in the East End by the early 1920s; and Charles 'Derby' Sabini, the London-born son of an Italian father and Irish mother, who, after starting out as a bouncer at a boxing establishment, ran a protection and extortion racket on the racecourses of southern England in the 1920s and 1930s (he is said to have been the prototype of the brutal Colleoni in Graham Greene's *Brighton Rock*, first published in 1938). Sabini and Emmanuel were to join forces against the 'Brummies' (the alliance was dissolved after the common enemy had been defeated), and the resulting 'Racecourse Wars' received much tabloid coverage at a time when films imported from Hollywood were chronicling the rise of the gangster.

The Krays' immediate forebears were men like Jacob Colmore or Comer (better known as Jack Spot), erstwhile bookie's runner and protection racketeer, and his rival Billy Hill, a former burglar and smash-and-grab raider in the 1930s turned Second World War racketeer.[14] In the 1950s Hill, by now the self-styled 'Boss of Britain's Underworld', pushed Spot into retirement, and subsequently acted as mentor to Reggie and Ronnie Kray in the early days of their criminal careers.[15]

And it's this disparate pattern of often deep-rooted crime that makes it so difficult to characterise, say, the 'violent sixties' or the 'violent seventies'. We can pinpoint specific problems – armed robbery, perhaps – and seek to explain why they should have become more prevalent in a particular period. In the case of armed robbery, for example, it seems likely that the move away from old-style banks with their thick grilles and high walls to a 'friendlier' open-plan look was sufficient to prompt the unwelcome attention of criminal gangs, that a relatively high level of police corruption in the 1970s made a bad situation worse, and that it only started to improve when bank security became more sophisticated, and robbers realised there was more money to be made from drug smuggling. But a series of such analyses does not necessarily build into a grand, overarching explanation of society's experience of violence at any given point in time.

Clearly, though, something was going on to cause a general rise in violent crime, and, as with previous eras, it's tempting to link that phenomenon, however tentatively, with contemporary social developments. From the 1960s onwards, England was changing very rapidly from a predominantly Victorian-style industrial society to what some have termed (a little misleadingly) a post-industrial economy. It was a period when large-scale industry went into decline, with mining, iron and steel production, ship- and car-building, and many other employers of large labour forces falling away at an ever-increasing rate. It was an era when new technologies increasingly automated processes once performed by workers, and when new approaches to old businesses – for example, containerised shipping – disrupted previous patterns of work and resulted in wide-scale layoffs. Heavy industry contracted; the population numbers in big cities fell. By the end of the 1990s it was hard to imagine that only forty years before the National Coal Board had employed 94,000 miners in Country Durham alone or that one in three of all London's workers had been employed in factories. It's arguable that the speed of this transition caused a degree of social dislocation that in turn sparked a rise in overall levels of aggressive behaviour.

The precise mechanism for this process is not at all clear: shifting patterns of work, a rise in unemployment or increased levels of poverty, do not in themselves make society more aggressive, as the 1930s demonstrated. But in the case of those transitional decades between the early 1960s and late 1990s, it does seem to be the case that the rapidity and extent of change undermined long-standing social relationships and norms as communities were unmade and remade. As a result, in some places and in some circumstances, a more violent culture became endemic. To be more precise or specific than that is to offer a hostage to fortune. Certainly the claims of some contemporary commentators that the rise in violence could be linked to such specific phenomena as the greater permissiveness ushered in by the 1960s, the rise of consumerism, the decline of organised religion, the rising number of divorces, the end of corporal and capital punishment, or the abolition of National Service, simply don't stand up to close scrutiny.

To that extent, the late-twentieth-century experience serves as a useful corrective to the 'civilising process' I have talked about previously, not only because it shows that there is no such thing as inexorable progress, but because it demonstrates that the behaviour of individuals and groups is too complex to be reduced to a single formula. It's possible to sustain the theory of the civilising process in general terms and over broad chronological sweeps of time, but that turbulent period from the late 1960s to the turn of the century reveals its limitations and drawbacks.

V

An added complication – or, at least, a reminder of how inadvisable it is to be too doctrinaire about patterns of violence in recent times – is that although our ability to gather information and statistics has increased massively over recent decades, when it comes to violence the data remain unstable and hard to interpret. Take the numbers of offences against the person recorded by the police, for example. At one level, the figures seem unequivocal enough: 41,088 cases in 1970, 97,246 by 1980, 184,655 by 1990, and 258,070 by 1998/9 (at which point the way in which the numbers were compiled and presented changed, making further comparison impossible).[16] It would be a very perverse statistician indeed who would suggest anything other than that these figures show a significant rise in interpersonal violence. But was the rate of increase actually as steep as it appears? For that to be the case one would have to believe that people in 1998 took precisely the same view of what merited reporting to the police as those a quarter of a century or so earlier. Evidence suggests this was not the case. A clip round the ear by a teacher that might have gone unremarked in 1970 would almost certainly have found its way into police statistics in 1998; a woman who in 1970 might have decided against reporting her violent partner was, by the end of the century, far more likely to do so. Society had changed greatly over a single generation. So while the statistics do certainly show an increase in the number of assaults, they also hint at a greater willingness on the part of victims to come forward. They therefore (certainly) support the image of a society that was becoming more violent over that handful of decades, but also (very definitely) show a society that by the turn of the twenty-first century was less prepared to accept certain types of violent behaviour.

This broadening of a front against violent activity is reflected in contemporary Parliamentary legislation. The basic framework for dealing with non-sexual violent offences remains the 1861 Offences Against the Person Act. A paper submitted to the government in October 2015 calling for its repeal and replacement pointed out that, annually, 26,000 people were being convicted under its provisions.[17] (Its continuing astonishingly wide applicability is demonstrated by the somewhat bizarre case brought before the Court of Appeal in 1996, when Section 47 of the Act was invoked to quash the conviction for assault causing actual bodily harm of a man who, at his wife's instigation, had branded his initials on her buttocks with a hot knife.[18]) But in other spheres, new laws have been introduced to define more tightly – and to legislate against – forms of behaviour that might once have been punished more leniently or have escaped official censure altogether.

Thus a stronger stance against domestic violence (see Chapter 14) was taken in the 1990s in the form of the Family Law Act of 1996 (later amended by Part 1 of the Domestic Violence, Crime and Victims Act 2004) and by the 1997 Protection from Harassment Act. As recently as 29 December 2015 new legislation came into force that made coercive or controlling behaviour against an intimate partner or family member a criminal offence. The Sexual Offences Act of 2003 overhauled earlier definitions of rape and created five distinct types of sexual offence against children. Section 58 of the Children Act of 2004, while not abolishing parents' rights to chastise their children, did place new restrictions on what constituted 'reasonable punishment', although what 'reasonable punishment' means in practice continues to elude precise definition. The Public Order Act of 1986, as well as refining official definitions of riot, violent disorder, and affray, and enacting new regulations covering demonstrations and processions, also made religiously or racially motivated assaults a distinct category of offence. Sometimes the toughening of a stance against violent behaviour lies buried in legislation ostensibly dealing with a completely different issue. The UK Borders Act of 2007, for example, which was largely concerned with asylum and immigration issues, also determined that any assault on an immigration officer would automatically be regarded as a criminal offence. It's not just that a wider range of violent activities has been brought within the purview of the criminal justice system over recent years; their relative seriousness too is subject to constant re-evaluation.

There are other complicating factors when it comes to trying to interpret the mass of statistics with which we are daily confronted. Because law and order is such a key political issue, crime figures have a tendency to be manipulated to prove a particular point. Since the police have been and are under constant pressure to improve clear-up rates, there is strong evidence to suggest that crimes are sometimes wrongly recorded or described. And as most of the statistics we read are compiled centrally, broad-brushstroke national trends do not necessarily reflect what is happening in a specific part of the country at any given point. Even a local statistic can be misleading. If the murder figures for 2010/11 are to be believed, the most dangerous area of England was Cumbria with 3.24 homicides per 100,000 as against London's 1.67 and Eastern England's 0.91. But that 3.24 figure includes Derrick Bird's murderous shooting spree on 2 June 2010 in the course of which he gunned down and killed 12 people and injured 11 others. In the normal run of events, Cumbria is very definitely not the murder centre of England.

VI

Modern crime statistics, then, are problematic and need to be handled with considerable caution. But to return to the vexed issue of the extent to which violence increased from the 1960s onwards, it is perhaps worth dwelling briefly on one particular dataset for that handful of decades – the homicide figures. As with the medieval period, so with modern times: homicide numbers may not tell us everything, but they are useful general indicators of the fundamental extent of violence at any given time. What's more they have the advantage of being pretty unambiguous. We might debate at what point an altercation becomes a criminal assault. We can argue about how a particular generation might have viewed a particular form of violence – whether it was accepting or disapproving. But while views might differ as to whether a specific homicide is murder or manslaughter, there can be no doubt whatsoever about the fact of its actually taking place. Moreover, its extreme nature is a fair guarantee of its being recorded. Homicide figures have a usefully robust aspect to them that is lacking in so many other areas of violent crime.

And certainly the homicide figures for the decades leading up to the millennium seem to confirm the overall trend of other crime statistics in the same period. In 1950 346 homicides were recorded in England and Wales. In 1967 the number exceeded 400 for the first time since the Second World War. Although levels were to fluctuate over the next few years the general trend remained upwards: to 508 in 1975, 621 in 1980, and then yet higher as the millennium approached. The peak year was 2002/3, when a total of 1,047 homicides were recorded, though a significant number of these (172) were laid at the door of the serial killer Harold Shipman. England's violent post-war climb had reached its summit.

VII

After that fateful year, though, the homicide rate dropped even faster than it had climbed. Indeed by 2013/14, the figure had fallen to 526 – about half the level of just over a decade earlier, and yielding a rate per 100,000 of population of just 0.92 (actual rates, of course, varied significantly from area to area: see Appendix, Table 11). As in those previous eras when the homicide rate fell, that decline can largely be explained in terms of fewer attacks by (male) strangers and acquaintances. Figures for attacks by family members and other intimates, by contrast, remained fairly constant, women, as usual, proving most likely to fall fatal victims to partners or ex-partners than men (54 per cent of female victims aged over 16 fell into this category as opposed to 7 per cent of males). Of those victims aged 16 and under, the majority were acquainted with their killers (27 out of 46, or 59 per cent), and 23 were killed by their parents or step-parents (the homicide rate among children aged under one year was, as usual, twice that of the population as a whole). Six per cent of all male homicide victims were aged less than 16, as opposed to 14 per cent of female victims. Where the precise circumstances of an attack are known and recorded, it emerges that almost exactly half of these homicides were the result of a quarrel or loss of temper. Only 35 accompanied the commission of a robbery or other crime.

In terms of race (taking data from 2008–11), the vast majority of homicide victims were white (75 per cent); 11 per cent were black, 8 per cent were Asian, and 3 per cent came from other minority groups. As for the weapons employed, the commonest were knives and other sharp instruments, followed by feet and fists. With black victims, though – who tended to be younger than white victims – firearms were quite commonly the cause of death (26 per cent of black victims as opposed to 5 per cent of white); 81 per cent of black victims lived in the heavily urban Metropolitan, Greater Manchester, or West Midlands police areas.[19] Overall, more men fell prey to a killer than women – 343 out of the total of 526 homicides in 2013/14, nearly two-thirds. (During the previous five years 68/9 per cent of victims had been male.)

VIII

And, as one would expect from the statistical patterns of previous periods, as homicide rates fell from the early 2000s, so did those for other forms of violence.[20] According to the new rules for presenting criminal statistics adopted in 1998/9, there were 708,742 reported offences against the person in 2002/3. This rose to a high of 845,673 in 2004/5, and then declined steadily to 601,134 in 2012/13.[21] Figures from the British Crime Survey (subsequently Crime Survey England and Wales), initiated by the Home Office in 1982 (a survey based on regular interviews with a sample of 50,000 people), confirm this overall impression;[22] as do the findings of Cardiff University's Violence Research Group which bases its research on violence-related injuries recorded at 54 Emergency Departments and Minor Injury Units across England and Wales.[23]

Within these general statistics, more specific trends can be traced. The figures for violent offences against the person for the year ending March 2013 show not just a continuing decline in homicide rates, but a sharp drop in attempted murder (down by 16 per cent on the previous year), violence with injury (8 per cent down), and firearms offences and offences involving a knife or sharp instrument (down by 15 per cent). It's perhaps worth emphasising that, whatever television and film might suggest to the contrary, firearms are in any case relatively rarely deployed in the commission of crimes in England

and Wales – there were a relatively modest 11,227 incidents recorded in 2010–11, resulting in 58 homicides. Some forms of violence, though, have proved stubbornly resistant, instances of rape recorded by the police being a case in point (16,327 in 2012–13 compared with 16,038 in 2011–12).

Experts disagree as to the causes of this overall decline in violence over the past decade or so, just as they disagree about the causes of the rise in the preceding few decades. Perhaps the most ingenious, though, I suspect, least convincing theory, suggests that it's due to the increased use of unleaded petrol in vehicles, the argument being that there is a link between exposure to lead in childhood and behavioural problems in later life. More plausible is the suggestion that the prevalence of CCTV, along with other technological advances that have served to make crime in general more easily detectable, has therefore had a deterrent effect – though, of course, it would hardly stop violence committed on the spur of the moment or in the privacy of people's homes. Some argue that the fact prison populations are higher than they were in, say, the 1970s means, quite simply, that a greater number of hard-core offenders are being kept off the streets. Others believe that as the population of England ages, so the relative proportion of that problematic, more violence-prone 16–24-year-old male group is falling. Others again are of the view that we've reached the latest stage in our endless civilising process, and that as society has adjusted to a 'post-industrial' world, a cultural shift has taken place that renders getting into fights less acceptable than it was twenty years ago. This last explanation seems to me the most plausible, though it doesn't preclude other factors.

The experience of the 1960s and 1970s, however, should be a safe-guard against complacency. Each era throws up its own problems and challenges. The armed gang of the 1960s has given way to the drugs gang of today. IRA terrorists have been replaced by Islamic terrorists. A marked increase in alcohol consumption in recent years, and the deregulation of the hours when alcohol can be sold and consumed, has had a discernible impact on the extent and nature of contemporary violence. Then there's the rise of what amounts to a modern equivalent of the traditional charivari or skimmington: trolling on the internet, a phenomenon now so widespread that it raises the question of whether at some point we will come to view extreme online bullying as our forebears regarded verbal insults – as a form of violence. Certainly, guidelines on cyber-bullying issued by the Director of Public Prosecutions in December 2012 and again in June 2013 show how seriously the legal establishment regards this new phenomenon. At a more fundamental, structural level, greatly increasing pay for a small percentage of the workforce and the ensuing social inequality threatens to exclude many from mainstream society, pushing them possibly to accept an alternative culture and to reject the world of formal employment for the rougher, casual economy of the streets.[24] In this context it's worth bearing in mind the findings of a recent study of the victims of violence, which demonstrates just how often the disadvantaged who turn to violence do so against their own peers: in 2013/14 women living in the lowest income bracket were over three times more likely to be victims than those living in the highest bracket (15.3 per cent compared to 4.2).

IX

The idea that violence might one day be virtually eliminated from society seems something of a Utopian dream – most of us are capable of it, and even the most pacific indulge in the occasional fantasy about it. Anyone who has watched the 1985 movie *Witness* will recall the scene in which the undercover cop, played by Harrison Ford, hits (and hits very hard) a young man who is taunting a member of the violence-avoiding Amish community, and will also doubtless guiltily recall how much they enjoyed that moment. Somehow, the cop's actions *felt* right, even though he was in the company of someone who strongly disapproved of them. As criminologist Simon Winlow puts it, 'Violence will never go out of fashion or lose its perceived uses, or its aesthetic and seductive qualities.'[25]

For some, aggression is the quickest and best route to righting wrongs and achieving status. Anthropologist Gillian Evans, who has conducted fieldwork in Bermondsey, South-east London, describes how 'Sophie', the 15-year-old daughter of one of her principal informants, 'Sharon', opted to deal with a gang of girls from another estate who had been causing her problems by agreeing to have a one-on-one fight with their leader. On the day, Sophie rapidly knocked the other girl unconscious and put her head through the windscreen of a parked car. She was arrested and accused of grievous bodily harm, but one suspects that she had few regrets: her difficulties with the girl gang were resolved, and she simultaneously acquired a useful reputation for hardness.[26] It's an experience that will be familiar to anyone who has taken on – and defeated – a bully at school.

It's not difficult to see, therefore, why it's so easy for a culture of violence to be a part of everyday life, to be accepted by some and enjoyed by others. Studying communities living on the fringes of organised crime in Sunderland – 'where violence is always on the agenda, for a multitude of reasons, and yet violence is not the affliction of their environment' – Simon Winlow concluded of those actively involved in violent acts:

> Most of them like it. They like the way it looks, sounds and ends; they appreciate quality, ferocity, cunning and cool conduct. Violence is an aspect of their lives which is comforting in its familiarity, a behavioural characteristic that everyone in this environment understands and respects, even if their involvement in it is minimal and they want to keep it that way.[27]

Beatrix Campbell's *Goliath*, which explores the riots that took place in various British cities in 1991, closes with a discussion between a number of Tyneside five year olds about how they see their futures. The girls want to be mothers, and enjoy what they regard as a normal family life. 'Then a boy dissented. "I don't want to be a dad, I want to be a robber."'[28]

Violence can even form an important element of what constitutes a good night out. One striking feature of the epidemic of binge drinking that swept across Britain from the late 1990s is the extent to which – admittedly a small minority of – young people clearly not only wanted to get blind drunk but have a fight, too. In central Manchester, for example, between 1998 and 2001 there was a 240 per cent increase in the number of licensed premises and a 225 per cent increase in cases of assault. As Criminologist Dick Hobbs and his co-authors put it: 'If you cram tens of thousands of individuals together from the age groups most prone to criminal behaviour and then fill them with alcohol, does anyone really believe that it won't occasionally "go off?".' It became an accepted part of the scene, even among those who were themselves anxious to avoid trouble. As one eye-witness expressed it:

> . . . it's not like you can avoid it, because it [trouble] just seems to find you. Usually it's nothing much, but mostly I'm not really the type to get into fights. I try to stay out of the way of those types of people . . . [who] you can tell like fighting . . . You pick the kind of bars you go to and the nightclubs and that. It's basic commonsense really. There's some bars and nightclubs where you know fights are going to happen, so you just don't go. And, you know, be careful in pizza shops and trying to get taxis and stuff. We usually don't go into those types of places anyway, so normally it's OK.

Two-thirds of the male and a fifth of the female respondents in this particular survey had experienced violence at first hand on nights out.[29] The relevant Crime Survey for England and Wales suggests that 704,000 (or 53 per cent) of violent incidents reported in 2013/14 were alcohol-related, that 62 per cent of all male and 38 per cent of all female victims of violence were involved in alcohol-related incidents, that these incidents were more likely to involve strangers than other types of violent attack, that three-quarters of them occurred at weekends, and that over 80 per cent of the incidents of violence reported between 10 p.m. and 6 a.m. had a link with alcohol.[30]

Violence of this type, while terrifying for the innocent victims caught up in it, is nevertheless transient. It's a hallmark of a certain type of adolescent and young adult, and it will become less likely to occur as that person gets older. Many other instances of violence are the consequence of isolated flare-ups. But there is also a much darker thread that runs through contemporary society. A significant proportion of prosecutions brought today are against people who come from that struggling 30 per cent of the population from the 40/30/30 split I mentioned in Chapter 17, people who have experienced tough childhoods, who have been largely untouched by education, and who emerge into the adult world with little chance of finding a good job or becoming settled.[31] Simon Winlow, surveying the rise of organised crime in the Sunderland area, concluded that 'crime is one of the few traditional trades that still offers an apprenticeship in the post-industrial North East' – and part of the stock in trade of crime is physical force.[32] *Criminal Justice: The Way Ahead*, a government White Paper published in 2001, stated that about half of all crimes (one can assume that a proportionate number of these were crimes of violence) were committed by a hard core of about 100,000 offenders, these forming about 10 per cent of all 'active criminals'. Half of these 100,000 were aged under 21, nearly two-thirds were drug users, three-quarters were out of work, and more than a third had been in care as children. Another White Paper, published the following year, reinforced the notion that many offenders were themselves, in a sense, victims: compared with ordinary citizens, it suggested, people in prison are thirteen times more likely to have been in care as a child, ten times more likely to have been a regular truant from school, thirteen times more likely to be unemployed, two and a half times more likely to have a close relative with a criminal conviction, and six times more likely to have been a young parent. A large proportion were drug users who committed crime to fund their habit. A third of active offenders were aged under 21. The peak offending age was 18.[33]

X

Given the many and often seemingly intractable factors that lead to violence, is there anything that can be done to reduce current levels of violent crime?

A major obstacle that society faces when it comes to taking sensible, practical steps is that it's actually very badly informed about violence. We certainly read or hear about it all the time;[34] and we learn about individual cases from programmes such as BBC1's *Crimewatch* (launched in 1984).[35] But what we infer from the torrent of information that confronts us is often mistaken. All the statistics show that in recent years violent crime has been on the decline – but that's not most people's perception. Thus the 2013/14 Crime Survey for England and Wales found that, in a period of falling prosecutions, 61 per cent of adult respondents thought that crime was rising nationally, 19 per cent thought they were very or fairly likely to become a victim of crime over the next twelve months, and 12 per cent were especially worried about violent crime. All the statistics show that we are highly *unlikely* to fall prey to the murderous stranger – but clearly that's not what many of us believe. All the statistics show that while organised crime (particularly drugs trafficking) is widespread, it is relatively non-violent:[36] of the 696 non-terrorist homicides recorded in England and Wales in 2005–6, a comparatively modest 42 were in some way – and of these 17 directly – related to organised crime, figures that pale against the 646 gang-related murders (18 per 100,000 of population) recorded in Los Angeles in 2006–8.[37] But that's not the popular perception.[38] Because we are regularly confronted by the exceptional reported in the media, we have an inevitable tendency to assume that it must be the everyday. One British Crime Survey concluded that readers of national tabloids were twice as likely to think that the national crime rate had increased significantly in the previous two years as did readers of broadsheets: it's surely no coincidence that tabloids tend to carry more crime stories than their broadsheet rivals. If our knowledge is so skewed, how can we hope to understand the true nature of the problems we face?

To make matters worse, we have a tendency to want to find simple explanations for complex problems. Steve Chibnall, author of the 1977 book *Law-and-Order News*, demonstrated convincingly that when confronted by the unfamiliar or the disturbing, the natural inclination of most commentators is to grasp at a conventional response. Thus the serial killer is explained away as 'evil' (a tricky enough term to employ in a secular society) rather than as anything more complex. It's recognisable shorthand among journalists. But they are far from being the only offenders in this respect. In his final comments to the court during the trial of James Bulger's killers, the presiding judge, Mr Justice Morland, considering what had prompted Jon Venables and Richard Thompson to murder a toddler, suggested that 'it is not for me to pass judgement on their upbringing, but I suspect that exposure to violent video films may in part be an explanation'. His speculation arose from a widely circulated rumour that either Venables and Thompson or both had seen a video of *Child's Play 3* in which the villainous doll Chucky is hit by a blue paintball fired by a child (James Bulger was spattered with blue paint) and finally meets his end at a ghost train attraction at a fairground (the little boy's corpse was found on a railway track). But since there is no firm evidence that either child did actually see the film (all we know is that Neil Venables, Jon's father, had rented *Child's Play 3* a few weeks before the killing), since the similarities between the film and the circumstances of James Bulger's death are slight, to say the least, and since (as I argued in Chapter 18) evidence for a firm link between fictional and actual violence is inconclusive, the judge's suggestion seems less than plausible. It was a perhaps understandable attempt to offer a simple explanation for the seemingly inexplicable, in an era when controversy raged over video nasties, but it sidestepped far tougher questions about the killers' state of mind and their backgrounds. That such an intelligent man should make such an unprovable assertion serves as a more general warning about the ease with which we all make assumptions.[39]

There are thus problems both with the way in which we hear about violence and how we then analyse it. Particular types of physical aggression come to the fore in popular consciousness when they are at the centre of a cause célèbre: the Victoria Climbié case, for example, sparked a national debate about one of the most disturbing and widespread of social problems – child abuse. Attention inevitably subsides despite the issue at the centre of the debate remaining a live one, and even exceptional cases come to public attention in a somewhat ad hoc way, their coverage depending as much on such quirks of fate as timing (what else is in the news at the time?) as anything else. Take for example the case of Trevor Joseph Hardy, convicted for the murder of three women in Manchester in May 1977. His life and career are the stuff of popular journalism: a juvenile delinquent, he became obsessed with 15-year-old Beverley Driver when he was released from prison at the age of 27 in 1973, was sent back to prison for assaulting a man in a pub with a pickaxe, vowed vengeance both on that man (who died while Hardy was in prison) and on Beverley (whose parents had persuaded her to break off any ties with him), and then, while on parole, attacked and killed another 15-year-old girl, apparently mistaking her for the one with whom he was obsessed. He buried the body, returned later to mutilate it, and then went on to murder two other teenagers, inflicting appalling injuries on them. He was sentenced to life imprisonment in 1978, and died in prison in 2012. Yet while the crimes of the 'Beast of Manchester', as he became known locally, received extensive coverage in his home town, they attracted scant attention from the national press (garnering just three short mentions in *The Times*).[40] Why that should have been the case is not at all clear, but it does serve as a reminder of how piecemeal and anecdotal our knowledge is.

The danger is that while our lack of true awareness of the patterns and nature of different types of violent crime is an excellent recipe for periodic bouts of moral panic, that's all it is. We condemn – understandably so – but we don't seek to understand. Fairly typical of our natural instincts when faced with stories about violence is this extract from an editorial piece in the *Daily Mirror* on 25 August 1971, written against the background of Angry Brigade bombings and the shooting of Police Superintendent Gerald Richardson a few days earlier:

> This newspaper has no intention of advocating a return to the obscenity of the noose and the cat. But the *Mirror* recognises that the modern wave of violence is in a different category from any other crime. The answer cannot be found in the extension of do-goodery and penal reform on behalf of the violent criminal. Let there be no doubt about what will happen if violence escalates at the present catastrophic rate. The streets of London and other major British cities will become as deadly for peaceful citizens and for policemen as the streets of New York. In those circumstances, society and the police will lose heart. Britain would become a battle ground. Mindless thuggery on the streets would be frontally opposed by coppers with guns . . . Somewhere a stand has to be made. The time is now . . .

It's a demonstration of the kind of public handwringing that could have been indulged in at any time over the past century; and as is generally the case with handwringing, it's hard to tell precisely what the editorial proposes should be done about an issue it only vaguely defines (beyond a vague side-swipe at 'do-goodery').

One can get a sense of just how profoundly the reporting of exceptional crimes can shape public perceptions by considering popular attitudes to the death penalty over the past half century. From mid-Victorian times onwards there was a general consensus that only people found guilty of murder should face the gallows, but rather less agreement as to whether the ultimate sanction should ever actually be invoked. Those in favour of retaining the death penalty argued that its use in exceptional and particularly appalling cases was a justified act of retribution, and that it had a certain deterrent effect on other would-be killers. Opponents argued that it was morally wrong for the State to take a life, that the death penalty punished not just the guilty but their families, too, and that there was always the risk of a miscarriage of justice. By the 1930s a fair number of lawmakers favoured abolition, in line with several other European countries, and a Royal Commission 'to consider and report whether the liability under the criminal law in Great Britain to suffer capital punishment for murder should be limited or modified' was appointed in 1949. The Commission's report of 1953 was couched in terms of 'limiting or modifying' the law relating to capital punishment for murder, but it recognised that its recommendations had disadvantages, and that should those recommendations prove unacceptable the debate had to shift to encompass either abolition or retention. Public opinion in 1953 was not yet ready for abolition. Three high-profile cases over the next handful of years, however, had a significant impact on popular attitudes.

In 1953, the arrest and then execution of John Christie for murdering eight women (including his own wife) at 10 Rillington Place, North Kensington, raised the question of whether the hanging of his tenant Timothy Evans three years before for murdering his own child had constituted a miscarriage of justice (Evans was posthumously pardoned in 1966). In the same year as Christie's, the hanging of Derek Bentley for being an accessory to the murder of a policeman also attracted considerable controversy, since it was not clear what precisely his role had been (his conviction was posthumously quashed in 1998). And two years later came the much-debated execution of Ruth Ellis, who had shot her lover, a twenty-five-year-old racing driver called David Blakely, but who, as her trial revealed, had suffered violent abuse at his hands.[41] Shortly afterwards, a bill to abolish capital punishment, passed by the Commons in 1955, was rejected by the House of Lords, though the Homicide Act of 1957 did further restrict the use of capital punishment. In 1965 the Murder (Abolition of Death Penalty) Act (made permanent in 1969) effectively removed capital punishment from the statute book.[42]

However, if these three high-profile cases helped the cause of abolition, other subsequent murders have had the opposite effect. Even at the time that the 1965 Act was passed, many still favoured the death penalty. In 1983, when the first NatCon British Social Attitudes Report was released, 75 per cent of respondents favoured the reintroduction of the death penalty for certain categories of murder. This had fallen to 45 per cent in 2014. But that general downward trend was momentarily and strikingly reversed in a 2003 poll, which reported that 67 per cent of respondents said that they favoured the death penalty for child killers, and 69 per cent supported it for serial killers. The reason for this? The same year saw the trial of Ian Huntley, who had abducted and murdered two ten year olds, Holly Wells and Jessica Chapman, from Soham in Cambridgeshire. It was a case that had received saturation media coverage.

XI

If the public's view of violent crime is all too often buffeted around by popular prejudice and partial knowledge, it has to be said that the approach taken by successive governments has not always been much more considered. Post-war politicians have never been able to reconcile the conflicting expectations we have of law and order: that we should want simultaneously to punish wrongdoers, keep them off the streets (at least, in the short term), achieve 'justice' for the victims, deter other would-be criminals – and while all this is going on, that we should also want to rehabilitate offenders, or, at least, persuade them not to reoffend. It is, admittedly, not the easiest of circles to square. But the task is made considerably more difficult by policy-makers' tendency to opt for what will play best with the electorate in the short term. 'Society needs to condemn a little more and understand a little less,' Prime Minister John Major had said in

1993 – making the rash assumption that there had been much under-standing beforehand. 'Tough on crime, tough on the causes of crime,' Tony Blair vowed in 1995, seeking with the first half of that statement to seize the law and order initiative from the Conserva-tives. 'We will put victims and witnesses at the heart of the criminal justice system and ensure they see justice done more often and more quickly,' the Home Office promised in 2002, setting to one side for the moment the issue of how to stop criminals reoffending.

Criminologist David Garland has noted how over the past thirty years in both the United Kingdom and the United States, policy-makers have reduced the reformative element of prison that operated between about 1890 and 1970 and increased its penal nature.[43] It's a trend that another criminologist, Michael Tonry, has also picked up on, leading to the following fairly bleak view of England's criminal justice system offered in 2004 from his vantage point as Director of the Institute of Criminology at the University of Cambridge:

> To an American, resident now in England for five years, who long admired the rationality, decency and moderation of Eng-land's criminal justice system, especially in comparison with the United States, all that I have described is perplexing. Until the early 1990s only America developed an hyperbolic law-and-order politics and cruel, simplistic policies that were based more on ideology and politicians' perceived self-interest than on evidence or acceptance of human frailty. And then in the early 1990s, England broke ranks with other Western countries and began to emulate American politics and policies.[44]

From the vantage point both of society in general and the victim in particular, it is entirely understandable why punishment and retri-bution are key. However, when it comes to seeking not simply to punish but to reduce violence, the history of the past five hundred years suggests that changing would-be perpetrators' attitudes is just as important. That's why I find it depressing that a document like *Justice for All* (a 2002 White Paper) should devote just 4 of its 181 pages to 'Turning Children and Young People Away from Crime'. It's why I find it a matter for concern that when 10-year-old Jon Venables and Robert Thompson were held on remand for nine months before their trial for the murder of James Bulger, they should have been offered no psychological treatment and that they should then have been tried as adults (something that would not have happened in most other European countries). It's why I find it puzzling that we place such emphasis on deterrence when we know in our heart of hearts that it rarely works: after all, if it did, then America, which still operates the death penalty in some states, would have a far lower homicide rate than Britain, when the reality is that between 2006 and 2008 England and Wales averaged a rate of 2.14 killings per 100,000 people, while the figure for the US stood at 5.6. I'm not suggesting for a moment that violence should go unpunished but if we actually want to reduce it where it is most deep-rooted, then punishment alone is an inadequate response.

Of late there have been some encouraging signs of a more sophisticated response. The research done in Hospital Emergency Departments by the University of Cardiff's Violence Research Group suggests that where different agencies – police, health practitioners, local government – combine their resources, levels of violence do actually decrease. This multi-agency approach also seems to be of central importance to one of the most recent anti-violence initiatives launched by the government, *Ending Gang and Youth Violence: A Cross-Government Report*, published in November 2011, and prompted by the riots of that year. In the introduction to the abridged version of the report, Home Secretary Theresa May commented: 'Our proposals are wide ranging . . . stopping such violence is not a task for police alone. Teachers, doctors and youth workers all have a vital role to play. Success will only come when local areas and local agencies like these work together and share information.' Iain Duncan Smith, Secretary of State for Work and Pensions, commented that although intensive police action was needed to arrest offenders and bring them to justice, there was also a need for robust support for those wishing to leave gang life, and an intensive prevention strategy. 'Violence', he stated, 'is a public health issue; we must start seeing and treating it as such.' It's only one piece in the jigsaw, but it does at least display a desire to change behaviour and not simply to punish it.[45] And earlier experiments suggest that it might meet with some success. The Home Office-sponsored multi-agency Kirkholt Project in the 1980s proved successful in reducing the number of burglaries,[46] and Cardiff's Multi-Agency Risk Assessment Conferences (MARACS) have reduced the number of repeat attacks against women who have been the victims of domestic violence.[47]

XII

If nothing else these new approaches to violent crime show just how far society has come since the killing of Roger Crockett at Nantwich in 1572, with which I opened this book. Then, the idea that the aggressive acts of individuals might betoken broader social problems was unthinkable. Now, while we still believe that people must ultimately take responsibility for their actions, most of us also accept that in many cases their actions may have been shaped, at least in part, by wider circumstances.

But recent experience also shows how fragile and inconsistent our retreat from violence has been. While it is unquestionably the case that England is a far safer and gentler country than it was, say, two centuries ago, the pattern of late-twentieth-century crime shows that resurgences are always possible. The civilising process is not an inexorable or inevitable one. Moreover, our propensity to violence can so easily be shaped by particular circumstance or location. I mentioned earlier, for example, how relatively restrained the army was in handling strike action in England and Wales in the 1920s, but, of course, this was the same army that was simultaneously committing acts of brutality during the Irish War of Independence and perpetrating the Amritsar Massacre in India. England in the 1950s was comparatively non-violent; English rule in Kenya in the same period was often savage.[48] The violence of empire is a book in itself but it serves to remind us how complex our relationship with aggression is, and how easily it can be switched on as well as how difficult it can be to switch it off altogether.

I don't feel able, therefore, to hazard an opinion on what the future holds. Nor do I think knowledge of our past record is likely to alter the way people approach the issue today, whether they are lawmakers, commentators, enforcers, victims or perpetrators. But I do believe that a history of violence provides what the Cambridge historian Peter Laslett, writing half a century ago, described as '[an] understanding [of] ourselves in time'.[49] We see how previous generations have grappled with issues that still concern us today. We come to appreciate how easy it has always been to be blown off course by moral panics and hasty judgements. We gain a sense of perspective about a fundamental conundrum: that we seem to be worrying about violence more than ever and yet live in an era when it is occurring at a comparatively low level. In reading about 'the violence we have lost', we might, perhaps, gain a clearer understanding of the violence we still encounter.

APPENDIX: CRIME STATISTICS

Table 1: Verdicts in Sussex Assize homicide indictments, 1560–1619

	Acquitted	Ignoramus*	Hanged	Clergy	Pregnancy	At large	Other	No details
Male	33	1	36	33	–	20	–	12
Female	12	–	4	–	15	1	1	–
Total	45	1	40	33	15	21	1	12

* 'not known'

Table 2: Murder and manslaughter verdicts in Sussex Coroners'
Inquests, 1485–1688

	1485–1558	1558–1603	1603–88
Total surviving inquests	244	582	521
Murder	65	53	96
Manslaughter	7	53	69
Self-defence	14	12	4

Table 3: Method of killing, Sussex Assize indictments, 1560–1619

Stabbing with knife	36
Sword	13
Staff	23
Cudgel	8
Firearms	9
Beating/kicking	19
Tools, etc.	17
Poison	4
Suffocation/strangling	6
Other	13

Table 4: Method of killing, Kent Assizes, selected periods, 1560–1799

	1560–99	1600–49	1650–99	1700–49	1750–99
Total recorded homicides	231	248	310	180	215
Sharp instrument	73 (32%)	68 (27%)	88 (28%)	26 (14%)	27 (13%)
Blunt instrument	74 (32%)	80 (32%)	51 (20%)	34 (19%)	29 (13%)
Hitting/kicking	14 (6%)	22 (9%)	39 (12%)	39 (22%)	65 (30%)
Shooting	5 (1%)	6 (2%)	26 (8%)	26 (14%)	45 (21%)

Table 5: Treatment of infanticide suspects at the Home Circuit
Assizes, 1560–1624

	Guilty to hang	Other guilty	Pleaded pregnancy	Reprieved/ pardoned	Acquitted	Other	No details
1560–69	3	3	5	1	6	–	–
1570–79	4	–	1	–	7	2	–
1580–89	15	–	8	–	19	–	1
1590–99	9	–	2	–	10	4	–
1600–09	7	–	2	4	8	2	–
1610–19	11	–	–	–	7	1	–
1620–24	4	–	–	–	13	–	1
Totals	53	3	18	5	70	9	2

Table 6: Treatment of infanticide suspects at the Kent Assizes,
1625–49, 1660–88

	Guilty to hang	Other guilty	Pleaded pregnancy	Reprieved/ pardoned	Acquitted	Other	No details
1625–29	6	–	–	–	4	–	–
1630–39	7	–	–	3	6	–	–
1640–49	2	–	–	–	2	–	–
1660–69	8	–	–	–	5	–	–
1670–79	9	–	–	–	14	3	1
1680–89	–	–	–	–	9	5	–
Totals	32	–	–	3	40	9	2

Table 7: Assault cases, 1861–70 and 1901–10

	Assaults on police	Common assault	Aggravated assault	Total rate per 100,000
1861–70	131,091	742,033	28,772	383.8*
1901–10	100,469	417,465	11,027	197.2*

*rates for 1861 and 1901

Taken from V. A. C. Gatrell, 'The Decline of Theft and Violence in Victorian and Edwardian England', in V. A. C. Gatrell, Bruce Lenman and Geoffrey Parker (eds.), *Crime and the Law: The Social History of Crime in Western Europe Since 1500* (London, 1980), Table A5, pp. 358–60.

Table 8: Sentencing in assault cases, Essex Quarter Sessions, 1748–52 and 1819–21 (percentages)

	1748–52	1819–21
Not guilty	12.5	20.8
Fined 1/- or less	73.2	13.2
Fined over 1/-	5.4	13.2
Imprisoned	3.6	51.6
Removed by certiorari	5.4	1.1

Adapted from Peter King, 'Punishing Assault: The Transformation of Attitudes in English Courts', *Journal of Interdisciplinary History*, 27 (1996), Table 1, p. 49. I have very much followed King's overall argument here; a *certiorari* was a writ removing a case to a higher court, normally King's Bench.

Table 9: Crimes known to the police and crime rates per 100,000 of population, England and Wales, 1901–65

	Crimes recorded by police	Rate per 100,000	Increase (1901 = 100)
1901	80,962	249	100
1911	97,171	269	108
1921	103,258	273	110
1931	159,278	399	162
1951	524,506	1,299	482
1961	806,900	1,748	702
1965	1,133,382	2,374	954

Based on F. H. McClintock and N. Howard Avison, *Crime in England and Wales* (London, 1968), Table 2.2, p. 23. Apart from 1965, census years were chosen to get as accurate an estimate of population as possible. Wartime conditions meant that there was no census in 1941.

Table 10: Annual averages of persons dealt with summarily for assault at magistrates' courts, England and Wales, selected periods, 1915–1959

	1915–19	1925–29	1935–39	1945–9	1955–59
Aggravated assault	354	347	154	131	62
Assault on police	3,596	3,564	3,896	2,525	5,218
Common assault	24,118	25,089	14,663	17,094	12,107

Taken from Clive Emsley, *Hard Men: Violence in England Since 1750* (London, 2005), Table 2, p. 23.

Table 11: Homicide rates by region per 100,000 of population, England and Wales, 2010–11

North East Region	1.04
North West Region	1.47
Yorkshire and Humber	1.26
East Midlands	0.98
West Midlands	1.36
East of England	0.91
London	1.67
South East	0.82
South West	0.82
Wales	0.77

FURTHER READING

Introduction: The Death of Roger Crockett

There are numerous works which explore theories of violence. A representative sample might include: Elizabeth A. Stanko (ed.), *The Meanings of Violence* (Abingdon, 2003); Neil L. Whitehead (ed.), *Violence* (Santa Fe, 2004); David Riches (ed.), *The Anthropology of Violence* (Oxford, 1986); Konrad Lorenz, *On Aggression* (London, 1966); Hannah Arendt, *On Violence* (London, 1970); and Slavoj Žižek, *Violence: Six Sideways Reflections* (London, 2009).

For evolutionary psychology and violence, see John Carter Wood, 'The Limits of Culture? Evolutionary Psychology and the History of Violence', *Cultural and Social History*, 4 (2007), pp. 95–114. An alternative approach to human violence, based on the study of primates, can be found in Linda Marie Fedigan, *Primate Paradigms: Sex Roles and Social Bonds* (Chicago, 1992).

For long-term studies of the history of violence, see Steven Pinker *The Better Angels of our Nature: A History of Violence and Humanity* (London, 2011), and Robert Muchembled, *A History of Violence* (Cambridge, 2012). Clive Emsley, *Hard Men: Violence in England since 1750* (London, 2005) focusses on the relatively recent English experience. Manuel Eisner, 'Modernisation, Self-control and Lethal Violence. The Long-term Dynamics of European Homicide Rates in Theoretical Perspective', *British Journal of Criminology*, 41 (2001), pp. 618–38, conversely, offers a bold synthesis crossing several centuries on a pan-European level.

Chapter 1: The Violent Middle Ages?

Although overtaken by modern scholarship, Johan Huizinga, *The Waning of the Middle Ages: A Study of the Forms of Art, Thought and Life in France and the Netherlands in the XIVth and XVth Centuries* (London, 1970), is a classic and is well worth reading. It has frequently been republished in English and other languages. A more recent popular work, which again can be read with pleasure, is Barbara W. Tuchman, *A Distant Mirror: The Calamitous Fourteenth Century* (Basingstoke, 1989).

An early work of systematic research on medieval violence, grounded soundly on court records, is James Buchanan Given, *Society and Homicide in Thirteenth-century England* (Stanford, 1977). Other studies include Carl I. Hammer Jr., 'Patterns of Homicide in a Medieval University Town: Fourteenth-century Oxford', *Past and Present*, 78 (1978), pp. 3–23, which suggests the city had extremely high homicide rates in that period. Barbara A. Hanawalt, 'Violent Death in Fourteenth- and Early Fifteenth-century England', *Comparative Studies in Society and History*, 18 (1976), pp. 297–320 probably gives a more typical impression.

Recent studies of the Peasants' Revolt of 1381 include Alastair Dunn, *The Great Rising of 1381: The Peasants' Revolt and England's Failed Revolution* (Stroud, 2002), and Juliet Barker, *England, Arise: The People, the King, and the Great Revolt of 1381* (London, 2014). R. B. Dobson, *The Peasants' Revolt of 1381* (London, 1970, and later editions), still provides an attractive starting point for those new to the subject, combining judicious analysis and commentary with a rich selection of documents. See also the essays gathered together in R. H. Hilton and Trevor Aston (eds.), *The English Rising of 1381* (Cambridge, 1984). Later risings are described in: I. M. W. Harvey, *Jack Cade's Rebellion of 1450* (Oxford, 1991); Anthony Fletcher and Diarmaid MacCulloch, *Tudor Rebellions* (5th edn., Harlow, 2004); and Andy Wood, *Riot, Rebellion and Popular Politics in Early Modern England* (Basingstoke, 2002).

On the Wars of the Roses, see A. J. Pollard, *The Wars of the Roses* (Basingstoke, 2nd edn., 2001), and Charles Ross, *The Wars of the Roses* (London, 1976). For the bloodiest battle in these wars, see A. W. Boardman, *The Battle of Towton* (Stroud, 1994). E. L. G. Stones, 'The Folvilles of Ashby-Folville, Leicestershire, and their Associates in Crime, 1326–1341', *Transactions of the Royal Historical Society*, 5th Series, 7 (1957), pp. 117–36, remains the classic article on medieval gentry criminals.

Chapter 2: Church and State: the Forces of Restraint.

On the 'Peace of God', see Thomas Head and Richard Landes (eds.), *The Peace of God: Social Violence and Religious Response in France around the Year 1000* (Ithaca & London, 1992). Timothy Gorringe, *God's Just Vengeance: Crime, Violence and the Rhetoric of Salvation* (Cambridge, 1996), provides another approach to the relationship between the Christian message and violence. Daniel Thiery, *Polluting the Sacred: Violence, Faith and the 'Civilising' of Parishioners in Late-Medieval England* (Brill, Leiden and Boston,

2009), provides fascinating evidence of how these matters worked themselves out on the ground.

On chivalry, the classic work is Maurice Keen, *Chivalry* (New Haven & London, 1984). Craig Taylor, *Chivalry and the Ideals of Knighthood in France during the Hundred Years' War* (Cambridge, 2013) is an important recent study. For the broader cultural influence of the concept, see Mark Girouard, *The Return to Camelot: Chivalry and the English Gentleman* (New Haven & London, 1981). On the related phenomenon of the tournament, good introductions are provided by Juliet R. V. Barker, *The Tournament in England, 1100–1400* (Woodbridge, 2003), and David Crouch, *Tournament* (London, 2005). The story is continued by Alan R. Young, *Tudor and Jacobean Tournaments* (London, 1987).

On medieval English law, see: Anthony Musson, *Medieval Law in Context: The Growth of Legal Consciousness from Magna Carta to the Peasants' Revolt* (Manchester, 2001); Anthony Musson, *Public Order and Law Enforcement: The Local Administration of Criminal Justice, 1294–1350* (Woodbridge, 1996); and Anthony Musson and W. M. Ormrod, *The Evolution of English Justice: Law, Politics and Society in the Fourteenth Century* (Basingstoke, 1999).

Chapter 3: The Retreat from Killing

The downward trend of homicide in England has been traced by a number of articles in scholarly journals. The pioneering publication was T. R. Gurr, 'Historical Trends in Violent Crime: A Critical Review of the Evidence', *Crime and Justice: An Annual Review of Research*, 3 (1981), pp. 295–353, which was brought to the attention of mainstream historians by Lawrence Stone, 'Interpersonal Violence in English Society 1300–1980', *Past and Present*, 101 (1983), pp. 22–33. This apparent decline in English homicide from between the middle ages and the late twentieth century was shown to be part of a broader northern European pattern in Manuel Eisner, 'Modernisation, Self-control and Lethal Violence'. For long-term trends in one English county, see J. S. Cockburn, 'Patterns of Violence in English Society: Homicide in Kent 1560–1985', *Past and Present*, 130 (1991), pp. 70–106. Another county's experience of homicide in the early modern period is explored in two articles published while this book was in press: James Sharpe and J. R. Dickinson, 'Revisiting the "Violence We Have Lost": Homicide in Seventeenth-Century Cheshire', *English Historical Review*, 131 (2016), pp. 293–323; and James Sharpe and J. R. Dickinson, 'Homicide in Eighteenth-century Cheshire', *Social History*, 41 (2016), pp. 192–209.

Chapter 4: Violence in Print: from Murder Pamphlets to Revenge Tragedies

Murder pamphlets form the basis of John Bellamy, *Strange, Inhuman Deaths: Murder in Tudor England* (Westport, CT, 2006), and are drawn upon heavily in Vanessa McMahon, *Murder in Shakespeare's England* (London & Hambledon, 2004). For shorter studies, see Peter Lake, 'Puritanism, Arminianism and a Shropshire Axe-Murder', *Midland History*, 15 (1990), pp. 37–64, and Peter Lake, 'Deeds Against Nature: Cheap Print, Protestantism and Murder in Early Modern England', in Kevin Sharpe and Peter Lake (eds.), *Culture and Politics in Early Stuart England* (Basingstoke, 1994). Randall Martin, 'Henry Goodcole, Visitor of Newgate: Crime, Conversion and Patronage', *The Seventeenth Century*, 20 (2005), pp. 153–84, discusses the oeuvre of perhaps the most important crime pamphlet writer of the seventeenth century.

Although not limiting its attention to the Sixth Commandment, Dominik Markl (ed.), *The Decalogue and its Cultural Influence* (Sheffield, 2013) provides a good introduction to the historical significance of the Ten Commandments. On revenge tragedy, see: Charles A. Hallett and Elaine S. Hallett, *The Revenger's Madness: A Study of Revenge Tragedy Motifs* (Lincoln, Nebraska, & London, 1980); Eileen Allman, *Jacobean Revenge Tragedy and the Politics of Virtue* (Newark, NJ & London, 1999); and Wendy Griswold, *Renaissance Revivals: City Comedy and Revenge Tragedy in the London Theatre 1576–1980* (Chicago & London, 1986).

Chapter 5: Domestic Violence: Wives, Husbands and Servants

For accounts of domestic violence between the sixteenth and nineteenth centuries see: Frances E. Dolan, *Marriage and Violence: The Early Modern Legacy* (Philadelphia, 2008); Laura Gowing, *Domestic Dangers: Women, Words and Sex in Early Modern London* (Oxford, 1996); Joanne Bailey, *Unquiet Lives: Marriage and Marital Breakdown in England, 1660–1800* (Cambridge, 2003); and Elizabeth Foyster, *Marital Violence: An English Family History, 1660–1857* (Cambridge, 2005). J. A. Sharpe, 'Domestic Homicide in Early Modern England', *Historical Journal*, 24 (1981), pp. 29–48 was an important early analysis of domestic violence, and Anna Clark, 'Domesticity and the Problem of Wife-Beating in Nineteenth-century Britain: Working-class Culture, Law and Politics', in Shani D'Cruze (ed.), *Everyday Violence in England, 1850–1950* (Harlow, 2000), takes the story through to the Victorian era.

On divorce, see Roderick Phillips, *Putting Asunder: Divorce in Western Society* (Cambridge, 1988), and Lawrence Stone, *Road to Divorce: England*

1530–1987 (Oxford, 1990). On 'popular divorce' through wife sale, see E. P. Thompson, *Customs in Common* (London, 1991), Chapter 7, 'The Sale of Wives', and Samuel Pyeatt Menefee, *Wives for Sale: An Ethnographic Study of British Popular Divorce* (Oxford, 1981).

Chapter 6: Mothers and Infanticide

R. W. Malcolmson, 'Infanticide in the Eighteenth Century', in J. S. Cockburn (ed.), *Crime in England 1550–1800* (London, 1977), was an important pioneering essay on the subject, and was followed by an early attempt at an overview, Peter C. Hoffer and N. E. H. Hull, *Murdering Mothers: Infanticide in England and New England, 1558–1803* (New York, 1981). The best work so far produced on the subject, albeit with an eighteenth-century focus, is Mark Jackson, *New-Born Child Murder: Women, Illegitimacy and the Courts in Eighteenth-century England* (Manchester, 1996). It was followed by Mark Jackson (ed.), *Infanticide: Historical Perspectives on Child Murder and Concealment, 1550–2000* (Aldershot, 2002), which contains a number of essays dealing with early modern England. Laura Gowing, 'Secret Births and Infanticide in Seventeenth-century England', *Past and Present*, 156 (1997), pp. 87–115, provides powerful reconstructions of the experiences of women charged with infanticide on the basis of contemporary court records. See also Garthine Walker, 'Just Stories: Telling Tales of Infant Death in Early Modern England', in Margaret Lael Mikesell and Adele F. Seeff (eds.), *Culture and Change: Attending to Early Modern Women* (Newark, NJ, 2003).

The history of infanticide is taken up to the twentieth century by Lionel Rose, *The Massacre of the Innocents: Infanticide in Britain, 1800–1939* (London, 1986). For comparison with Scotland, see Deborah A. Symonds's interesting study, *Weep Not for Me: Women, Ballads, and Infanticide in Early Modern Scotland* (University Park, PA, 1997).

Chapter 7: Verbal Violence: Scolding, Slander and Libel

One of the first works on early modern defamation was J. A. Sharpe, *Defamation and Sexual Slander in Early Modern England: the Church Courts at York* (Borthwick Paper 58, York, 1980), while ecclesiastical defamation cases were further discussed in Laura Gowing, *Domestic Dangers*. For written libels and similar documents, see Adam Fox, 'Ballads, Libels and Popular Ridicule in Jacobean England', *Past and Present*, 145 (1994), pp. 47–83. For changing cultural attitudes to defamation and related matters, see Robert B. Shoemaker, 'The Decline of Public Insult in London 1660–1800', *Past and Present*, 169 (2000), pp. 97–131.

On scolding, see: David Underdown, 'The Taming of the Scold: The Enforcement of Patriarchal Authority in Early Modern England', in

Anthony Fletcher and John Stevenson (eds.), *Order and Disorder in Early Modern England* (Cambridge, 1985); Martin Ingram, '"Scolding Women Cucked or Washed": A Crisis in Gender Relations in Early Modern England?', in J. L. Kermode and Garthine Walker (eds.), *Women, Crime and the Courts in Early Modern England* (London, 1994); and Lynda E. Boose, 'Scolding Brides and Bridling Scolds: Taming the Woman's Unruly Member', *Shakespeare Quarterly*, 42 (1991), pp. 179–213.

The classic introduction to the English charivari is Martin Ingram, 'Ridings, Rough Music and the "Reform of Popular Culture" in Early Modern England', *Past and Present*, 105 (1984), although mention should also be made of an earlier work, E. P. Thompson, '"Rough Music": Le Charivari Anglais', *Annales ESC*, 27 (1972), pp. 285–312. A particularly nasty example of public shaming forms the subject matter of Joan Kent, '"Folk Justice" and Royal Justice in Early Seventeenth-century England: A "Charivari" in the Midlands', *Midland History*, 8 (1983), pp. 70–85. See also Steve Hindle, 'The Shaming of Margaret Knowsley: Gossip, Gender and the Experience of Authority in Early Modern England', *Continuity and Change*, 9 (1994), pp. 391–419.

Chapter 8: The Rise and Fall of the Duel

Probably the most sophisticated work on duelling in England is Markku Peltonen, *The Duel in Early Modern England* (Cambridge 2003), although its focus is largely on the seventeenth century. The story is continued by Stephen Banks, *A Polite Exchange of Bullets: The Duel and the English Gentleman, 1750–1850* (Woodbridge, 2010). Some important comments on the connections between the duel and the developing military ethos of the seventeenth century are provided by Roger B. Manning, *Swordsmen: The Martial Ethos in the Three Kingdoms* (Oxford, 2003).

There is an extensive literature on the duel as a European phenomenon, perhaps the two key works here being V. G. Kiernan, *The Duel in European History: Honour and the Reign of Aristocracy* (Oxford, 1988), and François Billacois, *The Duel: Its Rise and Fall in Early Modern France* (New Haven & London, 1990). James Kelly, *'That Damn'd Thing Called Honour': Duelling in Ireland, 1570–1860* (Cork, 1995), demonstrates interesting points of contrast with the English experience.

On the decline of the duel, see: Donna T. Andrew, 'The Code of Honour and its Critics: The Opposition to Duelling in England, 1700–1850', *Social History*, 5 (1980), pp. 409–34; Robert B. Shoemaker, 'The Taming of the Duel: Masculinity, Honour and Ritual Violence in London, 1660–1800', *Historical Journal*, 45 (2002), pp. 525–45; and Anthony Simpson, 'Dandelions on the Field of Honour: Duelling, the Middle Classes, and the Law in Nineteenth-century England', *Criminal Justice History*, 9 (1988), pp. 99–155.

Chapter 9: Sport and the Decline of Casual Violence

Pre-industrial pastimes are discussed by Robert W. Malcolmson, *Popular Recreations in English Society 1700–1850* (Cambridge, 1973), and by a number of the essays in Eileen Yeo and Stephen Yeo (eds.), *Popular Culture and Class Conflict 1590–1914: Explorations in the History of Labour and Leisure* (Brighton, 1981).

On the history of football, see James Walvin, *The People's Game: A Social History of British Football* (London, 1975), and Tony Mason, *Association Football and English Society 1863–1915* (Hassocks, 1980). For rugby, Eric Dunning and Kenneth Sheard, *Barbarians, Gentlemen and Players: A Sociological Study of the Development of Rugby Football* (Oxford, 1979), and Jennifer Macrory, *Running with the Ball: The Birth of Rugby Football* (London, 1991). Derek Birley, *Sport and the Making of Britain* (Manchester, 1993), is a good overview of the interplay between sport and society in the relevant period. The rise of organised sport at the public schools is touched on by a number of essays in Brian Simon and Ian Bradley (eds.), *The Victorian Public School: Studies in the Development of an Educational Institution* (London, 1975).

Those with a taste for a more theoretical approach could consult Norbert Elias and Eric Dunning, *Quest for Excitement: Sport and Leisure in the Civilising Process* (Oxford, 1986), while Johan Huizinga, *Homo Ludens: A Study of the Play-Element in Culture* (London, 1938) remains a classic.

Chapter 10: Violence and Organised Crime: Highwaymen and Smugglers

Given the intrinsic interest of both subjects, there is surprisingly little by way of publications of real value on either highwaymen or smugglers.

Highwaymen fare better in this respect. For a long term overview, see Gillian Spraggs, *Outlaws and Highwaymen: The Cult of the Robber in England from the Middle Ages to the Nineteenth Century* (London, 2001), while James Sharpe, *Dick Turpin: The Myth of the English Highwayman* (London, 2004), offers not only an account of the life and legend of Turpin, but also of highway robbery more generally. Lincoln B. Faller, *Turned to Account: The Forms and Functions of Criminal Biography in Seventeenth- and Early Eighteenth-century England* (Cambridge, 1987), is a scholarly study of the formation of the image of the highwayman.

For smuggling, see the important pioneering essay, Cal Winslow, 'Sussex Smugglers', in Douglas Hay *et al.*, *Albion's Fatal Tree: Crime and Society in Eighteenth-century England* (London, 1975). Paul Muskett, 'Deal Smugglers in the Eighteenth Century', *Southern History*, 8 (1986), pp. 46–69 is a good local study. For an overview, see Frank McLynn, *Crime and Punishment in Eighteenth-century England* (Oxford, 1989), Chapter 10, 'Smuggling'.

On prostitution, see: Tony Henderson, *Disorderly Women in Eighteenth-century London: Prostitution and Control in the Metropolis, 1730–1830* (London, 1999); Judith R. Walkowitz, *Prostitution and Victorian Society: Women, Class and the State* (Cambridge, 1980); and Frances Finnegan, *Poverty and Prostitution: A Study of Victorian Prostitutes in York* (Cambridge, 1979).

Organised crime in London is touched on by two books which neatly frame the chronological span of this chapter: Gerald Howson, *Thief-taker General: Jonathan Wild and the Emergence of Crime and Corruption as a Way of Life in Eighteenth-century England* (London, 1970); and Raphael Samuel, *East End Underworld: Chapters in the Life of Arthur Harding* (London, 1981).

Chapter 11: The Georgian Mob

Among the many works now available on rioting in eighteenth-century England, the reader would probably find most useful: Nicholas Rogers, *Crowds, Culture and Politics in Georgian Britain* (Oxford, 1998); John Archer, *Social Unrest and Popular Protest in England, 1780–1840* (Cambridge, 2000); and John Stevenson, *Popular Disturbances in England, 1700–1832* (2nd edn., London, 1992). E. P. Thompson, 'The Moral Economy of the English Crowd in the Eighteenth Century', *Past and Present*, 50 (1971), pp. 76–136 remains essential reading.

Christopher Hibbert, *King Mob: The Story of Lord George Gordon and the Riots of 1780* (London, 1958), despite its age remains a good popular history of the Gordon Riots. It should be read in conjunction with the more recent approaches provided in the various essays in Ian Hayward (ed.), *The Gordon Riots: Politics, Culture and Insurrection in Late Eighteenth-century Britain* (Cambridge, 2012). George Rudé, 'The Gordon Riots: A Study of the Rioters and their Victims', *Transactions of the Royal Historical Society*, 5th series, 6 (1956), pp. 93–115 set new standards in the scholarship surrounding not only the Gordon Riots but also the eighteenth-century mob more generally.

On Peterloo, see: Joyce Marlow, *The Peterloo Massacre* (London, 1969); Donald Read, *Peterloo: The 'Massacre' and its Background* (Manchester, 1968); and Michael Bush, *The Casualties of Peterloo* (Lancaster, 2005).

Some idea of the breadth of mob action and popular disturbances in this period can be gained from consulting: Eric Hobsbawm, 'The Machine

Breakers', *Past and Present*, 1 (1952), pp. 57–70; Robert W. Malcolmson, 'A Set of Ungovernable People: The Kingswood Colliers in the Eighteenth Century', in John Brewer and John Styles (eds.), *An Ungovernable People: The English and their Law in the Seventeenth and Eighteenth Centuries* (London, 1980); and Eric Hobsbawm and George Rudé, *Captain Swing* (London, 1969).

Chapter 12: State Violence and the End of the Old Punishment Regime

For the operation of capital punishment in England, see: V. A. C. Gatrell, *The Hanging Tree: Execution and the English People 1770–1868* (Oxford, 1994); Peter Linebaugh, *The London Hanged: Crime and Civil Society in the Eighteenth Century* (2nd edn., London, 2003); and Andrea McKenzie, *Tyburn's Martyrs: Execution in England 1675–1775* (London, 2007). An early attempt to get to grips with the ideological significance of public execution was J. A. Sharpe, '"Last Dying Speeches": Religion, Ideology and Public Execution in Seventeenth-century England', *Past and Present*, 107 (1985), pp. 144–67. For the standard eighteenth-century alternative to capital punishment for serious crime, see A. Roger Ekirch, *Bound for America: The Transportation of British Convicts to the Colonies, 1718–1775* (Oxford, 1987).

On the gamut of pre-modern penal practices in play, see the various essays in S. Devereaux and P. Griffiths (eds.), *Penal Practice and Culture, 1500–1700: Punishing the English* (Basingstoke, 2004), and J. A. Sharpe, *Judicial Punishment in England* (London, 1990), Chapter 2, 'The Old Penal Regime'.

For the shift to a modern punishment system, consult Leon Radzinowicz and Roger Hood, *The Emergence of Penal Policy in Victorian and Edwardian England* (Oxford, 1990). Mention must also be made of Michel Foucault, *Discipline and Punish: The Birth of the Prison* (London, 1977), a bold attempt to reinterpret the switch from physical punishment to imprisonment in the years around 1800. Robert Hughes, *The Fatal Shore: A History of the Transportation of Convicts to Australia, 1787–1868* (London, 1987), is a reminder that imprisonment was not the only penal option being considered at the turn of the nineteenth century.

Chapter 13: An English Miracle?

For the concept of the 'English Miracle', see Radzinowicz and Hood, *Emergence of Penal Policy*, Chapter 5, 'The English Miracle'. For a more detailed discussion of crime levels in the relevant period, see V. A. C. Gatrell, 'The Decline of Theft and Violence in Victorian and Edwardian England', in V. A. C. Gatrell, Bruce Lenman and Geoffrey Parker (eds.), *Crime and the Law: The Social History of Crime in Western Europe since 1500*

(London, 1980). Clive Emsley, *Crime and Society in England 1750–1900* (Harlow, 1987), Chapter 6, 'A Midpoint Assessment: The Criminal Class and Professional Criminals', discusses one of the most important concepts to enter social debate in the nineteenth century, that of a 'criminal class'. See also Martin J. Wiener, *Reconstructing the Criminal: Culture, Law, and Policy in England, 1830–1980* (Cambridge, 1990).

Violence over the nineteenth century is discussed in John Carter Wood, *Violence and Crime in Nineteenth-century England: The Shadow of Our Refinement* (London & New York, 2004), and Martin J. Wiener, *Men of Blood: Violence, Manliness, and Criminal Justice in Victorian England* (Cambridge, 2004). See also Rosalind Crone, *Violent Victorians: Popular Entertainment in Nineteenth-century London* (Manchester, 2012).

Jennifer Davis, 'The London Garrotting Panic of 1862: A Moral Panic and the Creation of a Criminal Class in Mid-Victorian England', in Gatrell, Lenman and Parker (eds.), *Crime and the Law*, is an excellent introduction to the ways the media can amplify criminality, a theme which is also central to Geoffrey Pearson, *Hooligan: A History of Respectable Fears* (London, 1983). Andrew Davies, *The Gangs of Manchester: The Story of the Scuttlers, Britain's First Youth Cult* (Preston, 2008), is an important study of late-Victorian urban street gangs.

Chapter 14: Partners and Children, Victims and Killers

Among the numerous works now in print on domestic violence, perhaps the most useful introduction is Lynne Harne and Jill Radford, *Tackling Domestic Violence: Theories, Policies and Practice* (Maidenhead, 2008). Two important works published when domestic violence was first being identified as a serious issue are Erin Pizzey, *Scream Quietly or the Neighbours Will Hear* (London, 1974), and Janine Turner, *Behind Closed Doors: Advice for Families with Violence in the Home* (Wellingborough, 1988). On elder abuse, see Jacki Pritchard, *The Abuse of Older People: A Training Manual for Detection and Prevention* (2nd edn., London, 1995).

On child abuse, see: Lionel Rose, *The Erosion of Childhood: Child Oppression in Britain 1860–1918* (London, 1991); G. K. Behlmer, *Child Abuse and Moral Reform in England 1870–1908* (Stanford, 1982); and Nigel Parton, *The Politics of Child Abuse* (Basingstoke, 1985), this last a thoughtful analysis of the emergence of child abuse as a social issue since the 1960s. For an important early publication, see K. C. H. Kempe, F. N. Silverman, B. F. Steele, W. Droegmueller and H. K. Silver, 'The Battered-Child Syndrome', *Journal of the American Medical Association*, 181 (1962), pp. 17–24.

The murder of James Bulger is covered by: David James Smith, *The Sleep of Reason: the James Bulger Case* (London, 2011); Mark Thomas, *Every Mother's*

Nightmare: The Murder of James Bulger (New York, revised edn., 2011); and Blake Morrison, *As If* (London, 1988). Gitta Sereny, *The Case of Mary Bell: A Portrait of a Child Who Murdered* (London, revised edn., 1995), analyses another example of a child who killed another child.

Modern sensitivity to bullying is demonstrated in Peter K. Smith and Sonia Sharpe, *School Bullying: Insights and Perspectives* (London, 1994), and Ken Rigby, *New Perspectives on Bullying* (London, 2002).

Chapter 15: Women and Sexual Violence

Awareness of the issue of rape and sexual violence against women was raised to a new level by a major work of second-wave feminism, Susan Brownmiller, *Against Our Will: Men, Women and Rape* (London, 1975). There is now a massive literature on rape as a current cause for concern. Useful guides might include Ann J. Cahill, *Rethinking Rape* (Ithaca & London, 2001), and Nicole Gavey, *Just Sex? The Cultural Scaffolding of Rape* (Hove, 2005). Anne Llewellyn Barstow (ed.), *War's Dirty Secret: Rape, Prostitution and Other Crimes Against Women* (Cleveland, Ohio, 2000), explores the connection between war and sexual violence, a theme which warrants further investigation from an historical perspective, while the connection between rape and pornography is discussed in Diana E. H. Russell (ed.), *Making Violence Sexy: Feminist Views on Pornography* (New York & London, 1993).

On the law and reality of rape in the Middle Ages see: Caroline Dunn, *Stolen Women in Medieval England: Rape, Abduction and Adultery, 1100–1500* (Cambridge, 2013); Corinne Saunders, 'The Medieval Law of Rape', *King's Law Journal*, 11 (2000), pp. 19–48; and Shannon McSheffrey and Julia Pope, 'Ravishment, Legal Narratives, and Chivalric Culture in Fifteenth-century England', *Journal of British Studies*, 48 (2009), pp. 818–36.

Rape in later periods has received less detailed attention: see, however, Sylvana Tomaselli and Roy Porter, *Rape* (Oxford, 1986), and Anna Clark, *Women's Silence, Men's Violence: Sexual Assault in England, 1770–1845* (London, 1987). Garthine Walker is currently researching rape in the early modern period: for two important early publications see her 'Rereading Rape and Sexual Violence in Early Modern England', *Gender & History*, 10 (1998), pp. 1–25, and 'Everyman or a Monster? The Rapist in Early Modern England, c.1600–c.1750', *History Workshop Journal*, 76 (2013), pp. 5–31. The story is continued by Joanna Bourke, *Rape: A History from 1860 to the Present* (London, 2007).

Chapter 16: The Serial Killer: a Very Modern Murderer?

Good starting points for those interested in the recent history of serial killers are Anna Gekoski, *Murder by Numbers: British Serial Killers since 1950: Their Childhoods, Their Lives, Their Crimes* (London, 1998), and David

Wilson, *Serial Killers: Hunting Britons and their Victims, 1960–2006* (Winchester, 2007). David Wilson, *Mary Ann Cotton: Britain's First Serial Killer* (Hook, 2012) provides a well-researched account of the Mary Cotton case. Less prolific nineteenth-century serial killers are noted in Richard D. Altick, *Victorian Studies in Scarlet: Murders and Manners in the Age of Victoria* (London, 1972). Bernard Capp. 'Serial Killers in Seventeenth-century England', *History Today*, 46, 3 (March 1996), pp. 21–6 implies a challenge to Mary Ann Cotton's status as Britain's first serial killer.

On Jack the Ripper see especially: Philip Sugden, *The Complete History of Jack the Ripper* (New York, 1994); Paul Begg, Martin Fido and Keith Skinner, *The Jack the Ripper A to Z* (London, 1991); and L. Perry Curtis Jr., *Jack the Ripper and the London Press* (New Haven, 2001). For the context of the Ripper case, see Judith R. Walkowitz, *City of Dreadful Delights: Narratives of Sexual Danger in Late-Victorian London* (London, 1992).

Two contrasting but interesting perspectives on the Yorkshire Ripper are offered by Gordon Burn, *Somebody's Husband, Somebody's Son* (London, 1984), and Nicole Ward Jouve, *'The Streetcleaner': The Yorkshire Ripper Case on Trial* (London, 1986). On Harold Shipman see C. Peters, *Harold Shipman: Mind Set on Murder* (London, 2005).

Chapter 17: Public Violence: from Football Hooliganism to Inner-city Riots

On youth cults from the second half of the twentieth century see: Paul Rocke and Stanley Cohen, 'The Teddy Boys', in V. Bognador and R. Skidelsky (eds.), *The Age of Affluence, 1951–1961* (London, 1970); Stanley Cohen, *Folk Devils and Moral Panics* (London, 1972), which deals with the mod and rocker 'riots'; and for skinheads, Pat Doyle *et al.*, *The Paint House: Words from an East End Gang* (Harmondsworth, 1972).

Good overviews of football violence and the theoretical approaches to it are provided by: Eric Dunning, Patrick Murphy and John M. Williams, *The Roots of Football Hooliganism: An Historical and Sociological Study* (London, 1988); *Football on Trial: Spectator Violence and Development in the Football World* (London, 1990); and Steve Frosdick and Peter Marsh, *Football Hooliganism* (Cullompton, 2005). For two individual clubs, see Gary Armstrong, *Football Hooligans: Knowing the Score* (Oxford, 1998), and Garry Robson, *'No One likes Us, We Don't Care': The Myth and Reality of Millwall Fandom* (Oxford, 2000).

Trades union militancy is dealt with in H. A. Clegg, *A History of British Trades Unions Since 1889*, 3 volumes (Oxford, 1985). For the General Strike, see Patrick Renshaw, *The General Strike* (London, 1975), and Keith Laybourn, *The General Strike of 1926* (Manchester, 1993).

For the 1983–4 Miners' Strike, see: Geoffrey Goodman, *The Miners' Strike* (London, 1985); Huw Benyon (ed.), *Digging Deeper: Issues in the Miners' Strike* (London, 1985); and Bob Fine and Robert Millar (eds.), *Policing the Miners' Strike* (London, 1985). Other popular disturbances during the Thatcher years are dealt with by Martin Kettle and Lucy Hodges, *Uprising! The Police, The People, and the Riots in Britain's Inner Cities* (London, 1982), and David Butler, Andrew Adonis and Tony Travers, *Failure in British Government: the Politics of the Poll Tax* (Oxford, 1994).

For the 2011 riots, see Riots, Communities and Victims Panel, *5 Days in August: An Interim report on the 2011 English Riots* (London, 2012), and *Reading the Riots: Investigating England's Summer of Disorder* (London, 2011).

Chapter 18: A Culture of Violence? Film and Television

The impact of the *A Clockwork Orange* movie is discussed in Stuart Y. McDougal (ed.), *Stanley Kubrick's A Clockwork Orange* (Cambridge, 2003), and Alexander Walker, *Stanley Kubrick Directs* (Aylesbury, 1972). For the more general issue of violence and the movies, see Stephen Prince (ed.), *Screening Violence* (London, 2000), and J. David Slocum (ed.), *Violence and American Cinema* (New York & London, 2001). For the perspective from the other side, see James C. Robertson, *The British Board of Film Censors: Film Censorship in Britain, 1896–1950* (London, 1985).

Anybody wishing to gain a deeper understanding of the issues involved in assessing the impact of TV violence would benefit from reading: David Gauntlett, *Moving Experiences: Understanding Television's Influence and Effects* (London, 1995); Barrie Gunter and Jackie Harrison, *Violence on Television: An Analysis of Amount, Nature, Location and Origins of Violence in British Programmes* (London, 1998); and Barrie Gunter and Mallory Wober, *Violence on Television: What the Viewers Think* (London, 1998). These should be read in conjunction with Mary Whitehouse, *Cleaning Up TV: From Protest to Participation* (London, 1967).

On video nasties, see Martin Barker (ed.), *The Video Nasties: Freedom and Censorship in the Media* (London, 1984), and Kate Egan, *Trash or Treasure: Censorship and the Changing Meaning of the Video Nasties* (Manchester, 2007). For an overview of the alleged problems caused by the various media, see Martin Barker and Julian Petley (eds.), *Ill Effects: The Media Violence Debate* (London, 1997), and W. James Potter, *The 11 Myths of Media Violence* (Thousand Oaks, 2003).

Chapter 19: Peaks and Troughs: Patterns of Violence Today

A good general guide to crime in the twentieth century is provided by Clive Emsley, *Crime and Society in Twentieth-century England* (Harlow, 2011).

Studies of particular aspects of crime during the 1960s and 1970s include: Steve Chibnall, *Law-and-Order News: An Analysis of Crime Reporting in the British Press* (London, 1977); Stuart Hall, *Policing the Crisis: Mugging, the State and Law and Order* (London, 1978); and J. Ritchie, *Myra Hindley: Inside the Mind of a Murderess* (London, 1988).

For the connections between violence and organised crime in this period, see James Pearson, *The Profession of Violence: The Rise and Fall of the Kray Twins* (London, 1972). Other studies of the development of organised crime include: David Thomas, *An Underworld at War: Spivs, Deserters, Racketeers and Civilians in the Second World War* (London, 2003); Heather Shore, *London's Criminal Underworlds c.1720–c.1930: A Social and Cultural History* (Basingstoke, 2015); and James Morton, *East End Gangland* (London, 2000).

Aspects of current criminality and its relation to violence are touched on in: Simon Winlow, *Badfellas: Crime, Tradition and New Masculinities* (Oxford & New York, 2001); Dick Hobbs, Philip Hadfield, Stuart Lister and Simon Winlow, *Bouncers: Violence and Governance in the Night-time Economy* (Oxford, 2003); and Dick Hobbs, *Bad Business: Professional Crime in Modern Britain* (Oxford, 1995). Current ideas on crime control are discussed in David Garland, *The Culture of Control: Crime and Social Order in Contemporary Society* (London, 2001), while the social order from which our current criminality originates is analysed in Richard Wilkinson and Kate Pickett, *The Spirit Level: Why Equality is Better for Everyone* (London, 2010).

As the references for this chapter demonstrate, I have made use of government publications dealing with violent crime, and with criminal behaviour more generally. These are available on government websites, and I would advise the interested reader look online to find out more.

NOTES

Introduction: The Death of Roger Crockett

1. The source for the Roger Crockett incident is Cheshire Archives and Local Studies (hereafter CALS), Chester, DDX 196/1, 'Examinations touching the Death of Roger Crockett'. Specific references are: Margaret Parker, f. 48; Ralph Ince, f. 47; Ellen Ince, f. 48v; Alice Inpley, f. 57; John Gryffin, f. 46v; William Jackson, f. 26; Richard Bally, f. 55v; Thomas Palen, f. 10v; John Lovett, f. 23v; Ellen Turner, f. 23v; references to 'Joan of Love Lane', ff. 26v, 43; the incident forms the subject matter of Steve Hindle, 'Bleedinge, Afreshe? The Affray and Murder at Nantwich, 19 December 1572', in Angela McShane and Garthine Walker (eds.), *The Extraordinary and the Everyday in Early Modern England: Essays in Celebration of the Work of Bernard Capp* (Basingstoke, 2010).
2. For two major works on the history of violence see: Steven Pinker, *The Better Angels of our Nature: A History of Violence and Humanity* (London, 2011); and Robert Muchembled, *A History of Violence* (Cambridge, 2012). Clive Emsley, *Hard Men: Violence in England since 1750* (London, 2005) provides a more narrowly focussed overview, while Stuart Carroll (ed.), *Cultures of Violence: Interpersonal Violence in Historical Perspective* (Basingstoke, 2007), is a useful collection of essays.
3. There are many books discussing the nature and meaning of violence. I have found the following particularly useful: Elizabeth A. Stanko (ed.), *The Meanings of Violence* (Abingdon, 2003); Neil L. Whitehead (ed.), *Violence* (Santa Fe, 2004); David Riches (ed.), *The Anthropology of Violence* (Oxford, 1986); Pamela J. Stewart and Andrew Strathern (eds.), *Violence: Theory and Ethnography* (London & New York, 2002).
4. For the Australopithecines, Konrad Lorenz, *On Aggression* (London, 1966), p. 295.
5. Slavoj Žižek, *Violence: Six Sideways Reflections* (London, 2009).
6. The point about perpetrators, victims and audiences, and the importance of their interpretations of what they see and experience, is discussed in

David Riches' Introduction, 'The Phenomenon of Violence', in Riches (ed.), *Anthropology of Violence.*

7. Gary Armstrong, *Football Hooligans: Knowing the Score* (Oxford, 1998), p. 233.

8. George Gaskell and Robert Pearton, 'Aggression and Sport', in Jeffrey H. Goldstein (ed.), *Sports, Games and Play: Social and Psychological Viewpoints* (Hillsdale, 1979), p. 291.

9. Julian Pitt-Rivers, 'Honour and Social Status', in J. G. Peristiany (ed.), *Honour and Shame: The Values of Mediterranean Society* (Chicago, 1966), p. 29.

10. Details of indecent assault are given in Emsley, *Hard Men*, pp. 20–1.

11. Rethinking the riot as a historical phenomenon owed much to E. P. Thompson, 'The Moral Economy of the English Crowd in the Eighteenth Century', *Past and Present*, 50 (1971), pp. 76–136.

12. Dan Todman, *The Great War: Myth and Memory* (London, 2005), p. 9.

13. John Keegan, *The Face of Battle: A Study of Agincourt, Waterloo and the Somme* (London, 1976).

14. For details of battle fatigue in Normandy in 1944, Antony Beevor, *D-Day: The Battle for Normandy* (London, 2009), pp. 280–1.

15. On expectations of crime waves after the two world wars, Emsley, *Hard Men*, pp. 21–4.

16. For the classic exposition of Max Weber's views on violence and the state see Max Weber, 'The Profession and Vocation of Politics', in Peter Lassman and Ronald Spiers (eds.), *Weber: Political Writings* (Cambridge, 1994), pp. 310–11.

17. Frantz Fanon, *The Wretched of the Earth* (Harmondsworth, 2001), pp. 73–4.

18. Hannah Arendt, *On Violence* (London, 1970).

19. Thomas Hobbes, *Leviathan: or the Matter, Form, and Power of a Commonwealth, Ecclesiastical and Civil* (London, 1965), pp. 64–5.

20. John Bennett, *A Discourse Against the Fatal Practice of Duelling: Occasioned by a Late Melancholy Event and Preached at St Mary's Church in Manchester, on Sunday the 23rd of March, 1783* (Manchester, 1783), pp. 24–5.

21. John Carter Wood, 'The Limits of Culture? Society, Evolutionary Psychology and the History of Violence', *Cultural and Social History*, 4 (2007), pp. 95–114, quotation at p. 98.

22. Martin Daly and Margo Wilson, *Homicide* (Hawthorne, 1988).

23. Linda Marie Fedigan, *Primate Paradigms: Sex Roles and Social Bonds* (Chicago, 1992), p. 72.

24. The major works setting out the idea of the civilising process are: Norbert Elias, *The Civilising Process: Vol. 1: The History of Manners* (Oxford, 1978); and Norbert Elias, *The Civilising Process: Vol. 2: State Formation and Civilisation* (Oxford, 1982); Norbert Elias, *Reflections on a Life* (Cambridge, 1994), is the key biographical source.

25. Perhaps the best distillation of Pieter Spierenburg's views on Elias are given in his 'Violence and the Civilising Process: Does it Work?', *Crime, Histoire & Sociétés/Crime, History & Societies*, 5 (2001), pp. 87–105.
26. Manuel Eisner, 'Modernisation, Self-control and Lethal Violence. The Long-term Dynamics of European Homicide rates in Theoretical Perspective', *British Journal of Criminology*, 41 (2001), pp. 618–38.
27. For Elias on the middle ages, see especially *The History of Manners*, pp. 204–17; cf. Pinker, *The Better Angels of Our Nature*, pp. 65–72.
28. Sigmund Freud, *Civilisation and its Discontents*, translated Joan Riviere (London, 1957), pp. 85–6.
29. On strategies for violent and abusive men, see Alan Jenkins, *Invitations to Responsibility: The Therapeutic Engagement of Men Who are Violent and Abusive* (Adelaide, 1990); for a more general discussion of ways of dealing with violent individuals, see Hazel Kemshall and Jacki Pritchard (eds.), *Good Practice in Working with Violence* (London, 1999).
30. The best introduction to the working of the assizes is J. S. Cockburn, *A History of English Assizes 1558–1714* (Cambridge, 1972); for a discussion of the court system of the pre-modern period see J. A. Sharpe, *Crime in Early Modern England 1550–1750* (2nd edn., London, 1999), Chapter 2, 'Courts, Officers and Documents'.
31. The standard work on the medieval coroner is R. F. Hunnisett, *The Medieval Coroner* (Cambridge, 1961); publications on the coroner in later periods have included Carol Loar, 'Under Felt Hats and Worsted Stockings: The Uses of Conscience in Early Modern Coroners' Inquests', *Sixteenth-century Journal*, 41 (2010), pp. 303–414; and James Sharpe and J. R. Dickinson, 'Coroners' Inquests in an English County, 1600–1800: A Preliminary Survey', *Northern History*, 48, 2 (2011), pp. 253–69.
32. For the accidental deaths, Hunnisett, *Medieval Coroner*, p. 25; CALS, Chester City Quarter Sessions, ZQSE/7/15.
33. The Concannon case is discussed by John E. Archer, 'Researching Violence in the Past: Quantifiable and Qualitative Evidence', in Raymond M. Lee and Elizabeth A. Stanko (eds.), *Researching Violence: Essays on Methodology and Measurement* (London, 2003), p. 22.
34. On the filtering of assault cases in Islington, see Trevor Jones, Brian Maclean and Jock Young, *The Islington Crime Survey: Victimisation and Policing in Inner-city London* (Aldershot, 1986), p. 97.
35. For the Smiths of Eccles, TNA, Palatinate of Chester, Depositions, CHES 38/1, 'A Note of the outrageous Maner & Misdemayn[ou]rs of the p[er]sons hereunder named'. This and other Palatinate of Chester sources held by TNA were noted as part of a project funded by the Economic and Social Research Council, ESRC Award Number L133251012.

36. For Alice Compton's account of her rape, TNA, Palatinate of Lancaster Depositions, PL 27/1, Part 1, 'Alice Compton's Information ag[ainst] Murray & Wroe', 17 March 1728 [i.e. 1729].
37. Cited in R. B. Dobson, *The Peasants' Revolt of 1381* (London, 1970), p. 175.
38. Richard Brathwaite, *The English Gentleman: containing sundry excellent Rules or exquisite Observations, tending to Direction of every Gentleman of selecter Ranke and Qualities: how to demean or accommodate himself in the Manage of publike or private Affairs* (London, 1630), p. 206.
39. *The Diary of Samuel Pepys, MA, FRS*, Henry B. Wheatley (ed.), 9 volumes (London, 1893–7), Vol. 2, pp. 110–12; Vol. 4, pp. 119–200; Vol. 6, pp. 339–40; Vol. 4, p. 389.
40. Pierce Egan, *Boxiana: or, Sketches of Ancient and Modern Pugilism*, 4 volumes (London, 1818–24), Vol. 1, pp. 13–14.
41. On young men throwing punches, Armstrong, *Football Hooligans*, p. 317.
42. For William Moore's death, *Sussex Coroners' Inquests 1603–1688*, R. F. Hunnisett (ed.), (London, 1998), p. 138.

Chapter 1: The Violent Middle Ages?

1. Estimates of casualties in the First World War vary, but the figure of upwards of 9 million is given in two authoritative studies: Martin Gilbert, *The First World War* (London, 1994), p. xv; and Niall Ferguson, *The Pity of War* (London, 1998), p. xlii; Gilbert also estimates that there were 5 million civilian casualties that can be directly or indirectly attributed to the war.
2. The edition of Huizinga's work consulted was Johan Huizinga, *The Waning of the Middle Ages: A Study of the Forms of Art, Thought and Life in France and the Netherlands in the XIVth and XVth Centuries* (London, 1970).
3. The views of earlier generations of medievalists on the violence of the middle ages are listed by James Buchanan Given, *Society and Homicide in Thirteenth-century England* (Stanford, 1977), pp. 33–4.
4. John Keegan, *The Face of Battle: A Study of Agincourt, Waterloo and the Somme* (London, 1976), pp. 115–16.
5. Barbara W. Tuchman, *A Distant Mirror: The Calamitous Fourteenth Century* (Basingstoke, 1989), pp. 133–4.
6. Norbert Elias, *The Civilising Process: Volume 1: The History of Manners* (Oxford, 1978), p. 200.
7. Given, *Society and Homicide*, Table 2, p. 36 for estimated homicide rates; for family homicide, Chapter 3, 'Homicide and the Medieval Household'; for punishment, Chapter 5, 'The Accused Slayer in Court'; for violence at Honeydon, pp. 119–20; for Margery de Karl, p. 182; for adulteress, p. 56; for Goldington, p. 59.

8. Barbara A. Hanawalt, 'Violent Death in Fourteenth- and Early Fifteenth-century England', *Comparative Studies in Society and History*, 18 (1976), pp. 297–320.

9. Luke Owen Pike, *A History of Crime in England*, 2 volumes (London, 1873–6), Vol. 1, p. 155.

10. For an account of the St Scholastica's Day riot see *The Early Oxford Schools*, J. I. Catto (ed.), Vol. 1 of *The History of the University of Oxford* (Oxford, 1989), pp. 146–7.

11. Carl I. Hammer Jr., 'Patterns of Homicide in a Medieval University Town: Fourteenth-century Oxford', *Past and Present*, 78 (1978), pp. 3–23.

12. *Early Oxford Schools*, Catto (ed.), pp. 145–6; Hammer, 'Patterns of Homicide', p. 15.

13. Given, *Society and Homicide*, p.59.

14. Hanawalt, 'Violent Death in Fourteenth- and Early Fifteenth-century England', p. 312.

15. Hanawalt, 'Violent Death in Fourteenth- and Early Fifteenth-Century England'.

16. As might be expected, the Peasants' Revolt has long attracted attention. Important early studies include Charles Oman, *The Great Revolt of 1381* (Oxford, 1906); André Réville, *Le Soulèvement des Travailleurs d'Angleterre en 1381* (Paris, 1898); and E. Powell, *The Rising in East Anglia in 1381* (Cambridge, 1896). Overall, however, the most useful starting point will be R. B. Dobson, *The Peasants' Revolt of 1381* (London, 1970, and later editions), which contains a very useful Introduction and numerous extracts from contemporary documents. R. H. Hilton and Trevor Aston (eds.), *The English Rising of 1381* (Cambridge, 1984) contains a number of excellent essays dealing with various aspects of the revolt, while R. H. Hilton, *Bond Men Made Free: Medieval Peasant Movements and the English Rising of 1381* (London, 1973) provides context. Alastair Dunn, *The Great Rising of 1381: The Peasants' Revolt and England's Failed Revolution* (Stroud, 2002) is a good recent introduction.

17. For Thomas Walsingham's comments on the rebels in London, see Dobson, *Peasants' Revolt*, pp. 169–70.

18. Information for Essex is brought together in W. H. Liddell and R. G. E. Wood (eds.), *Essex and the Great Revolt of 1381* (Essex Record Office Publications, 84, Chelmsford, 1982); on John Gildesborough, see Anthony Musson, *Medieval Law in Context: The Growth of Legal Consciousness from Magna Carta to the Peasants' Revolt* (Manchester, 2001), p. 246.

19. For Cambridge and Cavendish 'kissing', Dobson, *Peasants' Revolt*, p. 245.

20. My analysis of the causes of the revolt is derived largely from Dobson, *Peasants' Revolt*, Introduction; Hilton and Aston (eds.), *English Rising of 1381*; Hilton, *Bond Men Made Free*; and John Hatcher, *Plague, Population and the English Economy 1348–1530* (London, 1977).

21. For Walsingham's comments on John Ball, Dobson, *Peasants' Revolt*, p. 375.
22. For William Grindecobbe's execution speech, Dobson, *Peasants' Revolt*, p. 277.
23. The standard work on the 1450 rising is I. M. W. Harvey, *Jack Cade's Rebellion of 1450* (Oxford, 1991).
24. The Cornish Rebellion of 1497 is described in Anthony Fletcher and Diarmaid MacCulloch, *Tudor Rebellions* (5ᵗʰ edn., Harlow, 2004), pp. 19–20; more generally, Fletcher and MacCulloch's book is an excellent introduction to sixteenth-century rebellions. It should be read together with Andy Wood, *Riot, Rebellion and Popular Politics in Early Modern England* (Basingstoke, 2002), which extends into the seventeenth century.
25. The extent of the disturbances of 1549 is revealed in Amanda Jones, *Commotion Time: The English Risings of 1549* (London, 2008); a distinctive slant on their deeper significance is provided by Andy Wood, *The 1549 Rebellions and the Making of Early Modern England* (Cambridge, 2007); the risings in the South West have received less recent attention than those in East Anglia, but anyone wishing to read a classic work of history might enjoy Frances Rose-Troup, *The Western Rebellion of 1549* (London, 1913).
26. There is extensive literature on the Wars of the Roses, in which, as I have hinted, there can be found a number of interpretations of the extent of the violence and disruption caused by the conflict. A. J. Pollard, *The Wars of the Roses* (Basingstoke, 2ⁿᵈ edn., 2001), is an excellent short introduction; Charles Ross, *The Wars of the Roses* (London, 1976), is succinct and well illustrated.
27. William Denton, *England in the Fifteenth Century* (London, 1888), especially pp. 115–26.
28. Edward IV's propaganda statement is quoted in Pollard, *The Wars of the Roses*, p. 8.
29. On Towton, see A. W. Boardman, *The Battle of Towton* (Stroud, 1994); Christopher Gravett, *Towton 1461: England's Bloodiest Battle* (Oxford, 2003); and Veronica Fiorato, Anthea Boylston and Christopher Knüsel (eds.), *Blood Red Roses: The Archaeology of a Mass Grave from the Battle of Towton, AD 1461* (Oxford, 2000).
30. On Plummer, see Pollard, *Wars of the Roses*, pp. 11–12.
31. The existence of these two gangs was established by E. L. G. Stones, 'The Folvilles of Ashby-Folville, Leicestershire, and their Associates in Crime, 1326–1341', *Transactions of the Royal Historical Society*, 5ᵗʰ series, 7 (1957), pp. 117–36; and J. G. Bellamy, 'The Coterel Gang: An Anatomy of a Band of Fourteenth-century Criminals', *English Historical Review*, 79 (1964), pp. 698–717; see also J. G. Bellamy, *Crime and Public Order in England in the Later Middle Ages* (London, 1973), Chapter 3, 'The Criminal Bands'.

32. Bellamy, *Crime and Public Order in England in the Later Middle Ages*, p. 70.
33. Lawrence Stone, *The Crisis of the Aristocracy, 1558–1641* (Oxford, 1965), p. 226; the incident is described in Stone's overview of changing aristocratic attitudes to violence, his Chapter 5, 'Power'.
34. Stone, *Crisis of the Aristocracy*, pp. 226, 236; *Oxford DNB*, 'Grey, Arthur, 14th Baron Grey of Wilton'.
35. Philippa C. Maddern, *Violence and Social Order: East Anglia 1422–1442* (Oxford, 1992), p. 4.
36. Philippa C. Maddern, 'Honour Among the Pastons: Gender and Integrity in Fifteenth-century Provincial Society', *Journal of Medieval History*, 14 (1988), pp. 357–71.

Chapter 2: Church and State: the Forces of Restraint

1. The full text is given in Daniel Lord Smail and Kelly Gibson, *Vengeance in Medieval Europe: A Reader* (Toronto, 2009), pp. 168–71.
2. Cited in Introduction to Thomas Head and Richard Landes (eds.), *The Peace of God: Social Violence and Religious Response in France around the Year 1000* (Ithaca & London, 1992); this collection of essays is an excellent introduction to the subject.
3. For these clerical interventions, Daniel Thiery, *Polluting the Sacred: Violence, Faith, and the 'Civilising' of Parishioners in Late-medieval England* (Brill, Leiden & Boston, 2009), pp. 107, 132, 146–7.
4. Wrath's statement is taken from George Economou (trs.), *William Langland's Piers Plowman: The C Version* (Philadelphia, 1996), pp. 51–2; *Jacob's Well, an English treatise on the cleansing of man's conscience*, Arthur Brandeis (ed.), (London, Early English Text Society, 1900), pp. 89–103.
5. This discussion is based on: Richard G. Newhauser and Susan J. Ridyard, *Sin in Medieval and Early Modern Culture: The Tradition of the Seven Deadly Sins* (Woodbridge, 2012); Roger Rosewell, *Medieval Wall Paintings* (Woodbridge, 2008); for an important re-evaluation of Christianity in late-medieval England, Eamon Duffy, *The Stripping of the Altars: Traditional Religion in England 1400–1580* (New Haven & London, 1992); and W. A. Pantin's important pioneering work, *The English Church in the Fourteenth Century* (Toronto, 1980).
6. Cited in Timothy Gorringe, *God's Just Vengeance: Crime, Violence and the Rhetoric of Salvation* (Cambridge, 1996), p. 85. See also *The Ecclesiastical History of Orderic Vitalis*, M. Chibnall (ed.), 6 volumes (Oxford, 1969–80), Vol. 2, p. 233; William's 'harrying of the North' seems to have been something which the chronicler especially held against the Conqueror in an otherwise favourable assessment of his qualities and abilities: therefore in a lengthy (and almost certainly) fictitious deathbed speech he attributed to the dying William, he has him express special repentance for his actions: *Ecclesiastical History*, Vol. 4, p. 95.

7. William Granger Ryan and Helmut Ripperger (eds.), *The Golden Legend of Jacobus de Voragine* (New York, 1941), pp. 144–5, 167, 246.
8. For le Despenser, *Oxford DNB*.
9. These incidents are described in Barbara A. Hanawalt, *Crime and Conflict in English Communities, 1300–1348* (Cambridge, Mass., 1979), pp. 205, 207; for general comments on clergy as members of criminal gangs, pp. 208, 268. For more on Godfrey of Crombe and Sir Malcolm Musard see R. H. Hilton, *A Medieval Society: The West Midlands at the end of the Thirteenth Century* (Cambridge, 1966), pp. 255–8.
10. Barbara A. Hanawalt, 'Violent Death in Fourteenth- and Early Fifteenth-century England', *Journal of Comparative Studies in Society and History*, 18 (1976), p. 309.
11. On de Lisle, see John Aberth, 'Crime and Justice under Edward III: The Case of Thomas de Lisle', *English Historical Review*, 107 (1992), pp. 283–301.
12. There is now an extensive literature on chivalry. The classic work is Maurice Keen, *Chivalry* (New Haven & London, 1984). Nigel Saul, *For Honour and Fame: Chivalry in England, 1066–1500* (London, 2011), as its title suggests, focusses on the phenomenon in England; Craig Taylor, *Chivalry and the Ideals of Knighthood in France during the Hundred Years War* (Cambridge, 2013), is an excellent study; two other useful works are Richard Barber, *The Knight and Chivalry* (Woodbridge, 1996), and Malcolm Vale, *War and Chivalry* (London, 1981). Richard W. Kaeuper, *Holy Warriors: The Religious Ideology of Chivalry* (Philadelphia, 2009) is a useful study of that aspect of the subject.
13. Taylor, *Chivalry and the Ideals of Knighthood*, p. 4.
14. Richard W. Kaeuper, 'Chivalry and the Civilising Process', in Kaeuper (ed.), *Violence in Medieval Society* (Woodbridge, 2000), p. 24.
15. The edition of Malory's work used here was Sir Thomas Malory, *Le Morte Darthur: The Winchester Manuscript*, Helen Cooper (ed.), (Oxford, 1998); on Arthurianism in the Elizabethan period, see Marco Nievergelt, 'The Chivalric Imagination in Elizabethan England', *Literature Compass*, 8, issue 5 (2011), pp. 256–79; and Richard C. McCoy, *The Rites of Knighthood: The Literature and Politics of Elizabethan Chivalry* (Berkeley & Los Angeles, 1989).
16. The broader cultural influence is discussed in Mark Girouard, *The Return to Camelot: Chivalry and the English Gentleman* (New Haven & London, 1981).
17. For specific references see *Le Morte Darthur*, Cooper (ed.), pp. 89–90 (Arthur fighting the giant); 109 (Lancelot and the two giants); 360–1 (Bors fighting Sir Pridam); 210–11 (Tristram and Sir Lamorak de Gales; 229 (Tristram kills Sir Palomides); 193 (Tristram and Sir Blamor); 219, 255 (Tristram and Sir Dinadan).

18. Sir Frank Dicksee's *Chivalry* is widely reproduced, for example in Christopher Wood, *The Pre-Raphaelites* (London, 1981), p. 138.
19. See Catherine Batt, 'Malory and Rape', *Arthuriana*, 7, issue 3 (1997), pp. 78–99; and Corinne J. Saunders, *Rape and Ravishment in the Literature of Medieval England* (Cambridge, 2001), Chapter 6, 'Malory's *Morte Darthur*: A Romance Retrospective': it should be noted that Saunders, p. 252, identifies 'different forms of coercion and varying nuances of the act of ravishment' in Malory's work.
20. Sir Thomas Malory, *Le Morte Darthur*, Cooper (ed.), pp. 57 (for the oath); 284–5 (Lancelot and Elaine); 89–91 (rape and the giant); 383 (brothers planning to rape their sister); 53 ('and half by force...'); 241 (Sir Gaheris killing his mother).
21. For discussions of Malory's portrayal of women see: Thelma S. Fenster (ed.), *Arthurian Women* (New York & London, 2000); and Bonnie Wheeler and Fiona Tolhurst, *On Arthurian Women: Essays in Memory of Maureen Fries* (Dallas, 2001).
22. James Buchanan Given, *Society and Homicide in Thirteenth-century England* (Stanford, 1977), pp. 56–7.
23. For Sir William Marmion's exploit and the English knights at Valenciennes, see Keen, *Chivalry*, pp. 117, 213.
24. M. H. Keen, *The Laws of War in the Late Middle Ages* (London & Toronto, 1965), pp. 156–64.
25. There are numerous accounts of the Battle of Agincourt: two excellent recent ones are Juliet R. V. Barker, *Agincourt: The King, the Campaign, the Battle* (London, 2005); and Anne Curry, *Agincourt: A New History* (Stroud, 2005); see also John Keegan, *The Face of Battle* (London, 1976), Chapter 2, 'Agincourt, October 25th, 1415'.
26. Keen, *Laws of War*, p. 243.
27. Details of the Towton corpses are given in Veronica Fiorato, Anthea Boylston and Christopher Knüsel (eds.), *Blood Red Roses: The Archaeology of a Mass Grave from the Battle of Towton, AD 1461* (Oxford, 2000).
28. On Talbot, see A. J. Pollard, *John Talbot and the War in France, 1427–1453* (London, 1983).
29. On Malory, *Oxford DNB*; J. C. Field, *The Life and Times of Sir Thomas Malory* (Cambridge, 1993).
30. On the tournament, see: Juliet R. V. Barker, *The Tournament in England, 1100–1400* (Woodbridge, 2003); and David Crouch, *Tournament* (London, 2005).
31. For the survival of the tournament into the post-medieval period, see Alan R. Young, *Tudor and Jacobean Tournaments* (London, 1987), and the important pioneering study by Frances A. Yates, 'Elizabethan Chivalry: The Romance of the Accession Day Tilts', *Journal of the Warburg and Courtauld Institutes*, 20 (1957), pp. 4–25.

32. There is now extensive literature on the law in medieval England. I have largely depended upon Anthony Musson, *Medieval Law in Context: The Growth of Legal Consciousness from Magna Carta to the Peasants' Revolt* (Manchester, 2001), which is especially interesting on law as a cultural phenomenon; Anthony Musson, *Public Order and Law Enforcement: The Local Administration of Criminal Justice, 1294–1350* (Woodbridge, 1996); Anthony Musson and W. M. Ormrod, *The Evolution of English Justice: Law, Politics and Society in the Fourteenth Century* (Basingstoke, 1999); Edward Powell, 'Law and Justice', in Rosemary Horrox (ed.), *Fifteenth-century Attitudes: Perceptions of Society in Late Medieval England* (Cambridge, 1994); and Richard W. Kaeuper, *War, Justice and Public Order in England and France in the Later Middle Ages* (Oxford, 1988).

33. Musson, *Law in Context*, pp. 91, 124.

34. For arbitration, see two important articles by Edward Powell: 'Arbitration and the Law in the Late Middle Ages', *Transactions of the Royal Historical Society*, 5th series, 33 (1983), pp. 49–67; and 'Settlement of Disputes by Arbitration in Fifteenth-century England', *Law and History Review*, 2 (1984), pp. 21–43; Simon J. Payling, 'Law and Arbitration in Nottinghamshire 1399–1461', in Joel Rosenthal and Colin Richmond (eds.), *People, Politics and Community in the Later Middle Ages* (Stroud, 1987); for the Macclesfield episode, Michael J. Bennett, *Community, Class and Careerism: Cheshire and Lancashire Society in the Age of Sir Gawain and the Green Knight* (Cambridge, 1983), pp. 22–4.

35. Paul Brand, *The Making of the Common Law* (London, 1992), Chapter 5, 'Edward I and the Judges: The "State Trials" of 1289–93'.

36. For the Scrope brothers, *Oxford DNB*.

37. Philippa C. Maddern, *Violence and Social Order: East Anglia 1422–1442* (Oxford, 1992), pp. 27–47.

38. These concluding paragraphs have drawn upon Anthony Musson, *Medieval Law in Context: The Growth of Legal Consciousness from Magna Carta to the Peasants' Revolt* (Manchester, 2001), and A. Harding, *The Law Courts of Medieval England* (London, 1973).

Chapter 3: The Retreat from Killing

1. Background on Sussex in this period is provided by Anthony Fletcher, *A County Community at Peace and War: Sussex 1600–1660* (London, 1975), while the broader workings of the criminal justice system in Sussex in the period in question are provided by Cynthia Herrup, *The Common Peace: Participation and the Criminal Law in Seventeenth-century England* (Cambridge, 1987). Indictments for homicide and other offences in Sussex are discussed briefly in J. S. Cockburn, 'The Nature and Incidence of Crime in England 1559–1625: A Preliminary Survey', in J. S. Cockburn (ed.), *Crime in England, 1550–1800* (London, 1977).

2. Figures for Sussex homicide indictments are derived from *A Calendar of Assize Records: Sussex Indictments Elizabeth I*, J. S. Cockburn (ed.), (London 1975), and *A Calendar of Assize Records: Sussex Indictments James I*, J. S. Cockburn (ed.), (London, 1975); individual cases cited include: *Assize Indictments Elizabeth I*, Cockburn (ed.), entries 149; 231; 294; 411; 412; 474; 593; 689; 690; 810; 856; 116; 1212; 1329; 1321; 1327; 1328; 1743; 1929; *Indictments James I*, Cockburn (ed.), entries 381; 1000. These are supplemented with information provided by: *Sussex Coroners' Inquests 1485–1558*, R. F. Hunnisett (ed.), (Sussex Record Society, 74, 1985); *Sussex Coroners' Inquests 1558–1603*, R. F. Hunnisett (ed.), (London, 1996); *Sussex Coroners' Inquests 1603–1668*, R. F. Hunnisett (ed.), (London, 1998).

3. On the emergence of the legal concept of manslaughter, see T. A. Green, 'The Jury and the English Law of Homicide, 1200–1600', *Michigan Law Review*, 74 (1976), pp. 413–99.

4. Figures for murder and manslaughter in the Sussex coroners' inquests are provided by: *Sussex Coroners' Inquests 1485–1558*, Hunnisett (ed.), Table 3, pp. xviii–xix; *Sussex Coroners' Inquests 1558–1603*, Hunnisett (ed.), Table 11, p. xxxiv; *Sussex Coroners' Inquests 1603–1688*, Hunnisett (ed.), Table 9, pp. xliv–xlv.

5. The estimated population of Sussex in 1600 is based on data given in E. A. Wrigley and R. S. Schofield, *The Population History of England 1541–1871: A Reconstruction* (London, 1981), Tables A3.1, pp. 528–9, A7.10, p. 621.

6. Richard Gough, *The History of Myddle*, David Hey (ed.), (Harmondsworth, 1981), pp. 71–2.

7. These figures come from Charles Carlton, *Going to the Wars: The Experience of the British Civil Wars 1638–1651* (London & New York, 1992), Chapter 9, 'To Slay and Be Slain'.

8. T. W. Moody, F. X. Martin and F. J. Byrne (eds.), *A New History of Ireland, Vol. III, Early Modern Ireland 1534–1691* (Oxford, 1976), p. 389, estimates that Ireland's population in 1671 was 1.7 million, compared to 2.1 million in 1641. Political violence in Ireland in the relevant period is discussed in David Edwards, Pádraig Lenihan and Clodagh Tait (eds.), *Age of Atrocity: Violence and Political Conflict in Early Modern Ireland* (Dublin, 2007).

9. *The Vindication of Richard Atkyns Esquire, as also a Relation of several Passages in the Western War, wherein he was concerned* (London, 1669), pp. 23, 38–40.

10. On Goring, Bodleian Library, Oxford, Western MSS, Herne Diaries 158–9 ('Analecta Ro. Plot').

11. For the violence at Kilsby, *A true Relation of the barbarous Crueltie of divers of the bloudy cavaleers, as in all Parts: so more especially and principally now in the County of Northampton* (London, 1642); for a very different account of this incident, which claims that the troops opened fire after being shot at by the townsfolk, see Peter Young, *Edgehill 1642: The Campaign and the Battle* (Kineton, 1967), p. 296.

12. *The Autobiography of Richard Baxter*, J. M. Lloyd Thomas (ed.), (London, 1931), p. 43.
13. Gough, *History of Myddle*, pp. 73-4.
14. Gough, *History of Myddle*, pp. 104-6.
15. For Cheshire, J. A. Sharpe, *Crime in Early Modern England 1550-1750* (2nd edn., Harlow, 1999), Figure 3, p. 87.
16. A number of publications have examined long-term trends in homicide prosecutions. For England, the pioneering work was T. R. Gurr, 'Historical Trends in Violent Crime: A Critical Review of the Evidence', *Crime and Justice: An Annual Review of Research*, 3 (1981), pp. 295-353; Gurr's findings were brought to a wider audience and commented upon by Lawrence Stone, 'Interpersonal Violence in English Society 1300-1980', *Past and Present*, 101 (1983), pp. 22-33; the English evidence is located in a broader European framework by Manuel Eisner, 'Modernisation, Self-control and Lethal Violence. The Long-term Dynamics of European Homicide Rates in Theoretical Perspective', *British Journal of Criminology*, 41 (2001), pp. 618-38. For a good overview of the legal and cultural background to homicide in the early modern period, see Malcolm Gaskill, *Crime and Mentalities in Early Modern England* (Cambridge, 2000), Part 3, 'Murder'.
17. J. M. Beattie, *Crime and the Courts in England, 1660-1800* (Oxford, 1986), Table 3.4, p. 108.
18. J. S. Cockburn, 'Patterns of Violence in English Society: Homicide in Kent 1560-1985', *Past and Present*, 130 (1991), pp. 70-106.
19. Figures abstracted from Cockburn, 'Patterns of Violence in English Society', Table 2, pp. 80-1.
20. For continental European developments, see Eisner, 'Modernisation, Self-control and Lethal Violence'.
21. J. A. Sharpe, *Crime in Seventeenth-century England: A County Study* (Cambridge, 1983), p. 131.
22. TNA, CHES 24/180/1.
23. TNA, CHES 38/41, depositions taken 13 September 1673 relating to the death of Richard Downes.
24. TNA. CHES 24/164/2.
25. TNA, CHES 24/179/6.
26. TNA, CHES 24/179/5. This last set of depositions, dealing with the death of Sarah Statham *alias* Malone, is complemented by a contemporary anonymous pamphlet, *the Evidence of the Trial of John Thornhill for the Murder of Sarah Statham at Lymm in Cheshire, for which he was executed at Chester on Monday the twenty-third of April 1798* (Chester, 1798).
27. John Cannon's encounters with violence are recorded in *The Chronicles of John Cannon, Excise Officer and Writing Master*, John Money (ed.), 2 volumes (British Academy, Records of Social and Economic History,

new series, Oxford, 2010), Vol. 1, pp. 70, 95–6, 175–6, 189, 194–5; Vol. 2, pp. 266, 294, 300–1, 332, 348, 361, 445, 356.

28. TNA, CHES 38/41, depositions relating to the death of John Venables, 8 November 1686.

29. Adam Smith, *An Inquiry into the Nature and Causes of the Wealth of Nations*, 3 vols (Dublin, 1776), Vol. 2, pp. 197–8.

30. I have based these concluding remarks on Eisner, 'Modernisation, Self-control and Lethal Violence', and Robert B. Shoemaker, 'Male Honour and the Decline of Public Violence in Eighteenth-century London', *Social History*, 26, 2 (2001), pp. 190–208. Politeness, as it was understood in eighteenth-century England, is one of the main themes of Paul Langford, *A Polite and Commercial People: England 1727–1783* (Oxford, 1989).

Chapter 4: Violence in Print: from Murder Pamphlets to Revenge Tragedies

1. Henry Goodcole, *The Adultresses Funerall Day: in flaming, scorching and consuming Fire: or, the Burning Downe to Ashes of Alice Clarke late of Uxbridge in the County of Middlesex . . . for the unnaturall Poisoning of Fortune Clarke her Husband* (London, 1635).

2. For the Arden of Faversham case, see John Bellamy, *Strange, Inhuman Deaths: Murder in Tudor England* (Westport, CT, 2006), Chapter 4, 'The Murder of Thomas Arden'.

3. The Enoch ap Evans case is explored in Peter Lake, 'Puritanism, Arminianism and a Shropshire Axe-Murder', *Midland History*, 15 (1990), pp. 37–64.

4. Henry Goodcole, *Heaven's Speedie Hue and Cry sent after Lust and Murther, Manifested upon the suddaine Apprehending of Thomas Sharwood and Elizabeth Evans, whose manner of Lives, Death and free Confessions, are here expressed* (London, 1635).

5. Early murder pamphlets are analysed in Bellamy, *Strange, Inhuman Deaths*, which discusses the George Saunders case in depth. Murder pamphlets are also drawn upon in Vanessa McMahon, *Murder in Shakespeare's England* (London, 2004); see also Malcolm Gaskill, 'Reporting Murder: Fiction in the Archives in Early Modern England', *Social History*, 23 (1998), pp. 1–30; and Peter Lake, 'Deeds Against Nature: Cheap Print, Protestantism and Murder in Early Modern England', in Kevin Sharpe and Peter Lake (eds.), *Culture and Politics in Early Stuart England* (Basingstoke, 1994).

6. On Goodcole, see *Oxford DNB*, and Randall Martin, 'Henry Goodcole, Visitor of Newgate: Crime, Conversion and Patronage', *The Seventeenth Century*, 20 (2005), pp. 153–84.

7. *A true relation of the most horrid and barbarous Murders committed by Abigail Hill of St. Olaves Southwark, on the persons of foure Infants . . .* (London, 1658, pp. 2, 3, 5–6, 8–9).

8. Keith Thomas, *Religion and the Decline of Magic: Studies in Popular Beliefs in Sixteenth-and-Seventeenth-century England* (London, 1971), p. 597.

9. *The Rest-less Ghost: Or, wonderful News from Northamptonshire, and Southwark* (London, 1675).

10. Malcolm Gaskill, *Crime and Mentalities in Early Modern England* (Cambridge, 2000), p. 232.

11. Anthony Munday, *A View of Sundry Examples: reporting many straunge Murthers, sundry Persons perjured, Signes and Tokens of God's Anger towards us* (London, 1580), sig. B1v.

12. *The Unnaturall Grand-Mother or, a true relation of a most barbarous Murther, committed by Elizabeth Hazard who sold Oranges and lemons neer Soper Land in Cheap-Side* (London, 1659).

13. *Murther, Murther, or a Bloody Relation of How Anne Hamton dwelling in Westminster nigh London, by Poison murdered her deare Husband* (London, 1641), *passim*.

14. *The Bloody Husband and Cruel Neighbour: or, a true Historie of two Murthers lately committed in Laurence Parish, in the Isle of Thanet in Kent, neer Sandwich* (London, 1653), pp. 2, 1, 13.

15. *The most cruell and bloody Murther committed by an Inkeepers Wife, called Annis Dell, and her Sonne George Dell, foure Yeares since. On the Bodie of a Childe, called Anthony Iames in Bishops Hatfield in the Countie of Hartford* (London, 1606), sig. C1; the indictment of the Dells survives, TNA, ASSI 35/48/2/11.

16. Goodcole, *Heaven's Speedie Hue and Cry after Lust and Murder*, sig. C3.

17. The transition was first spelled out by John Bossy, 'Moral Arithmetic: Seven Sins into Ten Commandments', in Edmund Leites (ed.), *Conscience and Casuistry in Early Modern Europe* (Cambridge, 1988).

18. For John Dod, *Oxford DNB*; *A Plaine and Familiar Exposition of the Ten Commandments* (London, 1607), pp. 256, 257, 271, 252, 264.

19. For Ezekiel Hopkins, *Oxford DNB*; Ezekiel Hopkins, 'The Sixth Commandment: "Thou shalt not kill"', in *An Exposition on the Ten Commandments; with other sermons* (London, 1692), *passim*.

20. There is extensive literature on revenge tragedy. Fredson Thayer Bowers, *Elizabethan Revenge Tragedy 1587–1642* (Gloucester, MA, 1959) is an interesting early study. Charles A. Hallett and Elaine S. Hallett, *The Revenger's Madness: A Study of Revenge Tragedy Motifs* (Lincoln, Nebraska & London, 1980), opens up a number of themes within the genre; Eileen Allman, *Jacobean Revenge Tragedy and the Politics of Virtue* (Newark, NJ & London, 1999), is especially good on gender issues; Wendy Griswold, *Renaissance Revivals: City Comedy and Revenge Tragedy in the London Theatre 1576–1980* (Chicago & London, 1986), at p. 57 usefully lists the works which might be regarded as being within the Revenge Tragedy canon, and examines later revival patterns; Eleanor Prosser, *Hamlet and Revenge*

(Stanford, CA, 1967) discusses this well-known work's status as a revenge tragedy.

21. There are numerous editions of many of the plays noted in the text. I would recommend *The Revenger's Tragedy*, Brian Gibbons (ed.), (New Mermaids, 3rd edn., London, 2008); Thomas Kyd, *The Spanish Tragedy*, Andrew Gurr and J. R. Mulryne (eds.), (New Mermaids, 3rd edn., London, 2009); John Marston, *Antonio's Revenge*, W. Reavley Gair (ed.), (Manchester, 1978), which could usefully be read with a work where the play is discussed at length, Peter B. Murray, *Thomas Kyd* (New York, 1969); Thomas Middleton and William Rowley, *The Changeling*, Michael Neill (ed.), (London, 2006); John Webster, *The White Devil*, Christina Luckyj (ed.), (New Mermaids, 2nd edn., London, 1996); and John Webster, *The Duchess of Malfi*, Leah S. Marcus (ed.), (London, 2009), the editor of this last having produced an exceptionally useful introduction.

22. *The Essays of Francis Bacon, Baron Verulam, Viscount St. Albans and Lord High Chancellor of England, on Civil, Moral, Literary and Political Subjects* (London, 1787), pp. 15–17.

23. Dod and Cleaver, *A Plaine and Familiar Exposition*, p. 263.

24. John Reynolds, *The Triumphs of Gods Revenge Against the Crying and Execrable Sin of Murther; expressed in thirty several tragical Histories* (6th edn., London, 1679), 'The Re-advertisement to the Christian Reader', unpaginated.

25. For Edward Nares, *Oxford DNB*; Edward Nares, *A Sermon on the Sixth Commandment: 'Thou shal't do no murder'* (Canterbury, 1799), *passim*.

26. James VI and I, *Daemonologie, in Forme of a Dialogue, divided into three Bookes* (Edinburgh, 1597), pp. 80–1; John Webster, *The Displaying of Supposed Witchcraft* . . . (London, 1677), pp. 304, 305–6; Jeremy Bentham quoted in Gaskill, *Crime and Mentalities*, p. 272, n. 134.

27. John Wingrave, *A Narrative of the many horrid cruelties inflicted by Elizabeth Brownrigg upon the Body of Mary Clifford* . . . (London, 1767), p. 18.

28. *An Appeal to Humanity, in an Account of the Life and cruel Actions of Elizabeth Brownrigg, who was tried at the Old Bailey on the 12th September 1767* (London, 1767), pp. 1–2.

29. *The cruel Mistress; being, the genuine Trial of Elizabeth Branch, and her own Daughter, for the Murder of Jane Buttersworth their serving Maid* (London, 1740), quotations at pp. 25, 8; see also *The Trial of Mrs Branch, and her daughter, for the Murder of Jane Buttersworth, before the Hon. Mr. Justice Chapple, at Somerset Assizes, March 31, 1740* (Dublin, 1741).

30. The cases listed here are recorded in a collection of single-sheet broadsides, probably pirated from contemporary newspapers, found in the Raymond Burton Collection, University of York Library. Those cited here include: *Particulars of a most horrid and unnatural Murder which was committed on Monday last, on the Body of a new born Child by Burning to Ashes*

in the Fire (Nottingham, 1822); *A Particular Account of that horrid and inhumane Murder, committed on the Body of Richard Walker, who was found murdered in a Field, between Scarboro and Leckonfield, on Monday, Jan the 6ᵗʰ, 1823* (Nottingham, 1823); *The full, true and particular Account of the most barbarous, cruel and inhumane Outrage and Murder committed on the Body of Mary M'Intosh, on Monday Last, near Bowes in Yorkshire* (York, 1820); and *A full true and particular Account of a most barbarous, cruel and inhumane Murder, which was committed on Thursday the 8ᵗʰ day of this instant January, 1818, at a Cottage on Grange Moor, near Leeds in the County of York, by James Cheeseborough, on the Body of his own Mother* (Nottingham, 1818).

Chapter 5: Domestic Violence: Wives, Husbands and Servants

1. The figures for the current situation are derived from Gavin Thompson, 'Domestic Violence Statistics' (House of Commons Library, Standard Note SN/SG/950, updated 10 March 2010); Alison Walker, John Flatley, Chris Kershaw and Debbie Moon (eds.), *Crime in England and Wales 2008/9: Volume 1, Findings of the British Crime Survey and Police Recorded Crime* (Home Office Statistical Bulletin, July 2009), p. 58; Aliyah Dar, *Domestic Violence Statistics* (House of Commons Library, December 2013), p. 3. See also Chapter 13 of this book.
2. The figures for the three south-eastern counties are derived from J. S. Cockburn, 'The Nature and Incidence of Crime in England 1558–1625: A Preliminary Survey', in J. S. Cockburn (ed.), *Crime in England 1550–1800* (London, 1977); for Essex, from J. A. Sharpe, *Crime in Seventeenth-century England: A County Study* (Cambridge, 1983), pp. 119–20, 126–7.
3. William Gouge, *Of Domesticall Duties: Eight Treatises* (London, 1622), p. 18.
4. For a history of the family which stresses the dreadfulness of family relations before the eighteenth century, when the arrival of middle-class values supposedly made things better, see Lawrence Stone, *The Family, Sex and Marriage in England 1500–1800* (London, 1977).
5. The classic statement of the lack of a clear concept of childhood before the eighteenth century is Philippe Ariès, *Centuries of Childhood* (London, 1973).
6. J. A. Sharpe, *Early Modern England: a Social History 1550–1760* (2ⁿᵈ edn., London, 1997), p. 218.
7. For well-informed and balanced work on the history of domestic violence over the period covered by this chapter, see: Joanne Bailey, *Unquiet Lives: Marriage and Marriage Breakdown in England, 1660–1800* (Cambridge, 2003); Elizabeth Foyster, *Marital Violence: An English Family History, 1660–1857* (Cambridge, 2005); and Laura Gowing, *Domestic Dangers: Women, Words and Sex in Early Modern London* (Oxford, 1996), Chapter 6, 'Domestic Disorders: Adultery and Violence'. Those wishing to read further into the subject could consult: Susan Dwyer Amussen, '"Being stirred to much Unquietness": Violence and Domestic Violence in Early Modern England',

Journal of Women's History, 6 (1994), pp. 70–89; J. A. Sharpe, 'Domestic Homicide in Early Modern England', *Historical Journal,* 24 (1981), pp. 29–48; and Anna Clark, 'Domesticity and the Problem of Wife Beating in Nineteenth-century Britain: Working-class Culture, Law and Politics', in Shani D'Cruze (ed.), *Everyday Violence in Britain, 1850–1950* (Harlow, 2000).

8. Simon White's opinion on his violence towards his wife is quoted in Gowing, *Domestic Dangers,* p. 219.

9. John Cannon's brushes with household violence are noted in *The Chronicles of John Cannon, Excise Officer and Writing Master,* John Money (ed.), 2 volumes (Oxford: British Academy Records of Social and Economic History, new series, 43, 2010), Vol. 1, pp. 47, 53.

10. For the Marylebone police court incident, Foyster, *Marital Violence,* p. 12, where Buller's alleged dictum is discussed more generally; William Blackstone, *Commentaries on the Laws of England,* 4 volumes (2nd edn., Oxford, 1765–9),Vol. 1, p. 432; Matthew Bacon, *A New Abridgement of the Law,* 7 volumes (5th edn., 1798), Vol. 1, p. 475.

11. Whately's changing views are noted by Foyster, *Domestic Violence,* pp. 64–5.

12. Gouge, *Domesticall Duties,* pp. 208, 209, 271, 272 on the need for mutual support, but the necessity of wifely subjection; pp. 355, 390–2 for his hostile attitude to wife-beating.

13. Joseph Green's death is recorded in a single-sheet broadside, *The Last Dying Speech and Confession of Charles Squire, who was executed at Stafford, on Monday the 29th Day of April, 1799, for the Murder of Joseph Green his Apprentice* (n.p., 1799).

14. Anne Nailor's death is reported in *God's Revenge Against Murder: or, the Genuine History of the Life, Trial and last Dying Words of Sarah Metyard, Widow, and Sarah Morgan Metyard, Spinster, for the Murder of Anne Nailor, an Infant, aged 13* (n.p., 1762).

15. For the death of Elizabeth Rainbow, *The Trial at large of John Bolton, Gent., of Bulmer, near Castle Howard, for the wilful Murder of Elizabeth Rainbow, his Apprentice Girl* (York, 1775), *passim.*

16. The cases of abuse to apprentices are given in *Western Circuit Assize Orders 1629–48: A Calendar,* J. S. Cockburn (ed.), (Camden Society, 4th series, 1976), pp. 114, 125, 185; *Essex Quarter Sessions Order Book 1652–1661,* D. H. Allen (ed.), (Essex Edited Texts, Chelmsford, 1974), pp. 43, 130, 28.

17. For statements concerning Mary Simpson's death, TNA, CHES 24/161/2.

18. The fullest analysis of wife sale is provided by E. P. Thompson, *Customs in Common* (London, 1991), Chapter 7, 'The Sale of Wives'.

19. The history of divorce in England is discussed and set in context by Roderick Phillips, *Putting Asunder: Divorce in Western Society* (Cambridge, 1988).

20. For Catherine Warburton, Bailey, *Unquiet Lives,* pp. 106–7.

21. Charles Arthur's comments survive in the Borthwick Institute for Archives, Cause Papers, York, CPI 631.

22. Borthwick Institute for Archives, York, Cause Papers, CPH 3000 (Chatsworth); CPH 4505 (Pighill); CPI 154 (Idelle).
23. Alexander George Sinclair's robust treatment at the hands of his in-laws is described in Foyster, *Marital Violence*, p. 175.
24. Samuel Pepys blacking his wife's eye is recorded in *The Diary of Samuel Pepys*, Henry B. Wheatley (ed.), 10 volumes (London, 1893–9), Vol. 4, pp. 309–10, 316.
25. The Surrey charivari is noted in Phillips, *Putting Asunder*, p. 335; the Kent incident in Foyster, *Marital Violence*, p. 216.
26. For a discussion of the spread of 'polite' values in the eighteenth century, see Paul Langford, *A Polite and Commercial People: England 1727–1783* (Oxford, 1989), especially Chapter 3, 'The Progress of Politeness'.
27. The committal of William White to Bedford gaol is noted in Bailey, *Unquiet Lives*, p. 42.
28. The comments from Sir John Nicholl and J. W. Kaye are given in Foyster, *Marital Violence*, pp. 79–80.
29. Sir William Scott's opinions are recorded in the *First Report of the Commissioners, Appointed by Her Majesty to Enquire into the Law of Divorce* (London, 1853), p. 13.
30. For Essex domestic homicides, Sharpe, *County Study*, p. 127; for Surrey, John M. Beattie, *Crime and the Courts in England 1660–1800* (Oxford, 1986), p. 97.
31. Gwenda Morgan and Peter Rushton, *Rogues, Thieves and the Rule of Law: The Problem of Law Enforcement in North-east England, 1718–1800* (London, 1998), pp. 112–13.
32. *Inhumanity and Barbarity not to be equal'd: being an impartial Relation of the barbarous Murder committed by Mrs Elizabeth Branch and her Daughter* (London, 1740), p. 31.
33. The death of Jane Buttersworth is recorded in *Inhumanity and Barbarity not to be equal'd* . . . which has been cited, *passim*, as well as the slightly shorter *The Cruel Mistress*.
34. *The last Speech and Confession of Sarah Elestone at the Place of execution who was Burned for Killing her Husband, April 24 1678. With her Deportment in Prison since her Condemnation* (London, 1678), pp. 2–3. The custom of burning women convicted of petty treason, which included husband murder, was ended in 1790: see Simon Devereaux, 'The Abolition of the Burning of Women in England Reconsidered', *Crime, Histoire & Sociétés/ Crime, History & Societies*, 9 (2005), pp. 73–95.

Chapter 6: Mothers and Infanticide

1. There is now an established body of writing on infanticide in early modern England. The best introduction is Mark Jackson, *New-Born Child Murder: Women, Illegitimacy and the Courts in Eighteenth-century England*

(Manchester, 1996); Mark Jackson (ed.), *Infanticide: Historical Perspectives on Child Murder and Concealment, 1550–2000* (Aldershot, 2002) is a wide-ranging collection of essays around the theme; R. W. Malcolmson, 'Infanticide in the Eighteenth Century', in J. S. Cockburn (ed.), *Crime in England 1550–1800* (London, 1977), was an important pioneering piece; Peter C. Hoffer and N.E.H. Hull, *Murdering Mothers: Infanticide in England and New England, 1558–1803* (New York, 1981), was an early attempt at an overview; Laura Gowing, 'Secret Births and Infanticide in Seventeenth-century England', *Past and Present*, 156 (1997), pp. 87–115, is a very rich analysis of the experience of infanticidal mothers.

2. The idea of an 'infanticide craze' was put forward by Alfred Soman, 'Deviance and Criminal Justice in Western Europe, 1300–1800: An Essay in Structure', *Criminal Justice History*, 1 (1980), pp. 22–3.

3. For Margaret Judge, J. S. Cockburn (ed.), *Kent Indictments Elizabeth I*, (London, 1979), entries 86–7, 104, 112, 153, 183, 209, 222, 257, 289.

4. The figures are derived from J. S. Cockburn (ed.), *A Calendar of Assize Records: Essex Indictments Elizabeth I* (London, 1978); *A Calendar of Assize Records: Essex Indictments James I* (London, 1982); *A Calendar of Assize Records: Hertfordshire Indictments Elizabeth I* (London, 1975); *A Calendar of Assize Records: Hertfordshire Indictments James I* (London, 1975); *A Calendar of Assize Records: Kent Indictments Elizabeth I* (London, 1979); *A Calendar of Assize Records: Kent Indictments James I* (London, 1980); *A Calendar of Assize Records: Surrey Indictments Elizabeth I* (London, 1980); *A Calendar of Assize Records: Surrey Indictments James I* (London, 1982); *A Calendar of Assize Records: Sussex Indictments Elizabeth I* (London, 1975); *A Calendar of Assize Records: Sussex Indictments James I* (London, 1975).

5. Henry Goodcole, *Nature's Cruell Step-Dames: or, matchless Monsters of the female Sex: Elizabeth Barnes, and Anne Willis. Whoe were executed the 26th day April, 1637, at Tyburne, for the unnaturall Murthering of their owne Children* (London, 1637), p. 17.

6. The sermon is referred to by William Tong, *An Account of the life and death of Mr Matthew Henry, Minister of the Gospel at Hackney, who dy'd June 22, 1714 in the 52d Year of his Age* (London, 1716), p. 177.

7. The statutes were 18 Elizabeth I, cap. 3, and 7 James I, cap. 4.

8. Joan Kent, 'Attitudes of Members of the House of Commons to the Regulation of 'Personal Conduct' in Late Elizabethan and Early Stuart England', *Bulletin of the Institute of Historical Research* 46 (1973), p. 69.

9. Statute 21 James I, cap. 27.

10. Old Bailey Online, case t16740909.

11. The figures are derived from: J. S. Cockburn (ed.), *A Calendar of Assize Records: Kent Indictments Charles I* (London, 1995); *A Calendar of Assize*

Records: Kent Indictments Charles II 1660–75 (London, 1995); *A Calendar of Assize Records: Kent Indictments Charles II 1676–88* (London, 1997).

12. For the Essex figures, J. A. Sharpe, *Crime in Seventeenth-century England: A County Study* (Cambridge, 1983), Table 15, p. 136; Table 12, p. 124; Table 4, p. 95; Table 6, p. 108.

13. For Marion Eridge, Cockburn (ed.), *Kent Indictments Charles I*, entry 1024; for Agnes Barnes, *Kent Indictments Elizabeth I*, entry 53; for Elizabeth Courthopp, *Kent Indictments Charles II 1676–88*, entry 508; for the other Kentish cases, *Kent Indictments Elizabeth I*, entries 141, 2074; for the brutal Essex case, *Essex Indictments Elizabeth I*, entry 2162; for Elizabeth Browne, *Kent Indictments Elizabeth I*, entry 2162; for Margaret Chandler, *Surrey Indictments Elizabeth I*, entry 2279.

14. For the Sibyl Ellyot case, Cockburn (ed.), *Sussex Indictments Elizabeth I*, entry 151; for Alice Hilley, *Kent Indictments Elizabeth I*, entry 1742.

15. *Deposition Book of Richard Wyatt, JP, 1767–76*, Elizabeth Silverthorne (ed.), (Surrey Record Society, 30, 1978), pp. 47–9.

16. For Mary Cliff, TNA, CHES 24/164/4.

17. Bernard de Mandeville, *The Fable of the Bees: or, Private Vices, Publick Benefits* (6th edn., London, 1732), pp. 66–8.

18. For the Anne Linscale case, *Depositions from the Castle of York*, James Raine (ed.), (Surtees Society, 40, 1861), pp. 131–2.

19. For the problems at Tonge and Sutton, Cockburn (ed.), *Kent Indictments Charles II 1660–75*, entries 1896, 1899, 1929–30.

20. For Hester Pixey, TNA, CHES 24/156/2.

21. For Mary Stockton, TNA, CHES 38/41, Depositions relating to the death of a child of Mary Stockton, 2 April 1681; for Elizabeth Holdinge, TNA, CHES 38/41, Depositions relating to the death of a child of Elizabeth Holdinge, 2 November 1686.

22. Gowing, 'Secret Births and Infanticide', p. 86.

23. For Martha Roberts, TNA, CHES 24/162/4.

24. For the declining convictions in Cheshire, J. R. Dickinson and James Sharpe, 'Infanticide in Early Modern England: The Court of Great Sessions at Chester', in Jackson (ed.), *Infanticide*, Table 3.1, p. 38; for the Northern Assize Circuit, Jackson, *New-born Child Murder*, p. 3.

25. William Eden, *Principles of Penal Law* (2nd edn., London, 1771), pp. 15–16; on the growing opposition to the 1624 act, Jackson, *New-Born Child Murder*, Chapter 7, 'Single Women, Bastardy and the Law: The Decline and Fall of the 1624 Statute'.

26. For Elizabeth Jackson, TNA, CHES 24/158/4.

27. Old Bailey Online, case t17370420-18; *Gentleman's Magazine* (October 1774), pp. 462–3.

28. For Erasmus Darwin's opinions, *The Collected Letters of Erasmus Darwin*, D. King-Hele (ed.), (Cambridge, 2007), p. 76.

29. William Hunter, quoted by Jackson, *New-born Child Murder*, p. 116; for background on Hunter, see W. F. Bynum and Roy Porter (eds.), *William Hunter and the Eighteenth-century Medical World* (Cambridge, 1985).
30. For Margaret Hedley, Jackson, *New-born Child Murder*, p. 121.
31. On Ellenborough, *Oxford DNB*; Jackson, *New-born Child Murder*, pp. 168–76.
32. Statute 53 George III, cap. 58.
33. Figures extracted from V. A. C. Gatrell, Bruce Lenman and Geoffrey Parker, *Crime and the Law: The Social History of Crime in Western Europe Since 1500* (London, 1980), Table A1, pp. 342–5.
34. I have been guided here by Lionel Rose, *The Massacre of the Innocents: Infanticide in Britain, 1800–1939* (London, 1986).
35. Cited in Rose, *Massacre of the Innocents*, p. 35.
36. Cited in Hilary Marland, 'Getting Away With Murder? Puerperal Insanity, Infanticide and the Defence Plea', in Jackson, *Infanticide*, p. 186.
37. For an excellent short introduction to the nineteenth- and early-twentieth-century legal position on infanticide, see Tony Ward, 'Legislating for Human Nature: Legal Responses to Infanticide, 1860–1938', in Jackson, *Infanticide*.
38. Rose, *Massacre of the Innocents*, p. 118.
39. For discussions of this issue, see Marland, 'Getting Away With Murder?'; and Cath Quinn, 'Images and Impulses: Representations of Puerperal Insanity in Late-Victorian England', in Jackson, *Infanticide*.
40. Statute 12/13 Geo V, cap. 18.

Chapter 7: Verbal Violence: Scolding, Slander and Libel

1. [Richard Allestree], *The Government of the Tongue, by the Author of the Whole Duty of Man, &c* (6th impression, Oxford, 1702), quotations at pp. 135, 174, 188, 214–5, 47, 125–6.
2. William Perkins, *A Direction for the Government of the Tongue According to God's Word* (London, 1638), p. 23. The work was first published in 1593.
3. For scolding to death, Bodleian Library, Oxford, Western MSS, Herne Diaries 158–9 ('Analecta Ro.' Plot').
4. *The Tragedy of Othello the Moor of Venice*, eds. Barbara A. Marat and Paul Werstine: folgerdigitaltexts.org, Act 2, Scene iii, 281–3.
5. John March, *Actions for Slaunder, or, A methodicall collection under certain grounds and heads of what words are actionable in the law, and what not?* (London, 1647), pp. 10–11.
6. Borthwick Institute for Archives, York, Cause Papers, CPH/4499.
7. Quoted in Laura Gowing, *Domestic Dangers: Women, Words and Sex in Early Modern London* (Oxford, 1996), p. 73.
8. Examples of Manx cursing, including those used here, are referenced and discussed in James Sharpe, 'Witchcraft in the Early Modern Isle of Man', *Cultural & Social History*, 4 (2007), pp. 11–28.

9. The case of Thomas Perne and the Bishop of Barcelona's curse are noted in Keith Thomas, *Religion and the Decline of Magic: Studies in Popular Beliefs in Sixteenth- and Seventeenth-century England* (London, 1971), pp. 501, 502; for William Lacey, Sharpe, 'Witchcraft in the Early Modern Isle of Man', p. 20.

10. For Julius Palmer, *The Actes and Monuments of John Foxe*, Josiah Pratt (ed.), 8 volumes (London, 1877), Vol. 8, pp. 201–19.

11. The cases of Helen Hiley and Anne Dixon are noted in J. A. Sharpe, *Crime in Early Modern England 1550–1750* (2nd edn., 1997), pp. 120–1; for Mary Weston, Cheshire Archives and Local Studies Service, Cause Papers, EDC 5 (1593); for John Smyth, Thomas, *Religion and the Decline of Magic*, p. 507.

12. Perkins, *Direction for the Government of the Tongue*, p. 42.

13. William Perkins, *A Discourse of the Damned Art of Witchcraft: so farre forth as it is revealed in the Scriptures, and manifest by true Experience* (Cambridge, 1608), p. 202; Thomas Cooper, *The Mystery of Witchcraft: Discovering the Truth, Nature, Occasions, Growth, and Power thereof: together with the Detection and Punishment of the Same* (London, 1617), pp. 208–9.

14. For Elizabeth Lowys, Essex Record Office, depositions at end of Archdeaconry of Essex Act Book, D/AEA/2.

15. For Elizabeth Bennett's troubles, W.W., *A true and just Recorde, of the Information, Examination and Confession, of all the Witches taken at St Oses in the Countie of Essex* (London, 1582), sig. B5v.

16. *The most strange and admirable Discoverie of the three Witches of Warboys* (London, 1593), sig. D4.

17. *Certaine Sermons or Homilies appointed to be read in Church* (London, 1623), p. 92. 'The Book of Homilies', written principally by Thomas Cranmer, first appeared in 1547.

18. *Borough Customs, Volume I*, Mary Bateson (ed.), (The Selden Society, 18, 1904), p. 80, for the Hereford order.

19. On scolds see David Underdown, 'The Taming of the Scold: The Enforcement of Patriarchal Authority in Early Modern England', in Anthony Fletcher and John Stevenson (eds.), *Order and Disorder in Early Modern England* (Cambridge, 1985); and Martin Ingram, '"Scolding Women Cucked or Washed": A Crisis in Gender Relations in Early Modern England?', in J. L. Kermode and Garthine Walker (eds.), *Women, Crime and the Courts in Early Modern England* (London, 1994).

20. Moses à Vauts, *The Husband's Authority Unvail'd: wherein it is moderately discussed whether it be fit or lawfull for a good man to beat his bad Wife* (London, 1650), p. 80.

21. *Court Rolls of the Manor of Acomb*, Vol. I, Harold Richardson (ed.), (Yorkshire Archaeological Society Record Series, 131, 1969), pp. 74–5, 145–6, 79, 126, 138, 129, 132.

22. For the Wiltshire man's opinion, Ingram, 'Scolding Women Cucked or Washed', p. 68.

23. For Mary Stracke, Paul Hair (ed.), *Before the Bawdy Court: Selections from Church Court and Other Records relating to the Correction of Moral Offences in England, Scotland and New England, 1300–1800* (London, 1972), p. 147.

24. *Macclesfield in the Later Fourteenth Century: Communities of Town and Forest*, A. M. Tonkinson, (Chetham Society, 3rd series, 42, 1999), pp. 207–9, 164, 166–7.

25. The instances of ducking are noted in Underdown, 'Taming of the Scold', p. 125.

26. Underdown, 'Taming of the Scold', p. 125.

27. The scold's bridle is discussed in Lynda E. Boose, 'Scolding Brides and Bridling Scolds: Taming the Woman's Unruly Member', *Shakespeare Quarterly*, 42 (1991), pp. 179–213; for Brushfield's pioneering contribution, 'On Obsolete Punishments, with particular reference to those of Cheshire: Part I, The Branks or Scold's Bridle', *Journal for the Architectural, Archaeological, and Historic Society for the City, County and Neighbourhood of Chester*, 2 (1864), pp. 41–7.

28. Robert Plot, *The Natural History of Staffordshire* (Oxford, 1686), p. 389.

29. Ralph Gardiner, *England's Grievance Discovered in Relation to the Coal Trade* (London, 1655), p. 110.

30. For Dorothy Waugh, *The Lamb's Defence against Lyes: and a true Testimony given concerning the Sufferings and Death of James Parnell* (London, 1656), pp. 29–30.

31. 'The Flyting of Dunbar and Kennedie' in *The Poems of William Dunbar*, Priscilla Bawcutt (ed.), 2 volumes (Glasgow, 1998), Vol. 1, pp. 200–18; Margaret Galway, 'Flyting in Shakspere [sic]', *Shakespearean Association Bulletin*, 10 (1935), pp. 183–91; for a more recent and comprehensive analysis of the role of verbal violence in Shakespeare's plays, see Kenneth Gross, *Shakespeare's Noise* (Chicago, 2001); and for discussion of flyting, or something like it, in another early modern context, see Donald Weinstein, 'Fighting or Flyting? Verbal Duelling in Mid-sixteenth-century Italy', in Trevor Dean and K. J. P. Lowe (eds.), *Crime, Society and the Law in Renaissance Italy* (Cambridge, 1994).

32. The Yorkshire church court defamation cases cited here and on pp. 241–2 are, with others, gathered together and analysed in J. A. Sharpe, *Defamation and Sexual Slander in Early Modern England: The Church Courts at York* (Borthwick Paper 58, York, 1980).

33. For the Goldhanger and Great Oakley cases, F. G. Emmison, *Elizabethan Life: Morals and the Church Courts* (Chelmsford, 1973), pp. 66–7.

34. For written libels and cognate documentation, see Adam Fox, 'Ballads, Libels and Popular Ridicule in Jacobean England', *Past and Present*, 145 (1994), pp. 47–83; the George Hawkins case is discussed at pp. 49–51, and the Southwark incident at p. 64.

35. For charivari, Martin Ingram, 'Ridings, Rough Music and the "Reform of Popular Culture" in Early Modern England', *Past and Present*, 105 (1984), pp. 79–113; the quotation concerning the Quemerford incident is at p. 82.
36. Joan R. Kent, '"Folk Justice" and Royal Justice in Early Seventeenth Century England: A "Charivari" in the Midlands', *Midland History*, 8 (1983), pp. 70–85.
37. TNA. Clerks of Assize Records, Northern Circuit Depositions, ASSI 45/8/2/113–15.
38. *A Vindication or Iustification of John Griffith esq. Against the horrid, malitious, and unconscionable verdict of the Coroners Iury in Cheshire; which was packt by the Means of that pocky, rotten, lying, cowardly and most perfidious Knave Sir Hugh Calverley Knight* (London, 1648), p. 5.
39. Robert B. Shoemaker, 'The Decline of Public Insult in London 1660–1800', *Past and Present*, 169 (2000), pp. 97–131.
40. Ibid., p. 111.
41. Erasmus Darwin, *Zoonomia, or, the Laws of Organic Life*, 2 volumes (London, 1794–6), Vol. 2, pp. 359, 356.
42. *Proverbs*, 18:21.

Chapter 8: The Rise and Fall of the Duel

1. Details of Reresby's life are taken from the Introduction to *Memoirs of Sir John Reresby*, Andrew Browning (ed.), (Glasgow, 1936), supplemented by the entry on Reresby in *Oxford DNB*: for a fuller discussion of Reresby's predilection for fighting, see James Sharpe, 'Violence and Sir Reresby', in Annika Sandén (ed.), *Demographi, Rätt och Hälsa-en Vänbok till Jan Sundin: Se Människan* (Linköping, 2008). It is a matter of regret that Reresby's forename disappeared from the title of this essay between proof-reading and publication.
2. Quotations come from *Memoirs of Sir John Reresby*, Browning (ed.), pp. 44–5, 46, 271–2, 21–2.
3. William Thomas, *The Historie of Italie: a Boke excedyng profitable to be redde* (London, 1549), pp. 3–4.
4. References to early fencing masters and their publications are taken from Lawrence Stone, *The Crisis of the Aristocracy 1558–1641* (Oxford, 1965), pp. 144–5; there are a number of general works on the duel, of which V. G. Kiernan, *The Duel in European History: Honour and the Reign of Aristocracy* (Oxford, 1988), probably remains the best overall introduction. Markku Peltonen, *The Duel in Early Modern England* (Cambridge, 2003) is a detailed and scholarly work which is especially interesting in linking the duel to the culture of upper-class civility. Peltonen's focus is on the history of the duel in England up to the early eighteenth century. The story is continued in Stephen Banks, *A Polite Exchange of Bullets: The Duel and the English Gentleman, 1750–1850* (Woodbridge, 2010).

5. Sir Philip Sidney's duel with Oxford is described and contextualised in Roger Howell, *Sir Philip Sidney: The Shepherd Knight* (London, 1968), pp. 68–70; there are numerous works on Sidney's cultural significance, of which Matthew Woodcock, *Sir Philip Sidney and the Sidney Circle* (Tavistock, 2010), constitutes a good up-to-date short guide.

6. The implications for duelling on a partly militarised elite are discussed in Roger B. Manning, *Swordsmen: The Martial Ethos in the Three Kingdoms* (Oxford, 2003).

7. *Memoirs of Sir John Reresby*, Browning (ed.), pp. 318, 263–4.

8. Peltonen, *Duel in Early Modern England*, p. 13.

9. Vincentio Saviolo, *Vincentio Saviolo, His Practise* (London, 1595), sig, R4r.

10. Joseph Addison, *The Spectator*, 23 June 1711.

11. Bernard de Mandeville, *The Fable of the Bees: or, Private Vices, Publick Benefits* (6th edn., London, 1732), p. 244.

12. For the Montgomery–Macnamara affair, Robert Baldick, *The Duel: A History of Duelling* (London, 1965), pp. 97–8.

13. On fatality rates and the use of pistols, see Robert B. Shoemaker, 'The Taming of the Duel: Masculinity, Honour and Ritual Violence in London, 1660–1800', *Historical Journal*, 45 (2002), pp. 525–45.

14. Samuel Stanton, *The Principles of Duelling: With Rules to be Observed in Every Particular Respecting It* (London, 1790), p. 69.

15. On Wellington's duel with Winchilsea see the account at http://www.kingscollections.org/exhibitions/archives/wellington/duel/background; on the duel between Wilkes and Martin, Arthur H. Cash, *John Wilkes: The Scandalous Father of Civil Liberty* (New Haven, 2006), pp. 154–8.

16. For a number of stories of women duellists, see Baldick, *The Duel*, Chapter 11, 'Women Duellists'.

17. *The Western County Magazine for the Year 1790* (Salisbury, 1790), p. 136; Baldick, *The Duel*, p. 175; All Things Georgian, https://georgianera.wordpress.com/2014/08/05/the-petticoat-duellists-of-1792.

18. César de Saussure, *A Foreign View of England in the Reigns of George I and George II*, M. Van Muyden (ed.), (London, 1902), pp. 112–13; de Saussure is quoted and these informal boxing matches discussed further in Robert Shoemaker, *The London Mob: Violence and Disorder in Eighteenth-century England* (London, 2004), pp. 194–200.

19. Lodowick Bryskett, *A Discourse of Civill Life: Containing the Ethicke part of Morall Philosophie. Fit for the Instructing of a Gentleman in the Course of a Vertuous Life* (London, 1606), pp. 79–80, 70.

20. *The Diary of Samuel Pepys*, Henry B. Wheatley (ed.), 10 volumes (London, 1893–9), Vol. 7, pp. 47, 66, 283–4.

21. This account of the decline of duelling is based on the arguments put forward by: Donna T. Andrew, 'The Code of Honour and its Critics: The

Opposition to Duelling in England, 1700–1850', *Social History*, 5 (1980), pp. 409–34; Robert B. Shoemaker, 'Taming of the Duel'; Robert B. Shoemaker, 'Male Honour and the Decline of Public Violence in Eighteenth-century London', *Social History*, 26 (2001), pp. 190–208; and Anthony Simpson, 'Dandelions on the Field of Honour: Duelling, the Middle Classes, and the Law in Nineteenth-century England', *Criminal Justice History*, 9 (1988), pp. 99–155, and the closing chapters of Banks, *Polite Exchange of Bullets*. I have also drawn on Kiernan, *Duel in European History*, Chapter 12, 'Britain: The Final Decades', and Clive Emsley, *Hard Men: Violence in England since 1750* (London, 2005), pp. 43–5.

22. *An Essay on Duelling* (London, 1792), pp. 17, 29–30.
23. Edmund Chishull, *Against Duelling. A Sermon Preach'd before the Queen in the Royal Chapel at Windsor-Castle on November the 23rd, 1712* (London, 1712), pp. 5, 16, 23–4.
24. Granville Sharp, *A tract on duelling: wherein the opinions of some of the most celebrated writers on crown laws are examined and corrected* . . . (London, 1773), pp. iii, vi.
25. Stanton, *Principles of Duelling*, pp. iv, 5, 18, 19.
26. John Bennett, *A Discourse Against the Fatal Practice of Duelling; Occasioned by a Late Melancholy Event, and Preached at St Mary's Church, in Manchester, on Sunday the 23rd of March, 1783* (Manchester, 1783), pp. 9–10. On Pitt's duel with Tierney, see William Hague, *William Pitt the Younger* (London, 2004), pp. 424–7.
27. Stanton, *Principles of Duelling*, p. 36.
28. Bennett, *Discourse Against the Fatal Practice of Duelling*, p. ii.
29. These arguments are developed in Banks, *Polite Exchange of Bullets*.
30. Giles Hunt, *The Duel: Castlereagh, Canning and Deadly Cabinet Rivalry* (London, 2008), provides a good popular account of the Castlereagh–Canning duel and its background.

Chapter 9: Sport and the Decline of Casual Violence

1. I first became alerted to the traditional football at Ashbourne when advising on a York History BA dissertation, Ashley Coxon, 'Popular Culture and Changing Attitudes towards Ashbourne Shrovetide Football, 1860–1891' (2009); Lindsey Porter has written a number of books on the subject, of which *Ashbourne Royal Shrovetide Football: The Official History* (1992) is perhaps the best overview.
2. On pre-industrial pastimes in general, see Robert W. Malcolmson, *Popular Recreations in English Society 1700–1850* (Cambridge, 1973).
3. Folk football at Derby is a major theme of Anthony Delves, 'Popular Recreation and Social Conflict at Derby, 1800–1850', in Eileen Yeo and Stephen Yeo (eds.), *Popular Culture and Class Conflict 1590–1914: Explorations in the History of Labour and Leisure* (Brighton, 1981).

4. For Fifth of November celebrations, see: Robert D. Storch, '"Please to Remember the Fifth of November": Conflict, Solidarity and Public Order in Southern England, 1815–1900', in Storch (ed.), *Popular Culture and Custom in Nineteenth-century England* (London & New York, 1982); and James Sharpe, *Remember Remember the Fifth of November: A Cultural History of Guy Fawkes Day* (Cambridge, Mass., 2005), Chapter 5, 'The Triumph and Taming of Bonfire Night'; for a detailed study of events in Guildford, see Gavin Morgan, *The Guildford Guy Riots: Being an Exact Description of the Terrible Disturbances in the County Town of Surrey* (London, 1992).

5. Alun Howkins, 'The Taming of Whitsun: The Changing Face of a Nineteenth-century Rural Holiday', in Yeo and Yeo (eds.), *Popular Culture and Class Conflict*: the quotation on the celebration at Cranfield is on p. 195.

6. On public schools, see T. W. Bamford, *Rise of the Public Schools: A Study of Boys' Public Boarding Schools in England and Wales from 1837 to the Present Day* (London, 1967); David Newsome, *Godliness & Good Learning: Four Studies on a Victorian Ideal* (London, 1961); Brian Simon and Ian Bradley (eds.), *The Victorian Public School: Studies in the Development of an Educational Institution* (London, 1975); and J. R. de S. Honey, *Tom Brown's Universe: The Development of the Victorian Public School* (London, 1977). Christopher Tyerman, *A History of Harrow School 1324–1991* (Oxford, 2000), is an excellent study of one of the major public schools.

7. Tyerman, *A History of Harrow School*, pp. 159–60.

8. My account of football at various public schools in the early nineteenth century is based on James Walvin, *The People's Game: A Social History of British Football* (London, 1975), pp. 32–4.

9. Thomas Arnold, cited in de S. Honey, *Tom Brown's Universe*, p. 6.

10. On Hughes, see Edward C. Mack and W. H. G. Armytage, *Thomas Hughes: The Life of the Author of Tom Brown's Schooldays* (London, 1952); Chapter 6, '"Tom Brown's Schooldays", 1857–1858', provides information on the book's initial reception; Isabel Quigly, *The Heirs of Tom Brown: The English School Story* (London, 1984), provides a good overview of the subject, while Jenny Holt, *Public School Literature, Civic Education and the Politics of Male Adolescence* (Farnham, 2008), is a good analysis of the wider importance of the public-school novel. On the readership of the Billy Bunter stories, George Orwell, *Collected Essays, Journalism and Letters*, eds. Sonia Orwell and Ian Angus (London, 1968), 'Boys' Weeklies'.

11. Thomas Hughes, *Tom Brown's School Days* (9th edn., 1869), pp. 140, 116.

12. Thomas Hughes, *Tom Brown's School Days*, Preface.

13. See T. W. Bamford, *Thomas Arnold* (London, 1960), Chapter 6, 'Flogging'.

14. Tyerman, *A History of Harrow School*, p. 400.

15. Holt, *Public School Literature*, pp. 125–7.

16. The origins of the practice of carrying the ball at Rugby, which was eventually to lead to the modern sport of rugby football, remains debatable. It seems that the practice developed, while not initially being regarded as legitimate, over the 1820s and 1830s, and was finally formally accepted in 1841; see Jennifer Macrory, *Running with the Ball: The Birth of Rugby Football* (London, 1991), which has a balanced discussion of the contribution of the Rugby schoolboy William Webb Ellis to the invention of the game.
17. Hughes, *Tom Brown's School Days*, Preface.
18. Hughes, *Tom Brown's School Days*, p. 355.
19. Norman Vance, 'The Ideal of Manliness', in Simon and Bradley (eds.), *Victorian Public School*, p. 123.
20. On muscular Christianity, see Donald E. Hall (ed.), *Muscular Christianity: Embodying the Victorian Age* (Cambridge, 1994).
21. Cited by J. A. Mangan, 'Athleticism: A Case Study of the Evolution of an Educational Ideology', in Simon and Bradley (eds.), *Victorian Public School*, p. 166.
22. Both quoted in Tyerman, *History of Harrow School*, pp. 398, 468.
23. My account of boxing is based on Robert Shoemaker, *The London Mob: Violence and Disorder in Eighteenth-century England* (London, 2004), pp. 194–213; Derek Birley, *Sport and the Making of Britain* (Manchester, 1993), especially pp. 193–6, 234–6, 286–90; and *Oxford DNB* entries on James Figg, Jack Broughton, Daniel Mendoza and Tom Cribb. The flavour of early boxing is captured in Pierce Egan, *Boxiana: or, Sketches of Ancient & Modern Pugilism from the Days of the renowned Broughton and Slack to the Championship of Cribb*, 4 volumes (London, 1830).
24. Egan, *Boxiana*, Vol. 1, pp. 2–3; *A New Song Concerning the Boxing Match Between that Ancient British Boxer John Bull and that Elf, Bonaparte* (single-sheet broadside ballad, London, 1799).
25. I have based my account of the Queensberry Rules on the entries for Queensberry and Chambers in the *Oxford DNB*.
26. The history of the development of football given in this section is based on Walvin, *People's Game*; Tony Mason, *Association Football and English Society 1863–1915* (Hassocks, 1980), this being by far the fullest account; and Eric Dunning, 'The Origins of Modern Football and the Public School Ethos', in Simon and Bradley (eds.), *The Victorian Public School*.
27. On the fortunes of rugby, see Eric Dunning and Kenneth Sheard, *Barbarians, Gentlemen and Players: A Sociological Study of the Development of Rugby Football* (Oxford, 1979), a book which places the history of rugby firmly within the framework of a civilising process; Macrory, *Running with the Ball*, is an entertaining collection of extracts relating to the early history of rugby football.

28. Dunning and Sheard, *Barbarians, Gentlemen and Players*, quotations at pp. III, II4, II7; injuries in Yorkshire and the unwilling insurance company, pp. 220–1.
29. The attendance at St James' Park in 1908 is noted in Mason, *Association Football and English Society*, p. 143.
30. On 'flat-footed Robertos', Mason, *Association Football and English Society*, p. 167.
31. For the quotation on the disciplines of industrial society, Walvin, *People's Game*, p. 67.
32. Johan Huizinga, *Homo Ludens: A Study of the Play-Element in Culture* (London, 1938).
33. These themes are elaborated in the various essays collected together in Norbert Elias and Eric Dunning, *Quest for Excitement: Sport and Leisure in the Civilising Process* (Oxford, 1986).
34. James Buchanan Given, *Society and Homicide in Thirteenth-century England* (Stanford, 1977), p. 50.
35. Norbert Elias, Introduction, in Elias and Dunning, *Quest for Excitement* (Oxford, 1986), p. 20.

Chapter 10: Violence and Organised Crime: Highwaymen and Smugglers

1. *Tudor Economic Documents*, R. H. Tawney and Eileen Power (eds.), 3 volumes (London, 1924), Vol. 2, pp. 337–8.
2. On Jonathan Wild, see Gerald Howson, *Thief-taker General: Jonathan Wild and the Emergence of Crime and Corruption as a Way of Life in Eighteenth-century England* (London, 1970).
3. This account is based on J. M. Beattie, *Crime and the Courts in England 1660–1800* (Oxford, 1986), pp. 156–69.
4. For two typical accounts of well-known highwaymen, see: *The Mémoires of Monsieur du Vall: containing the History of his Life and Death. Whereunto are Annexed his Last Speech and Epitaph* (London, 1670: reprinted, 1744); and *The complete History of James MacLean, the gentleman highwayman, who was executed at Tyburn on Wednesday, October 3, 1750, for robbery on the highway* (London, 1750). Gillian Spraggs, *Outlaws and Highwaymen: The Cult of the Robber in England from the Middle Ages to the Nineteenth Century* (London, 2001), places highwaymen in a broader context, while Lincoln B. Faller, *Turned to Account: The Forms and Functions of Criminal Biography in Seventeenth- and Early Eighteenth-century England* (Cambridge, 1987), is a scholarly study of the formation of the highwayman image, focussing on James Hind and Claude Duvall.
5. William Harrison Ainsworth, *Rookwood* (Bentley's Standard Novel Series, London, 1837), quotations at pp. 62–3, 64, 196–7.

6. Turpin's career and his subsequent legend form the subject matter of James Sharpe, *Dick Turpin: The Myth of the English Highwayman* (London, 2004); materials relating to Turpin and his associates are gathered together in Derek Barlow, *Dick Turpin and the Gregory Gang* (London & Chichester, 1973).

7. Ralph Wilson, *A full and impartial Account of all the Robberies committed by John Hawkins, George Sympson (lately executed for Robbing the Bristol Mail) and their Companions* (London, 1722).

8. Highwaymen's careers are detailed in G. T. Crook (ed.), *Complete Newgate Calendar*, 5 volumes (London, 1926). The biographies of the various miscreants listed in the Calendar are arranged by date of execution: for the highwaymen mentioned in the text: Vol. 3, pp. 261–4 (William Page); Vol. 4, pp. 232–6 (Richard Ferguson); Vol. 2, pp. 28–33 (William Davis); Vol. 2, pp. 4–7 (Patrick O'Bryan); Vol. 2, pp. 202–5 (Jack Ovet); Vol. 3, pp. 76–9 (William Udall and Raby); Vol. 2, pp. 155–7 (Jack Blewitt); Vol. 1, pp. 275–9 (Richard Dudley); Vol. 3, pp. 71–3 (the Hallam brothers); Vol. 2, pp. 82–4 (Jocelin Harwood).

9. As with all of Dickens's works, there is extensive critical literature on *Oliver Twist*; for a good sample of it, see Charles Dickens, *Oliver Twist*, Fred Kaplan (ed.), (New York & London, 1993), 'Criticism', pp. 419–608.

10. Susan Magarey, 'The Invention of Juvenile Delinquency in Early Nineteenth-century Britain', *Labour History*, 34 (1978), pp. 11–27; see also Peter King and Joan Noel, 'Origins of "The Problem of Juvenile Delinquency"', *Criminal Justice History*, 14 (1993), pp. 17–41; and Heather Shore, *Artful Dodgers: Youth and Crime in Early Nineteenth-century London* (Woodbridge, 1999).

11. *Newgate Calendar*, accessed at http://www.exclassics.com/newgate/ng859.htm; *Oxford DNB*.

12. Henry Goddard, *Memoirs of a Bow Street Runner* (London, 1956), pp. 37–41.

13. This notebook forms the basis of the discussion in Leon Radzinowicz, *A History of English Criminal Law and Its Administration from 1750, Vol. 2: The Clash Between Private Initiative and Public Interest in the Enforcement of the Law* (London, 1956), pp. 298–306, which in turn forms the basis for my account.

14. Peter Quennell (ed.), *London's Underworld: Being Selections from 'Those That Will Not Work', the Fourth Volume of 'London Labour and the London Poor', by Henry Mayhew* (London, 1950), quotation on p. 305; for a useful commentary on Mayhew's social reportage, see Richard Maxwell, 'Henry Mayhew and the Life of the Streets', *Journal of British Studies*, 17, 2 (1978), pp. 87–105; details on Mayhew from *Oxford DNB*.

15. There are now a number of excellent studies of prostitution in the nineteenth century, although they direct little of their attention to the issue of prostitution as an aspect of organised crime, or to violence

within the sex trade. I have consulted: Tony Henderson, *Disorderly Women in Eighteenth-century London: Prostitution and Control in the Metropolis, 1730–1830* (London, 1999); Judith R. Walkowitz, *Prostitution and Victorian Society: Women, Class and the State* (Cambridge, 1980); Paula Bartley, *Prostitution: Prevention and Reform in England, 1860–1914* (Abingdon, 2000); and Frances Finnegan, *Poverty and Prostitution: A Study of Victorian Prostitutes in York* (Cambridge, 1979). The last title is an excellent example of how a local study can illuminate the broader picture.

16. Quennell (ed.), *London's Underworld*, pp. 48–9.
17. Quennell (ed.), *London's Underworld*, p. 109.
18. Raphael Samuel, *East End Underworld: Chapters in the Life of Arthur Harding* (London, 1981).
19. Arthur George Morrison, *A Child of the Jago* (London, 1896). Morrison, born in Poplar, was a journalist and author who wrote extensively on conditions in the East End, and this novel was a bestseller which cemented his reputation.
20. Sam Newens, 'The Genesis of *East End Underworld: Chapters in the Life of Arthur Harding* by Raphael Samuel', *History Workshop Journal*, 64 (2007), pp. 347–53.
21. The starting point for a discussion of eighteenth-century smuggling is Cal Winslow, 'Sussex Smugglers', in Douglas Hay *et al.*, *Albion's Fatal Tree: Crime and Society in Eighteenth-century England* (London, 1975). Frank McLynn, *Crime and Punishment in Eighteenth-century England* (Oxford, 1989), Chapter 10, 'Smuggling', provides a good overview for the general reader. Considerable material is gathered together, and some interesting ideas put forward, in Paul Muskett, 'English Smuggling in the Eighteenth Century' (unpublished PhD thesis, Open University, 1996) – Chapter 3 of this work, 'Violence and the Smuggling Trade', has proved especially useful; Muskett's 'Deal Smugglers in the Eighteenth Century', *Southern History*, 8 (1986), pp. 46–69, is a good local study.
22. For the economic background to smuggling, see: W. A. Cole, 'Trends in Eighteenth-century Smuggling', in W. E. Minchinton (ed.), *The Growth of English Overseas Trade in the Seventeenth and Eighteenth Centuries* (London, 1969); and Robert Nash, 'The English and Scottish Tobacco Trades in the Seventeenth and Eighteenth Centuries: Legal and Illegal Trade', *Economic History Review*, second series, 35 (1982), pp. 354–72.
23. For details on tea imports, McLynn, *Crime and Punishment*, p. 179; see also Hoh-Cheung and Lorna H. Mui, 'Smuggling and the British Tea Trade before 1784', *American Historical Review*, 74, 1 (1968), pp. 44–73.
24. For Lady Holderness's silk gowns, McLynn, *Crime and Punishment*, p. 183.
25. For Arthur Young's calculations, McLynn, *Crime and Punishment*, p. 183.
26. The murders of Galley and Chater are described in *The genuine history of the inhuman and unparallell'd murders committed on the bodies of Mr William*

Galley, a custom-house officer in the Port of Southampton, and Mr Daniel Chater, a shoemaker of Fordingbridge in Hampshire (London, 1749), written by an anonymous 'Gentleman in Chichester': quotation at p. 23.

27. On violence against informers, Muskett, 'English Smuggling', pp. 226–8.
28. Winslow, 'Sussex Smugglers', p. 133; Muskett, 'English Smuggling', pp. 226–8.
29. The 1662 statute was 14 Charles II, cap. 11.
30. The 1733 Committee is quoted in Muskett, 'English Smuggling', p. 119.
31. For Charles Fleet on the state of anarchy, Winslow, 'Sussex Smugglers', p. 119.
32. *Genuine history of the inhuman and unparallell'd murders*, p. 41.
33. For these disorders, Winslow, 'Sussex Smugglers', p. 133.

Chapter 11: The Georgian Mob

1. An opinion voiced by Colin Haydon in his entry on Gordon in *Oxford DNB*.
2. There is an excellent recent introduction to perspectives on the Gordon Riots, Ian Hayward (ed.), *The Gordon Riots: Politics, Culture and Insurrection in Late Eighteenth-century Britain* (Cambridge, 2012); for a good popular narrative, Christopher Hibbert, *King Mob: The Story of Lord George Gordon and the Riots of 1780* (London, 1958); there is still much of value in J. P. de Castro, *The Gordon Riots* (Oxford, 1926); scholarly reappraisal of the events of 1780 began with George Rudé, 'The Gordon Riots: A Study of the Rioters and their Victims', *Transactions of the Royal Historical Society*, 5th series, 6 (1956), pp. 93–115; see also Colin Haydon, *Anti-Catholicism in Eighteenth-century England c. 1714–80: A Political and Social Study* (Manchester, 1993).
3. Rudé, 'The Gordon Riots', pp. 113, 111.
4. For the quotations on eighteenth-century riots: J. H. Plumb, *The First Four Georges* (London, 1956), pp. 14–15; J. H. Plumb, *England in the Eighteenth Century* (Harmondsworth, 1950); Max Beloff, *Public Order and Popular Disturbances, 1660–1714* (London, 1963), p. 29.
5. There is extensive literature on eighteenth-century rioting: I have drawn on John Archer, *Social Unrest and Popular Protest in England, 1780–1840* (Cambridge, 2000); Ian Gilmour, *Riots, Rising and Revolution: Governance and Violence in Eighteenth-century England* (London, 1992); Mark Harrison, *Crowds in History: Mass Phenomena in English Towns, 1790–1835* (Oxford, 1998); Adrian Randall, *Riotous Assemblies: Popular Protest in Hanoverian England* (Oxford, 2006); Nicholas Rogers, *Crowds, Culture and Politics in Georgian Britain* (Oxford, 1998); George Rudé, *The Crowd in History: A Study of Popular Disturbances in France and England, 1730–1848* (London, 1964); and John Stevenson, *Popular Disturbances in England, 1700–1832* (2nd edn., London, 1992); an important aspect of the subject is discussed by

Tony Hayter, *The Army and the Crowd in Mid-Georgian England* (London, 1978).

6. For the background to the Riot Act, Gilmour, *Riot, Rising and Revolution*, pp. 61–4.

7. On the Porteous Riots, Gilmour, *Riots, Rising and Revolution*, pp. 94–6; H. T. Dickinson and Kenneth Logue, 'The Porteous Riot, 1736: Events in a Scottish Protest against the Act of Union with England', *History Today*, 22 (1972), pp. 272–81.

8. On the St George's Fields Massacre and its aftermath, Gilmour, *Riots, Rising and Revolution*, pp. 314–7; for the broader disturbances associated with Wilkes, Stevenson, *Popular Disturbances*, pp. 64–76.

9. Lord Hervey's opinions on the military's difficulties come from John, Lord Hervey, *Some Materials Towards Memoirs of the Reign of King George II*, Romney Sedgwick (ed.), 3 volumes (London, 1931), p. 566; see also Gilmour, *Riot, Risings and Revolution*, Chapter 6, 'The Army and the Riot Act'.

10. Sir Charles Napier, *Remarks on Military Law and the Punishment of Flogging* (London, 1837), p. 47.

11. Hayter, *Army and Crowd Control*, p. 50.

12. Nathaniel Cholmley is cited by Hayter, *Army and Crowd Control*, p. 18.

13. For the Hexham incident, Hayter, *Army and Crowd Control*, pp. 176–7; Gilmour, *Riots, Risings and Revolution*, p. 299.

14. For the demolition of the calendar rioting myth, see Robert Poole, *Time's Alteration: Calendar Reform in Early Modern England* (London, 1998), Chapter 1, '"Give us our eleven days": The English Calendar Riots of 1752'.

15. E. P. Thompson, 'The Moral Economy of the English Crowd in the Eighteenth Century', *Past and Present*, 50 (1971), pp. 76–136; the quotation is at p. 76.

16. For crowd action at Banbury and Chipping Norton, Thompson. 'Moral Economy', p. 110; for the women at Bath, Gilmour, *Riots, Rising and Revolution*, p. 140; for the Gloucester sheriff, Thompson, 'Moral Economy', p. 111.

17. Eric Hobsbawm, 'The Machine Breakers', *Past and Present*, 1 (1952), pp. 57–70; the quotation is at p. 57. This article influenced later studies, e.g. Malcolm I. Thomis, *The Luddites: Machine-breaking in Regency England* (Newton Abbot, 1970); and Adrian Randall, *Before the Luddites: Custom, Community and Machinery in the English Woollen Industry, 1776–1809* (Cambridge, 1991).

18. For rioting in Colchester, J. A. Sharpe, *Crime in Seventeenth-century England: A County Study* (Cambridge, 1983), pp. 80–2, 85–6; J. A. Sharpe, *Crime in Early Modern England 1550–1750* (2nd edn., London, 1999), pp. 193–8.

19. On legitimation, Thompson, 'Moral Economy', p. 78.

20. For Kingswood Forest, see Robert W. Malcolmson, 'A Set of Ungovernable People: The Kingswood Colliers in the Eighteenth Century', in John

Brewer and John Styles (eds.), *An Ungovernable People: The English and Their Law in the Seventeenth and Eighteenth Centuries* (London, 1980).

21. *The Autobiography of Samuel Bamford*, 2 volumes (London, 1839–41), Vol. 1, p. 7.

22. For Peterloo, see: Joyce Marlow, *The Peterloo Massacre* (London, 1969); Donald Read, *Peterloo: The 'Massacre' and its Background* (Manchester, 1968); Michael Bush, *The Casualties of Peterloo* (Lancaster, 2005); Robert Poole, 'By the Law or the Sword: Peterloo Revisited', *History*, 91 (2006), pp. 254–76.

23. Quoted in John Saville, *1848: The British State and the Chartist Movement* (Cambridge, 1987), p. 25.

24. For a full, if somewhat dated, account of events at Newport, Frank F. Rosenblatt, *The Chartist Movement in its Social and Economic Aspects* (London, 1967), Chapter 12, 'The Newport Riots'.

25. Sir William Napier, *The Life and Opinions of General Sir Charles James Napier*, 3 volumes (London, 1857), Vol. 2, pp. 42, 71–2.

26. The key work is Saville, *1848: The British State and the Chartist Movement*; the significance of 1848 for Chartism is discussed and contextualised in a number of general works on the movement, e.g. Edward Royle, *Chartism* (London & New York, 1980), and Dorothy Thompson, *The Chartists* (London, 1984). For the quotation from *Alton Locke*, Charles Kingsley, *Alton Locke, Tailor and Poet: An Autobiography*, 2 volumes (London, 1881) Vol. 2, p. 265

Chapter 12: State Violence and the End of the Old Punishment Regime

1. For background to the Babington Plot, Conyers Read, *Mr Secretary Walsingham and the Policy of Queen Elizabeth*, 3 volumes (Oxford, 1925), Vol. 3, Chapter 12, 'The Babington Plot'; for Coke on the penalty for treason, *A true and perfect Relation of the Proceedings at the severall Arraignments of the late most barbarous Traitors* (London, 1606), sigs. K2–K2v: George Whetstone, The *Censure of a Loyall Subiect: upon certain noted Speech and Behaviours, of those that were notable Traitors, in the Place of their Executions, the xx, and xxi, of September last past* (London, 1587), Sig. A4v.

2. The punishment of Robert Archer is noted in Paul Griffiths, 'Bodies and Souls in Norwich: Punishing Petty Crime, 1540–1700', in S. Devereaux and P. Griffiths (eds.), *Penal Practice and Culture, 1500–1700: Punishing the English* (Basingstoke, 2004), p. 92.

3. London shaming punishments are discussed in Martin Ingram, 'Shame and Pain: Themes and Variations in Tudor Punishment', in Devereaux and Griffiths (eds.), *Penal Practice and Culture*: specific references are at pp. 40–1, 45–6.

4. For Elizabeth Hollande, *Middlesex County Records*, J. C. Jefferson (ed.), 4 volumes (Middlesex County Record Society, Clerkenwell, 1886–92), Vol. 1, p. 234.

5. Paul Hair, *Before the Bawdy Court: Selections from Church Court and Other Records Relating to the Correction of Moral Offences in England, Scotland and New England, 1300–1800* (London, 1972), pp. 156–7.
6. For an overview of pre-modern punishments, see J. A. Sharpe, *Judicial Punishment in England* (London, 1990), Chapter 2, 'The Old Penal Regime'.
7. On the pillorying of Daniel Defoe, Paula R. Backscheider, *Daniel Defoe: His Life* (Baltimore, 1989), pp. 118–19.
8. Major works on capital punishment for this period include: V. A. C. Gatrell, *The Hanging Tree: Execution and the English People 1770–1868* (Oxford, 1994); Peter Linebaugh, *The London Hanged: Crime and Civil Society in the Eighteenth Century* (2nd edn., London, 2003); and Andrea McKenzie, *Tyburn's Martyrs: Executions in England 1675–1775* (London, 2007); for a more narrowly focussed study, see Simon Devereaux, 'Recasting the Theatre of Execution: The Abolition of the Tyburn Ritual', *Past and Present*, 202 (2009), pp. 127–74.
9. For the total number of hangings between 1805 and 1832, Gatrell, *Hanging Tree*, p. 618.
10. For Jack Ketch, see *Oxford DNB*, where Evelyn is cited.
11. For Turpin's executioner, James Sharpe, *Dick Turpin: The Myth of the English Highwayman* (London, 2004), p. 28.
12. See *The Times*, 24 April 1821.
13. Jack Sheppard's career and execution are discussed in Linebaugh, *The London Hanged*, Chapter 1, 'The Common Discourse of the Whole Nation: Jack Sheppard and the Art of Escape'.
14. For MacLaine, see *A Complete History of James MacLean, the Gentleman Highwayman, who was executed at Tyburn on Wednesday, October 3 1750, for Robbery on the Highway* (London, 1750).
15. For Turpin in prison, see Sharpe, *Dick Turpin*, pp. 5–7.
16. For Renwick Williams, see Robert Shoemaker, *The London Mob: Violence and Disorder in Eighteenth-century England* (London, 2004), Chapter 10, 'The Monster'.
17. Bernard de Mandeville, *An Enquiry into the Causes of the Frequent Executions at Tyburn* (London, 1725), p. 26.
18. De Mandeville, *An Enquiry*, pp. 18–23.
19. Crowd reactions at executions figure prominently in McKenzie, *Tyburn's Martyrs*, Chapter 5, 'Dying Well: Martyrs and Penitents', and Chapter 7, 'Dying Game: Bridegrooms and Highwaymen'.
20. On the burial of Turpin, see Sharpe, *Dick Turpin*, pp. 34–5.
21. On Turpin's execution, Sharpe, *Dick Turpin*, pp. 1–3.
22. John Kettlewell, *An Office for Prisoners for Crimes together with another for Prisoners for Debt* (London, 1697), pp. 21–2.
23. For an early reassessment of the gallows speech and execution crowd reactions, see J. A. Sharpe, '"Last Dying Speeches": Religion, Ideology and

Public Execution in Seventeenth-century England', *Past and Present*, 107 (1985), pp. 144–67.

24. *The Diary of Ralph Thoresby*, Rev. Joseph Hunter (ed.), 2 volumes (London, 1830), Vol. 1, p. 131.

25. On the decline of penance, Robert B. Shoemaker, 'Streets of Shame? The Crowd and Public Punishments in London, 1700–1800', in Devereaux and Griffiths (eds.), *Penal Practice and Culture*, p. 237.

26. Smith's death was widely reported in the contemporary press, e.g. by the Chester paper *Adams's Weekly Courant*, 18 April 1780.

27. Talfourd is quoted by Shoemaker, 'Streets of Shame?', p 247; the statute quoted was 56 George III, cap. 168.

28. On Norwich, Griffiths, 'Bodies and Souls in Norwich'; for an overview of the disappearance of the old penal regime see J. A. Sharpe, 'The Decline of Public Punishment in England, Sixteenth to Nineteenth Centuries: Law, Public Opinion, and Modernity', in Reiner Schulze, Thomas Vormbaum, Christine D. Schmidt and Nicola Willenburg (eds.), *Strafzweck und Strafform zwischen religiöser und weltlicher Wertevermittlung* (Münster, 2008).

29. Leon Radzinowicz and Roger Hood, *The Emergence of Penal Policy in Victorian and Edwardian England* (Oxford, 1990), pp. 692, 717.

30. On the decline of whipping in London, Simon Devereaux, 'The Abolition of the Burning of Women in England Reconsidered', *Crime, Histoire & Sociétés/Crime, History & Societies*, 9 (2005), p. 83; for the later use of flogging, Radzinowicz and Hood, *Emergence of Penal Policy*, pp. 689–96.

31. My account of flogging in the British Army is based on: Peter Burroughs, 'Crime and Punishments in the British Army, 1815–1870', *English Historical Review*, 100 (1985), pp. 545–71; and J. R. Dinwiddy, 'The Early Nineteenth-century Campaign Against Flogging in the Army', *English Historical Review*, 97 (1982), pp. 308–31; for flogging during the Chindit campaigns, David Rooney, *Wingate and the Chindits: Redressing the Balance* (London, 1994), p. 97.

32. I have based this account on Devereaux, 'The Abolition of the Burning of Women', pp. 73–98.

33. On the execution of the Cato Street conspirators and the Derby hangings see Gatrell, *Hanging Tree*, Chapter 11, 'Executing Traitors'.

34. On the end of gibbeting, see Leon Radzinowicz, *A History of English Criminal Law and its Administration from 1750: The Movement for Reform* (London, 1948), pp. 213–29; Gatrell, *Hanging Tree*, pp. 268–9.

35. For high levels of hanging in earlier periods, Philip Jenkins, 'From Gallows to Prison? The Execution Rate in Early Modern England', *Criminal Justice History*, 7 (1986), pp. 51–71.

36. For Devon, A. H. A. Hamilton, *Quarter Sessions from Queen Elizabeth to Queen Anne* (London, 1878), p. 131; for the Western Circuit, Clive Emsley, *Crime and Society in England 1750–1900* (Harlow, 1987), p. 211.

37. The objections to hanging from More, Coke and Cromwell cited in J. A. Sharpe, 'Civility, Civilising Processes, and the End of Public Punishment in England', in Peter Burke, Brian Harrison and Paul Slack (eds.), *Civil Histories: Essays Presented to Sir Keith Thomas* (Oxford, 2000), p. 230.

38. For an important commentary on this issue by an expert in the field, see Randall McGowen, 'The Problem of Punishment in Eighteenth-century England', in Devereaux and Griffiths, *Penal Practice and Culture*.

39. Richard Gough, *The History of Myddle*, David Hey (ed.), (Harmondsworth, 1981), pp. 145–6.

40. For a discussion of benefit of clergy and the undervaluing of stolen goods, Sharpe, *Judicial Punishment in England*, pp. 23–4; for the Essex figures, J. A. Sharpe, *Crime in Seventeenth-century England: A County Study* (Cambridge, 1983), Table 4, p. 95.

41. On transportation to the American colonies, see A. Roger Ekirch, *Bound for America: The Transportation of British Convicts to the Colonies, 1718–1775* (Oxford, 1987).

42. Sharpe, *Judicial Punishment in England*, pp. 51–61, provides a brief overview of Transportation to Australia; for an in-depth study, see Robert Hughes, *The Fatal Shore: A History of the Transportation of Convicts to Australia, 1787–1868* (London, 1987).

43. Radzinowicz, *History of English Criminal Law*, pp. 523–4.

44. William Paley quoted in Gatrell, *The Hanging Tree*, p. 202.

45. On the restrictions of offences liable to capital punishment, Gatrell, *Hanging Tree*, pp. 570–2.

46. On execution of murderers in England and Wales, 1857–1868, Gatrell, *Hanging Tree*, p. 594.

47. For a brief introduction to the emergence of the prison as the main method of punishing serious criminals, see Sharpe, *Judicial Punishment in England*, pp. 61–87; those wishing to read further into the subject should turn to Michael Ignatieff, *A Just Measure of Pain: The Penitentiary in the Industrial Revolution 1750–1850* (London, 1978), and for an important but disputed book, Michel Foucault, *Discipline and Punish: The Birth of the Prison* (London, 1977); although some of its assumptions have been challenged by more recent research, Leon Radzinowicz, *A History of English Criminal Law and its Administration from 1750: The Movement for Reform* (London, 1948) was a remarkable pioneering work, which gathered together a mass of information.

48. This is the central idea of Foucault, *Discipline and Punish*.

49. On paying to watch the Cato Street conspirators hang, Gatrell, *Hanging Tree*, p. 309.

50. For the story of those wishing to become executioner after Marwood, see Greg T. Smith, 'I Could Hang Anything You Bring Before Me:

England's Willing Executioners 1883', in Devereaux and Griffiths, *Penal Practice and Culture*.

51. This is certainly the view of a historian of comparable changes in the Netherlands: Pieter Spierenburg, *The Spectacle of Suffering: Execution and the Evolution of Repression: From a preindustrial Metropolis to the European Experience* (Cambridge, 1984).
52. Cited in Gatrell, *Hanging Tree*, p. 593.
53. Richard J. Evans, *Rituals of Retribution: Capital Punishment in Germany, 1600–1987* (Harmondsworth, 1997), pp. 305–47.
54. On the executions of the girl in Bristol and of William Bousfield, Gatrell, *Hanging Tree*, pp. 39, 606–8.
55. Radzinowicz and Hood, *Emergence of Penal Policy*, p. 423; other sources give the number of fatalities as fifteen.
56. For the execution of Thomas Wells, Gatrell, *Hanging Tree*, pp. 600–1.
57. For Binns, Smith, 'I Could Hang Anything', pp. 295–6, 299–300.

Chapter 13: An English Miracle?

1. Leon Radzinowicz and Roger Hood, *The Emergence of Penal Policy in Victorian and Edwardian England* (Oxford, 1990), Chapter 5, 'The English Miracle'.
2. L. O. Pike, *A History of Crime in England*, 2 volumes (London, 1873–6), Vol. 2, pp. 480–1.
3. Criminal statistics for the relevant period are provided by V. A. C. Gatrell, 'The Decline of Theft and Violence in Victorian and Edwardian England', in V. A. C. Gatrell, Geoffrey Parker and Bruce Lenman (eds.), *Crime and the Law: The Social History of Crime in Western Europe Since 1500* (London, 1980), and figures given in this chapter are derived from this essay unless otherwise indicated: NB section on Criminal Violence, pp. 284–310; Table A1, pp. 342–5, Homicide; Table A2, pp. 346–8, Felonious and Malicious Wounding; and Table A5, pp. 358–60, Assaults.
4. Sir John Macdonell is quoted in Radzinowicz and Hood, *Emergence of Penal Policy*, p. 676; the male–female ratio of perpetrators and the rising proportion of domestic homicides is noted ibid., p. 675.
5. Peter King, 'The Impact of Urbanisation on Murder Rates and on the Geography of Homicide in England and Wales 1780–1850', *Historical Journal*, 53 (2010), pp. 1–28.
6. Alexis de Tocqueville, *Journeys to England and Ireland*, J. P. Mayer (ed.), (London, 1958), pp. 106, 107–8.
7. P. Gaskell, quoted in John Carter Wood, *Violence and Crime in Nineteenth-century England: The Shadow of our Refinement* (London & New York, 2004), p. 38.
8. Mayhew is quoted in Clive Emsley, *Crime and Society in England 1750–1900* (Harlow, 1987), p. 61; the concept of the criminal class is discussed ibid.,

Chapter 6, 'A Mid-point Assessment: The Criminal Class and Professional Criminals'; see also Radzinowicz and Hood, *Emergence of Penal Policy*, pp. 73–84.

9. For a brief introduction to Lombroso see Mary S. Gibson, 'Cesare Lombroso and Italian Criminology: Theory and Politics', in Peter Becker and Richard F. Wetzell (eds.), *Criminals and their Scientists: The History of Criminology in International Perspective* (Cambridge, 2006); for an overview of the importance of physiognomy in the Victorian period, see Sharrona Pearl, *About Faces: Physiognomy in Nineteenth-century Britain* (Cambridge, Mass. & London, 2010).

10. Henry Maudsley, *Responsibility in Mental Disease* (London, 1874), p. 35.

11. These processes are admirably described in Martin Wiener, *Reconstructing the Criminal: Culture, Law, and Policy in England, 1830–1914* (Cambridge, 1990).

12. For comments on wife-beating, Martin J. Wiener, *Men of Blood: Violence, Manliness, and Criminal Justice in Victorian England* (Cambridge, 2004), p. 173; on adultery by a wife as provocation to murder, ibid., Chapter 6, 'Bad Wives II: Adultery and the Unwritten Law'.

13. John Carter Wood, *Violence and Crime in Nineteenth-century England: The Shadow of Our Refinement* (London & New York, 2004), pp. 3–4; this is an exceptionally stimulating and insightful study.

14. Carter Wood, *Violence and Crime in Nineteenth-century England*.

15. Richard D. Altick, *Victorian Studies in Scarlet: Murders and Manners in the Age of Victoria* (London, 1972), p. 115.

16. Judith Flanders, *The Invention of Murder* (London, 2011); see also Rosalind Crone, *Violent Victorians: Popular Entertainment in Nineteenth-century London* (Manchester, 2012).

17. For an introduction to the story of Spring-heeled Jack, see Peter Haining, *The Legend and Bizarre Crimes of Spring-heeled Jack* (London, 1977).

18. The development and significance of criminal statistics in England is discussed in Radzinowicz and Hood, *Emergence of Penal Policy*, Chapter 4, 'Devising Indices of Crime'.

19. For the Chatham and Portland prison disturbances, Radzinowicz and Hood, *Emergence of Penal Policy*, pp. 522–5.

20. The key introduction to the garrotting panic is Jennifer Davis, 'The London Garrotting Panic of 1862: A Moral Panic and the Creation of a Criminal Class in Mid-Victorian England', in Gatrell, Lenman and Parker, *Crime and the Law*; see also Geoffrey Pearson, *Hooligan: A History of Respectable Fears* (London, 1983), Chapter 6, 'A New Variety of Crime', and, for context, the broader study by Rob Sindall, *Street Violence in the Nineteenth Century: Media Panic or Real Danger?* (Leicester, 1990); evidence from the 1850s is deployed in Emelyne Godfrey, 'Stranglehold on Victorian Society', *History Today*, 59, 7 (2009), pp. 54–9.

21. For the 'Science of Garrotting', Pearson, *Hooligan*, p. 129.
22. For Redwood and other specific incidents relating to the garrotting scare, Davis, 'London Garrotting Panic', pp. 295, 207.
23. For the penalties imposed, Radzinowicz and Hood, *Emergence of Penal Policy*, pp. 703–6; for the Earl of Carnarvon and later legislation, Davies, 'London Garrotting Panic', p. 207.
24. Ambivalent attitudes to the early police are examined in Robert D. Storch, 'The Plague of the Blue Locusts: Police Reform and Popular Resistance in Northern England', *International Review of Social History*, 20 (1975), pp. 61–90.
25. Harold Taylor, 'Rationing Crime: The Political Economy of Criminal Statistics Since the 1850s', *Economic History Review* 2nd series, 51 (1998), pp. 568–90: quotations at pp. 574 (Wilmot Seton); 586 (*Judicial Statistics*); 587–8 (Horatio Nelson Hardy).
26. The 1901 views of the Criminal Registrar are quoted in Gatrell, 'Decline of Theft and Violence', p. 241; Alfred Marshall, 'The Future of the Working Classes', in *Memorials of Alfred Marshall*, A. C. Pigou (ed.), (New York, 1956), p. 116.
27. Joe Toole, quoted in Andrew Davies, *The Gangs of Manchester: The Story of the Scuttlers, Britain's First Youth Cult* (Milo, Preston, 2008), p. 257.
28. William Bowen quoted in Davies, *The Gangs of Manchester*, p. 258.
29. For scuttlers, Andrew Davies, *Gangs of Manchester*; for girl scuttlers, Davies, 'These Viragoes are no less cruel than the Lads: Young Women, Gangs and Violence in late-Victorian Manchester and Salford', *British Journal of Criminology*, 39 (1999), pp. 72–89.
30. For the August Bank Holiday 1898 troubles and the emergence of the concept of the hooligan, Pearson, *Hooligan*, Chapter 5, 'Victorian Boys, we are here'; Thomas Holmes and Patrick McIntyre are quoted ibid., p. 77.
31. For 5 November disturbances at Oxford, James Sharpe, *Remember Remember the Fifth of November: A Cultural History of Guy Fawkes Day* (Cambridge, Mass. 2005), pp. 165–6; for the upper-class young men at Cremorne Gardens, Pearson, *Hooligan*, pp. 153–5.
32. On the development of the M'Naghten Rules, Radzinowicz and Hood, *Emergence of Penal Policy*, pp. 681–5, where the impact of the insanity plea on homicide conviction rates is also discussed; see also Wiener, *Reconstructing the Criminal*, pp. 269–76; on McNaughtan, *Oxford DNB*: I have followed the version of his surname given in this source.
33. The disposition of cases of wife murder is given in Wiener, *Men of Blood*, Table 1, p. 166.
34. On nineteenth-century rape, Wiener, *Men of Blood*, Chapter 3, 'Sexual Violence'; on changing attitudes to rape victims, ibid., pp. 93–7.

Chapter 14: Partners and Children, Victims and Killers

1. There is now extensive literature on domestic violence. Useful introductory works include: Lynne Harne and Jill Radford, *Tackling Domestic Violence: Theories, Policies and Practice* (Maidenhead, 2008); Chris Bazell and Bryan Gibson, *Domestic Violence and Occupation of the Family Home* (Winchester, 1999); Zvi Eisikovits and Eli Buchbinder, *Locked in a Violent Embrace: Understanding and Intervening in Domestic Violence* (Thousand Oaks, 2000); and Richard J. Gelles, *Intimate Violence in Families* (3rd edn., Thousand Oaks, 1997), these last two being written from an American perspective but raising important general issues (Gelles in particular is an acknowledged expert in the field).

2. J. W. Kaye, 'Outrages on Women', *North British Review*, 25 (1856), pp. 233–56, quotation at pp. 233–4; Frances Power Cobbe was a noted anti-vivisectionist and campaigner for women's rights, and her career has recently been re-assessed in Lori Williamson, *Power and Protest: Frances Power Cobbe and Victorian Society* (London, 2005); her article on wife torture appeared in the *Contemporary Review*, 32 (1878), pp. 55–87.

3. This story is discussed in an excellent survey of the subject, Lisa Surridge, *Bleak Houses: Marital Violence in Victorian Fiction* (Athens, Ohio, 2005).

4. These figures are taken from Richard D. Altick, *Victorian Studies in Scarlet: Murders and Manners in the Age of Victoria* (London, 1972), p. 286.

5. I have based this paragraph on Krista Cowman, *Women in British Politics, c.1689–1979* (Basingstoke, 2010), Part 3, 'Women's Politics after the Vote', and Julie V. Gottlieb and Richard Toye (eds.), *The Aftermath of Suffrage: Women, Gender, and Politics in Britain, 1918–1945* (Basingstoke, 2013).

6. Cited in Cowman, *Women in British Politics*, p. 144.

7. This account is based on: A. F. Young and E. T. Ashton, *British Social Work in the Nineteenth Century* (London, 1956); Eileen Younghusband, *Social Work in Britain 1950–1975*, 2 volumes (London, 1978); and Kathleen Jones, *Eileen Younghusband: A Biography* (London, 1984).

8. Erin Pizzey, *Scream Quietly or the Neighbours Will Hear* (London, 1974) was a key work in drawing attention to wife-battering. Her thoughts were developed in the later *Prone to Violence* (London, 1982).

9. The mood of the early Women's Aid Movement is captured in a short report, *Battered Women, Refuges and Women's Aid* (n.p., c.1976).

10. The story of Mandy is given in Janine Turner, *Behind Closed Doors: Advice for Families with Violence in the Home* (Wellingborough, 1988), p. 39.

11. For Janine Turner on her husband, *Behind Closed Doors*, p. 16.

12. This situation was remedied by the Housing Act of 1996, which set out clearly the duties of a housing authority for rehoming victims of domestic abuse and other forms of violence.

13. Pizzey, *Prone to Violence*, Chapter 2, 'Is It Love or Is It Addiction?'
14. Although dealing mainly with the United States, Susan L. Miller, *Victims as Offenders: The Paradox of Women's Violence in Relationships* (New Brunswick, 2005) opens up some important general issues about men as victims of domestic violence.
15. There is a growing body of publications on elder abuse. Two useful introductions to the British situation are: Jacki Pritchard, *The Abuse of Older People: A Training Manual for Detection and Prevention* (2nd edn., London, 1995); and Simon Biggs, Chris Phillipson and Paul Kingston, *Elder Abuse in Perspective* (Buckingham, 1995); The case of Mrs E is taken from Pritchard, *Abuse of Older People*, p. 31; estimates on the sex of elder abusers are based on figures given ibid., Table 4.4. I have also drawn on information from Simon Biggs, Jill Manthorpe, Anthea Tinker, Melanie Doyle and Bob Erens, 'Mistreatment of Older People in the United Kingdom: Findings from the First National Prevalence Study', *Journal of Elder Abuse and Neglect*, 21 (2009), pp. 1–14.
16. *God's dreadful Judgement on cruel, wicked and disobedient Children to their Parents* (Wolverhampton, c.1780).
17. I have based the following two paragraphs on two works by Lionel Rose: *The Massacre of the Innocents: Infanticide in Britain, 1800–1939* (London, 1986); and *The Erosion of Childhood: Child Oppression in Britain 1860–1918* (London, 1991).
18. The case is discussed by Angela Brabin, 'The Black Widows of Liverpool', *History Today*, 52 (October, 2002), pp. 40–6.
19. Rose, *Massacre of the Innocents*, p. 140.
20. Rose, *Massacre of the Innocents*, p. 98.
21. For the development of policies directed at abused children, see Harry Ferguson, *Protecting Children in Time: Child Abuse, Child Protection and the Consequences of Modernity* (Basingstoke, 2004); those seeking a more detailed account should turn to G. K. Behlmer, *Child Abuse and Moral Reform in England 1870–1908* (Stanford, 1982). Nigel Parton, *The Politics of Child Abuse* (Basingstoke, 1985), supplements the historical account given by the two previous works, and also provides a thought-provoking critical account of the development of child abuse as a social issue and policies towards it in the 1960s, 1970s and 1980s.
22. K. C. H. Kempe, F. N. Silverman, B. F. Steele, W. Droegemueller and H. K. Silver, 'The Battered-Child Syndrome', *Journal of the American Medical Association*, 181 (1962), pp. 17–24.
23. D. L. Griffiths and F. J. Moynihan, 'Multiple Epiphysial Injuries in Babies ("Battered Baby" Syndrome)', *British Medical Journal*, 2 (1963), pp. 1558–61.
24. Peter Reder, Sylvia Duncan and Moira Gray, *Beyond Blame: Child Abuse Tragedies Revisited* (London, 1993).

25. Reder, Duncan and Gray, *Beyond Blame*, p. 44, where details of the cases noted above are given.

26. On the death of Victoria Climbié, see *The Victoria Climbié Inquiry: Report of an Inquiry by Lord Laming* (London, 2003: this publication is Crown Copyright); the quotation comes on p. 2.

27. The cases listed here are taken from David James Smith, *The Sleep of Reason: The James Bulger Case* (London, 2011), pp. 2–5.

28. *The Preston Gazette*, 25 August 1855, one of a number of contemporary newspaper reports.

29. On the Mary Bell case, see two works by Gitta Sereny: *The Case of Mary Bell: A Portrait of a Child Who Murdered* (London, revised edn., 1995); and *Cries Unheard: The Story of Mary Bell* (London & Basingstoke, 1998). For an overview of child murderers in the late twentieth century, see Paul Cavadino (ed.), *Children Who Kill* (Winchester, 1996).

30. There is an official report on the Edlington affair, *The Edlington Case: A Review by Lord Carlile of Berriew, CBE, QC, at the Request of the Rt. Hon. Michael Gove, Secretary of State for Education* (London, 2012), which is mainly concerned with recommendations for improving the relevant social services; David Cameron's speech was widely reported, e.g. the *Guardian*, 22 January 2010.

31. I have based my account of the death of James Bulger on David James Smith, *The Sleep of Reason*; Mark Thomas, *Every Mother's Nightmare: The Murder of James Bulger* (New York, revised edn., 2011); and Blake Morrison, *As If* (London, 1998); see also the entry on Patrick James Bulger in *Oxford DNB*. David A. Green, *When Children Kill Children: Penal Populism and Political Culture* (Oxford, 2008), compared the Bulger case and reactions to it to the murder of five-year-old Silje Marie Redergård by two slightly older boys in Norway in 1994.

32. On this transition, see Peter King, 'The Rise of Juvenile Delinquency in England 1780–1840: Changing Patterns of Perception and Prosecution', *Past and Present*, 160 (1998), pp. 116–66.

33. Historical instances of children killing children are marshalled in Smith, *Sleep of Reason*, pp. 2–7; on the George Burgess case, see: Judith Rowbotham, Kim Stevenson and Samantha Peg, 'Children of Misfortune: The Parallels in the Cases of Child Murderers Thompson and Venables, Barratt and Bradley', *Howard Journal*, 42 (2003), pp. 107–22; Gitta Sereny, 'A Child Murdered by Children' (1995: accessed at http://www.independent.co.uk/arts-entertainment/a-child-murdered-by-children-1616746.html).

34. Peter K. Smith and Sonia Sharpe, *School Bullying: Insights and Perspectives* (London, 1994), sums up the main relevant issues and has an excellent bibliography; see also Ken Rigby, *New Perspectives on Bullying* (London, 2002).

35. For representative policy statements, see: Union and College Union, 'Stopping Bullying and Harassment at Work' (2008), accessed at www. ucu.org.uk; Unite, 'Zero Tolerance – Dignity and Equality at Work – Dealing with Harassment, Discrimination and Bullying' (2014), accessed at www.unitetheunion.org. On the bullying of adults more generally, see: Peter Randall, *Bullying in Adulthood: Assessing the Bullies and their Victims* (London, 2001); and Andrea Adams and Neil Crawford, *Bullying at Work: How to Confront and Overcome It* (London, 1992).

Chapter 15: Women and Sexual Violence

1. Susan Brownmiller, *Against Our Will: Men, Women and Rape* (London, 1975); quotations are on pp. 404, 15. There is now extensive modern literature on rape as a current issue. I have consulted: Lee Ellis, *Theories of Rape: Inquiries into the Causes of Sexual Aggression* (New York, 1989); Joan McGregor, *Is it Rape? On Acquaintance Rape and Taking Women's Consent Seriously* (Aldershot, 2005); Jan Jorden, *Serial Survivors: Women's Narratives of Surviving Rape* (Sydney, 2008); Nicole Gavey, *Just Sex? The Cultural Scaffolding of Rape* (Hove, 2005); Ann J. Cahill, *Rethinking Rape* (Ithaca & London, 2001). The connections between pornography and rape are considered in many of the essays gathered together in Diana E. H. Russell (ed.), *Making Violence Sexy: Feminist Views on Pornography* (New York & London, 1993). The connection between war and rape in the modern world is analysed in Anne Llewellyn Barstow (ed.), *War's Dirty Secret: Rape, Prostitution and Other Crimes Against Women* (Cleveland, Ohio, 2000).

2. Curiously, it has been claimed that rape carried out by troops was not a major phenomenon in the English Civil War: Charles Carlton, *Going to the Wars: The Experience of the British Civil Wars, 1638–1651* (London & New York, 1992), p. 259; references (admittedly usually non-specific) to 'ravishments' carried out by soldiers (notably when besieged towns were taken) in contemporary documentation do, however, suggest that further research might modify this conclusion.

3. See Richard Bessel, *Germany 1945: From War to Peace* (London, 2009), especially Chapter 6, 'Revenge'.

4. Sections of Barstow (ed.), *War's Dirty Secrets*, are devoted to rape in the former Yugoslavia and Rwanda; see also Beverly Allen, *Rape Warfare: The Hidden Genocide of Bosnia-Herzegovina and Croatia* (Minneapolis and London, 1996).

5. Catharine A. MacKinnon, *Toward a Feminist Theory of the State* (Cambridge, Mass., 1989), p. 124.

6. For balanced discussions of this issue, see Cahill, *Rethinking Rape*, Chapter 1, 'Feminist Theories of Rape: Sex or Violence?', and Gavey, *Just Sex?*, pp. 30–5.

7. The full title of Thornhill and Palmer's book is *A Natural History of Rape: Biological Bases of Sexual Coercion* (Cambridge, Mass., 2000).
8. For a critique of Thornhill and Palmer, see Gavey, *Just Sex?*, pp. 94–7.
9. On the medieval law of rape, see: Corinne Saunders, 'The Medieval Law of Rape', *King's Law Journal*, 11 (2000), pp. 19–48, which is especially strong on the Anglo-Saxon and immediate post-Conquest periods; Corinne Saunders, 'A Matter of Consent: The Law of *Raptus* and Middle English Romance' and Kim M. Phillips, 'Written on the Body: Reading Rape from the Twelfth to the Fifteenth Centuries', both in N. J. Menuge (ed.), *Medieval Women and the Law* (Woodbridge, 2000); J. B. Post, 'Ravishment of Women and the Statute of Westminster', in J. H. Baker (ed.), *Legal Records and the Historian* (London, 1978); J. B. Post, 'Sir Thomas West and the Statute of Rapes, 1382', *Bulletin of the Institute of Historical Research*, 53 (1980), pp. 24–30; Suzanne Edwards, 'The Rhetoric of Rape and the Politics of Gender in The Wife of Bath's Tale and the 1382 Statute of Rapes', *Exemplaria*, 23 (2011), pp. 3–26; Shannon McSheffrey and Julia Pope, 'Ravishment, Legal Narratives, and Chivalric Culture in Fifteenth-century England', *Journal of British Studies*, 48 (2009), pp. 818–36; E. W. Ives, 'Agaynst Taking Awaye of Women: The Inception and Operation of the Abduction Act of 1487', in E. W. Ives, R. J. Knecht and J. J. Scarisbrick (eds.), *Wealth and Power in Tudor England: Essays Presented to S. T. Bindoff* (London, 1978); Jeremy Goldberg, *Communal Discord, Child Abduction, and Rape in the Later Middle Ages* (Basingstoke, 2008), pp. 168–72; Caroline Dunn, *Stolen Women in Medieval England: Rape, Abduction and Adultery, 1100–1500* (Cambridge, 2013), is an excellent introduction to the complexity of the issues covered by rape and abduction prosecutions in the medieval period.
10. The statute redefining rape was 18 Elizabeth I, cap. 7.
11. The quotations from Glanvill and Bracton are cited by Saunders, 'Medieval Law of Rape', p. 31.
12. The early-thirteenth-century cases demonstrating violence in rape are cited by Phillips, 'Written on the Body', p. 130.
13. The relevant complexities are discussed in depth in Dunn, *Stolen Women in Medieval England*.
14. Details of rape cases on the Home Circuit were gathered from: *A Calendar of Assize Records: Essex Indictments Elizabeth I*, J. S. Cockburn (ed.), (London, 1978); *A Calendar of Assize records: Hertfordshire Indictments Elizabeth I*, J. S. Cockburn (ed.), (London, 1975); *A Calendar of Assize Records: Kent Indictments Elizabeth I*, J. S. Cockburn (ed.), (London, 1979); *A Calendar of Assize Records: Surrey Indictments Elizabeth I*, J. S. Cockburn (ed.), (London. 1980); *A Calendar of Assize Records: Sussex Indictments Elizabeth I*, J. S. Cockburn (ed.), (London, 1975). Cases specifically referred to are: *Essex Indictments Elizabeth I*, entries 1143, 1445, 1916, 2130, 2225, 2271;

Kent Indictments Elizabeth I, entries 1041, 2050; *Sussex Indictments Elizabeth I*, entries 346–7; *Sussex Indictments Elizabeth I*, entries 251, 304, 612, 1929.

15. The legal definition of rape comes from Michael Dalton, *The Countrey Justice: Containing the Practice of the Justices of the Peace out of their Sessions* (6ᵗʰ edn., London, 1643), pp. 348–9.

16. I have taken the stories of rape in ancient myth from Jenny March, *Cassell's Dictionary of Classical Mythology* (London, 2001); see also Froma Zeitlin, 'Configurations of Rape in Greek Myth' in Sylvana Tomaselli and Roy Porter (eds.), *Rape* (Oxford, 1986).

17. There is now an extensive body of writing on rape in late medieval and early modern literature. I have drawn in particular on Elizabeth Robertson and Christine M. Rose (eds.), *Representing Rape in Medieval and Early Modern Literature* (New York, 2001); and Jocelyn Catty, *Writing Rape, Writing Women in Early Modern England: Unbridled Speech* (Basingstoke, 1999).

18. The quotation from *Ars Amatoria* is from Ovid, *Art of Love*, Rolfe Humphries (trs.), (Bloomington, 1955), p. 126.

19. The attempted rape of Adam Fisher's daughter is recounted in *A blazing Starre seene in the West at Totneis in Devonshire, on the fourteenth of this instant November 1642* (London, 1642); for the Civil War background, see Mark Stoyle, *Loyalty and Locality: Popular Allegiance in Devon During the English Civil War* (Exeter, 1994).

20. For Elizabeth Tarrier, Old Bailey Online, case t17840225-19; for the Bedfordshire incident, Anna Clark, *Women's Silence, Men's Violence: Sexual Assault in England 1770–1845* (London, 1987), p. 50.

21. These statistics are derived from: J. A. Sharpe, *Crime in Seventeenth-century England: A County Study* (Cambridge, 1983), p. 63; J. M. Beattie, *Crime and the Courts in England 1660–1800* (Oxford, 1986), pp. 124–32; Martin J. Wiener, *Men of Blood: Violence, Manliness, and Criminal Justice in Victorian England* (Cambridge, 2004), Chapter 3, 'Sexual Violence'.

22. Ministry of Justice/Home Office/Office for National Statistics, *An Overview of Sexual Offending in England and Wales* (10 January 2013), Figure 1.1, p. 7, showing 2,910 persons stood trial for rape on a three-year average to 2013 of whom 1,070, or 37 per cent, were convicted.

23. Sir Matthew Hale, *The History of the Pleas of the Crown*, T. Dogerty (ed.), 2 Volumes (1678: London, 1800), Vol. 1, p. 634.

24. Depositions concerning the rape of Patience Ditchfield are given in TNA, CHES 24/180/2.

25. Old Bailey Online, cases t1797092-12 (Jane Bell); t17960914-12 (Mary Homewood).

26. Beattie, *Crime and the Courts in England*, pp. 124–32; Table 8.3, p. 411.

27. Garthine Walker, 'Everyman or a Monster? The Rapist in Early Modern England, c.1600–c.1750', *History Workshop Journal*, 76 (2013), pp. 21–2.

28. The case of Margaret Allen is recorded in TNA, CHES 24/162/7.

29. Brownmiller, *Against Our Will*, p. 316; for a useful contextualising work, see Mari Jo Buhle, *Feminism and its Discontents: A Century of Struggle with Psychoanalysis* (Cambridge, Mass., 1998). Deutsch, of Jewish descent, left Germany for Boston in 1935, and her ideas appeared in English as *The Psychology of Women*, published in two volumes, 1943 and 1945.

30. *Overview of Sexual Offending in England and Wales*, Figure 1.1, p. 7; Figure 2.1, p. 16.

31. On the 1982 TV programme, see Joe Sieder's comments on www. screenonline.org.uk. The case featured in a 2006 *Panorama* programme, 'Rape on Trial', broadcast on 25 June.

32. I have based the following paragraphs on: Joanna Bourke, *Rape: A History from 1860 to the Present* (London, 2007), which is an excellent guide to the subject's more recent history, very much connecting with current concerns over the issue; Edward Shorter, 'On Writing the History of Rape', *Signs: Journal of Women in Culture and Society*, 3 (1977), pp. 471–82, which is an interesting pioneering piece written in response to Brownmiller's book, although Shorter's interpretation of developments in the early modern period is rather simplistic; Tomaselli and Porter's *Rape* is an important collection of essays on rape's history. Other works dealing with rape in the post-medieval period are: Nazife Bashar, 'Rape in England between 1550 and 1700', and Anna K. Clark, 'Rape or Seduction? A Controversy over Sexual Violence in the Nineteenth Century', both in the London Feminist History Group, *The Sexual Dynamics of History: Men's Power, Women's Resistance* (London, 1983); Clark, *Women's Silence, Men's Violence*; Miranda Chaytor, 'Husband(ry): Narratives of Rape in the Seventeenth Century', *Gender & History*, 7 (1995), pp. 378–407; and Garthine Walker, 'Rereading Rape and Sexual Violence in Early Modern England', *Gender History*, 10 (1998), pp. 1–25. The treatment of rape cases before the courts in the eighteenth century is discussed in Beattie, *Crime and the Courts in England*, pp. 124–32.

33. Figures from Bourke, *Rape*, p. 45, citing Neil M. Malamuth and James V. P. Check, 'Sex Role Stereotyping and Reactions to Depictions of Stranger versus Acquaintance Rape', *Journal of Personality and Social Psychology*, 45 (1983), pp. 344–56; for a more recent study which indicates depressingly similar attitudes, see Susan R. Edwards, Kathryn A. Bradshaw and Verlin B. Hinsz, 'Denying Rape but Endorsing Forceful Intercourse: Exploring Differences Among Responders', *Violence and Gender*, 1 (2014), pp. 188–93.

34. For a good overview of the relevant issues, see Ronald J. Berger, Patricia Searles and Charles E. Cottie, *Feminism and Pornography* (Westport, Conn., and London, 1991).

35. For a strong assertion of the connection, and a critique of some of the social scientists who have denied it, see Diana E. H. Russell, 'The Experts

Cop Out', in Russell (ed.), *Making Violence Sexy*; the evidence from rape victims is discussed in Mimi H. Silbert and Ayala M. Pines, 'Pornography and Sexual Abuse of Women', ibid.

36. Brownmiller, *Against Our Will*, p. 346.
37. Walker, 'Everyman or a Monster', p. 11; see also Walker's 'Rape, Acquittal and Culpability in Popular Crime Reports in England, 1670–1750', *Past and Present*, 220 (2013), pp. 115–42.

Chapter 16: The Serial Killer: a Very Modern Murderer?

1. The Gloucestershire killings are described in *The Bloody Innkeeper; or, sad and barbarous News from Gloucester-Shire: being a true Relation of how the Bodies of seven Men and Women were found murdered in a Garden belonging to a House in Putley near Gloucester* (London, 1675). Unfortunately the author of the piece does not name the killer 'merely that I may not seem to prejudice him'; this and other early examples of serial killing and mass murder are noted in Bernard Capp, 'Serial Killers in Seventeenth-century England', *History Today*, 46, 3 (March, 1996), pp. 21–6.
2. This case is described in Henry Goodcole, *Heaven's speedie Hue and Cry after Lust and Murder. Manifested upon the suddaine Apprehending of Thomas Sherwood and Elizabeth Evans, whose Lives, Death and free Confession are here expressed* (London, 1635).
3. Capp, 'Serial Killers in Seventeenth-century England', p. 22.
4. For an engaging semi-fictionalised account of Wainewright's life see Andrew Motion, *Wainewright the Poisoner: The True Confession of a Charming and Ingenious Criminal* (London, 2000).
5. The Mary Ann Cotton case has recently been analysed by David Wilson, *Mary Ann Cotton: Britain's First Serial Killer* (Hook, 2012), which replaces Arthur Appleton, *Mary Ann Cotton; Her Story and Trial* (London, 1973); I have also consulted Judith Flinders, *The Invention of Murder* (London, 2011), pp. 387–94; I have taken the version of the skipping song quoted here and the comment from the *Newcastle Chronicle* from the brief discussion of the case in Clive Emsley, *Hard Men: Violence in England Since 1750* (London, 2005), pp. 57–8.
6. Wilson, *Mary Ann Cotton*, p. 49.
7. Wilson, *Mary Ann Cotton*, p. 159.
8. Wilson, for example, makes good use of letters written by Cotton from her cell, which have since disappeared but were published in the press: see, for example, her remarkable letter to James Robinson, Wilson, *Mary Ann Cotton*, p. 143.
9. For William Palmer I have depended heavily upon: Flinders, *Invention of Murder*, pp. 258–68, which is especially interesting on the medical evidence offered at the trial and the media attention which the case provoked; Richard D. Altick, *Victorian Studies in Scarlet: Murders and*

NOTES TO PAGES 516–521

Manners in the Age of Victoria (London, 1972), pp. 152–60; and *Oxford DNB*, where a number of earlier works on the case are noted. For further information on the media treatment of homicide in the nineteenth century, see Rosalind Crone, *Violent Victorians: Popular Entertainments in Nineteenth-century London* (Manchester, 2012).

10. Jonathon Green, *Green's Dictionary of Slang*, 3 volumes (London, 2010), Vol. 3, p. 240. The first recorded use in the US is dated 1876, so it is conceivable that the phrase originated with the Palmer case and crossed the Atlantic before being recorded.

11. There is extensive literature, of varying quality, on the Whitechapel murders and Jack the Ripper: in my account I have drawn on: Philip Sugden, *The Complete History of Jack the Ripper* (New York, 1994); Paul Begg, *Jack the Ripper: The Definitive History* (London, 2005); Paul Begg, Martin Fido and Keith Skinner, *The Jack the Ripper A to Z* (London, 1991), which is a very useful reference work; and Stewart P. Evans and Keith Skinner (eds.), *The Ultimate Jack the Ripper Sourcebook: An Illustrated Encyclopaedia* (London, 2001), which provides very full documentation on the period of the killings and slightly beyond. There are also a number of websites devoted to the Ripper murders, of which I found 'Casebook: Jack the Ripper', www.casebook.org, the most useful: this site, incidentally, lists and provides short reviews of over 150 non-fiction books relating to the murders.

12. For the details of Kelly's injuries, Evans and Skinner (eds.), *Ultimate Jack the Ripper Sourcebook*, pp. 742–50.

13. Press reactions to the Whitechapel murders are dealt with superbly by L. Perry Curtis Jr., *Jack the Ripper and the London Press* (New Haven, 2001), from which most of the detailed information here is taken. The 'Casebook: Jack the Ripper' website contains 5,449 fully transcribed articles from contemporary newspapers, which demonstrate that as well as the interest generated in the British press, the murders were avidly reported in the United States, and were even mentioned in Polish and Swedish newspapers. There is now well-developed literature on the arrival of mass newspaper readership in late-Victorian England: a good introduction is Joel H. Wiener (ed.), *Papers for the Millions: The New Journalism in Britain, 1850s to 1914* (New York, 1988), while an essay of special relevance is Kevin Williams, *Get Me a Murder a Day! A History of Mass Communication in Britain* (London, 1998), Chapter 3, 'Get Me a Murder a Day: The Northcliffe Revolution and the Rise of the Popular Press'.

14. For an impression of the range of people suspected as the Ripper, see Christopher J. Morley, *Jack the Ripper, 150 Suspects* (n.p., 2004).

15. The East End and other contextual issues around the Whitechapel murders are discussed with great insight in Judith R. Walkowitz, *City of*

707

Dreadful Delights: Narratives of Sexual Danger in Late-Victorian London (London, 1992); Alex Werner (ed.), *Jack the Ripper and the East End* (London, 2008), contains a number of excellent essays which also help contextualise the murders.

16. For a discussion of the 'Dear Boss' letters, see Begg, *Jack the Ripper*, Chapter 12, 'Dear Boss'.

17. For John Littlechild on the origins of the name 'Jack the Ripper', Begg, *Jack the Ripper*, p. 275.

18. Alan Moore and Eddie Campbell, *From Hell* (London, 2000), Chapter 10, p. 33, panel 2.

19. This typology is developed in Ronald M. Holmes and James De Burger, *Serial Murder* (Newbury Park, Calif., 2008), pp. 55–60.

20. There is extensive literature on serial killing, much of it originating from the United States. For Britain, I have found two books especially useful: Anna Gekoski, *Murder by Numbers: British Serial Killers since 1950: Their Childhoods, Their Lives, Their Crimes* (London, 1998); and David Wilson, *Serial Killers: Hunting Britons and Victims, 1960–2006* (Winchester, 2007). The title of this latter work reflects that of one of the more influential North American works on the subject, Elliott Leyton, *Hunting Humans: The Rise of the Modern Multiple Murderer* (Toronto, 1986). See also: James A. Fox and Jack Levine, *Extreme Killing: Understanding Serial and Mass Murder* (Thousand Oaks, 2005); Martin Fido, *A History of British Serial Killing* (London, 2001); and Philip Jenkin, 'Serial Murder in England, Germany and the USA: 1900–1940', in Thomas O'Reilly Fleming (ed.), *Serial and Mass Murder: Theory, Research and Policy* (Toronto, 1996).

21. For Peter Sutcliffe I have depended heavily upon Gordon Burn, *Somebody's Husband, Somebody's Son* (London, 1984); M. Bilton, *Wicked Beyond Belief: The Hunt for the Yorkshire Ripper* (London, 2003); Gekoski, *Murder by Numbers*, Chapter 5, 'Peter Sutcliffe'; Wilson, *Serial Killers*, Chapter 3, 'Women Who Are Involved in Prostitution'; and a remarkable feminist interpretation of Sutcliffe, Nicole Ward Jouve, *'The Streetcleaner': The Yorkshire Ripper Case on Trial* (London, 1986). Further feminist interpretations are provided by Lucy Bland, 'The Case of the Yorkshire Ripper: Mad, Bad, Beast or Male?', in Phil Scraton and Paul Gordon (eds.), *Cause for Concern: British Criminal Justice On Trial* (Harmondsworth, 1984), and Wendy Hollway, '"I Just Wanted to Kill a Woman": Why? The Yorkshire Ripper and Male Sexuality', *Feminist Review*, 9 (1981), pp. 33–40. Hilary Kinnell, *Violence and Sex Work in Britain* (Cullompton, 2008), is an important contribution to our overall understanding of that issue, while Chapter 1, 'Peter Sutcliffe: A Long Shadow', provides both a lucid account of the killings and a critique of the use of the label 'prostitute' to cover some of Sutcliffe's victims and of the initial Women's Movement's reactions to the killings. Although some of the interpretations of D. A.

Yallop, *Deliver Us From Evil* (London, 1981) have been questioned by subsequent research, the work does benefit from a contemporaneity in its treatment of the Yorkshire Ripper killings.

22. There is an excellent Yorkshire Ripper website at http://www.execulink. com/-kbrannen which, among other things, provides a list of Sutcliffe's victims and possible victims.

23. Those interested in the police investigation are particularly directed to *The Yorkshire Ripper Case: Review of the Police Investigation of the Case by Lawrence Byford, Esq., CBE, QPM, Her Majesty's Inspector of Constabulary* (London, December 1981); the passage on the fears of the female population of the North comes from p. 7 of this, while the description of Sutcliffe as 'an otherwise unremarkable young man' comes from p. 6.

24. Wilson, *Serial Killers*.

25. Wilson, *Serial Killers*, p. 23.

26. For sensationalist approaches, highlighting the supposed 'serial killing epidemic' in the United States, see: Mark Seltzer, *Wound Cultures: Death and Life in America's Wound Culture* (New York & London, 1998); and Joel Norris, *Serial Killers: A Controversial Look at a Horrifying Trend* (London, 1990).

27. On Harold Shipman I have consulted C. Peters, *Harold Shipman: Mind Set on Murder* (London, 2005); Wilson, *Serial Killers*, Chapter 2, 'The Elderly'; Kenneth V. Iserven, *Demon Doctors: Physicians as Serial Killers* (Tucson, 2002), Chapter 9, 'The Dr Jekyll of Hyde: Harold Frederick Shipman'; and two important official sources: the six *Reports on the Shipman Inquiry*, presided over by Dame Janet Smith, released between 10 July 2002 and 27 January 2005, available at www.shipman-inquiry.org.uk/reports.asp; and *Harold Shipman's Clinical Practice 1974–1998: A Clinical Audit Commissioned by the Chief Medical Officer* (London, Department of Health, 2001).

28. This account follows Dame Janet Smith, *The Shipman Report: Second Report. The Police Investigation of March 1998* (Parliamentary Papers: Command Paper Cm 5853, Session 2002–3).

29. Steven A. Egger, *The Killers Among Us: An Examination of Serial Murder and its Investigation* (2nd edn., Upper Saddle River, 2012), p. 3.

Chapter 17: Public Violence: from Football Hooliganism to Inner-city Riots

1. On teddy boys, Paul Rocke and Stanley Cohen, 'The Teddy Boys', in V. Bognador and R. Skidelsky (eds.), *The Age of Affluence, 1951–1961* (London, 1970); and Robert J. Cross, 'The Teddy Boy as Scapegoat', *Doshisha Studies in Language and Culture*, 1 (1998), pp. 263–91; quotation is at p. 1.

2. On mods and rockers, see Stanley Cohen, *Folk Devils and Moral Panics* (London, 1972).

3. On skinheads, see Pat Doyle *et al.*, *The Paint House: Words from an East End Gang* (Harmondsworth, 1972); Chapter 8, 'Violence', is especially relevant.

4. Football hooliganism is another topic that has generated an enormous literature. The various interpretations of the phenomenon are set out in: Eric Dunning, Patrick Murphy and John M. Williams, *The Roots of Football Hooliganism: An Historical and Sociological Study* (London, 1988); idem, *Football on Trial: Spectator Violence and Development in the Football World* (London, 1990); Steve Frosdick and Peter Marsh, *Football Hooliganism* (Cullompton, 2005); and Anastassia Tsoukala, *Football Hooliganism in Europe: Security and Civil Liberties in the Balance* (Basingstoke, 2009); see also the books on individual teams by Gary Armstrong and Garry Robson cited below.

5. Evidence on early-twentieth-century football-related disorder is marshalled in Dunning, Murphy and Williams, *Roots of Football Hooliganism*, Chapter 2, 'The Football Fever (1)'.

6. *Leicester Mercury*, 23 April 1928, cited in Dunning, Murphy and Williams, *Football on Trial*, p. 77.

7. For a succinct guide to government reports on football hooliganism, and the various academic interpretations of the phenomenon, see Frosdick and Marsh, *Football Hooliganism*, Chapter 6, 'An Overview of British Theories of Football Hooliganism', and Chapter 7, 'British Theoretical Perspectives in Detail'.

8. Taylor's ideas on football hooliganism are discussed in Dunning, Murphy and Williams, *Roots of Football Hooliganism*, pp. 23–5; for a more general appraisal, see his obituary in the *Guardian*, 24 January 2001.

9. See, for example, the Centre's 'Fact Sheet 1: Football and Football Hooliganism' (Leicester, n.d.).

10. Sir Norman Chester Centre for Football Research, 'Football and Football Hooliganism', p. 9.

11. On onion bhajis, Gary Armstrong, *Football Hooligans: Knowing the Score* (Oxford, 1998), p. 103.

12. Armstrong, *Hooligans*, passim: quotations are at pp. 233 and 252, and details of injuries inflicted at pp. 229–30.

13. In 2016 a coroner's jury, at the conclusion of a two-year inquest, brought in a verdict of unlawful killing on the Hillsborough victims.

14. On the Bradford disaster, Paul Firth, *Four Minutes to Hell: The Story of the Bradford City Fire* (Manchester, 2005); on Hillsborough, the most important document is *The Report of the Hillsborough Independent Panel* (House of Commons HC581: London, HMSO, 12 September 2012).

15. For a summary of the main features of legislation on football hooliganism and details of Banning Orders see the Football Association's 'Summary of Measures Taken to Prevent Football Violence' (June 2012).

16. Garry Robson, *'No One Likes Us, We Don't Care': The Myth and Reality of Millwall Fandom* (Oxford, 2000); the quotation from *The Lion Roars* is at p. 110.

17. Home Office, 'Football-related Arrests and Football Banning Order Statistics Season 2013–14' (Home Office, 11 September 2014).
18. On young men taking a punch, Armstrong, *Hooligans*, p. 317.
19. I have based this account largely upon H. A. Clegg, *A History of British Trades Unions Since 1889*, 3 volumes (Oxford, 1985), Volume 2, which deals with the years 1911–1933. Those seeking a lively, if now dated, introduction to the period and the role of labour unrest in it should consult George Dangerfield, *The Strange Death of Liberal England* (London, 1935, new edition 1966).
20. Figures in this section are taken from Clegg, *History of British Trade Unions*, Vol. 3, Table 1, p. 26; and Table 7, p. 568.
21. Sir George Askwith, *Industrial Problems and Disputes* (London, 1920), p. 150.
22. I am grateful to Professor Krista Cowman for information on the Garston bobbin-makers' strike.
23. On Major-General Macready, *Oxford DNB*; for the specific incidents mentioned here, Dangerfield, *Strange Death of Liberal England*, pp. 200, 219–20.
24. Among the numerous works on the General Strike I have consulted Patrick Renshaw, *The General Strike* (London, 1975); G. A. Phillips, *The General Strike: The Politics of Industrial Conflict* (London, 1976); and Keith Laybourn, *The General Strike of 1926* (Manchester, 1993); Anthony Mason, *The General Strike in the North East* (Hull, 1970), pp. 165–78, describes violence on the picket lines and elsewhere in that region.
25. Much has been written on the 1983–4 miners' strike. I have drawn on: Geoffrey Goodman, *The Miners' Strike* (London, 1985); Huw Benyon (ed.), *Digging Deeper: Issues in the Miners' Strike* (London, 1985); Martin Adeney and John Lloyd, *The Miners' Strike 1984–5: Loss Without Limit* (London, 1986); Andrew J. Richards, *Miners on Strike: Class Solidarity and Division in Britain* (Oxford, 1996); and Bob Fine and Robert Millar (eds.), *Policing the Miners' Strike* (London, 1985).
26. George Moores's views on the Metropolitan Police are quoted by Sarah Spencer, 'The Eclipse of the Police Authority', in Fine and Millar (eds.), *Policing the Miners' Strike*, p. 45.
27. On events at Armthorpe, see: Goodman, *Miners' Strike*, pp. 79–88; and Adeney and Lloyd, *Miners' Strike*, pp. 119–22.
28. On Orgreave, see: Goodman, *Miners' Strike*, pp. 106–9; Adeney and Lloyd, *Miners' Strike*, pp. 111–19; Richards, *Miners on Strike*, pp. 127–8; for media reporting, Maggie Wykes, *News, Crime and Culture* (London, 2001), pp. 71–3.
29. The Wapping dispute is discussed in Richard Belfield, Christopher Hird and Sharon Kelly, *Murdoch: The Decline of an Empire* (London, 1994), Chapter 4, 'Wapping'. It is contextualised in Brian McNair, *News and*

Journalism in the UK (4th edn., London, 2003), Chapter 7, 'Before and After Wapping: The Changing Political Economy of the British Press'.

30. On the community charge and related unrest, see: David Butler, Andrew Adonis and Tony Travers, *Failure in British Government: The Politics of the Poll Tax* (Oxford, 1994); David Deacon and Peter Golding, *The Media, Political Communication and the Poll Tax* (London, 1994); Eric J. Evans, *Thatcher and Thatcherism* (London, 1997), pp. 62–4, 112; and Alan Watkins, *A Conservative Coup: The Fall of Margaret Thatcher* (London, 1991), Chapter 3, 'The Poll Tax'.

31. There is a large and growing literature on the Thatcher years, much of it hagiographic. Hugo Young, *One of Us: A Biography of Margaret Thatcher* (London, 1989), is well informed and appropriately critical, while John Campbell, *Margaret Thatcher: Volume Two, The Iron Lady* (London, 2003), is a full and balanced account of her time in office as Prime Minister; for a useful short analytical work, see Evans, *Thatcher and Thatcherism*.

32. Martin Kettle and Lucy Hodges, *Uprising! The Police, the People and the Riots in Britain's Inner Cities* (London, 1982) is a good guide to the 1981 riots, and should be read in conjunction with *The Brixton Disorders 10–12 April 1981* (Report of an Inquiry by the Right Hon. the Lord Scarman, London, 1981).

33. Margaret Simey is quoted in Kettle and Hodges, *Uprising!*, p. 172; the Brixton petrol-bomber, ibid., p. 203.

34. This account of the 2011 riots is based on: Riots, Communities and Victims Panel, *5 Days in August: An Interim Report on the 2011 English Riots* (London, 2012 – interim report published 2011, final 2012); Metropolitan Police Service, *4 Days in August: Strategic Review into the Disorder of 2011: Final Report March 2012* (London, 2012); *After the Riots: The Final Report of the Riots, Communities and Victims Panel* (London, 2012); and *Reading the Riots: Investigating England's Summer of Disorder* (London, 2011), this last the report of an investigation commissioned by the *Guardian* and the London School of Economics.

35. Quotations from the rioters are given in *Reading the Riots*, pp. 20, 23, 25.

Chapter 18: A Culture of Violence? Film and Television

1. George Orwell, *Essays*, Bernard Crick (ed.) (Harmondsworth, 1968).

2. Orwell, Crick (ed.), *Essays*, 'The Decline of the English Murder', citations at pp. 346, 348. The case is the subject of a book, R. Alwyn Raymond's *The Cleft Chin Murder* (London, 1945), and served as the basis for the 1990 movie *Chicago Joe and the Showgirl* (directed by Bernard Rose).

3. Leslie Stephen, 'The Decay of Murder', *Cornhill Magazine*, 20 (1869), citations at pp. 724, 726.

4. Thomas de Quincey, 'On Murder, Considered as One of the Fine Arts', *Blackwood's Magazine*, 20 (1827), pp. 211–12.

5. Orwell, 'Raffles and Miss Blandish', p. 260.

6. Cited in Richard D. Altick, *Victorian Studies in Scarlet: Murders and Manners in the Age of Victoria* (London, 1972), pp. 300–1.

7. An issue discussed in Keith Hollingsworth, *The Newgate Novel, 1830–1847* (Detroit, 1963), Chapter 5, 'The Newgate Novel and the Moral Argument'.

8. Hollingsworth, *Newgate Novel*, pp. 145–7; there were, apparently, four theatrical productions based on Ainsworth's novel running at the time. Following the furore about *Jack Sheppard*, Ainsworth desisted from writing novels featuring historic criminals.

9. Film censorship in Britain in the first half of the twentieth century is described in James C. Robertson, *The British Board of Film Censors: Film Censorship in Britain, 1896–1950* (London, 1985), while the story is taken up to 1971 by John Trevelyan, *What the Censor Saw* (London, 1973): Chapter 11 of this book, 'Violence', provides an interesting view of movie censorship from the censor's perspective; see also the detailed discussion, which includes a consideration of local censorship, in Guy Phelps, *Film Censorship* (London, 1975); and the BBFC website at http:www.bbfc. co.uk

10. Robertson, *British Board of Film Censors*, p. 57. There are numerous publications dealing with violence and the movies. I have made use of two good short guides: Stephen Prince (ed.), *Screening Violence* (London, 2000); and J. David Slocum (ed.), *Violence and American Cinema* (New York & London, 2001).

11. Phelps, *Film Censorship*, p. 41; on the pre-war situation, see Robertson, *The British Board of Film Censors*, Chapter 4, 'The Talkies: Some Films, Genres and Themes, 1929–1939', which implies that there was little concern over violence, although violent behaviour could figure in wider concerns over more general issues with crime or gangster movies.

12. *A Clockwork Orange* is discussed in Stuart Y. McDougal (ed.), *Stanley Kubrick's A Clockwork Orange* (Cambridge, 2003), and Alexander Walker, *Stanley Kubrick Directs* (Aylesbury, 1972); Christian Bugge, 'A Clockwork Controversy', at http://www.visual-memory.co.uk/amk/doc/0012.html is an invaluable guide to the movie's impact; on Burgess, see *Oxford DNB*.

13. There are a number of booklets produced by TV companies discussing and setting out guidelines for the use of violence in television programmes. I have consulted *The Portrayal of Violence in Television Programmes: Suggestions for a Revised Note of Guidance* (BBC, March 1979); *The Portrayal of Violence in Television Programmes: The Reissue of a Note of Guidance* (BBC, September 1983); and *Violence on Television: Guidelines for Production Staff – 1987* (BBC, 1987).

14. A clear statement of Mary Whitehouse's view can be found in her *Cleaning Up TV: From Protest to Participation* (London, 1967); for biographical details and interpretation of her career I have used Michael Tracy and David Morrison, *Whitehouse* (London & Basingstoke, 1979), supplemented by the entry on Whitehouse in *Oxford DNB*.

15. Tracy and Morrison, *Whitehouse*, p. 60, note that Buchman made statements to this effect in 1936 in an interview for the *New York World Telegram*.

16. Quoted in Tracy and Morrison, *Whitehouse*, p. 85.

17. The various essays gathered together in Martin Barker (ed.), *The Video Nasties: Freedom and Censorship in the Media* (London, 1984), constitute an effectively critical analysis of the moral panic; Kate Egan, *Trash or Treasure: Censorship and the Changing Meaning of the Video Nasties* (Manchester, 2007), takes the story further; see also Nigel Wingrove and Marc Morris (eds.), *The Art of the Nasty* (London, 1998), and Julian Petley, *Film and Video Censorship in Contemporary Britain* (Edinburgh, 2011).

18. The text of the editorial is reproduced in Martin Barker, 'Nasty Politics or Video Nasties', in Barker (ed.), *The Video Nasties*.

19. There is now a massive literature on television and violence. The main issues are explained clearly and cogently in David Gauntlett, *Moving Experiences: Understanding Television's Influence and Effects* (London, 1995), while Barrie Gunter and Jackie Harrison, *Violence on Television: An Analysis of Amount, Nature, Location, and Origins of Violence in British Programmes* (London, 1998), is a very solid piece of research, which can be complemented by Barrie Gunter and Mallory Wober, *Violence on Television: What the Viewers Think* (London, 1988). An older work, William A. Belson, *Television Violence and the Adolescent Boy* (Farnborough, 1978), is meticulously researched and constitutes a good guide to thinking on the subject at that time, while Dennis Howitt and Guy Cumberbatch, *Mass Media, Violence and Society* (London, 1975), is an interesting early statement of the sceptical position. The more recent David Gauntlett and Annette Hall, *TV Living: Television, Culture and Everyday Life* (London, 1999), is a sensitive and well-researched attempt to get to grips with the reality of TV viewing: Chapter 9 of this work, 'Television Violence and Other Controversies' is very relevant to our argument; another excellent collection of essays is Martin Barker and Julian Petley (eds.), *Ill Effects: The Media Violence Debate* (London, 1997).

20. Cited by Barker, 'Nasty Politics or Video Nasties', p. 20.

21. Graham Murdock's views are expressed in his 'Figuring out the Arguments', and Brian Brown's in his 'Exactly What We Wanted', both in Barker (ed.), *The Video Nasties*. Murdock's earlier publication

mentioned in the text was *Mass Media and the Secondary School* (London, 1973). It should be noted that Barker was involved in the enquiry as a representative of Methodism.

22. W. James Potter, *The 11 Myths of Media Violence* (Thousand Oaks, 2003), although a work dealing with the US media, does explore issues relevant to the British situation.

23. This paragraph depends heavily upon the excellent overview given by Gauntlett, *Moving Experiences*, Chapter 3, 'Television and Violence'.

24. As in the text, Philip Schlesinger *et al.*, *Women Viewing Violence* (London, 1992) is indicative of the range of possible responses to TV and film violence, and also opens up gender issues effectively; these latter are analysed in greater depth in Karen Boyle, *Media and Violence: Gendering the Debates* (London, 2005).

25. For an overview of some of the negative reactions, see 'Controversies Surrounding *Grand Theft Auto IV*, http://en.wikipedia.org/wiki/Controversies_surrounding_Grand_Theft_Auto_IV

26. Cited in James Newman, *Playing with Videogames* (London & New York, 2008), p. 3.

27. Simon Egenfeldt-Nielsen, Jonas Heide Smith and Susana Pajares Tosca, *Understanding Video Games: The Essential Introduction* (New York & London, 2008), p. 137; for an early report of the killing asserting the connection, BBC News Channel, 29 July 2004.

28. For a balanced discussion which focusses on the link between computer games and violence, see Egenfeldt-Nielsen, Smith and Tosca, *Understanding Video Games*, Chapter 10, 'Video Games and Risks'; I have also consulted Newman, *Videogames*, especially Chapter 4, 'Videogame Players: Who Plays, For How Long and What It's Doing to Them'.

29. http://www.lionlamb.org/violent_toys.html

30. Gisela Wegener-Spöhring, 'War Toys and Aggressive Play Scenes', in Jeffrey H. Goldstein (ed.), *Toys, Play, and Child Development* (Cambridge, 1994), p. 93.

31. Peter K. Smith, 'The War Play Debate', in Goldstein (ed.), *Toys, Play, and Child Development*, pp. 82–3.

32. Edward Bulwer-Lytton, *England and the English*, 2 volumes (London, 1833), Vol. 1, pp. 76–7.

33. On the Hungerford Massacre, see Jeremy Josephs, *Hungerford: One Man's Massacre* (London, 1993); for the media-made connections between Michael Ryan and *Rambo*, see Duncan Webster, '"Whodunnit? America Did": *Rambo* and Post-Hungerford Rhetoric', *Cultural Studies*, 3 (1989), pp. 173–93.

34. The quotation from Mike Purdy is cited in Bugge, 'A Clockwork Controversy'.

Chapter 19: Peaks and Troughs: Patterns of Violence Today

1. Reports on violence in Yorkshire are derived from the *Yorkshire Post* and the *York Press*, and the BBC News York and North websites between January and July 2013; for the Alan Greaves case I have also drawn on the BBC News Sheffield and South Yorkshire website.
2. For Lee Rigby: BBC News website, 22 May 2013; 23 May 2013; 12 July 2013; 27 May 2013; *London Evening Standard*, 23 May 2013; *Independent*, 28 May 2013.
3. For a good summary of the trends, see F. H. McClintock and N. Howard Avison, *Crime in England and Wales* (London, 1968), Chapter 2, 'Trends in Crime'; see also Clive Emsley, *Crime and Society in Twentieth-century England* (Harlow, 2011), Chapter 2, 'The Pattern of Crime'.
4. These figures are derived from Terence Morris and Louis Blom-Cooper, *A Calendar of Murder: Criminal Homicide in England Since 1957* (London, 1964), pp. 277–82, 373–86.
5. D. J. West, *Murder Followed by Suicide: An Inquiry Carried Out for the Institute of Criminology, Cambridge* (London, 1965); for the United States, James Alan Fox and Marianne W. Zawitz, *Homicide Trends in the United States* (United States Bureau of Justice Statistics, n.d.).
6. *Criminal Statistics for England and Wales 1992* (London, 1993), p. 76.
7. On mugging and responses to it, see Stuart Hall, *Policing the Crisis: Mugging, the State and Law and Order* (London, 1978).
8. On the IRA, see Tommy McKearney, *The Provisional IRA: From Insurrection to Parliament* (London, 2011).
9. On the Angry Brigade, see Gordon Carr, John Barker and Stuart Christie, *The Angry Brigade: A History of Britain's First Urban Guerrilla Group* (London, 1975).
10. James Pearson, *The Profession of Violence: The Rise and Fall of the Kray Twins* (London, 1972), is the best introduction to the story of the Krays, which Pearson followed with *The Cult of Violence: The Untold Story of the Krays* (London, 2001). Their rise is contextualised by P. Jenkins and G. W. Potter, 'Before the Krays: Organised Crime in London, 1920–1960', *Criminal Justice History: An International Annual*, 9 (1988), pp. 209–30.
11. On the Moors Murders, J. Ritchie, *Myra Hindley: Inside the Mind of a Murderess* (London, 1988).
12. I have based my account of the creation of the concept of the 'violent society' on Steve Chibnall, *Law-and-Order News: An Analysis of Crime Reporting in the British Press* (London, 1977); NB Chapter 4, 'Bombers, Muggers and Thugs: The Press and the Violent Society'; the *Sunday Times* dubbing 1972 'The Year of Violence' is noted at p. 141.

13. Lord Hailsham quoted in Chibnall, *Law-and-Order News*, p. 75.
14. On the impact of the black market, see Mark Roodhouse, *Black Market: Britain 1935–1955* (Oxford, 2013); for a general overview of wartime criminality, see David Thomas, *An Underworld at War: Spivs, Deserters, Racketeers and Civilians in the Second World War* (London, 2003).
15. On Sabini, see the entry on Charles 'Derby' Sabini in *Oxford DNB*. There has so far been little scholarly research on inter-war organised crime, but for an important exception see Heather Shore, *London's Criminal Underworlds c.1720–c.1930: A Social and Cultural History* (Basingstoke, 2015), Chapter 8, '"The Terror of the People": Organised Crime in Interwar London'; see also Dr Shore's earlier publications, 'Criminality and Englishness in the Aftermath: The Racecourse Wars of the 1920s', *Twentieth-Century British History*, 22 (2011), pp. 474–97, and '"Undiscovered Country": Towards a History of the "Criminal Underworld"', in *Crimes and Misdemeanours: Deviance and the Law in Historical Perspective*, 1 (2007), pp. 41–68. For information on the Sabinis, Billy Hill and Jack Spot see James Morton, *East End Gangland* (London, 2000); see also Billy Hill, *Boss of Britain's Underworld* (London, 1955).
16. *A Summary of Recorded Crime Data from 1892 to 2001/2*, Home Office dataset. When changes were made to police recording methods in the late 1990s the number of violent crimes appeared to increase significantly – evidence again of the problematic nature of statistics.
17. http://www.lawcom.gov.uk/project/offences-against-the-person/
18. Michael J. Allen, *Textbook on Criminal Law* (13th edition, Oxford, 2015), p. 394.
19. The major specific points touched on in the above discussion are drawn from Kevin Smith (ed.), *Homicides, Firearms Offences and Intimate Violence, 2010/11; Supplementary Volume 2 to Crime in England and Wales 2010/11* (Home Office Statistical Bulletin, January 2012): notably pp. 18 (international comparisons); 24 (ethnic background of victims); 53 (homicide by region, forming the basis of Table 11, see Appendix; 42 (circumstances of killing).
20. I have based my comments on statistics in the following paragraphs on three government documents: *Crime in England and Wales, Year Ending March 2013* (Office for National Statistics, London, 18 July 2013), which offers both police and CSEW figures; *Focus on Violent Crime and Sexual Offences* (Office for National Statistics, London, 2015); Smith (ed.), *Homicides, Firearm Offences and Intimate Violence 2010/11*.
21. These figures are derived from *A Summary of Recorded Crime data from 1892 to 2001/2* and *Offences Recorded by the Police in England and Wales: by Offence and Police Force Area, 1990 to 2012/3*, both of these Home Office datasets accessed at www.gov.uk/government/publications/historical-crime-data

22. The British Crime Survey evolved into the Crime Survey England and Wales (CSEW), now conducted annually (there are separate ones for Northern Ireland and Scotland). This has its critics: the fact that it imposes a cap of five reported crimes per person means that some persistent crimes – domestic violence, for example – may go under-reported. It also doesn't cover crimes against businesses (9.2 million were recorded by the 2012 Commercial Victimisation Survey, although, in fairness, it should be noted that very few of these would have been crimes involving violence). What the survey does do, though, is give a good sense of overall patterns of crime, and an insight into the sort of violent events that don't get reported to the police, either because victims think that they are too trivial to make an official complaint about, or because they fear reprisals, or because they know that they themselves bear some of the blame. The CSEW figures for the year ending March 2013 estimated that 8.6 million crimes had been committed in England and Wales against persons aged 16 or over – a decrease of 9 per cent on the previous year and very much in line with police figures.

23. For the Cardiff University Violence Research Group's findings, see V. Sivarajasingam, J. P. Wells, S. Moore, N. Page, P. Morgan, K. Matthews and J. P. Shepherd, 'Violence in England and Wales 2012: An Accident and Emergency Perspective' (Cardiff University Violence and Society Research Group, 2012); I am grateful to the group's leader, Professor J. Shepherd, for permission to reproduce a figure from this paper; for a more detailed overview of the group's findings, see V. Sivarajasingam *et al.* 'Trends in Community Violence in England and Wales 2005–2009', *Injury*, 45 (2014), pp. 592–8. The data gathered by the Cardiff Violence Research Group suggests that 267,291 people with violence-related injuries attended Emergency Units and Minor Injury Units in England and Wales in 2012, a drop of 40,706, or 25 per cent, on the previous year. Those most likely to attend A&E with injuries sustained during a violent altercation were males aged between 18 and 30 (overall, male victims outnumbered females by about three to one). As might be expected, Saturdays and Sundays were the busiest days for A&E departments.

24. On this transition see Jock Young, *The Exclusive Society: Social Exclusion, Crime and Difference in Late Modernity* (London & Thousand Oaks, Calif., 1999); Young has developed his ideas further in his *The Vertigo of Late Modernity* (Thousand Oaks, Calif., 2007); for another discussion of the implications of inequality in modern Britain, see Richard Wilkinson and Kate Pickett, *The Spirit Level: Why Equality is Better for Everyone* (London, 2010).

25. Simon Winlow, *Badfellas: Crime, Tradition and New Masculinities* (Oxford & New York, 2001), p. 171.

26. Gillian Evans, *Educational Failure and Working Class White Children in Britain* (Basingstoke, 2006), pp. 52–3.

27. Winlow, *Badfellas*, p. 271.

28. Beatrix Campbell, *Goliath: Britain's Dangerous Places* (London, 1993), p. 324.

29. Dick Hobbs, Philip Hadfield, Stuart Lister and Simon Winlow, *Bouncers: Violence and Governance in the Night-time Economy* (Oxford, 2003), quotation at p. 11; figures for Manchester, p. 39. For 'mass volume vertical drinkers', Simon Winlow and Steve Hall, *Violent Night: Urban Leisure and Contemporary Culture* (Oxford & New York, 2006), p. 175; for comments on violence, p. 118; for overall figures, p. 115.

30. *Focus on Violent Crime and Sexual Offences*, Chapter 5, 'Violent Crime and Sexual Offences – Alcohol related Violence'.

31. On the transition from an inclusive to an exclusive society, see Young, *Exclusive Society*; also *Vertigo of Late Modernity*. For a further discussion of inequality in modern Britain, see Wilkinson and Pickett, *The Spirit Level*. For the 40/30/30 argument, see Will Hutton, *The State We're In* (London, 1995).

32. Winlow, *Badfellas*, p. 170.

33. *Criminal Justice: The Way Ahead* (Secretary of State for the Home Department, February 2001); *Justice for All* (Crown Prosecution Service, July 2002).

34. An analysis of *The Times* and the *Daily Mirror* between 1945 and 1991 demonstrated an increase in the number of stories concerned with crime, from under 10 per cent of the papers' column space in the 1940s to over 20 per cent in the 1990s, with the most marked rise coming in the 1960s; murder became the most-reported crime: Hazel Croall, *Crime and Society in Britain* (2nd edn., Harlow, 2011), pp. 17–18.

35. For *Crimewatch*, Philip Schlesinger and Howard Tumber, *Reporting Crime: The Media Politics of Criminal Justice* (Oxford, 1994), pp. 129, 141–2, 248–70.

36. My thoughts on violence and organised crime were focussed by Dick Hobbs, *Bad Business: Professional Crime in Modern Britain* (Oxford, 1995), especially pp. 121–4 (a section entitled 'Whacking People'); and Winlow, *Badfellas*, Chapter 4, 'Summary and Conclusion'.

37. Matt Hopkins, Nick Tilley and Kate Gibson, 'Homicide and Organised Crime in England', *Homicide Studies* 17 (2012), pp. 291–313; for recent thinking on organised crime, Dick Hobbs, *Lush Life: Constructing Organised Crime in the UK* (Oxford, 2013).

38. These issues, along with the whole concept of 'the gang' in the modern United Kingdom, are discussed in the various contributions to Barry Goldson (ed.), *Youth in Crisis?: 'Gangs'. Territoriality and Violence* (Abingdon, 2011).

39. The connection between video nasties and the Bulger murder case is discussed by: Blake Morrison, *As If* (London, 1997), pp. 154–6; and David

James Smith, *The Sleep of Reason: The James Bulger Case* (London, 2011), p. 277.

40. For Trevor Joseph Hardy, David Wilson, *Looking for Laura: Public Criminology and Hot News* (Hook, 2011), Chapter 5, 'Serial Killers: Now You See Them, Now You Don't'.

41. On Timothy Evans, Michael Eddowes, *The Man on Your Conscience: An Investigation of the Evans Murder Trial* (London, 1955); on Derek Bentley, David Yallop, *To Encourage the Others* (London, 1991); on Ruth Ellis, R. Hancock, *Ruth Ellis: The Last Woman to be Hanged* (London, 1963); for the background to the abolition of capital punishment in Britain, J. A. Sharpe, *Judicial Punishment in England* (London, 1991), pp. 100–8.

42. Causing a fire or explosion in a Royal Navy dockyard, ship, magazine or warehouse remained a capital offence until 1971; espionage until 1981; piracy with violence, treason, and a number of purely military offences affecting the armed forces until 1998. No executions under any of these headings were carried out post-1965. These 1998 removals of the death penalty were part of the Crime and Disorder Act 1998, perhaps most likely to be remembered for the Introduction of Anti-Social Behaviour Orders.

43. David Garland, *The Culture of Control: Crime and Social Order in Contemporary Society* (London, 2001).

44. Michael Tonry, *Punishment and Politics: Evidence and Emulation in the Making of English Crime Control Policy* (Collumpton, 2004), p. ix.

45. *Ending Gang and Youth Violence: A Cross-Government Report* (HM Government, London, November 2011), quotations from Teresa May and Iain Duncan Smith, pp. 3–4.

46. For a review of the work of one of the leading exponents of this approach, see Adam Crawford and Matthew Jones, 'Inter-Agency Co-operation and Community-Based Crime Prevention: Some Reflections on the Work of Pearson and Colleagues', *British Journal of Criminology*, 35 (1995), pp. 17–33.

47. Amanda L. Robinson, 'Reducing Repeat Victimisation among High-risk Victims of Domestic Violence: The Benefits of Co-ordinated Community Responses, Cardiff, Wales', *Violence Against Women*, 12 (2006), pp. 761–88.

48. One of a number of recent books exploring this theme is Caroline Elkin, *Britain's Gulag: The Brutal End of Empire in Kenya* (London, 2005).

49. Peter Laslett, *The World We Have Lost* (Oxford, 1965) Chapter 10, 'Understanding Ourselves in Time'.

INDEX

Page numbers in *italics* denote illustrations

Abel *see* Cain and Abel
Abercromby, Mrs and Helen, 509
abortion, 206
The Accused (film), 596
Acomb, 234–5
Act for the Better Prevention and
　Punishment of Aggravated Assaults
　upon Women and Children (1853), 190
Act for the Prevention of Cruelty to, and
　Protection of, Children (1889), 458
Acton, 239
Adderley, Charles, 426
Adebolajo, Michael, 607–8
Adebowale, Michael, 607–8
Admiralty court *see* courts
adoption, 206–7, 218–19
adultery, 92, 199, 376–7
advice books, 36–7
African Australopithecines, 10
Agarr, Elizabeth, 207–8
Agincourt, Battle of (1415), 93–4
Agnew, Thomas, 457–8
agriculture, 58–60, 288
Ainsworth, William Harrison,
　313–14, 581
Akers, Anne, 235
alcohol: and football hooliganism, 548,
　551; and modern violence levels,
　624–5, 627–8; nineteenth-century
　attitudes, 288, 289; and pre-1800
　violence levels, 51, 128, 133–4
Aldershot, 613

Alderton, Thomas, 108–9
Alfred the Great, 481
Algeria, 16
Allen, Thomas and Margaret, 499
Allen, William, 350–1
Allestree, Richard, 223–5
Allitt, Beverly, 531
Almond, James, 179–80
ambition, as revenge tragedy
　theme, 155
American colonies, transportation
　to, 396
American War of Independence
　(1777–83), 338
Anderton, James, 589
anger *see* wrath
Angry Brigade, 613, 632
animals: cruelty to, 150, 160;
　impounding of stray, 235
Anjou, Duc d', 260
Anne, Queen, 274
anti-colonialism, 16–17
Antonio's Revenge, 154–5
*An Appeal to Humanity in an Account of
　the Life and Cruel Actions of Elizabeth
　Brownrigg*, 164
Appleton, William, 54
Applin, John, 133
apprentices, 10–11, 108, 171–2, 176–80, 346
Apps, Scott, 605
arbitration, 101
Archer, Robert, 376

archery, 110–11
Arde(r)n, Thomas, 139
Arendt, Hannah, 17
aristocracy *see* class issues
Aristotle, 5
Armstrong, Gary, 548–50, 552
Armthorpe, 561–2
Army Act (1881), 390
Arnold, Thomas, 292–4, 296
arson, 378, 379, 397–8, 568, 571, 572
Arthurian legends, 89–93
Arthurs, John, 119
Ascott-under-Wychwood, 284–5
Ashbourne, 283–4, 285
Ashcroft, Henry, 210
Ashley, Ralph, 490–1
Ashworth, John, 365
Askwith, Sir George, 553–4
assault: measuring rates, 31; modern
    causes, 625–9; nineteenth-century
    decline in rate, 409–10; nineteenth-
    century hardening of attitudes,
    419–28; nineteenth-century
    statistics and sentences, 642;
    premeditated, 130–1; twentieth- and
    twenty-first-century statistics,
    609–10, 612, 618–20, 643; *see also*
    sexual assault
assizes *see* courts
Aston, John, 395–6
Aston Villa, 303
Atherton, Anthony, 134
Atkyns, Richard, 120–1
Augustine, St, 84
Australia, transportation to, 396–7,
    420–2

Babington, Anthony, 373–4
Bacon, Francis, 156
Bacon, Matthew, 174–5
Bailey, Mary, 204–6
Bailey, Michael, 568
Ball, John, 61–2
Ballard, Lucy, 482–3
Bally, Richard, 6

Bambroffe, Deborah and David, 535
Bamford, Samuel, 361–2
Banbury, 356
Bandura, Albert, 593–4
bank holidays, 288, 434–5
Bann, Thomas, 129–30
Barfoote, Henry, 122–3
Barid, Roger de, 482
Barnes, Agnes, 203
Barratt, Peter Henry, 470–2
Barrett, Michael, 403
The Barriers (celebration), 99
bastard feudalism, 68, 72
Bates, Paul, 592
Bath, 356
Baxter, Elizabeth, 226
Baxter, Richard, 123
Bealknap, Sir Robert, 61
Bean, James, wife of, 244
Beavans, Richard ap, 110, 487
Beccaria, Cesare, 394–5
Beccles, 331
Becket, Thomas, Archbishop of
    Canterbury, 86–7
Bedfordshire, 46, 492
beheading, 379–80
Bel(l)ers, Roger, 70
Bell, Jane, 494–5, 499
Bell, Mary, 464–5
Bell, Norma, 464–5
bell, book and candle ritual, 228
Bellasis (Belasyse), Sir Henry,
    257–8, 273
Bellfield, Levi, 539
Beloff, Max, 345
Benedik, László, 583
Bennett, Elizabeth, 231
Bennett, John, 18, 277, 278
Bentham, Jeremy, 162
Bentley, Derek, 633
The Best Little Whorehouse in Texas
    (film), 389
Beverley, 243
Beyond Blame (child abuse study),
    460–1

Bible: Cain and Abel, *viii*, 9–10; on divine vengeance, 84; lay reading of, 147–8; passages on wrath, 80
Billing, James, 174
Binns, Bartholomew, 404
biology, and violence, 19
Bird, Derrick, 621
Birdsall, Trevor, 527
Birmingham, 303, 361, 434, 440, 572, 616
Birmingham pub bombing (1974), 613
Birmingham University Centre for Contemporary Cultural Studies, 547
Black Death, 59
Black Prince *see* Edward the Black Prince
Blackboard Jungle (film), 541, 583
Blackburn Rovers, 303, 304
Blackburn Olympic, 303
Blackheath, 301
Blackout Ripper *see* Cummins, Gordon Frederick
Blackpool FC, 303
Blackstone, Sir William, 137, 174
Bladen, Leonard, 517
Blair, Tony, 635
Blakely, David, 633
Blewitt, Jack, 314
Bloch, Marc, 44
Bloody Sunday (1972), 613
Boleyn, Anne, 379
Bolton, John, 178–9
Bond, Dr Thomas, 520–1
Bonetti, Rocco, 261
Bonfire Night, 286–8, 436
Bonner, William, 231
Bonnie and Clyde (film), 583
Bonville, William, 69–70
Booth, Charles, 433
borough courts *see* courts
Bosanquet, Helen, 446
Bosnian War (1992–5), 478
Bousfield, William, 402–3
Bowen, William, 432
Bowes, Emmanuel, 178
Bowkley, William, 123

Bowling, Jonathan, 606–7
boxing, 297–301; *see also* fights
Boy's Own Paper, 293
Bracton, Henry de; works by, 76, 482
Braddock, Lady Almeria, 269–70
Bradford, 525, 528
Bradford City fire (1985), 550
Bradley, James, 470–2
Brady, Ian, 524, 614–15
Bramwell, Mr Justice Baron, 426
Branch, Elizabeth and Mary, 164–5, 192–3
branks *see* scold's bridle
Brathwaite, Richard, 36
Breen, John, 464, 468
Brentwood, 56, 61
Briant, John, 494–5
Brides in the Bath Murders, 523
Brighton, 287, 542
Brinkhurst, Robert, 40
Bristol, 47, 402, 567
British army: and British Empire, 637–8; floggings, 389–90; and riot control, 339–43, 349–53, 363–7, 368; and smuggling, 333–4; and strikes, 555, 556
British Board of Film Censors, 582–3
British Board of Film Classification, 590
British Empire, 637–8
British Union of Fascists, 565
Brixton riots (1981), 567–9, 570
Brontë, Ann, 444
Brooke, Sir John, 259–60, 263
Brooke, William, 247
brothels, 323, 324, 376
Broughton, Jack, 298, 299, 300
Brown, Brian, 592
Brown, Martin, 465
Browne, Elizabeth, 203
Browne, George, 139
Browne, Tracy, 526, 528
Brownmiller, Susan, 477–80, 499, 500–1, 502, 504
Brownrigg, Elizabeth, 162–4
Brownrigg, James, 163

Brushfield, T. N., 239
Bryskett, Lodowick, 271
Buchman, Frank, 587
Buckingham, Humphrey Stafford, 1st
    Duke of, 96
Buckingham, George Villiers, 2nd
    Duke of, 258, 273
Buckinghamshire, 72
Buckley, John, 470
Buckley, Tim, 314
Bulger, Denise, 466
Bulger, James, 466–70, 472–3, 630–1, 636
Buller, Judge Sir Francis, 174
Bulling, Thomas J., 522
bullying, 13, 290, 293–4, 473–4; cyber-
    bullying, 625
Bulwer-Lytton, Edward George
    Earle, 599
Bunne, William, 117
Bunter, Billy, 293
Burcher, Richard, 109
Burden, Mr (JP), 342
Burgess, Anthony, works by, 27, 574,
    584–6, 602
Burgess, George, 470–2
Burgess, Ralph, 470
Burghley, William Cecil, Lord, 310
burglary see robbery and theft
Burke, Edmund, 341, 387
burning at stake, 139, 194, 390–1
Burroughs, Sir Nehemiah, 317–18
Burton, John, 117
Burton on Trent, 247
Bury, 361
Butler, Henry, 165
Butley, 129–30
Buttersworth, Jane, 165, 192–3
Byford Report (1981), 326
Byng, General Sir John, 364
Byron, George Gordon, Lord, 291
Bywater, Brian, 243

Cade's rebellion (1450), 63–4
Cain and Abel, *viii*, 9–10
Caird, Monica, 444

Calcraft, William, 403, 513
Calendar, Gregorian, 354–5
Calverley (brawler), 257
Calverley, Sir Hugh, 248–9
Cambodia, 43–4
Cambridge, 57, 63
Cambridge, John, 57
Cambridge Rules, 301
Cambridge University, 102
Cambridgeshire, 227
Cameron, David, 467
Campbell, Beatrix, 626–7
Campbell, F. W., 302
Campion, William, 376
Compton, Alice, 33
Canbery Besse see Evans, Elizabeth
Cancellor, Reginald, 294–5
Cannibal Holocaust (film), 589
Canning, George, 280
Cannon, John, 131–5, 173–4
Capel, 82
capital punishment, 372; abolition,
    632–4; abolition's effect on crime
    rates, 618; beheading, 379–80;
    benefit of clergy, 113, 116, 395, 480,
    484; burning at stake, 139, 194, 390–1;
    Christian attitude, 150–1, 159;
    claiming pregnancy, 113–14, 198–9,
    202–3, 395; dying speeches, 384–5; in
    eighteenth and nineteenth
    centuries, 390–8, 399–404; hanging,
    379, 380, 383–4, 393, 400, 403–4;
    hanging, drawing and quartering,
    373–4, 391–2; in middle ages, 115;
    other loopholes in potentially
    capital cases, 395; public executions,
    381–5, 390, 400, 401–3; public
    exhibition of corpses, 393; spiritual
    preparation, 140; statistics, 378; in
    twentieth century, 611; twentieth-
    century popular attitudes, 632–4
capitalism, 24, 356
car industry, 557
car ownership, 558
Cardiff, 637

CARE *see* Christian Act Research and Education
care homes, 453
Carey, Dr Nathaniel, 463
Carlton, Charles, 119, 120
Carmarthen, 352
Carnarvon, Henry Howard Molyneux Herbert, 4th Earl of, 427
Carr, Robert, 613
Carrington, 239
Carter, William, 329
Carter Wood, John, 20, 415–16
carting, 376
Case, Anthony, 486–7
Casement, John, 227
Castlereagh, Lord, 280
Caterall, Laurence, 80
Catholics: Babington plot, 373–4; discrimination against, 337–45; *see also* religion
Cato Street conspiracy (1820), 392, 400
Cavendish, Sir John, 57
Caxton, William, 89
Cecil, William *see* Burghley, William Cecil, Lord
celebrations and holidays, traditional, 283–90, 434–6
censorship, 580–6, 589–90
Challener, Margaret, 123–4
Challener, Richard, 118
Chambers, John Graham, 300
Chancery court *see* courts
Chandler, Margaret, 203
chansons de geste, 88–93
Chapman, Annie, 520
Chapman, Jessica, 634
Charity Organisation Society, 446, 447
charivari, 187, 245–9, 286
Charles VII, King of France, 95
Charterhouse, 291, 303
Chartism, 366–9, 392, 411, 418
Chase, James Hadley, 575–6, 577, 579
Chater, Daniel, 329–30
Chatham gaol, 422
Chatsworth, Lady Grace, 185

Cheeseborough, James, 166–7
Chelmsford, 287–8
Cherry, Henry, 485
Cheshire: arbitration, 101; charivari, 248–9; domestic violence, 180–1; fights and murders, 127–30, 135; infanticide, 206, 208–12, 213; murder rates, 125, 410; rape, 493–4, 499; scolding, 236–7, 239
Chester, 200, 229, 239
Chesterfield, 555
Chetulton, Sir William de, 71
chevauchées, 94
Chibnall, Steve, 630
Chichester, 107
Child's Play 3 (film), 630
children: adoption, 206–7, 218–19; age of legal responsibility, 468, 471; baby farming, 218–19, 442, 457; child abuse, 454–63; child labour, 455; childhood concept, 171; and corporal punishment, 389; effect of computer games, 597–8; effect of cultural depictions of violence, 589, 591–4; effect of violent toys, 598–9; infant mortality, 218, 455; infanticide, 108, 166, 196, 197–221, 622, 641; juvenile delinquency, 458, 471; Moors murders, 524, 614–15; murders committed by, 463–73; nineteenth-century attitudes to, 219; parents' right to punish, 620; sexual abuse, 480, 481, 485, 486, 493–8, 499, 500, 620; as victims of serial killers, 510–14, 516, 517, 524, 531; *see also* families
Children Act (1908), 456–7, 458
Children Act (1948), 459
Children Act (2004), 620
Children and Young Persons Act (1933), 459
China, 43
Chipping Norton, 356
Chishull, Edmund, 274–5
Chistleton, 130

Chiswick Women's Aid Group, 447–8
chivalry, 87–99
Cholle, Joan and Henry, 109
Cholmley, Nathaniel, 353
Christian Act Research and Education (CARE), 592
Christianity *see* religion
Christie, Agatha, 507
Christie, John, 633
Chrysostom, St John, 83
church wall paintings, 82, 147
cinema *see* films
Cinematograph Act (1909), 581
Cinthio, Giovani Battista Giraldi, 271
cities *see* towns and cities
civilising process, 23–6, 45, 136, 305–6, 430, 547, 618, 637
Clarendon, Constitutions of (1164), 86–7
Clarendon Commission (1864), 295
Clarke, Alice, 139
Clarke, Thomas, 508–9
Clarke, William, 142
class issues: aristocracy and Wars of the Roses, 66–7, 68; and compensation payments, 481; and domestic violence, 445; and football violence, 546–7, 549; gentry criminal bands, 70–3; and hooliganism, 541; middle class and honour codes, 278–9; middle–working-class relations, 288, 369–70; and murder in Elizabethan and Jacobean England, 109–10, 111, 116–17, 131–3; and murder perpetrators, 409; and nineteenth-century crime, 414–17, 430; origins of middle class, 64–5; and public executions, 402; and punishments, 387, 436–7; and rape, 503; and sport, 285–6, 288, 298–9, 304–5; and wife-beating, 188–9
classical mythology and literature, rape theme, 488–90
Claxton, Marcella, 525–6
Cleaver, Robert, 148–50, 156

Cleft Chin Murder, 577
Cliff, Mary, 206
Clifford, Mary, 162–4
Climbié, Victoria, 462–3, 631
A Clockwork Orange (film), 574, 584–6, 602
A Clockwork Orange (novel) *see* Burgess, Anthony
Closing Ranks (TV programme), 596
Clough, Arthur Hugh, 219
Clough, Isobel, 241–2
Clyst, 69
Coal Mines (Minimum Wage) Act (1912), 555
coalminers *see* miners' strikes
Coastguard, 334
Cobbe, Frances Power, 444
Cobbett, William, 362
Cochrane, Thomas, Lord, 387
Cockburn, J. S., 125–6
Cohen, Stanley, 542–3
Coke, Sir Edward, Lord, 373–4, 394
Colchester, 358–9
Cole, Agnes, 486
Collins, William Wilkie, 518
Collins (soldier), 123–4
Collinson, Joseph, 427
Colmore (or Comer), Jacob (Jack Spot), 616
Colnbrook, 508
colonialism *see* anti-colonialism
Colquhoun, Patrick, 311
Colwell, Maria, 460
Common Pleas court *see* courts
Community Charge *see* Poll Tax Riots
Compton, Sir Charles, 462
computer games, 597–8
Concannon, Ann, 30–1
Congleton, 239, 347
Contagious Diseases Acts (1864–9), 325
Cook, James (murderer), 393
Cook, John Parsons, 517
Cooper, Edward, 112
Cooper, Thomas, 230
Corden, William, 580
Cornell, George, 614

Cornwall, 64, 333, 410, 482–3
coroners' inquests, 30
corporal punishment *see* punishment
corruption, 60, 100, 322, 326, 617
Cortonwood colliery, 560
Cosmides, Leda, 20
Coterel, James, 70–1
Coterel gang, 70–2
Cottier, Catherine (alias Kneale), 227
Cotton, Charles Edward, 512–13, 514
Cotton, Frederick, 512
Cotton, Margaret, 512
Cotton, Mary Ann, 510–15, 518–19
counterfeiting and forgery, 372, 378, 390–1, 502
Country Tom *see* Sherwood, Thomas
County Durham, 162
Court, Joan, 460
Courtenay, Thomas, 5th Earl of Devon, 68–70
Courtenay, Thomas, 6th Earl of Devon, 70
Courthopp, Elizabeth, 203
courtly love, 91–2
courts: Admiralty, 99; assizes, 28–9; borough, 29, 99; Chancery, 100; Common Pleas, 100; court records as sources, 33; ecclesiastical, 29, 99, 240–1, 249–50, 376–7, 385–6; Equity, 100; eyres, 46–7; King's Bench, 100, 103; manor, 29, 99; quarter sessions, 29; Star Chamber, 100, 245
Courvoisier, François, 401–2
Couton, Adrian *see* Edes, Adrian
Coventry City, 303–4
Cowle, Jony, 228
Cowper, Roger, 243–4
Crabbe, George, 538
Cramlington, 556
Cranfield, 289–90
Cream, Thomas Neill (Lambeth Poisoner), 523–4
Crewe, Edmund, 7–8
Crewe, Peers, 6, 7, 18
Crewe Alexandra, 303

Cribb, Tom, 298–9
cricket, 111, 291, 295, 304
crime, organised *see* gangs, criminal
Crime and Disorder Act (1998), 392
crime and punishment *see* capital punishment; courts; justice system; punishment
crime statistics: early periods, 38–30; history of, 27–8; manipulation, 620–1; nineteenth-century improvement, 408–33; problems with using, 30–2, 618–21; sixteenth and seventeenth centuries, 639; twentieth and twenty-first centuries, 609–12, 618–25, 643
crimes of passion, 415
Criminal Justice Act (1948), 500
Criminal Justice: The Way Ahead (White Paper), 628–9
criminology, 413–14
Crockett, Bridget, 3, 4–5, 8
Crockett, Roger, 1–8, 18
Cromwell, Lady, 232
Cromwell, Oliver, 119, 394
Cronkshay, John, Emma and Richard, 376–7
Curry, William (or John), 380
culture, and violence, 21–2
culture, popular: depiction of violence, 575–602; effect on real-life violence, 590–602; serial killers in, 507, 538–9
Cumberbatch, Guy, 592
Cumberland, 410
Cumberland, William Augustus, Duke of, 298
Cumbria, 621
Cummins, Gordon Frederick (Blackout Ripper), 524
curses, 226–32, 251–2
Cusack, Hannah, 495

Daily Mirror (newspaper), 632
Dalton, Michael, 487–8
Daly, Martin, 21–2

Danby, Thomas Osborne, Earl of, 255
Daniel, Phoebe, 130–1
Darky the Coon, 326
Darwin, Charles, 215
Darwin, Erasmus, 214–15, 251–2
Davenant, Nicholas, 56
Davenport, Richard, 129
Davey, William, 485–6
Davies, Andrew, 434
Davis, Robert, 453
Davis, William (Golden Farmer), 318
Day, Mr Justice, 426–7
Daye, John, 486
De Burger, James, 523, 529
Death Trap (film), 588–9
defamation, 223–6, 232–45, 249–51
Defoe, Daniel, 214, 377
Del Ponte, Carla, 43–4
Dell, Annis (Agnes) and George, 146
Deloney, Thomas, 508
Denson, Elizabeth and William, 209
Denton, William, 66
depositions, 33
Derby, 285–6, 392
Derbyshire, 188, 288
Despenser, Henry le, Bishop of
    Norwich, 63, 85
Detroit, 21
Deutsch, Helene, 500–1
Devon, 393–4, 490–1
DHSS see Health and Social Security,
    Department of
Diamond, John, 328, 329
diaries, 37–8
Dickens, Charles, 219, 319–20, 344,
    401–2, 411, 518
Dicksee, Frank, 91
Dickson, Thomas and Elizabeth,
    208–9
dissection, 383
Ditchfield, Patience, 493–4
divorce, 182, 189–91, 446
Dixon, Anne, 229
Dobin, Hugh and Marjorie, 49
dockers' strike (1911), 553–4

Dr Who (TV programme), 588
Dod, John, 148–50, 156
Dodd, William, 248–9
Domestic Proceedings and
    Magistrates' Courts Act (1978), 449
domestic violence, 168; against
    apprentices and servants, 176–80,
    192–3; changing attitudes, 10, 13, 37,
    186–9; changing future attitudes, 637;
    child abuse, 454–63; husband-killing,
    49, 109, 193–4, 390–1; against men,
    452–3; modern statistics, 169, 443–4;
    pre-1800, 108–9, 134, 169–94; twentieth-
    and twenty-first-century statistics and
    types, 610–12, 619–20, 622; against
    women, 108–9, 127, 134, 169–91, 414–15,
    439, 443–52; by women, 191–4
Domestic Violence and Matrimonial
    Proceedings Act (1976), 449
Domestic Violence, Crime and
    Victims Act (2004), 449, 620
Donaldson, Professor Liam, 538
Dore, Daniel, 180
Douglas, Alfred, 300
Dowler, Milly, 539
Downer, Samuel, 329–30
Downes, Richard, 129
Downey, Lesley Ann, 615
Doyle, Sir Arthur Conan, 444–5
Dracott, John, 179
drama see plays
Driller Killer (film), 588–9
Driver, Beverley, 631
Driver, Samuel, 40
drugs, and violent crime, 628–9
Drummond, Edward, 437
Drury, Anne, 139
Du Cane, Edmund, 427–8
Duby, Georges, 44
ducking stools, 222, 237–8, 247
Dudley, Richard, 314–15
duels, 254; contemporary attitudes, 10,
    36, 271–80; Elizabethan and
    Jacobean, 109–10; and family ties,
    18; overview, 255–80; verbal, 242–3

Duggan, Mark, 571
Dunbar, William, 242
Duncan Smith, Iain, 636–7
Dundee, 361–2
Dunning, Eric, 547
Durand-Deacon, Mrs, 523
Dürer, Albrecht, engravings by, *viii*
Duval, Claude, 314
Dyer, Adam, 56

East Anglia, 64, 74
East India Company, 327
Eaton, Daniel, 397
Eccles, 32
ecclesiastical courts *see* courts
Eddowes, Catherine, 520
Eden, William, 212
Edes (or Couton), Adrian, 485
Edinburgh, 349–50
education: bullying in schools, 473–4;
    and football hooliganism, 548;
    increase in availability, 430; public
    schools, 282, 290–7, 301, 303
Edward I, 98, 102
Edward II, 100
Edward III, 60, 98
Edward IV, 66, 96–7
Edward VIII, 284
Edward of Hales, 48
Edward the Black Prince, 98
Edwards, John, 485
Edwards, Richard, 130
Egan, Pierce, 38–9, 299–300
Egremont, Thomas Percy, Baron, 80
Eisner, Manuel, 23–4
Elcock, Alexander, 180
elder abuse, 453–4
elections and voting systems, 360, 363,
    366–9, 431, 445–6
Elestone, Sarah and Thomas, 194
Elias, Norbert, 23–6, 45, 306, 547
Elizabeth I, 98, 147, 262, 373–4
Ellenborough, Lord Chief Justice
    William Law, 1st Baron, 217
Ellis, Brett Easton, 538

Ellis, Edmund, 375–6
Ellis, Ruth, 633
Ellyot, Sibyl and William, 203–4
Elphinstone, Howard, 190
Elphinstone, Mrs (dueller), 269–70
Ely, 361
Emmanuel, Edward, 616
employment: in 1930s, 557; effect of
    pattern changes on crime rates,
    617–18, 628–9; and football
    hooliganism, 150; and riots, 567–8, 573
*Ending Gang and Youth Violence: A
    Cross-Government Report*, 636
Engels, Friedrich, 412
English Civil War (1642–51), 118–25, 136,
    490–1
Equity court *see* courts
Eridge, Marion and William, 197–8
Erskine, Thomas, 345
An Essay on Duelling, 273–4
Essex: domestic violence, 170, 176–7,
    179, 180; female murderers, 191;
    infanticide, 198, 202, 203; murder
    rates, 410; nineteenth-century
    increase in intolerance of assault,
    419; and Peasants' Revolt, 52, 54,
    55–6, 61; punishments, 396; rape,
    484, 485, 486, 491–2; robbery, 202;
    witchcraft, 202, 230–1
Eton College, 290, 303
Eudoxia, Byzantine empress, 83
Eulogius, Prefect of Nicodemia, 83
Evans, Elizabeth (Canbery Besse), 140,
    146, 508–9
Evans, Enoch ap, 140
Evans, Gillian, 626
Evans, John, 352
Evans, Timothy, 633
Evelyn, John, 380
Everitt, Samuel, 179–80
Everton FC, 303, 544
Evesham, 244–5
evolutionary psychology *see*
    psychology
excommunication, 228, 376

executions *see* capital punishment
Exeter, 69, 286, 287
The Exorcist (film), 590
eyres *see* courts

factories, 471, 493–4
Fagin, 319–20
fags, 291, 292, 293
Fairfax, Sir Thomas, 248
Falmouth, Viscount, 267–8
families: child abuse, 454–63; elder
    abuse, 453–4; and football
    hooliganism, 548; murders within,
    49, 108–9, 127, 139–40, 143–5, 166–7,
    443–5, 610–12; pre-modern, 170–1; as
    restraint upon violence, 18–19; *see
    also* domestic violence
Family Law Act (1996), 449, 620
Fanon, Frantz, 16–17
farming *see* agriculture
Farnecombe, Joan and Leonard, 109
Faversham, 139
Fedigan, Linda Marie, 22
felony, appeals of, 8, 482
fencing, 254, 261–2
Ferguson, Richard (Galloping
    Dick), 318
feudalism *see* bastard feudalism
Fielding, Sir John, 341
Figg, James, 297–8
fights: boxing, 297–301; conventions
    governing, 270–1; minor fights,
    133–5; prize fights, 37–8; *see also*
    assault
Fildes, Ann and William, 364
films: depiction of violence, 581–6,
    588–90; effect on real-life violence,
    590–7, 600–2; football hooligan
    theme, 546; video nasties, 588–9,
    590–3, 630
firearms *see* weapons
The Firm (film), 546
First Blood (film), 601
First Catholic Relief Act (Papist Act;
    1778), 338–45

First World War (1914–18), 14–15, 43,
    119, 582
Fisher, Adam, daughter of, 490–1, 499
Fisher, Samuel, 130
Fitz, Alfred, 464, 468
Flanders, 85; Flemish in England, 34,
    53–54
Flanders, Judith, 417
Flannagan, Catherine, 456
flash houses, 311, 321–2
Fleeson, James, 464
Fleetwood, William, 310
Fletcher, Amice, 236
flogging *see* whipping and flogging
Fludde, David, 485
Flying Scotsman, 556
flyting, 242–3
Folville, Eustace de, 70–1, 72
Folville, Richard de, 70, 71
food *see* grain riots
football, 38, 111, 282, 283–6, 288–9, 301–5
Football Association, 301, 304, 545
Football Association Cup, 303
football hooliganism, 11–12, 305, 540,
    543–52
football stadia, 550–1
forensic science, 514, 517, 523
Forfeiture Act (1870), 392
forgery *see* counterfeiting and forgery
Formeston, Thomas, 118
Fortescue, John, 72–3
Fortin, Robert, 93
Foster, Ashley, 606–7
fox-hunting, 289
Foxe, Mary, 209–10
Foyster, Elizabeth, 188
France: 1848 revolutions, 368; British
    attitude to, 337; crimes of passion,
    415; duels, 256–7; Hundred Years'
    War, 60, 85, 93–4, 95–6; infanticide,
    198; medieval, 48; murder rates, 127;
    Peace of God movement, 78–9;
    Thirty Years' War, 122
Frankenstein (film), 582
Freemason, Thomas, 203

French Revolution, 362–3
Freud, Sigmund, 24–5, 26–7, 500–1
Friendly Societies Act (1793), 456
From the Manger to the Cross (film), 582
Fry, Elizabeth, 401
Fulham FC, 303
funeral insurance, 456

Gale, Elizabeth, 230–1
Galley, William, 329–30
Galloping Dick *see* Ferguson, Richard
Galway, Margaret, 242–3
gangs, criminal: aristocratic, 70–3;
   clerical, 85–7; government report
   on deterring, 636–7; medieval,
   49–50; nineteenth-century youth
   gangs, 433–7; overview, 309–35;
   twentieth-century, 614, 616, 626
gaols *see* prison
Gardiner, Ralph, 239
Gargrave, 80
Garland, David, 635
garrotters, 406, 423–8
Garter, Order of the, 98
Gascoigne Wood drift mine, 560
Gascoyne (Guards ensign), 341
Geering, Thomas, 109
Gem (magazine), 293
gender issues: charivari, 187, 245–9,
   286; computer games, 598; courtly
   love, 91–2; elder abuse, 454; family
   murders, 443; murder, 108, 622–3;
   public whipping, 388; sexual assault,
   13; *see also* domestic violence; men;
   women
General Strike (1926), 556–7
genetics, and violence, 19
George I, 347–8
George III, 280, 339, 343
George IV, 298, 299
Germany, 43, 122, 127, 275, 402, 478
ghosts, 141–2, 154–5, 160
gibbeting, 393
Gilbert de Mordone, 51
Gildesborough, Sir John, 56, 61

Gill, George and Margaret, 234–5
Gillingham, 237
Given, James Buchanan, 46–7, 48–9, 52
Glaber, Rodulphus, 78–9
Glamorgan, 410
Glanvill, Ranulf de, 481–2
Glasgow, 15, 434
Glastonbury, 131–5
Glorious Revolution (1688), 346–7, 360
Gloucestershire, 357, 399
Goddard, Henry, 320
Godfrey, William, wife of, 244
Godfrey of Crombe, 86
Golden Farmer *see* Davis, William
Goldfinch, Thomas, 204
Goldhanger, 243–4
Golding, Arthur, 140
Goodcole, Henry, 139, 140, 199–200
Gordon, Lord George, 338–9, 344–5
Gordon Riots (1780), 14, *336*, 337–45
Goring, Charles, 413
Goring, George, 122
Gorleston, 330–1
gossip *see* defamation; scolding
Goudhurst, 332–3
Gouge, William, 170, 175–6
Gough, Richard, 118–19, 123–5, 395–6
The Government of the Tongue see
   Allestree, Richard
Gower, Nicholas, 110
Graef, Roger, 502
grain riots, 356–7, 361–2, 368
Grand Theft Auto (computer game), 597
Grange, John, 210
Grantham, Christine, 204
Grassi, Giacomo di, 261–2
Graves, Robert, 518
Gray, Arthur, 331
Great Waltham, 230–1
Greaves, Alan, 606–7
Green, Henry, 242
Green, Joseph, 177
Greene, Graham, 616
Greenwood, Thomas, 498
Gregory, Ronald, 526

Gregory brothers, 315
Grey, Lord, of Wilton, 72–3
Griffith, Anne, 241
Griffiths, D. L., 459
Griffiths, George Edwards, 509
Griffiths, John, 248–9
Grindecobbe, William, 57–8, 63
Grindill, Margaret, 210
Grosvenor Square protest (1968), 565
Grunwick Dispute (1976–8), 558–9
Grundy, Kathleen, 536
Gryffin, John, 5
Guildford, 287
Guillam, Samuel, 350–1
Gull, Sir William, 522
guns see weapons
Guy Fawkes Night see Bonfire Night
Gwyn, Nell, 316
Gyles, Joan, 109

Hadfield, Thomas, 380
Haigh, John George, 523
Hailsham, Lord, 615
Hale, Sir Matthew, 493
Hales, Sir Robert, 54–5
Halifax, 527
Hall, John, 178
Hallam, Isaac and Thomas, 317
Halliday, Harriet, 440
Halsall, Anne, 8
Halsall, Richard, and family, 2–8
Halsall, William, 2, 7, 8
Hamilton, William, 425
Hammer, Carl I., Jr., 47–9
Hampshire, 329
Hamton, Anne, 144–5
Hanawalt, Barbara, 50–1, 52
hanging, 379, 380, 383–4, 393, 400, 403–4
hanging, drawing and quartering, 373–4, 391–2
Harcourt, John, 204
Harcourt, Margaret, 205
Harding, Arthur, 325–7
Hardinge, Henry, 267–8
Hardy, Horatio Nelson, 430

Hardy, Thomas, 181, 246
Hardy, Trevor Joseph, 631
Hardye, John, 486
Harman, William, 110
Harris, Phoebe, 391
Harrow School, 291, 294, 297
harrying of the North, 83
Hart, Richard, 614
Harwood, Jocelin, 317–18
Haselrig, Sir Arthur, 121
Havers, Sir Michael, 530
Haward, Richard, 110
Hawkhurst Gang, 328–30, 333
Hawkins (naturalist), 421
Hawkins, George, 244–5
Hayes, Jerry, 590–1
Hayes, Katherine, 391
Hayter, Tony, 352
Hayward, John, 110–11
Hayward, Thomas, 119
Hazard, Elizabeth, 143–4
Health and Social Security, Department of (DHSS), 460
Heath, George Edward, 577
Hedley, Margaret, 216
Helling, Christian, 210
Hempnall, 236
Henley-in-Arden, 237
Henrietta Maria, Queen, 255
Henry II, 86–7, 99–100
Henry III, 84
Henry VI, 95
Henry VIII, 98, 147
Henry, Prince (son of James I and VI), 98–9
Henry, Matthew, 200
Henshaw, John, 486
Henslowe, Philip, 152
heraldry, 97
Hereford, 229, 233–4, 238
Hertfordshire, 146, 198, 484
Hervey, Lord, 351
Hesketh, Mary, 209
Hexham, 353–4
Heys, Mary, 365

Heysel stadium disaster (1985), 544–5
Higgins, Margaret and Thomas, 456
High Leigh, 127–9
High Rip Gang, 427
highwaymen, 312–19
Hiley, Helen, 229
Hill, Abigail, 140–1
Hill, Billy, 616
Hill, Octavia, 446
Hilley, Alice and Robert, 203
Hills, Graham, 613
Hills, Rebecca, 208
Hillsborough disaster (1989), 545–6, 550–1
Hindley, Myra, 524, 614–15
Hinton, Katharine, 114
Hobbes, Thomas, 17, 137
Hobbs, Dick, 627
Hobsbawm, Eric, 357–8
Hogarth, William, 355; engravings
    by, 106
Hoker, Stephen, 482–3
Holdernesse, Lady, 328
Holdinge, Elizabeth, 209–10
Holford Report (1811), 399
holidays: annual paid, 558; see also
    celebrations and holidays, traditional
Holland, Sir Thomas, 94
Hollande, Elizabeth, 376
Hollingworth, John, 129–30
Holloway, William, 180
Holmes, Alice, 110
Holmes, Ronald M., 523, 529
Holmes, Thomas, 435
Holocaust, 43
Holroyd, Justice, 440
Homewood, Mary, 495–8
homicide see murder
Homicide Act (1957), 611, 633–4
'Homily against Strife and
    Contention', 233–4
homosexuality see LGBT issues
Honeydon, 50
honour codes: accusation of lying,
    264–5; chivalry, 87–99; in eighteenth
    century, 137; and football violence,
550; in middle ages, 74; and middle
    class, 278–9; muscular Christianity
    and fair play, 296–7, 303; revenge
    tragedies, 138, 151–8; and violence,
    12–13; working-class respectability,
    430–1, 433; see also duels
Hood, Robin, 72
Hood, Roger, 407
Hood, Samuel, Lord, 265
hoodies, 542
hooligans, 11–12, 305, 435–7, 540, 541–52
Hopkins, Ezekiel, 150–1
Hopley, Thomas, 294–5
Hopton Castle, 119
Hornung, E. W., 575, 577
horse racing, 436
Horsted Keynes, 111
Hosmer, George, 111
housing, 557–8
How, John, 162
Howard, John, 399, 400–1
Howard, Michael, 469
Howard Association, 401
Howe, Brian, 465
Howkins, Bridget, 486
Hudson, Hannah, 129
Hudson, John, 130
Hughes, Thomas, 292–4, 295–6
Huizinga, Johan, 25, 44–5, 305
Hull, 242, 553–4
Hulten, Karl, 577
Hulton, William, 364
Hume, David, 161
Hume, Dr John, 267–8
Hundred Years War (1337–1453), 60, 85,
    93–4, 95–6
Hungerford massacre (1987), 507–8,
    600–1
Hunt, Henry 'Orator', 363–4
Hunt, Peter, 135
Hunter, William, 215–16
Huntingdon, 35
Huntley, Ian, 634
Hyde, 534–8
Hyde, William, 341

I.D. (film), 546
Idelle, William and Elizabeth, 185
identity, national, and boxing, 299–300
illegitimacy, and infanticide, 197–221
Illustrated Times, 518
Ince, Ralph and Ellen, 2
incest, 155
industrial disputes *see* strikes and industrial disputes
Industrial Revolution: factories as seminaries of crime, 471; Luddites, 357–8, 361; and urbanisation of crime, 410–13
infant mortality *see* children
infanticide *see* children
Infanticide Act (1922), 221
Ingram, Sir Robert, 71
inns of court, 102
Inpley, Alice, 2
insanity *see* mental health
insurance fraud, 219, 455–7, 509–14, 516–17
internet trolling, 625
IRA, 613
Iraq War protests (2003), 565
Ireland: court records, 39–40; Edwardian era, 554; Fenians, 403; in nineteenth century, 267, 410–11; Northern Ireland in twentieth century, 613; in seventeenth century, 119–20
Islam, radicalised, 607–8
Italy: duelling, 261–2, 264, 271; Elizabethan and Jacobean attitude to, 154; Italians in England, 53–4; medieval wars, 85

Jack the Stripper, 530
Jackson, Elizabeth, 213
Jackson, John and Mabel, 235
Jackson, Mark, 214, 217
Jackson, William, 6, 329–30
Jacobite Rebellion (1715), 348
Jacob's Well, 81
Jacobus de Voragine, 83

James I and VI, 98, 161, 271–2
James IV, King of Scotland, 242
James, Anne, 192–3
James, Anthony, 146
Jeffraies, Martin, 242
Jennings, Margaret, 456
Jessop, Francis, 258–9, 263
Joan of Love Lane/the Lane, 7
Jobling, William, 393
John, King, 84
John de Bamptoun, 61
John of Gaunt, Duke of Lancaster, 53, 57, 60, 61, 483
Johnson, Boris, 597
Johnson, Lyndon B., 16
Johnson, Dr Samuel, 345
Johnston, Raymond, 592
Jolly Boys (smuggling cutter), 333
Jones, Elizabeth, 577
Jones, Mary, 163
Jones, Sarah, 365
Jones, Tom, 314
Jonson, Ben, 488
Jordan, Jean, 526
Joseph, Sir Keith, 460
jousts, 98–9
Juden, Richard, 109
Judge, Margaret, 199
Juliana, St, 83
Justice for All (White Paper), 635
justice system: and duelling, 275, 279; medieval penances for murder, 77–8; in middle ages, 51–2, 99–104; nineteenth-century financing, 429–30; nineteenth-century hardening of attitudes, 419–28; nineteenth-century reforms, 437–41; and rape, 480–2, 492–500, 501–2; *see also* capital punishment; courts; punishment
justices of the peace, 100–1

Kaeuper, Richard W., 88–9
Kaye, J. W., 444
Keate, John, 290

Keating, Mr Justice, 426
Keegan, John, 15, 44
Keeling, Alice and Agnes, 486
Keen, Maurice, 94
Keighley, 606
Kelly, Mary Jane, 519, 520–1, 522
Kelly, William, 393
Kemp, M. C., 294
Kempe, C. Henry, 459
Kennedy, Walter, 242
Kennet, John, 109–10
Kennett, Brackley, 340, 341, 342
Kennington Common meeting (1848),
    367–9
Kent: Cade's rebellion, 63–4; domestic
    violence, 186, 187; infanticide, 197–8,
    202, 203, 208; murder rates, 46,
    125–6; and Peasants' Revolt, 52–3,
    54, 55, 56, 60, 61; rape, 484, 486;
    smuggling, 333, 334
Kenya, 637–8
Kerby, Joan, 485
Ketch, Jack, 379–80
Kettlewell, John, 384
Kett's rebellion (1549), 64
Khmer Rouge, 43–4
Kilsby, 122–3
Kimber, William, 616
Kind Hearts and Coronets (film), 507
King, Benjamin, 499
King's Bench court see courts
kingship see monarchy
Kingsley, Charles, 293, 368–9
Kingswood Forest, 359
Kipling, Rudyard, 293
Kirkholt Project, 637
Kneale, Catherine see Cottier,
    Catherine
knife amnesty, 604
Knight, Mr (minister), 243
Knutsford, 239
Kouao, Marie-Therese, 462–3
Kray, Ronnie and Reggie, 309,
    614, 616
Kubrick, Stanley, 574, 584–6, 602

Kyd, Thomas, The Spanish Tragedie, 138,
    151–2, 154, 156–7

Laburn, Thomas, wife of, 235
Lacey, William, 228
Lambeth Poisoner see Cream, Thomas
    Neill
Laming, Lord, 463
Lancashire, 71, 357–8, 376–7, 410
Lancaster, Thomas, 509
Lancelot romance cycle, 88–9
land ownership, 56, 58–60, 62
Langland, William, 80–1
Langton, Stephen, Archbishop of
    Canterbury, 84
Larton, Mary, 209
Laslett, Peter, 638
Latham, John, 128–9
Latimer, William, 60
Lawrence, Joseph, 315
lawyers see legal profession
Le Mans, 96
Leadbeater, John, 209
Leah, Elizabeth, 180
Leblanc, Warren, 597
Lee, Bruce George Peter, 524
Lee, Margaret, 35
Leeds, 247–8, 524, 525, 528
Leeds United, 529
Lees, John, 365
legal profession, 101–4
legal system see capital punishment;
    courts; justice system; punishment
Legett, Roger, 53, 58
Legge, John, 54
Leicester, 393, 597
Leicester City, 303, 543–4
Leicester University Sociology
    Department, 547, 549
Leicestershire, 70–1, 543
Leigh, Edward, 1
Lester, Thomas, 40
L'Estrange, Lieutenant-Colonel
    Guy, 364
Levick, Ann, 464

Lewes, 40, 107, 331

Lewis, Peter, 537

LGBT issues: domestic violence, 444, 449, 452; gay men as victims of serial killers, 531; punishments for homosexuality, 378, 386–7, 397

libel, 244–5; *see also* defamation

liberty concept, 62–3

Lichfield Cathedral, 71

life insurance *see* insurance fraud

Lincolnshire, 317, 393, 410

Linscale, Anne, 207

Linscale, Em, 207–8

Linscale, Jane, 207

Linscale, Pegg, 207

Linscale, Sissilye, 207–8

Linwood, Joseph, 35

Lisbye, Mr (minister), 226

Lisle, Thomas de, Bishop of Ely, 86

Lister, John, 242

literature: *chansons de geste*, 88–93; flyting, 242–3; imaginative, 37; rape theme in classical, 488–90; *see also* novels; plays

Litster, Geoffrey, 56

Littlechild, John George, 522

Liverpool: child abuse charities, 457; child murders, 464, 466–70; crime levels, 410–11; early football teams, 303; murders, 456; nineteenth-century punishments, 426–7; prostitutes, 323; strikes, 554–5; Toxteth riots, 569–70; youth gangs, 434

Liverpool FC, 544–5, 545–6

living standards, 557–8

Livy, 489

Llanelli, 555

Lloyd (alehouse customer), 130

Lloyds Weekly, 521

Lockhart, Thomas, 216

Lomax (rugby player), 302

Lombroso, Cesare, 413

London: Angry Brigade activities, 613; assaults, 421; baby farming, 457; Bethnal Green Bonfire Night, 286;

boxing arenas and matches, 298; child abuse charities, 458; clergy as perpetrators and victims of murder, 86; Clerkenwell prison bomb attack, 403; defamation, 245, 249–51; duels, 266, 267–8, 278; during the Commonwealth, 260; examples of medieval violence, 72, 80; executions, 378–82, 391, 402–3, 404; fights, 297; Foundling Hospital, 206; gangs, 310–12, 315, 318–27, 614, 616, 626; garrotters, 423–8; hooligans, 435, 436; infant mortality, 455; infanticide, 218, 220–1; inns of court, 102; Kennington Common, 347–9; King's College, 267; Mayhew on street people, 413; Millbank Prison, 399; murders and murder rates, 47, 50–1, 139, 144–5, 146, 162–4, 410, 417, 607–8, 613, 614, 621, 633; Newgate gaol, 140, 341; nineteenth-century crime, 431–2, 433; Pentonville, 399; prostitutes, 323–5, 375, 376; punishments, 375–6, 386–8; Peasants' Revolt, 14, 34, 42, 52–5; Pepys on violence in, 37–8; rape, 492, 494–8; riots and protests, 14, 336, 337–46, 347–8, 350–1, 361, 541, 564, 565, 566–9, 570–2; serial killers, 508–9, 514, 519–22, 524, 530; in seventeenth and eighteenth centuries, 137; Southwark, 52–3, 125, 245, 339, 343, 350–1; Spring-heeled Jack, 417–18; strikes, 554, 556–7, 558–9, 563; Teddy Boys, 541

Longly, Richard, 111

Lovatt, Simon Fraser, 11th Lord, 390

Lovett, John, 7

Lowe, Michael, 508–9

Lowys, Elizabeth, 230–1

Lucas, Catherine, 112

Luchaire, Achille, 44

Luddites, 357–8, 361

Luke de Horton, 48

Lunn, Louisa, 220–1

Lush, Mr Justice, 426
lust, as revenge tragedy theme, 155
Lydd, 333
Lymm, 130–1
Lyons, Richard, 60

Maberley, Mr (Gordon Riots), 340
McCann, Wilma, 524
Macclesfield, 236–7, 239
Macdemar (dueller), 257–8
Macdonell, Sir John, 409
MacGregor, Ian, 559, 560
Machiavelli, Niccolò, 154, 155
McIntyre, Patrick, 435
MacKinnon, Catherine, 479
MacLaine, James, 318, 381
Macnamara, Captain James, 264, 265
McNaughtan, Daniel, 437–8
M'Naghten (McNaughton) Rules,
    437–9
Macready, Major-General C. F. N., 555
McVitie, Jack 'The Hat', 309
Madame Tussaud's, 417, 515, 518
Maddern, Philippa, 73–4
Maddock, Dorothy, 213
madness see mental health
Magna Carta, 84
Magnet (magazine), 293
Maidstone, 403–4
Maisterson, John, 4–5
Major, John, 469, 566–7, 634–5
Maldon, 56
Mallard, George, 359
Malmesbury, Lord, 403
Malo, James, 340
Malory, Sir Thomas, 89–93, 96–7
Man, Isle of, 226–7, 228
Manchester: alcohol consumption
    and assault levels, 627; crime levels,
    410–11; garrotting, 426; murders, 631;
    nineteenth-century atmosphere,
    411–12; Peterloo, 363–6; prostitutes,
    323; rape, 33; riots, 348, 569; serial
    killers, 525; youth gangs, 434–5
Manchester Observer (newspaper), 365

Manchester Police, 561–2
Manchester United, 303
Mandeville, Bernard de, 206, 265, 382
Manhunt (computer game), 597
Mann, Tom, 553, 554
manners see honour codes
Mannheim, Karl, 23
Manning, Carl John, 462–3
Manning, Frederick and Maria, 402
Manning, Richard, 123–4
Manningtree, 56
manor courts see courts
Mansfield, Lord Chief Justice,
    339, 342
manslaughter, 114–17
Mao Zedong, 43
March, John, 225–6
Margaret of Anjou, 70, 95
Margate, 542
Margery de Karl, 50
Maria Marten, or the Murder in the Red
    Barn, 580
Marina (rape victim), 482
Marlborough College, 290
Marmion, Sir William, 93
marriage: average pre-modern length,
    172; charivari, 187, 245–9, 286;
    divorce, 182, 189–91, 446; marital
    rape, 501; as portrayed in murder
    pamphlets, 144–5; scolding, 222,
    232–5; wife sales, 181; women's
    rights within, 181–3, 445; see also
    domestic violence; families
Married Women's Property Acts (1870,
    1882 and 1893), 445
Marshall, Alfred, 431
Marshall, James, 331
Marshall, Leonard, 242
Marston Moor, Battle of (1644), 119
Marten, Maria, 580
Martin, Samuel, 268
martyr concept, 63
Marwood, William, 400
Mary, Queen of Scots, 373, 379
Massey, Alan, 535

Maternity and Child Welfare Act (1918), 459
Matrimonial Causes Act (1857), 190
Matrimonial Causes Act (1937), 446
Maudsley, Henry, 414
Maurice, Prince (Charles I's nephew), 120
May, Theresa, 636
Mayhew, Henry, 322–4, 413
Meades, Peter, 123
Meadowe, Roland, 110
Meaker, Jacob, 134
media: and copycat rioting, 570, 571; influence on public attitudes, 417–18, 423–4; social, 571, 625; see also films; newspapers; television
medieval chronicles, 34
Meeting Point (TV programme), 587
Melbourne, William, Lord, 190
melees, 97
men: male rape, 500; propensity for sexual violence, 503; verbal attacks on, 242–5; violence and masculinity, 12–13, 20–1, 26, 48, 50, 137; see also gender issues
Mendoza, Daniel, 298, 299
mental health: and criminal responsibility, 437–9; and curses, 251–2; and infanticide, 221; madness as revenge tragedy theme, 155; wife-beating and mental cruelty, 174–6, 180–91, 620
Merthyr Tydfil, 361, 410–11
Merthyr Vale Colliery, 560–1
Metcalfe, John, 229
Metropolitan Police, 450, 558–9, 561
Metyard, Sarah and Sarah Morgan, 177–8
middle class see class issues
Middleton, Thomas, 153, 155, 157, 580
Milan, 85
Mill, John Stuart, 401
Mills, John, 128–9
Mills, Richard, 330
Mills, Thomas and Agnes, 246–7

Millwall FC, 543, 546, 551–2
Millward, Vera, 525
Milner, Ann, 241–2
Milošević, Slobodan, 43–4
miners' strike (1910–11), 553, 555
miners' strike (1974), 558
miners' strike (1984–5), 552, 559–62
M'Intosh, Mary, 166
miracles, 161
Mitchell, Mary, 163
mods and rockers, 542–3
monarchy: absolute, 84; medieval attitudes, 84; royal justice, 99–104
Monmouth, James Scott, Duke of, 379–80
Montgomery, Lieutenant-Colonel, 264
Moore, John, 522
Moore, William, 40
Moores, George, 561
Moors murders, 524, 614–15
moral panics, 460, 467, 542–3, 580–1, 614–15, 629–34
Moral Re-Armament (MRA), 587
morality plays, 82
morals: attitudes to alcohol, 288, 289; attitudes to bullying, 473–4; attitudes to child murderers, 472–3; attitudes to domestic violence, 186–9, 444–5, 619–20; attitudes to duelling, 271–80; attitudes to infanticide, 199–203, 214–21; attitudes to rape, 488–90, 499, 500–5; attitudes to smuggling, 327–8; attitudes to violence, 77–87, 147–51, 158–67, 413–17, 430–3; as basis for eighteenth-century riots, 356–7; modern attitudes to capital punishment, 632–4; punishments for fornication and adultery, 376–7; sex and violence in popular culture, 575–97; sexual, 199, 206, 226; twentieth- and twenty-first-century concerns about national moral welfare, 460, 467, 542–3, 587–90, 614–15, 629–34
More, Thomas, 394

Morland, Mr Justice, 630
Morland, Sir Michael, 469
Morris dancing, 284–5
Morrison, Arthur, 325
Mould, John, 119
Mowbray, William, 510
Moynihan, F. J., 459
MRA *see* Moral Re-Armament
mugging, 612–13
Mulcaster, Richard, 152
mumming plays, 288
Munday, Anthony, 142–3
murder: changes in attitude in
   sixteenth to nineteenth centuries,
   147–51, 158–67; by children, 463–73;
   clergy as perpetrators and victims,
   86; cultural depiction, 88–93, 151–8,
   575–602; culture's effect on rate,
   21–2; degrees of culpability, 114–17;
   divine retribution, 140–1; European
   rates, 127; favourite murder
   weapons, 51, 117, 126–7, 622–3, 640;
   fictitious killers, 112, 198; first
   Biblical, 9–10; infanticide, 108, 166,
   196, 197–221, 641; insanity pleas,
   437–9; manslaughter, 114–17;
   measuring rates, 28–31; medieval
   attitude, 77–87; medieval penances
   for, 77–8; methods of killing, 640;
   miraculous detection, 146, 161–2,
   514; murderers committing suicide,
   611–12; nineteenth-century change
   in rates and type, 408–9, 410;
   nineteenth-century 'invention' of,
   417; premeditated assault, 130–1;
   rates and types after Civil War,
   125–37; rates and types in
   Elizabethan and Jacobean England,
   107–18; rates and types in middle
   ages, 46–52; reliability of statistics,
   429–30, 621–3; self-defence, 115–17;
   and Ten Commandments, 147–51;
   twentieth- and twenty-first-century
   statistics and types, 609–25, 644; *see
   also* domestic violence; serial killers

Murder (Abolition of Death Penalty)
   Act (1965), 634
murder pamphlets, 34–5, 139–46, 162–7
Murdoch, Rupert, 573
Murdock, Graham, 591–2
Murray (soldier), 33
Musard, Sir Malcolm, 86
Myddle, 118–19, 123–5, 395–6

Nailor, Anne and Mary, 177–8
Nantwich, 1–8, 18
Napier, General Sir Charles, 351–2,
   366–7
Narbonne, Council of (1054), 79
Nares, Edward, 158–60
Nash, Anne, 179
National Service, 618
National Society for the Prevention of
   Cruelty to Children (NSPCC), 458,
   459–60
National Union of Societies for Equal
   Citizenship, 446
National Viewers' and Listeners'
   Association (NVLA), 587–90
Nattrass, Joseph, 510, 512
Nazis, 43
Nehru, Jawaharlal, 297
Nelson, Horatio, Lord, 265
Nermit, Fulk, 48
Netherlands, 127
Nettleton, 237–8
Neville family, 80
Newarke, Mrs, 235
Newcastle-under-Lyme, 238
Newcastle United, 305
Newcastle upon Tyne, 239, 361, 556
Newe, Agnes, 110, 487
Newport, 366, 392
newspapers: and mods and rockers,
   542; and perceptions of violence, 35,
   417–18, 423–4, 630–4; and serial
   killers, 506, 514–15, 518, 521–2;
   Wapping dispute, 563
Newton, John, 40
Nicholl, Sir John, 189

Nicholls, William, 135
Nichols, Mary Ann ('Polly'), 519–20
Nichols, William, 519
Nilsen, Dennis, 524, 531, 532, 533
Norfolk, 46, 56, 61, 63, 71, 236, 330–1
Northamptonshire, 50–1, 52, 288
Northumberland, Hugh Percy, Duke
    of, 339
Norton, Caroline and George, 189–90
Norwich, 56, 376, 386
Nottingham, 361, 541, 556, 566
Nottinghamshire, 410
novels: depictions of violence, 575–7,
    579–80; domestic violence theme,
    444–5; Newgate Novels, 580; about
    public schools, 292–4; serial killers
    in, 507, 538
Nowell, Charles, 71
NSPCC see National Society for the
    Prevention of Cruelty to Children
NVLA see National Viewers' and
    Listeners' Association

O'Bryan, Patrick, 316–17
Ockenden, Ken, 532
Offences against the Person Act (1828),
    190, 419–20
Offences against the Person Act
    (1837), 420
Offences against the Person Act (1861),
    500, 619
Oldefield, John, 236
Oldfield, George, 525
Olivier, J., works by, 254
Olweus, Dan, 473
Ordinance of Labourers (1349), 59
Orgreave, 562
Orwell, George, 575–9
Ovet, Jack, 314
Ovid, 489–90
Owen, Nathaniel, 118–19
Oxford, 47–9, 102, 348, 436
Oxford, Edward, 438
Oxford, Edward de Vere, Earl of, 262
Oxfordshire, 46, 72, 288, 355

Page, Mistress, 140
Page, William, 318
Paine, Elizabeth, 329
Paine, Tom, 397
Pakeerah, Stefan, 597
Palen, Thomas, 6
Paley, Archdeacon William, 397
Pall Mall Gazette, 521, 522
Palmer, Craig, 479
Palmer, James, 586
Palmer, John, 116–17
Palmer, Julius, 228
Palmer, Philippa, 244
Palmer, Thomas, 117
Palmer, Walter, 516
Palmer, William (Rugeley Poisoner),
    417, 515–18
Papist Act see First Catholic Relief Act
Parfet, William, 133–4
Parker, Charles, 133, 135
Parker, Margaret, 1
Parliament (Qualification of Women)
    Act (1918), 445
Parry, Captain, 285
Parsons, John, 133
Partridge, Christopher, 180
Paul, Sir George Onesiphorus, 399
Peace of God movement, 78–9
Peasants' Revolt (1381), 14, 34, 42,
    52–63
Peckinpah, Sam, 583
Peel, Sir Robert, 275, 419–20, 428, 437
Peele, Thomas, 32
Peeping Tom (film), 507
Peers, Thomas, 213
peine forte et dure, 485
Peirce (English Civil War veteran),
    124–5
Peirson, Margery, 129
Pellyng, Henry, 109
Penal Servitude Act (1857), 499–500
Penal Servitude Act (1864), 427
penitentiaries, 420–1
penny dreadfuls, 35

People (newspaper), 521
Pepys, Samuel, 37–8, 186, 273
Percy, Richard, 80
performance, violence as, 11–12, 549–50
Perkins, William, 172, 224, 230
Perne, Thomas, 227
Perrers, Alice, 60
Perrin, Richard, 328–9
Peterloo massacre (1819), 363–6
Petty, William, 120
petty treason, 193–4, 390–1
Pevere, Marion, 236–7
Phippes, Mathea, 485
Piers Plowman see Langland, William
Pighill, John and Elizabeth, 184–5
Pike, Luke Owen, 46, 407–8, 411
Pilkington, Hugh, 421–5
pillories, 377–8, 386–8
pimps, 323–5
pinders, 235
piracy, 397–8
Pitt, William, the Younger, 276–7, 280
Pitt-Rivers, Julian, 12–13
Pixey, Hester, 208
Pizzey, Erin, 447–8, 452
Place, Francis, 219
plague, 59
Platt, Mr Justice Baron, 464
plays: depiction of violence, 580–1;
    morality plays, 82; mumming plays,
    288; revenge tragedies, 138, 151–8
Plot, Robert, 225, 238, 239
Plough Monday, 288
Plumb, J. H., 345–6
Plummer, Charles, 68
Plymouth, 556
poisoning: in *chansons de geste*, 89; in
    detective novels, 577, 579–80; in
    nineteenth century, 239, 456, 457;
    pre-1800, 114, 117, 126, 139, 144–5, 192,
    213, 640; in revenge tragedies, 153,
    155; by serial killers, 509, 510–18,
    523–4, 533
police: and Bulger case, 468; and child
    abuse, 463; corruption, 322, 326, 617;

and domestic violence, 448–9, 450;
and football, 305, 540, 548, 550, 552;
and garrotters, 425–6; and industrial
disputes, 553, 554–5, 556–7, 558–63;
manipulation of statistics, 620;
murders of, 614, 632; nineteenth-
century attitude, 422;
nineteenth-century development
and effectiveness, 428–9;
professionalisation, 370; and rape,
502; and riots and protests, 368, 565,
566–7, 568–72; and serial killers, 521,
524–7, 535–6; and sus laws, 568; and
traditional celebrations, 285–6, 287;
twentieth-century attacks on, 610
Poll Tax Riots (1990), 565–7
Pollard, John, 535
Pollard, Sarah and Samuel, 495, 499
Pontefract, 534, 536
Poole, 328–9
population, 59
pornography, and rape, 503–4
Porteous Riots (1736), 349–50
Porter, Thomas, 273
Portland gaol, 422
post-traumatic stress, 15, 124–5
Powderham Castle, 69
Pownall, John, 128
Preece, William and Francis, 119
Prentice, William, 179
press, popular *see* newspapers
Preston, 361, 556
Prevention of Cruelty to Children Act
    (1904), 458
Price, Esther, 211
primate studies, 22
prison, 398–400, 420–2, 427, 628–9, 635
prison hulks, 398
Prisons Act (1877), 427
prize fights *see* fights
prostitutes and prostitution: murder
    of, 50; in nineteenth century, 323–5;
    punishments, 375, 376; and rape, 440,
    488, 502; as victims of serial killers,
    519–22, 523, 524, 528, 530, 531

Protection from Harassment Act
(1997), 449–50, 620
Protestant Association, 339
protests *see* riots and protests
psychoanalysis, and violence, 26–7
psychology: evolutionary, 19–23; and
violence, 19–27; *see also* mental
health
Public Order Act (1986), 620
Pudlicote House, 284–5
Pultoe, 508
punishment: compensation payments,
481; corporal, 10–11, 16, 290, 294–5,
378, 386, 388–90, 406; as deterrence,
397, 403, 427–8, 636; modern policy-
makers' attitude, 634–5;
nineteenth-century hardening of
attitudes in sentencing, 419–28;
peine forte et dure, 485; prison,
398–400, 420–2, 427; for rape, 480–2,
484–5, 490–2, 498, 499–500; as
rehabilitation, 399, 420–1; shaming,
375–8, 385–8; transportation, 396–7,
398, 420–2; whipping and flogging,
378, 386, 388–90, 406, 426–7; *see also*
capital punishment
Purdy, Mike, 602

Quakers, 240, 401
quarter sessions *see* courts
Queen's Park Rangers, 303
Queensberry, John Sholto Douglas,
9th Marquess of, 300–1
Queensberry Rules, 300–1
Quemerford, 246–7
Quincey, Thomas de, 578–9

Raby, Thomas, 314
race issues: and football, 551; murder
statistics, 622–3; race riots, 541, 567–72;
racially motivated assault, 620
Racecourse Wars, 616
Radford, Nicholas, 69
radicalism, 61–2, 361–70
Radzinowicz, Sir Leon, 407

Raffles, 575, 577
railway strike (1911), 554, 555
railways, 370
Rainbow, Elizabeth, 178–9
Rainforth, Samson, 340
Rambo films, 601
Ramsden, William, 243
rape *see* sexual assault and rape
Ratsey, Lancelot, 244–5
Reader, Elizabeth, 112
Rebel Without a Cause (film), 583
rebellions: in general, 14; Jacobite
Rebellion (1715), 348; Kett's rebellion
(1549), 64; Peasants' Revolt and
other medieval rebellions, 14, 34, 42,
52–65
receivers, 70
recidivism, 32
Red Barn murder, 580
Redfern, Peter, 606
Redgrave, Samuel, 418
Redwood, John 'Boney', 425
religion: advice books, 36–7;
Babington plot, 373–4; benefit of
clergy, 113, 116, 395, 480, 484; Church
and curses, 227–9; criminal clergy,
70, 71, 85–7; and cultural depictions
of violence, 582, 587; discrimination
against Catholics, 337–45; divine
retribution for murder, 140–1; and
duelling, 274–5, 277, 278, 279; effect
of decline in organised religion on
crime rates, 618; eighteenth-century
notions of wrongdoing, 160–6;
excommunication, 228, 376; and
executions, 384–5; female bishops,
605; and infanticide, 199–200; 'just
war' concept, 84–5, 151; muscular
Christianity, 296–7, 303; nineteenth-
century notions of wrongdoing,
166–7; and nineteenth-century
reduction in violence, 430–1;
Non-conformism, evangelical
Anglicanism and leisure activities,
289; and penal reform, 400–1, 420;

penances for murder, 77–8;
Quakers, 240, 401; radicalised Islam,
607–8; radicalism and the Peasants'
Revolt, 61–2; Reformation, 147, 199;
religious tone of murder pamphlets,
140–4, 145–6; religiously motivated
assault, 620; riots re Protestant
dissenters, 347; Sabbatarianism and
sport, 304; sixteenth- and
seventeenth-century notions of
wrongdoing, 146–51, 158–62;
traditional celebrations in Christian
calendar, 283–6; verbal attacks on
clergy, 242; and violence, 18, 77–87;
see also Bible; courts: ecclesiastical
Renshaw, William, 493–4
Representation of the People Act
(1918), 445
Representation of the People (Equal
Franchise) Act (1928), 445–6
Reresby, Sir John, 255–60, 263
revenge *see* plays; revenge tragedies;
vengeance
Reynolds, John, 158
Reynolds, Dr Linda, 535
Rhondda Valley, 553
Richard II, 54, 55, 60, 62, 65–6, 85
Richards, Thomas, 135
Richardson, Gerald, 632
Richardson gang, 309, 614
riding *see* charivari
Rigby, Lee, 607–8
Riley, Thomas, 512–13
Rillington Place murders, 633
Riot Act (1715), 346, 348–9, 350–4
riots and protests: agents
provocateurs, 567; Georgian, 336,
337–70; grain riots, 356–7, 361–2, 368;
medieval, 47; overview, 14; race
riots, 541, 567–72; twentieth and
twenty-first centuries, 564–73
Ripper murders *see* Whitechapel
murders
ritual, as aspect of violence, 12, 270, 547,
549–50

robbery and theft: medieval, 50, 51;
mugging, 612–13; punishment, 379,
394–6, 397, 426–7; twentieth-century
rise in armed, 614, 616–17; *see also*
gangs, criminal
Robert, son of Bernard (knight), 306
Robert of Flamborough, 77–8
Roberts, Harry, 614
Roberts, Martha, 210–11
Roberts, Thomas, 109
Robertson, Elizabeth, 210–11
Robinson, James, 511, 519
Robson, Garry, 551–2
Rock Around the Clock (film), 583
rockers *see* mods and rockers
Rockingham, Lord, 338
Roffe, Susan and Jane, 114
Romilly, Colonel, 275
rookeries, 411
Rooney, Christopher, 606
Roses, Wars of the (1455–85), 65–70,
94–5, 96–7
Rossetti, Dante Gabriel, 89
Rosslyn, Alexander Wedderburn, 1st
Earl of, 343
Rossy, Thomas de, 84
Roulfe, Richard, 485
Roundway Down, Battle of (1643), 121
Rowley, William, 155, 580
Rowson, Elizabeth, 486
Royle, Hannah, 181
Royle, Lydia, 180
Rudé, George, 344
rugby, 282, 295, 301–3
Rugby School, 282, 292–4, 295–6
Rugeley Poisoner *see* Palmer, William
rule of thumb expression, 174
Russell, Lord John, 366
Russell, Lord William, 379, 401, 581
Rwandan genocide (1994), 478
Ryan, Michael, 507–8, 600–1
Rye, 331

Sabini, Charles 'Derby', 616
Sacheverell, Dr Henry, 347

St Albans, 34, 57–8
St Albans, first Battle of (1455), 66–7
St Osyth, 56, 231
St Scholastica's Day riots (1355), 47
Salford, 432–3, 434, 572
Salle, Sir Robert, 56
Samuel, Alice, 232
Sampson, Eve, 208
San Antonio, Texas, 22
Sandys, Robert and Ann, 219, 456
Sant, Sarah, 211–12
Saunders, George and Ann, 139
Saussure, César de, 270, 271
Savage, Susan, 179
Savile, Sir George, 338, 339, 341
Saviolo, Jeronimo and Vincentio,
    261, 264–5
Sayton, 248–9
Scandinavia, 127
Scargill, Arthur, 559, 560
Scarman Report (1986), 568, 570
Scattergood, Dr Thomas, 514
schools see education
scold's bridle, 237, 238–40
scolding, 222, 232–40, 250
Scotland: civil war fatalities, 119; court
    records, 39–40; flyting, 242; Poll
    Tax, 566; Richard II's invasion, 85;
    riots, 338; scolding, 239; strikes, 556
Scott, David, 495–8
Scrope, Sir Geoffrey, 102
Scrope, Sir Henry, 102
scuttlers, 434
seamen's strike (1911), 553
Second World War (1939–45), 43,
    390, 478
Security from Violence Bill (1863),
    426–7
Segar, William, 262
Serbia, 43
Sereny, Gitta, 465
serfdom, 59
serial killers, 506; definition, 507–8;
    modern statistics, 530; motives,
    527–30, 531–3, 537; origins of term,

538; overview, 507–39; popular
    conception, 630; types, 523
servants, 10–11, 108, 164–5, 171–2, 173–4,
    176–80, 192–3
Seton, Wilmot, 429
Seven Deadly Sins, 81, 82, 146–7
sexual assault and rape: and benefit of
    clergy, 113; causes and motives,
    477–9, 502–4; date rape, 501, 503;
    difficulty of getting conviction,
    492–500; Elizabethan and Jacobean
    era, 484–90; examples, 33, 35;
    historical attitudes, 13; male rape,
    500; marital rape, 501; measuring
    rates, 31; in medieval literature, 89,
    91–2; modern era, 500–5; nineteenth-
    century reforms, 439–41; overview,
    477–505; and pornography, 503–4;
    post-English Civil War era, 492–500;
    pre-Elizabethan era, 479–84; protests
    against, 476; punishment, 397–8; rape
    as abduction, 480–4, 487, 488;
    relationship between perpetrator
    and victim, 444; in revenge
    tragedies, 155; statistics, 408; in
    twenty-first century, 620; see also
    gangs, criminal
sexual morality see morals
Sexual Offences Act (1956), 500
Sexual Offences Act (2003), 500, 620
Shaftesbury, Lord, 403
Shakespeare, William, 66, 140, 153, 225,
    243, 488–9, 580
Sharp, Granville, 275
Sharpe, Edward, 486
Shaw, John, 535
Shearer, Mr (customs collector), 329
Sheffield, 606–7
Sheffield United, 11–12, 548–50
Sheffield Wednesday, 549
Sheppard, Jack, 381, 581
Sheppard, Thomas, 109
Sheppard, William, 237
Sherwood, Thomas (Country Tom),
    140, 146, 508–9

Shipman, Dr Harold, 530, 531, 533–8, 622
Shoemaker, Robert B., 249–50, 266
Shotter, Alice, 485–6
Shrewsbury, 458
Shrewsbury, John Talbot, 1st Earl of, 95–6
Shrewsbury, 11th Earl of, 273
Shrewsbury School, 292
Shropshire, 118–19, 317–18
Shrove Tuesday, 283–4, 286
Sibba (rape victim), 483
Sidney, Sir Philip, 262
Simey, Margaret, 570
Simi Valley, California, 22
Simpson, J. H., 296–7
Simpson, Keith, 523
Simpson, Mary and David, 180–1, 186, 187
sin see religion
Sinclair, Alexander George, 186
Sinter, John, 4
Sir Norman Chester Centre for Football Research, 547
skimmington see charivari
skinheads, 542
Slack, John, 298
slander see defamation
Smethurst, Dr Thomas, 401
Smith, Adam, 136
Smith, Captain Alexander, 312
Smith, George Joseph, 523
Smith, Dame Janet, 536, 537
Smith, Peter K., 599
Smith, Rebecca, 220
Smith, William, 386–7
Smith family, 32
smugglers, 327–35
Smyth, Alice, 110
Smyth, George, 275
Smyth, John, 229
Smyth, Judith, 486–7
Smythe, Ralph, 486
social learning theory, 593–4
social workers, 447, 460, 463
sociology, and violence, 19

Soham murders, 634
Sole, Henry, 207
Solomon, Isaac ('Ikey'), 319–21
Somenour, Richard, 54
Somers, Anne, 165
Somerset, 180
South Yorkshire Police, 562
Southampton, 553
Southampton FC, 303
Southchurch, 56
Southsea, 556
Soviet Union, 43
Sowden, John, 606
Spacye, Robert, 235
Spain, 228, 337
Spargo, J. W., 237
Spencer, Mr (brawler), 256
Spenser, Edmund, 89
spielers, 325, 326
Spierenburg, Pieter, 23–4
Spilsbury, Bernard, 523
sport, 38, 110–11, 282, 283–6, 288–9, 295–306, 431, 436; see also football hooliganism
Spot, Jack see Colmore (or Comer), Jacob
Sprackling, Adam, 145
Spring-heeled Jack, 417–18
Spynner, Nicholas, 110–11
Squire, Charles, 177
Staffordshire, 71, 410
Stalin, Joseph, 43
Stanbridge, William, 109
Standish, Richard, 55
Stanton, Samuel, 266, 275–6, 278
Star (newspaper), 521
Star Chamber see courts
Starkye, Edward, 179
the state: legitimacy of violence against, 15–16; as restraint upon violence, 16–17, 24; state-sponsored violence, 15; see also monarchy
Statham, Mary (alias Malone), 130–1
Statute of Labourers (1351), 59
Statute of Rapes (1382), 483

Statutes of Westminster (1275 and 1285), 483, 484
Stead, W. T., 522
Stephen, Sir Leslie, 578–9
Stevens, Elizabeth, 205
Stevens, Mary, 417
Stewart, Charles, 502
Stockport, 239, 364, 410–11, 456, 470–2
Stockton, Mary, 208–9
Stoke, Battle of (1487), 67
Stoke City, 303
Stone, Lawrence, 72
Stowell, Sir William Scott, Lord, 190–1
Stracke, Mary, 236
Straw Dogs (film), 590
Street, Dorothy, 315
Stride, Elizabeth, 520
strikes and industrial disputes, 362, 552–64
Stuart, Prince James Francis Edward, the Old Pretender, 347, 348
Substitution of Punishments for Death Act (1841), 499
Sudbury, Simon, Archbishop of Canterbury, 53, 54–5
Suffield, Edward Harbord, 3rd Baron, 393
Suffolk, 56, 61, 63, 85, 410, 463, 580
suffrage see elections and voting systems
Sullivan, Margaret, 391
Sun newspaper, 469, 545–6
Sunderland, 510–15, 626, 628
Surrey: domestic violence, 187; female murderers, 191; infanticide, 198, 203, 204–6; murder rates, 125, 410; rape, 484, 492, 498
sus laws, 568
Sussex: infanticide, 198, 203–4; murder rates, 125, 410; murders, 107–18; prisons, 398; rape, 484, 485–6; smuggling, 331, 332–3, 334
Sutcliffe, Peter (Yorkshire Ripper), 506, 524–30, 533
Sutton, Anthony, 132–3

Swansea, 556
Swetnam, Joseph, 235
Swindon Town, 303
Symes, Ann, 226
Symon, John, 110–11
Synderford, Thomas, 486

Tadcaster, 242
Talbot, John see Shrewsbury, John Talbot, 1st Earl of
Talfourd, Thomas, 387
Tallack, William, 401
Tapper, Sir Thomas, 109–10
Tarantino, Quentin, 583
Tarrier, Elizabeth, 492
Tarver, David, 244
taxation: customs duties, 327; Hearth Tax, 358; middle ages, 60–1; Poll Tax Riots, 565–7
Taylor, Benjamin, 180
Taylor, Craig, 87
Taylor, Elizabeth, 213
Taylor, Howard, 429
Taylor, Ian, 546–7
Taylor, Thomas, 119
Taylor, Tommy, 326
tea, 327, 328, 329
Teddy Boys, 541
telegraph, 370
television, 586–90, 593–7
Temperance movement, 289
Ten Commandments, 147–51, 158–60
terrorism, 16–17, 607–8, 613
textile industry, 357–9, 361
Thames Valley Police, 502
Thanet, Isle of, 145
Thatcher, Margaret, 545, 559, 565, 567
theft see robbery and theft
Thirty Years War (1618–48), 122
Thomas, Alice and Robert, 110
Thomas, William, 261
Thompson, Ann, 467
Thompson, Edward, 355–6, 359
Thompson, Robert, 466–70, 472–3, 630–1, 636

Thoresby, Ralph, 385
Thornhill, John, 130–1
Thornhill, Randy, 479
Thring, J. C., 301
Tierney, George, 276–7, 280
The Times, 518
Tindal, Chief Justice, 438
Tindall (brawler), 257
Tocqueville, Alexis de, 411–12
Todman, Dan, 15
Todmorden, 534
Tom and Jerry (cartoons), 595
Tonry, Michael, 635
Tonypandy, 553
Tooby, John, 20
Toole, Joe, 432, 433
Tories, 347
tournaments, 89, 97–9
Tourneur, Cyril, 153
Tout, T. F., 44
towns and cities: crime as urban
    phenomenon, 410–13; mugging,
    612–13; youth gangs, 433–7
Towton, Battle of (1461), 67–8, 94–5
Toxteth riots (1981), 569–70
toys, violent, 598–9
trades unions: and industrial disputes,
    553, 555, 558, 559–64; inter-war era,
    557; legislation regulating, 562;
    modern weakness, 563–4; and
    nineteenth-century reduction in
    violence, 430–1; origins, 357–8, 362,
    369, 370
transportation, 396–7, 398, 420–2
treason, 70, 354, 379, 390–2, 397–8; petty
    treason, 193–4, 390–1
Treason Felony Act (1848), 392
trials: expert witnesses, 437–8, 517, 518,
    523; medics called as witnesses, 131;
    rape, 439–40, 494–8, 501
*A True Relation of the Most Horrid and
    Barbarous Murders Committed by
    Abigail Hill*, 140–1
Truce of God movement, 79
Tuchman, Barbara W., 44

Tunbridge Wells, 566
Tuppen, Alice, 112
Turner, Ellen, 7
Turner, Janine, 448–9, 451
Turpin, Dick, 313, 315–16, 380, 381, 383–4
Tye, Edward, 111
Tyler, Wat, 54, 55, 57, 58, 62–3

Udall, William, 314
UK Borders Act (2007), 620
unemployment *see* employment
United Kingdom Carnegie Trust, 447
The Unnaturall Grand-Mother, 143–4
Uppingham School, 301
Urban V, Pope, 85
Urban VI, Pope, 85
USA: murder rates, 21–2; Orwell on
    influence, 577; prison policy, 635;
    punishment as deterrence, 636;
    rape, 502, 503, 504; twentieth-
    century murder types, 612

Vachell, H. A., 293
vagrants, 378
Vaughan, Reece, 119
Vauts, Moses à, 234
Venables, John, 135
Venables, Jon, 466–70, 472–3, 630–1, 636
Venables, Neil, 630
Venables, Piers, 72
vengeance: Christian attitude, 77–8,
    84; Elizabethan attitude, 155–8; *see
    also* plays: revenge tragedies
Victoria, Queen, 438
video nasties, 588–9, 590–3, 630
Video Recordings Act (1984), 590
Vietnam War protests, 564–5
Vinall, Jasper, 111
Violation of the Bitch (film), 529
violence: the abused becoming
    abusers, 461, 465–7; academic
    explanations, 19–27; changing
    future attitudes, 634–8; collective,
    14; definitions, 10; meaningfulness,
    12; measuring rates, 27–32; modern

attitudes and misconceptions, 8–9, 629–36; modern ongoing attraction, 625–9; nineteenth-century 'invention' of, 416–17; reasons for decline, 23–6, 136–7, 430, 624; reasons for twentieth-century rise, 617–18; restraints upon, 17–18, 24, 26–7, 77–104, 134–5; sources for early cases, 32–9; types and aspects, 10–17; verbal, 223–52
Vitalis, Orderic, 83
Vitalis, St, 83
voting see elections and voting systems

wages, 59
Wainewright, Thomas Griffiths and Ann, 509
Wake, Blanche, Lady, 86
Wake, Thomas, Lord, 86
Wakefield, Battle of (1460), 70
Walker, Agnes, 485
Walker, Edward, 519
Walker, Garthine, 505
Walker, Richard, 166
Walpole, Horace, 342
Walsingham, Sir Francis, 373
Walsingham, Thomas, 34, 53, 62, 63
Walter de Benington, 51
Walter de Cantilupe, Bishop of Worcester, 84
Walton, Robert, 242
Walton, William, 229
Walvin, Jim, 305
Walworth, William, 55
Wapping, 563
war: conduct of medieval, 93–7; conduct of seventeenth-century, 120–5; and everyday violence, 14–15; 'just war' concept, 84–5, 151; and sexual assault, 478
Warboys, Witches of, 232
Warburton, Catherine and Robert, 183–4
Ward, George, 511
Ward Jouve, Nicole, 528

Warren, Sarah Ann, 470
Warwickshire, 46, 410
Waters, John and Mary, 179
Waters, Margaret, 442, 457
Wath-upon-Dearne, 606
Waugh, Dorothy, 239–40
weapons: sixteenth century prevalence, 6; duelling, 265–7; favourite murder weapons, 51, 117, 126–7, 622–3, 640; first, 10; gun culture, 127, 600–1; knife amnesty, 604; rarity of firearm use, 127, 623–4; see also poisoning
Weber, Max, 16
Webster, John (clergyman turned doctor), 161
Webster, John (playwright), 152–3, 143, 156, 157, 586–7
Webster, Nesta, 446
Welfare State, 446–7
Wellington, Arthur Wellesley, Duke of, 267–8
Wells, Holly, 634
Wells, Thomas, 403–4
Wennington, 56
West, D. J., 611
West, Frederick and Rosemary, 524, 531, 533
West, Sir Thomas and Eleanor, 483
West Ham United, 546
West Yorkshire Police, 450, 526
Westminster School, 291
Westmorland, 410
Weston, Mary, 229
Wettenhall, Roger, 2–3, 5, 7, 8
Wettenhall, Thomas, 2, 4, 8
Whately, William, 175
Whigs, 347
whipping and flogging, 378, 386, 388–90, 406, 426–7
Whitacre, John, 298
Whitby, 606
White, Simon and Elizabeth, 173
White, Thomas, 179
White, William, 132–3
White, William and Mary, 188

Whitechapel murders (1888), 417, 514, 519–22
Whitehouse, Ernest, 587
Whitehouse, Mary, 587–90
Whiteleg, George, 128–9
Whitsun, 284, 288, 289–90
The Whole Duty of Man see Allestree, Richard
Wiatt, William, 247
Wilberforce, Samuel, Bishop of Oxford, 289
Wilbraham, Richard, 3, 4–5, 7, 8
Wild, Jonathan, 310–11
The Wild Bunch (film), 583
The Wild One (film), 583
Wilde, Oscar, 300
Wilkes, John, 268, 346, 350
Wilkes, Richard, 6
Wilkie, David, 560–1
Wilkinson, Matthew, 290
William (alleged rapist), 483
William I, the Conqueror, 83
William III, 347
William of Wenden, 306
Williams, Renwick, 381–2
Williamson, Robert, 242
Willis, Anne, 196, 199–200
Wilmot, Lancelot, 316
Wilmslow, 129
Wilson, Andrew, 349–50
Wilson, Professor David, 530–2, 538
Wilson, Margot, 21–2
Wilson, Ralph, 312, 318–19
Wilson, Thomas, 2–3, 6, 7
Wiltshire, 179, 235, 316–17
Winchester gaol, 427
Winchester School, 291–2
Winchilsea, George Finch-Hatton, 10th Earl of, 267–8
Wingham, 333
Wingrove, John, 162–4
Winlow, Simon, 625–6, 628
Winter of Discontent (1978–9), 558
witchcraft, 161, 202, 228, 230–2, 237, 251, 379

Witness (film), 625
women: claiming pregnancy to escape hanging, 113–14, 198–9, 202–3, 395; duelling, 268–70; female bishops, 605; and infanticide, 196, 197–221; modern increased capacity for aggression, 595; as peacemakers, 7; petty treason crime, 193–4, 390–1; reaction to violence in TV and films, 596; rights within marriage, 181–3; twentieth-century misogyny, 529; and verbal violence, 226, 232–40, 241–2; Victorian view, 221; voting rights and other advances, 445–6; wife sales, 181; *see also* domestic violence; gender issues; sexual assault and rape
Women Viewing Violence (study), 596
Wood, Baron, 440
Wood, John, 229
Wood, Phoebe, 180, 181, 186, 187
Woodford, Lieutenant-Colonel John, 342
Woodforde, James, 328
Woodgate, Isabel and Robert, 109
Woodruff, Angela, 536
Woodward, John, 32
Woodworth, Mary, 180–1
Worboise, Emma Jane, 579–80
Worcestershire, 498
Wordsworth, William, 251
World War I *see* First World War
World War II *see* Second World War
Wotton (gang leader), 310
Wrangle, 331
wrath, Christian attitude, 80–2, 148–51, 159–60
Wrawe, John, 56–7
Wright, William, 317
Wroe (soldier), 33
Wroe, James, 365–6
Wyatt, Richard, 204
Wyclif(fe), John, 61–2
Wylughby, Sir Richard, 70, 71

York, 323, 381, 383–4, 605–6
York, Richard, Duke of, 69, 70
York, William, 463
York Minster, 82, 259–60, 605
Yorkshire: child violence, 465; curses, 229; domestic violence, 178–9, 183–5; infanticide, 166, 207–8; Luddites, 357–8; murder rates, 46; murders, 166; rape, 483; riots and discontent, 58, 353; scolding, 234–5; strikes, 559–62; verbal abuse, 241
Yorkshire Ripper *see* Sutcliffe, Peter
Younghusband, Eileen, 447

Zachreson, DCI David, 525
Žižek, Slavoj, 10

PICTURE ACKNOWLEDGMENTS

———————⊃⊂———————

Black and white images are reproduced by kind permission of:

Alamy: 282 (Chronicle), 476 (© Homer Sykes), 540 (© Janine Wiedel Photolibrary), 574 (© sjbooks). The British Library: 42, 76, 138, 168, 308, 442 (© The British Library Board). Folger Shakespeare Library: 196. Getty: 222 (Culture Club), 254 (Florilegius), 336 (Universal Images Group), 372 (Hulton Archive), 406 (Print Collector), 506 (© Popperfoto). National Archives/Home Office: 604 (© Crown copyright). National Gallery of Art, Washington D.C.: viii. Yale Center for British Art: 106

Colour images are reproduced by kind permission of:

Inset 1

Alamy: Rowlandson: *Dr Syntax with the Skimmington Riders* (Chronicle), Sussex smugglers (Chronicle), Elizabeth Brownrigg (Chronicle). The Bridgeman Art Library: William Marsh execution (Private Collection), Earl of Lancaster execution (The British Library), misericord (photograph © Neil Holmes), knights jousting (© Lambeth Palace Library), Battle of Barnet (Centrale Bibliotheek van de Universiteit, Ghent, Belgium), vagabond engraving (Private Collection), Windsor Martyrs (Private Collection), execution of witches (The Stapleton Collection), fencing school (Private Collection), English Civil War